CHILTON *BOOK COMPANY*

REPAIR MANUAL
DATSUN/NISSAN 200SX, 240SX, 510, 610, 710, 810, Maxima 1973-89

All U.S. and Canadian models of 200SX • 240SX • 510, 610, 710, 810 • Maxima

Sr. Vice President	Ronald A. Hoxter
Publisher and Editor-In-Chief	Kerry A. Freeman, S.A.E.
Managing Editors	Peter M. Conti, Jr. □ W. Calvin Settle, Jr., S.A.E.
Assistant Managing Editor	Nick D'Andrea
Senior Editors	Richard J. Rivele, S.A.E. □ Ron Webb
Director of Manufacturing	Mike D'Imperio
Manager of Manufacturing	John F. Butler
Editor	Anthony C. Tortorici, A.S.E., S.A.E.

CHILTON *BOOK COMPANY*

*ONE OF THE DIVERSIFIED PUBLISHING COMPANIES,
A PART OF CAPITAL CITIES/ABC, INC.*

CONTENTS

SAFETY NOTICE

Proper service and repair procedures are vital to the safe, reliable operation of all motor vehicles, as well as the personal safety of those performing repairs. This book outlines procedures for servicing and repairing vehicles using safe, effective methods. The procedures contain many NOTES, CAUTIONS and WARNINGS which should be followed along with standard safety procedures to eliminate the possibility of personal injury or improper service which could damage the vehicle or compromise its safety.

It is important to note that repair procedures and techniques, tools and parts for servicing motor vehicles, as well as the skill and experience of the individual performing the work vary widely. It is not possible to anticipate all of the conceivable ways or conditions under which vehicles may be serviced, or to provide cautions as to all of the possible hazards that may result. Standard and accepted safety precautions and equipment should be used when handling toxic or flammable fluids, safety goggles or other protection should be used during cutting, grinding, chiseling, prying, or any other process that can cause material removal or projectiles.

Some procedures require the use of tools specially designed for a specific purpose. Before substituting another tool or procedure, you must be completely satisfied that neither your personal safety, nor the performance of the vehicle will be endangered.

Although the information in this guide is based on industry sources and is as complete as possible at the time of publication, the possibility exists that the manufacturer made later changes which could not be included here. While striving for total accuracy, Chilton Book Company cannot assume responsibility for any errors, changes, or omissions that may occur in the compilation of this data.

PART NUMBERS

Part numbers listed in this reference are not recommendations by Chilton for any product by brand name. They are references that can be used with interchange manuals and aftermarket supplier catalogs to locate each brand supplier's discrete part number.

SPECIAL TOOLS

Special tools are recommended by the vehicle manufacturer to perform their specific job. Use has been kept to a minimum, but where absolutely necessary, they are referred to in the text by the part number of the tool manufacturer. Datsun special tools referred to in this guide are available through Kent-Moore Corporation, 29784 Little Mack, Roseville, Michigan 48066. For Canada, contact Kent-Moore of Canada, LTD., 2395 Cawthra Mississauga, Ontario, Canada L5A 3Ps., or an equivalent tool can be purchased locally from a tool supplier or parts outlet.

ACKNOWLEDGMENTS

Chilton Book Company expresses appreciation to the Nissan Motor Corporation in the U.S.A., Carson, California 90248 for their generous assistance.

Copyright © 1989 by Chilton Book Company
All Rights Reserved
Published in Radnor, Pennsylvania 19089, by Chilton Book Company

Manufactured in the United States of America
    67890   876543

Chilton's Repair Manual: Datsun/Nissan 200SX, 240SX, 510, 610, 710, 810, Maxima 1973–89
ISBN 0-8019-7852-1 pbk.
Library of Congress Catalog Card No. 87-47922

General Information and Maintenance

HOW TO USE THIS BOOK

Chilton's Repair Manual for Datsun and Nissan 510, 610, 710, 810, 200SX, 240SX and Maxima cars is intended to help you learn more about the inner workings of your vehicle and save you money on its upkeep and operation.

The first two chapters will be the most used, since they contain maintenance and tune-up information and procedures. Studies have shown that a properly tuned and maintained car can get at least 10% better gas mileage than an out-of-tune car. The other chapters deal with the more complex systems of your car. Operating systems from engine through brakes are covered to the extent that the average do-it-yourselfer becomes mechanically involved. This book will not explain such things as rebuilding the differential for the simple reason that the expertise required and the investment in special tools make this task uneconomical. It will give you detailed instructions to help you change your own brake pads and shoes, replace spark plugs, and do many more jobs that will save you money, give you personal satisfaction, and help you avoid expensive problems.

A secondary purpose of this book is a reference for owners who want to understand their car and/or their mechanics better. In this case, no tools at all are required.

Before removing any bolts, read through the entire procedure. This will give you the overall view of what tools and supplies will be required. There is nothing more frustrating than having to walk to the bus stop on Monday morning because you were short one bolt on Sunday afternoon. So read ahead and plan ahead. Each operation should be approached logically and all procedures thoroughly understood before attempting any work.

All chapters contain adjustments, maintenance, removal and installation procedures, and repair or overhaul procedures. When repair is not considered practical, we tell you how to remove the part and then how to install the new or rebuilt replacement. In this way, you at least save the labor costs. Backyard repair of such components as the alternator is just not practical.

Two basic mechanic's rules should be mentioned here. One, whenever the left side of the car or engine is referred to, it is meant to specify the driver's side of the car. Conversely, the right side of the car means the passenger's side. Secondly, most screws and bolt are removed by turning counterclockwise, and tightened by turning clockwise.

Safety is always the most important rule. Constantly be aware of the dangers involved in working on an automobile and take the proper precautions. (See the section in this chapter Servicing Your Vehicle Safely and the SAFETY NOTICE on the acknowledgement page.)

Pay attention to the instructions provided. There are 3 common mistakes in mechanical work:

1. Incorrect order of assembly, disassembly or adjustment. When taking something apart or putting it together, doing things in the wrong order usually just costs you extra time; however, it CAN break something. Read the entire procedure before beginning disassembly. Do everything in the order in which the instructions say you should do it, even if you can't immediately see a reason for it. When you're taking apart something that is very intricate (for example, a carburetor), you might want to draw a picture of how it looks when assembled at one point in order to make sure you get everything back in its proper position. (We will supply exploded views whenever possible). When making adjustments, especially tune-up adjustments, do them in order; often, one adjustment affects another, and you cannot expect even satisfactory results unless each adjustment is made

only when it cannot be changed by any order.

2. Overtorquing (or undertorquing). While it is more common for over-torquing to cause damage, undertorquing can cause a fastener to vibrate loose causing serious damage. Especially when dealing with aluminum parts, pay attention to torque specifications and utilize a torque wrench in assembly. If a torque figure is not available, remember that if you are using the right tool to do the job, you will probably not have to strain yourself to get a fastener tight enough. The pitch of most threads is so slight that the tension you put on the wrench will be multiplied many, many times in actual force on what you are tightening. A good example of how critical torque is can be seen in the case of spark plug installation, especially where you are putting the plug into an aluminum cylinder head. Too little torque can fail to crush the gasket, causing leakage of combustion gases and consequent overheating of the plug and engine parts. Too much torque can damage the threads, or distort the plug which changes the spark gap.

There are many commercial products available for ensuring that fasteners won't come loose, even if they are not torqued just right (a very common brand is Loctite®). If you're worried about getting something together tight enough to hold, but loose enough to avoid mechanical damage during assembly, one of these products might offer substantial insurance. Read the label on the package and make sure the products is compatible with the materials, fluids, etc. involved before choosing one.

3. Crossthreading. This occurs when a part such as a bolt is screwed into a nut or casting at the wrong angle and forced. Cross threading is more likely to occur if access is difficult. It helps to clean and lubricate fasteners, and to start threading with the part to be installed going straight in. Then, start the bolt, spark plug, etc. with your fingers. If you encounter resistance, unscrew the part and start over again at a different angle until it can be inserted and turned several turns without much effort. Keep in mind that many parts, especially spark plugs, used tapered threads so that gentle turning will automatically bring the part you're treading to the proper angle if you don't force it or resist a change in angle. Don't put a wrench on the part until its's been turned a couple of turns by hand. If you suddenly encounter resistance, and the part has not seated fully, don't force it. Pull it back out and make sure it's clean and threading properly.

Always take your time and be patient; once you have some experience, working on your car will become an enjoyable hobby.

TOOLS AND EQUIPMENT

The service procedures in this book presuppose a familiarity with hand tools and their proper use. However, it is possible that you may have a limited amount of experience with the sort of equipment needed to work on an automobile. This section is designed to help you assemble a basic set of tools that will handle most of the jobs you may undertake.

In addition to the normal assortment of screwdrivers and pliers, automotive service work requires an investment in wrenches, sockets and the handles needed to drive them, plus various measuring tools such as torque wrenches and feeler gauges.

You will find that virtually every nut and bolt on your vehicle is metric. Therefore, despite a few close size similarities, standard inch-size tools will not fit and must not be used. You will need a set of metric wrenches as your most basic tool kit, ranging from about 6-22mm in size. High quality forged wrenches are available in three styles: open end, box end and combination open/box end. The combination tools are generally the most desirable as a starter set; the wrenches shown in the accompanying illustration are of the combination type.

The other set of tools inevitably required is a ratchet handle and socket set. This set should have the same size range as your wrench set. The ratchet, extensions and flex drives for the sockets are available in many sizes; it is advisable to choose a ⅜″ drive set initially. One break in the inch/metric sizing war is that metric sized sockets sold in the U.S. have inch-sized drive (¼″, ⅜″, ½″ and etc.). Thus, if you already have an inch-sized socket set, you need only buy new metric sockets in the sizes needed. Sockets are available in 6- and 12-point versions; six point types are stronger and are a good choice for a first set. The choice of a drive handle for the sockets should be made with some care. If this is your first set, take the plunge and invest in a flex-head ratchet; it will get into many places otherwise accessible only through a long chain of universal joints, extensions and adapters. An alternative is a flex handle, which lacks the ratcheting feature but has a head which pivots 180°; such a tool is shown below the ratchet handle in the illustration. In addition to the range of sockets mentioned, a rubber lined spark plug socket should be purchased. The correct size for the plugs in your vehicle's engine is $^{13}\!/_{16}$″.

The most important thing to consider when purchasing hand tools is quality. Don't be misled by the low cost of bargain tools. Forged wrenches, tempered screwdriver blades and

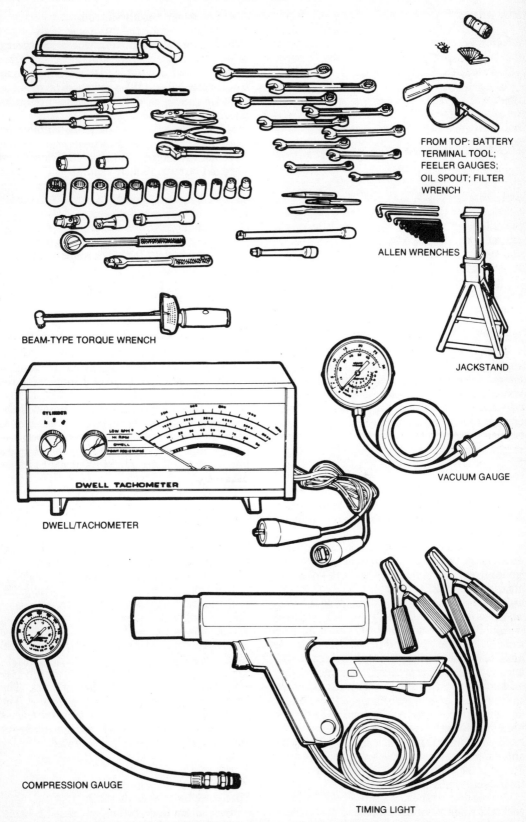

FROM TOP: BATTERY
TERMINAL TOOL;
FEELER GAUGES;
OIL SPOUT; FILTER
WRENCH

ALLEN WRENCHES

BEAM-TYPE TORQUE WRENCH

JACKSTAND

DWELL TACHOMETER

VACUUM GAUGE

DWELL/TACHOMETER

COMPRESSION GAUGE

TIMING LIGHT

You need only a basic assortment of hand tools and test instruments for most maintenance and repair jobs

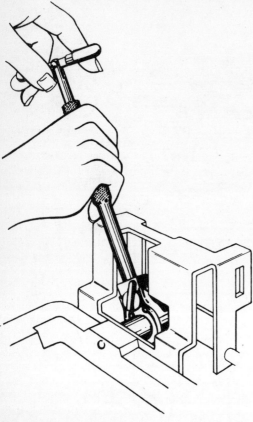

New design speedwrench

fine tooth ratchets are much better investments than their less expensive counterparts. The skinned knuckles and frustration inflicted by poor quality tools make any job an unhappy chore. Another consideration is that quality tools come with an unbeatable replacement guarantee; if the tool breaks, you get a new one, no questions asked.

Most jobs can be accomplished using the tools on the accompanying lists. There will be an occasional need for a special tool, such as snap ring pliers; that need will be mentioned in the text. It would not be wise to buy a large assortment of tools on the premise that someday they will be needed. Instead, the tools should be acquired one at a time, each for a specific job, both to avoid unnecessary expense and to be certain that you have the right tool.

The tools needed for basic maintenance jobs, in addition to the wrenches and sockets mentioned, include:

1. Jackstands, for support.
2. Oil filter wrench.
3. Oil filter spout or funnel.
4. Grease gun.
5. Battery post and clamp cleaner.

6. Container for draining oil.
7. Many rags for the inevitable spills.

In addition to these items there are several others which are not absolutely necessary but handy to have around. These include a transmission funnel and filler tube, a drop (trouble) light on a long cord, an adjustable (crescent) wrench and slip joint pliers.

A more advanced list of tools, suitable for tune-up work, can be drawn up easily. While the tools are slightly more sophisticated, they need not be outrageously expensive. The key to these purchases is to make them with an eye towards adaptability and wide range. A basic list of tune-up tools could include:

1. Tachometer/dwell meter.
2. Spark plug gauge and gapping tool.
3. Feeler gauges for valve adjustment.
4. Timing light.

Note that if your vehicle has electronic ignition, you will have no need for a dwell meter and of course a tachometer is provided on the instrument panel of the vehicle. You will need both the wire type (spark plugs) and the flat type (valves) feeler gauges. The choice of a timing light should be made carefully. A light which works on the DC current supplied by the vehicle battery is the best choice; it should have a xenon tube for brightness. Since most of the vehicles have electronic ignition or will have it in the future, the light should have an inductive pickup which clamps around the No. 1 spark plug cable (the timing light illustrated has one of these pickups).

In addition to these basic tools, there are several other tools and gauges which you may find useful. These include:

1. A compression gauge. The screw-in type is slower to use but eliminates the possibility of faulty reading due to escaping pressure.
2. A manifold vacuum gauge.
3. A test light.
4. A combination volt/ohmmeter.
5. An induction meter, used to determine whether or not there is current flowing in a wire, an extremely helpful tool for electrical troubleshooting.

Finally, you will find a torque wrench necessary for all but the most basic of work. The beam type models are perfectly adequate. The newer click type (breakaway) torque wrenches are more accurate but are much more expensive and must be periodically recalibrated.

Special Tools

Special tools are available from:
Kent-Moore Corporation
29784 Little Mack
Roseville, Michigan 48066

In Canada:
Kent-Moore of Canada, Ltd.,
2395 Cawthra
Mississauga, Ontario
Canada L5A 3P2

SERVICING YOUR CAR SAFELY

It is virtually impossible to anticipate all of the hazards involved with automotive maintenance and service, but care and common sense will prevent most accidents.

The rules of safety for mechanics range from don't smoke around gasoline, to use the proper tool for the job. The trick to avoiding injuries is to develop safe work habits and take every possible precaution. Always think through what you do before doing it!

Dos

• Do keep a fire extinguisher and first aid kit within easy reach.

• Do wear safety glasses or goggles when cutting, drilling, grinding or prying, even if you have 20/20 vision. If you wear glasses for the sake of vision, they should be made of hardened glass that can serve also as safety glasses, or wear safety goggles over your regular glasses.

• Do shield your eyes whenever you work around the battery. Batteries contain sulphuric acid. In case of contact with the eyes or skin, flush the area with water or a mixture of water and baking soda and get medical attention immediately.

• Do use safety stands for any undercar service. Jacks are for raising vehicles; safety stands are for making sure the vehicle stays raised until you want it to come down. Whenever the car is raised, block the wheels remaining on the ground and set the parking brake.

• Do use a hydraulic floor jack of at least 1½ ton capacity when working on your Datsun or Nissan. That little jack supplied with the car is only designed for changing tires out on the rod.

• Do use adequate ventilation when working with any chemicals or hazardous materials. Like carbon monoxide, the asbestos dust resulting from brake lining wear can be poisonous in sufficient quantities.

• Do disconnect the negative battery cable when working on the electrical system. The secondary ignition system can contain up to 40,000 volts.

• Do follow manufacturer's directions whenever working with potentially hazardous materials. Both brake fluid and antifreeze are poisonous if taken internally.

• Do properly maintain your tools. Loose

Always support the car securely with jackstands; don't use cinder blocks, tire-changing jacks or the like

hammerheads, mushroomed punches and chisels, frayed or poorly grounded electrical cords, excessively worn screwdrivers, spread wrenches (open end), cracked sockets, slipping ratchets, or faulty droplight sockets can cause accidents.

• Do use the proper size and type of tool for the job being done.

• Do when possible, pull on a wrench handle rather than push on it, and adjust your stance to prevent a fall.

• Do be sure that adjustable wrenches are tightly closed on the nut or bolt and pulled so that the face is on the side of the fixed jaw.

• Do select a wrench or socket that fits the nut or bolt. The wrench or socket should sit straight, not cocked.

• Do strike squarely with a hammer. Avoid glancing blows.

• Do set the parking brake and block the drive wheels if the work requires the engine running.

Don'ts

• Don't run an engine in a garage or anywhere else without proper ventilation – EVER! Carbon monoxide is poisonous. It takes a long time to leave the human body and you can build up a deadly supply of it in your system by simply breathing in a little every day. You may not realize you are slowly poisoning yourself. Always use power vents, windows, fans or open the garage doors.

• Don't work around moving parts while wearing a necktie or other loose clothing. Short sleeves are much safer than long, loose sleeves. Hard-toed shoes with neoprene soles protect your toes and give a better grip on slippery surfaces. Jewelry such as watches, fancy belt buckles, beads or body adornment of any kind is not safe working around a car. Long hair should be hidden under a hat or cap.

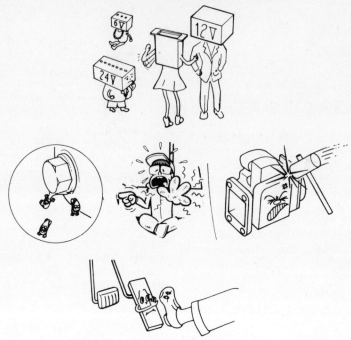

Never work on a car for so long that you begin to lose your sense of reality

• Don't use pockets for toolboxes. A fall or bump can drive a screwdriver deep into your body. Even a wiping cloth hanging from the back pocket can wrap around a spinning shaft or fan.

• Don't use cinderblocks to support a car! When you get the car jacked up (with a hydraulic floor jack), support it with jackstands.

• Don't smoke when working around gasoline, cleaning solvent or other flammable material.

• Don't smoke when working around the battery. When the battery is being charged, it gives off explosive hydrogen gas.

• Don't use gasoline to wash your hands. There are excellent soaps available. Gasoline may contain lead, and lead can enter the body through a cut, accumulating in the body until you are very ill. Gasoline also removes all the natural oils from the skin so that bone dry hands will suck up oil and grease.

• Don't service the air conditioning system unless you are equipped with the necessary tools and training. The refrigerant, R-12, is compressed and in liquid form, and when released into the air will instantly freeze any surface it contacts, including your eyes. Although the refrigerant is normally non-toxic, R-12 becomes a deadly poisonous gas (phosgene) in the presence of an open flame. One good whiff of the vapors from burning refrigerant can be fatal.

SERIAL NUMBER IDENTIFICATION

Vehicle

The vehicle identification plate is located on the cowl at the rear of the engine compartment. The plate contains the model type, engine capacity, maximum horsepower, wheelbase and the engine and chassis serial numbers.

The vehicle or chassis serial number is broken down as shown in the illustration and described below. The vehicle identification number is also reproduced on a plate on the upper left surface of the instrument panel and can be seen from the outside through the windshield.

The V.I.N. is broken down as follows:

• First three digits/letters: Manufacturer

Vehicle identification plate

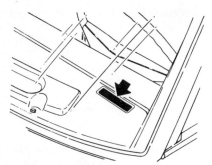

The vehicle identification number is visible through the windshield

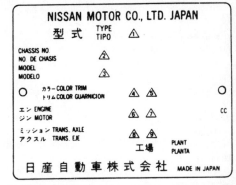

1   Type
2   Vehicle identification number (Chassis number)
3   Model
4   Body color code
5   Trim color code
6   Engine model
7   Engine displacement
8   Transmission model
9   Axle model

Vehicle identification plate

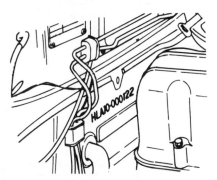

The vehicle serial number is stamped into the firewall

● Fourth letter: Engine type
● Fifth letter: Vehicle line
● Sixth digit: Model change number (0-9)
● Seventh digit: Body type (sedan or wagon)
● Eighth letter: Restraint system. S means standard
● Ninth digit: Check digit 0-9 or X to verify that the serial number is being read off the car itself
● Tenth letter: Model year in a letter code

● Eleventh letter: Manufacturing plant code
● Last six digits: Vehicle serial (chassis) number

Engine

The engine serial number is stamped on the right side top edge of the cylinder block on all rear wheel drive models except the 1980 and later 200SX, 1980-83 200SX engine (Z20, Z22) numbers are stamped on the left side top edge of the cylinder block. The 1984 and later 200SX engines (CA20, CA18ET) are stamped on the left side rear edge of the block, next to the bellhousing. The engine serial number is preceeded by the engine model code. The 240SX

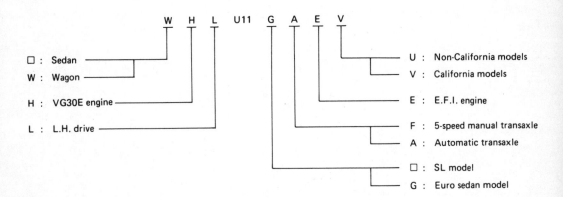

Note: ☐ means no indication.

Serial number breakdown for models to 1985

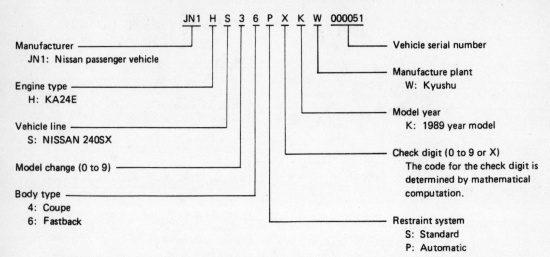

JN1 H S 3 6 P X K W 000051

Manufacturer
    JN1: Nissan passenger vehicle

Engine type
    H: KA24E

Vehicle line
    S: NISSAN 240SX

Model change (0 to 9)

Body type
    4: Coupe
    6: Fastback

Vehicle serial number

Manufacture plant
    W: Kyushu

Model year
    K: 1989 year model

Check digit (0 to 9 or X)
    The code for the check digit is
    determined by mathematical
    computation.

Restraint system
    S: Standard
    P: Automatic

Vehicle identification number arrangement—1986–89 Maxima, 1989 240SX and 1986–88 200SX

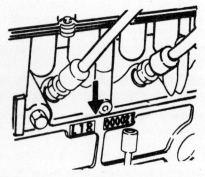

Typical engine serial number location gasoline engines

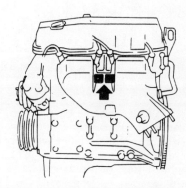

Engine serial number location—1989 240SX

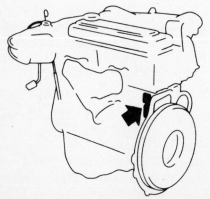

1984 and later 200SX engine (CA20E, CA18ET) serial number location

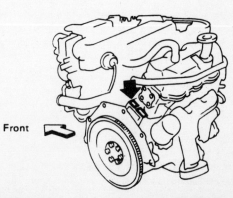

Front

Engine serial number location—1985–89 Maxima

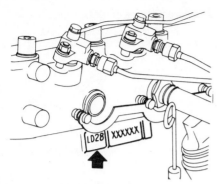

Engine serial number—diesel

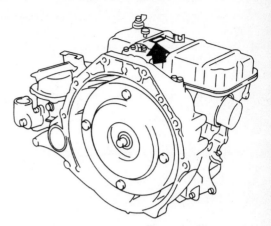

Transaxle serial number location automatic

engine serial number is stamped on the left side top edge of the cylinder block between No. 2 and No. 3 cylinders. On the 1985-89 Maxima, the number can be found on the driver's side edge of the front cylinder bank, looking from the driver's seat.

Transmission

The transmission serial number is stamped on the front upper face of the transmission case on manual transmissions, or on the lower right side of the case on automatic transmissions except for the 1989 240SX model which is on the right side but in the tailshaft area.

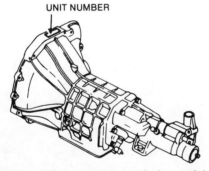

UNIT NUMBER

Location of the manual transmission serial number

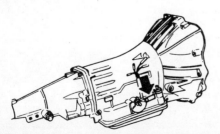

Location of the automatic transmission serial number

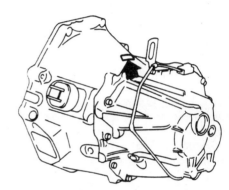

Transaxle serial number location manual

Transaxle

On the manual transaxle the serial number is stamped on the front upper face of the transaxle case. On the automatic transaxle the serial number is stamped on the transmission oil pan except on the 1989 model which is stamped on the upper lip of the transaxle case near the bolt mounting holes.

ROUTINE MAINTENANCE

Routine maintenance is the self-explanatory term used to describe the sort of periodic work necessary to keep a car in safe and reliable working order. A regular program aimed at monitoring essential systems ensure that the car's components are functioning correctly (and will continue to do so until the next inspection, one hopes), and can prevent small problems from developing into major headaches. Routine maintenance also pays off big dividends in keeping major repair costs at a mini-

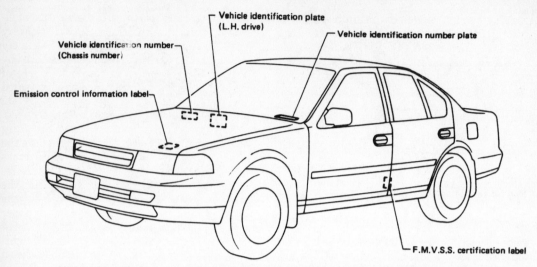

Various identification and emission label locations—1989 Maxima—other models similar

mum, extending the life of the car, and enhancing resale value, should you ever desire to part with your Datsun/Nissan.

A very definite maintenance schedule is provided by Nissan, and must be followed, not only to keep the new car warranty in effect, but also to keep the car working properly. The Maintenance Intervals chart in this chapter outlines the routine maintenance which must be performed according to intervals based on either accumulated mileage or time. Your car also came with a maintenance schedule provided by Nissan. Adherence to these schedules will result in a longer life for your car, and will, over the long run, save you money and time.

The checks and adjustments in the following sections generally require only a few minutes of attention every few weeks. The services to be

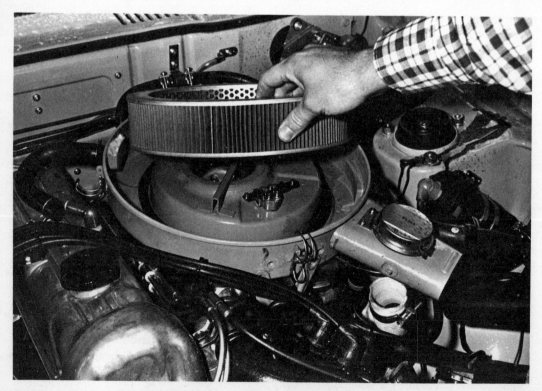

Your engine breathes too, don't strangle it with a dirty air filter

performed can be easily accomplished in a morning. The most important part of any maintenance program is regularity. The few minutes or occasional morning spent on these seemingly trivial tasks will forestall or eliminate major problems later.

Air Cleaner

An air cleaner is used to keep airborne dirt and dust out of the air flowing through the engine. Proper maintenance is vital, as a clogged element will undesirably enrichen the fuel mixture, restrict air flow and power, and allow excessive contamination of the oil with abrasives.

All models covered in this book are equipped

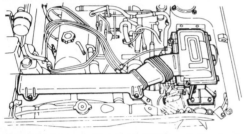

810 and Maxima air filter box. 200SX and diesels similar

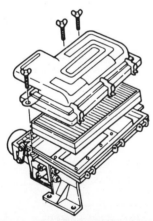

Exploded view of the 810 and Maxima air cleaner showing filter element; 1980 and later 200SX similar

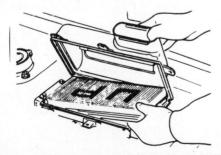

When installing the filter element on fuel injected engines, make sure that the word "UP" is facing up

with a disposable, paper cartridge air cleaner element. The filter should be checked at every tune-up (sooner if the car is operated in a dusty area). Loose dust can sometimes be removed by striking the filter against a hard surface several times or by blowing through it with compressed air. The filter should be replaced every 24,000 miles (30,000 miles, 1979 and later).

To remove the filter, unscrew the wing nut(s), lift off the housing cover and remove the filter element. There are four thumb latches which will also have to be released before removing the housing cover. Before installing the original or the replacement filter, wipe out the inside of the housing with a clean rag or paper towel. Install the paper air cleaner filter, seat the top cover on the bottom housing and tighten the wing nut(s). Clip on the thumb latches if so equipped.

NOTE: *Certain models (810, Maxima, and 1980 and later 200SX) utilize a flat, cartridge type air cleaner element. Although removal and installation procedures for these models are the same as for those with round air cleaners, make sure that the word UP is facing up when you install the filter element.*

Air Induction Valve Filter

Certain later models use an air induction valve filter. It is located in the side of the air cleaner housing and is easily replaced. Unscrew

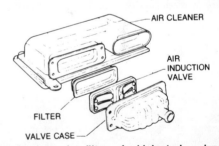

Air induction valve filter—fuel injected engines

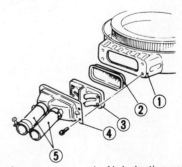

1. Air cleaner
2. Filter
3. Air induction valve
4. Air induction valve case
5. Rubber hose

Air induction valve filter—carbureted engines

the mounting screws and remove the valve filter case. Pull the air induction valve out and remove the filter that lies underneath it. Install the new filter and then the valve. Pay particular attention to which way the valve is facing so that the exhaust gases will not flow backward through the system. Install the valve case. Replacement intervals are every 30,000 miles.

Gasoline Fuel Filters

The fuel filter on all models is a disposable plastic unit. It's located on the right inner fender. The filter should be replaced at least every 24,000 miles. A dirty filter will starve the engine and cause poor running.

REMOVAL AND INSTALLATION

510, 610, 710 and 1977-79 200SX

1. Locate fuel filter on right side of the engine compartment.
2. Disconnect the inlet and outlet hoses from the fuel filter. Make certain that the inlet hose (bottom) doesn't fall below the fuel tank level or the gasoline will drain out.
3. Pry the fuel filter from its clip and replace the assembly.
4. Replace the inlet, outlet lines and hose clamps. Secure the hose clamps to prevent leaks.
5. Start the engine and check for leaks.

1977-79 810

These models utilize an electric fuel pump. The pressure on these models must be released before removing the fuel filter.
1. Disconnect the negative cable from the battery.

2. Disconnect the cold start valve harness connector.
NOTE: *See Chapter 5 for illustration.*
3. Use two jumper wires and connect one side of each to a terminal on the cold start valve connector.
NOTE: *Be sure to keep both terminals separate in order to avoid short circuiting.*
4. Connect the two remaining terminals of the jumper wires to the negative and positive battery terminals in order to release the pressure in the fuel system.
5. Unfasten the clamps securing the fuel lines to the inlet and outlet sides of the fuel filter and then remove the fuel lines.
6. Remove the fuel filter.
7. Install new fuel filter with new hose clamps. Replace fuel lines if necessary.
8. Reconnect the cold start valve harness connector.
9. Connect the negative cable to the battery.
10. Start engine and check for leaks

1980 and Later 810, Maxima, 200SX and 240SX

These models utilize an electric fuel pump. The pressure must be released on these models before removing the fuel filter. On later years, the fuel pump fuse should be removed, instead of the relay. Crank the engine a couple times to

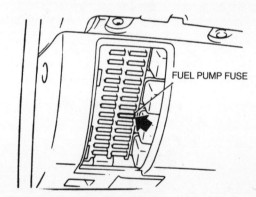

Fuel pump fuse location—Maxima

Fuel filter (arrow), mounted on inner fender inside engine compartment. This is a 1978 510; others are similar

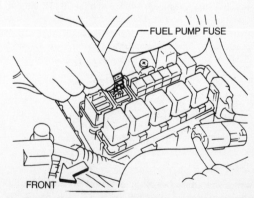

Fuel pump fuse location—240SX

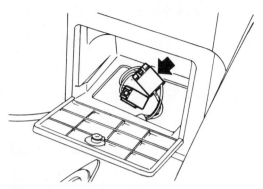

The fuel pump harness connector is in the tool box on the rear right-hand side on the 1984 and later 200SXs

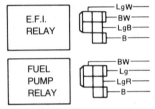

Both of the above relays are green, but can be distinguished by the color of harness.

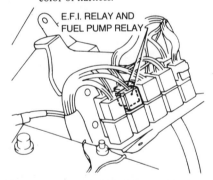

The Maxima fuel pump relay is located in the engine compartment near the battery

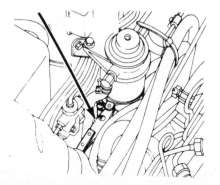

Remove the diesel fuel filter with a strap wrench (arrow)

release pressure before removing the fuel filter. On some late models the "Check Engine Light" will stay on after installation is completed. The memory code in the control unit must be erased. To erase the code disconnect the battery cable for 10 seconds then reconnect after installation of fuel filter. Refer to Chapter 5 for more information.

1. Start the engine.

2. Disconnect the #2 fuel pump relay harness connector with the engine running.

NOTE: *See Chapter 5 for illustrations.*

3. After the engine stalls, crank it two or three times.

4. Turn the ignition off and reconnect the #2 fuel pump relay harness connector.

5. Unfasten the clamps securing the fuel lines to the inlet and outlet side of the fuel filter and then disconnect the fuel lines.

6. Remove the fuel filter.

7. Install the fuel filter and new hose clamps. Replace fuel lines if necessary.

8. Start the engine and check for leaks.

Diesel Fuel Filter

The fuel filter on all diesel models is located on the right inner fender. The filter should be replaced at least every 30,000 miles. It should also be drained of water periodically.

REMOVAL AND INSTALLATION

1. Locate the filter on the right side of the engine compartment.

2. Place a small pan or glass jar under the filter, unscrew the fuel filter sensor on the bottom and drain any fuel that is in the filter.

3. Using Datsun/Nissan special tool SP193200000 or a strap wrench, unscrew the filter from the mount.

4. Connect the fuel filter sensor to the new filter and then install the new filter.

NOTE: *The new fuel filter should be screwed on hand tight. DO NOT use the wrench to tighten the filter.*

5. Bleed the fuel system as detailed in Chapter 5.

DRAINING WATER FROM THE FUEL FILTER

1. Place a small pan or glass jar under the bottom of the fuel filter.

2. Unscrew the fuel filter sensor and let the filter drain.

NOTE: *There is a round primer pump on top of the filter mount. Pumping it will quicken the draining process.*

3. The diesel fuel and the water will separate themselves in the container. The water is heavier and will therefore be on the bottom.

4. Allow the filter to drain until all the water has dripped out.

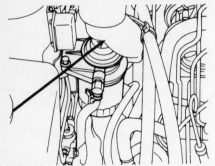

Pump the priming pump (underneath hand at tip of arrow) to speed the draining process

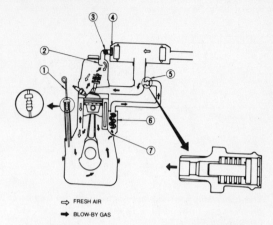

⇨ FRESH AIR
➡ BLOW-BY GAS

1. Seal type oil level gauge
2. Baffle plate
3. Flame arrester
4. Filter
5. P.C.V. valve
6. Steel net
7. Baffle plate

PCV valve location—610, 710, 1978–79 510 and 1980 510 (Canada)

5. Replace the fuel sensor and then bleed the fuel system as detailed in Chapter 5.

Positive Crankcase Ventilation Valve

REMOVAL AND INSTALLATION

Gas Engines

This valve feeds crankcase blow-by gases into the intake manifold to be burned with the normal air/fuel mixture. The PCV valve should be replaced every 24,000 miles on models through 1979. On 1980 and later models, no strict interval for maintenance is specified. However, it is wise to check the system occasionally in case of clogging, especially if you know that you have a vehicle that has been neglected. Make sure that all PCV connections are tight. Check that the connecting hoses are clear and not clogged. Replace any brittle or broken hoses.

To check the valve's operation, remove the valve's ventilation hose with the engine idling. If the valve is working, a hissing noise will be heard as air passes through the valve, and a strong vacuum will be felt when you place a finger over the valve opening.

To replace the valve, which is located in the side or bottom of the intake manifold:

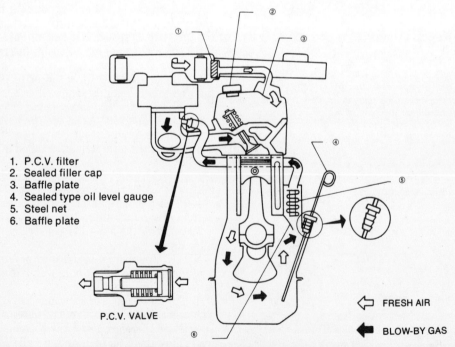

1. P.C.V. filter
2. Sealed filler cap
3. Baffle plate
4. Sealed type oil level gauge
5. Steel net
6. Baffle plate

P.C.V. VALVE

⇦ FRESH AIR
⬅ BLOW-BY GAS

PCV valve location—1980 and later 510 (except Canada)

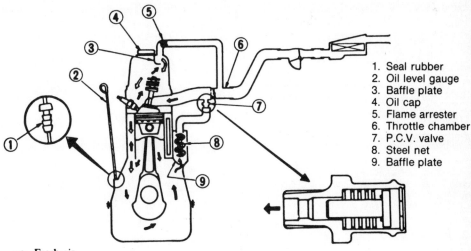

1. Seal rubber
2. Oil level gauge
3. Baffle plate
4. Oil cap
5. Flame arrester
6. Throttle chamber
7. P.C.V. valve
8. Steel net
9. Baffle plate

⇨ Fresh air

➡ Blow-by gas

PCV valve location—810, Maxima and 1980–81 200SX

1. Squeeze the hose clamp with pliers and remove the hose.

2. Using a wrench, unscrew the PCV valve and remove the valve.

3. Disconnect the ventilation hoses and flush with solvent.

4. Install the new PCV valve and replace the hoses and clamp.

NOTE: *On the 1989 240SX model the PCV vavlve is located on the side of the collector as-sembly. On the VG30E engine the PCV valve is located in the end of the ventilation hose coming from the rocker cover.*

Diesel Engines

These engines use a crankcase emission control valve in place of the PCV valve. Although different in configuration it is similar in function.

To replace the valve which is located inline

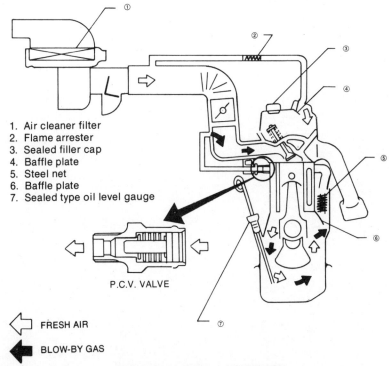

1. Air cleaner filter
2. Flame arrester
3. Sealed filler cap
4. Baffle plate
5. Steel net
6. Baffle plate
7. Sealed type oil level gauge

P.C.V. VALVE

⇦ FRESH AIR

⬅ BLOW-BY GAS

PCV valve location—1982 200SX

CA20E ENGINE   CA18ET ENGINE

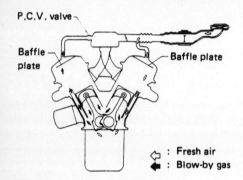

P.C.V VALVE

STEEL NET

BAFFLE PLATE

SEAL TYPE OIL LEVER GAUGE

OIL SEPARATOR

⇦ : FRESH AIR

⬅ : BLOW-BY GAS

PCV systems, 1984 and later 200SX. Turbo engine on right

P.C.V. valve

Baffle plate

Baffle plate

⇦ : Fresh air

⬅ : Blow-by gas

P.C.V. valve location—VG30E engine

between the cylinder head cover and the intake manifold:

1. Locate the valve. There should be three hoses attached to it.

2. Use a pair of pliers and squeeze the hose clamp on each hose so that you can remove the hose from the valve.

3. Install the new valve and reconnect all the hoses..

Evaporative Emission Control System

SERVICING

Gasoline Engines Only

Check the evaporation control system every 12,000 miles (15,000 miles, 1980 and later).

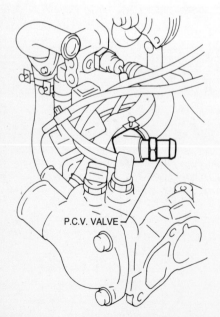

P.C.V. VALVE

200SX turbo (CA18ET engine) PCV valve location

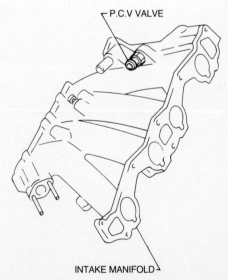

P.C.V VALVE

INTAKE MANIFOLD

PCV valve location, CA20E engine, 1984 and later

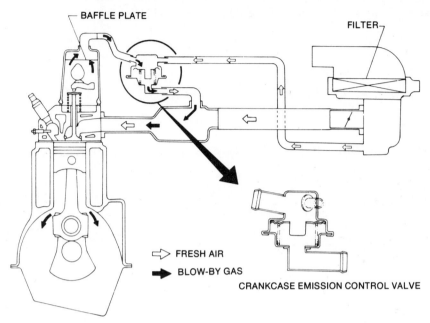

BAFFLE PLATE

FILTER

⇨ FRESH AIR

➡ BLOW-BY GAS

CRANKCASE EMISSION CONTROL VALVE

Diesel crankcase emission control valve location

Check the fuel and vapor lines for proper connections and correct routing as well as condition. Replace damaged or deteriorated parts as necessary. Remove and check the operation of the check valve on pre-1975 models in the following manner.

1. With all the hoses disconnected from the valve, apply air pressure to the fuel tank side of the valve. The air should flow through the valve and exit the crankcase side of the valve. If the valve does not behave in the above manner, replace.

2. Apply air pressure to the crankcase side valve. Air should not pass to either of the two outlets.

3. When air pressure is applied to the carburetor side of the valve, the air should pass through to exit out the fuel tank and/or the crankcase side of the valve.

On 1975 and later models, the flow guide

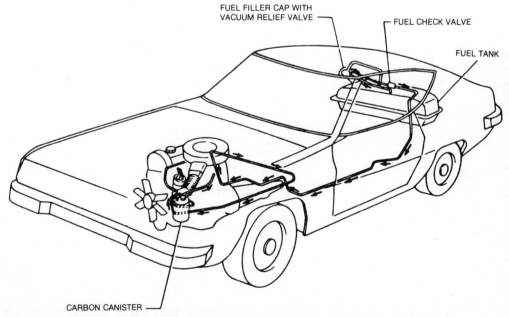

FUEL FILLER CAP WITH
VACUUM RELIEF VALVE

FUEL CHECK VALVE

FUEL TANK

CARBON CANISTER

1975 and later evaporative emissions control system; most models similar

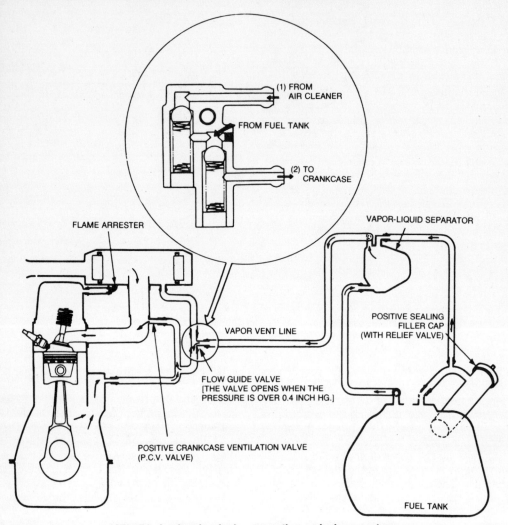

(1) FROM
AIR CLEANER

FROM FUEL TANK

(2) TO
CRANKCASE

FLAME ARRESTER

VAPOR-LIQUID SEPARATOR

VAPOR VENT LINE

POSITIVE SEALING
FILLER CAP
(WITH RELIEF VALVE)

FLOW GUIDE VALVE
[THE VALVE OPENS WHEN THE
PRESSURE IS OVER 0.4 INCH HG.]

POSITIVE CRANKCASE VENTILATION VALVE
(P.C.V. VALVE)

FUEL TANK

1973–74 check valve fuel evaporative emissions system

valve is replaced with a carbon filled storage canister which stores fuel vapors until the engine is started and the vapors are drawn into the combustion chambers and burned.

On those vehicles built through 1983, you should check the operation of the carbon canister purge valve. To do this, disconnect the rubber hose between the canister control valve and

1. Cover
2. Diaphragm
3. Retainer
4. Diaphragm spring

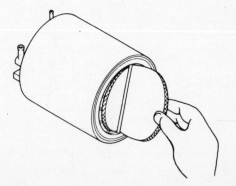

1975 and later carbon canister

The carbon canister has a replaceable filter in the bottom

the T-fitting, at the T-fitting. Apply vacuum to the hose leading to the control valve. The vacuum condition should be maintained indefinitely. If the control valve leaks, remove the top cover of the valve and check for a dislocated or cracked diaphragm. If the diaphragm is damaged, a repair kit containing a new diaphragm, retainer, and spring is available and should be installed.

The carbon canister has an air filter in the bottom of the canister. On models built in years up to and including 1982, the filter element should be checked every two years or 30,000 miles; more frequently if the car is operated in dusty areas. Replace the filter by pulling it out of the bottom of the canister and installing a new one.

Battery

SPECIFIC GRAVITY (EXCEPT MAINTENANCE FREE BATTERIES)

At least once a year, check the specific gravity of the battery. It should be between 1.20 and 1.26 at room temperature.

The specific gravity can be checked with the use of a hydrometer; an inexpensive instrument available from many sources, including auto parts stores. The hydrometer has a squeeze bulb at one end and a nozzle at the other. Battery electrolyte is sucked into the hy-

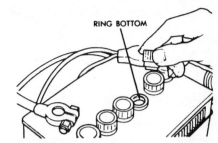

Fill each battery cell to the bottom of the split ring with distilled water

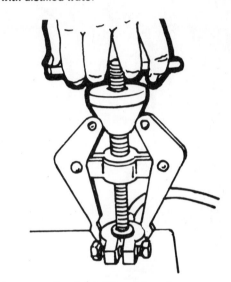

Pullers make clamp removal easier

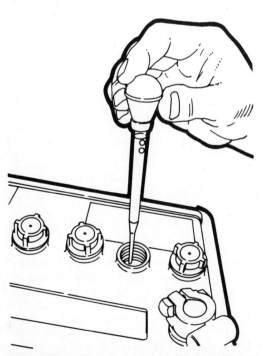

Specific gravity can be checked with an hydrometer

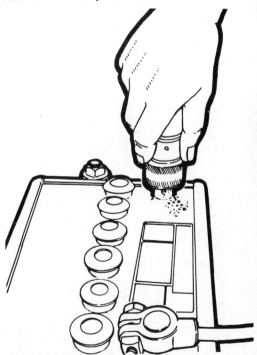

Clean the posts with a wire brush, or a terminal cleaner made for the purpose (shown)

Clean the inside of the clamps with a wire brush, or the special tool

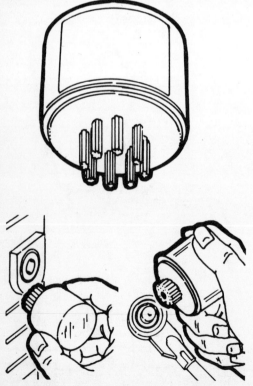

Special tools are also available for cleaning the posts and clamps on side terminal batteries

drometer until the float is lifted from its seat. The specific gravity is then read by noting the position of the float. Generally, if after charging, the specific gravity between any two cells varies more than 50 points (0.050), the battery is bad and should be replaced.

NOTE: *If the battery level is low add distilled water than operate vehicle for about 1 hour than test the specific gravity.*

It is not possible to check the specific gravity in this manner on sealed (maintenance free) batteries. Instead, the indicator built into the top of the case must be relied on to display any signs of battery deterioration. If the indicator is dark, the battery can be assumed to be OK. If the indicator is light, the specific gravity is low, and the battery should be charged or replaced.

Cables And Clamps

Once a year, the battery terminals and the cable clamps should be cleaned. Loosen the clamps and remove the cables, negative cable first. On batteries with posts on top, the use of a puller specially made for the purpose is recommended. These are inexpensive, and available in auto parts stores. Side terminal battery cables are secured with a bolt.

Clean the cable clamps and the battery terminal with a wire brush, until all corrosion, grease, etc., is removed and the metal is shiny. It is especially important to clean the inside of the clamp thoroughly, since a small deposit of foreign material or oxidation there will prevent a sound electrical connection and inhibit either starting or charging. Special tools are available for cleaning these parts, one type for conventional batteries and another type for side terminal batteries.

Before installing the cables, loosen the battery holddown clamp or strap, remove the battery and check the battery tray. Clear it of any debris, and check it for soundness. Rust should be wire brushed away, and the metal given a coat of anti-rust paint. Replace the battery and tighten the holddown clamp or strap securely, but be careful not to overtighten, which will crack the battery case.

After the clamps and terminals are clean, reinstall the cables, negative cable last. Do not hammer on the clamps to install. Tighten the clamps securely, but do not distort them. Give the clamps and terminals a thin external coat of grease after installation, to retard corrosion.

Check the cables at the same time that the terminals are cleaned. If the cable insulation is cracked or broken, or if the ends are frayed, the cable should be replaced with a new cable of the same length and gauge.

NOTE: *Keep flame or sparks away from the battery. It gives off explosive hydrogen gas.*

Battery electrolyte contains sulphuric acid. If you should splash any on your skin or in your eyes, flush the affected area with plenty of clear water. If it lands in your eyes, get medical help immediately.

REPLACEMENT

When it becomes necessary to replace the battery, select a battery with a rating equal to or greater than the battery originally installed. Deterioration, embrittlement and just plain aging of the battery cables, starter motor, and associated wires makes the battery's job harder in successive years. The slow increase in electrical resistance over time makes it prudent to install a new battery with a greater capacity than the old. Details on battery removal and installation are covered in Chapter 3.

E.F.E. System (Heat Riser)

SERVICING

Gasoline Engines Only

The heat riser, or Early Fuel Evaporative System, is a thermostatically operated valve in the exhaust manifold. It closes when the engine is warming up to direct hot exhaust gases to the intake manifold, in order to preheat the incoming air/fuel mixture. It is used on carbureted engines only. If it sticks shut, the result will be frequent stalling during warmup, especially in cold or damp weather. If it sticks open, the result will be a rough idle after the engine is warm.

The heat control valve should be checked for free operation every six months or 6,000 miles. Simply give the counterweight a twirl (engine cold) to make sure that no binding exists. If the valve sticks, apply a heat control solvent to the ends of the shaft. This type of solvent is available in auto parts stores. Sometimes lightly rapping the end of the shaft with a rubber hammer (engine hot) will break it loose. If this fails, the components will have to be removed from the car for repair.

NOTE: *The 1980 and later carbureted engines do not use the heat control valve. Instead, these engines warm the fuel mixture by a coolant passage under the carburetor. No maintenance is required.*

Belts

INSPECTION AND ADJUSTING

Check the belts driving the fan, air pump, air conditioning compressor, and the alternator for cracks, fraying, wear, and tension every 12 months or 12,000 miles (15,000 miles, 1980 and later). Replace as necessary.

Belt deflection at the midpoint of the longest span between pulleys should be not more than ½" with 22 lbs. of pressure applied to the belt.

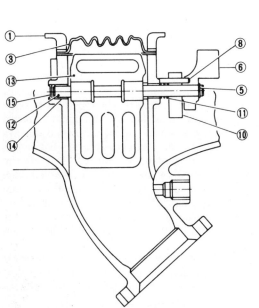

1. Intake manifold	5. Snap ring	9. Screw	13. Heat control valve
2. Stove gasket	6. Counterweight	10. Thermostat spring	14. Bushing
3. Manifold stove	7. Key	11. Coil spring	15. Cap
4. Heat shield plate	8. Stopper pin	12. Control valve shaft	16. Exhaust manifold

EFE system—L-series (both 4 and 6-cyl.) engines

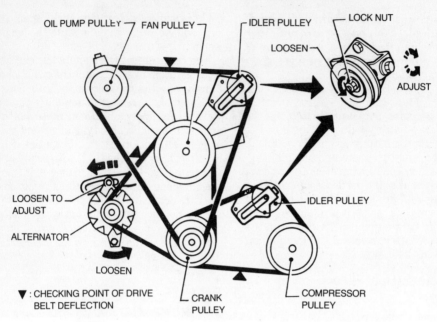

200SX Z-series 4-cylinder engine accessories and belt adjustments

To adjust the tension on all components except the air conditioning compressor, power steering pump, and some late model air pumps, loosen the pivot and mounting bolts of the component which the belt is driving, then, using a wooden lever, pry the component toward or away from the engine until the proper tension is achieved. Tighten the component mounting bolts securely.

NOTE: *An overly tight belt will wear out the pulley bearings on the assorted components*

Belt tension adjustments for the factory installed air conditioning compressor and power steering pump are made at the idler pulley. The idler pulley is the smallest of the three pulleys. At the top of the slotted bracket holding the idler pulley there is a bolt which is used to either raise or lower the pulley. To free the bolt for adjustment, it is necessary to loosen the lock nut in the face of the idler pulley. After adjusting

the belt tension, tighten the lock nut in the face of the idler pulley.

NOTE: *1980 California Datsuns come equipped with special fan belts which, if loose, generate friction heat by slipping and shrink, taking up the slack. The air conditioning drive belt on those cars so equipped is adjusted in a similar fashion.*

REMOVAL AND INSTALLATION

The replacement of the inner belt on multi-belted engines may require the removal of the outer belts. To replace a drive belt loosen the pivot and mounting bolts of the component which the belt is driving, then, using a wooden lever or equivalent pry the component inward to relieve the tension on the drive belt, always be careful where you locate the pry bar not to damage the component. Slip the belt off the component pulley, match up the new belt with the old belt for length and width, these measurement must be the same or problems will occur when you go to adjust the new belt. After new belt is installed correctly adjust the tension of the new belt.

NOTE: *When replacing more than one belt it is a good idea, to make note or mark what belt goes around what pulley. This will make installation fast and easy.*

On air conditioning compressor and power steering pump belt replacements loosen the lock bolt for the adjusting bolt on idler pulley or power steering pump and then loosen the adjusting bolt. Pry pulley or pump inward to re-

Drive Belt Deflection	Adjust Deflection of Used Belt	Set Deflection of New Belt
Cooling fan mm(in)	12–15 (0.47–0.59)	8–11 (0.31–0.43)
Air conditioner compressor mm(in)	10–13 (0.39–0.51)	7–10 (0.28–0.39)
Power steering oil pump mm(in)	15–18 (0.59–0.71)	12–15 (0.47–0.59)
Aplied pushing force N (kg, lb)	98 (10, 22)	

Z-series 4-cyl. drive belt tensions

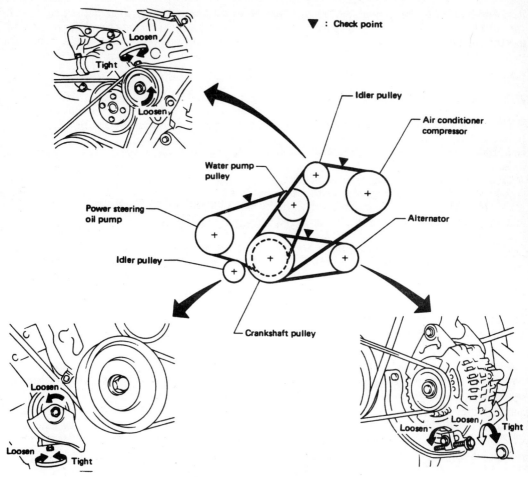

Checking drive belts—Maxima

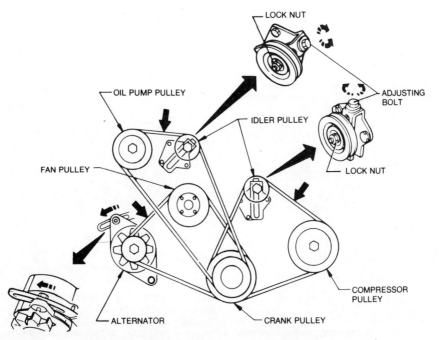

Maxima and 810 fan belt configuration. Note idler pulleys

lieve the tension on the drive belt, always be careful where you locate the pry bar not to damage the component or pulley.

Hoses
REMOVAL AND INSTALLATION

The upper and lower radiator hoses and all heater hoses should be checked for deterioration, leaks and loose hose clamps every 15,000 miles.

CAUTION: *When draining the coolant, keep in mind that cats and dogs are attracted by the ethylene glycol antifreeze, and are quite likely to drink any that is left in an uncovered container or in puddles on the ground. This will prove fatal in sufficient quantity. Always drain the coolant into a sealable container. Coolant should be reused unless it is contaminated or several years old.*

After engine is cold, remove the radiator cap and drain the radiator into a clean pan if you are going to reuse the old coolant. Remove the hose clamps and remove the hose by either cutting it off or twisting it to break its seal on the radiator and engine coolant inlets. When installing the new hose, do not overtighten the hose clamps or you might cut the hose or destroy the neck of the radiator. Refill the radiator with coolant, run the engine with the radiator cap on and then recheck the coolant level after engine has reached operating temperature which is about 5 minutes.

NOTE: *It always is good idea, to replace hose clamps when replacing radiator hoses.*

Air Conditioning System
SAFTEY WARNINGS

Because of the importance of the necessary safety precautions that must be exercised when working with air conditioning systems and R-12 refrigerant, a recap of the safety precautions are outlined.

1. Avoid contact with a charged refrigeration system, even when working on another part of

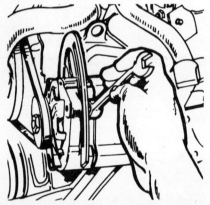

To adjust the belt tension or replace the belts, first loosen the component's (in this case, the alternator) mounting and adjusting bolts slightly

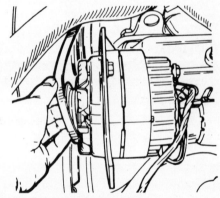

Slip the new belt over the pulleys

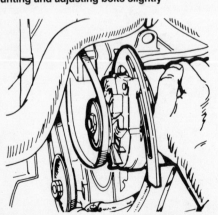

Next, push the component toward the engine and slip off the belt

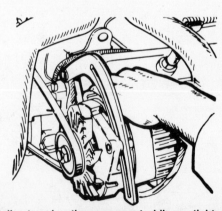

Pull outward on the component while you tighten the mounting bolts. Make sure the belt has proper deflection; a belt too tight will cause premature bearing failure in whatever component it drives, as well as premature belt wear

HOW TO SPOT WORN V-BELTS

V-Belts are vital to efficient engine operation—they drive the fan, water pump and other accessories. They require little maintenance (occasional tightening) but they will not last forever. Slipping or failure of the V-belt will lead to overheating. If your V-belt looks like any of these, it should be replaced.

Cracking or weathering

This belt has deep cracks, which cause it to flex. Too much flexing leads to heat build-up and premature failure. These cracks can be caused by using the belt on a pulley that is too small. Notched belts are available for small diameter pulleys.

Softening (grease and oil)

Oil and grease on a belt can cause the belt's rubber compounds to soften and separate from the reinforcing cords that hold the belt together. The belt will first slip, then finally fail altogether.

Glazing

Glazing is caused by a belt that is slipping. A slipping belt can cause a run-down battery, erratic power steering, overheating or poor accessory performance. The more the belt slips, the more glazing will be built up on the surface of the belt. The more the belt is glazed, the more it will slip. If the glazing is light, tighten the belt.

Worn cover

The cover of this belt is worn off and is peeling away. The reinforcing cords will begin to wear and the belt will shortly break. When the belt cover wears in spots or has a rough jagged appearance, check the pulley grooves for roughness.

Separation

This belt is on the verge of breaking and leaving you stranded. The layers of the belt are separating and the reinforcing cords are exposed. It's just a matter of time before it breaks completely.

HOW TO SPOT BAD HOSES

Both the upper and lower radiator hoses are called upon to perform difficult jobs in an inhospitable environment. They are subject to nearly 18 psi at under hood temperatures often over 280°F., and must circulate nearly 7500 gallons of coolant an hour—3 good reasons to have good hoses.

A good test for any hose is to feel it for soft or spongy spots. Frequently these will appear as swollen areas of the hose. The most likely cause is oil soaking. This hose could burst at any time, when hot or under pressure.

Swollen hose

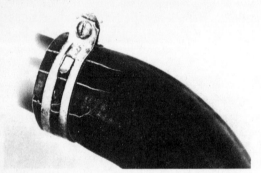

Cracked hoses can usually be seen but feel the hoses to be sure they have not hardened; a prime cause of cracking. This hose has cracked down to the reinforcing cords and could split at any of the cracks.

Cracked hose

Weakened clamps frequently are the cause of hose and cooling system failure. The connection between the pipe and hose has deteriorated enough to allow coolant to escape when the engine is hot.

Frayed hose end (due to weak clamp)

Debris, rust and scale in the cooling system can cause the inside of a hose to weaken. This can usually be felt on the outside of the hose as soft or thinner areas.

Debris in cooling system

the air conditioning system or vehicle. If a heavy tool comes into contact with a section of copper tubing or a heat exchanger, it can easily cause the relatively soft material to rupture.

2. When it is necessary to apply force to a fitting which contains refrigerant, as when checking that all system couplings are securely tightened, use a wrench on both parts of the fitting involved, if possible. This will avoid putting torque on refrigerant tubing. (It is advisable, when possible, to use tube or line wrenches when tightening these flare nut fittings.)

3. Do not attempt to discharge the system by merely loosening a fitting, or removing the service valve caps and cracking these valves. Precise control is possibly only when using the service gauges. Place a rag under the open end of the center charging hose while discharging the system to catch any drops of liquid that might escape. Wear protective gloves when connecting or disconnecting service gauge hoses.

4. Discharge the system only in a well ventilated area, as high concentrations of the gas can exclude oxygen and act as an anesthesia. When leak testing or soldering, this is particularly important, as toxic gas is formed when R-12 contacts any flame.

5. Never start a system without first verifying that both service valves are backseated, if equipped, and that all fittings are throughout the system are snugly connected.

6. Avoid applying heat to any refrigerant line or storage vessel. Charging may be aided by using water heated to less than +125°F (+51°C) to warm the refrigerant container. Never allow a refrigerant storage container to sit out in the sun, or near any other source of heat, such as a radiator.

7. Always wear goggles when working on a system to protect the eyes. If refrigerant contacts the eye, it is advisable in all cases to see a physician as soon as possible.

8. Frostbite from liquid refrigerant should be treated by first gradually warming the area with cool water, and then gently applying petroleum jelly. A physician should be consulted.

9. Always keep refrigerant can fittings capped when not in use. Avoid sudden shock to the can which might occur from dropping it, or from banging a heavy tool against it. Never carry a can in the passenger compartment of a car.

10. Always completely discharge the system before painting the vehicle (if the paint is to be baked on), or before welding anywhere near the refrigerant lines.

SYSTEM INSPECTION

CAUTION: *The compressed refrigerant used in the air conditioning system expands into the atmosphere at a temperature of −2°F (−19°C) or lower. This will freeze any surface, including your eyes, that it contacts. In addition, the refrigerant decomposes into a poisonous gas in the presence of a flame. Do not open or disconnect any part of the air conditioning system.*

Sight Glass Check

You can safely make a few simple checks to determine if your air conditioning system needs service. The tests work best if the temperature is warm (about 70°F).

NOTE: *If your vehicle is equipped with an aftermarket air conditioner, the following system check may not apply. You should contact the manufacturer of the unit for instructions on systems checks.*

1. Place the automatic transmission in **PARK** or the manual transaxle in **NEUTRAL**. Set the parking brake.

2. Run the engine at a fast idle (about 1,500 rpm) either with the help of a friend or by temporarily readjusting the idle speed screw.

The sight glass is located in the head of the receiver-dryer (arrow)

3. Set the controls for maximum cold with the blower on High.

4. Locate the sight glass in one of the system lines. Usually it is on the left alongside the top of the radiator.

5. If you see bubbles, the system must be recharged. Very likely there is a leak at some point. If it is determined that the system has a leak, it should be corrected as soon as possible. Leaks may allow moisture to enter and cause a very expensive rust problem.

6. If there are no bubbles, there is either no refrigerant at all or the system is fully charged. Feel the 2 hoses going to the belt-driven compressor. If they are both at the same temperature, the system is empty and must be recharged.

7. If one hose (high-pressure) is warm and the other (low-pressure) is cold, the system may be all right. However, you are probably making these tests because you think there is something wrong, so proceed to the next step.

8. Have an assistant in the car, turn the fan control on and off to operate the compressor clutch. Watch the sight glass.

9. If bubbles appear when the clutch is disengaged and disappear when it is engaged, the system is properly charged.

10. If the refrigerant takes more than 45 seconds to bubble when the clutch is disengaged, the system is overcharged. This usually causes poor cooling at low speeds.

NOTE: *Run the air conditioner for a few minutes, every 2 weeks or so, during the cold months. This avoids the possibility of the compressor seals drying out from lack of lubrication.*

GAUGE SETS

Most of the service work performed in air conditioning requires the use of a set of 2 gauges, one for the high (head) pressure side of the system, the other for the low (suction) side.

The low side gauge records both pressure and vacuum. Vacuum readings are calibrated from 0 to 30 in.Hg and the pressure graduations read from 0 to no less than 60 psi.

The high side gauge measures pressure from 0 to at last 600 psi.

Both gauges are threaded into a manifold that contains two hand shut-off valves. Proper manipulation of these valves and the use of the attached test hoses allow the user to perform the following services:

1. Test high and low side pressures.
2. Remove air, moisture, and contaminated refrigerant.
3. Purge the system (of refrigerant).
4. Charge the system (with refrigerant).

The manifold valves are designed so that they have no direct effect on gauge readings, but serve only to provide for, or cut off, flow of refrigerant through the manifold. During all testing and hook-up operations, the valves are kept in a close position to avoid disturbing the refrigeration system. The valves are opened only to purge the system or refrigerant or to charge it.

DISCHARGING THE SYSTEM

1. Close the high and low pressure valves of the manifold gauge fully.
2. Connect the 2 charging hoses of the manifold gauge to their respective service valves.
3. Slowly open both manifold gauge valves and discharge the refrigerant from the system. NOTE: *Do not allow the refrigerant to rush out. Otherwise, compressor oil will be discharged along with the refrigerant.*

EVACUATING THE SYSTEM

NOTE: *This procedure requires the use of a vacuum pump.*
1. Connect the manifold gauge set.
2. Discharge the system.
3. Connect the center service hose to the inlet fitting of the vacuum pump.
4. Turn both gauge set valves to the wide open position.
5. Start the pump and note the low side gauge reading.

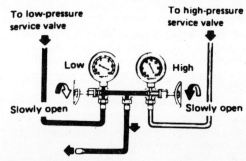

Discharging A/C system

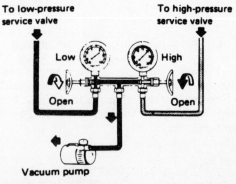

Evacuating A/C system

6. Operate the pump for a minimum of 30 minutes after the lowest observed gauge reading.

7. Leak test the system. Close both gauge set valves. Turn off the pump and note the low side gauge reading. The needle should remain stationary at the point at which the pump was turned off. If the needle drops to 0 rapidly, there is a leak in the system which must be repaired.

8. If the needle remains stationary for 3 to 5 minutes, open the gauge set valves and run the pump for at least 30 minutes more.

9. Close both gauge set valves, stop the pump and disconnect the gauge set. The system is now ready for charging.

CHARGING THE SYSTEM

CAUTION: *Never charge refrigerant through high-pressure side (discharge side) of the system since this will force refrigerant back into can and it may exploded.*

1. Close (clockwise) both gauge set valves.

2. Connect the gauge set.

3. Connect the center hose to the refrigerant can opener valve.

4. Make sure the can opener valve is closed, that is, the needle is raised, and connect the valve to the can. Open the valve, puncturing the can with the needle.

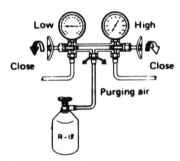

Purge air from center hose

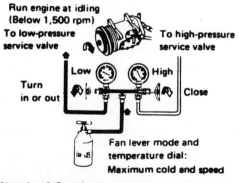

Charging A/C system

5. Loosen the center hose fitting at the pressure gauge, allowing refrigerant to purge the hose of air.

NOTE: *Always keep refrigerant can in upright position.*

6. Open the low side gauge set valve and the can valve.

7. Start the engine and turn the air conditioner to the maximum cooling mode. The compressor will operate and pull refrigerant gas into the system.

NOTE: *To help speed the process, the can may be placed, upright, in a pan of warm water, not exceeding 104°F (40°C).*

8. If more than one can of refrigerant is needed, close the can valve and gauge set low side valve when the can is empty and connect a new can to the opener. Repeat the charging process until the sight glass indicates a full charge.

9. When the charging process has been completed, close the gauge set valve and can valve. Run the system for at least 5 minutes to allow it to normalize.

10. Loosen both service hoses at the gauges to allow any refrigerant to escape. Remove the gauge set and install the dust caps on the service valves.

NOTE: *Multi-can dispensers are available which allow a simultaneous hook-up of up to four 1 lb. cans of R-12.*

CAUTION: *Never exceed the recommended maximum charge for the system. The maximum charge for systems is 2.4 lbs. The maximum charge for 1989 models systems is 2.2 lbs.*

Windshield Wipers

For maximum effectiveness and longest element life, the windshield and wiper blades should be kept clean. Dirt, tree sap, road tar and so on will cause streaking, smearing and blade deterioration if left on the glass. It is advisable to wash the windshield carefully with a commercial glass cleaner at least once a month. Wipe off the rubber blades with the wet rag afterwards. Do not attempt to move the wipers back and forth by hand; damage to the motor and drive mechanism will result.

If the blades are found to be cracked, broken or torn, they should be replaced immediately. Replacement intervals will vary with usuage, although ozone deterioration usually limits blade life to about one year. If the wiper pattern is smeared or streaked, or if the blade chatters across the glass, the blades should be replaced. It is easiest and most sensible to replace them in pairs.

There are basically three different types of wiper blade refills, which differ in their method

Troubleshooting Basic Air Conditioning Problems

Problem	Cause	Solution
There's little or no air coming from the vents (and you're sure it's on)	• The A/C fuse is blown • Broken or loose wires or connections • The on/off switch is defective	• Check and/or replace fuse • Check and/or repair connections • Replace switch
The air coming from the vents is not cool enough	• Windows and air vent wings open • The compressor belt is slipping • Heater is on • Condenser is clogged with debris • Refrigerant has escaped through a leak in the system • Receiver/drier is plugged	• Close windows and vent wings • Tighten or replace compressor belt • Shut heater off • Clean the condenser • Check system • Service system
The air has an odor	• Vacuum system is disrupted • Odor producing substances on the evaporator case • Condensation has collected in the bottom of the evaporator housing	• Have the system checked/repaired • Clean the evaporator case • Clean the evaporator housing drains
System is noisy or vibrating	• Compressor belt or mountings loose • Air in the system	• Tighten or replace belt; tighten mounting bolts • Have the system serviced

Sight glass condition
  Constant bubbles, foam or oil streaks
  Clear sight glass, but no cold air
  Clear sight glass, but air is cold
  Clouded with milky fluid
	
	• Undercharged system
	
	• No refrigerant at all
	• System is OK
	• Receiver drier is leaking dessicant
		
		• Charge the system
		
		• Check and charge the system
		
		• Have system checked

Large difference in temperature of lines	• System undercharged	• Charge and leak test the system
Compressor noise	• Broken valves • Overcharged • Incorrect oil level • Piston slap • Broken rings • Drive belt pulley bolts are loose	• Replace the valve plate • Discharge, evacuate and install the correct charge • Isolate the compressor and check the oil level. Correct as necessary. • Replace the compressor • Replace the compressor • Tighten with the correct torque specification
Excessive vibration	• Incorrect belt tension • Clutch loose • Overcharged • Pulley is misaligned	• Adjust the belt tension • Tighten the clutch • Discharge, evacuate and install the correct charge • Align the pulley
Condensation dripping in the passenger compartment	• Drain hose plugged or improperly positioned • Insulation removed or improperly installed	• Clean the drain hose and check for proper installation • Replace the insulation on the expansion valve and hoses
Frozen evaporator coil	• Faulty thermostat • Thermostat capillary tube improperly installed • Thermostat not adjusted properly	• Replace the thermostat • Install the capillary tube correctly • Adjust the thermostat
Low side low—high side low	• System refrigerant is low • Expansion valve is restricted	• Evacuate, leak test and charge the system • Replace the expansion valve
Low side high—high side low	• Internal leak in the compressor—worn	• Remove the compressor cylinder head and inspect the compressor. Replace the valve plate assembly if necessary. If the compressor pistons, rings or

Troubleshooting Basic Air Conditioning Problems (cont.)

Problem	Cause	Solution
Low side high—high side low (cont.)		cylinders are excessively worn or scored replace the compressor
	• Cylinder head gasket is leaking	• Install a replacement cylinder head gasket
	• Expansion valve is defective	• Replace the expansion valve
	• Drive belt slipping	• Adjust the belt tension
Low side high—high side high	• Condenser fins obstructed	• Clean the condenser fins
	• Air in the system	• Evacuate, leak test and charge the system
	• Expansion valve is defective	• Replace the expansion valve
	• Loose or worn fan belts	• Adjust or replace the belts as necessary
Low side low—high side high	• Expansion valve is defective	• Replace the expansion valve
	• Restriction in the refrigerant hose	• Check the hose for kinks—replace if necessary
	• Restriction in the receiver/drier	• Replace the receiver/drier
	• Restriction in the condenser	• Replace the condenser
Low side and high side normal (inadequate cooling)	• Air in the system	• Evacuate, leak test and charge the system
	• Moisture in the system	• Evacuate, leak test and charge the system

of replacement. One type has two release buttons, approximately one-third of the way up from the ends of the blade frame. Pushing the buttons down releases a lock and allows the rubber blade to be removed from the frame. The new blade slides back into the frame and locks in place.

The second type of refill has two metal tabs which are unlocked by squeezing them together. The rubber blade can then be withdrawn from the frame jaws. A new one is installed by inserting it into the front frame jaws and sliding it rearward to engage the remaining frame jaws. There are usually four jaws. Be certain when installing that the refill is engaged in all of them. At the end of its travel, the tabs will lock into place on the front jaws of the wiper blade frame.

The third type is a refill made from polycarbonate. The refill has a simple locking device at one end which flexes downward out of the groove into which the jaws of the holder fit, allowing easy release. By sliding the new refill through all the jaws and pushing through the slight resistance when it reaches the end of its travel, the refill will lock into position.

Regardless of the type of refill used, make sure that all of the frame jaws are engaged as the refill is pushed into place and locked. The metal blade holder and frame will scratch the glass if allowed to touch it.

Tire and Wheels
TIRE ROTATION

Tires should be rotated periodically to get the maximum tread lift available. A good time to do this is when changing over from regular tires to snow tires, or about once per year. If front end problems are suspected have them corrected before rotating the tires.

NOTE: *Mark the wheel position or direction of rotation on radial, or studded snow tires before removing them.*

Avoid overtightening the lug nuts to prevent damage to the brake disc or drum. Alloy wheels can also be cracked by overtightening. Tighten the lug nuts in a criss-cross sequence.

TIRE DESIGN

All 4 tires should be of the same construction type. Radial, bias, or bias-belted tires should not be mixed. The wheels must be the correct width for the tire. Tire dealers have charts of tire and rim compatibility. A mismatch can cause sloppy handling and rapid tire wear. The tread width should match the rim width (inside bead to inside bead) within an inch. For radial tires, the rim width should be 80% or less of the tire (not tread) width. The height (mounted diameter) of the new tires can greatly change speedometer accuracy, engine speed at a given road speed, fuel mileage, acceleration, and ground clearance. Tire manufacturers furnish full measurement specifications.

TIRE INFLATION

The tires should be checked frequently for proper air pressure. Make sure that the tires are cool, as you will get a false reading when the tires are heated because air pressure increases with temperature. A chart in the glove compartment or on the driver's door pillar gives the recommended inflation pressure. Maximum fuel economy and tire life will result if pressure is maintained at the highest figure given on chart. When checking pressures, do not neglect the spare tire. The tires should be checked before driving since pressure can increase as much as 6 pounds per square inch (psi) due to heat buildup.

NOTE: *Some spare tires require pressures considerably higher than those used in other tires.*

While you are checking the tire pressure, take a look at the tread. The tread should be wearing evenly across the tire. Excessive wear in the center of the tread could indicate over-inflation. Excessive wear on the outer edges could indicate underinflation. An irregular wear pattern is usually a sign of incorrect front wheel alignment or wheel balance. A front end that is out of alignment will usually pull the car to one side of a flat road when the steering wheel is released. Incorrect wheel balance will produce vibration in the steering wheel, while unbalanced rear wheels will result in floor or trunk vibration.

It is a good idea to have your own accurate

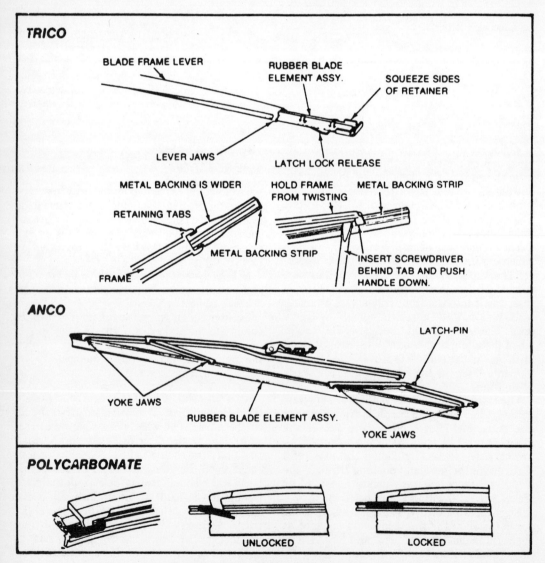

The three types of wiper blade retention

Tread wear indicators will appear when the tire is worn out

A penny works as well as anything for checking tire tread depth; when you can see the top of Lincoln's head, it's time for a new tire

Tread depth can be checked with an inexpensive gauge

gauge, and to check pressures weekly. Not all gauges on service station air pumps can be trusted.

Tires should be replaced when a tread wear indicator appears as a solid band across the tread.

CARE OF SPECIAL WHEELS

Aluminum wheels should be cleaned and waxed regularly. Do not use abrasive cleaners, as they could damage the protective coating. Inspect wheel rims regularly for dents or corrosion, which may cause loss of pressure, damage the tire bead, or sudden wheel failure.

FLUIDS AND LUBRICANTS

Oil and Fuel Recommendations

OIL

The SAE (Society of Automotive Engineers) grade number indicates the viscosity of the en-

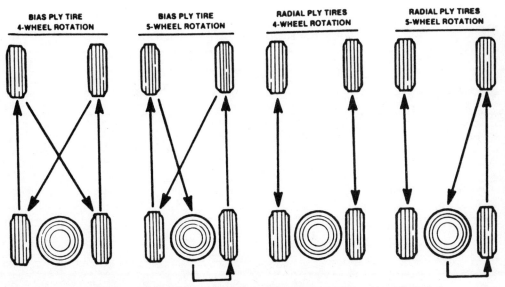

| BIAS PLY TIRE 4-WHEEL ROTATION | BIAS PLY TIRE 5-WHEEL ROTATION | RADIAL PLY TIRES 4-WHEEL ROTATION | RADIAL PLY TIRES 5-WHEEL ROTATION |

Tire rotation diagrams; note that radials should not be cross-switched

gine oil and thus its ability to lubricate at a given temperature. The lower the SAE grade number, the lighter the oil. The lower the viscosity, and the easier it is to crank the engine in cold weather.

Oil viscosities should be chosen from those oils recommended for the lowest anticipated temperatures during the oil change interval.

Multi-viscosity oils (10W-30, 20W-50, etc.) offer the important advantage of being adaptable to temperature extremes. They allow easy starting at low temperatures, yet they give good protection at high speeds and engine temperatures. This is a decided advantage in changeable climates or in long distance touring.

Choose the viscosity range carefully, based upon the lowest expected temperature for the time of year. If the lowest expected temperature is 0°F (−18°C), you should use 10W-30. If it is 50°F (10°C), as in spring and fall, you can use 20W-40 and 20W-50 for their extra guarantee of sufficient viscosity at high temperatures.

Troubleshooting Basic Wheel Problems

Problem	Cause	Solution
The car's front end vibrates at high speed	• The wheels are out of balance • Wheels are out of alignment	• Have wheels balanced • Have wheel alignment checked/adjusted
Car pulls to either side	• Wheels are out of alignment • Unequal tire pressure • Different size tires or wheels	• Have wheel alignment checked/adjusted • Check/adjust tire pressure • Change tires or wheels to same size
The car's wheel(s) wobbles	• Loose wheel lug nuts • Wheels out of balance • Damaged wheel • Wheels are out of alignment • Worn or damaged ball joint • Excessive play in the steering linkage (usually due to worn parts) • Defective shock absorber	• Tighten wheel lug nuts • Have tires balanced • Raise car and spin the wheel. If the wheel is bent, it should be replaced • Have wheel alignment checked/adjusted • Check ball joints • Check steering linkage • Check shock absorbers
Tires wear unevenly or prematurely	• Incorrect wheel size • Wheels are out of balance • Wheels are out of alignment	• Check if wheel and tire size are compatible • Have wheels balanced • Have wheel alignment checked/adjusted

Troubleshooting Basic Tire Problems

Problem	Cause	Solution
The car's front end vibrates at high speeds and the steering wheel shakes	• Wheels out of balance • Front end needs aligning	• Have wheels balanced • Have front end alignment checked
The car pulls to one side while cruising	• Unequal tire pressure (car will usually pull to the low side) • Mismatched tires • Front end needs aligning	• Check/adjust tire pressure • Be sure tires are of the same type and size • Have front end alignment checked
Abnormal, excessive or uneven tire wear See "How to Read Tire Wear"	• Infrequent tire rotation • Improper tire pressure • Sudden stops/starts or high speed on curves	• Rotate tires more frequently to equalize wear • Check/adjust pressure • Correct driving habits
Tire squeals	• Improper tire pressure • Front end needs aligning	• Check/adjust tire pressure • Have front end alignment checked

The API (American Petroleum Institute) designation indicates the classification of engine oil used under certain given operating conditions. Only oils designated for use Service SE should be used. Oils of the SE type perform a variety of functions inside the engine in addition to the basic function as a lubricant. Through a balanced system of metallic detergents and polymeric dispersants, the oil prevents the formation of high and low temperature deposits and also keeps sludge and particles of dirt in suspension. Acids, particularly sulfuric acid, as well as other byproducts of combustion, are neutralized. Both the SAE grade number and the API designation can be found on top of the oil can.

Diesel engines all require SE engine oil. In addition, the oil must qualify for ACC rating.

The API has a number of different diesel engine ratings, including CB, CC and CD. Any of these other oils are fine as long as the designation CC appears on the can along with them. Do not use oil labeled only SE or only CC. Both designations must always appear together.

NOTE: *As of late 1980, the API has come out with a new designation of motor oil, SF. Oils designated for use Service SF are equally acceptable in your Datsun/Nissan. Non-detergent or straight mineral oils should not be used in your car.*

SYNTHETIC OIL

There are excellent synthetic and fuel efficient oils available that, under the right circumstances, can help provide better fuel mileage and better engine protection. However, these

Tire Size Comparison Chart

| | "Letter" sizes | | | Inch Sizes | Metric-inch Sizes | | |
"60 Series"	"70 Series"	"78 Series"	1965–77	"60 Series"	"70 Series"	"80 Series"
		Y78-12	5.50-12, 5.60-12 6.00-12	165/60-12	165/70-12	155-12
		W78-13	5.20-13	165/60-13	145/70-13	135-13
		Y78-13	5.60-13	175/60-13	155/70-13	145-13
			6.15-13	185/60-13	165/70-13	155-13, P155/80-13
A60-13	A70-13	A78-13	6.40-13	195/60-13	175/70-13	165-13
B60-13	B70-13	B78-13	6.70-13 6.90-13	205/60-13	185/70-13	175-13
C60-13	C70-13	C78-13	7.00-13	215/60-13	195/70-13	185-13
D60-13	D70-13	D78-13	7.25-13			
E60-13	E70-13	E78-13	7.75-13			195-13
			5.20-14	165/60-14	145/70-14	135-14
			5.60-14	175/60-14	155/70-14	145-14
			5.90-14			
A60-14	A70-14	A78-14	6.15-14	185/60-14	165/70-14	155-14
	B70-14	B78-14	6.45-14	195/60-14	175/70-14	165-14
	C70-14	C78-14	6.95-14	205/60-14	185/70-14	175-14
D60-14	D70-14	D78-14				
E60-14	E70-14	E78-14	7.35-14	215/60-14	195/70-14	185-14
F60-14	F70-14	F78-14, F83-14	7.75-14	225/60-14	200/70-14	195-14
G60-14	G70-14	G77-14, G78-14	8.25-14	235/60-14	205/70-14	205-14
H60-14	H70-14	H78-14	8.55-14	245/60-14	215/70-14	215-14
J60-14	J70-14	J78-14	8.85-14	255/60-14	225/70-14	225-14
L60-14	L70-14		9.15-14	265/60-14	235/70-14	
	A70-15	A78-15	5.60-15	185/60-15	165/70-15	155-15
B60-15	B70-15	B78-15	6.35-15	195/60-15	175/70-15	165-15
C60-15	C70-15	C78-15	6.85-15	205/60-15	185/70-15	175-15
	D70-15	D78-15				
E60-15	E70-15	E78-15	7.35-15	215/60-15	195/70-15	185-15
F60-15	F70-15	F78-15	7.75-15	225/60-15	205/70-15	195-15
G60-15	G70-15	G78-15	8.15-15/8.25-15	235/60-15	215/70-15	205-15
H60-15	H70-15	H78-15	8.45-15/8.55-15	245/60-15	225/70-15	215-15
J60-15	J70-15	J78-15	8.85-15/8.90-15	255/60-15	235/70-15	225-15
	K70-15		9.00-15	265/60-15	245/70-15	230-15
L60-15	L70-15	L78-15, L84-15	9.15-15			235-15
	M70-15	M78-15				255-15
		N78-15				

Note: Every size tire is not listed and many size comparisons are approximate, based on load ratings. Wider tires than those supplied new with the vehicle, should always be checked for clearance.

advantages come at a price, which can be three or four times the price per quart of conventional motor oils.

Before pouring any synthetic oils into your car's engine, you should consider the condition of the engine and the type of driving you do. Also, check the car's warranty conditions regarding the use of synthetics.

Generally, it is best to avoid the use of synthetic oil in both brand new and older, high

Capacities

Year	Model	Engine Crankcase (qts)		Transmission (pts)			Drive Axle (pts)●	Fuel Tank (gals)●	Cooling System (qts)
		With Filter	Without Filter	4-Spd	5-Spd	Automatic (total capacity)			
1973	610	5.0	4.5	4.25	—	11.8	1.75/2.75	13.8/14.5	9.0
1974	610	4.5	—	4.25	—	10.9	1.75/2.2	14.5/13.5	6.88
	710	4.45	—	4.25	—	10.9	2.75	13.25	7
1975	610	4.5	4.0	4.25	—	11.8	1.75/2.75	14.5/13.7	7.25
	710	5.0	4.5	4.25	—	11.8	2.75	13.2/11.8	7.25
1976	610	4.5	4.0	4.25	—	11.8	1.75/2.2	14.5/13.75	7.25
1976–77	710	4.5	4.0	4.25 ①	—	11.8	2.75	13.25/11.8	7.25
1977–78	810	6.0	5.5	3.6	—	11.8	2.75/2.2	15.9/14.5	11
1977–79	200SX	4.5	4.0	—	3.6	11.8	2.75	15.9	7.9
1978–79	510	4.5	4.0	3.6	3.6	11.8	2.4	13.2	9.4
1979–80	810	5.9	5.25	3.7	4.25	11.8	2.0	15.9/14.5	11
1980	510	4.5	4.0	3.15	3.6	11.8	2.4	13.25	9.25
	200SX	4.4	4.1	—	4.25	11.8	2.4	14/15.9	10
1981	810	5.25	4.75	—	4.25	11.8	2.1	16.4/15.9	11.6
	510	4.6	4.1	3.1	3.6	11.8	2.4	13.25	9.25
	200SX	4.6	4.1	—	4.25	11.8	2.4	14/15.9	10
1982	810	5.0②	4.5②	—	4.25	11.8	2.1	16.4/15.9	11.6③
	200SX	4.5	3.9	—	4.25	11.8	2.1	14.0/15.9	10
1983–84	Maxima	5.25②	4.75②	—	4.25	14.75	2.1	16.5/16.0	11.5③
	200SX	⑦	⑧	—	4.25	⑥	⑤	14	④
1985–88	Maxima	4.5	4.125	—	10	14¾	—	15⅞	9¾
	200SX	3.875	3.375	—	4½	14¾	⑨	14	9.1
1989	Maxima	4.5	4.125	—	10	15.5	—	15⅞	8¾
	240SX	3.5	3.2	—	5⅛	17.5	5.5	15⅞	7⅛

●When two numbers are given, first number is sedan and second number is station wagon or hatchback
① 3.6 pts., 1977
② Figures are for gasoline engine. For diesel engine: w/filter—6.5 qts., w/o filter—6.0 qts.
③ Figure is for gasoline engine. For diesel engine: 11.0 qts.
④ 1983: 10 qt. w/heater; 9¼ qts. w/out heater
   1984: 9⅛ qt.
⑤ Solid rear axle: 2⅛ pt.
   IRS: 2¾ pt.
⑥ 1983: 11.6 pts.
   1984: 14.75 pts.
⑦ 1983: 4.5
   1984: 4.25
⑧ 1983: 3.9
   1984: 3.75
⑨ R180—2⅛
   R200—2¾

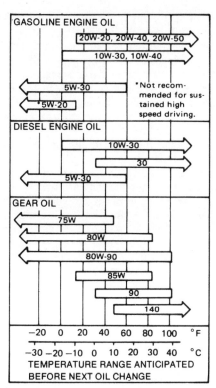

Oil viscosity chart, all except CA20E, CA18ET

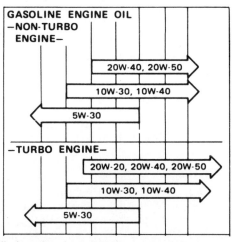

Oil viscosity chart, CA20E and CA18ET (turbo) engines, 200SX

Recommended Lubricants

Item	Lubricant
Engine Oil	API "SE" or "SF" API "SE/CC" or "SF/CC" (diesel)
Manual Transmission	SAE 80W GL-4 or SAE 80W/90 GL-4
Automatic Transmission	DEXRON® ATF
Rear Axle	SAE 80W GL-5 or SAE 80W/90 GL-5
Power Steering Reservoir	DEXRON® ATF
Brake and Clutch Fluid	DOT 3
Antifreeze	Ethylene Glycol
Chassis Lubrication	NLGI #2
Steering Gear	SAE 80W GL-4 or SAE 80W/90 GL-4

will leak and use more with a slippery synthetic oil inside.

Consider your type of driving. If most of your accumulated mileage is on the highway at higher, steadier speeds, a synthetic oil will reduce friction and probably help deliver better fuel mileage. Under such ideal highway conditions, the oil change interval can be extended, as long as the oil filter will operate effectively for the extended life of the oil. If the filter can't do its job for this extended period, dirt and sludge will build up in your engine's crankcase, sump, oil pump and lines, no matter what type of oil is used. If using synthetic oil in this manner, you should continue to change the oil filter at the recommended intervals.

Cars used under harder, stop-and-go, short hop circumstances should always be serviced more frequently, and for these cars synthetic oil may not be a wise investment. Because of the necessary shorter change interval needed for this type of driving, you cannot take advantage of the long recommended change interval of most synthetic oils.

Finally, most synthetic oils are not compatible with conventional oils and cannot be added to them. This means you should always carry a couple of quarts of synthetic oil with you while on a long trip, as not all service stations carry this oil.

FUEL

All Datsun gasoline engined models covered in this book have been designed to run on regular low-lead or unleaded fuel, 1973-79, with the exception of those models built for use in California (1975 and later) which require the use of unleaded fuel. All 1980 and later models must

mileage engines. New engines require a proper break-in, and the synthetics are so slippery that they can prevent this. Most manufacturers recommend that you wait at least 5,000 miles before switching to a synthetic oil. Conversely, older engines are looser and tend to use more oil. Synthetics will slip past worn parts more readily than regular oil, and will be used up faster. If your car already leaks and/or uses oil (due to worn parts and bad seals or gaskets), it

also use only unleaded fuel. 1975 and later California cars and all 1980 and later models utilize a catalytic converter. The use of leaded fuel will plug the catalyst, rendering it inoperative, and will increase the exhaust back pressure to the point where engine output will be severely reduced. The minimum octane requirement for all engines using unleaded fuel is 91 RON (87 CLC). All unleaded fuels sold in the U.S. are required to meet this minimum octane rating.

The use of a fuel too low in octane (a measurement of anti-knock quality) will result in spark knock. Since many factors such as altitude, terrain, air temperature and humidity affect operating efficiency, knocking may result even though the recommended fuel is being used. If persistent knocking occurs, it may be necessary to switch to a higher grade of fuel. Continuous or heavy knocking may result in engine damage.

NOTE: *Your engine's fuel requirement can change with time, mainly due to carbon buildup, which will in turn increase the temperatures in the combustion chamber and change the compression ratio. If your engine pings, knocks, or runs on, switch to a higher grade of fuel. Sometimes just changing brands will cure the problem. If it becomes necessary to retard the timing from specifications, don't change it more than about two degrees. Retarded timing will reduce power output and fuel mileage, in addition to increasing the engine temperature.*

Datsun diesels require the exclusive use of diesel fuel. At NO time should gasoline be substituted or mixed with diesel fuel. Two grades of diesel fuel are manufactured, #1 and #2, although #2 is generally more available. Better fuel economy results from the use of #2 grade fuel. In some northern parts of the U.S. and in most parts of Canada, #1 grade fuel is available in the winter or, if not, a winterized blend of #2 grade is supplied. When the temperature falls below 20°F (–7°C), #1 grade or winterized #2 grade fuel are the only fuels that can be used. Temperatures below 20° F. cause unwinterized #2 to thicken (it actually gels), blocking the fuel lines and preventing the engine from running.

Diesel Cautions:

• Do not use heating oil in your car. While in some cases, home heating refinement levels equal those of diesel fuel, at times they are far below diesel engine requirements. The result of using dirty home heating oil will be a clogged fuel system, in which case the entire system may have to be dismantled and cleaned. There may also be engine running problems such as ignition lag (see below).

• Do not use ether or starting assist fluids in your car.

• Do not use any fuel additives recommended for use in gasoline engines.

It is normal that the engine noise level is louder during the warm-up period in winter. This occurs due to a normal diesel phenomenon known as ignition lag. It relates to the lower temperatures reached through compression if the combustion chambers are cold, and normally does not indicate any engine abnormality. It is also normal that whitish-blue smoke may be emitted from the exhaust shortly after starting and during warm-up. The amount of smoke depends upon the outside temperature.

If the increases in noise and smoke levels at cold temperatures seem extreme, you may wish to check on the fuel's cetane rating (you may have to ask your fuel dealer what the rating is). This is a measurement of the fuel's ability to ignite at low temperatures. The rating should be at least 42 (higher cetane numbers are more desirable).

Engine

OIL LEVEL CHECK

The best time to check the engine oil is before operating the engine or after it has been sitting for at least 10 minutes in order to gain an accurate reading. This will allow the oil to drain back in the crankcase. To check the engine oil level, make sure that the vehicle is resting on a level surface, remove the oil dipstick, wipe it clean and reinsert the stick firmly for an accurate reading. The oil dipstick has two marks to indicate high and low oil level. If the oil is at or below the "low level" mark on the dipstick, oil should be added as necessary. The oil level should be maintained in the safety margin, neither going above the "high level" mark or below the "low level" mark.

OIL AND FILTER CHANGE

The Datsun/Nissan factory maintenance intervals (every 7,500 miles or 6 months) specify changing the oil filter at every second oil change after the initial service. We recommend replac-

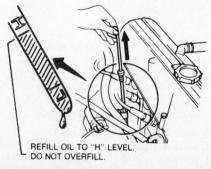

REFILL OIL TO "H" LEVEL.
DO NOT OVERFILL.

Oil dipstick markings

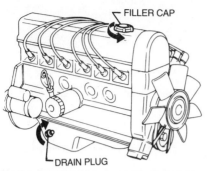

Oil filler cap and drain plug locations, six cylinder engines shown. Four cylinder engines similar. Note filter location on side of block

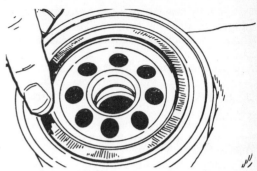

Coat the new oil filter gasket with clean oil

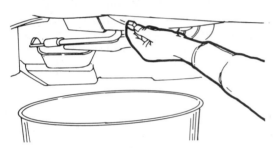

By keeping an inward pressure on the plug as you unscrew it, oil won't escape past the threads

Install the new oil filter by hand

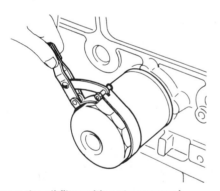

Remove the oil filter with a strap wrench

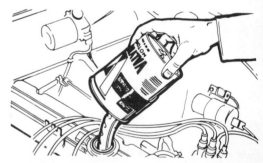

Add oil through the capped opening in the camshaft (valve) cover

ing the oil filter with every oil change. For the small price of an oil filter, it's cheap insurance to replace the filter at every oil change. One of the larger filter manufacturers points out in its advertisements that not changing the filter leaves 1 quart of dirty oil in the engine. This claim is true and should be kept in mind when changing your oil.

NOTE: *On turbocharged engines factory maintenance intervals are every 5,000 miles/ 6 months and diesel maintenance intervals are 7,500 miles/6 months.*

1. Run the engine until it reaches normal operating temperature.

2. Jack up the front of the car and support it on safety stands if necessary to gain access to the filter.

3. Slide a drain pan of at least 6 quarts capacity under the oil pan.

CAUTION: *The EPA warns that prolonged contact with used engine oil may cause a number of skin disorders, including cancer! You should make every effort to minimize your exposure to used engine oil. Protective gloves should be worn when changing the oil. Wash your hands and any other exposed skin areas as soon as possible after exposure to used engine oil. Soap and water, or waterless hand cleaner should be used.*

4. Loosen the drain plug. Turn the plug out

by hand. By keeping an inward pressure on the plug as you unscrew it, oil won't escape past the threads and you can remove it without being burned by hot oil.

5. Allow the oil to drain completely and then install the drain plug. Don't overtighten the plug or you'll be buying a new pan or a trick replacement plug for damaged threads.

6. Using a strap wrench, remove the oil filter. Keep in mind that it's holding about one quart of dirty, hot oil.

7. Empty the old filter into the drain pan and dispose of the filter and old oil.

NOTE: *One ecologically desirable solution to the used oil disposal problem is to find a cooperative gas station owner who will allow you to dump your used oil into his tank or take the oil to a reclamation center (often at garages and gas stations.*

8. Using a clean rag, wipe off the filter adapter on the engine block. Be sure that the rag doesn't leave any lint which could clog an oil passage.

9. Coat the rubber gasket on the filter with fresh oil. Spin it onto the engine *by hand*; when the gasket touches the adapter surface give it another ½–¾ turn. No more or you'll squash the gasket and it will leak.

10. Refill the engine with the correct amount of fresh oil. See the Capacities chart.

11. Crank the engine over several times and then start it. If the oil pressure indicator light doesn't go out or the pressure gauge shows zero, shut the engine down and find out what's wrong.

12. If the oil pressure is OK and there are no leaks, shut the engine off and lower the car.

Manual Transmission/Transaxle
FLUID RECOMMENDATION

For manual transmission/transaxles be sure to use fluid with an API GL-4 rating.

LEVEL CHECK

You should inspect the manual transmission gear oil at 7,500 miles or 6 months (12 months or 15,000 miles 1980 and later), at this point you should correct the level or replace the oil as necessary. The lubricant level should be even with the bottom of the filler hole. Hold in on the filler plug when unscrewing it. When you are sure that all of the threads of the plug are free of the transaxle case, move the plug away from the case slightly. If lubricant begins to flow out of the transmission, then you know it is full. If not, add the correct gear oil as necessary

Inspect the manual transaxle gear oil at 12 months or 15,000 miles at this point you should

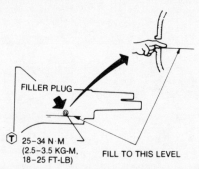

FILLER PLUG

25–34 N·M
(2.5–3.5 KG-M,
18–25 FT-LB)   FILL TO THIS LEVEL

Transmission oil should be level with the bottom of the filler plug on manual transmissions

also correct the level. To check the oil level in the manual transaxle you have to remove speedometer cable at the clutch housing and look in the transaxle case to determine if fluid is needed. Refer below to the picture of the speedometer pinion for the correct level.

Only on the 1989 Maxima model you do not check it with the above procedure. On this year it is checked like a manual transmission by removing the filler plug to determine the fluid level.

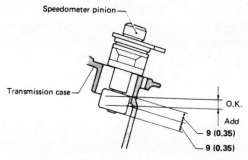

Speedometer pinion

Transmission case

O.K.
Add
9 (0.35)
9 (0.35)
Unit: mm (in)

Checking oil level manual transaxle

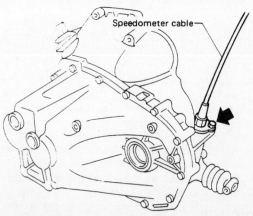

Speedometer cable

Remove speedometer cable to check manual transaxle level

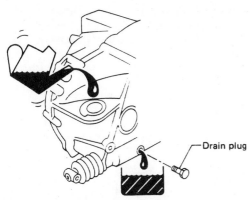

Drain plug location on manual transaxle

DRAIN AND REFILL

NOTE: *It is recommended that the manual transmission/transaxle fluid be changed every 30,000 miles if the vehicle is used in severe service. You may also want to change it if you have bought your car used or if it has been driven in water deep enough to reach the transaxle case.*

1. Run the engine until it reaches normal operating temperature then turn key to the **OFF** position.

2. Jack up the front of the car and support it on safety stands level, if necessary to gain access.

3. Remove the filler plug from the left-side of the transmission/transaxle to provide a vent.

4. The drain plug is located on the bottom of the transmission/transaxle case. Place a pan under the drain plug and remove it.

CAUTION: *The oil will be HOT. Push up against the threads as you unscrew the plug to prevent leakage.*

5. Allow the oil to drain completely. Clean off the plug and replace it. DO NOT OVERTIGHTEN PLUG.

6. Fill the transmission/transaxle with gear oil through the filler plug hole. Use API service GL-4 gear oil of the proper viscosity . This oil usually comes in a squeeze bottle with a long nozzle. If yours isn't, use a plastic squeeze bottle (the type used in the kitchen). Refer to the "Capacities" chart for the amount of oil needed.

7. The oil level should come up to the edge of the filler hole. You can stick your finger in to verify this. Watch out for sharp threads.

8. Replace the filler plug. Lower the vehicle, dispose of the old oil in the same manner as old engine oil.

9. Test drive the vehicle, stop and check for leaks.

Automatic Transmission/Transaxle
FLUID RECOMMENDATIONS

All automatic transmission/transaxle, use Dexron®II ATF (automatic transmission fluid)

LEVEL CHECK

The fluid level in the automatic transmission (or transaxle on late model Maximas) should be checked every 6 months or 7,500 miles (12 months or 15,000 miles, 1980 and later), whichever comes first. The transmission/transaxle has a dipstick for fluid level checks.

1. Drive the car until it is at normal operating temperature. The level should not be checked immediately after the car has been driven for a long time at high speed, or in city traffic in hot weather. In those cases, the transaxle should be given a half hour to cool down.

2. Stop the car, apply the parking brake, then shift slowly through all gear positions, ending in Park. Let the engine idle for about five minutes with the transmission/transaxle in Park. The car should be on a level surface.

3. With the engine still running, remove the dipstick, wipe it clean, then reinsert it, pushing it fully home.

4. Pull the dipstick again and, holding it horizontally, read the fluid level.

5. Cautiously feel the end of the dipstick to determine the temperature. Note that on Datsuns/Nissans there is a scale on each side, HOT on one, COLD on the other. If the fluid level is not in the correct area, more will have to be added.

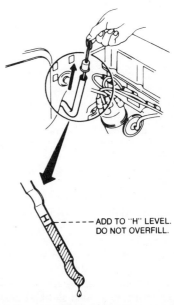

ADD TO "H" LEVEL.
DO NOT OVERFILL.

Remove the automatic transmission dipstick with engine warm and idling in Park

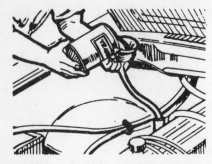

Add automatic transmission fluid through the transmission dipstick tube. You'll probably need a funnel

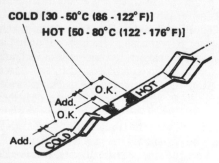

COLD [30 - 50°C (86 - 122°F)]

HOT [50 - 80°C (122 - 176°F)]

Dipstick from late model automatic transaxle

6. Fluid is added through the dipstick tube. You will probably need the aid of a spout or a long necked funnel. Be sure that whatever you pour through is perfectly clean and dry. Use an automatic transmission fluid marked DEXRON®II. Add fluid slowly, and in small amounts, checking the level frequently between additions. Do not overfill, which will cause foaming, fluid loss, slippage, and possible transmission damage. It takes only one pint to raise the level from L to H when the transaxle is hot.

DRAIN AND REFILL

NOTE: *It is recommended that the automatic transmission/transaxle fluid be changed every 30,000 miles if the vehicle is used in severe service. You may also want to change it if you have bought your car used or if it has been driven in water deep enough to reach the transaxle case.*

Transmission

1. There is no drain plug. The fluid pan must be removed. Partially remove the pan screws until the pan can be pulled down at one corner. Place a container under the transmission, lower a rear corner of the pan, and allow the fluid to drain.

2. After draining, remove the pan screws completely, and remove the pan and gasket.

3. Clean the pan thoroughly and allow it to air dry. If you wipe it out with a rag you risk

leaving bits of lint in the pan which will clog the tiny hydraulic passages in the transmission.

NOTE: *It is very important to clean the old gasket from the oil pan, to prevent leaks upon installation, a razor blade does a excellent job at this.*

4. Install the pan using a new gasket. If you decide to use sealer on the gasket apply it only in a very thin bead running to the outside of the pan screw holes. Tighten the pan screws evenly

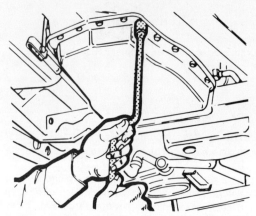

Remove the pan to drain the automatic transmission

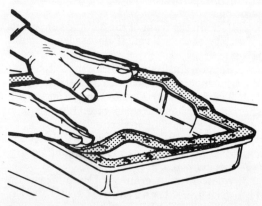

Install a new gasket

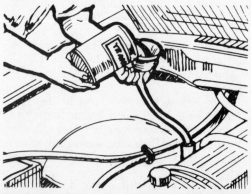

Add fluid through the transmission dipstick tube

in rotation from the center outwards, to 36-60 in. lbs.

5. It is a good idea to measure the amount of fluid drained to determine how much fresh fluid to add. This is because some part of the transmission, such as the torque converter, will not drain completely, and using the dry refill amount specified in the Capacities chart may lead to overfilling. Fluid is added through the dipstick tube. Make sure that the funnel, hose, or whatever you are using is completely clean and dry before pouring transmission fluid through it. Use DEXRON®II automatic transmission fluid.

6. Replace the dipstick after filling. Start the engine and allow it to idle. Do NOT race the engine. Check the installation of the new pan gasket for leaks.

7. After the engine has idled for a few minutes, shift the transmission slowly through the gears, then return the lever to Park. With the engine idling, check the fluid level on the dipstick. It should be between the H and L marks. If below L, add sufficient fluid to raise the level to between the marks.

8. Drive the car until it is at operating temperature. The fluid should be at the H mark. If not, add sufficient fluid until this is the case. Be careful not to overfill. Overfilling causes slippage, overheating, and seal damage.

NOTE: *If the drained fluid is discolored (brown or black), thick, or smells burnt, serious transmission problems due to overheating should be suspected. Your car's transmission should be inspected by a transmission specialist to determine the cause.*

Transaxle

To change the the transaxle fluid on early models the transaxle fluid oil pan must be removed and the gasket must be replaced. This procedure is similar to the transmission procedure with the exception of the oil pan location. On late models there is a drain plug located on the side of the transaxle case. Remove the drain plug and allow the fluid to drain then refill with new fluid, start engine and correct the fluid level as necessary. Before attempting this service read the complete section above on "DRAIN AND RFILL" procedure.

Rear Drive Axle

FLUID RECOMMENDATIONS

Use only standard GL-5 hypoid type gear oil: SAE 80W or SAE 80W/90.

LEVEL CHECK

The oil in the differential should be checked at least every 7,500 miles (15,000 miles, 1980 and later).

1. With the car on a level surface, remove the filler plug from the back side of the differential.

2. If the oil begins to trickle out of the hole, there is enough. Otherwise, carefully insert your finger (watch out for sharp threads) into the hole and check that the oil is up to the bottom edge of the filler hole.

3. If not, add oil through the hole until the level is at the edge of the hole. Most gear oils come in a plastic squeeze bottle with a nozzle; making additions is simple. You can also use a common kitchen baster. Use only the specified fluid.

4. Replace the plug and check for leaks.

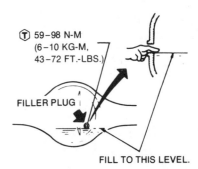

Ⓣ 59–98 N-M
(6–10 KG-M,
43–72 FT.-LBS.)

FILLER PLUG

FILL TO THIS LEVEL.

Checking the fluid level in the differential on models with a solid rear axle

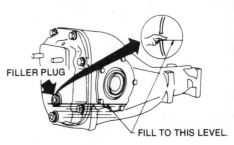

FILLER PLUG

FILL TO THIS LEVEL.

Ⓣ 39–59 N-M
(4–6 KG-M, 29–43 FT. LBS.)

Checking the fluid level in the differential on models with independent rear suspension

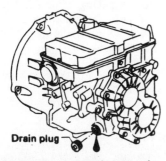

Drain plug

Drain plug location automatic transaxle

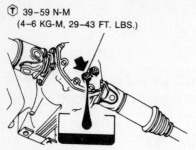

39–59 N-M
(4–6 KG-M, 29–43 FT. LBS.)

Draining the differential fluid on models with independent rear suspension

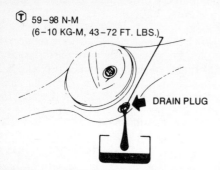

59–98 N-M
(6–10 KG-M, 43–72 FT. LBS.)

DRAIN PLUG

Draining the differential fluid on models with a solid rear axle

DRAIN AND REFILL

The axle lubricant should be changed according to the schedule in the Maintenance Intervals chart. You may also want to change it if you have bought your car used, or if it has been driven in water deep enough to reach the axle.

1. Park the car on a level surface. Place a pan of at least two quarts capacity underneath the drain plug. The drain plug is located on the center rear of the differential carrier, just below the filler plug on some models, on others it can be found at the bottom of the carrier. Remove the drain plug.

2. Allow the lubricant to drain completely.

3. Install the drain plug. Tighten it so that it will not leak, but do not overtighten. If you have a torque wrench, recommended torque is 29-43 ft. lbs.

4. Refill the differential housing with API GL-5 gear oil of the proper viscosity. The correct level is to the edge of the filler hole.

5. Install the filler plug. Tighten to 29-43 ft. lbs.

Cooling System

FLUID RECOMMENDATION

The cooling fluid or antifreeze, should be changed every 30,000 miles or 24 months. When replacing the fluid, use a mixture of 50% water and 50% ethylene glycol antifreeze.

Coolant protection can be checked with a simple, float-type tester

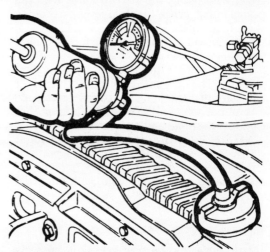

The system should be pressure tested at least once a year

Check the freezing protection rating at least once a year, preferably just before the winter sets in. This can be done with an antifreeze tester (most service stations will have one on hand and will probably check it for you, if not, they are available at an auto parts store). Maintain a protection rating of at least −20°F (−29°C) to prevent engine damage as a result of freezing and to assure the proper engine operating temperature.

It is also a good idea to have the the cooling system check for leaks. A pressure test gauge is available to perform such a task. Checking and repairing a coolant leak in the early stages while save time and money.

LEVEL CHECK

Check the coolant level every 3,000 miles or once a month. In hot weather operation, it may be a good idea to check the level once a week. Check for loose connections and signs of deterioration of the coolant hoses. Maintain the coolant level ¾-1¼" below the level of the filler neck when the engine is cold. If the engine is equipped with a coolant recovery bottle check the coolant level in the bottle when the engine is cold, the level should be up to the MAX mark. If the bottle is empty, check the level in the radiator and refill as necessary, then fill the bottle up to the MAX level.

CAUTION: *Never remove the radiator cap when the vehicle is hot or overheated. Wait until it has cooled. Place a thick cloth over the radiator cap to shield yourself from the heat and turn the radiator cap, SLIGHTLY, until the sound of escaping pressure can be heard. DO NOT turn any more; allow the pressure to release gradually. When no more pressure can be heard escaping, remove the cap with the heavy cloth, CAUTIOUSLY.*

NOTE: *Never add cold water to an overheated engine while the engine is not running.*

After filling the radiator, run the engine until it reaches normal operating temperature, to make sure that the thermostat has opened and all the air is bled from the system.

If the engine is hot, cover the radiator cap with a rag

Some radiator caps have pressure release levers

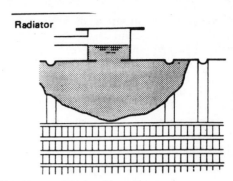

Checking coolant level in radiator

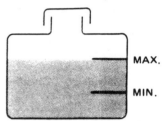

Checking coolant level in recovery bottle

DRAIN AND REFILL

To drain the cooling system, allow the engine to cool down **BEFORE ATTEMPTING TO REMOVE THE RADIATOR CAP.** Then turn the cap until it hisses. Wait until all pressure is off the cap before removing it completely.

CAUTION: *To avoid burns and scalding, always handle a warm radiator cap with a heavy rag.*

1. At the dash, set the heater TEMP control lever to the fully HOT position. If the vehicle is equipped with automatic air conditioning turn ignition switch ON and set temperature at MAXIMUM. Then turn the ignition swith OFF.

2. With the radiator cap removed, drain the radiator by loosening the petcock at the bottom of the radiator.

CAUTION: *When draining the coolant, keep in mind that cats and dogs are attracted by the ethylene glycol antifreeze, and are quite likely to drink any that is left in an uncovered container or in puddles on the ground. This will prove fatal in sufficient quantity. Always drain the coolant into a sealable container. Coolant should be reused unless it is contaminated or several years old.*

3. Close the petcock. Be careful not to damage the petcock when closing.

NOTE: *On Maxima models (1985-89) and 240SX (1989) model slowly pour coolant through coolant filler neck to release air in the system with the air relief bolt or plug loosen.*

4. Refill the system with a 50/50 mix of ethylene glycol antifreeze; fill the system to ¾-1¼″ from the bottom of the filler neck. Reinstall the radiator cap.

NOTE: *If equipped with a fluid reservoir tank, fill the reservior tank up to the MAX level.*

5. Operate the engine at 2,000 rpm for a few minutes and check the system for signs of leaks and for the correct level.

FLUSHING AND CLEANING THE SYSTEM

To flush the system you must first, drain the cooling system but do not close the petcock valve on the bottom of the radiator. You can insert a garden hose, in the filler neck, turn the

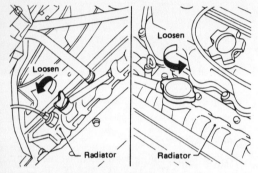

Petcock and radiator cap location

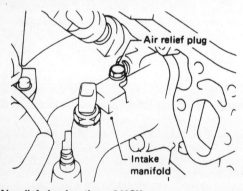

Air relief plug location—240SX

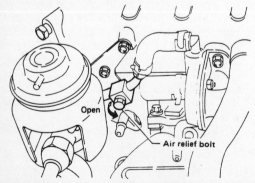

Air relief bolt location—1985–89 Maxima

water pressure on moderately then start the engine. After about 10 minutes or less the water coming out of the bottom of the radiator should be clear. Shut off the engine and water supply, allow the radiator to drain then refill and bleed the system as necessary.

NOTE: *DO NOT allow the engine to overheat. The supply of water going in the top must be equal in amount to the water draining from the bottom, this way the radiator will always be full when the engine us running.*

Usually flushing the radiator using water is all that is necessary to maintain the proper condition in the cooling system.

Radiator flush is the only cleaning agent that can be used to clean the internal portion of the radiator. Radiator flush can be purchased at any auto supply store. Follow the directions on the label.

Brake and Clutch Master Cylinder
FLUID RECOMMENDATION

When adding or changing the fluid in the systems, use a quality brake fluid of the DOT 3 specifications.

NOTE: *Never reuse old brake fluid.*

LEVEL CHECK

The brake and clutch master cylinders are located under the hood, in the left rear section of the engine compartment. They are made of translucent plastic so that the levels may be checked without removing the tops. The fluid level in both reservoirs should be checked at least every 7,500 miles (15,000 miles, 1980 and later). The fluid level should be maintained at the upper most mark on the side of the reservoir. Any sudden decrease in the level indicates a possible leak in the system and should be checked out immediately.

NOTE: *Some models may have two reservoirs for the brake master cylinder, while other models (those with an automatic transmis-*

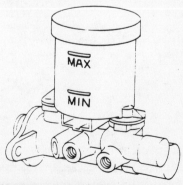

Typical brake master cylinder

sion/transaxle) will not have a clutch master cylinder at all.

When making additions of brake fluid, use only fresh, uncontaminated brake fluid meeting or exceeding DOT 3 standards. Be careful not to spill any brake fluid on painted surfaces, as it eats the paint. Do not allow the brake fluid container or the master cylinder reservoir to remain open any longer than necessary. Brake fluid absorbs moisture from the air, reducing its effectiveness and causing corrosion in the lines.

Power Steering System

FLUID RECOMMENDATION

When adding or changing the power steering fluid, use Dexron®II ATF (Automatic Transmission Fluid).

LEVEL CHECK

The power steering hydraulic fluid level is checked with a dipstick inserted into the pump reservoir cap. The level can be checked with the fluid either warm or cold. The car should be parked on a level surface. Check the fluid level every 6 months or 7,500 miles (12 months or 15,000 miles, 1980 and later), whichever comes first.

1. With the engine off, unscrew the dipstick and check the level. If the engine is warm, the level should be within the proper range on the HOT scale. If the engine is cold, the level should be within the proper range on the COLD scale (see illustrations).

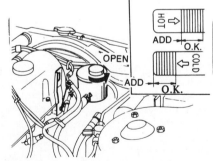

Power steering reservoir dipstick markings on all models but the 1981 and later 200SX

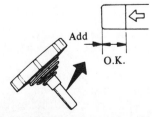

1981 and later 200SX power steering dipstick markings

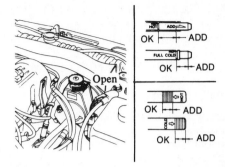

Power steering reservoir dipstick markings on the 1981 and later 810 and Maxima

2. If the level is low, add DEXRON®II ATF until correct. Be careful not to overfill, which will cause fluid loss and seal damage.

STEERING GEAR BOX EXCEPT RACK AND PINION TYPE

FLUID RECOMMENDATIONS

When fill the steering gear box use only standard GL-4 hypoid type gear oil, SAE 80W or SAE 80W/90.

LEVEL CHECK

Check the level of the lubricant in the steering gear every 12,000 miles (15,000 miles, 1979 and later). If the level is low, check for leakage. Any oily film is not considered a leak; solid grease must be present. The lubricant is added and checked through the filler plug hole in the top of the steering gearbox.

Chassis Greasing

The manufacturer doesn't install lubrication fittings in lube points on the steering linkage or suspension. You can buy metric threaded fit-

💧 : CHECK FLUID LEAKS.

🫗 : ADD FLUID.

Check the fluid level in the steering gearbox through the filler hole in the top

tings to grease these points or use a pointed, rubber tip end on your grease gun. Lubricate all joints equipped with a plug, every 15,000 miles or once a year with NLGI No. 2 (Lithium base) grease. Replace the plugs after lubrication.

Body Lubrication

Lubricate all locks and hinges with multipurpose grease every 6,000 miles (7,500 miles, 1980 and later).

Wheel Bearings

Clean and repack wheel bearings every 30,000 miles on rear wheel drive vehicles. In order to clean and repack the front wheel bearings on the rear wheel drive vehicle the wheel bearings must be removed from the wheel hub. You should also check that the wheel bearings operate smoothly and their is no excess amount of play (looseness) in the bearing assemnbly before removing the wheel bearing. To remove the wheel bearing refer to Chapter 8.

On front wheel drive vehicles the front wheel bearings are different than on rear wheel drive vehicles the front hub must be removed. The rear wheel bearings on front wheel drive vehicles are similar to the front bearings on rear wheel drive vehicles. Refer to Chapter 8 for both of the above procedures.

TRAILER TOWING

General Recommendations

Your car was primarily designed to carry passengers and cargo. It is important to remember that towing a trailer will place additional loads on your vehicle's engine, drive train, steering, braking and other systems. However, if you find it necessary to tow a trailer, using the proper equipment is a must.

Local laws may require specific equipment such as trailer brakes or fender mounted mirrors. Check your local laws.

NOTE: *A trailering brochure with information on trailer towing, special equipment required and optional equipment available can be obtained from your Nissan dealer*

Trailer Weight

Never allow the total trailer load to exceed 1,000 lbs. The total trailer load equals trailer weight plus its cargo weight.

Hitch Weight

Figure the hitch weight to select a proper hitch. Hitch weight is usually 9-11% of the trailer gross weight and should be measured with the trailer loaded. Hitches fall into three types: those that mount on the frame and rear bumper or the bolt-on or weld-on distribution type used for larger trailers. Axle mounted or clamp-on bumper hitches should never be used.

Check the gross weight rating of your trailer. Tongue weight is usually figured as 10% of gross trailer weight. Therefore, a trailer with a maximum gross weight of 1,000 lb. will have a maximum tongue weight of 100 lb. Class I trailers fall into this category.

When you've determined the hitch that you'll need, follow the manufacturer's installation instructions, exactly, especially when it comes to fastener torques. The hitch will subjected to a lot of stress and good hitches come with hardened bolts. Never substitute an inferior bolt for a hardened bolt.

Cooling
ENGINE

One of the most common, if not THE most common, problems associated with trailer towing is engine overheating.

If you have a standard cooling system, without an expansion tank, you'll definitely need to get an aftermarket expansion tank kit, preferably one with at least a 2 quart capacity. These kits are easily installed on the radiator's overflow hose, and come with a pressure cap designed for expansion tanks.

Another helpful accessory is a Flex Fan. These fan are large diameter units are designed to provide more airflow at low speeds, with blades that have deeply cupped surfaces. The blades then flex, or flatten out, at high speed, when less cooling air is needed. These fans are far lighter in weight than stock fans, requiring less horsepower to drive them. Also, they are far quieter than stock fans.

If you do decide to replace your stock fan with a flex fan, note that if your car has a fan clutch, a spacer between the flex fan and water pump hub will be needed.

Aftermarket engine oil coolers are helpful for prolonging engine oil life and reducing overall engine temperatures. Both of these factors increase engine life.

While not absolutely necessary in towing Class I and some Class II trailers, they are recommended for heavier Class II and all Class III towing.

Engine oil cooler systems consist of an adapter, screwed on in place of the oil filter, a remote filter mounting and a multi-tube, finned heat exchanger, which is mounted in front of the radiator or air conditioning condenser.

TRANSMISSION

An automatic transmission is usually recommended for trailer towing. Modern automatics have proven reliable and, of course, easy to operate, in trailer towing.

The increased load of a trailer, however, causes an increase in the temperature of the automatic transmission fluid. Heat is the worst enemy of an automatic transmission. As the temperature of the fluid increases, the life of the fluid decreases.

It is essential, therefore, that you install an automatic transmission cooler.

The cooler, which consists of a multi-tube, finned heat exchanger, is usually installed in front of the radiator or air conditioning compressor, and hooked inline with the transmission cooler tank inlet line. Follow the cooler manufacturer's installation instructions.

Select a cooler of at least adequate capacity, based upon the combined gross weights of the car and trailer.

Cooler manufacturers recommend that you use an aftermarket cooler in addition to, and not instead of, the present cooling tank in your radiator. If you do want to use it in place of the radiator cooling tank, get a cooler at least two sizes larger than normally necessary.

NOTE: *A transmission cooler can, sometimes, cause slow or harsh shifting in the transmission during cold weather, until the fluid has a chance to come up to normal operating temperature. Some coolers can be purchased with or retrofitted with a temperature bypass valve which will allow fluid flow through the cooler only when the fluid has reached operating temperature, or above.*

Handling A Trailer

Towing a trailer with ease and safety requires a certain amount of experience. It's a good idea to learn the feel of a trailer by practicing turning, stopping and backing in an open area such as an empty parking lot.

PUSHING AND TOWING

Push Starting

This is the last recommended method of starting a car and should be used only in an extreme case. Chances of body damage are high, so be sure that the pushcar's bumper does not override your bumper. If your Nissan/Datsun has an automatic transmission it cannot be push started. In an emergency, you can start a manual transmission car by pushing. With the bumpers evenly matched, get in your car, switch on the ignition, and place the gearshift in Second or Third gear. Do not engage the clutch. Start off slowly. When the speed of the car reaches about 15-20 mph, release the clutch gradually enough to avoid a lot of shock to the drivetrain.

NOTE: *Although they may have manual transmissions, 1976 and later California models and all models made in 1980 and later should never be push started. These models are all equipped with a catalytic converter which will be severely damaged if they are push started.*

Towing

On rear wheel drive vehicles the car can be flat-towed safely (with the transmission in Neutral) from the front at speeds of 20 mph or less. The car must either be towed with the rear wheels off the ground or the driveshaft disconnected if: towing speeds are to be over 20 mph, or towing distance is over 50 miles, or transmission or rear axle problems exist.

When towing the car on its front wheels, the steering wheel must be secured in a straight-ahead position and the steering column unlocked. Tire-to-ground clearance should not exceed 6″ during towing.

On front wheel drive vehicles never tow with rear wheels raised (with front drive wheels on the ground) as this may cause serious and expensive damage to the the transaxle. On front wheel drive models Datsun/Nissan recommends that the vehicle be towed with the driving (front) wheels off the ground.

On all models there are towing hooks under the vehicle to attact tow hooks. If any question concerning towing are in doubt, check with the "Towing Procedure Manual" at your local Datsun/Nissan dealer.

JACKING

Never use the tire changing jack (the little jack supplied with the car) for anything other than changing a flat out on the road. These jacks are simply not safe enough for any type of vehicle service except tire changing!

The service operations in this book often require that one end or the other, or both, of the car be raised and safely supported. For this reason a hydraulic floor jack of at least 1½ ton capacity is as necessary as a spark plug socket to you, the do-it-yourself owner/mechanic. The cost of these jacks (invest in a good quality unit) is actually quite reasonable considering how they pay for themselves again and again over the years.

Along with a hydraulic floor jack should be at

JUMP STARTING A DEAD BATTERY

The chemical reaction in a battery produces explosive hydrogen gas. This is the safe way to jump start a dead battery, reducing the chances of an accidental spark that could cause an explosion.

Jump Starting Precautions

1. Be sure both batteries are of the same voltage.
2. Be sure both batteries are of the same polarity (have the same grounded terminal).
3. Be sure the vehicles are not touching.
4. Be sure the vent cap holes are not obstructed.
5. Do not smoke or allow sparks around the battery.
6. In cold weather, check for frozen electrolyte in the battery. Do not jump start a frozen battery.
7. Do not allow electrolyte on your skin or clothing.
8. Be sure the electrolyte is not frozen.

CAUTION: *Make certain that the ignition key, in the vehicle with the dead battery, is in the OFF position. Connecting cables to vehicles with on-board computers will result in computer destruction if the key is not in the OFF position.*

Jump Starting Procedure

1. Determine voltages of the two batteries; they must be the same.
2. Bring the starting vehicle close (they must not touch) so that the batteries can be reached easily.
3. Turn off all accessories and both engines. Put both cars in Neutral or Park and set the handbrake.
4. Cover the cell caps with a rag—do not cover terminals.
5. If the terminals on the run-down battery are heavily corroded, clean them.
6. Identify the positive and negative posts on both batteries and connect the cables in the order shown.
7. Start the engine of the starting vehicle and run it at fast idle. Try to start the car with the dead battery. Crank it for no more than 10 seconds at a time and let it cool off for 20 seconds in between tries.
8. If it doesn't start in 3 tries, there is something else wrong.
9. Disconnect the cables in the reverse order.
10. Replace the cell covers and dispose of the rags.

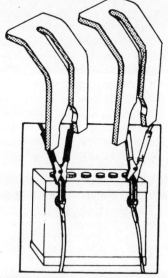

Side terminal batteries occasionally pose a problem when connecting jumper cables. There frequently isn't enough room to clamp the cables without touching sheet metal. Side terminal adaptors are available to alleviate this problem and should be removed after use.

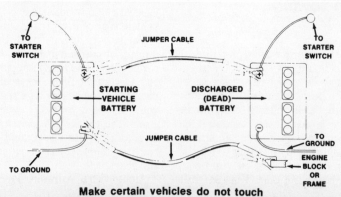

Make certain vehicles do not touch

This hook-up for negative ground cars only

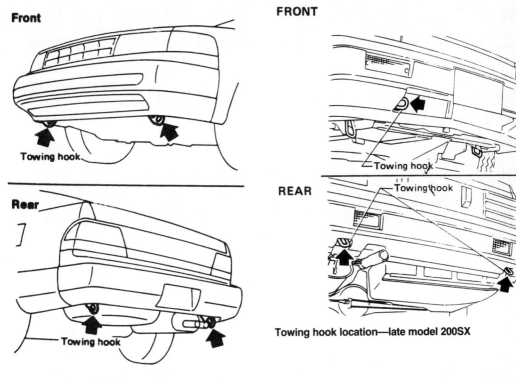

Front

Towing hook

Rear

Towing hook

Towing hook location—front wheel drive model

FRONT

Towing hook

REAR

Towing hook

Towing hook location—late model 200SX

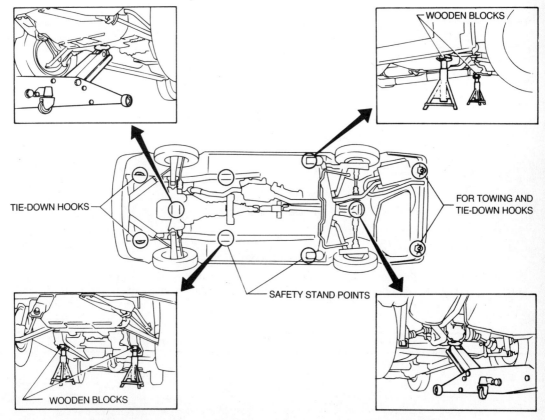

WOODEN BLOCKS

TIE-DOWN HOOKS

FOR TOWING AND
TIE-DOWN HOOKS

SAFETY STAND POINTS

WOODEN BLOCKS

200SX jacking points, 1984 independent rear suspension (IRS) model shown

least two sturdy jackstands. These are a necessity if you intend to work underneath the car. Never work under the car when it is only supported by a jack!

Drive-on ramps are an alternative method of raising the front end of the car. They are commercially available or can be fabricated from heavy lumber or steel. Be sure to always block the wheels when using ramps.

CAUTION: *NEVER use concrete cinder blocks to support the car. They are likely to break if the load is not evenly distributed. They should never be trusted when you are underneath the car!*

SEDAN

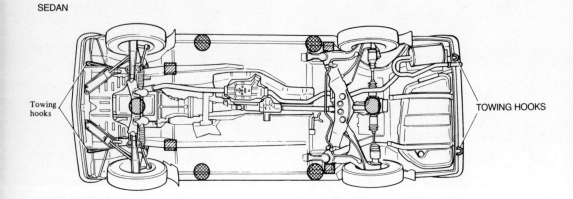

WAGON

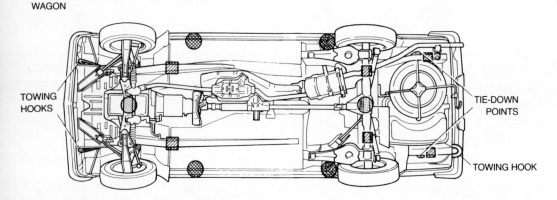

⊛ : JACK-UP POINT FOR PANTOGRAPH JACK

◉ : JACK-UP POINT FOR GARAGE JACK

▨ : SUPPORTABLE POINT FOR SAFETY STAND

810 and Maxima jacking points

Maintenance Intervals Chart

Intervals are for number of months or thousands of miles, whichever comes first.

NOTE: Heavy-duty operation (trailer towing, prolonged idling, severe stop and start driving) should be accompanied by a 50% increase in maintenance. Cut the interval in half for these conditions.

Maintenance	Service Interval
Air Cleaner (Replace)	24,000 miles 1973–78 30,000 miles 1979 and later
Air Induction Valve Filter (Replace) ①	30,000 miles
PCV Valve (Replace)	24,000 miles (No service interval for cars built in 1980 and later years)

Maintenance Intervals Chart (cont.)

Maintenance	Service Interval
Diesel Crankcase Emission Control Valve (Replace)	30,000 miles
Evaporative Emissions System Check Fuel/Vapor Lines Carbon Canister Filter (Replace)	12,000 miles 1973–79 30,000 miles 1980 and later 24,000 miles 1973–79
Battery Fluid Level (Check) Specific Gravity (Check) Cables and Clamps (Check)	Once a Month Once a Year Once a Year
Belt Tension (Adjust)	12 mo./12,000 miles 1973–79 12 mo./24,000 miles 1980–83 12 mo./30,000 miles 1984–89
Hoses (Check)	15,000 miles
Radiator Coolant Check Change	Weekly 24 mo./30,000 miles
Engine Oil and Filter Check Oil Level Change	Weekly 6 mo./7,500 mi. gasoline 3,000 mi. diesel 6 mo./5,000 mi.
Manual Transmission Check Change	6 mo./7,500 mi. 1973–79 12 mo./15,000 mi. 1980 and later 30,000 mi. Heavy Duty operation
Automatic Transmission Check Change	6 mo./7,500 mi. 1973–79 12 mo./15,000 mi. 1980 and later 30,000 mi. Heavy Duty operation
Brake and Clutch Fluid Check	7,500 mi. 1973–79 15,000 mi. 1980 and later
Rear Axle Check Change	6 mo./7,500 mi. 1973–79 12 mo./15,000 mi. 1980 and later 30,000 mi. Heavy Duty operation
Steering Gear Check	12,000 mi. 1973–78 15,000 mi. 1979 and later
Power Steering Fluid Check	6 mo./7,500 mi. 1973–78 12 mo./15,000 mi. 1980 and later
Power Steering Lines and Hoses	12 mo./15,000 mi.
Tires Rotate	6,000 mi.
Fuel Filter Change (gasoline) Change (diesel)	24,000 mi. 1973–78 ② 30,000 mi. 1979 and later ② 30,000 mi. ②
Chassis Lubrication Lubricate Inspect seals	12 mo./15,000 mi. 1973–76 12 mo./24,000 mi. 1977–79

① On models so equipped
② Change the filter as soon as there is any indication of clogging by abnormal dirt in the fuel

Engine Performance and Tune-Up

T2

TUNE-UP PROCEDURES

In order to extract the full measure of performance and economy from your engine it is essential that it is properly tuned at regular intervals. A regular tune-up will keep your Datsun's engine running smoothly and will prevent the annoying breakdowns and poor performance often associated with an unmaintained engine.

NOTE: *All 1973-77 models use the conventional breaker point ignition system except for 1975-77 California cars and 1977 810's which use an electronic system. All models made in 1978 and later (except diesels) utilize this system also.*

On 1979 and earlier cars, a complete tune-up should be performed at least every 15,000 miles (24,000 km) or twelve months, whichever comes first.

On 1980 and later models the interval is 30,000 miles (48,000 km).

This interval should be halved if the car is operated under severe conditions such as trailer towing, prolonged idling, start-and-stop driving, or if starting or running problems are noticed. It is assumed that the routine maintenance described in Chapter 1 has been kept up, as this will have a decided effect on the results of a tune-up. All of the applicable steps of a tune-up should be followed in order, as the result is a cumulative one.

If the specifications on the underhood tune-up sticker in the engine compartment of your car disagree with the Tune-Up Specifications chart in this chapter, the figures on the sticker must be used. The sticker often reflects changes made during the production run.

Other than the periodic changing of oil, air and fuel filters as outlined in Chapter 1, diesel engines do not require a tune-up, as there is no ignition system.

Spark Plugs

A typical spark plug consists of a metal shell surrounding a ceramic insulator. A metal electrode extends downward through the center of the insulator and protrudes a small distance. Located at the end of the plug and attached to the side of the outer metal shell is the side electrode. This side electrode bends in a 90° so its tip is even with, parallel to, the tip of the center electrode. This distance between these two electrodes is called spark plug gap. The spark plug in no way produces a spark but merely provides a gap across which the current can arc. The coil produces 20,000-25,000 V (transistorized ignition produces considerably more voltage than the standard type, approximately 50,000 volts), which travels to the distributor where it is distributed through the spark plug wires to the plugs. The current passes along the center electrode and jumps the gap to the side electrode and, in so doing, ignites the air/fuel mixture in the combustion chamber. All plugs used in Datsun/Nissan have a resistor built into the center electrode to reduce interference to any nearby radio and television receivers. The resistor also cuts down on erosion of plug electrodes caused by excessively long sparking. Resistor spark plug wiring is original equipment on all Datsun/Nissan.

Spark plug life and efficiency depend upon the condition of the engine and the temperatures to which the plug is exposed. Combustion chamber temperatures are affected by many factors such as compression ratio of the engine, fuel/air mixtures, exhaust emission equipment, and the type of driving you do. Spark plugs are designed and classified by number according to the heat range at which they will operate most efficiently. The amount of heat that the plug absorbs is determined by the length of the lower insulator. The longer the insulator (it ex-

Tune-Up Specifications

When analyzing compression test results, look for uniformity among cylinders, rather than specific pressures.

Year	Model	Spark Plug Type	Gap (in.)	Distributor Point Dwell (deg)	Point Gap (in.)	Ignition Timing (deg) ● MT	AT	Fuel Pump Pressure (psi)	Idle Speed (rpm) MT	AT▲	Valve Clearance (in.) In	Ex	Percentage of CO at Idle
1973	610	BP-6ES	0.028–0.031	49–55	0.018–0.022	5B	5B	2.6–3.4	800	650	0.008 COLD 0.010 HOT	0.010 COLD 0.012 HOT	1.5
1974	610	B6ES	0.028–0.031	49–55	0.018–0.022	12B	12B	3.0–3.8	750	650	0.008 COLD 0.010 HOT	0.010 COLD 0.012 HOT	3.0
	710	B6ES	0.028–0.031	49–55	0.018–0.022	12B	12B	2.6–3.4	800	650	0.008 COLD 0.010 HOT	0.010 COLD 0.012 HOT	1.5
1975	610	BP-6ES	0.031–0.035	49–55 ①	0.018–② 0.022	12B	12B	3.8	750	650	0.010 HOT	0.012 HOT	2.0
	710	BP-6ES	0.031–0.035	49–55 ①	0.018–② 0.022	12B	12B	3.8	750	650	0.010 HOT	0.012 HOT	2.0
1976	610	BP-6ES	0.031–③ 0.035	49–55 ①	0.018–② 0.022	12B	12B	3.8	750	650	0.008 COLD 0.010 HOT	0.010 COLD 0.012 HOT	2.0
	710	BP-6ES	0.031–③ 0.035	49–55 ①	0.018–② 0.022	12B	12B	3.8	750	650	0.008 COLD 0.010 HOT	0.010 COLD 0.012 HOT	2.0
1977	710	BP-6ES	0.039–④ 0.043	49–55 ①	0.018–② 0.022	12B	12B	3.8	600 ⑤	600 ⑥	0.008 COLD 0.010 HOT	0.010 COLD 0.012 HOT	1.0 ⑦
	810	BP-6ES	0.039–0.043	ELECTRONIC	②	10B	10B	35 EFI	700	650	0.008 COLD 0.010 HOT	0.010 COLD 0.012 HOT	1.0 ⑧
	200SX	BP-6ES	0.039–④ 0.043	49–55 ①	0.018–② 0.022	9B ⑨	12B	3.8	600 ⑤	600 ⑥	0.008 COLD 0.010 HOT	0.010 COLD 0.012 HOT	1.0 ⑦
1978	510	BP-6ES	0.039–④ 0.043	ELECTRONIC	②	12B	12B	3.8	600	600	0.010 HOT	0.012 HOT	1.0
	810	B6ES	0.039–0.043	ELECTRONIC	②	8B ⑩	8B ⑩	36 EFI	700	650	0.010 HOT	0.012 HOT	1.0 ⑧
	200SX	BP-6ES	0.039–④ 0.043	ELECTRONIC	②	12B	12B	3.8	600	600	0.010 HOT	0.012 HOT	1.0

Tune-Up Specifications (cont.)

When analyzing compression test results, look for uniformity among cylinders, rather than specific pressures.

Year	Model	Spark Plug Type	Gap (in.)	Distributor Point Dwell (deg)	Point Gap (in.)	Ignition Timing (deg)● MT	AT	Fuel Pump Pressure (psi)	Idle Speed (rpm) MT	AT▲	Valve Clearance (in.) In	Ex	Percentage of CO at Idle
1979	510	BP-6ES	0.039–[4] 0.043	ELECTRONIC	[2]	11B[9]	12B	3.8	600	600	0.010 HOT	0.012 HOT	1.0
	810	B6ES	0.039– 0.043	ELECTRONIC	[2]	10B	10B	37[22] EFI	700	650	0.010 HOT	0.012 HOT	2.0[8]
	200SX	BP-6ES	0.039–[4] 0.043	ELECTRONIC	[2]	9B[9]	12B	3.8	600	600	0.010 HOT	0.012 HOT	1.0
1980	510 (L20B)	BPR6ES	0.031– 0.035	ELECTRONIC	[2]	12B	12B	3.8	600	600	0.010 HOT	0.012 HOT	1.0
	510 (Z20S)	BP-6ES	0.031– 0.035	ELECTRONIC	[2]	8B[11]	8B[11]	3.8	600	600	0.012 HOT	0.012 HOT	1.5[12]
	810	BP6ES-11	0.039– 0.043	ELECTRONIC	[2]	10B	10B	37[22] EFI	700	650	0.010 HOT	0.012 HOT	1.0[12]
	200SX	BP-6ES	0.031– 0.035	ELECTRONIC	[2]	8B[11]	8B[11]	37[22] EFI	700	700	0.012 HOT	0.012 HOT	1.3[12]
1981	510	BP-6ES[13]	0.031– 0.035	ELECTRONIC	[2]	6B	6B	3.8	600	600	0.012 HOT	0.012 HOT	[14]
	810	BP6ES-11	0.039– 0.043	ELECTRONIC	[2]	10B	10B	37[22] EFI	700	650	0.010 HOT	0.012 HOT	[14]
	200SX	BP-6ES[13]	0.031– 0.035	ELECTRONIC	[2]	6B[15]	6B[15]	37[22] EFI	750	700	0.012 HOT	0.012 HOT	[16]
1982–84	810 Maxima	BPR-6ES-11	0.039– 0.043	ELECTRONIC	[2]	8B	8B	37[22] EFI	700	650	0.010 HOT	0.012 HOT	[14]
	200SX	[17]	0.031– 0.035[20]	ELECTRONIC	[2]	8B[19]	8B[19]	37[22] EFI	750	700[18]	0.012 HOT	0.012 HOT	[14]
1985–88	Maxima	BCPR-6ES-11 [21]	.039– .043	ELECTRONIC	[2]	20B	20B [26]	37[22]	700	650	N.A.	N.A.	[14]
	200SX	[23]	.039– .043	ELECTRONIC	[2]	[24] 15B	[24] 15B	37[22]	750	700	.012 [27]	.012 [27]	[14]

1989	Maxima	BKR6ES-11	.039–.043	ELECTRONIC	②	15B	15B	37②	750	750㉖	N.A.	N.A.	⑭
	240SX	ZFR50-11	.039–.043	ELECTRONIC	②	15B	15B	37②	750	750㉖	N.A.	N.A.	⑭

● At idle
▲ In drive
N.A. Nonadjustable
① California cars are equipped with electronic ignition—dwell is pre-set and non-adjustable
② Electronic ignition—Air gap: 0.008–0.016 in. (1975–78)
   0.012–0.020 in. (1979 and later)
③ All models with electronic ignition—0.039–0.043 in.
④ 0.031–0.035 in.—Canada
⑤ 750—Canada
⑥ 650—Canada
⑦ 2%—Canada
⑧ 0.5%—California
⑨ 12B—California and Canada
⑩ 10B—California
⑪ 6B—California
⑫ Idle mixture screw is pre-set and nonadjustable on California cars
⑬ BPR6ES—Canada
⑭ Idle mixture screw is pre-set and nonadjustable
⑮ 8B—Canada
⑯ U.S.A.—idle mixture screw is pre-set and nonadjustable. Canada—1.3%
⑰ 1982–83: Intake side BPR–6ES; exhaust side BPR–5ES
   1984 and later: Intake side BCPR6ES-11
      Exhaust side BCPR5ES-11
⑱ 630 rpm high altitudes
⑲ CA20E (1984 and later): 0° BTDC w/vacuum hose disconnected
   CA18ET (1984 and later): 15° BTDC
⑳ 0.039–0.043 in.—1984 and later
㉑ Hot BCPR5ES-11 and cold BCPR7ES-11 are also approved
㉒ Note that fuel pressure is 37 p.s.i. above intake manifold pressure. Pressure must be measured in conjunction with a vacuum gauge.
㉓ Intake Side—BCPR6ES-11
   Exhaust Side—BCPR5ES-11
㉔ VG30E engine is 20° BTDC
㉕ For 18ET (Turbo) Engine, idle speed is 750 at sea level and 680 at high altitude.
㉖ On 1988 Maxims manual transmission is 15° B.T.D.C.

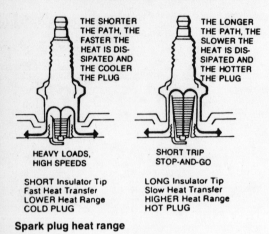

THE SHORTER THE PATH, THE FASTER THE HEAT IS DISSIPATED AND THE COOLER THE PLUG

THE LONGER THE PATH, THE SLOWER THE HEAT IS DISSIPATED AND THE HOTTER THE PLUG

HEAVY LOADS, HIGH SPEEDS

SHORT TRIP STOP-AND-GO

SHORT Insulator Tip
Fast Heat Transfer
LOWER Heat Range
COLD PLUG

LONG Insulator Tip
Slow Heat Transfer
HIGHER Heat Range
HOT PLUG

Spark plug heat range

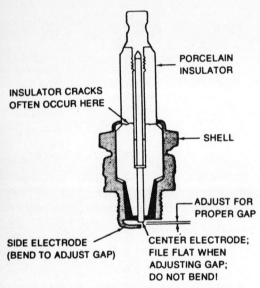

PORCELAIN INSULATOR

INSULATOR CRACKS OFTEN OCCUR HERE

SHELL

ADJUST FOR PROPER GAP

SIDE ELECTRODE (BEND TO ADJUST GAP)

CENTER ELECTRODE; FILE FLAT WHEN ADJUSTING GAP; DO NOT BEND!

Cross section of a spark plug

tends farther into the engine), the hotter the plug will operate. A plug that has a short path for heat transfer and remains too cool will quickly accumulate deposits of oil and carbon since it is not hot enough to burn them off. This leads to plug fouling and consequently to misfiring. A plug that has a long path for heat transfer will have no deposits but, due to the excessive heat, the electrodes will burn away

quickly and, in some instances, pre-ignition may result.

Preignition takes place when plug tips get so hot that they glow sufficiently to ignite the fuel/air mixture before the spark does. This early ignition will usually cause a pinging during low speeds and heavy loads. In sever cases, the heat may become enough to start the fuel/air mixture burning throughout the combustion chamber rather than just to the front of the plug as in normal operation. At this time, the piston is rising in the cylinder making its compression stroke. The burning mass is compressed and an explosion results producing tremendous pressure. Something has to give, and it does. Pistons are often damaged. Obviously, this detonation (explosion) is a destructive condition that can be avoided by installed a spark plug designed and specified for your particular engine.

A set of spark plugs usually requires replacement after 12,000 miles (19,000 km) depending on the type of driving for 1979 and earlier models, or 30,000 miles (48,000 km) for all 1980 and later models. The electrode on a new spark plug has a sharp edge but, with use, this edge becomes rounded by erosion causing the plug gap to increase. In normal operation, plug gap increases about 0.001″ in every 1,000-2,000 miles (1,600-3,200 km). As the gap increases, the plug's voltage requirement also increases. It requires a greater voltage to jump the wider gap and about two to three times as much voltage to fire a plug at high speeds and acceleration than at idle.

The higher voltage produced by the ignition coil is one of the primary reasons for the prolonged replacement interval for spark plugs in later cars. A consistently hotter spark prevents the fouling of plugs for much longer than could normally be expected. This spark is also able to jump across a larger gap more efficiently than a spark from a conventional system.

Worn plugs become obvious during acceleration. Voltage requirement is greatest during acceleration and a plug with an enlarged gap may require more voltage than the coil is able to produce. As a result, the engine misses and sput-

Diesel Tune-Up Specifications

Year Model	Engine Displacement cu. in. (cc)	Warm Valve Clearance (in.)		Intake Valve Opens (deg)	Injection Pump Setting (deg)	Injection Nozzle Pressure (psi)		Idle Speed (rpm)	Compression Pressure (psi)
		In	Ex			New	Used		
1981–83	170 (2,793)	0.010	0.012	NA	align marks	1,920–2,033	1,778–1,920	650	455 @ 200 rpm

ters until acceleration is reduced. Reducing acceleration reduces the plug's voltage requirement and the engine runs smoother. Slow, city driving is hard on plugs. The long periods of idle experienced in traffic creates an overly rich gas mixture. The engine isn't running fast enough to completely burn the gas and, consequently, the plugs are fouled with gas deposits and engine idle becomes rough. In many cases driving under right conditions can effectively clean these fouled plugs.

NOTE: *There are several reasons why a spark plug will foul and you can usually learn which is at fault by just looking at the plug. A few of the most common reasons for plug fouling, and a description of the fouled plug's appearance, can be found in the color insert of this book.*

Accelerate your car to the speed where the engine begins to miss and then slow down to the point where the engine smooths out. Run at this speed for a few minutes and then accelerate again to the point of engine miss. With each repetition this engine miss should occur at increasingly higher speeds and then disappear altogether. Do not attempt to shortcut this procedure by hard acceleration. This approach will compound problems by fusing deposits into a hard permanent glaze. Dirty, fouled plugs may be cleaned by sandblasting. Many shops have a spark plug sandblaster. After sandblasting, the electrode should be filed to a sharp, square shape and then gapped to specifications. Gapping a plug too close will produce rough idle while gapping it too wide will increase its voltage requirement and cause missing at high speeds and during acceleration.

The type of driving you do may require a change in spark plug heat range. If the majority of your driving is done in the city and rarely at high speeds, plug fouling may necessitate changing to a plug with a heat range number one lower than that specified by the car manufacturer. For example, a 1980 810 requires a BP6ES-11 plug. Frequent city driving may foul these plugs making engine operation rough. A BP5ES-11 is the next hottest plug and its insulator is longer than the BP6ES-11 so that it can absorb and retain more heat than the shorter BP6ES-11. This hotter BPES-11 burns off deposits even at low city speeds but would be too hot for prolonged turnpike driving. Using this plug at high speeds would create dangerous pre-ignition. On the other hand, if the aforementioned 810 were used almost exclusively for long distance high speed driving, the specified BP6ES-11 might be too hot resulting in rapid electrode wear and dangerous pre-ignition. In this case, it might be wise to change to a colder BP7ES-11. If the car is used for abnormal driv-

ing (as in the examples above), or the engine has been modified for higher performance. Then a change to a plug of a different heat range may be necessary. For a modified car it is always wise to go to a colder plug as a protection against pre-ignition. It will require more frequent plug cleaning, but destructive detonation during acceleration will be avoided.

REMOVAL

NOTE: *Some 1980 Calif. and all 1981 and later 510 and 200SX models equipped with the Z20, Z22, CA20E and CA18ET engine have two plugs for each cylinder. All eight plugs should be replaced at every tune-up for maximum fuel efficiency and power.*

When you're removing spark plugs, you should work on one at a time. Don't start by removing the plug wires all at once because unless you number them, they're going to get mixed up. On some models though, it will be more convenient for you to remove all the wires before you start to work on the plugs. If this is necessary, take a minute before you begin and number the wires with tape before you take them off. The time you spend here will pay off later on.

1. Twist the spark plug boot and remove the boot from the plug. You may also use a plug

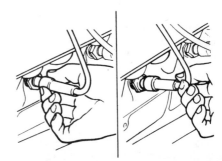

Twist and pull on the rubber boot to remove the spark plug wires; never pull on the wire itself

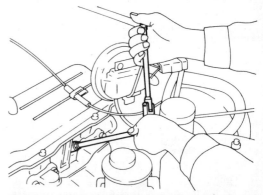

Plugs are removed using the proper combination of socket wrench, universals, and extensions

wire removal tool designed especially for this purpose. Do not pull on the wire itself. When the wire has been removed, take a wire brush and clean around the plug. Make sure that all the grime is removed so that none will enter the cylinder after the plug has been removed.

2. Remove the plug using the proper size socket, extensions, and universals as necessary. The Datsun/Nissan cylinder head is aluminum, which is easily stripped. Remove plugs ONLY when the engine is cold.

3. If removing the plug is difficult, drip some penetrating oil on the plug threads, allow it to work, then remove the plug. Also, be sure that the socket is straight on the plug, especially on those hard to reach plugs.

INSPECTION

Check the plugs for deposits and wear. If they are not going to be replaced, clean the plugs thoroughly. Remember that any kind of deposit will decrease the efficiency of the plug. Plugs can be cleaned on a spark plug cleaning machine, which can sometimes be found in service stations, or you can do an acceptable job of cleaning with a stiff brush. If the plugs are cleaned, the electrodes must be filed flat. Use an ignition points file, not an emery board or the like, which will leave deposits. The electrodes must be filed perfectly flat with sharp edges. Rounded edges reduce the spark plug voltage by as much as 50%.

Check the spark plug gap before installation. The ground electrode (the L-shaped one connected to the body of the plug) must be parallel to the center electrode and the specified size wire gauge (see Tune-Up Specifications) should pass through the gap with a slight drag. Always check the gap on new plugs, too. They are not always set correctly at the factory. Wire gapping tools usually have a bending tool attached. Use that to adjust the side electrode until the proper distance is obtained. Absolutely never bend the center electrode. Also, be careful not to bend the side electrode too far or too often. It may weaken and break off within the engine, requiring removal of the cylinder head to retrieve it.

INSTALLATION

1. Lubricate the threads of the spark plugs with drop of oil. Install the plugs and tighten them hand tight. Take care not to crossthread them.

2. Tighten the spark plugs with the socket. Do not apply the same amount of force you would use for a bolt; just snug them in. If a torque wrench is available, tighten to 11-15 ft.

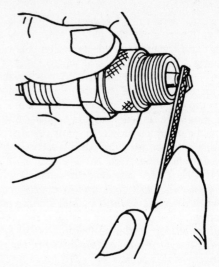

Plugs that are in good condition can be filed and re-used

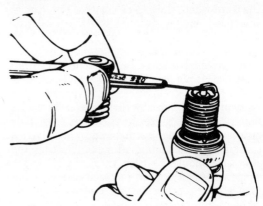

Always use a wire gauge to check the electrode gap

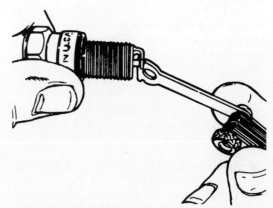

Adjust the electrode gap by bending the side electrode

lbs. On models from 1984-89 tighten spark plugs to 14-22 ft. lbs.

3. Install the wires on their respective plugs. Make sure the wires are firmly connected. You will be able to feel them click into place.

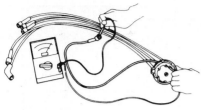

RESISTANCE:
LESS THAN 30,000 OHMS

Checking the spark plug wire resistance. 30,000 ohms is the absolute limit of acceptability

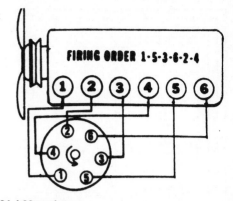

L24, L28 engines
Firing order: 1–5–3–6–2–4
Distributor rotation: counterclockwise

Spark Plug Wires
REPLACING AND TESTING

Every 15,000 miles (24,000 km), inspect the spark plug wires for burns, cuts, or breaks in the insulation. Check the boots and the nipples on the distributor cap. Replace any damaged wiring.

Every 45,000 miles (72,000 km) or so, the resistance of the wires should be checked with an ohmmeter. Wires with excessive resistance will cause misfiring, and may make the engine difficult to start in damp weather. Generally, the useful life of the cables is 45,000-60,000 miles (72,000-96,000 km).

To check resistance, remove the distributor cap, leaving the wires in place. Connect one lead of an ohmmeter to an electrode within the cap. Connect the other lead to the corresponding spark plug terminal (remove it from the spark plug for this test). Replace any wire which shows a resistance over $30,000\Omega$. Resistance should not be over $25,000\Omega$, and $30,000\Omega$ must be considered the outer limit of acceptability.

It should be remembered that resistance is also a function of length; the longer the wire, the greater the resistance. Thus, if the wires on your car are longer than the factory originals, resistance will be higher, quite possibly outside these limits.

When installing new wires, replace them one at a time to avoid mixups. Start by replacing the longest one first. Install the boot firmly over the spark plug. Route the wire over the same path as the original. Insert the nipple firmly onto the tower on the distributor cap, then install the cap cover and latches to secure the wires.

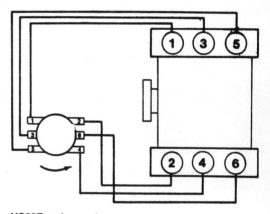

VG30E series engine
Firing order: 1–2–3–4–5–6
Distributor rotation: counterclockwise

Firing Orders

NOTE: *To avoid confusion, remove and tag the wires one at a time, for replacement.*

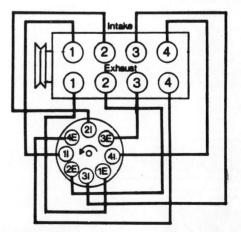

Z-series engines
Firing order: 1–3–4–2
Distributor rotation: counterclockwise

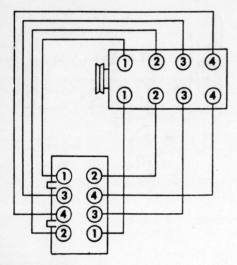

C-series engines
Firing order: 1–3–4–2
Distributor rotation: counterclockwise

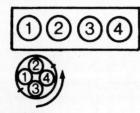

Firing order: 1-3-4-2
Distributor rotation: counterclockwise 1973 L18

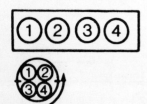

Firing order: 1-3-4-2
Distributor rotation: counterclockwise 1974 L18

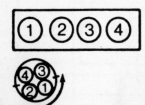

Firing order: 1-3-4-2
Distributor rotation: counterclockwise L20B

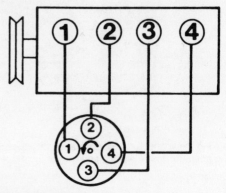

Firing order: 1-3-4-2
Distributor rotation: counterclockwise
1980 Z20 (49 states)

POINT TYPE IGNITION

Breaker Points and Condenser

NOTE: *Certain 1975-77 and virtually all 1978 and later Datsuns are equipped with electronic, breakerless ignition systems. See the following section for maintenance procedures.*

The points function as a circuit breaker for the primary circuit of the ignition system. The ignition coil must boost the 12 volts of electrical pressure supplied by the battery to as much as 25,000 volts in order to fire the plugs. To do this, the coil depends on the points and the condenser to make a clean break in the primary circuit.

The coil has both primary and secondary circuits. When the ignition is turned on, the battery supplies voltage through the coil and onto the points. The points are connected to ground, completing the primary circuit. As the current passes through the coil, a magnetic field is created in the iron center core of the coil. When the cam in the distributor turns, the points open, breaking the primary circuit. The magnetic field in the primary circuit of the coil then collapses and cuts through the secondary circuit windings around the iron core. Because of the physical principle called electromagnetic induction, the battery voltage is increased to a level sufficient to fire the spark plugs.

When the points open, the electrical charge in the primary circuit tries to jump the gap created between the two open contacts of the points. If this electrical charge were not transferred elsewhere, the metal contacts of the points would start to change rapidly.

The function of the condenser is to absorb excessive voltage from the points when they open and thus prevent the points from becoming pitted or burned.

If you have ever wondered why it is necessary to tune-up your engine occasionally, consider the fact that the ignition system must complete the above cycle each time a spark plug fires. On a 4-cylinder, 4-cycle engine, two of the four plugs must fire once for every engine revolution. If the idle speed of your engine is 800 revolutions per minutes (800 rpm), the breaker points open and close two times for each revolution. For every minute your engine idles, your points open and close 1,600 times (2 × 800 = 1,600). And that is just at idle. What about at 60 mph?

There are two ways to check breaker point gap: with a feeler gauge or with a dwell meter. Either way you set the points, you are adjusting the amount of time (in degrees of distributor rotation) that the points will remain open. If you adjust the points with a feeler gauge, you are setting the maximum amount the points will open when the rubbing block on the points is on a high point of the distributor cam. When you adjust the points with a dwell meter, you are measuring the number of degrees (of distributor cam rotation) that the points will remain closed before they start to open as a high point of the distributor cam approaches the rubbing block of the points.

If you still do not understand how the points function, take a friend, go outside, and remove the distributor cap from your engine. Have your friend operate the starter (make sure that the transmission is not in gear) as you look at the exposed parts of the distributor.

There are two rules that should always be followed when adjusting or replacing points. The points and condenser are a matched set. Never replace one without replacing the other. If you change the point gap or dwell of the engine, you also change the ignition timing. Therefore, if you adjust the points, you must also adjust the timing.

INSPECTION

A dual breaker point distributor was used on the 610 in 1973 as part of the emissions control system. The point sets are wired parallel in the primary ignition circuit. The two sets have a phase difference of 7°, making one a retard set and the other an advance. Ignition timing is advanced or retarded depending on which set is switching. Which set the engine operates on is controlled by a relay which in turn is connected to throttle position, temperature, and transmission switches. The dual points are adjusted with a feeler gauge in the same manner as the single point distributor.

1. Mark and disconnect the high tension wire from the top of the distributor and the coil.

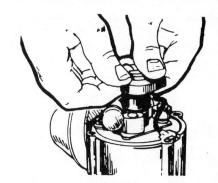

Pull the rotor straight up to remove it

2. Remove the distributor cap by prying off the spring clips on the sides of the cap.

3. Remove the rotor from the distributor shaft by pulling it straight up. Examine the condition of the rotor. If it is cracked or the metal tip is excessively worn or burned, it should be replaced. Clean the tip with fine emery paper.

NOTE: *It is a good idea at this time, to check the distributor cap for small cracks as this will affect the performance of the engine.*

4. Pry open the contacts of the points with a screwdriver and check the condition of the contacts. If they are excessively worn, burned or pitted, they should be replaced.

5. If the points are in good condition, adjust them and replace the rotor and the distributor cap. If the points need to be replaced, follow the replacement procedure given below.

REMOVAL AND INSTALLATION

1. Mark or tag then remove the coil high tension wire from the top of the distributor cap. Remove the distributor cap and place it out of the way. Remove the rotor from the distributor shaft by pulling up.

2. On single point distributors, remove the condenser from the distributor body. On early dual point distributors, you will find that one condenser is virtually impossible to reach without removing the distributor from the engine. To do this, first note and mark the position of the distributor on the small timing scale on the front of the distributor. Then mark the position of the rotor in relation to the distributor body. Do this by simply replacing the rotor on the distributor shaft and marking the spot on the distributor body where the rotor is pointing. Be careful not to turn the engine over while performing this operation.

3. Remove the distributor on dual point models by removing the small bolt at the rear of the distributor. Lift the distributor out of the block. It is now possible to remove the rear con-

On dual point distributors, #1 and #2 are the mounting screws. Do not loosen #3, the phase adjusting screw

denser. Do not crank the engine with the distributor removed.

4. On single point distributors, remove the points assembly attaching screws and then remove the points. A magnetic screwdriver or one with a holding mechanism will come in handy here, so that you don't drop a screw into the distributor and have to remove the entire distributor to retrieve it. After the points are removed, wipe off the cam and apply new cam lubricant. If you don't, the points will wear out in a few thousand miles.

5. On dual point distributors, you will probably find it easier to simply remove the points assemblies while the distributor is out of the engine. Install the new points and condensers. You can either set the point gap now or later after you have reinstalled the distributor.

6. On dual point models, install the distributor, making sure the marks made earlier are lined up. Note that the slot for the oil pump drive is tapered and will only fit one way.

7. On single point distributors, slip the new set of points onto the locating dowel and install the screws that hold the assembly onto the plate. Don't tighten them all the way yet, since you'll only have to loosen them to set the point gap.

8. Install the new condenser on single point models and attach the condenser lead to the points.

9. Set the point gap and dwell (see the following sections).

ADJUSTMENT OF THE BREAKER POINTS WITH A FEELER GAUGE

Single Point Distributor

1. If the contact points of the assembly are not parallel, bend the stationary contact so that they make contact across the entire surface of the contacts. Bend only the stationary bracket part of the point assembly; not the movable contact.

2. Turn the engine until the rubbing block of the points is on one of the high points of the distributor cam. You can do this by either turning the ignition switch to the start position and releasing it quickly (bumping the engine) or by using a wrench on the bolt which holds the crankshaft pulley to the crankshaft.

3. Place the correct size feeler gauge between the contacts (see the Tune-Up chart). Make sure that it is parallel with the contact surfaces.

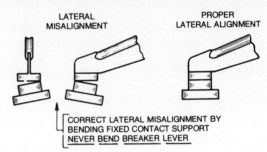

Check the points for proper alignment after installation

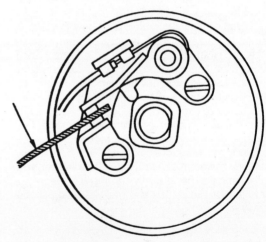

The arrow indicates the feeler gauge used to check the point gap

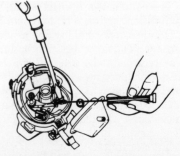

All single point distributor gaps are adjusted with the eccentric screw

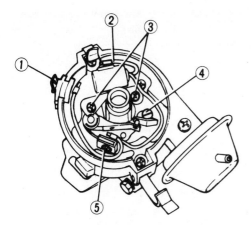

1. Primary lead terminal
2. Ground lead wire
3. Set screw
4. Adjuster
5. Screw

Single point distributor

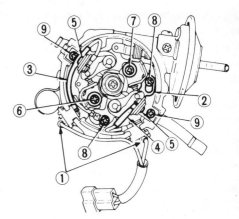

1. Lead wire terminal set screws
2. Adjuster plate
3. Primary lead wire—advanced points
4. Primary lead wire—retarded points
5. Primary lead wire set screw
6. Set screw—advanced points
7. Set screw—retarded points
8. Adjuster plate set screws
9. Breaker plate set screws

Dual point distributor. This view shows two screws (8) which must not be disturbed when adjusting or replacing points

4. With your free hand, insert a screwdriver into the eccentric adjusting screw, then twist the screwdriver to either increase or decrease the gap to the proper setting.

5. Tighten the adjustment lockscrew and recheck the contact gap to make sure that didn't change when the lockscrew was tightened.

6. Replace the rotor and distributor cap, and the high tension wire which connects the top of the distributor and the oil. Make sure that the rotor is firmly seated all the way onto the distributor shaft and that the tab of the rotor is aligned with notch in the shaft. Align the tab in the base of the distributor cap with the notch in the distributor body. Make sure that the cap is firmly seated on the distributor and that the retainer clips are in place. Make sure that the end of the high tension wire is firmly placed in the top of the distributor and the coil.

Dual Point Distributor

The two sets of breaker points are adjusted with a feeler gauge in the same manner as those in a single point distributor, except that you do the actual adjusting by twisting a screwdriver in the point set notch. Check the Tune-up Specifications chart for the correct setting. Both are set to the same opening.

Dwell Angle

The dwell angle or cam angle is the number of degrees that the distributor cam rotates while the points are closed. There is an inverse relationship between dwell angle and point gap. Increasing the point gap will decrease the dwell

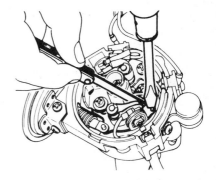

Point gap on the dual point distributor is adjusted by twisting a screwdriver in the notch

angle and vice versa. Checking the dwell angle with a meter is a far more accurate method of measuring point opening than the feeler gauge method.

After setting the point gap to specification with a feeler gauge as described above, check the dwell angle with a meter. Attach the dwell meter according to the manufacturer's instruction sheet. The negative lead is grounded and the positive lead is connected to the primary wire terminal which runs from the coil to the distributor. Start the engine, let it idle and reach operating temperature, and observe the dwell on the meter. The reading should fall within the allowable range. If it does not, the gap will have to be reset or the breaker points will have to be replaced.

ADJUSTMENT OF THE BREAKER POINTS WITH A DWELL METER

Dwell can be checked with the engine running or cranking. Decrease dwell by increasing the point gap; increase by decreasing the gap. Dwell angle is simply the number of degrees of distributor shaft rotation during which the points stay closed. Theoretically, if the point gap is correct, the dwell should also be correct or nearly so. Adjustment with a dwell meter produces more exact, consistent results since it is a dynamic adjustment. If dwell varies more than 3° from idle speed to 1,750 engine rpm, the distributor is worn.

Single Point Distributor

1. Adjust the points with a feeler gauge as previously described.
2. Connect the dwell meter to the ignition circuit as according to the manufacturer's instructions. One lead of the meter is connected to a ground and the other lead is connected to the distributor post on the coil. An adapter is usually provided for this purpose.
3. If the dwell meter has a set line on it, adjust the meter to zero the indicator.
4. Start the engine.

NOTE: *Be careful when working on any vehicle while the engine is running. Make sure that the transmission is in Neutral and that the parking brake is applied. Keep hands, clothing, tools and the wires of the test instruments clear of the rotating fan blades.*

5. Observe the reading on the dwell meter. If the reading is within the specified range, turn off the engine and remove the dwell meter.

NOTE: *If the meter does not have a scale for 4-cylinder engines, multiply the 8-cylinder reading by two.*

6. If the reading is above the specified range, the breaker point gap is too small. If the reading is below the specified range, the gap is too large. In either case, the engine must be stopped and the gap adjusted in the manner previously covered. After making the adjustment, start the engine and check the reading on the dwell meter. When the correct reading is obtained, disconnect the dwell meter.
7. Check the adjustment of the ignition timing.

Dual Point Distributor

Adjust the point gap of a dual point distributor with a dwell meter as follows:
1. Mark and disconnect the wiring harness of the distributor from the engine wiring harness.
2. Using a jumper wire, connect the black wire of the engine side of the harness to the black wire of the distributor side of the harness (advance points).

Use the terminals provided (arrows) for jumper wire connections

3. Start the engine and observe the reading on the dwell meter. Shut the engine off and adjust the points accordingly as previously outlined for single point distributors.
4. Disconnect the jumper wire from the black wire of the distributor side of the wiring harness and connect it to the yellow wire (retard points).
5. Adjust the point gap as necessary.
6. After the dwell of both sets of points is correct, remove the jumper wire and connect the engine-to-distributor wiring harness securely.

ELECTRONIC IGNITION

In 1975, in order to comply with California's tougher emission laws, Datsun/Nissan introduced electronic ignition systems for all models sold in that state. Since that time, the Datsun electronic ignition system has undergone a metamorphosis from a standard transistorized circuit (1975-78) to an Integrated Circuit system (IC), 1979 and later, to the special dual spark plug system used in 1980 and later 510 and 200SX models with the Z20 and CA20 series engine.

The electronic ignition system differs from the conventional breaker points system in form only. Its function is exactly the same: to supply a spark to the spark plugs at precisely the right moment to ignite the compressed gas in the cylinders and create mechanical movement.

NOTE: *On Maxima and some late model 200SX and 240SX a crankangle sensor mounted in the distributor is the basic component of the entire E.C.C.S. (Electronic Concentrated Control System). There are no adjustments necessary.*

Located in the distributor, in addition to the normal rotor cap, is a spoked rotor (reluctor) which fits on the distributor shaft where the breaker points cam is found on nonelectronic

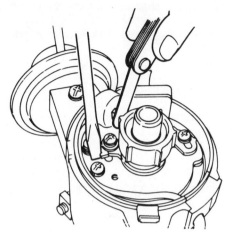

Checking the air gap—1975–78

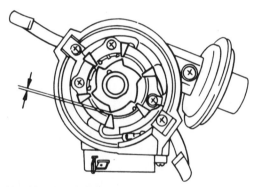

Checking the air gap—1979 and later

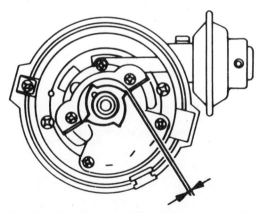

Checking the air gap—1980 and later models with the Z20 engine

ignitions. The rotor (reluctor) revolves with the top rotor cap and, as it passes a pickup coil inside the distributor body, breaks a high flux phase which occurs while the space between the reluctor spokes passes the pickup coil. This allows current to flow to the pickup coil. Primary ignition current is then cut off by the electronic ignition unit, allowing the magnetic field in the ignition coil to collapse, creating the spark which the distributor passes on to the spark plug.

The 1979 and later IC ignition system uses a ring type pickup coil which surrounds the reluctor instead of the single post type pickup coil on earlier models.

The dual spark plug ignition system used on some 1980 and later uses two ignition coils and each cylinder has two spark plugs which fire simultaneously. In this manner the engine is able to consume large quantities of recirculated exhaust gas which would cause a single spark plug cylinder to misfire and idle roughly.

Because no points or condenser are used, and because dwell is determined by the electronic unit, no adjustments are necessary. Ignition timing is checked in the usual way, but unless the distributor is disturbed it is not likely to ever change very much.

ADJUSTMENT

The adjustment service consists of inspection of the distributor cap, rotor, and ignition wires, replacing when necessary. These parts can be expected to last for at least 40,000 miles (64,000 km). In addition, the reluctor air gap should be check periodically.

1. The distributor cap is held on by two clips. Release them with a screwdriver and lift the cap straight up and off, with the wires attached. Inspect the cap for cracks, carbon tracks, or a worn center contact. Replace it if necessary, transferring the wires one at a time from the old cap to the new.

2. Pull the ignition rotor (not the spoked reluctor) straight up to remove. Replace it if its contacts are worn, burned, or pitted. Do not file the contacts. To replace, press it firmly onto the shaft. It only goes on one way, so be sure it is fully seated.

3. Before replacing the ignition rotor, check the reluctor air gap. Use a non-magnetic feeler gauge. Rotate the engine until a reluctor spoke is aligned with the pick-up coil (either bump the engine around with the starter, or turn it with a wrench on the crankshaft pulley bolt). The gap should measure 0.20-0.40mm through 1978, or 0.30-0.50mm for 1979 and later. Adjustment, if necessary, is made by loosening the pickup coil mounting screws and shifting the coil either closer to or farther from the reluctor. On 1979 and later models, center the pickup coil (ring) around the reluctor. Tighten the screws and recheck the gap.

4. Inspect the wires for cracks or brittleness. Replace them one at a time to prevent crosswiring, carefully pressing the replacement wires into place. The cores of electronic wires

are more susceptible to breakage than those of standard wires, so treat them gently.

NOTE: *On models that use IC ignition unit and no pickup coil measure the air gap between the reluctor and stator. If not within specifications (0.30-0.50mm), loosen stator retaining screws and adjust.*

PICK-UP COIL AND RELUCTOR REPLACEMENT

1975-78

The reluctor cannot be removed on some early models. It is an integral part of the distributor shaft. Non-removable reluctors can be distinguished by the absence of a roll pin (retaining pin) which locks the reluctor in place on the shaft.

To replace the pick-up coil on all 1975-78 models:

1. Remove the distributor cap by releasing the two spring clips. Remove the ignition rotor by pulling it straight up and off the shaft.

2. Disconnect the distributor wiring harness at the terminal block.

3. Remove the two pick-up coil mounting screws. Remove the screws retaining the wiring harness to the distributor.

4. Remove the pick-up coil.

When replacing the the pick-up coil leave the mounting screws slightly loose to facilitate air gap adjustment.

To replace the reluctor on models with a roll pin:

1. Remove the distributor cap, ignition rotor and the pick-up coil.

2. Use two screwdrivers or pry bars to pry the reluctor from the distributor shaft. Be extremely careful not to damage the reluctor teeth. Remove the roll pin.

3. To replace, press the reluctor firmly onto the shaft. Install a new roll pin with the slit facing away from the distributor shaft. Do not reuse the old roll pin.

1979 and Later

NOTE: *The 1980 200SX and 510 models (Calif. only) and 1981 200SX and 510 models (ex. Canada) use the Z20 engine. This engine is equipped with a slightly different ignition system and does not utilize a pick-up coil.*

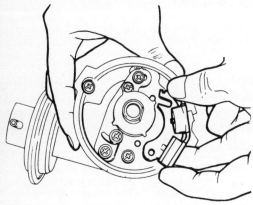

Removing the pick up coil—1975–78

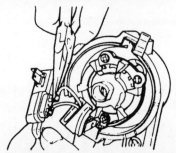

Removing the pickup coil on all models except twin-plug (Z-series and CA-series) engines

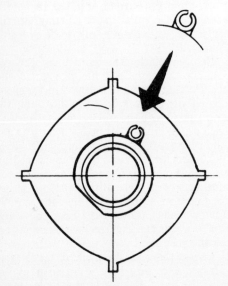

Roll pin installation—1975–80

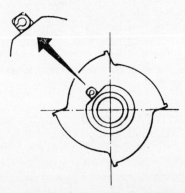

Roll pin installation—all models except the 1980–84 810 and Maxima and the 1984 and later 200SX

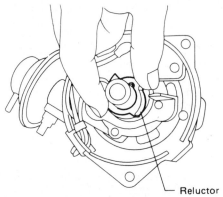

On the 1984 and later 200SX distributors, pry off the reluctor after first removing the distributor cap and rotor head

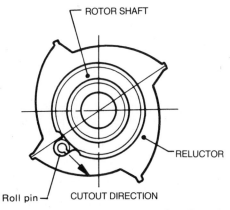

ROTOR SHAFT

RELUCTOR

Roll pin   CUTOUT DIRECTION

Roll pin installation, 1984 and later CA20E engines (200SX)

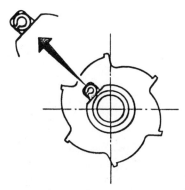

Roll pin installation—1980 and later 810 and Maxima

The 1984 and later CA20E and CA18ET Turbo engines (200SX) also do not utilize a pick-up coil.

1. Remove the distributor cap. Remove the ignition rotor by pulling the rotor straight up and off the shaft. On 1984 and later 200SX distributors, remove the round rotor head by first removing the set screw, then carefully pry off the rotor (see the exploded view of this distributor in this book for more detail).

2. On all models except the 1984 and later 200SX, use a pair of needle nose pliers to disconnect the pick-up coil spade connectors from the ignition unit. Do not pull on the pick-up coil wires themselves.

3. Remove the toothed stator and the ring magnet underneath it by removing the three mounting screws.

4. Remove the reluctor by prying it from the distributor shaft with two small pry bars or a small puller. Be careful not to damage any of the reluctor teeth. Remove the roll pin.

5. On all models except the 1984 and later 200SX, remove the screw retaining the pick-up coil wiring harness to the distributor. Remove the pick-up coil.

6. On all models except the 1984 and later 200SX, install the pick-up coil into place in the distributor body. Replace the wiring harness retainer.

7. Press the reluctor firmly into place on the shaft. Install a new roll pin with the slit in the pin parallel to the flat on the shaft.

8. Install the magnet and stator, and center the stator around the reluctor. Air gap is 0.30-0.50mm.

9. Press the pick-up coil spade connectors onto the ignition unit terminals with your fingers. The proper connections can be determined from the color code marked on the grommet. Replace the ignition rotor and the distributor cap.

RELUCTOR AND IC IGNITION UNIT

1. Remove the distributor cap and rotor. The rotor is held to the distributor shaft by a retaining screw, which must be removed.

2. Remove the wiring harness and the vacuum controller from the housing.

3. Using 2 flat bladed screwdrivers, place one on each side of the reluctor and pry it from the distributor shaft.

NOTE: *When removing the reluctor, be careful not to damage or distort the teeth.*

4. Remove the roll pin from the reluctor.

NOTE: *To remove the IC unit, mark and remove the breaker plate assembly and separate the IC unit from it. Be careful not to loose the spacers when you remove the IC unit.*

5. Install the IC unit to the breaker plate assembly.

6. Install the wiring harness and the vacuum controller to the distributor housing. When you install the roll pin into the reluctor position the cutout direction of the roll pin in parallel with the notch in the reluctor. Make sure that the harness to the IC ignition unit is tightly secured, then adjust the air gap between the

reluctor and the stator to 0.30-0.50mm. Refer to the exploded views of the distributor in this book.

IGNITION TIMING

Gasoline Engines

Ignition timing is the measurement in degrees of crankshaft rotation, of the point at which the spark plugs fire in each of the cylinders. It is measured in degrees before or after Top Dead Center (TDC) of the compression stroke.

Because it takes a fraction of a second for the spark plug to ignite the mixture in the cylinder, the spark plug must fire a little before the piston reaches TDC. Otherwise, the mixture will not be completely ignited as the piston passes TDC and the full power of the explosion will not be used by the engine.

The timing measurement is given in degrees of crankshaft rotation before the piston reaches TDC (BTDC). If the setting for the ignition timing is 5° BTDC, the spark plug must fire 5° before each piston reaches TDC. This only holds true, however, when the engine is at idle speed.

As the engine speed increases, the pistons go faster. The spark plugs have to ignite the fuel even sooner if it is to be completely ignited when the piston reaches TDC. To do this, the distributor has two means to advance the timing of the spark as the engine speed increases: a set of centrifugal weights within the distributor, and a vacuum diaphragm, mounted on the side of the distributor.

NOTE: *On all Maxima models, late model 200SX (all turbo versions) and 240SX model a crankangle sensor in the distributor is used. This sensor controls ignition timing and has other engine control functions. There is no vacuum or centrifugal advance all timing settings are controlled by the E.C.U.*

If the ignition is set too far advanced (BTDC), the ignition and expansion of the fuel in the cylinder will occur too soon and tend to force the piston down while it is still traveling up. This causes engine ping. If the ignition spark is set too far retarded, after TDC (ATDC), the piston will have already passed TDC and started on its way down when the fuel is ignited. This will cause the piston to be forced down for only a portion of its travel. This will result in poor engine performance and lack of power.

Timing marks consist of a notch on the rim of the crankshaft pulley and a scale of degrees attached to the front of the engine. The notch corresponds to the position of the piston in the number 1 cylinder. A stroboscopic (dynamic) timing light is used, which is hooked into the circuit of the No. 1 cylinder spark plug. Every time the spark plug fires, the timing light flashes. By aiming the timing light at the timing marks, the exact position of the piston within the cylinder can be read, since the stroboscopic flash makes the mark on the pulley appear to be standing still. Proper timing is indicated when the notch is aligned with the correct number on the scale.

There are three basic types of timing light available. The first is a simple neon bulb with two wire connections (one for the spark plug and one for the plug wire, connecting the light in series). This type of light is quite dim, and must be held closely to the marks to be seen, but it is inexpensive. The second type of light operates from the car battery. Two alligator clips connect to the battery terminals, while a third wire connects to the spark plug with an adapter. This type of light is more expensive, but the xenon bulb provides a nice bright flash which can even be seen in sunlight. The third type replaces the battery source with 110 volt house current. Some timing lights have other functions built into them, such as dwell meters, tachometers, or remote starting switches. These are convenient, in that they reduce the tangle of wires under the hood, but may duplicate the functions of tools you already have.

If your Datsun has electronic ignition, you should use a timing light with an inductive pickup. This pickup simply clamps onto the No. 1 plug wire, eliminating the adapter. It is not prone to crossfiring or false triggering, which may occur with a conventional light, due to the

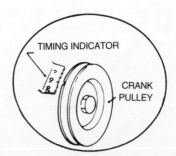

Typical timing indicator-to-pulley relationship

Typical Datsun timing marks

greater voltages produced by electronic ignition.

ADJUSTMENT

All with Single Points and all Electronic Ignition except 1983 and Later 200SX

NOTE: *Nissan does not give ignition timing adjustments for 1980 California models or for any 1981-82 200SXs and for 1981 and later 810s, Maxima and 240SX models. If timing requires adjustment, please refer to the underhood specifications sticker for applicable procedures.*

1. Set the dwell of the breaker points to the proper specification.

2. Locate the timing marks on the crankshaft pulley and the front of the engine.

3. Clean off the timing marks, so that you can see them.

4. Use chalk or white paint to color the mark on the crankshaft pulley and the mark on the scale which will indicate the correct timing when aligned with the notch on the crankshaft pulley.

5. Attach a tachometer to the engine.

6. Attach a timing light to the engine, according to the manufacturer's instructions. If the timing light has three wires, one, usually green or blue, is attached to the No. 1 spark plug with an adapter. The other wires are connected to the battery. The red wire goes to the positive side of the battery and the black wire is connected to the negative terminal of the battery.

7. Leave the vacuum hose connected to the distributor advance vacuum diaphragm on all models through 1979.

On 1980 models: disconnect the throttle valve switch harness connector (810 only). Disconnect and plug the canister purge hose from the intake manifold (810 only). Plug the opening in the intake manifold. On 1980 49 States models, also disconnect the hoe from the air induction pipe and cap the pipe, and disconnect and plug the vacuum advance hose at the distributor. Note that the disconnect and plug instructions for the air induction pipe and the distributor vacuum advance do not apply to 1980 models sold in Canada.

8. Check that all of the wires clear the fan, pulleys, and belts, and then start the engine. Allow the engine to reach normal operating temperature.

CAUTION: *Block the front wheels and set the parking brake. Shift the manual transmission to Neutral or the automatic transmission to Drive. Do not stand in front of the car when making adjustments!*

9. Adjust the idle to the correct setting. See

1980 throttle valve switch (1)

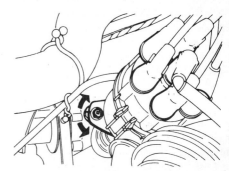

Loosen the distributor lockbolt and turn the distributor slightly to advance (upper arrow) or retard (lower arrow) the timing

the Idle Speed and Mixture section later in this chapter.

10. Aim the timing light at the timing marks. If the marks which you put on the pulley and the engine are aligned when the light flashes, the timing is correct. Turn off the engine and remove the tachometer and the timing light. If the marks are not in alignment, proceed with the following steps.

11. Turn off the engine.

12. Loosen the distributor lockbolt just enough so that the distributor can be turned with a little effort.

13. Start the engine. Keep the wires of the timing light clear of the fan.

14. With the timing light aimed at the pulley and the marks on the engine, turn the distributor in the direction of rotor rotation to retard the spark, and in the opposite direction of rotor rotation to advance the spark. Align the marks on the pulley and the engine with the flashes of the timing light.

15. Tighten the distributor lockbolt and recheck the timing.

Models with Dual Points

PHASE DIFFERENCE

1. Disconnect the wiring harness of the distributor from the engine harness.

2. Connect the black wire of the engine harness to the black wire of the distributor harness with a jumper wire. This connects the advanced set of points.

3. With the engine idling, adjust the ignition timing by rotating the distributor.

4. Disconnect the jumper wire from the black wire of the distributor harness and connect it to the yellow wire of the distributor harness. The retarded set of points is now activated.

5. With the engine idling, check the ignition timing. The timing should be retarded from the advanced setting 7°.

6. To adjust the out of phase angle of the ignition timing, loosen the adjuster plate set screws on the same side as the retarded set of points.

7. Place the blade of a screwdriver in the adjusting notch of the adjuster plate and turn the adjuster plate as required to obtain the correct retarded ignition timing specification. The ignition timing is retarded when the adjuster plate is turned counterclockwise. There are graduations on the adjuster plate to make the adjustment easier. One graduation is equal to 4° of crankcase rotation.

8. Replace the distributor cap, start the engine and check the ignition timing with the retarded set of points activated (yellow wire of the

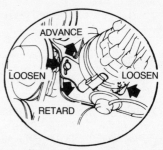

Ignition timing adjustments on 1983 and later 200SX

distributor wiring harness connected to the black wire of the engine wiring harness).

9. Repeat the steps above as necessary to gain the proper retarded ignition timing.

1983 and Later 200SX

NOTE: *When checking ignition timing on air conditioner equipped cars, make sure that the air conditioner is off when proceeding with the check. Refer to Idle Speed And Mixture Adjustments section in this chapter.*

CAUTION: *Automatic transmission equipped models should be shifted into D for idle speed checks. When in Drive, the parking brake must be fully applied and both front and rear wheels chocked. When racing the engine on automatic transmission equipped models, make sure that the shift lever is in the N or P position and remove the wheel chocks.*

1. Run the engine up to normal operating temperature.

2. Open the hood, and run the engine up to 2,000 rpm for about 2 minutes under no-load (all accessories off).

3. Run the engine at idle speed. Disconnect the hose from the air induction pipe, and cap the pipe.

4. Race the engine two or three times under no-load, then run the engine for one minute at idle.

5. Check the idle speed. Adjust the idle speed to specifications by turning the idle speed adjusting screw. Refer to the Tune Up Specifications Chart.

6. Connect a timing light according to the light manufacturer's instructions. Adjust the timing by loosening the distributor holddown bolts and turning the distributor clockwise to advance and counterclockwise to retard.

7. Reconnect the air induction pipe hose.

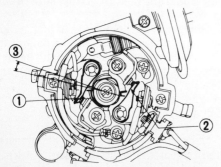

(1) Advance point set (2) Retarded point set (3) Phase difference

INJECTION PUMP TIMING

Diesel Engines

For information and procedures regarding injection pump timing, please refer to Chapter 5.

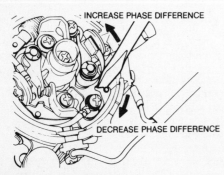

Adjusting phase difference

Valve Lash

Valve adjustment determines how far the valves enter the cylinder and how long they stay open and closed.

If the valve clearance is too large, part of the lift of the camshaft will be used in removing the excessive clearance. Consequently, the valve will not be opening for as long as it should. This condition has two effects: the valve train components will emit a tapping sound as they take up the excessive clearance and the engine will perform poorly because the valves don't open fully and allow the proper amount of gases to flow into and out of the engine.

If the valve clearance is too small, the intake valves and the exhaust valves will open too far and they will not fully seat on the cylinder head when they close. When a valve seats itself on the cylinder head, it does two things: it seals the combustion chamber so that one of the gases in the cylinder escape and it cools itself by transferring some of the heat it absorbs from the combustion in the cylinder to the cylinder head and to the engine's cooling system. If the valve clearance is too small, the engine will run poorly because of the gases escaping from the combustion chamber. The valves will also become overheated and will warp, since they cannot transfer heat unless they are touching the valve seat in the cylinder head.

NOTE: *While all valve adjustments must be made as accurately as possible, it is better to have the valve adjustment slightly loose than slightly tight, as a burned valve may result from overly tight adjustments.*

ADJUSTMENT

610, 710 and 1977-80 510, 200SX (Single Plug Engine)

1. The valves are adjusted with the engine at normal operating temperature. Oil temperature, and the resultant parts expansion, is much more important than water temperature. Run the engine for at least fifteen minutes to ensure that all the parts have reached their full expansion. After the engine is warmed up, shut it off.

2. Purchases either a new gasket or some silicone gasket seal before removing the camshaft cover. Note the location of any wires and hoses which may interfere with cam cover removal, disconnect them and move them aside. Then remove the bolts which hold the cam cover in place and remove the cam cover.

3. Place a wrench on the crankshaft pulley bolt and turn the engine over until the valves for No. 1 cylinder are closed. When both cam lobes are pointing up, the valves are closed. If

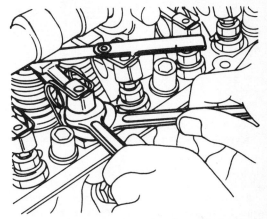

Loosen the locknut and turn the pivot adjuster to adjust the valve clearance—all models except those with twin-plug engines

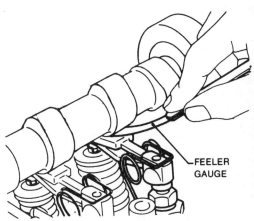

FEELER GAUGE

Checking the valve clearance with a flat feeler gauge—all models except those with twin-plug engines

you have not done this before, it is a good idea to turn the engine over slowly several times and watch the valve action until you have a clear idea of just when the valve is closed.

4. Check the clearance of the intake and exhaust valves. You can differentiate between them by lining them up with the tubes of the intake and exhaust manifolds. The correct size feeler gauge should pass between the base circle of the cam and the rocker arm with just a slight drag. Be sure the feeler gauge is inserted straight and not on an angle.

5. If the valves need adjustment, loosen the locking nut and then adjust the clearance with the adjusting screw. You will probably find it necessary to hold the locking nut while you turn the adjuster. After you have the correct clearance, tighten the locking nut and recheck the clearance. Remember, it's better to have them too loose than too tight, especially exhaust valves.

6. Repeat this procedure (Steps 3-5) until

you have checked and/or adjusted all the valves. (Be sure to adjust in the firing order.) Keep in mind that all that is necessary is to have the valves closed and the camshaft lobes pointing up.7. Install the cam cover gasket, the cam cover, and any wires and hoses which were removed.

810 and Maxima Through 1984

NOTE: *The 810 and Maxima engine valves are adjusted hot.*

1. Note the locations of all hoses or wires that would interfere with valve cover removal, disconnect them and move them aside. Then, remove the six bolts which hold the valve cover in place.

2. Bump one end of the cover sharply to loosen the gasket and then pull the valve cover off the engine vertically.

3. Place a wrench on the crankshaft pulley bolt and turn the engine over until the first cam lobe is pointing straight up. The timing marks on the crankshaft pulley should be lined up approximately where they would be when the No. 1 spark plug fires.

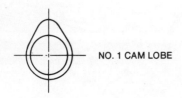

NO. 1 CAM LOBE

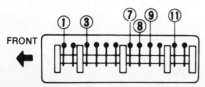

FRONT

Primary valve adjustment, No. 1 cam lobe pointing up—810 and Maxima

NO. 1 CAM LOBE

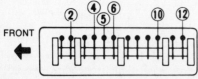

FRONT

Secondary valve adjustment, No. 1 cam lobe pointing down—810 and Maxima

NOTE: *If you decide to turn the engine by bumping it with the starter, be sure to disconnect the high tension wire from the coil to prevent the engine from accidentally starting and spewing oil all over the engine compartment. Never attempt to turn the engine by using a wrench on the camshaft sprocket bolt. This would put a tremendous strain on the timing chain.*

4. See the illustration for primary adjustment and check the clearance for valves (1), (3), (7), (8), (9) and (11) using a flat bladed feeler gauge. The feeler gauge should pass between the cam and the cam follower with a very slight drag. Insert the feeler gauge straight, not at an angle.

NOTE: *A narrow angled feeler gauge blade should be used to fit in the slot of the cam follower. Do not angle the feeler gauge when checking the clearance.*

5. If the clearance is not within the specified limits, loosen the pivot locking nut and then insert the feeler gauge between the cam and the cam follower. Adjust the pivot screw until there is a very slight drag on the gauge, tighten the locking nut, recheck the adjustment and correct as necessary.

6. Turn the engine over so that the first cam lobe is pointing straight down. See the illustration for secondary adjustment and then check the clearance on valves (2), (4), (5), (6), (10) and (12). If clearance is not within specifications, adjust as detailed in Step 5.

7. Clean all traces of old gasket material from the valve cover and the head. Install the new gasket in the valve cover with sealer and install the valve cover. Tighten the valve cover bolts evenly in several stages going around the cover to ensure a good seal. Reconnect all hoses and wires securely and operate the engine to check for leaks.

8. Road test the vehicle for proper operation.

1985 and Later 3.0 Liter V6

These engines use hydraulic valve adjusters which cannot be adjusted in any way. If the engine exhibits valve noise, this indicates either excessive wear of valve train parts or clogged hydraulic tensioners, due to inadequate engine maintenance. You may also wish to check the torque of rocker shaft retaining bolts. See Chapter 3.

1980-83 510 and 200SX (Twin Plug Engines)

1. The valves must be adjusted with the engine warm, so start the car and run the engine until the needle on the temperature gauge reaches the middle of the gauge. After the engine is warm, shut it off.

2. Purchase either a new gasket or some sili-

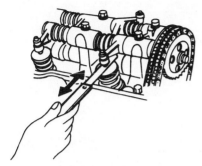

Checking the valve clearance with a flat feeler gauge—
Z20 and Z22 (twin-plug) series engines

NO. 1 CAM LOBE

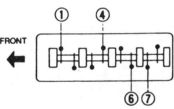

FRONT ←

Primary valve adjustment, No. 1 cam lobe pointing
down—Z20 and Z22 series engines

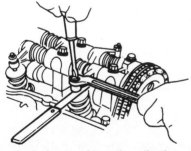

Loosen the locknut and turn the adjusting screw to
adjust the valve clearance—Z20 and Z22 series engines

cone gasket sealer before removing the camshaft cover. Counting on the old gasket to be in
good shape is a losing proposition. Always use
new gaskets. Note the location of any wires and
hoses which may interfere with cam cover removal, disconnect them and move them to one
side. Remove the bolts holding the cover in
place and remove the cover. Remember, the engine will be hot, so be careful.

3. Place a wrench on the crankshaft pulley
bolt and turn the engine over until the first cam

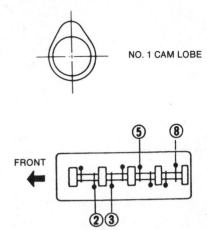

NO. 1 CAM LOBE

FRONT ←

Secondary valve adjustment, No. 1 cam lobe pointing up—Z20 and Z22 series engines

lobe behind the camshaft timing chain sprocket
is pointing straight down.

NOTE: *If you decide to turn the engine by
bumping it with the starter, be sure to disconnect the high tension wire from the coil(s) to
prevent the engine from accidentally starting
and spewing oil all over the engine compartment. Never attempt to turn the engine by using a wrench on the camshaft sprocket bolt.
There is a one to two turning ratio between
the camshaft and the crankshaft which will
put a tremendous strain on the timing chain.*

4. See the illustration for primary adjustment and check the clearance of valves (1), (4),
(6), and (7) using a flat bladed feeler gauge. The
feeler gauge should pass between the valve
stem end and the rocker arm screw with a very
slight drag. Insert the feeler gauge straight, not
at an angle.

5. If the clearance is not within specified value, loosen the rocker arm lock nut and turn the
rocker arm screw to obtain the proper clearance. After correct clearance is obtained, tight-
en the lock nut.

6. Turn the engine over so that the first cam
lobe behind the camshaft timing chain sprocket
is pointing straight up and check the clearance
of the valves marked (2), (3), (5), and (8) in the
secondary adjustment illustration. They, too,
should be adjusted to specifications as in Step 5.

7. Install the cam cover gasket, the cam cover and any wires and hoses which were
removed.

1984 and Later 200SX

NOTE: *Starting in mid year 1986-88 the
CA20E engine in the 200SX model valves are
non-adjustable. On V6 equipped 200SX models and 240SX models the valves are also
non-adjustable. Refer to Valve Clearance column in the Tune-Up Specifications Chart.*

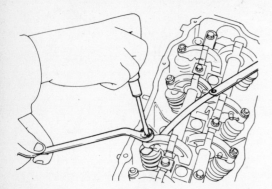

Adjusting the CA20E and CA18ET valves. Clearance is 0.012 in.

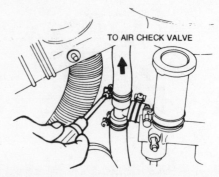

Disconnecting air hose between three way connector and check valve, 1978 510 shown

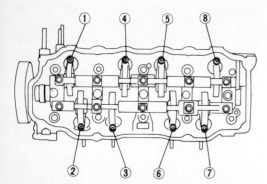

Valve location, 1984 and later 200SX (CA20E and CA18ET engines). See text for sequence

Follow the procedure above for 1980-83 models, with the following exceptions: on step 4, check and adjust the clearance valves 1, 2, 4 and 6 as shown in the accompanying illustration. This is with No. 1 cylinder at TDC on compression. On step 6, check and adjust the clearance on valves 3, 5, 7 and 8 with the No. 4 cylinder at TDC on compression.

IDLE SPEED AND MIXTURE ADJUSTMENTS

This section contains only tune-up adjustment procedures for carburetors. Descriptions, adjustments, and overhaul procedures for fuel systems can be found in Chapter 5.

Caurbureted Engines

When the engine is running, the air/fuel mixture from the carburetor is being drawn into the engine by a partial vacuum which is created by the movement of the pistons downward on the intake stroke. The amount of air/fuel mixture that enters into the engine is controlled by the throttle plate(s) in the bottom of the carburetor. When the engine is not running the

Mixture screw (arrow). Note limiter tab

throttle plate(s) is closed, completely blocking off the bottom of the carburetor from the inside of the engine. The throttle plates are connected by the throttle linkage to the accelerator pedal in the passenger compartment of the vehicle. When you depress the pedal, you open the throttle plates in the carburetor to admit more air/fuel mixture to the engine.

When the engine is not running, the throttle plates are closed. When the engine is idling, it is necessary to have the throttle plates open slightly. To prevent having to hold your foot on the pedal when the engine is idling, an idle speed adjusting screw was added to the carburetor linkage.

The idle adjusting screw contacts a lever (throttle lever) on the outside of the carburetor. When the screw is turned, it either opens or closes the throttle plates of the carburetor, raising or lowering the idle speed of the engine.

This screw is called the curb idle adjusting screw.

ADJUSTMENT PROCEDURE

NOTE: *The l980 model Datsun/Nissan require a CO meter to adjust their mixture ratios, therefore, no procedures concerning this adjustment are given. Also, many California model Datsun/Nissan have a plug over their mixture control screw. It is suggested that in both of these cases, mixture adjustment be left to a qualified technician.*

1. Start the engine and allow it to run until it reaches normal operating temperature.

2. Allow the engine idle speed to stabilize by running the engine at idle for at least two minutes.

3. If you have not done so already, check and adjust the ignition timing to the proper setting.

4. Shut off the engine and connect a tachometer as per the manufacturer's instructions.

5. Disconnect and plug the air hose between the three way connector and the check valve, if equipped. On 1980 models with the Z20S engine, disconnect the air induction hose and plug the pipe, also disconnect and plug the vacuum hose at the distributor. With the transmission in Neutral, check the idle speed on the tachometer. If the reading is correct, continue on to Step 6 for 1973-79 models. For 1980 and later, and certain California models, proceed to step 10 below if the idle is correct. If the idle is not correct, for all models, turn the idle speed adjusting screw clockwise with a screwdriver to increase idle speed or counterclockwise to decrease it.

6. With the automatic transmission in Drive (wheels blocked and parking brake on) or the manual transmission in Neutral, turn the mixture screw out until the engine rpm starts to drop due to an overly rich mixture.

7. Turn the screw until just before the rpm starts to drop due to an overly lean mixture. Turn the mixture screw in until the idle speed drops 60-70 rpm with manual transmission, or 15-25 rpm with automatic transmission (in Drive) for 1975-76 610 and 710 models; 45-55 rpm for all 1977 710's, and 1978-79 510's and 200SX's. If the mixture limited cap will not allow this adjustment, remove it, make the adjustment, and install it. Go on to Step 10 for all 1975-79 models.

8. On 1973-74 models, turn the mixture screw back out to the point midway between the two extreme positions where the engine began losing rpm to achieve the fastest and smoothest idle.

9. Adjust the curb idle speed to the proper specification, on 1973-74 models, with the idle speed adjusting screw.

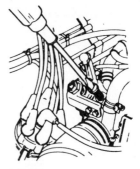

810 idle speed screw

Idle speed screw (arrow)

10. Install the air hose (if so equipped). If the engine speed increases, reduce it with the idle speed screw.

Electronic Fuel Injection (E.F.I.)

These cars use a rather complex electronic fuel injection system which is controlled by a series of temperature, altitude (for California) and air flow sensors which feed information into a central control unit. The control unit then relays an electronic signal to the injector nozzle at each cylinder, which allows a predetermined amount of fuel into the combustion chamber. To adjust the mixture controls on these units requires a CO meter and several special Datsun/Nissan tools. Therefore, we will confine ourselves to idle speed adjustment.

IDLE SPEED ADJUSTMENT

Fuel Injected Models up to 1984

1. Start the engine and run it until the water temperature indicator points to the middle of the temperature gauge. It might be quicker to take a short spin down the road and back.

2. Open the engine hood. Run the engine at about 2,000 rpm for a few minutes with the transmission in Neutral and all accessories off. If you have not already done so, check the ignition timing and make sure it is correct. Hook up a tachometer as per the manufacturer's instructions. For automatic transmission, set the parking brake, block the wheels and set the shift selector in the Drive position.

3. Run the engine at idle speed and disconnect the hose from the air induction pipe, then plug the pipe. Allow the engine to run for about a minute at idle speed.

4. Check the idle against the specifications given earlier in this chapter. Adjust the idle speed by turning the idle speed adjusting screw,

Idle speed adjusting screw—200SX

Idle speed adjusting screw—1977–80 810

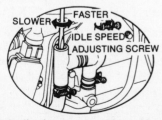

Idle speed adjusting screw—1981 and later 810 and Maxima

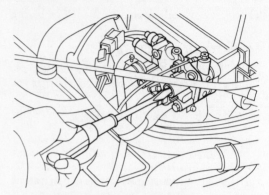

Adjusting idle speed 1985–88 Maxima

located near the air cleaner on the 200SX and the throttle chamber on the 810. Turn the screw clockwise for slower idle speed and counterclockwise for faster idle speed.

5. Connect the hose and disconnect the tachometer. If idle speed increases, adjust it with the idle speed adjusting screw.

1985-88 Maxima Models

1. Turn off the: headlights, heater blower, air conditioning, and rear window defogger. If the car has power steering, make sure the wheel is in the straight ahead position. The ignition timing must be correct to get an effective idle speed adjustment. Adjust the timing if do not know it to be correct. Connect a tachometer (a special adapter harness may be needed) according to the instrument manufacturer's directions.

Idle up solenoid harness location—1985–88 Maxima

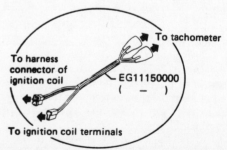

Special tool-adapter harness for tachometer installation

2. Start engine and warm up until water temperature indicator points to the middle of the gauge.

3. Run engine at about 2,000 rpm for about 2 minutes under no load.

4. Disconnect idle up solenoid harness connector and then race engine 2 or 3 times under no load, then run engine at idle speed.

5. Apply the parking brake securely and then put the transmission into Drive, if the car has an automatic. Adjust the idle speed to the figure shown in the Tune-Up Specifications Chart by turning the idle speed adjusting screw shown in the appropriate illustration.

6. Stop engine and connect idle up solenoid harness connector.

7. Remove tachometer and road test for proper operation.

1989 Maxima Model

1. Before adjusting the idle speed on the engine you must visually check the following items first: air cleaner for being clogged, hoses and ducts for leaks, EGR valve for proper operation, all electrical connectors, gaskets and idle switch.

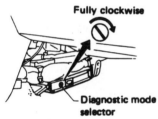

Closing A.A.C. valve before idle speed adjustment—1989 Maxima

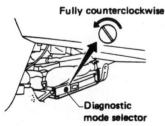

Opening A.A.C. valve after idle speed adjustment—1989 Maxima

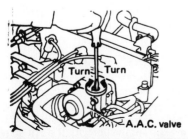

Idle speed adjusting screw location—1989 Maxima

2. Start the engine and warm the engine so it reaches normal operating temperature. The water temperature indicator should be in the middle of the gauge.

3. Then race the engine to 2,000-3,000 rpm a few times under no load and then allow it to return to the idle speed.

4. Connect a tachometer according to the instrument manufacturer's directions.

5. Check the idle speed in the Neutral position for both manual and automatic transaxle models.

6. If the idle speed has to be adjusted you must close the A.A.C. valve (Auxiliary Air Control) by turning the diagnostic mode selector on the E.C.U. fully clockwise.

7. Adjust the idle speed by turning the idle speed adjusting screw with transaxle in the Neutral position.

8. Operate the A.A.C. valve by turning the diagnostic mode selector on the E.C.U. fully conterclockwise.

9. Stop the engine. Remove the tachometer and road test vehicle for proper operation.

1984-86½ 200SX Models

1. Start the engine and warm the engine so it reaches normal operating temperature. The water temperature indicator should be in the middle of the gauge.

2. Then race the engine to 2,000-3,000 rpm a few times under no load and then allow it to return to the idle speed.

3. Connect a tachometer according to the instrument manufacturer's directions.

4. Check the idle speed on the manual transmission model in Neutral and on the automatic transmission model check in Drive.

NOTE: *For automatic transmission, set the*

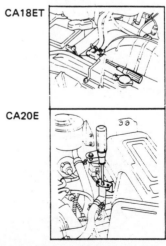

Adjusting idle speed—1984–86½ 200SX

parking brake, block the wheels and set the shift selector in the Drive position.

5. Adjust the idle speed to the figure shown in the Tune-Up Specifications Chart by turning the idle speed adjusting screw shown in the appropriate illustration.

6. Stop the engine. Remove the tachometer and road test for proper operation.

1986½-88 200SX (Exc. V6)

NOTE: *On 200SX models that are equipped with a V6 engine refer to the 1985-88 Maxima procedures.*

1. Before adjusting the idle speed on the engine you must visually check the following items first: air cleaner for being clogged, hoses and ducts for leaks, EGR valve for proper operation, all electrical connectors, gaskets and the throttle valve and throttle valve switch.

2. Start the engine and warm the engine so it reaches normal operating temperature. The water temperature indicator should be in the middle of the gauge.

3. Then race the engine to 2,000-3,000 rpm a few times under no load and then allow it to return to the idle speed.

4. Connect a tachometer according to the instrument manufacturer's directions.

5. Check the idle speed on the manual trans-

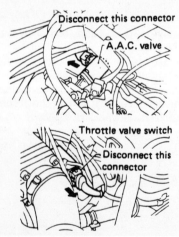

Disconnect A.A.C. valve connector and throttle valve switch connector 1986½—88

Adjusting idle speed—1986½—88 200SX

mission model in Neutral and on the automatic transmission model check in Drive.

NOTE: *For automatic transmission, set the parking brake, block the wheels and set the shift selector in the Drive position.*

6. If the idle speed has to be adjusted you must disconnect the A.A.C. valve harness connector (Auxiliary Air Control) and the throttle valve switch harness connector.

7. Adjust the idle speed to the figure shown in the Tune-Up Specifications Chart by turning the idle speed adjusting screw shown in the appropriate illustration.

8. Stop the engine. Connect the A.A.C. valve harness connector (Auxiliary Air Control) and the throttle valve switch harness connector.

9. Remove the tachometer and road test for proper operation.

1989 240SX Models

1. Before adjusting the idle speed on the engine you must visually check the following items first: air cleaner for being clogged, hoses and ducts for leaks, EGR valve for proper operation, all electrical connectors, gaskets and the throttle valve and throttle valve switch operation.

2. Start the engine and warm the engine so it reaches normal operating temperature. The water temperature indicator should be in the middle of the gauge.

3. Then race the engine to 2,000-3,000 rpm a few times under no load and then allow it to return to the idle speed.

4. Connect a tachometer according to the instrument manufacturer's directions.

5. Check the idle speed in the Neutral position for both manual and automatic transmission models.

6. If the idle speed has to be adjusted you must disconnect the throttle sensor harness connector.

7. Adjust the idle speed to the figure shown in the Tune-Up Specifications Chart by turning the idle speed adjusting screw.

8. Stop the engine. Connect the the throttle sensor harness connector.

9. Remove the tachometer and road test for proper operation.

Diesel Fuel Injection
IDLE SPEED ADJUSTMENT

NOTE: *A special diesel tachometer will be required for this procedure. A normal tachometer will not work.*

1. Make sure all electrical accessories are turned off.

2. Start the engine and run it until it reaches the normal operating temperature.

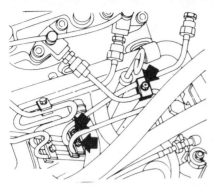

You may wish to remove all the clamps on the No. 1 injection tube to obtain a more accurate rpm reading

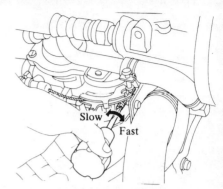

Idle speed adjusting screw—diesel

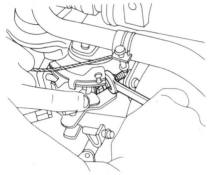

Loosen the idle screw locknut while holding the control lever

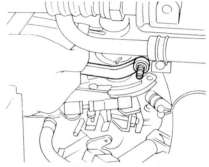

Tighten the idle adjusting screw lock nut when the adjustment is completed

3. The automatic transmission (if so equipped) should be in D with the parking brake on and the wheels blocked.

4. Attach the diesel tachometer's pick-up to the No. 1 injection tube.

NOTE: *In order to obtain a more accurate reading of the idle speed, you may wish to remove all the clamps on the No. 1 injection tube.*

5. Run the engine at about 2,000 rpm for two minutes under no-load conditions.

6. Slow the engine down to idle speed for about 1 min. and then check the idle.

7. If the engine is not idling at the proper speed, turn it off and disconnect the accelerator wire from the injection pump control lever.

8. Move the control lever to the full acceleration side, and then loosen the idle screw lock nut while still holding the control lever.

9. Start the engine again and turn the adjusting screw until the proper idle is obtained. Stop the engine.

10. Tighten the idle adjusting screw lock nut while still holding the control level to the full acceleration side and then connect the accelerator wire.

Engine and Engine Overhaul

3

UNDERSTANDING THE ENGINE ELECTRICAL SYSTEM

The engine electrical system can be broken down into three separate and distinct systems: the starting system, the charging system, and the ignition system.

Battery and Starting System

The battery is the first link in the chain of mechanisms which work together to provide cranking of the automobile engine. In most modern cars, the battery is a lead-acid electrochemical device consisting of six 2v subsections connected in series so the unit is capable of producing approximately 12 V of electrical pressure. Each subsection, or cell, consists of a series of positive and negative plates held a short distance apart in a solution of sulfuric acid and water. The two types of plates are of dissimilar metals. This causes a chemical reaction to be set up, and it is this reaction which produces current flow from the battery when its positive and negative terminals are connected to an electrical appliance such as a lamp or motor. The continued transfer of electrons would eventually convert the sulfuric acid in the electrolyte to water, and make the two plates identical in chemical composition. As electrical energy is removed from the battery, its voltage output tends to drop. Thus, measuring battery voltage and battery electrolyte composition are two ways of checking the ability of the unit to supply power. During the starting of the engine, electrical energy is removed from the battery. However, if the charging circuit is in good condition and the operating conditions are normal, the power removed from the battery will be replaced by the generator (or alternator) which will force electrons back through the battery, reversing the normal flow, and restoring the battery to its original chemical state.

The battery and starting motor are linked by very heavy electrical cables designed to minimize resistance to the flow of current. Generally, the major power supply cable that leaves the battery goes directly to the starter, while other electrical system needs are supplied by a smaller cable. During the starter operation, power flows from the battery to the starter and is grounded through the car's frame and the battery's negative ground strap.

The starting motor is a specially designed, direct current electric motor capable of producing a very great amount of power for its size. One thing that allows the motor to produce a great deal of power is its tremendous rotating speed. It drives the engine through a tiny pinion gear (attached to the starter's armature), which drives the very large flywheel ring gear at a greatly reduced speed. Another factor allowing it to produce so much power is that only intermittent operation is required of it. Thus, little allowance for air circulation is required, and the windings can be built into a very small space.

The starter solenoid is a magnetic device which employs the small current supplied by the starting switch circuit of the ignition switch. This magnetic action moves a plunger which mechanically engages the starter and electrically closes the heavy switch which connects it to the battery. The starting switch circuit consists of the starting switch contained within the ignition switch, a transmission neutral safety switch or clutch pedal switch, and the wiring necessary to connect thee with the starter solenoid or relay.

A pinion, which is a small gear, is mounted to a one way drive clutch. This clutch is splined to the starter armature shaft. When the ignition switch is moved to the start position, the solenoid plunger slides the pinion toward the flywheel ring gear via a collar and spring. If the teeth on the pinion and flywheel match properly, the pinion will engage the flywheel immediately. If the gear teeth butt one another, the spring will be compressed and will force the gears to mesh as soon as the starter turns far enough to allow them to do so. As the solenoid plunger reaches the end of its travel, it closes the contacts that connect the battery and starter and then the engine is cranked.

As soon as the engine starts, the flywheel ring gear begins turning fast enough to drive the pinion at an extremely high rate of speed. At this point, the one way clutch begins allowing the pinion to spin faster than the starter shaft so that the starter will not operate at excessive speed. When the ignition switch is released from the starter position, the solenoid is de-energized, and a spring contained within the solenoid assembly pulls the gear out of mesh and interrupts the current flow to the starter.

Some starters employ a separate relay, mounted away from the starter, to switch the motor and solenoid current on and off. The relay thus replaces the solenoid electrical switch, but does not eliminate the need for a solenoid mounted on the starter used to mechanically engage the starter drive gears. The relay is used to reduce the amount of current the starting switch must carry.

The Charging System

The automobile charging system provides electrical power for operation of the vehicle's ignition and starting systems and all the electrical accessories. The battery serves as an electrical surge or storage tank, storing (in chemical form) the energy originally produced by the engine driven generator. The system also provides a means of regulating generator output to protect the battery from being overcharged and to avoid excessive voltage to the accessories.

The storage battery is a chemical device incorporating parallel lead plates in a tank containing a sulfuric acid-water solution. Adjacent plates are slightly dissimilar, and the chemical reaction of the two dissimilar plates produces electrical energy when the battery is connected to a load such as the starter motor. The chemical reaction is reversible, so that when the generator is producing a voltage (electrical pressure) greater than that produced by the battery, electricity is forced into the battery, and the battery is returned to its fully charged state.

The vehicle's generator is driven mechanically, through V belts, by the engine crankshaft. It consists of two coils of fine wire, one stationary (the stator), and one movable (the rotor). The rotor may also be known as the armature, and consists of fine wire wrapped around an iron core which is mounted on a shaft. The electric-ity which flows through the two coils of wire (provided initially by the battery in some cases) creates an intense magnetic field around both rotor and stator, and the interaction between the two fields creates voltage, allowing the generator to power the accessories and charge the battery.

There are two types of generators; the earlier is the direct current (DC) type. The current produced by the DC generator is generated in the armature and carried off the spinning armature by stationary brushes contacting the commutator. The commutator is a series of smooth metal contact plates on the end of the armature. The commutator plates, which are separated from one another by a very short gap, are connected to the armature circuits so that current will flow in one direction only in the wires carrying the generator output. The generator stator consists of two stationary coils of wire which draw some of the output current of the generator to form a powerful magnetic field and create the interaction of fields which generates the voltage. The generator field is wired in series with the regulator.

Newer automobiles use alternating current generators or alternators because they are more efficient, can be rotated at higher speeds, and have fewer brush problems. In an alternator, the field rotates while all the current produced passes only through the stator windings. The brushes bear against continuous slip rings rather than a commutator. This causes the current produced to periodically reverse the direction of its flow. Diodes (electrical one way switches) block the flow of current from traveling in the wrong direction. A series of diodes is wired together to permit the alternating flow of the stator to be converted to a pulsating, but unidirectional flow at the alternator output. The alternator's field is wired in series with the voltage regulator.

The regulator consists of several circuits. Each circuit had a core, or magnetic coil of wire, which operates a switch. Each s witch is connected to ground through one or more resistors. The coil of wire responds directly to system voltage. When the voltage reaches the required level, the magnetic field created by the winding of wire closes the switch and inserts a resistance into the generator field circuit, thus reducing the output. The contacts of the switch cycle open and close many times each second to precisely control voltage.

While alternators are self limiting as far as maximum current is concerned, DC generators employ a current regulating circuit which responds directly to the total amount of current flowing through the generator circuit rather than to the output voltage. The current regulator is similar to the voltage regulator except that all system current must flow through the energizing coil on its way to the various accessories.

SAFETY PRECAUTIONS

Observing these precautions will ensure safe handling of the electrical system components, and will avoid damage to the vehicle's electrical system:

• Be absolutely sure of the polarity of a booster battery before making connections. Connect the cables positive to positive, and negative to negative. Connect positive cables first and then make the last connection to a ground on the body of the booster vehicle so that arcing cannot ignite hydrogen gas that may have accumulated near the battery. Even momentary connection of a booster battery with the polarity reversed will damage alternator diodes.

• Disconnect both vehicle battery cables before attempting to charge a battery.

• Never ground the alternator or generator output or battery terminal. Be cautious when using metal tools around a battery to avoid creating a short circuit between the terminals.

• Never ground the field circuit between the alternator and regulator.

• Never run an alternator or generator without load unless the field circuit is disconnected.

• Never attempt to polarize an alternator.

• Keep the regulator cover in place when taking voltage and current limiter readings.

• Use insulated tools when adjusting the regulator.

• Whenever DC generator-to-regulator wires have been disconnected, the generator must be repolarized. To do this with an externally grounded, light duty generator, momentarily place a jumper wire between the battery terminal and the generator terminal of the regulator. With an internally grounded heavy duty unit, disconnect the wire to the regulator field terminal and touch the regulator battery terminal with it.

ENGINE ELECTRICAL

Electronic Ignition System Coil/ Module

TESTING

1975-78

The main differences between the 1975-77 and 1978 systems are: (1) the 1975-77 system uses an external ballast resistor located next to the ignition coil, and (2) the earlier system uses a wiring harness with individual eyelet connectors to the electronic unit, while the later system uses a multiple plug connector. You will need an accurate voltmeter and ohmmeter for these tests, which must be performed in the order given.

1. Check all connections for corrosion, looseness, breaks, etc., and correct if necessary. Clean and gap the spark plugs.

2a. Disconnect the harness (connector of plug) from the electronic unit. Turn the ignition switch On. Set the voltmeter to the DC 50v range. Connect the positive (+) voltmeter lead to the black/white wire terminal, and the negative (−) lead to the black wire terminal. Battery, voltage should be obtained. If not, check the black/white and black wires for continuity; check the battery terminals for corrosion; check the battery state of charge.

2b. Next, connect the voltmeter (+) lead to the blue wire and the (−) lead to the black wire. Battery voltage should be obtained. If not check the blue wire for continuity; check the ignition coil terminals for corrosion or looseness; check the coil for continuity. On 1975-77 models, also check the external ballast resistor.

3. Disconnect the distributor harness wires from the ignition coil ballast resistor on 1975-77 models, leaving the ballast resistor-to-coil wires attached. On 1978 models, disconnect the ignition coil wires. Connect the leads of an ohmmeter to the ballast resistor outside terminals (at each end) for 1975-77, and to the two coil terminals for 1978. With the ohmmeter set in the X1 range, the following model years should show a reading of 1.6-2.0Ω: 1976 710, 610; 1977 810, 710.

The following models should show a reading of approximately 0Ω: 1975 710; 1978 810, 200SX. The maximum allowable limit for the 1.6-2.0Ω range models is 2.0Ω. The limit for the 0Ω models is 1.8Ω. If a reading higher than the limit is received, replace the ignition coil assembly.

4. Disconnect the harness from the electronic control unit. Connect an ohmmeter to the red and the green wire terminals. Resistance should be 720Ω. If far more or far less, replace the distributor pick-up coil.

5. Disconnect the anti-dieseling solenoid connector. Connect a voltmeter to the red and green terminals of the electronic control harness. When the starter is cranked, the needle should deflect slightly. If not, replace the distributor pick-up coil.

6. Reconnect the ignition coil and the electronic control unit. Leave the anti-dieseling solenoid wire disconnected. Unplug the high ten-

sion lead (coil to distributor) from the distributor and hole it 1/8-1/4" from the cylinder head with a pair of insulated pliers and a heavy glove. When the engine is cranked, a spark should be observed. If not, check the lead, and replace if necessary. If still no spark, replace the electronic control unit.

7. Reconnect all wires.

1976-77: connect the voltmeter (+) lead to

the blue electronic control harness connector and the (−) lead to the black wire. The harness should be attached to the control unit.

1978: Connect the voltmeter (+) lead to the (−) terminal of the ignition coil and the (−) lead to ground.

As soon as the ignition switch is turned ON, the meter should indicate battery voltage. If not, replace the electronic control unit.

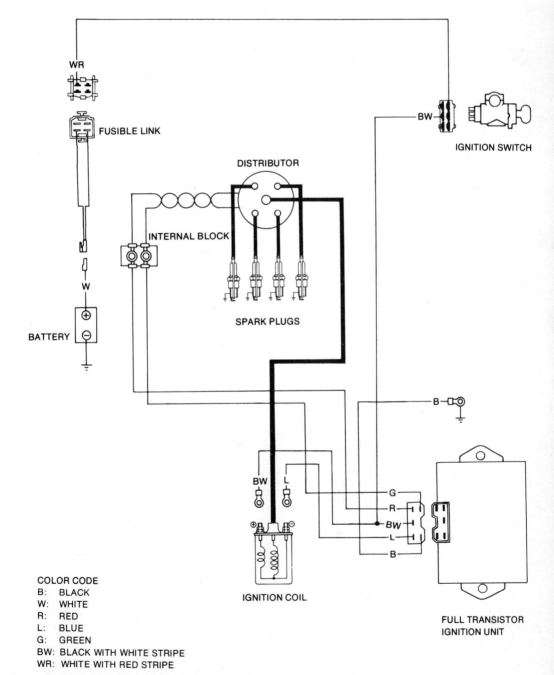

Electronic ignition schematic—1975–78 4 cylinder models (510 shown, other models similar)

1979-84

810 AND MAXIMA
510
200SX (SINGLE PLUG ENGINE ONLY)

1. Make a check of the power supply circuit. Turn the ignition OFF, Disconnect the connector from the top of the IC unit. Turn the ignition ON. Measure the voltage at each terminal of the connector in turn by touch the probe of the positive lead of the voltmeter to one of the terminals, and touching the probe of the negative lead of the voltmeter to a ground, such as the engine. In each case, battery voltage should

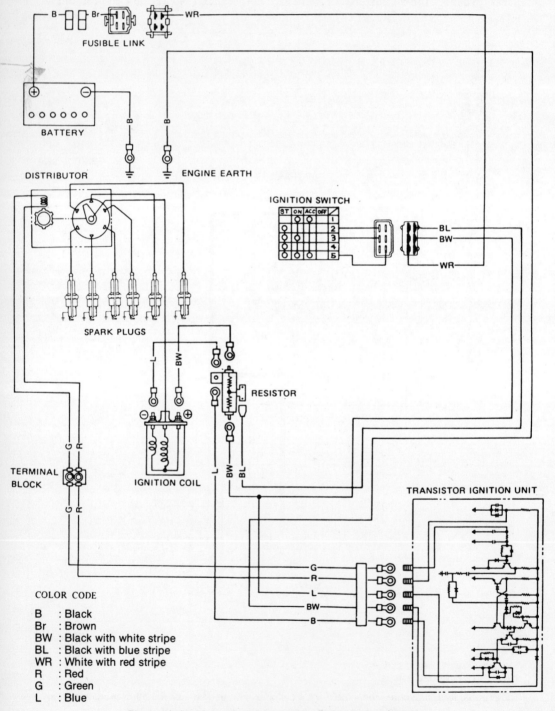

COLOR CODE

B   : Black
Br   : Brown
BW   : Black with white stripe
BL   : Black with blue stripe
WR   : White with red stripe
R   : Red
G   : Green
L   : Blue

Electronic ignition schematic—1975–78 6 cylinder models

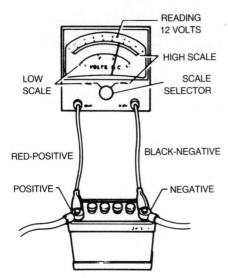

Testing battery voltage with a D.C. voltmeter

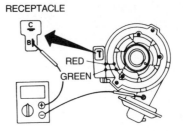

Testing the power supply circuit, 1983 200SX

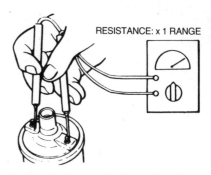

Checking the ignition coil primary circuit

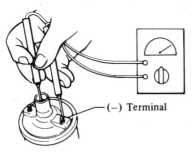

Testing the 1983 200SX ignition coil secondary circuit

be indicated. If not, check all wiring, the ignition switch, and all connectors for breaks, corrosion, discontinuity, etc., and repair as necessary.

2. Check the primary windings of the ignition coil. Turn the ignition OFF. Disconnect the

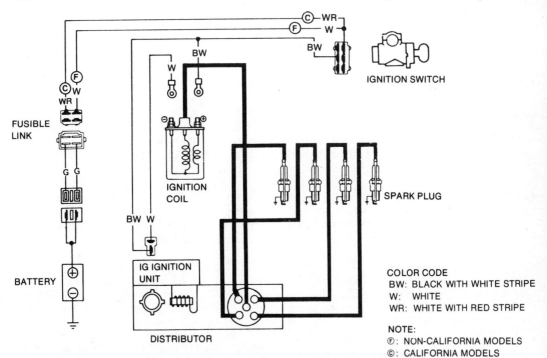

COLOR CODE
BW: BLACK WITH WHITE STRIPE
W: WHITE
WR: WHITE WITH RED STRIPE

NOTE:
Ⓕ: NON-CALIFORNIA MODELS
Ⓒ: CALIFORNIA MODELS

Electronic ignition schematic—1979 510 (200SX similar)

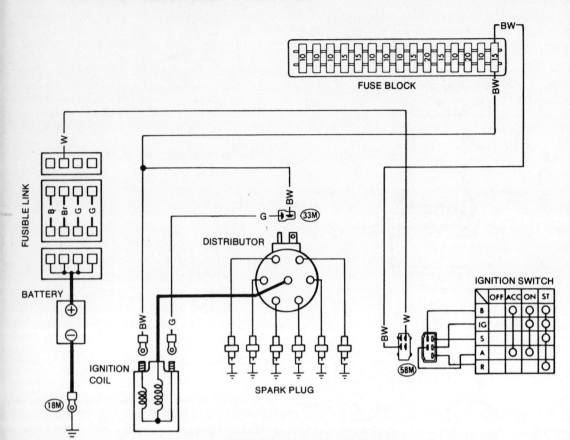

Electronic ignition schematic—1979–82 810

harness connector from the negative coil terminal. Use an ohmmeter to measure the resistance between the positive and negative coil terminals. If resistance is 0.84-1.02Ω the coil is OK. Replace if far from this range. If the power supply, circuits, wiring, and coil are in good shape, check the IC unit and pick-up coil, as follows:

3. Turn the ignition OFF. Remove the distributor cap and ignition rotor. Use an ohmmeter to measure the resistance between the two terminals of the pick-up coil, where they attach to the IC unit. Measure the resistance by reversing the polarity of the probes. If approximately 400Ω are indicated, the pick-up coil is OK, but the IC unit is bad and must be replaced. If other than 400Ω are measured, go to the next step.

4. Be certain the two pin connector to the IC unit is secure. Turn the ignition ON. Measure the voltage at the ignition coil negative terminal. Turn the ignition OFF.

CAUTION: *Remove the tester probe from the coil negative terminal before switching the ignition OFF, to prevent burning out the tester.* If zero voltage is indicated, the IC unit is bad

and must be replaced. If battery voltage is indicated, proceed.

5. Remove the IC unit from the distributor:

a. Disconnect the battery ground (negative) cable.

b. Remove the distributor cap and ignition rotor.

c. Disconnect the harness connector at the top of the IC unit.

d. Remove the two screws securing the IC unit to the distributor.

e. Disconnect the two pick-up coil wires from the IC unit.

CAUTION: *Pull the connectors free with a pair of needlenosed pliers. Do not pull on the wires to detach the connectors.*

f. Remove the IC unit.

6. Measure the resistance between the terminals of the pick-up coil. It should be approximately 400Ω. If so, the pick-up coil is OK, and the IC unit is bad. If not approximately 400Ω, the pick-up coil is bad and must be replaced.

7. With a new pick-up coil installed, install the IC unit. Check for a spark at one of the spark plugs. If a good spark is obtained, the IC unit is OK. If not, replace the IC unit.

1980-83 510, 200SX (TWIN PLUG ENGINE)

Complete Step 1-2 of the previous procedure; the resistance should be between 1.04-1.27Ω. If not, replace ignition coil(s).

NOTE: *The manufacturer does not give a complete system of tests for the 1980 200SX/510 California ignition system. Therefore, before attempting anything else, try this spark performance test:*

1. Turn the ignition switch to the OFF position.

2. On the 510 cut off the fuel supply to the engine. On the 200SX, disconnect the electronic fuel injection (EFI) fusible link.

3. Disconnect the high tension cable from the distributor. Hold the cable with insulated pliers to avoid getting shocked. Position the wire about a ¼" from the engine block and have an assistant turn over the engine using the

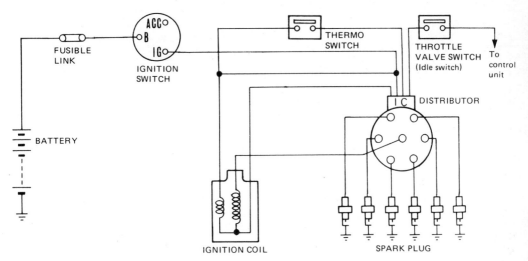

1983–84 810 and Maxima ignition schematic

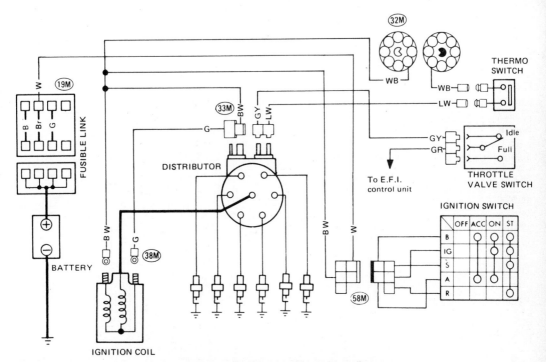

1983–84 810 and Maxima ignition wiring diagram

starter. A spark should jump from the cable to the engine block. If not, there is probably something wrong with the ignition system. Further testing should be left to an authorized service technician with the proper test equipment.

NOTE: *The 1985-89 Maxima, 1984-88 200SX and 1989 240SX vehicles use a highly complex computerized ignition system. Complete testing, flow charts and engine code diagnostic procedures will not be provided because of the extensive specialized training and equipment that would be required. We suggest that you do not try handling these kinds of repairs unless you have extreme skill*

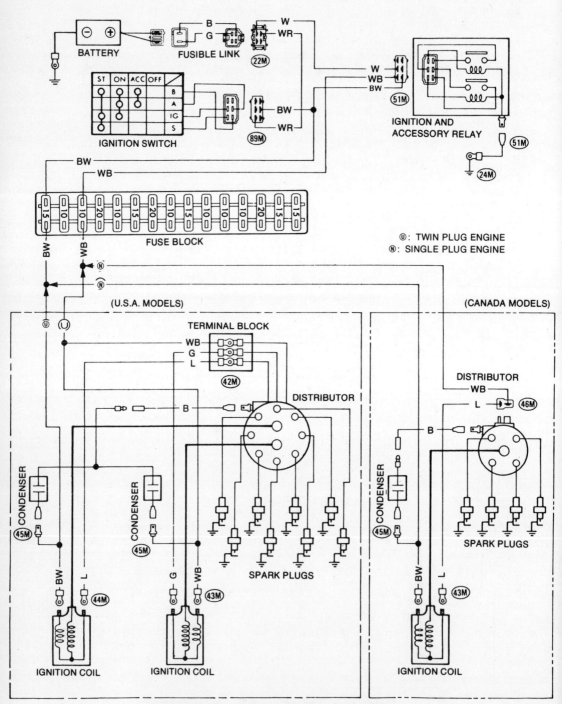

Electronic ignition schematic—1980–82 510/200SX

and experience with automotive electrical troubleshooting. If you want more information in this area refer to "Chilton's Electronic Engine Controls Maunual" for import car and trucks part No.#7800

Diesel Engine Auto-Glow System

The glow plug circuit is used on diesel engines to initially start the engine from cold. The glow plugs heat up the combustion chambers

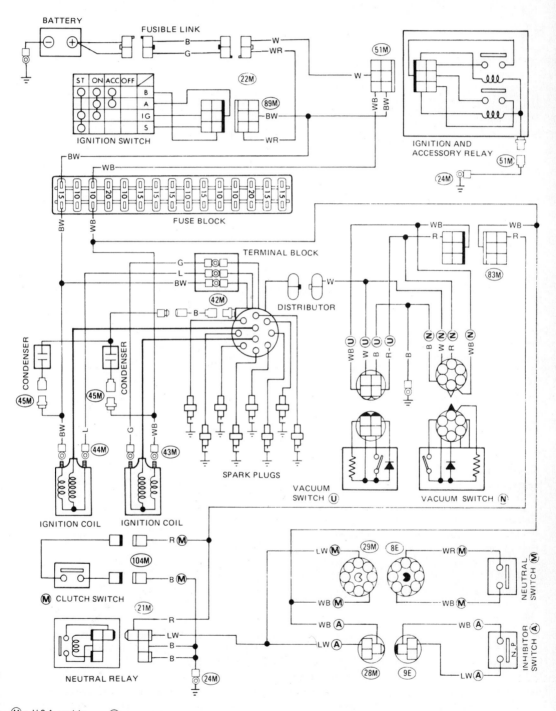

Ignition wiring diagram—1983 200SX

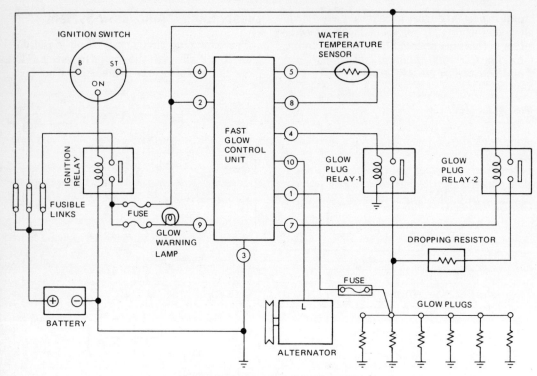

Diesel glow plug electrical schematic

prior to cranking the engine. This heat, combined with the first squirt of fuel from the injectors and the extremely high cylinder pressures, fires the engine during cold starts. After normal operating temperature is reached, the water temperature sensor wired in the glow plug system changes the system's electrical resistance and cancels glow plug operation during hot starting.

GLOW PLUG REMOVAL

LD28 Diesel

1. Disconnect the glow plug electrical leads. Remove the glow plug connecting plate.
2. Remove the glow plugs by unscrewing them from the cylinder head.
3. Inspect the tips of the plugs for any evidence of melting. If even one glow plug tip looks bad, all the glow plugs must be replaced. This is a general rule-of-thumb which applies to all diesel engines.

TESTING

Glow plugs are tested by checking their resistance with an ohmmeter. The plugs can be tested either while removed from the cylinder head or while still in position. To test them while removed, connect the ground side of the ohmmeter to the threaded section of the plug, and the other side to the plug's tip as shown in the illus-

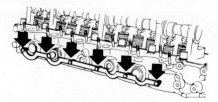

Remove the glow plug connecting plate

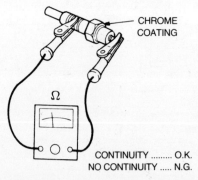

Check glow plug continuity with an ohmmeter (glow plug removed here; connect the ground wire to the threaded portion)

tration. If a minimum of continuity is shown on the meter, the plug is OK. If no continuity whatsoever is shown the plug must be replaced. To check the glow plugs without removing them from the cylinder head, connect the ground side of the ohmmeter to the engine block (or any other convenient ground) and the other end to the glow plug tip. Likewise, a minimum of continuity shown signifies that the plug is OK; a lack of continuity and the plug must be replaced.

INSTALLATION

To install the glow plugs, screw the glow plugs into the cylinder head just like spark plugs. Install the glow plug connecting plate. Torque the glow plugs to 14-18 ft. lbs., and the glow plug connecting plate bolts to 12 in. lbs.

CHECKING GLOW PLUG CONNECTIONS

A diesel engine's reluctance to start can often be traced to the glow plug busbar (the wire connections to the plugs.) Because diesel engines have a certain degree of vibration when running, they tend to loosen the glow plug busbars. This causes hard starting, as the plugs are not receiving their full current. Periodically tighten the wire connection to all glow plugs.

CAUTION: *The Datsun/Nissan glow plug system is a 12 volt system equipped with a dropping resistor and fast glow control unit. The resistor reduces the amount of current flowing through the plugs during the after-glow period, and the glow plug control unit stops the after-glow when more than 7 volts is detected flowing through the glow plugs. Never apply a full 12 volts directly to any part of the glow plug system, especially the glow plugs themselves.*

FAST GLOW CONTROL UNIT OPERATION

The fast glow control unit on 810 and Maxima diesels has multiple functions, controlling various components of the glow plug system. It has a total of ten terminals:

• No.1 Terminal: A terminal at which voltage being applied to the glow plug is measured. It serves two functions:

a. Determines the pre-glow time (approx. 4 to 12 seconds)

b. Stops after-glow operations when a voltage of more than 7 volts is detected after pre-glow operation

• No.2 Terminal: Control unit's power source terminal

• No.3 Terminal: Control unit's ground terminal

• No.4 Terminal: A terminal that controls the ON/OFF operation of glow plug relay 1.

• No.5 Terminal: A terminal connected to the water temperature sensor to serve three functions:

a. Determines the period that the warning lamp remains illuminated (approx. 1 to 9 seconds)

b. Determines the after-glow time (approx. 5 to 32 seconds)

c. Stops pre-glow operation when coolant temperature is higher than 50°C (122°F)

• No.6 Terminal: A terminal connected to the START position of the ignition switch (When the ignition key is returned from START to ON, after-glow operation begins.)

• No.7 Terminal: Controls the ON/OFF operation of glow plug relay 2.

• No.8 Terminal: A grounding terminal for the water temperature sensor

Engine Coolant Temperature °C (°F)	Glow Plug Terminal Voltage	Time (sec.)
Below 50 (122)	8V	Approx. 13
	10.5V	Approx. 6
Above 50 (122)	—	Approx. 0

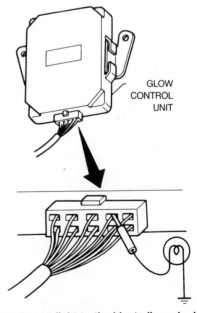

GLOW CONTROL UNIT

Connect a test light to the blue/yellow wire leading into the fast glow control unit

Fast glow control unit connections

- No.9 Terminal: A terminal for the flow/ fuel filter warning lamp
- No.10 Terminal: A terminal used to determine whether the engine has started or not (Glow plug relay is turned OFF by means of terminal (4) immediately after the engine has started.)

CHECKING PRE-GLOW SYSTEM

1. Connect a test light to the blue/yellow wire leading to the glow control unit. Measure the length of time that the test light is lighted.

2. Standard operation (except restart operation within 60 seconds):
Restart operation (within 80 seconds): The length of time the light is ON should be less than 6.5 seconds. For example, when restarting the engine 5 seconds after the ignition switch is turned off, the lamp should be ON for 1.5 seconds (with engine coolant temperature below 122°F and glow plug voltage 10.5 volts).

AFTER-GLOW OPERATION

1. Connect a test light to the blue/red wire leading to the glow control unit. Measure the length of time that the light is lighted. In the

Engine Coolant Temperature °C (°F)	Time (sec.)
Below −25 (−13) (approx.)	Approx. 31
Approx. 20 (68)	Approx. 17
Approx. 40 (104)	Approx. 9
Above 50 (122) (approx.)	0

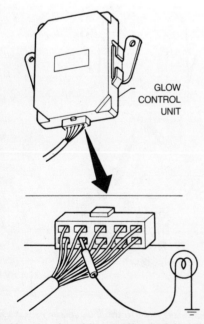

Checking the after-glow operation (terminal 7)

Glow Plug Terminal Voltage	Test Lamp ②
Above 7V	OFF
Below 7V	ON

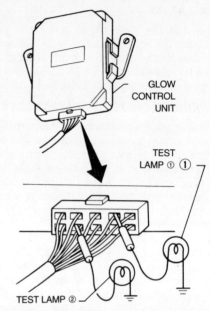

Testing the on/off operation of the glow plug relays 1 and 2

normal condition, when the ignition switch is turned ON from ST or OFF, and the ignition switch in ST, the test light is on continuously. Refer to the accompanying illustration.

2. After the pre-glow system turns off, check the operation of the test light (2) in the accompanying illustration; (test light no. (1) in the illustration is OFF).

WATER TEMPERATURE SENSOR OPERATION

The water temperature sensor is connected to the fast glow control unit. Sensor resistance varies with changes in the temperature of the engine coolant.

TESTING

The sensor is tested by measuring resistance while removed from the engine and inserted in a vessel of water as shown in the illustration. Replace the sensor if resistance figures vary greatly from those shown.

Distributor

REMOVAL

1. Unfasten the retaining clips and lift the distributor cap straight up. It will be easier to

TEMPERATURE ˇC ((°F)	RESISTANCE kΩ
10(50)	3.25 – 4.15
20(68)	2.25 – 2.75
50(122)	0.74 – 0.94
80(176)	0.29 – 0.36

Testing the water temperature sensor with an ohmmeter

install the distributor if the spark plug wires are not disconnected from the cap. If the wires must be removed from the cap remove the wires one at a time, mark or tag their positions to aid in installation.

2. Disconnect the distributor wiring harness and or the electrical connection if so equipped.

NOTE: *On late model Datsun/Nissan a crankangle sensor is the basic component of the distributor. No vacuum lines are used just one electrical connection.*

3. Disconnect the vacuum lines if so equipped.

4. Note the position of the rotor in relation to the base. Scribe a mark on the base of the distributor and on the engine block to facilitate reinstallation. Align the marks with the direction the metal tip of the rotor is pointing.

5. Remove the bolt(s) which holds the distributor to the engine.

6. Carefully lift the distributor assembly from the engine.

INSTALLATION

1. Insert the distributor shaft and assembly into the engine. Line up the mark on the distributor and the one on the engine with the metal tip of the rotor. Make sure that the vacuum advance diaphragm if so equipped is pointed in the same direction as it was pointed originally. This will be done automatically if the marks

on the engine and the distributor are lined up with the rotor.

2. Install the distributor holddown bolt and clamp. Leave the screw loose enough so that you can move the distributor with heavy hand pressure.

3. Connect the primary wire to the coil and or the electrical connection. Install the distributor cap on the distributor housing. Secure the distributor cap with the spring clips.

4. Install the spark plug wires if removed. Make sure that the wires are pressed all the way into the top of the distributor cap and firmly onto the spark plug. Make sure the correct firing order is maintained.

5. Adjust the point dwell if so equipped and set the ignition timing.

NOTE: *If the crankshaft has been turned or the engine disturbed in any manner (i.e., disassembled and rebuilt) while the distributor was removed, or if the marks were not drawn, it will be necessary to initially time the engine. Follow the procedure given below.*

INSTALLATION – CRANKSHAFT OR CAMSHAFT ROTATED

1. It is necessary to place the No. 1 cylinder in the firing position to correctly install the distributor. To locate this position, the ignition timing marks on the crankshaft front pulley are used.

2. Remove the No. 1 cylinder spark plug. Turn the crankshaft until the piston in the No. 1 cylinder is moving up on the compression stroke. This can be determined by placing your thumb over the spark plug hole and feeling the air being forced out of the cylinder. Stop turning the crankshaft when the timing marks that are used to time the engine are aligned.

3. Oil the distributor housing lightly where the distributor bears on the cylinder block.

4. Install the distributor so that the rotor, which is mounted on the shaft, points toward the No. 1 spark plug terminal tower position when the cap is installed. Of course you won't be able to see the direction in which the rotor is pointing if the cap is on the distributor. Lay the cap on the top of the distributor and make a mark on the side of the distributor housing just below the No. 1 spark plug terminal. Make sure that the rotor points toward that mark when you install the distributor.

5. When the distributor shaft has reached the bottom of the hole, move the rotor back and forth slightly until the driving lug on the end of the shaft enters the slots cut in the end of the oil pump shaft and the distributor assembly slides down into place.

6. When the distributor is correctly installed, the breaker points should be in such a position

that they are just ready to break contact with each other; or, on engines with electronic ignition, the reluctor teeth should be aligned with the pick-up coil. This can be accomplished by rotating the distributor body after it has been installed in the engine. Once again, line up the marks that you made before the distributor was removed.

7. Install the distributor holddown bolt.

8. Install the spark plug into the No. 1 spark plug hole and continue from Step 3 of the preceding distributor installation procedure.

If your engine has a distributor with a crankangle sensor set up read the above section and then you will be able to remove and install the distributor.

Basically, you have to remove the distributor cap, mark or tag all the spark plug wires and the electrical connections then remove them. Next, mark the postion of the base of the distributor with relation to the engine mounting location and the rotor position as opposed to the the base of the distributor.

When installing the distributor, line up your

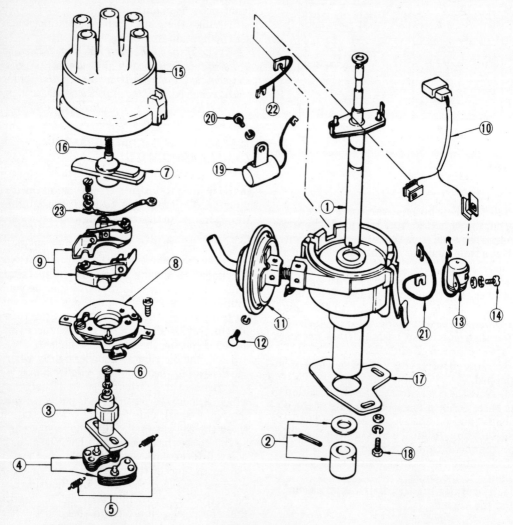

1. Shaft assembly
2. Collar set assembly
3. Cam assembly
4. Governor weight assembly
5. Governor spring set
6. Screw
7. Rotor
8. Breaker plate
9. Breaker points
10. Connector assembly
11. Vacuum control assembly
12. Screw
13. Condenser
14. Screw
15. Distributor cap
16. Carbon point assembly
17. Retaining plate
18. Bolt
19. Condenser
20. Screw
21. Lead wire
22. Lead wire
23. Ground wire

Exploded view of the dual point distributor

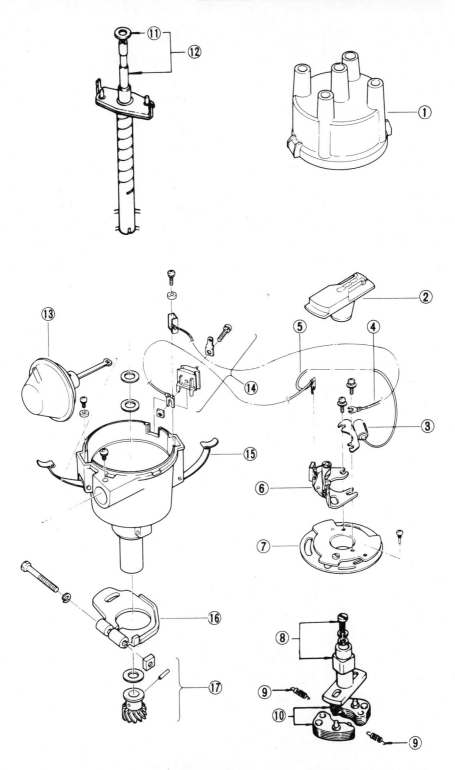

1. Cap
2. Rotor
3. Condenser
4. Ground wire
5. Lead wire
6. Breaker points
7. Breaker plate
8. Cam assembly
9. Governor spring
10. Governor weight
11. Thrust washer
12. Shaft assembly
13. Vacuum control assembly
14. Terminal assembly
15. Clamp
16. Retaining plate
17. Gear set

Exploded view of the single point distributor

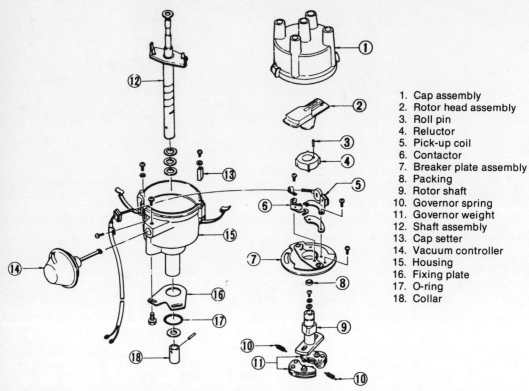

1. Cap assembly
2. Rotor head assembly
3. Roll pin
4. Reluctor
5. Pick-up coil
6. Contactor
7. Breaker plate assembly
8. Packing
9. Rotor shaft
10. Governor spring
11. Governor weight
12. Shaft assembly
13. Cap setter
14. Vacuum controller
15. Housing
16. Fixing plate
17. O-ring
18. Collar

Exploded view of the distributor—1975–77 California models, 610, 710 and 200SX; 1977–78 510, 200SX and 810

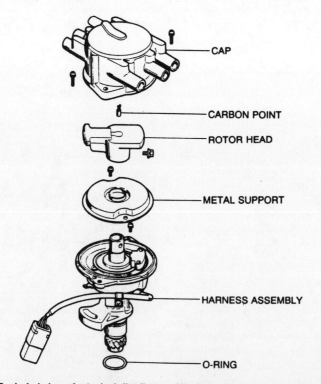

— CAP

— CARBON POINT

— ROTOR HEAD

— METAL SUPPORT

— HARNESS ASSEMBLY

— O-RING

Exploded view of a typical distributor—V6 shown (most late models similar)

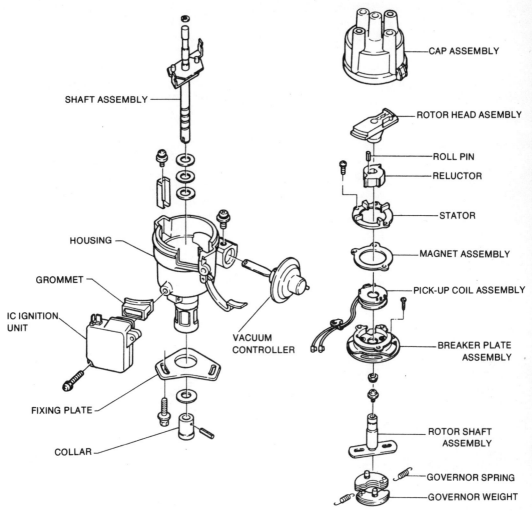

SHAFT ASSEMBLY

HOUSING

GROMMET

IC IGNITION
UNIT

FIXING PLATE

COLLAR

VACUUM
CONTROLLER

CAP ASSEMBLY

ROTOR HEAD ASEMBLY

ROLL PIN

RELUCTOR

STATOR

MAGNET ASSEMBLY

PICK-UP COIL ASSEMBLY

BREAKER PLATE
ASSEMBLY

ROTOR SHAFT
ASSEMBLY

GOVERNOR SPRING

GOVERNOR WEIGHT

Exploded view of the distributor—1979 510 (Canada); 1979 510 and 200SX; 1980 510 and 200SX (49-states). 1979 and later 810 and Maxima similar

marks and gently install the distributor and reconnect all spark wires and electrical connections. If you disturb the engine while the distributor is removed you will have to set inital timing.

Alternator

ALTERNATOR PRECAUTIONS

To prevent damage to the alternator and regulator, the following precautionary measures must be taken when working with the electrical system.

1. Never reverse battery connections.
2. Booster batteries for starting must be connected properly. Make sure that the positive cable of the booster battery is connected to the positive terminal of the battery that is getting the boost. This applies to both negative and ground cables.

3. Disconnect the battery cables before using a fast charger; the charger has a tendency to force current through the diodes in the opposite direction for which they are designed. This burns out the diodes.
4. Never use a fast charger as a booster for starting the vehicle.
5. Never disconnect the voltage regulator while the engine is running.
6. Do not ground the alternator output terminal.
7. Do not operate the alternator on an open circuit with the field energized.
8. Do not attempt to polarize an alternator.

REMOVAL AND INSTALLATION

1. Disconnect the negative battery terminal.
2. Disconnect the two lead wires and connector from the alternator.

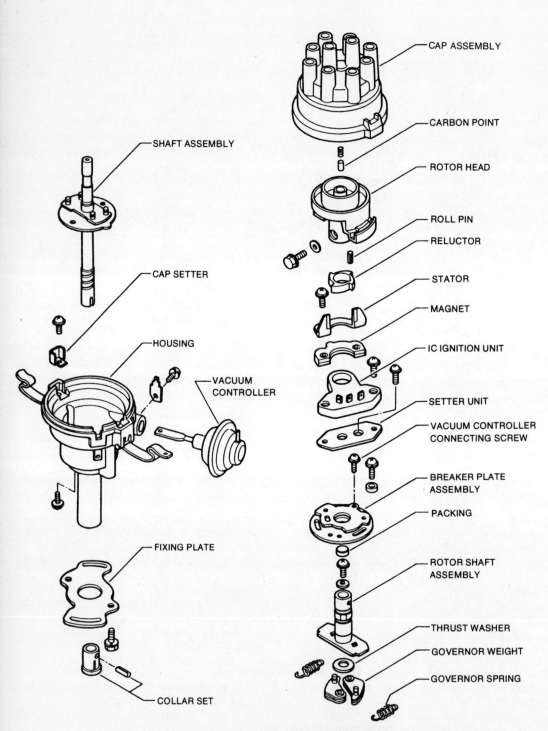

SHAFT ASSEMBLY

CAP ASSEMBLY

CARBON POINT

ROTOR HEAD

ROLL PIN

RELUCTOR

STATOR

MAGNET

CAP SETTER

IC IGNITION UNIT

HOUSING

VACUUM
CONTROLLER

SETTER UNIT

VACUUM CONTROLLER
CONNECTING SCREW

BREAKER PLATE
ASSEMBLY

PACKING

FIXING PLATE

ROTOR SHAFT
ASSEMBLY

THRUST WASHER

GOVERNOR WEIGHT

GOVERNOR SPRING

COLLAR SET

Exploded view of the distributor—1980–82 510/200SX with the twin plug engine

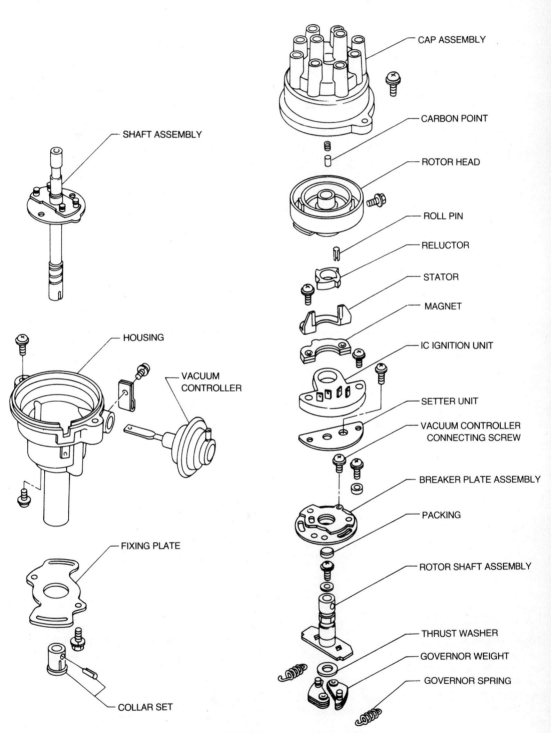

SHAFT ASSEMBLY

HOUSING

VACUUM CONTROLLER

FIXING PLATE

COLLAR SET

CAP ASSEMBLY

CARBON POINT

ROTOR HEAD

ROLL PIN

RELUCTOR

STATOR

MAGNET

IC IGNITION UNIT

SETTER UNIT

VACUUM CONTROLLER CONNECTING SCREW

BREAKER PLATE ASSEMBLY

PACKING

ROTOR SHAFT ASSEMBLY

THRUST WASHER

GOVERNOR WEIGHT

GOVERNOR SPRING

1983 200SX distributor, U.S. models

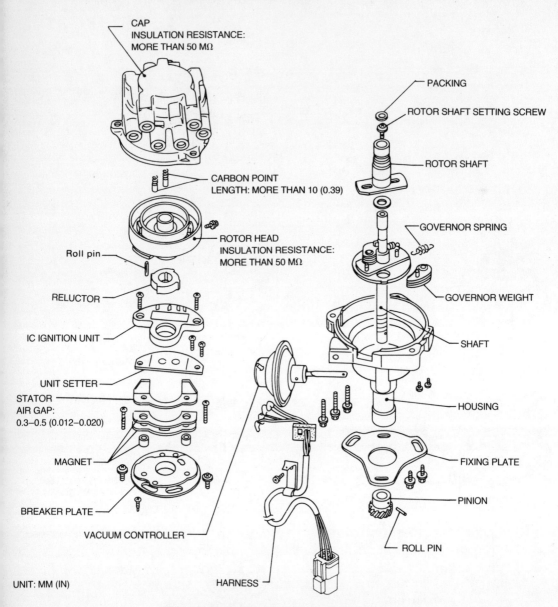

CAP
INSULATION RESISTANCE:
MORE THAN 50 MΩ

PACKING

ROTOR SHAFT SETTING SCREW

ROTOR SHAFT

CARBON POINT
LENGTH: MORE THAN 10 (0.39)

GOVERNOR SPRING

Roll pin

ROTOR HEAD
INSULATION RESISTANCE:
MORE THAN 50 MΩ

RELUCTOR

GOVERNOR WEIGHT

IC IGNITION UNIT

SHAFT

UNIT SETTER

STATOR
AIR GAP:
0.3–0.5 (0.012–0.020)

HOUSING

MAGNET

FIXING PLATE

BREAKER PLATE

PINION

VACUUM CONTROLLER

ROLL PIN

UNIT: MM (IN)

HARNESS

1984 and later 200SX distributor, CA20E engines

3. Loosen the drive belt adjusting bolt and remove the belt.

4. Unscrew the alternator attaching bolts and remove the alternator from the vehicle.

5. Mount the alternator to the engine and partially tighten the attaching bolts.

6. Reconnect the lead wires and connector to the alternator.

7. Install the alternator drive belt.

8. Adjust the alternator belt correctly and completely tighten the mounting bolts.

9. Connnect the battery cable. Start the engine and check for proper operation.

NOTE: *The alternator belt tension is quite critical. A belt that is too tight may cause alternator bearing failure; one that is too loose will cause a gradual battery discharge.*

Regulator

REMOVAL AND INSTALLATION

NOTE: *1978 and later models are equipped with integral regulator alternators. Since the regulator is part of the alternator no adjustments are possible or necessary.*

1. Disconnect the negative battery terminal.

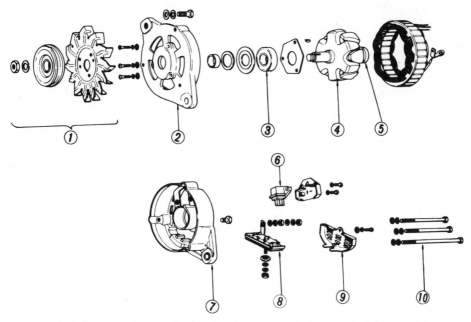

1. Pulley assembly
2. Front cover
3. Front bearing
4. Rotor
5. Rear bearing
6. Brush assembly
7. Rear cover
8. Diode set plate assembly
9. Diode cover
10. Through-bolts

Exploded view of the alternator used on pre-1978 510, 610, 710 and 200SX

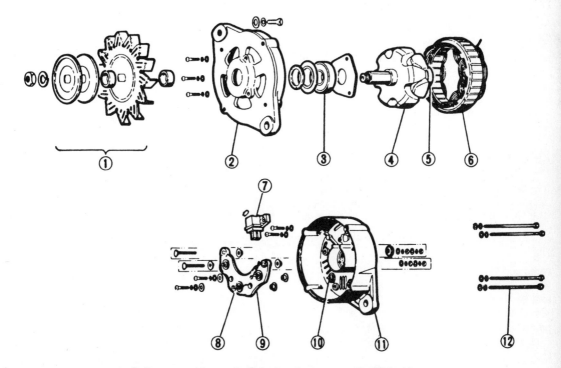

1. Pulley assembly
2. Front cover
3. Front bearing
4. Rotor
5. Rear bearing
6. Stator assembly
7. Brush assembly
8. Diode
9. SR holder
10. Diode
11. Rear cover
12. Through bolts

Exploded view of 1977 810 alternator

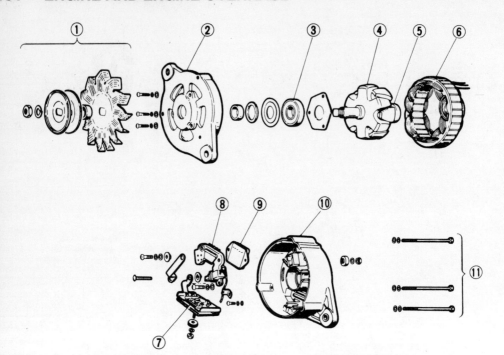

1. Pulley assembly
2. Front cover
3. Front bearing
4. Rotor
5. Rear bearing
6. Stator
7. Diode (Set plate) assembly
8. Brush assembly
9. IC voltage regulator
10. Rear cover
11. Through bolt

Integral regulator-type alternator—most models similar

2. Disconnect the electrical lead connector of the regulator.

3. Remove the two mounting screws and remove the regulator from the vehicle.

4. Install the regulator in the reverse order of removal.

ADJUSTMENT

1. Adjust the voltage regulator core gap on regulators that are adjustable by loosening the screw which is used to secure the contact set on the yoke, and move the contact up or down as

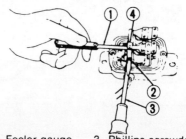

1. Feeler gauge
2. Screw
3. Phillips screwdriver
4. Upper contact

Adjust the point gap

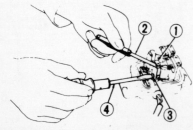

1. Contacts
2. Feeler gauge
3. Adjusting screw
4. Phillips screwdriver

Adjusting the core gap

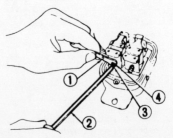

1. Wrench
2. Phillips screwdriver
3. Adjusting screw
4. Locknut

Adjust the regulated voltage

Alternator and Regulator Specifications

Year	Model	Alternator Identification Number	Rated Output @ 5000 RPM	Output @ 2500 RPM (not less than)	Brush Length (in.)	Brush Spring Tension (oz)	Regulated Voltage
1973	610	LT150-05B	50	37.5	0.571	8.8–12.32	14.3–15.3
1974	610	LT150-05B	50	37.5	0.571	8.8–12.32	14.3–15.3
	710	LT150-13	50	37.5	0.571	8.80	14.3–15.3
1975	610	LT150-13	50	37.5	0.310	9.0–12.2	14.3–15.3
	710	LT150-13	50	37.5	0.571	8.80	14.3–15.3
1976	610	LT150-13	50	37.5	0.310	9.0–12.2	14.3–15.3
	710	LT150-13	50	37.5	0.295	9.0–12.2	14.3–15.3
1977	710	LT150-25	50	37.5	0.295	9.0–12.2	14.3–15.3
	810	LT160-39	60	40	0.310	9.0–12.2	14.3–15.3
	200SX	LT150-35 ①	50	40	0.295	8.99–12.17	14.4–15.0
1978	810	LR160-42 ①	60	40	0.280	8.99–12.17	14.4–15.0
	510	LR150-35 ①	50	40	0.295	8.99–12.17	14.4–15.0
		LR160-47 ① ②	60	41	0.295	8.99–12.17	14.4–15.0
	200SX	LR150-35 ①	50	40	0.295	8.99–12.17	14.4–15.0
1979	810	LR160-42 ①	60	40	0.280	8.99–12.17	14.4–15.0
	510	LR150-35 ①	50	40	0.295	8.99–12.17	14.4–15.0
		LR160-47 ① ②	60	41	0.295	8.99–12.17	14.4–15.0
	200SX	LR150-35 ①	50	40	0.295	8.99–12.17	14.4–15.0
1980	810	LR160-42B ①	60	50	0.295	8.99–12.17	14.4–15.0
	510	LR150-52 ①	50	40	0.295	8.99–12.17	14.4–15.0
	200SX	LR160-47 ①	60	45	0.295	8.99–12.17	14.4–15.0
1981	810 (L24)	LR160-82 ①	60	50	0.280	8.99–12.17	14.4–15.0
	810 (LD28)	LR160-97 ①	60	52	0.240	10.79–14.60	14.4–15.0
	510	LR150-98 ①	50	40	0.295	8.99–12.17	14.4–15.0
		LR160-78 ① ②	60	50	0.276	8.99–12.17	14.4–15.0
	200SX	LR160-78 ①	60	50	0.280	8.99–12.17	14.4–15.0
1982	810 (L24)	LR160-82B ①	60	50	0.280	8.99–12.17	14.4–15.0
	810 (LD28)	LR160-97B ①	60	52	0.240	10.79–14.60	14.4–15.0
	200SX	LR160-78B ①	60	50	0.280	8.99–12.17	14.4–15.0
1983–84	Maxima (L24E)	LR160-82B ①	60	50	0.280	8.99–12.17	14.4–15.0
	Maxima (LD28)	LR160-97C ①	60	50	0.280	8.99–12.17	14.4–15.0
	200SX (Z22E)	LR160-109 ①	60	50	0.280	8.99–12.17	14.4–15.0
	200SX (CA20E)	LR160-104 ①	60	50	0.276	8.99–12.17	14.4–15.1
	200SX (CA18ET)	LR170-706 ①	70	50	0.217	5.29–12.70	14.4–15.0
1985–86	Maxima	LR190-704	87	65	0.217	5.29–12.70	14.1–14.7
	200SX (CA20E)	LR160-104	60	50	0.276	8.99–12.17	14.4–15.1
	200SX (CA18ET)	LR170-706	70	50	0.217	5.29–12.70	14.4–15.0
1987	Maxima	LR190-704	87	65	0.217	5.29–12.70	14.1–14.7
	200SX (CA20E)	LR170-717	67	50	0.28	9.88–14.11	14.1–14.7
	200SX (CA18ET)	LR170-717	67	50	0.28	9.88–14.11	14.1–14.7

Alternator and Regulator Specifications (cont.)

Year	Model	Alternator Identification Number	Rated Output @ 5000 RPM	Output @ 2500 RPM (not less than)	Brush Length (in.)	Brush Spring Tension (oz)	Regulated Voltage
	200SX (VG30E)	A2T46395	—	50	0.31	10.93–15.17	14.1–14.7
1988	Maxima	LR190-709B	87	65	0.276	9.88–14.11	14.1–14.7
	200SX (CA20E)	LR170-717	67	50	0.28	9.88–14.11	14.1–14.7
	200SX (VG30E)	A2T46395B	—	50	0.31	10.93–15.17	14.1–14.7
1989	Maxima	LR190-711	84	63	0.276	3.88–9.17	14.1–14.7
	240SX	LR180-715	77	58	0.236	5.29–11.99	14.1–14.7
		A2T14094	—	60	0.315	10.93–15.17	14.1–14.7

① Uses integral voltage regulator
② Optional in U.S., standard in Canada

necessary. Retighten the screw. The gap should be 0.60-1.00mm.

2. Adjust the point gap of the voltage regulator coil by loosening the screw used to secure the upper contact and move the upper contact up or down. The gap for 1973-75 models is 0.30-0.40mm. The point gap for all other models is 0.35-0.45mm.

3. The core gap and point gap on the charge relay coil is or are adjusted in the same manner as previously outlined for the voltage regulator coil. The core gap is to be set at 0.80-1.00mm and the point gap adjusted to 0.40-0.60mm.

4. The regulated voltage is adjusted by loosening the locknut and turning the adjusting screw clockwise to increase, or counterclockwise to decrease the regulated voltage. The voltage should be between 14.3-15.3 volts at 68°F.

Battery

REMOVAL AND INSTALLATION

1. Disconnect the negative (ground) cable from the terminal, and then the positive cable. Special pullers are available to remove the cable clamps.

NOTE: *To avoid sparks, always disconnect the ground cable first, and connect it last.*

2. Remove the battery holddown clamp.

Troubleshooting Basic Charging System Problems

Problem	Cause	Solution
Noisy alternator	· Loose mountings · Loose drive pulley · Worn bearings · Brush noise · Internal circuits shorted (High pitched whine)	· Tighten mounting bolts · Tighten pulley · Replace alternator · Replace alternator · Replace alternator
Squeal when starting engine or accelerating	· Glazed or loose belt	· Replace or adjust belt
Indicator light remains on or ammeter indicates discharge (engine running)	· Broken fan belt · Broken or disconnected wires · Internal alternator problems · Defective voltage regulator	· Install belt · Repair or connect wiring · Replace alternator · Replace voltage regulator
Car light bulbs continually burn out—battery needs water continually	· Alternator/regulator overcharging	· Replace voltage regulator/alternator
Car lights flare on acceleration	· Battery low · Internal alternator/regulator problems	· Charge or replace battery · Replace alternator/regulator
Low voltage output (alternator light flickers continually or ammeter needle wanders)	· Loose or worn belt · Dirty or corroded connections · Internal alternator/regulator problems	· Replace or adjust belt · Clean or replace connections · Replace alternator or regulator

3. Remove the battery, being careful not to spill the acid.

NOTE: *Spilled acid can be neutralized with a baking soda/water solution. If you somehow get acid into your eyes, flush it out with lots of water and get to a doctor.*

Clean the battery posts thoroughly before re-installing, or when installing a new battery.

5. Clean the cable clamps, using a wire brush, both inside and out.

6. Install the battery and the holddown clamp or strap. Connect the positive, and then the negative cable. Do not hammer them in place. The terminals should be coated lightly (externally) with grease to prevent corrosion. There are also felt washers impregnated with an anti-corrosion substance which are slipped over the battery posts before installing the cables; these are available in auto parts stores.

NOTE: *Make absolutely sure that the battery is connected properly before you turn on the ignition switch. Reversed polarity can burn out your alternator and regulator within a matter of seconds.*

Starter

Datsun/Nissan began using a reduction gear starter in 1978 on the 810 and in the Canadian versions of the 510 and 200SX. They were also available as an option on the U.S. 510 and 200SX. The differences between the gear reduction and conventional starters are: the gear reduction starter has a set of ratio reduction gears while the conventional starter does not; the brushes on the gear reduction starter are located on a plate behind the starter drive housing, while the conventional starter's brushes are located in its rear cover. The extra gears on the gear reduction starter make the starter pinion gear turn at about half the speed of the starter, giving the starter twice the turning power of a conventional starter.

REMOVAL AND INSTALLATION

1. Disconnect the negative battery cable from the battery.

2. Disconnect the starter wiring at the starter, taking note of the positions for correct installation.

3. Remove the bolts attaching the starter to the engine and remove the starter from the vehicle.

4. Install the starter to the engine.

5. Tighten the attaching bolts. Be careful not overtorque the mounting bolts as this will crack the nose of the starter case.

6. Install the starter wiring in the correct location.

Note the wire locations before removing the starter

7. Connect the negative battery cable.

8. Start the engine a few times to make sure of proper operation.

SOLENOID REPLACEMENT

NOTE: *The starter solenoid is also know as the magnetic switch assembly.*

1. Remove the starter from the engine as outlined above.

2. Place the starter in a vise or equivalent to hold the starter in place while you are working on the solenoid. DO NOT tighten the vise to tight around the case of the starter. The case will crack if you tighten the vise to much.

3. Loosen the locknut and remove the connection from the starter motor going to the **M** terminal of the solenoid or bottom terminal of the solenoid.

4. Remove the securing screws and remove the solenoid.

5. Install the solenoid to the starter and tighten the securing screws.

6. Install the connection and locknut at bottom terminal of the starter.

OVERHAUL

Brush Replacement

NON-REDUCTION GEAR TYPE

1. With the starter out of the vehicle, remove the bolts holding the solenoid to the top of the starter and remove the solenoid.

2. To remove the brushes, remove the 2 through-bolts, the 2 rear cover attaching screws (some models) and the rear cover.

NOTE: *Remove the dust cover, E-ring and thrust washers from the armature shaft before the rear cover.*

3. Using a wire hook, lift the brush springs

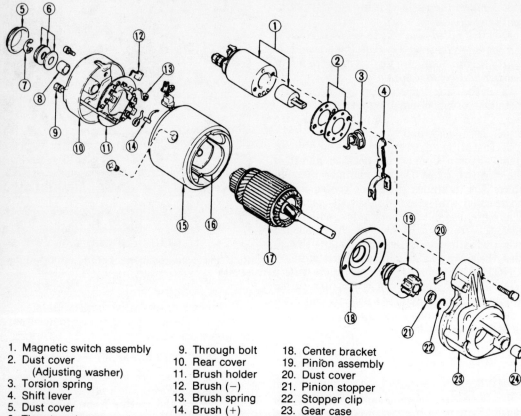

1. Magnetic switch assembly
2. Dust cover
   (Adjusting washer)
3. Torsion spring
4. Shift lever
5. Dust cover
6. Thrust washer
7. E-ring
8. Rear cover metal

9. Through bolt
10. Rear cover
11. Brush holder
12. Brush (−)
13. Brush spring
14. Brush (+)
15. Yoke
16. Field coil
17. Armature

18. Center bracket
19. Pinion assembly
20. Dust cover
21. Pinion stopper
22. Stopper clip
23. Gear case
24. Gear case metal

Exploded view of non-reduction gear starter

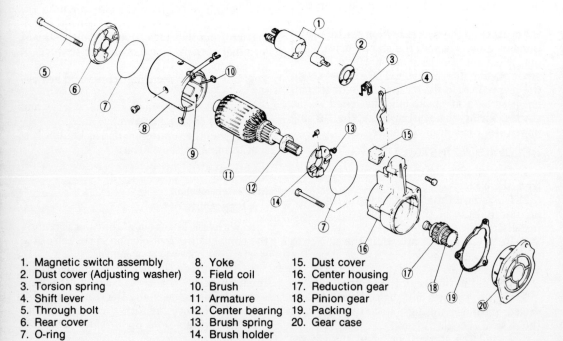

1. Magnetic switch assembly
2. Dust cover (Adjusting washer)
3. Torsion spring
4. Shift lever
5. Through bolt
6. Rear cover
7. O-ring

8. Yoke
9. Field coil
10. Brush
11. Armature
12. Center bearing
13. Brush spring
14. Brush holder

15. Dust cover
16. Center housing
17. Reduction gear
18. Pinion gear
19. Packing
20. Gear case

Gear reduction starter

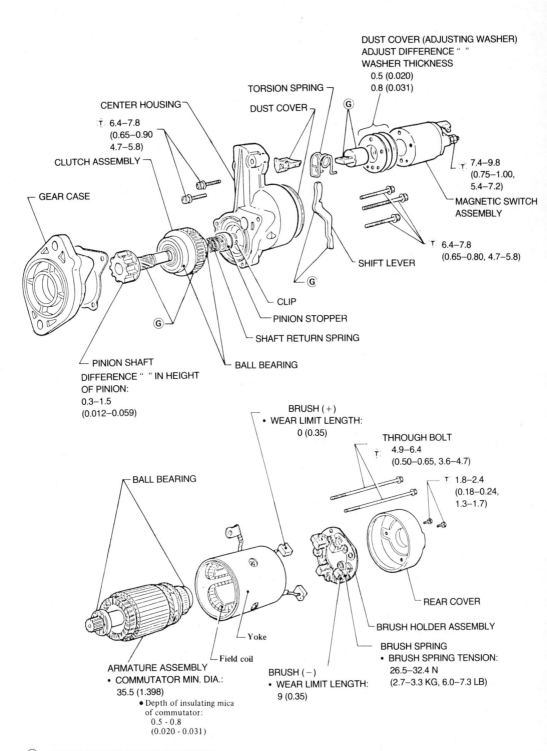

DUST COVER (ADJUSTING WASHER)
ADJUST DIFFERENCE " "
WASHER THICKNESS
0.5 (0.020)
0.8 (0.031)

TORSION SPRING

CENTER HOUSING
Ⓣ 6.4–7.8
(0.65–0.90
4.7–5.8)

DUST COVER

CLUTCH ASSEMBLY

GEAR CASE

Ⓣ 7.4–9.8
(0.75–1.00,
5.4–7.2)

MAGNETIC SWITCH
ASSEMBLY

Ⓣ 6.4–7.8
(0.65–0.80, 4.7–5.8)

SHIFT LEVER

CLIP

PINION STOPPER

SHAFT RETURN SPRING

BALL BEARING

PINION SHAFT
DIFFERENCE " " IN HEIGHT
OF PINION:
0.3–1.5
(0.012–0.059)

BRUSH (+)
• WEAR LIMIT LENGTH:
  0 (0.35)

THROUGH BOLT
Ⓣ 4.9–6.4
(0.50–0.65, 3.6–4.7)

Ⓣ 1.8–2.4
(0.18–0.24,
1.3–1.7)

BALL BEARING

REAR COVER

BRUSH HOLDER ASSEMBLY

BRUSH SPRING
• BRUSH SPRING TENSION:
  26.5–32.4 N
  (2.7–3.3 KG, 6.0–7.3 LB)

Yoke

Field coil

ARMATURE ASSEMBLY
• COMMUTATOR MIN. DIA.:
  35.5 (1.398)
  • Depth of insulating mica
    of commutator:
    0.5 - 0.8
    (0.020 - 0.031)

BRUSH (−)
• WEAR LIMIT LENGTH:
  9 (0.35)

Ⓖ : HIGH-TEMPERATURE GREASE POINTS
Ⓣ : N·M (KG-M, FT-LB)
UNIT: MM (IN)

LD28 diesel gear reduction starter

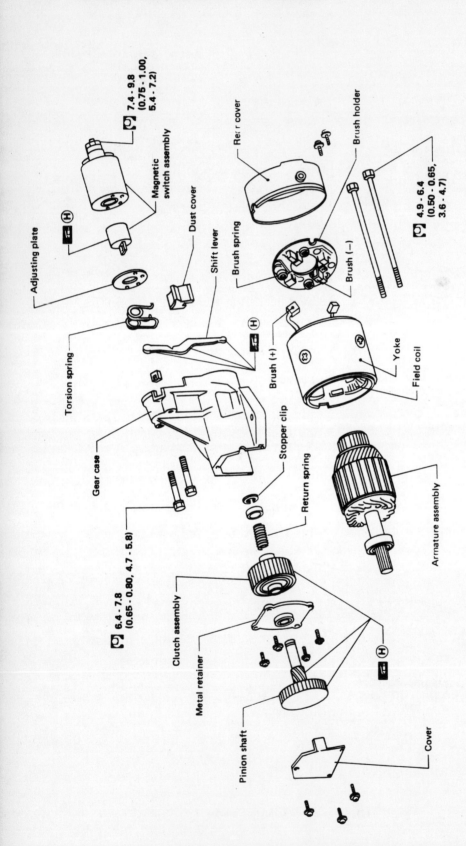

Adjusting plate

Magnetic switch assembly

7.4 - 9.8 (0.75 - 1.00, 5.4 - 7.2)

Dust cover

Shift lever

Torsion spring

Gear case

Rea r cover

Brush spring

Brush holder

Brush (–)

4.9 - 6.4 (0.50 - 0.65, 3.6 - 4.7)

Brush (+)

Yoke

Field coil

Stopper clip

Return spring

Armature assembly

6.4 - 7.8 (0.65 - 0.80, 4.7 - 5.8)

Clutch assembly

Metal retainer

Pinion shaft

Cover

: N·m (kg-m, ft-lb)
(H) : High-temperature grease points

Exploded view of Maxima (FWD) starter assembly

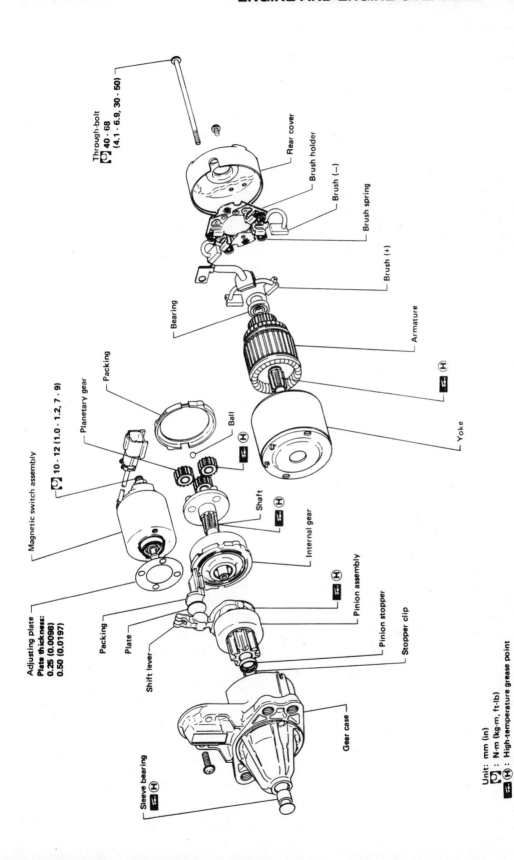

Through-bolt
🔧 40 - 68
(4.1 - 6.9, 30 - 50)

Rear cover

Brush holder

Brush (−)

Brush spring

Brush (+)

Bearing

Armature

Packing

Planetary gear

Ball

Yoke

Magnetic switch assembly

🔧 10 - 12 (1.0 - 1.2, 7 - 9)

Shaft

Internal gear

Adjusting plate
Plate thickness:
0.25 (0.0098)
0.50 (0.0197)

Pinion assembly

Pinion stopper

Stopper clip

Packing

Plate

Shift lever

Gear case

Sleeve bearing

Unit: mm (in)
🔧 : N·m (kg-m, ft-lb)
🅗 : High-temperature grease point

Exploded view of 240SX starter assembly

to separate the brushes from the commutator.

4. Install the brushes in the reverse order of removal and reasssemble the rear cover to the starter.

REDUCTION GEAR TYPE

1. Remove the starter, then the solenoid or magentic switch.

2. Remove the dust cover, E-ring and thrust washers.

3. Remove the starter through-bolts and brush holder setscrews.

4. Remove the rear cover. The rear cover can be pried off with a screwdriver, be careful not to damage the O-ring or gasket if equipped.

5. Remove the starter housing, armature and brush holder from the center housing. They can be removed as an assembly.

6. Using a wire hook on the spring, lift the spring then remove the positive side brush from its holder. The positive brush is insulated from the brush holder and its lead wire is connected to the field coil.

7. Using a wire hook on the spring, lift the spring and remove the negative brush from the holder.

8. Replace all the brushes in the starter assembly.

9. Insert the new brushes in the brush holder.

10. Install the starter housing, armature and brush holder to the center housing.

11. Install the brush holder setscrews, rear cover and starter through-bolts.

12. Install the thrust washers, E-ring and dust cover.

13. Install the solenoid or magnetic switch.

Starter Drive Replacement

NON-REDUCTION GEAR TYPE

1. With the starter motor removed from the vehicle, remove the solenoid from the starter.

2. Remove the 2 through-bolts at the rear cover but do not disassemble the entire starter. Mark the front gear cover with relationship to the yoke housing.

3. Separate the front gear case from the yoke housing, then the shift lever from the armature, without removing the armature from starter assembly.

4. Push the pinion stopper toward the rear cover, then remove the pinion stopper clip and the pinion stopper.

5. Slide the starter drive from the armature shaft.

6. Install the starter drive on the armature shaft.

7. Install pinion stopper and stopper clip.

8. Reassemble the front gear case to the yoke and the shift lever to the armature.

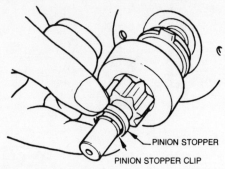

Pinion stopper removal

9. Install the rear cover through-bolts.

10. Install the solenoid or the magnetic switch.

REDUCTION GEAR TYPE

1. Remove the starter.

2. Remove the solenoid and the torsion spring. Mark the front housing with relationship to the center housing.

3. Remove the center housing-to-front housing bolts, then separate the front housing from the center housing . Do not disassemble the entire starter.

4. Remove the pinion/reduction gear assembly from the armature shaft.

NOTE: *It may be necessary to remove the shift lever pivot pin, to disconnect the pinion/reduction gear assembly from the armature shaft.*

5. Installation is the reverse of the removal procedures. The best idea is to try not to disassemble the entire starter when removing the pinion/reduction gear. Do not disturb the brush assembly in the rear cover.

NOTE: *On 1985-89 Maxima models remove the pinion inspection cover, pinion shaft then remove the clutch assembly by removing the screws that hold the metal retainer to the main housing.*

ENGINE MECHANICAL

Engine Overhaul Tips

Most engine overhaul procedures are fairly standard. In addition to specific parts replacement procedures and complete specifications for your individual engine, this chapter also is a guide to accepted rebuilding procedures. Examples of standard rebuilding practice are shown and should be used along with specific details concerning your particular engine.

Competent and accurate machine shop services will ensure maximum performance, reliability and engine life.

In most instances it is more profitable for the

TOOLS

The tools required for an engine overhaul or parts replacement will depend on the depth of your involvement. With a few exceptions, they will be the tools found in a mechanic's tool kit (see Chapter 1). More in-depth work will require any or all of the following:

- a dial indicator (reading in thousandths) mounted on a universal base
- micrometers and telescope gauges
- jaw and screw-type pullers
- scraper
- valve spring compressor
- ring groove cleaner
- piston ring expander and compressor
- ridge reamer
- cylinder hone or glaze breaker
- Plastigage®
- engine stand

do-it-yourself mechanic to remove, clean and inspect the component, buy the necessary parts and deliver these to a shop for actual machine work.

On the other hand, much of the rebuilding work (crankshaft, block, bearings, piston rods, and other components) is well within the scope of the do-it-yourself mechanic.

Troubleshooting Basic Starting System Problems

Problem	Cause	Solution
Starter motor rotates engine slowly	· Battery charge low or battery defective	· Charge or replace battery
	· Defective circuit between battery and starter motor	· Clean and tighten, or replace cables
	· Low load current	· Bench-test starter motor. Inspect for worn brushes and weak brush springs.
	· High load current	· Bench-test starter motor. Check engine for friction, drag or coolant in cylinders. Check ring gear-to-pinion gear clearance.
Starter motor will not rotate engine	· Battery charge low or battery defective	· Charge or replace battery
	· Faulty solenoid	· Check solenoid ground. Repair or replace as necessary.
	· Damage drive pinion gear or ring gear	· Replace damaged gear(s)
	· Starter motor engagement weak	· Bench-test starter motor
	· Starter motor rotates slowly with high load current	· Inspect drive yoke pull-down and point gap, check for worn end bushings, check ring gear clearance
	· Engine seized	· Repair engine
Starter motor drive will not engage (solenoid known to be good)	· Defective contact point assembly	· Repair or replace contact point assembly
	· Inadequate contact point assembly ground	· Repair connection at ground screw
	· Defective hold-in coil	· Replace field winding assembly
Starter motor drive will not disengage	· Starter motor loose on flywheel housing	· Tighten mounting bolts
	· Worn drive end busing	· Replace bushing
	· Damaged ring gear teeth	· Replace ring gear or driveplate
	· Drive yoke return spring broken or missing	· Replace spring
Starter motor drive disengages prematurely	· Weak drive assembly thrust spring	· Replace drive mechanism
	· Hold-in coil defective	· Replace field winding assembly
Low load current	· Worn brushes	· Replace brushes
	· Weak brush springs	· Replace springs

The use of most of these tools is illustrated in this chapter. Many can be rented for a one-time use from a local parts jobber or tool supply house specializing in automotive work.

Occasionally, the use of special tools is called for. See the information on Special Tools and Safety Notice in the front of this book before substituting another tool.

INSPECTION TECHNIQUES

Procedures and specifications are given in this chapter for inspecting, cleaning and assessing the wear limits of most major components. Other procedures such as Magnaflux® and Zyglo® can be used to locate material flaws and stress cracks. Magnaflux® is a magnetic process

Battery and Starter Specifications

All cars use 12 volt, negative ground electrical systems

Year	Model	Battery Amp Hour Capacity	Starter						Brush Spring Tension (oz)	Min Brush Length (in.)
			Lock Test			No Load Test				
			Amps	Volts	Torque (ft. lbs.)	Amps	Volts	RPM		
1973–77	610, 710	50, 60	430 MT	6.0	6.3	60	12	7,000	49–64	0.47
			540 AT	5.0	6.0	60	12	6,000	49–64	0.47
1977–78	200SX, 510	60	—	—	—	60 MT	12	7,000	49–64	0.47
						60 AT	12	6,000	49–64	0.47
						100 RG	12	4,300	56–70	0.43
1979–82	200SX, 510	60 ①	—	—	—	60 MT	11.5	7,000	49–64	0.47
						60 AT	11.5	6,000	49–64	0.47
						100 RG	11.0	3,900	56–70	0.43
1977–79	810	60 ②	—	—	—	100 RG	12	4,300	56–70	0.43
1980–82	810 (L24)	60 ②	—	—	—	100 RG	11	3,900	56–70	0.43
	810 (LD28)	80	—	—	—	100 RG	11	3,900	96–116.8	0.35
1983–84	Maxima (L24E)	60 ②	—	—	—	100 RG	11	3,900	56–70	0.43
	Maxima (LD28)	80	—	—	—	140 RG	11	3,900	96–116.8	0.35
	200SX (Z22E)	60	—	—	—	60 AT	11.5	6,000	64–78.4	0.47
	200SX (Z22E)	60	—	—	—	60 MT	11.5	7,000	64–78.4	0.47
	200SX (Z22E) ③	70	—	—	—	100 RG	11	3,900	56–70	0.43
	200SX ④	60 ②	—	—	—	60	11.5	7,000	64–78.4	0.43
	200SX ④	60 ②	—	—	—	100 RTG	11	3,900	56–70	0.43
1985–86	Maxima	60 ②	—	—	—	100 ⑤	11	3,900	3.5–4.4	0.43
	200SX	60 ①	—	—	—	100 ⑤	11	3,900	3.5–4.4	0.43
1987	Maxima	60 ⑥	—	—	—	100 ⑤	11	3,000	3.68–4.96	0.31
	200SX	60 ①	—	—	—	100 ⑤	11	3,900	3.5–4.4	0.43
1988	Maxima	60 ⑥	—	—	—	100 ⑤	11.5	3,000	3.7–5.1	0.37
	200SX	60 ⑦	—	—	—	100 ⑤	11	3,900	3.5–4.4	0.43
1989	Maxima	50 ⑧	—	—	—	100 ⑤	11	3,000	4.0–4.9	0.47
	240SX (Hitachi)	60 ①	—	—	—	85 ⑤	11	2,750	4.0–4.9	0.43
	(Mitsubishi)	60 ①	—	—	—	50–75 ⑤	11	3,500	3.1–5.7	0.47

MT: Manual Transmission
AT: Automatic Transmission
RG: Reduction Gear Starter
—: Not Recommended
① Canada—65
② Canada, optional U.S.—70
③ Canada

④ 1984 and later
⑤ Maximum
⑥ Optional 70
⑦ Optional 65, 70 U.S.A.
   Canada models 65
⑧ 65 optional
   Canada models 80

applicable only to ferrous materials. The Zyglo® process coats the material with a fluorescent dye penetrant and can be used on any material. Check for suspected surface cracks can be more readily made using spot check dye. The dye is sprayed onto the suspected area, wiped off and the area sprayed with a developer. Cracks will show up brightly.

OVERHAUL TIPS

Aluminum has become extremely popular for use in engines, due to its low weight. Observe the following precautions when handling aluminum parts:

• Never hot tank aluminum parts (the caustic hot tank solution will eat the aluminum.

• Remove all aluminum parts (identification tag, etc.) from engine parts prior to the tanking.

• Always coat threads lightly with engine oil or anti-seize compounds before installation, to prevent seizure.

• Never overtorque bolts or spark plugs especially in aluminum threads.

Stripped threads in any component can be repaired using any of several commercial repair kits (Heli-Coil®, Microdot®, Keenserts®, etc.).

When assembling the engine, any parts that will be frictional contact must be prelubed to provide lubrication at initial start-up. Any product specifically formulated for this purpose can be used, but engine oil is not recommended as a prelube.

When semi-permanent (locked, but removable) installation of bolts or nuts is desired, threads should be cleaned and coated with Loctite® or other similar, commercial nonhardening sealant.

REPAIRING DAMAGED THREADS

Several methods of repairing damaged threads are available. Heli-Coil® (shown here), Keenserts® and Microdot® are among the most widely used. All involve basically the same principle—drilling out stripped threads, tapping the hole and installing a prewound insert—making welding, plugging and oversize fasteners unnecessary.

Two types of thread repair inserts are usually supplied: a standard type for most Inch Coarse, Inch Fine, Metric Course and Metric Fine thread sizes and a spark lug type to fit most spark plug port sizes. Consult the individual manufacturer's catalog to determine exact applications. Typical thread repair kits will contain a selection of prewound threaded inserts, a tap (corresponding to the outside diameter threads of the insert) and an installation tool. Spark plug inserts usually differ because they require a tap equipped with pilot threads and a

combined reamer/tap section. Most manufacturers also supply blister-packed thread repair inserts separately in addition to a master kit containing a variety of taps and inserts plus installation tools.

Before effecting a repair to a threaded hole, remove any snapped, broken or damaged bolts or studs. Penetrating oil can be used to free frozen threads. The offending item can be removed with locking pliers or with a screw or stud extractor. After the hole is clear, the thread can be repaired, as shown in the series of accompanying illustrations.

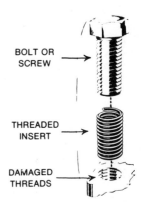

Damaged bolt holes can be repaired with thread repair inserts

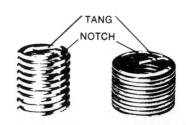

Standard thread repair insert (left) and spark plug thread insert (right)

Drill out the damaged threads with specified drill. Drill completely through the hole or to the bottom of a blind hole

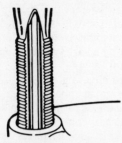

With the tap supplied, tap the hole to receive the thread insert. Keep the tap well oiled and back it out frequently to avoid clogging the threads

The screw-in type compression gauge is more accurate

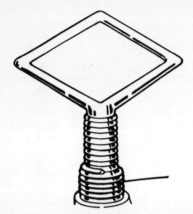

Screw the threaded insert onto the installation tool until the tang engages the slot. Screw the insert into the tapped hole until it is ¼–½ turn below the top surface. After installation break off the tang with a hammer and punch

ignition coil or the distributor harness connection if so equipped.

4. On carbureted cars fully open the throttle either by operating the carburetor throttle linkage by hand or by having an assistant floor the accelerator pedal. On fuel injected cars, disconnect the cold start valve and all injector connections.

5. Screw the compression gauge into the No.1 spark plug hole until the fitting is snug.

NOTE: *Be careful not to crossthread the plug hole. On aluminum cylinder heads use extra care, as the threads in these heads are easily ruined.*

Checking Engine Compression

A noticeable lack of engine power, excessive oil consumption and/or poor fuel mileage measured over an extended period are all indicators of internal engine war. Worn piston rings, scored or worn cylinder bores, blown head gaskets, sticking or burnt valves and worn valve seats are all possible culprits here. A check of each cylinder's compression will help you locate the problems.

As mentioned in the Tools and Equipment section of Chapter 1, a screw-in type compression gauge is more accurate that the type you simply hold against the spark plug hole, although it takes slightly longer to use. It's worth it to obtain a more accurate reading. Follow the procedures below.

Gasoline Engines

1. Warm up the engine to normal operating temperature.
2. Remove all the spark plugs.
3. Disconnect the high tension lead from the

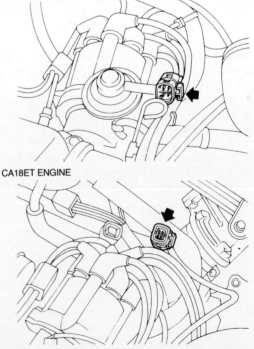

CA20E ENGINE

CA18ET ENGINE

Distributor harness connector locations, 1984 and later 200SX engines

Standard Torque Specifications and Fastener Markings

In the absence of specific torques, the following chart can be used as a guide to the maximum safe torque of a particular size/grade of fastener.

- There is no torque difference for fine or coarse threads.
- Torque values are based on clean, dry threads. Reduce the value by 10% if threads are oiled prior to assembly.
- The torque required for aluminum components or fasteners is considerably less.

U.S. Bolts

SAE Grade Number	1 or 2			5			6 or 7		
Number of lines always 2 less than the grade number.									
Bolt Size (Inches)—(Thread)	Maximum Torque			Maximum Torque			Maximum Torque		
	Ft./Lbs.	Kgm	Nm	Ft./Lbs.	Kgm	Nm	Ft./Lbs.	Kgm	Nm
¼ —20	5	0.7	6.8	8	1.1	10.8	10	1.4	13.5
—28	6	0.8	8.1	10	1.4	13.6			
⁵⁄₁₆ —18	11	1.5	14.9	17	2.3	23.0	19	2.6	25.8
—24	13	1.8	17.6	19	2.6	25.7			
⅜ —16	18	2.5	24.4	31	4.3	42.0	34	4.7	46.0
—24	20	2.75	27.1	35	4.8	47.5			
⁷⁄₁₆ —14	28	3.8	37.0	49	6.8	66.4	55	7.6	74.5
—20	30	4.2	40.7	55	7.6	74.5			
½ —13	39	5.4	52.8	75	10.4	101.7	85	11.75	115.2
—20	41	5.7	55.6	85	11.7	115.2			
⁹⁄₁₆ —12	51	7.0	69.2	110	15.2	149.1	120	16.6	162.7
—18	55	7.6	74.5	120	16.6	162.7			
⅝ —11	83	11.5	112.5	150	20.7	203.3	167	23.0	226.5
—18	95	13.1	128.8	170	23.5	230.5			
¾ —10	105	14.5	142.3	270	37.3	366.0	280	38.7	379.6
—16	115	15.9	155.9	295	40.8	400.0			
⅞ — 9	160	22.1	216.9	395	54.6	535.5	440	60.9	596.5
—14	175	24.2	237.2	435	60.1	589.7			
1— 8	236	32.5	318.6	590	81.6	799.9	660	91.3	894.8
—14	250	34.6	338.9	660	91.3	849.8			

Metric Bolts

Relative Strength Marking	4.6, 4.8			8.8		
Bolt Markings						
Bolt Size Thread Size x Pitch (mm)	Maximum Torque			Maximum Torque		
	Ft./Lbs.	Kgm	Nm	Ft./Lbs.	Kgm	Nm
6 x 1.0	2–3	.2–.4	3–4	3–6	.4–.8	5–8
8 x 1.25	6–8	.8–1	8–12	9–14	1.2–1.9	13–19
10 x 1.25	12–17	1.5–2.3	16–23	20–29	2.7–4.0	27–39
12 x 1.25	21–32	2.9–4.4	29–43	35–53	4.8–7.3	47–72
14 x 1.5	35–52	4.8–7.1	48–70	57–85	7.8–11.7	77–110
16 x 1.5	51–77	7.0–10.6	67–100	90–120	12.4–16.5	130–160
18 x 1.5	74–110	10.2–15.1	100–150	130–170	17.9–23.4	180–230
20 x 1.5	110–140	15.1–19.3	150–190	190–240	26.2–46.9	160–320
22 x 1.5	150–190	22.0–26.2	200–260	250–320	34.5–44.1	340–430
24 x 1.5	190–240	26.2–46.9	260–320	310–410	42.7–56.5	420–550

6. Ask an assistant to depress the accelerator pedal fully on both carbureted and fuel injected vehicles. Then, while you read the compression gauge, ask the assistant to crank the engine four times in short bursts using the ignition switch.

7. Read the compression gauge at the end of each series of cranks, and record the highest of these readings. Repeat this procedure for each of the engine's cylinders. Compare the highest reading of each cylinder to the compression pressure specification in the Tune-Up Specifications chart in Chapter 2.

A cylinder's compression pressure is usually acceptable if it is not less than 80% of maximum. The difference between any two cylinders should be no more than 12-14 pounds.

8. If a cylinder is unusually low, pour a tablespoon of clean engine oil into the cylinder through the spark plug hole and repeat the compression test. If the compression comes up after adding the oil, it appears that the cylinder's piston rings or bore are damaged or worn. If the pressure remains low, the valves may not be seating properly (a valve job is needed), or the head gasket may be blown near that cylinder. If compression in any two adjacent cylinders is low, and if the addition of oil doesn't help the compression, there is leakage past the head gasket. Oil and coolant water in the combustion chamber can result from this problem. There may be evidence of water droplets on the engine dipstick when a head gasket has blown.

NOTE: *Maximum cylinder compression for all Datsun/Nissan gasoline engines covered in this guide (except the L24 engine in the 1977-78 810) is 171 psi at 350 rpm. Minimum cylinder compression is 128 psi at 350 rpm. Maximum compression pressure for the 1977-78 810 L24 is 185 psi at 350 rpm. Maximum compression pressure for the V6 engine is 173 psi and the minimum is 128 psi; both are measured at 300 rpm. On the KA24E engine the compression pressure is 192 psi and the minimum is 142 psi measured at 300 rpm. Compression pressures for the LD28 diesel are 455 psi maximum, 356 psi minimum, at 200 rpm. When analyzing compression test results, look for uniformity among cylinders, rather than specific pressures.*

Diesel Engines

Checking compression on the Datsun/Nissan LD28 diesel engine is the same procedure as on the gasoline engines, except for the following:

1. A special compression gauge adaptor suitable for diesel engines must be used.

2. Begin the procedure by removing the spill tube assembly, the injection tubes on the nozzle side, and nozzle assemblies.

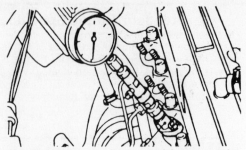

Diesel engines require a special compression gauge adaptor

NOTE: *Remove the nozzle washer with a pair of tweezers. Don't forget to remove this washer; otherwise, it may get lost when the engine is cranked.*

3. When fitting the compression gauge adaptor to the cylinder head, make sure the bleeder of the gauge is closed.

4. When reinstalling the injector assemblies, install new nozzle washers.

Engine

REMOVAL AND INSTALLATION

Rear Wheel Drive

The engine and transmission are removed together and then separated when out of the car. Always observe the following cautions:

● Make sure the vehicle is on a flat and leveel surface and that wheels are tightly chocked. Use the chocks on both sides of the rear wheels on front wheel drive cars.

● Allow the exhaust system to cool completely before starting work to prevent burns and possible fire as fuel lines are disconnected.

● Release fuel pressure from the fuel system before attempting to disconnect any fuel lines.

● When lifting the engine out, guide it carefully to avoid hitting parts such as the master cylinder.

● Mount the engine securely and then release the tension of lifting chains to avoid injury as you work on the engine.

1. Mark the location of the hinges on the hood. Unbolt and remove the hood.

2. Disconnect the battery cables. Remove the battery from the models with the L16 engine and Z20E models with air conditioning.

3. Drain the coolant and automatic transmission fluid.

NOTE: *When draining the coolant, keep in mind that cats and dogs are attracted by the ethylene glycol antifreeze, and are quite likely to drink any that is left in an uncovered container or in puddles on the ground. This will prove fatal in sufficient quantity. Always*

Troubleshooting Engine Mechanical Problems

Problem	Cause	Solution
External oil leaks	• Fuel pump gasket broken or improperly seated	• Replace gasket
	• Cylinder head cover RTV sealant broken or improperly seated	• Replace sealant; inspect cylinder head cover sealant flange and cylinder head sealant surface for distortion and cracks
	• Oil filler cap leaking or missing	• Replace cap
	• Oil filter gasket broken or improperly seated	• Replace oil filter
	• Oil pan side gasket broken, improperly seated or opening in RTV sealant	• Replace gasket or repair opening in sealant; inspect oil pan gasket flange for distortion
	• Oil pan front oil seal broken or improperly seated	• Replace seal; inspect timing case cover and oil pan seal flange for distortion
	• Oil pan rear oil seal broken or improperly seated	• Replace seal; inspect oil pan rear oil seal flange; inspect rear main bearing cap for cracks, plugged oil return channels, or distortion in seal groove
	• Timing case cover oil seal broken or improperly seated	• Replace seal
	• Excess oil pressure because of restricted PCV valve	• Replace PCV valve
	• Oil pan drain plug loose or has stripped threads	• Repair as necessary and tighten
	• Rear oil gallery plug loose	• Use appropriate sealant on gallery plug and tighten
	• Rear camshaft plug loose or improperly seated	• Seat camshaft plug or replace and seal, as necessary
	• Distributor base gasket damaged	• Replace gasket
Excessive oil consumption	• Oil level too high	• Drain oil to specified level
	• Oil with wrong viscosity being used	• Replace with specified oil
	• PCV valve stuck closed	• Replace PCV valve
	• Valve stem oil deflectors (or seals) are damaged, missing, or incorrect type	• Replace valve stem oil deflectors
	• Valve stems or valve guides worn	• Measure stem-to-guide clearance and repair as necessary
	• Poorly fitted or missing valve cover baffles	• Replace valve cover
	• Piston rings broken or missing	• Replace broken or missing rings
	• Scuffed piston	• Replace piston
	• Incorrect piston ring gap	• Measure ring gap, repair as necessary
	• Piston rings sticking or excessively loose in grooves	• Measure ring side clearance, repair as necessary
	• Compression rings installed upside down	• Repair as necessary
	• Cylinder walls worn, scored, or glazed	• Repair as necessary
	• Piston ring gaps not properly staggered	• Repair as necessary
	• Excessive main or connecting rod bearing clearance	• Measure bearing clearance, repair as necessary
No oil pressure	• Low oil level	• Add oil to correct level
	• Oil pressure gauge, warning lamp or sending unit inaccurate	• Replace oil pressure gauge or warning lamp
	• Oil pump malfunction	• Replace oil pump
	• Oil pressure relief valve sticking	• Remove and inspect oil pressure relief valve assembly
	• Oil passages on pressure side of pump obstructed	• Inspect oil passages for obstruction

Troubleshooting Engine Mechanical Problems (cont.)

Problem	Cause	Solution
No oil pressure (cont.)	• Oil pickup screen or tube obstructed	• Inspect oil pickup for obstruction
	• Loose oil inlet tube	• Tighten or seal inlet tube
Low oil pressure	• Low oil level	• Add oil to correct level
	• Inaccurate gauge, warning lamp or sending unit	• Replace oil pressure gauge or warning lamp
	• Oil excessively thin because of dilution, poor quality, or improper grade	• Drain and refill crankcase with recommended oil
	• Excessive oil temperature	• Correct cause of overheating engine
	• Oil pressure relief spring weak or sticking	• Remove and inspect oil pressure relief valve assembly
	• Oil inlet tube and screen assembly has restriction or air leak	• Remove and inspect oil inlet tube and screen assembly. (Fill inlet tube with lacquer thinner to locate leaks.)
	• Excessive oil pump clearance	• Measure clearances
	• Excessive main, rod, or camshaft bearing clearance	• Measure bearing clearances, repair as necessary
High oil pressure	• Improper oil viscosity	• Drain and refill crankcase with correct viscosity oil
	• Oil pressure gauge or sending unit inaccurate	• Replace oil pressure gauge
	• Oil pressure relief valve sticking closed	• Remove and inspect oil pressure relief valve assembly
Main bearing noise	• Insufficient oil supply	• Inspect for low oil level and low oil pressure
	• Main bearing clearance excessive	• Measure main bearing clearance, repair as necessary
	• Bearing insert missing	• Replace missing insert
	• Crankshaft end play excessive	• Measure end play, repair as necessary
	• Improperly tightened main bearing cap bolts	• Tighten bolts with specified torque
	• Loose flywheel or drive plate	• Tighten flywheel or drive plate attaching bolts
	• Loose or damaged vibration damper	• Repair as necessary
Connecting rod bearing noise	• Insufficient oil supply	• Inspect for low oil level and low oil pressure
	• Carbon build-up on piston	• Remove carbon from piston crown
	• Bearing clearance excessive or bearing missing	• Measure clearance, repair as necessary
	• Crankshaft connecting rod journal out-of-round	• Measure journal dimensions, repair or replace as necessary
	• Misaligned connecting rod or cap	• Repair as necessary
	• Connecting rod bolts tightened improperly	• Tighten bolts with specified torque
Piston noise	• Piston-to-cylinder wall clearance excessive (scuffed piston)	• Measure clearance and examine piston
	• Cylinder walls excessively tapered or out-of-round	• Measure cylinder wall dimensions, rebore cylinder
	• Piston ring broken	• Replace all rings on piston
	• Loose or seized piston pin	• Measure piston-to-pin clearance, repair as necessary
	• Connecting rods misaligned	• Measure rod alignment, straighten or replace
	• Piston ring side clearance excessively loose or tight	• Measure ring side clearance, repair as necessary
	• Carbon build-up on piston is excessive	• Remove carbon from piston

Troubleshooting Engine Mechanical Problems (cont.)

Problem	Cause	Solution

Valve actuating component noise	• Insufficient oil supply	• Check for:
		  (a) Low oil level
		  (b) Low oil pressure
		  (c) Plugged push rods
		  (d) Wrong hydraulic tappets
		  (e) Restricted oil gallery
		  (f) Excessive tappet to bore clearance

	• Push rods worn or bent	• Replace worn or bent push rods
	• Rocker arms or pivots worn	• Replace worn rocker arms or pivots
	• Foreign objects or chips in hydraulic tappets	• Clean tappets
	• Excessive tappet leak-down	• Replace valve tappet
	• Tappet face worn	• Replace tappet; inspect corresponding cam lobe for wear
	• Broken or cocked valve springs	• Properly seat cocked springs; replace broken springs
	• Stem-to-guide clearance excessive	• Measure stem-to-guide clearance, repair as required
	• Valve bent	• Replace valve
	• Loose rocker arms	• Tighten bolts with specified torque
	• Valve seat runout excessive	• Regrind valve seat/valves
	• Missing valve lock	• Install valve lock
	• Push rod rubbing or contacting cylinder head	• Remove cylinder head and remove obstruction in head
	• Excessive engine oil (four-cylinder engine)	• Correct oil level

Troubleshooting the Cooling System

Problem	Cause	Solution
High temperature gauge indication—overheating	• Coolant level low	• Replenish coolant
	• Fan belt loose	• Adjust fan belt tension
	• Radiator hose(s) collapsed	• Replace hose(s)
	• Radiator airflow blocked	• Remove restriction (bug screen, fog lamps, etc.)
	• Faulty radiator cap	• Replace radiator cap
	• Ignition timing incorrect	• Adjust ignition timing
	• Idle speed low	• Adjust idle speed
	• Air trapped in cooling system	• Purge air
	• Heavy traffic driving	• Operate at fast idle in neutral intermittently to cool engine
	• Incorrect cooling system component(s) installed	• Install proper component(s)
	• Faulty thermostat	• Replace thermostat
	• Water pump shaft broken or impeller loose	• Replace water pump
	• Radiator tubes clogged	• Flush radiator
	• Cooling system clogged	• Flush system
	• Casting flash in cooling passages	• Repair or replace as necessary. Flash may be visible by removing cooling system components or removing core plugs.
	• Brakes dragging	• Repair brakes
	• Excessive engine friction	• Repair engine
	• Antifreeze concentration over 68%	• Lower antifreeze concentration percentage
	• Missing air seals	• Replace air seals
	• Faulty gauge or sending unit	• Repair or replace faulty component

Troubleshooting the Cooling System (cont.)

Problem	Cause	Solution
High heating gauge indication—overheating (cont.)	• Loss of coolant flow caused by leakage or foaming • Viscous fan drive failed	• Repair or replace leaking component, replace coolant • Replace unit
Low temperature indication—undercooling	• Thermostat stuck open • Faulty gauge or sending unit	• Replace thermostat • Repair or replace faulty component
Coolant loss—boilover	• Overfilled cooling system • Quick shutdown after hard (hot) run • Air in system resulting in occasional "burping" of coolant • Insufficient antifreeze allowing coolant boiling point to be too low • Antifreeze deteriorated because of age or contamination • Leaks due to loose hose clamps, loose nuts, bolts, drain plugs, faulty hoses, or defective radiator • Faulty head gasket • Cracked head, manifold, or block • Faulty radiator cap	• Reduce coolant level to proper specification • Allow engine to run at fast idle prior to shutdown • Purge system • Add antifreeze to raise boiling point • Replace coolant • Pressure test system to locate source of leak(s) then repair as necessary • Replace head gasket • Replace as necessary • Replace cap
Coolant entry into crankcase or cylinder(s)	• Faulty head gasket • Crack in head, manifold or block	• Replace head gasket • Replace as necessary
Coolant recovery system inoperative	• Coolant level low • Leak in system • Pressure cap not tight or seal missing, or leaking • Pressure cap defective • Overflow tube clogged or leaking • Recovery bottle vent restricted	• Replenish coolant to FULL mark • Pressure test to isolate leak and repair as necessary • Repair as necessary • Replace cap • Repair as necessary • Remove restriction
Noise	• Fan contacting shroud • Loose water pump impeller • Glazed fan belt • Loose fan belt • Rough surface on drive pulley • Water pump bearing worn • Belt alignment	• Reposition shroud and inspect engine mounts • Replace pump • Apply silicone or replace belt • Adjust fan belt tension • Replace pulley • Remove belt to isolate. Replace pump. • Check pulley alignment. Repair as necessary.
No coolant flow through heater core	• Restricted return inlet in water pump • Heater hose collapsed or restricted • Restricted heater core • Restricted outlet in thermostat housing • Intake manifold bypass hole in cylinder head restricted • Faulty heater control valve • Intake manifold coolant passage restricted	• Remove restriction • Remove restriction or replace hose • Remove restriction or replace core • Remove flash or restriction • Remove restriction • Replace valve • Remove restriction or replace intake manifold

NOTE: *Immediately after shutdown, the engine enters a condition known as heat soak. This is caused by the cooling system being inoperative while engine temperature is still high. If coolant temperature rises above boiling point, expansion and pressure may push some coolant out of the radiator overflow tube. If this does not occur frequently it is considered normal.*

drain the coolant into a sealable container. Coolant should be reused unless it is contaminated or several years old.

4. Remove the grille on the 510, 610, and 710 models. Remove the radiator and radiator shroud after disconnecting the automatic transmission coolant tubes.

5. Remove the air cleaner.

6. Remove the fan and pulley.

7. Disconnect:

    a. water temperature gauge wire;

    b. oil pressure sending unit wire;

    c. ignition distributor primary wire;

    d. starter motor connections;

    e. fuel hose;

CAUTION: *On all fuel injected models, the fuel pressure must be released before the fuel lines can be disconnected. See the pressure releasing procedure under Gasoline Engine Fuel Filter in Chapter 1.*

    f. alternator leads;

    g. heater hoses;

    h. throttle and choke connections;

    i. engine ground cable;

    j. thermal transmitter wire;

    k. wire to fuel cut-off solenoid;

    l. vacuum cut solenoid wire.

NOTE: *A good rule of thumb when disconnecting the rather complex engine wiring of today's cars is to put a piece of masking tape on the wire and on the connection you removed the wire from, then mark both pieces of tape 1, 2, 3, etc. When replacing wiring, simply match the pieces of tape.*

CAUTION: *On models with air conditioning, it is necessary to remove the compressor and the condenser from their mounts. DO NOT ATTEMPT TO UNFASTEN ANY OF THE AIR CONDITIONER HOSES. See Chapter 1 for additional warnings.*

8. Disconnect the power brake booster hose from the engine.

Valve Specifications

Model/Year	Seat Angle (deg)	Face Angle (deg)	Spring Test Pressure (lbs. @ in.)		Spring Installed Height (in.)		Stem to Guide Clearance (in.)		Stem Diameter (in.)	
			Outer	Inner	Outer	Inner	Intake	Exhaust	Intake	Exhaust
L18, L20B	45	45	108 @ 1.161	56.2 @ 0.965	1.575	1.378	0.0008–0.0021	0.0016–0.0029	0.3136–0.3142	0.3128–0.3134
Z20E, Z20S	45	45	115.3 @ 1.18	57 @ 0.98	1.575	1.378	0.0008–0.0021	0.0016–0.0029	0.3136–0.3142	0.3128–0.3434
Z22E	45	45	115.3 @ 1.18	57 @ 0.98	1.575	1.378	0.0008–0.0021	0.0016–0.0029	0.3136–0.3142	0.3128–0.3134
CA20E, CA18ET	45	45	118.2 @ 1.00	66.6 @ 1.00	②	②	0.0008–0.0021	0.0016–0.0029	0.2742–0.2748	0.2734–0.2740
CA20E, CA18ET	45	45	118.2 ③	66.6 ③	1.9677	1.7636	0.0008–0.0021	0.0016–0.0029	0.2742–0.2748	0.2734–0.2740
L24	45	45	108 @ 1.161 ①	56.2 @ 0.965 ①	1.575	1.378	0.0008–0.0021	0.0016–0.0029	0.3136–0.3142	0.3128–0.3134
LD28	45	45	115.3 @ 1.181	—	1.575	—	0.0008–0.0021	0.0016–0.0029	0.3136–0.3142	0.3128–0.3134
VG30E	45	45	117.7 @ 1.181	57.3 @ 0.984	2.016 ④	1.736 ④	0.0008–0.0021	0.0016–0.0029	0.2742–0.2748	0.3128–0.3134
KA24E	45	45	135.8 @ 1.480 ⑤	63.9 @ 1.283 ⑤	2.2614 ⑥	2.1000 ⑥	0.0008–0.0021	0.0016–0.0028	0.2742–0.2748	0.3129–0.3134

① Figure is for Exhaust; for Intake: Outer 105.2 @ 1.181
Inner 54.9 @ 0.984
② Free height: 1.967 Outer, 1.736 Inner
③ Figures are lbs./in. of compression
④ Figures are for free height
⑤ These figures are intake valves; for exhaust valves 144 @ 1.343 (outer) 73.9 @ 1.146 (inner)
⑥ These figures are intake valves; for exhaust valves 2.0949 (outer) 1.8878 (inner)

General Engine Specifications

Year	Car Model	Engine Model	Engine Displacement Cu. In. (cc)	Carburetor Type	Horsepower (@ rmp)	Torque (@ rpm (ft. lbs.)	Bore x Stroke (in.)	Compression Ratio	Oil Pressure @ rpm (psi)
1973	610	L18	108.0 (1770)	2 BBL	105 @ 6000	108 @ 3600	3.35 x 3.307	8.5:1	50-57
1974	610	L20B	119.1 (1952)	2 BBL	110 @ 3500	112 @ 3600	3.35 x 3.39	8.5:1	50-57
	710	L18	108.0 (1770)	2 BBL	105 @ 6000	108 @ 3600	3.35 x 3.307	8.5:1	50-57
1975	610	L20B	119.1 (1952)	2 BBL	110 @ 5600	112 @ 3600	3.35 x 3.39	8.5:1	50-57
	710	L20B	119.1 (1952)	2 BBL	100 @ 5600	100 @ 3600	3.35 x 3.39	8.5:1	50-57
1976	610	L20B	119.1 (1952)	2 BBL	112 @ 5600	108 @ 3600	3.35 x 3.39	8.5:1	50-57
	710	L20B	119.1 (1952)	2 BBL	110 @ 5600	112 @ 5600	3.35 x 3.39	8.5:1	50-57
1977	200SX	L20B	119.1 (1952)	2 BBL	97 @ 5600	102 @ 3200	3.35 x 3.39	8.5:1	50-57
	710	L20B	119.1 (1952)	2 BBL	110 @ 5600	112 @ 5600	3.35 x 3.39	8.5:1	50-57
	810	L24	146.0 (2393)	EFI	154 @ 5600	155 @ 4400	3.27 x 2.90	8.6:1	50-57
1978	200SX	L20B	119.1 (1952)	2 BBL	97 @ 5600	102 @ 3200	3.35 x 3.39	8.5:1	50-57
	510	L20B	119.1 (1952)	2 BBL	97 @ 5600	102 @ 3200	3.35 x 3.39	8.5:1	50-57
	810	L24	146.0 (2393)	EFI	154 @ 5600	155 @ 4400	3.27 x 2.90	8.6:1	50-57
1979	200SX	L20B	119.1 (1952)	2 BBL	92 @ 5600	107 @ 3200	3.35 x 3.39	8.5:1	50-57
	510	L20B	119.1 (1952)	2 BBL	92 @ 5600	107 @ 3200	3.35 x 3.39	8.5:1	50-57
	810	L24	146.0 (2393)	EFI	120 @ 5200	125 @ 4400	3.27 x 2.90	8.9:1	50-60
1980	200SX	Z20E	119.1 (1952)	EFI	100 @ 5200	112 @ 3200	3.35 x 3.39	8.5:1	50-60
	510	L20B ② Z20E ③	119.1 (1952)	2 BBL	92 @ 5200	112 @ 2800	3.35 x 3.39	8.5:1	50-60
1981	810	L24	119.1 (1952)	EFI	120 @ 5200	125 @ 4400	3.27 x 2.90	8.9:1 ①	50-60
	200SX	Z20E	119.1 (1952)	EFI	100 @ 5200	112 @ 3200	3.35 x 3.39	8.5:1	50-60
	510	Z20S	119.1 (1952)	2 BBL	92 @ 5200	112 @ 2800	3.35 x 3.39	8.5:1	50-60
	810	L24E	146.0 (2393)	EFI	120 @ 5200	134 @ 2800	3.27 x 2.90	8.9:1	50-60
	810 Diesel	LD28	170.0 (2793)	DFI	80 @ 4600	120 @ 2400	3.33 x 3.27	22.7:1	NA

Year	Model	Engine	Displacement cu in (cc)	Fuel System	Horsepower @ rpm	Torque @ rpm	Bore x Stroke	Compression Ratio	Oil Pressure
1982–83	200SX	Z22E	133.4 (2181)	EFI	102 @ 5200	129 @ 2800	3.43 x 3.62	8.5:1	50–60
	810 Maxima	L24E	146.0 (2393)	EFI	120 @ 5200	134 @ 2800	3.27 x 2.90	8.9:1	50–60
	810 Diesel	LD28	170.0 (2793)	DFI	80 @ 4600	120 @ 2400	3.33 x 3.27	22.7:1	NA
1984	200SX	CA20E	120.4 (1974)	EFI	102 @ 5200	116 @ 3200	3.33 x 3.46	8.5:1	57 @ 4000
	200SX Turbo	CA18ET	110.3 (1809)	EFI	120 @ 5200	134 @ 3200	3.27 x 3.29	8.0:1	71 @ 4000
	Maxima	L24E	146.0 (2393)	EFI	120 @ 5200	134 @ 2800	3.27 x 2.90	8.9:1	50–60
1985–86	200SX	CA20E	120.4 (1974)	EFI	102 @ 5200	116 @ 3200	3.33 x 3.46	8.5:1	57 @ 4000
	200SX Turbo	CA18ET	110.3 (1809)	EFI	120 @ 5200	134 @ 3200	3.27 x 3.29	8.0:1	71 @ 4000
	Maxima	VG30E	180.6 (2960)	EFI	152 @ 5200	167 @ 3600	3.43 x 3.27	9.0:1	57 @ 4000
1987	200SX	CA20E	120.4 (1974)	EFI	102 @ 5200	116 @ 3200	3.33 x 3.46	8.5:1	43 @ 2000
		CA18ET	110.3 (1809)	EFI	120 @ 5200	134 @ 3200	3.27 x 3.29	8.0:1	43 @ 2000
		VG30E	180.6 (2960)	EFI	160 @ 5200	174 @ 4000	3.43 x 3.27	9.0:1	43 @ 2000
	Maxima	VG30E	180.6 (2960)	EFI	160 @ 5200	174 @ 4000	3.43 x 3.27	9.0:1	43 @ 2000
1988	200SX	CA20E	120.4 (1974)	EFI	99 @ 5200	116 @ 2800	3.33 x 3.46	8.5:1	60.5 @ 3200
		VG30E	180.6 (2960)	EFI	165 @ 5200	168 @ 3600	3.43 x 3.27	9.0:1	59 @ 3200
	Maxima	VG30E	180.6 (2960)	EFI	157 @ 5200	168 @ 3600	3.43 x 3.27	9.0:1	59 @ 3200
1989	240SX	KA24E	145.8 (2389)	EFI	135 @ 5600	142 @ 4400	3.50 x 3.78	9.0:1	65 @ 3000
	Maxima	VG30E	180.6 (2960)	EFI	160 @ 5200	182 @ 2800	3.43 x 3.27	9.0:1	59 @ 3200

NA: Not Available
DFI: Diesel Fuel Injection
① 8.6 in California
② Canadian models
③ U.S. models

Crankshaft and Connecting Rod Specifications

All measurements given in inches

Engine Model	Crankshaft				Connecting Rod Bearings		
	Main Brg Journal Dia	Main Brg Oil Clearance	Shaft End-Play	Thrust on No.	Journal Dia	Oil Clearance	Side Clearance
L18	2.1631–2.1636	0.001–0.002	0.002–0.007	3	1.9670–1.9675	0.001–0.002	0.008–0.012
L18 (710)	2.3599–2.360	0.0008–0.002	0.002–0.007	3	1.967–1.9675	0.001–0.002	0.008–0.012
L20B	2.3599–2.360	0.0008–0.0024	0.002–0.007	3	1.9660–1.9670	0.001–0.002	0.008–0.012
Z20S, Z20E, Z22E	2.1631–2.1636	0.0008–0.0024	0.002–0.0071	3	1.967–1.9675	0.001–0.0022	0.008–0.012
CA20E	2.0847–2.0852	0.0016–0.0024	0.012	3	1.7701–1.7706	0.0008–0.0024	0.008–0.012
CA18ET	2.0847–2.0852	0.0016–0.0024	0.0020–0.0071	3	1.7701–1.7706	0.0008–0.0024	0.008–0.012
L24	2.1631–2.1636	0.0008–0.0026	0.002–0.0071	Center	1.9670–1.9675	0.001–0.003	0.008–0.012
L24E	2.1631–2.1636	0.0008–0.0026	0.0020–0.0071	Center	1.7701–1.7706	0.0009–0.0024	0.008–0.012
LD28	2.1631–2.1636	0.0008–0.0024	0.0020–0.0071	Center	1.9670–1.9675	0.0008–0.0024	0.008–0.012
VG30E	①	0.0011–0.0022	0.0020–0.0067	4	1.9670–1.9675	0.0004–0.0020	0.0079–0.0138
KA24E	②	0.0008–0.0019	0.0020–0.0071	3	③	0.0004–0.0014	0.008–0.016

① Grade No. 0 2.4790–2.4793
Grade No. 1 2.4787–2.4790
Grade No. 2 2.4784–2.4787
② Grade No. 0 2.3609–2.3612
Grade No. 1 2.3606–2.3609
Grade No. 2 2.3603–2.3606
③ Grade No. 0 1.9672–1.9675
Grade No. 1 1.9670–1.9672
Grade No. 2 1.9668–1.9670

Piston and Ring Specifications
All measurements in inches

Engine Model/Year	Piston Clearance	Ring Gap			Ring Side Clearance		
		Top Compression	Bottom Compression	Oil Control	Top Compression	Bottom Compression	Oil Control
L18	0.001–0.002	0.014–0.022	0.012–0.020	0.012–0.035	0.002–0.003	0.002–0.003	—
L20B	0.001–0.002	0.010–0.016	0.012–0.020	0.012–0.035	0.002–0.003	0.001–0.003	—
Z20E, Z20S	0.001–0.002	0.0098–0.016	0.006–0.012	0.012–0.035	0.002–0.003	0.001–0.0025	—
Z22E	0.001–0.0018	0.0098–0.0157	0.0059–0.0118	0.0118–0.0354	0.0016–0.0029	0.0012–0.0025	—
CA20E '84	0.0010–0.0018	0.0098–0.0138	0.0059–0.0098	0.0079–0.0236	0.0016–0.0029	0.0012–0.0025	—
CA20E '85–'86	0.0010–0.0018	0.0098–0.0201	0.0059–0.0122	0.0079–0.0299	0.0016–0.0029	0.0012–0.0025	—
CA18ET '84	0.0010–0.0018	③	0.0059–0.0098	0.0079–0.0236	0.0016–0.0029	0.0012–0.0025	—
CA18ET '85–'86	0.0010–0.0018	④	0.0059–0.0122	0.0079–0.0299	0.0016–0.0029	0.0012–0.0025	—
L24	0.001–0.002	0.010–0.016	0.006–0.012	0.012–0.035	0.002–0.003	0.001–0.003	①
LD28	0.0020–0.0028	②	0.0079–0.0138	0.0118–0.0177	0.0024–0.0039	0.0016–0.0031	0.0012–0.0028
VG30E	0.0010–0.0018	0.0083–0.0173	0.0071–0.0173	0.0079–0.0299	0.0016–0.0029	0.0012–0.0025	0.0006–0.0075
KA24E	0.0008–0.0016	0.0110–0.0169	0.0177–0.0236	0.0079–0.0236	0.0016–0.0031	0.0012–0.0028	0.0026–0.0053

—Not applicable
① 1977–80—combined
　1981—0.009–0.0028
　1982—0.010
② Without mark—0.0079–0.0114
　With mark—0.0055–0.0087
③ Piston grades #1 and #2: 0.0098–0.0126 in.
　Piston grades #3, 4 and 5: 0.0075–0.0102 in.
④ Piston grades #1 and #2: 0.0098–0.0150
　Piston grades #3, 4, and 5: 0.0110–0.0165

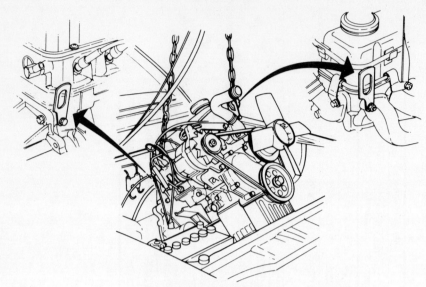

Removing the engine

Torque Specifications
All readings in ft. lbs.

Engine Model	Cylinder Head Bolts	Main Bearing Bolts	Rod Bearing Bolts	Crankshaft Pulley Bolts	Flywheel to Crankshaft Bolts	Manifold	
						Intake	Exhaust
L18	47–62	33–40	33–40	87–116	101–116	9–12	9–12
L20B	51–61	33–40	33–40	87–116	101–116	9–12	9–12
Z20E, Z20S, Z22E	51–58	33–40	33–40	87–116	101–116	12–15	12–15
CA20E	③	33–40	24–27	90–98	72–80	14–19	14–22
CA18ET	③	33–40	24–27	90–98	72–80	14–19	14–22
L24	51–61	33–40	33–40	101–116	94–108	①	
LD28	87–94	51–61	33–40	101–116	101–116	②	
VG30E	④	67–74	33–40 ⑤	90–98	72–80	12–14	13–16
KA24E	⑥	34–38	⑦	87–116	105–112	12–15	12–15

① M10 bolt: 25–35 ft. lbs.
  M8 bolt: 11–18 ft. lbs.
  M8 nut: 9–12 ft. lbs.
② Upper bolt (M10): 24–27 ft. lbs.
  Lower nut and bolt (M8): 12–18 ft. lbs.
③ Torque all bolts to 22 ft. lbs.; then to 58 ft. lbs. Loosen all bolts completely, then torque all bolts to 22.
④ Torque all bolts in the proper sequence to 22 ft. lbs.
  Torque all bolts in the proper sequence to 43 ft. lbs.
  Loosen all bolts completely.
  Torque all bolts in the proper sequence to 22 ft. lbs.
  Torque all bolts in the proper sequence to 40–47 ft. lbs.
⑤ 1988–89 model
  Tighten in 2 steps:
  1ST 10–12 ft. lbs.
  2ND 28–33 ft. lbs.
⑥ Tighten all bolts in numerical order to 22 ft. lbs. Then tighten all bolts to 58 ft. lbs. Loosen all bolts completely. Tighten all bolts to 22 ft. lbs. Then tighten to 54–61 ft. lbs. Always tighten and loosen bolts in numerical order—see text.
⑦ 2 steps:
  Tighten to 10–12 ft. lbs. Then tighten to 28–33 ft. lbs.

9. Remove the clutch operating cylinder and return spring.

10. Disconnect the speedometer cable from the transmission. Disconnect the backup light switch and any other wiring or attachments to the transmission. On cars with the L18 models, remove the boot, withdraw the lock pin, and remove the lever from inside the car.

12. Detach the exhaust pipe from the exhaust manifold. Remove the front section of the exhaust system. Be careful not to break the retaining bolts to manifold. If the bolts or studs break in the manifold remove the manifold and drill and tap the hole.

13. Mark the relationship of the driveshaft flanges and remove the driveshaft.

14. Place a jack under the transmission. Remove the rear crossmember.

15. Attach a hoist to the lifting hooks on the engine (at either end of the cylinder head). Support the engine.

NOTE: *On 1984 and later 200SX models, do not loosen the front engine mounting insulator cover securing nuts. When the cover is removed, the damper oil will flow out and the mounting insulator will not function.*

16. Unbolt the front engine mounts. Tilt the engine by lowering the jack under the transmission and raising the hoist.

17. With the engine/transmission assembly mounted safely on the engine hoist slowly lower the engine/transmission assembly into place.

Gearshift lever removal—1980 and later 510 and 200SX

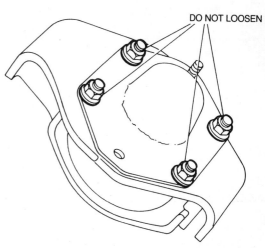

On 1984 and late 200SXs, do not loosen the front engine mounting insulation cover securing bolts

Camshaft Specifications
(All measurements in inches)

| Engine/Year | Journal Diameter | | | | | Bearing Clearance | Lobe Lift | | Camshaft End Play |
	1	2	3	4	5		Intake	Exhaust	
L18, L20B	1.8878– 1.8883	1.8878– 1.8883	1.8878– 1.8883	1.8878– 1.8883	—	0.0015– 0.0026	0.276	0.276	0.0031– 0.0150
Z20E, Z20S, Z22E	1.2967– 1.2974	1.2967– 1.2974	1.2967– 1.2974	1.2967– 1.2974	—	0.0018– 0.0035	NA	NA	0.008
L24, LD28	1.8878– 1.8883	1.8878– 1.8883	1.8878– 1.8883	1.8878– 1.8883	1.8878– 1.8883	0.0015– 0.0026	0.262	0.276	0.0031– 0.0150
CA20E, CA18ET '84	1.8085– 1.8092	1.8085– 1.8092	1.8085– 1.8092	1.8085– 1.8092	1.8077– 1.8085	0.004 ①	0.354	0.354	0.0028– 0.0055
	1.8085– 1.8092	1.8085– 1.8092	1.8085– 1.8092	1.8085– 1.8092	1.8077– 1.8085	0.004 ①	0.394 ②	0.394	0.0028– 0.0055
VG-30E	1.8472– 1.8480	1.8472– 1.8480	1.8472– 1.8480	—	—	0.0059 ①	1.5566– 1.5640	1.5566– 1.5640	0.0012– 0.0024
KA24E	1.2967– 1.2974	1.2967– 1.2974	1.2967– 1.2974	1.2967– 1.2974	1.2967– 1.2974	0.0047 ①	0.409	0.409	0.008 ①

① Clearance limit
② On CA18ET, intake lift is 0.354
③ Refers to total cam height from lobe tip to opposite side of shaft

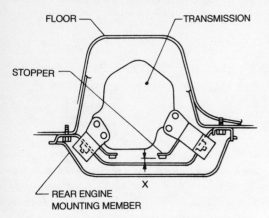

FLOOR — TRANSMISSION

STOPPER

REAR ENGINE
MOUNTING MEMBER

X

When installing the 1984 and later 200SX engine, adjust the rear mounting stopper clearance ("x") to 0.51 in.

NOTE: *When installing the CA20E and CA18ET engines into 1984 and later 200SXs, the rear engine mounting bracket must be adjusted. Using the accompanying illustration as a guide, adjust the rear mounting stopper clearance (X in the illustration) to 13mm.*

18. Support the transmission with a jack or equivalent until the crossmember is installed.

19. Tighten the front engine mounts. It may be necessary to lower or raise the engine hoist to correctly position the engine assembly to line up with the mount holes. Remove the engine hoist.

20. Install the crossmember then remove the jack or equivalent supporting the transmission.

21. Install the driveshaft in the correct marked position.

22. Reconnect the front exhaust system to the exhaust manifold. Be careful not to tighten retaining bolts to manifold to tight. If the bolts or studs break in the manifold remove the manifold and drill and tap the hole.

23. Reconnect all wiring at the transmission and the speedometer cable.

24. On cars with the L18 engine, install the lever, lock pin and shift boot.

25. Install the clutch cylinder and return spring. Reconnect the power brake hose to the engine if so equipped.

26. Install all wiring, brackets, vacuum hoses and water hoses to the engine. Make sure all connections are tight and in the correct location. It is always a good idea to replace all the old water hoses when installing the engine.

27. Install the fan and fan pulley.

28. Install the radiator shroud than the radiator reconnect the transmission lines if so equipped. Install the front grille if it was removed.

29. Refill the radiator and all other fluid levels.

30. Install the air cleaner, battery and reconnect the battery cables.

31. Install the hood in the same location as you removed it from.

32. Check all fluids, start engine, let it warm up and check for leaks.

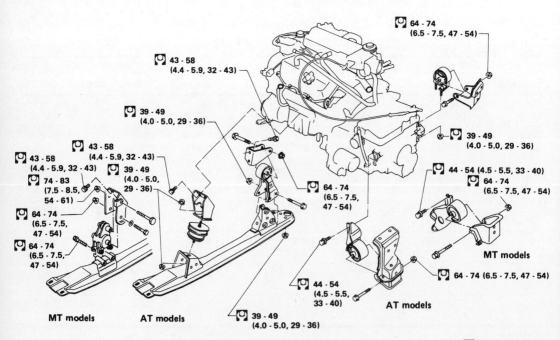

43 - 58
(4.4 - 5.9, 32 - 43)

39 - 49
(4.0 - 5.0, 29 - 36)

43 - 58
(4.4 - 5.9, 32 - 43)

43 - 58
(4.4 - 5.9, 32 - 43)

74 - 83
(7.5 - 8.5, 54 - 61)

39 - 49
(4.0 - 5.0, 29 - 36)

64 - 74
(6.5 - 7.5, 47 - 54)

64 - 74
(6.5 - 7.5, 47 - 54)

64 - 74
(6.5 - 7.5, 47 - 54)

64 - 74
(6.5 - 7.5, 47 - 54)

39 - 49
(4.0 - 5.0, 29 - 36)

64 - 74
(6.5 - 7.5, 47 - 54)

39 - 49
(4.0 - 5.0, 29 - 36)

44 - 54 (4.5 - 5.5, 33 - 40)
64 - 74
(6.5 - 7.5, 47 - 54)

MT models

64 - 74 (6.5 - 7.5, 47 - 54)

44 - 54
(4.5 - 5.5, 33 - 40)

AT models

MT models   AT models

: N·m (kg-m, ft-lb)

Mounting of the V6 engine used in the Maxima

33. Road test vehicle after you are sure there are no leaks.

Front Wheel Drive

On these models no standard engine removal and installation procedures are given by the manufacturer Datsun/Nissan. However it is recommended the engine and transaxle be removed as a single unit. Always release the fuel pressure in the system before disconnecting the fuel lines. Situate the vehicle on as flat and solid a surface as possible. Place chocks or equivalent at front and rear of rear wheels to stop vehicle from rolling while working on the vehicle.

To remove the engine and transaxle assembly the front halfshafts will have to be removed from the transaxle refer to Chapter 7 in this book.

Rocker Cover/Shaft
REMOVAL AND INSTALLATION

Rocker Cover/Shaft removal and installation procedures are included in the Camshaft Removal and Installation section in this chapter.

Thermostat
REMOVAL AND INSTALLATION

NOTE: *On V6 engines it may be necessary to remove radiator shroud, coolant fan assembly and water suction pipe retaining bolts to gain access to the thermostat housing.*

1. Drain the engine coolant into a clean container so that the level is below the thermostat housing.

CAUTION: *When draining the coolant, keep in mind that cats and dogs are attracted by the ethylene glycol antifreeze, and are quite likely to drink any that is left in an uncovered container or in puddles on the ground. This*

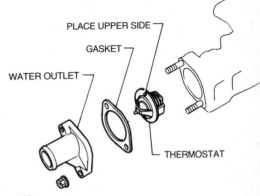

18–22 N·M (1.8–2.2 KG-M, 13–16 FT.LB.)

CA20E, CA18ET thermostat location

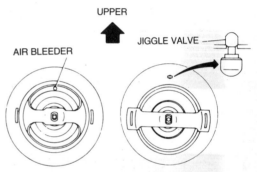

Always install the thermostat with the spring facing "down" and the jiggle valve facing "up"

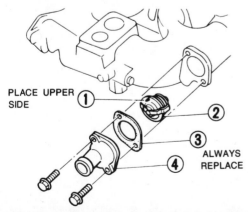

Z20 engine (carbureted) thermostat location. Note jiggle valve (1)

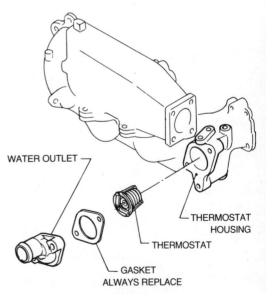

Thermostat location, Z22E (fuel injected) engines

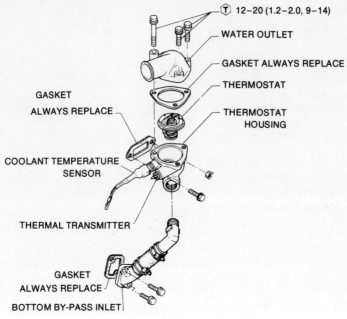

12–20 (1.2–2.0, 9–14)

WATER OUTLET

GASKET ALWAYS REPLACE

THERMOSTAT

GASKET ALWAYS REPLACE

THERMOSTAT HOUSING

COOLANT TEMPERATURE SENSOR

THERMAL TRANSMITTER

GASKET ALWAYS REPLACE

BOTTOM BY-PASS INLET

Diesel engine thermostat housing

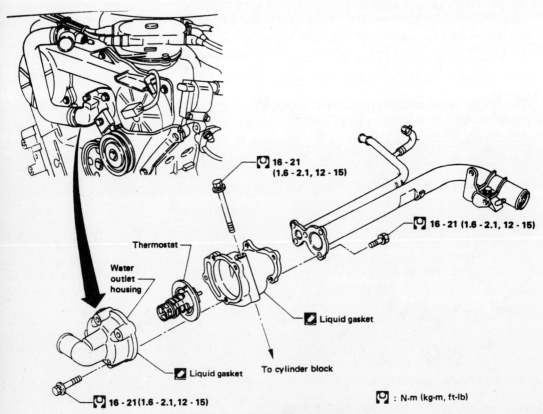

16 - 21 (1.6 - 2.1, 12 - 15)

16 - 21 (1.6 - 2.1, 12 - 15)

Thermostat

Water outlet housing

Liquid gasket

Liquid gasket

To cylinder block

16 - 21 (1.6 - 2.1, 12 - 15)

: N·m (kg-m, ft-lb)

Thermostat and housing assembly V6 engine

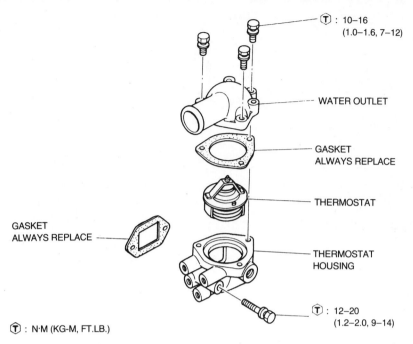

Ⓣ : 10–16
(1.0–1.6, 7–12)

WATER OUTLET

GASKET
ALWAYS REPLACE

THERMOSTAT

GASKET
ALWAYS REPLACE

THERMOSTAT
HOUSING

Ⓣ : 12–20
(1.2–2.0, 9–14)

Ⓣ : N·M (KG-M, FT.LB.)

L24 thermostat installation and torque specs

will prove fatal in sufficient quantity. Always drain the coolant into a sealable container. Coolant should be reused unless it is contaminated or several years old.

2. Disconnect the upper radiator hose at the water outlet.

3. Loosen the two securing nuts and remove the water outlet, gasket, and the thermostat from the thermostat housing.

4. Install the thermostat to the engine, using a new gasket with sealer and with the thermostat spring toward the inside of the engine.

5. Reconnect the upper radiator hose.

6. Refill the cooling system. Refer to Chapter 1 for Drain And Refill procedures if necessary. Make sure to let the engine reach normal operating temperature then check coolant for the correct level.

Intake Manifold

REMOVAL AND INSTALLATION

All Early Years Except 810, 1980-83 200SX/510, 1984-88 200SX, 240SX and Maxima

NOTE: *When unplugging wires and hoses, mark each hose and its connection with a piece of masking tape, then match code the 2 pieces of tape with the numbers 1, 2, 3, etc. When assembling, simply match up the pieces of tape.*

1. Remove the air cleaner assembly together with all of the attending hoses.

2. Disconnect the throttle linkage and fuel and vacuum lines from the carburetor.

3. The carburetor can be removed from the manifold at this point or can be removed as an assembly with the intake manifold.

4. Loosen the intake manifold attaching nuts, working from the two ends toward the center, and then remove them.

5. Remove the intake manifold from the engine.

6. Using a putty knife or equivalent, clean the gasket mounting surfaces.

7. Install the intake manifold and gasket on the engine. Always use a new gasket. Tighten the mounting bolts from the, center working to the end, in two or three stages. Torque the intake manifold bolts to 14-19 ft. lbs. or the nuts 12-15 ft. lbs.

8. Install throttle linkage, fuel and vacuum lines and the air cleaner assembly.

9. Start engine and check for leaks.

L-series engine intake manifold (4 cylinder)

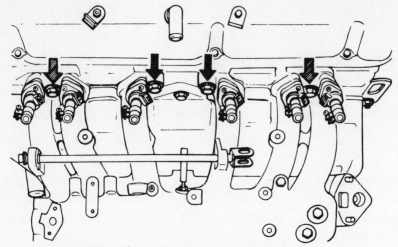

810 intake manifold mounting bolt locations—gasoline engine

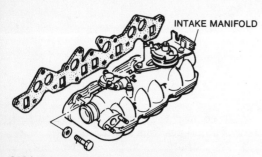

INTAKE MANIFOLD

810 intake manifold—diesel engine

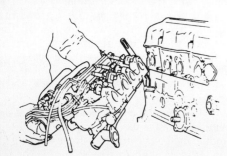

Z20E: remove the manifold with injectors, etc., still attached

810

NOTE: *Certain procedures may apply only to the gasoline engine. Always release the fuel pressure on fuel injected engines before removing any fuel system component.*

1. Disconnect all hoses to the air cleaner and remove the air cleaner.

2. Disconnect all air, water vacuum and fuel hoses to the intake manifold. Remove the cold start valve and fuel pipe as an assembly. Remove the throttle linkage.

3. Remove the B.P.T. valve control tube from the intake manifold. Remove the EGR hoses.

4. Disconnect all electrical wiring to the fuel injection unit. Note the location of the wires and mark them in some manner to facilitate reinstallation.

5. Make sure all wires, hoses, lines, etc. are removed. Unscrew the intake manifold bolts. Keep the bolts in order since they are of two different sizes. Remove the manifold.

6. Install the intake manifold to the engine. Use a new gasket, clean both sealing surfaces, and torque the bolts in several stages, working from the center outward.

7. Reconnect all electrical wiring to the fuel injection unit.

8. Install the EGR valve hose and B.P.T. valve control.

9. Reconnect the throttle linkage.

10. Install the fuel pipe assembly and the cold start valve.

11. Reconnect all air, water vacuum and fuel hoses to the intake manifold.

12. Install the air cleaner reconnect all hoses to the correct location.

13. Start engine and check for leaks.

1980-83 200SX/510

NOTE: *Always release the fuel pressure on fuel injected engines before removing any fuel system component.*

1. Drain the coolant and disconnect the battery cable.

CAUTION: *When draining the coolant, keep in mind that cats and dogs are attracted by the ethylene glycol antifreeze, and are quite likely to drink any that is left in an uncovered container or in puddles on the ground. This will prove fatal in sufficient quantity. Always drain the coolant into a sealable container. Coolant should be reused unless it is contaminated or several years old.*

2. On the fuel injected engine, remove the air cleaner hoses. On the carbureted engine, remove the air cleaner.

3. Remove the radiator hoses from the manifold.

4. For the carbureted engine, remove the fuel, air and vacuum hoses from the carburetor. Remove the throttle linkage and remove the carburetor.

5. Remove the throttle cable and disconnect the fuel pipe and the return fuel line on fuel injection engines. Plug the fuel pipe to prevent spilling fuel.

NOTE: *When unplugging wires and hoses, mark each hose and its connection with a piece of masking tape, then match code the two pieces of tape with the numbers 1, 2, 3, etc. When assembling, simply match the pieces of tape.*

6. Remove all remaining wires, tubes, the air cleaner bracket (carbureted engines) and the E.G.R. and P.C.V. tubes from the rear of the intake manifold. Remove the air induction pipe from the front of the carbureted engine. Remove the manifold supports on the fuel injected engine.

7. Unbolt and remove the intake manifold. On fuel injected engines, remove the manifold with injectors, E.G.R. valve, fuel tubes, etc., still attached.

8. Clean the gasket mounting surfaces then install the intake manifold on the engine. Always use a new intake manifold gasket.

9. Connect all electrical connections, tubes, the air cleaner bracket (carbureted engines) and the E.G.R. and P.C.V. tubes to the rear of the intake manifold. Install the air induction pipe to the front of the carbureted engine. Install the manifold supports on the fuel injected engine.

10. Install the throttle cable and reconnect the fuel pipe and the return fuel line on fuel injection engines.

11. Install the carburetor and throttle linkage. Reconnect the fuel, air and vacuum hoses to the carburetor on these models.

12. Install the radiator hoses to the intake manifold.

13. On the fuel injected engine, install the air cleaner hoses. On the carbureted engine, install the air cleaner.

14. Refill the coolant level and connect the battery cable. Start the engine and check for leaks.

1984-88 200SX
1989 240SX

NOTE: *Always release the fuel pressure before starting any repairs on the fuel system. On the 240SX the procedure may vary slightly use the procedure below as a guide. On the V6 200SX refer to the Maxima procedure. The collector assembly and intake manifold are removed as an assembly on these models.*

1. Remove the air duct between the air flow meter and the throttle body. Remove the throttle linkage.

2. Disconnect the fuel line(s) from the fuel injector assembly.

3. Disconnect and label all of the electrical connectors and the vacuum hoses to the throttle, the intake manifold/collector assembly and the related components. Remove the high tension wires from the spark plugs.

4. Disconnect the EGR valve tube from the exhaust manifold. Remove the intake manifold mounting brackets.

5. Remove the mounting bolts and separate the intake manifold from the cylinder head.

6. Using a putty knife, clean the gasket mounting surfaces.

7. Install the intake manifold/collector assembly and gasket on the engine. Always use a new gasket. Tighten the mounting bolts from the, center working to the end, in two or three stages. Torque the intake manifold mounting bolts to 14-19 ft. lbs. on the CA20 engine (200SX) and 12-15 ft. lbs . on the KA24E (240SX) engine.

8. Install intake manifold mounting brackets and reconnect the EGR valve tube to the exhaust manifold.

9. Install the spark plug wires, electrical connectors and the vacuum hoses to the throttle, the intake manifold assembly and the related components.

10. Reconnect the fuel line(s) to the fuel injector assembly.

11. Install the air duct between the air flow meter and the throttle body. Connect the throttle linkage.

12. Start engine and check for leaks.

1985-89 MAXIMA V6

NOTE: *The 1989 Maxima has a slightly different collector/intake manifold assembly as used in (1985-88) front wheel drive models, use this procedure as a guide for the 1989 year. The collector assembly and intake manifold are removed separately on all models.*

1. Release the fuel pressure and disconnect the battery cables.

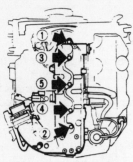

Removing collector—loosen bolts in this order

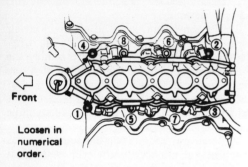

Front

Loosen in numerical order.

Removing intake manifold—loosen bolts in this order

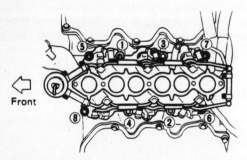

Front

Installing intake manifold—tighten bolts in this order

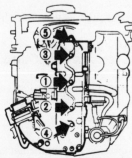

Installing collector to intake manifold—tighten bolts in this order

2. Drain coolant by removing the drain plug on the left side of the cylinder block into a suitable container for later use.

CAUTION: *When draining the coolant, keep*

in mind that cats and dogs are attracted by the ethylene glycol antifreeze, and are quite likely to drink any that is left in an uncovered container or in puddles on the ground. This will prove fatal in sufficient quantity. Always drain the coolant into a sealable container. Coolant should be reused unless it is contaminated or several years old.

3. Disconnect all valves, lines, hoses, cables and or brackets to gain access to the collector cover and collector assembly retaining bolts.

4. Remove the collector cover. Remove the collector to intake manifold bolts in numerical order.

5. Remove the intake manifold and fuel tube assembly. Loosen intake manifold bolts in numerical order.

6. Install the intake manifold and fuel tube assembly with a new gasket to the engine. Tighten the manifold bolts and nuts in two or three stages in the reverse order of removal.

7. Install the collector and collector cover with new gaskets. Tighten collector to intake manifold bolts in two or three stages in the reverse order of removal.

8. Connect all valves, lines, hoses, cables and or brackets to the collector cover and collector assembly.

9. Refill the cooling system. Refer to chapter 1 if necessary, reconnect the battery cables.

10. Check fluid levels , start the engine and check for leaks.

Exhaust Manifold

REMOVAL AND INSTALLATION

All Except V6

NOTE: *You may find that removing the intake manifold will provide better access to the exhaust manifold on some early models.*

1. Remove the air cleaner assembly, if necessary for access. Remove the heat shield.

2. Disconnect and tag the high tension wires from the spark plugs on the exhaust side of the engine.

3. Disconnect the exhaust pipe from the exhaust manifold. On turbocharged engines remove the exhaust pipe from the turbocharger assembly.

NOTE: *Soak the exhaust pipe retaining bolts with penetrating oil if necessary to loosen them.*

4. On the carbureted models, remove the air induction and/or the EGR tubes from the exhaust manifold. On the fuel injected models, disconnect the exhaust gas sensor electrical connector.

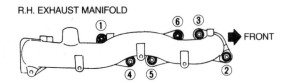

R.H. EXHAUST MANIFOLD

FRONT

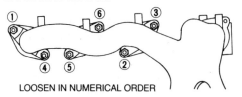

L.H. EXHAUST MANIFOLD

LOOSEN IN NUMERICAL ORDER

5. Remove the exhaust manifold mounting nuts and the manifold from the cylinder head.

6. Using a putty knife, clean the gasket mounting surfaces.

7. Install the manifold onto the engine, use new gaskets and from the, center working to the end. Torque the exhaust manifold nuts/ bolts to 14-22 ft. lbs.

8. Install the air induction and/or the EGR tubes to the exhaust manifold or the exhaust gas sensor electrical connector.

9. Reconnect exhaust pipe. On turbocharged engines reconnect the exhaust pipe to the turbocharger assembly.

10. Connect spark plug wires and air cleaner and any related hoses.

11. Start engine and check for exhaust leaks.

V6

1. Remove the exhaust manifold sub-cover and manifold cover. Remove the E.G.R. tube from the right side exhaust manifold. Remove the exhaust manifold stay.

2. Disconnect the left side exhaust manifold at the exhaust pipe by removing retaining nuts and disconnect the right side manifold from the connecting pipe.

NOTE: *Soak the exhaust pipe retaining bolts with penetrating oil if necessary to loosen them.*

3. Remove bolts for each manifold in the order shown.

4. Clean all gasket surfaces. Install new gaskets.

5. Install the manifold to the engine, torquing manifold bolts alternately in two stages in the exact reverse order of removal to 13-16 ft. lbs.

6. Reconnect the exhaust pipe and the connecting pipe. Be careful not break these bolts.

7. Install the exhaust manifold stay and the E.G.R. tube to the right side manifold.

8. Install the exhaust manifold covers. Start the engine and check for exhaust leaks.

Turbocharger

REMOVAL AND INSTALLATION

CA18ET Engine

1984-88 200SX

1. Drain the engine coolant.

CAUTION: *When draining the coolant, keep in mind that cats and dogs are attracted by the ethylene glycol antifreeze, and are quite likely to drink any that is left in an uncovered container or in puddles on the ground. This will prove fatal in sufficient quantity. Always drain the coolant into a sealable container. Coolant should be reused unless it is contaminated or several years old.*

2. Remove the air duct and hoses, and the air intake pipe.

3. Disconnect the front exhaust pipe at the exhaust manifold end (exhaust outlet in the illustration).

4. Remove the heat shield plates.

5. Tag and disconnect the oil delivery tube and return hose.

6. Disconnect the water inlet tube.

7. Unbolt and remove the turbocharger from the exhaust manifold.

NOTE: *The turbocharger unit should only be serviced internally by an engine specialist trained in turbocharger repair.*

8. Install the turbocharger to the exhaust manifold torque these bolts evenly and to 22-25 ft. lbs. Torque the turbocharger outlet to housing 16-22 ft. lbs. if the outlet was removed.

9. Reconnect the water inlet tube.

10. Connect the oil delivery tube and return hose.

11. Connect the front exhaust pipe at the exhaust manifold end and install the heat shields.

12. Connect the air duct and hoses, and the air intake pipe.

13. Refill the cooling system, start the engine and check for leaks.

Air Conditioning Compressor

NOTE: *Refer to Chapter 1 for Charging and Discharging procedures.*

REMOVAL AND INSTALLATION

All Models

CAUTION: *The compressed refrigerant used in the air conditioning system expands into the atmosphere at a temperature of $-2°F$ ($-19°C$) or lower. This will freeze any surface, including your eyes, that it contacts. In addition, the refrigerant decomposes into a poisonous gas in the presence of a flame. Do not open or disconnect any part of the air conditioning system until you have read the SAFETY WARNINGS section in Chapter 1.*

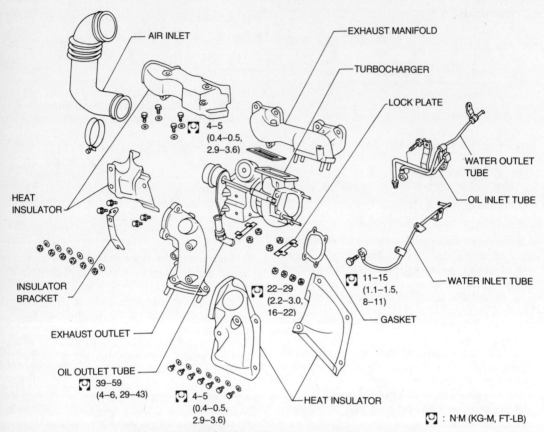

AIR INLET

EXHAUST MANIFOLD

TURBOCHARGER

LOCK PLATE

4–5
(0.4–0.5,
2.9–3.6)

WATER OUTLET
TUBE

OIL INLET TUBE

HEAT
INSULATOR

INSULATOR
BRACKET

11–15
(1.1–1.5,
8–11)

WATER INLET TUBE

22–29
(2.2–3.0,
16–22)

GASKET

EXHAUST OUTLET

OIL OUTLET TUBE
39–59
(4–6, 29–43)

4–5
(0.4–0.5,
2.9–3.6)

HEAT INSULATOR

: N·M (KG-M, FT-LB)

1984 and later 200SX (CA18ET engine) turbocharger assembly

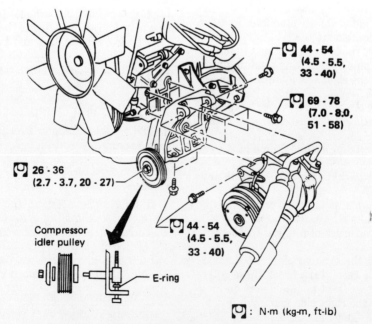

44 - 54
(4.5 - 5.5,
33 - 40)

69 - 78
(7.0 - 8.0,
51 - 58)

26 - 36
(2.7 - 3.7, 20 - 27)

Compressor
idler pulley

E-ring

44 - 54
(4.5 - 5.5,
33 - 40)

: N·m (kg-m, ft-lb)

Compressor mounting—200SX with CA20 engine—others similar

1. Disconnect the negative battery cables.

2. Remove all the necessary equipment in order to gain access to the compressor mounting bolts.

3. Remove the compressor drive belt.

NOTE: *To facilitate removal of the compressor belt, remove the idler pulley and bracket as an assembly beforehand from the underside of the car.*

4. Discharge the air conditioning system.

5. Disconnect and plug the refrigerant lines with a clean shop towel.

NOTE: *Be sure to use 2 wrenches (one to loosen fitting—one to hold fitting in place) when disconnecting the refrigerant lines.*

6. Disconnect and tag all electrical connections.

7. Remove the compressor mounting bolts. Remove the compressor from the vehicle.

8. Install the compressor on the engine and evenly torque all the mounting bolts the same.

9. Connect all the electrical connections and unplug and reconnect all refrigerant lines.

10. Install all the necessary equipment in order to gain access to the compressor mounting bolts.

11. Install and adjust the drive belt.

12. Connect the negative battery cable.

13. Evacuate and charge the system as required. Make sure the oil level is correct for the compressor.

NOTE: *Do not attempt to the leave the com-pressor on its side or upside down for more than a couple minutes, as the oil in the compressor will enter the low pressure chambers. Be sure to always replace the O-rings.*

Radiator

REMOVAL AND INSTALLATION

All Models Except Maxima (1985-89)

NOTE: *On some models, it may be necessary to remove the front grille to remove the radiator. The cooling system can be drained from opening the drain cock at the bottom of the radiator or by removing the bottom hose at the radiator. Be careful not to damage the fins or core tubes when removing and installing the radiator to the vehicle. NEVER OPEN THE RADIATOR CAP WHEN HOT!*

1. Drain the engine coolant into a clean container. On fuel injected models, remove the air cleaner inlet pipe.

CAUTION: *When draining the coolant, keep in mind that cats and dogs are attracted by the ethylene glycol antifreeze, and are quite likely to drink any that is left in an uncovered container or in puddles on the ground. This will prove fatal in sufficient quantity. Always drain the coolant into a sealable container. Coolant should be reused unless it is contaminated or several years old.*

2. Disconnect the upper and lower radiator hoses and the coolant reserve tank hose.

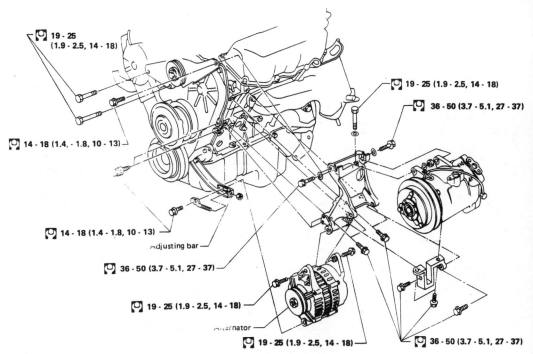

19 - 25 (1.9 - 2.5, 14 - 18)

19 - 25 (1.9 - 2.5, 14 - 18)

36 - 50 (3.7 - 5.1, 27 - 37)

14 - 18 (1.4, - 1.8, 10 - 13)

14 - 18 (1.4 - 1.8, 10 - 13)

Adjusting bar

36 - 50 (3.7 - 5.1, 27 - 37)

19 - 25 (1.9 - 2.5, 14 - 18)

Alternator

19 - 25 (1.9 - 2.5, 14 - 18)

36 - 50 (3.7 - 5.1, 27 - 37)

: N·m (kg-m, ft-lb)

Compressor mounting—Maxima with VG30 engine—others similar

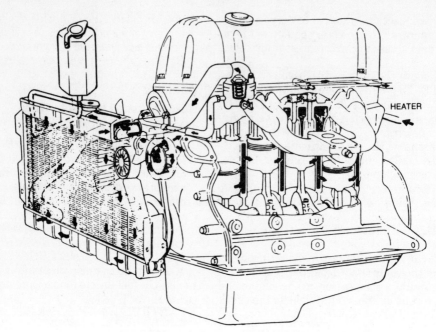

L-series engine cooling system (4 cylinder)

3. Disconnect the automatic transmission oil cooler lines if so equipped. Cap the lines to keep dirt out of them.

4. If the fan has a shroud, unbolt the shroud and move it back, hanging it over the fan.

5. Remove the radiator mounting bolts and the radiator.

6. Install the radiator in the vehicle and torque the mounting bolts evenly.

7. If equipped with an automatic transmission, connect the cooling lines at the radiator.

8. Connect the upper and lower hoses and the coolant reserve tank hose.

9. Refill the cooling system (refer to Chapter

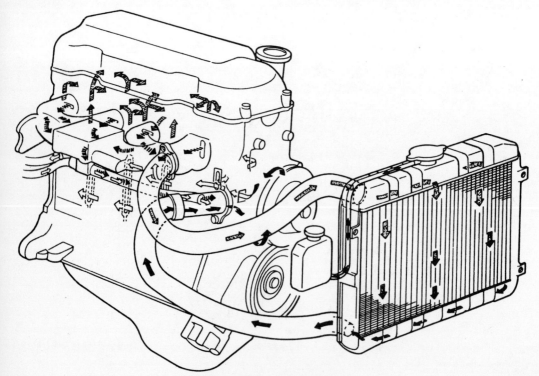

Cooling system—Z20 engines

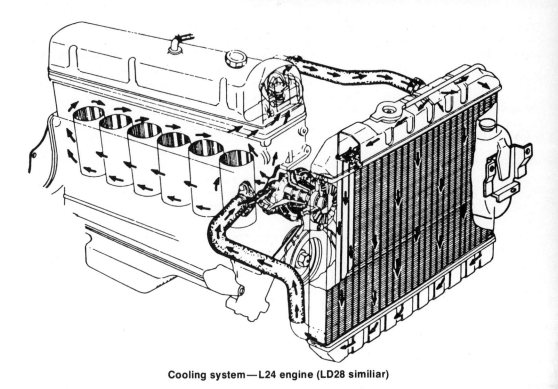

Cooling system—L24 engine (LD28 similiar)

CA20E ENGINE

THROTTLE CHAMBER

THERMOSTAT

INTAKE MANIFOLD

HEATER
UNIT

RADIATOR

CA18ET ENGINE

THROTTLE CHAMBER

TO TURBOCHARGER

THERMOSTAT

TO HEATER
UNIT

RADIATOR

OIL COOLER
(A/T MODEL)

CA20E and CA18ET cooling system schematics showing thermostat and oil cooler (CA18ET) locations

1) and automatic transmission if necessary, operate the engine until warm and then check the coolant level and for leaks.

Maxima (1985-89)

1. Remove the front bumper. Remove the cap and drain the radiator via the drain plug in the bottom tank.

CAUTION: *When draining the coolant, keep in mind that cats and dogs are attracted by the ethylene glycol antifreeze, and are quite likely to drink any that is left in an uncovered container or in puddles on the ground. This will prove fatal in sufficient quantity. Always drain the coolant into a sealable container. Coolant should be reused unless it is contaminated or several years old.*

2. Disconnect upper and lower radiator hoses and the water temperature switch connectors at top and bottom tanks of the radiator.

3. Remove the fan/shroud assembly from the radiator.

4. Remove the two bolts that mount the top of the radiator via grommets, and the two at the bottom which fasten the radiator to the mounts. Remove the radiator.

5. Position the fan/shroud assembly in the vehicle before installing the radiator.

6. Install the radiator in the vehicle and torque the mounting bolts evenly.

7. Connect the upper and lower radiator hoses and the water temperature switch connectors at the top and bottom tanks of the radiator.

8. Refill the cooling system with 50/50 antifreeze/water mix, and bleed the system. Refer to Chapter 1 if necessary.

9. Run engine and check the cooling system for leaks.

NOTE: *To remove the electrical cooling fan unplug the fan electrical connection and remove the fan/shroud as an assembly. If vehicle is equipped with an automatic transaxle disconnect and plug the transaxle cooling lines at the radiator.*

Air Conditioning Condenser

NOTE: *Refer to Chapter 1 for Charging and Discharging procedures.*

REMOVAL AND INSTALLATION

All Models

CAUTION: *The compressed refrigerant used in the air conditioning system expands into the atmosphere at a temperature of $-2°F$ ($-19°C$) or lower. This will freeze any surface, including your eyes, that it contacts. In addition, the refrigerant decomposes into a poisonous gas in the presence of a flame. Do not open or disconnect any part of the air*

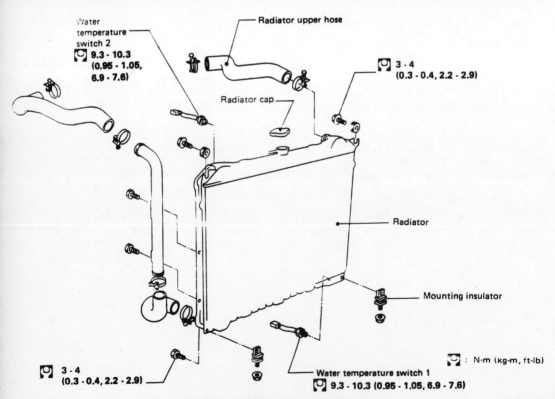

Radiator assembly mounting—Maxima

conditioning system until you have read the SAFTEY WARNINGS section in Chapter 1.

1. Disconnect the negative battery cables.

2. Remove the necessary components in order to gain access to the condenser retaining bolts. If equipped, remove the condenser fan motor, as necessary.

3. Discharge the system. Remove the condenser refrigerant lines and plug them with a clean shop towel.

NOTE: *On the 200SX models the receiver drier assembly should be removed before removing the condenser.*

4. Remove the condenser retaining bolts. Remove the condenser from the vehicle.

5. Install the condenser in the vehicle and evenly torque all the mounting bolts the same.

NOTE: *Always use new O-rings in all refrigerant lines.*

6. Reconnect all the refrigerant lines.

7. Install all the necessary equipment in order to gain access to the condenser mounting bolts. If removed, install the condenser fan motor.

8. Connect the negative battery cable.

9. Evacuate and charge the system as required.

Water Pump

REMOVAL AND INSTALLATION

Except Maxima (1985-89)

1. Drain the engine coolant into a clean container.

CAUTION: *When draining the coolant, keep in mind that cats and dogs are attracted by the ethylene glycol antifreeze, and are quite likely to drink any that is left in an uncovered container or in puddles on the ground. This will prove fatal in sufficient quantity. Always drain the coolant into a sealable container.*

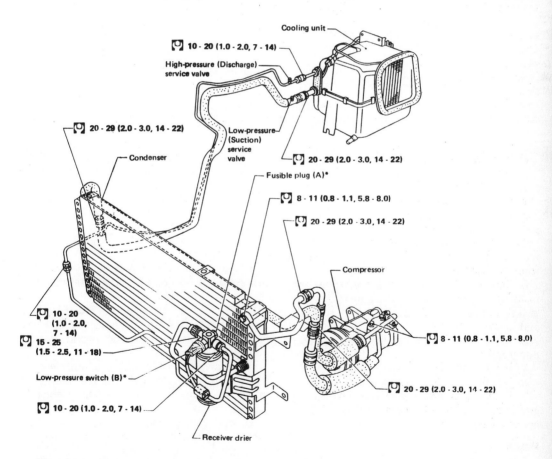

Condenser location—1988 200SX—others similar

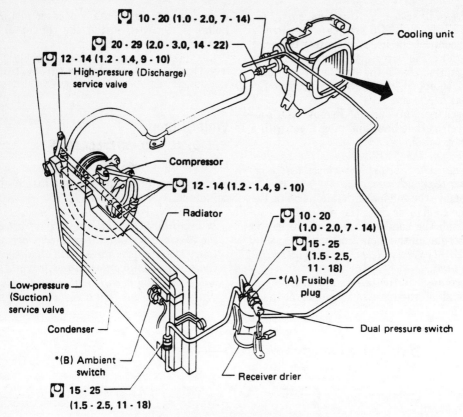

10 - 20 (1.0 - 2.0, 7 - 14)

20 - 29 (2.0 - 3.0, 14 - 22)

12 - 14 (1.2 - 1.4, 9 - 10)
High-pressure (Discharge)
service valve

Cooling unit

Compressor

12 - 14 (1.2 - 1.4, 9 - 10)

Radiator

**10 - 20
(1.0 - 2.0, 7 - 14)**

**15 - 25
(1.5 - 2.5,
11 - 18)**

*(A) Fusible
plug

Low-pressure
(Suction)
service valve

Condenser —

*(B) Ambient
switch

Dual pressure switch

Receiver drier

15 - 25
(1.5 - 2.5, 11 - 18)

Condenser location—1988 Maxima—others similar

Coolant should be reused unless it is contaminated or several years old.

2. Loosen the four bolts retaining the fan shroud to the radiator and remove the shroud.

3. Loosen the belt, then remove the fan and pulley from the water pump hub.

4. Remove the bolts retaining the pump and remove the pump together with the gasket from the front cover.

5. Remove all traces of gasket material and install the water pump to the engine with a new gasket and sealer. Tighten the bolts uniformly and to specifications.

6. Install the fan and pulley to the water pump hub.

7. Install and adjust the drive belt.

8. Install the radiator fan shroud.

9. Refill the cooling system and start the engine and check for leaks. Refer to Chapter 1 for necessary procedure.

Maxima

1. Drain the cooling system through the cocks at the bottom of the radiator and on the left hand side of the block. Remove the upper radiator hose.

CAUTION: *When draining the coolant, keep in mind that cats and dogs are attracted by*

the ethylene glycol antifreeze, and are quite likely to drink any that is left in an uncovered container or in puddles on the ground. This will prove fatal in sufficient quantity. Always drain the coolant into a sealable container. Coolant should be reused unless it is contaminated or several years old.

2. Loosen the tensioner and remove the A/C belt. Then, unbolt and remove the tensioner bracket while leaving the compressor mounted to its hinged bracket.

3. If the car is equipped with cruise control, remove the unit from the fender well to improve access. Remove the thermostat housing and gasket for access.

4. Remove the water pump mounting bolts (noting different lengths) and remove the pump, being careful to keep coolant off the timing belt.

5. Scrape the gasket surfaces, supply a new gasket, and reinstall the pump, torquing the bolts evenly to 12-15 ft. lbs.

6. Install the thermostat housing wih a new gasket. Install the cruise control unit if removed.

7. Install the tensioner, tensioner bracket, AC belt and adjust the belt correctly.

8. Install the upper radiator hose.

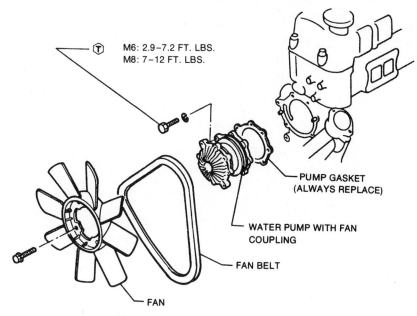

M6: 2.9–7.2 FT. LBS.
M8: 7–12 FT. LBS.

PUMP GASKET
(ALWAYS REPLACE)

WATER PUMP WITH FAN
COUPLING

FAN BELT

FAN

Removing the Z-series water pump

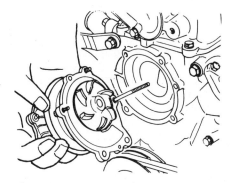

L-series water pump removal

9. Refill the cooling system, refer to Chapter 1 for necessary procedures. Start the engine, run to normal operating temperature and check for the correct coolant level and for leaks.

Cylinder Head
REMOVAL AND INSTALLATION

NOTE: *To prevent distortion or warping of the cylinder head, allow the engine to cool completely before removing the head bolts.*

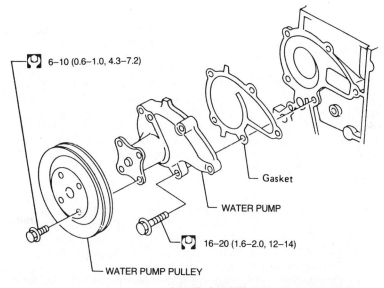

6–10 (0.6–1.0, 4.3–7.2)

Gasket

WATER PUMP

16–20 (1.6–2.0, 12–14)

WATER PUMP PULLEY

: N·M (KG-M, FT.LB.)

CA20E, CA18ET water pump installation

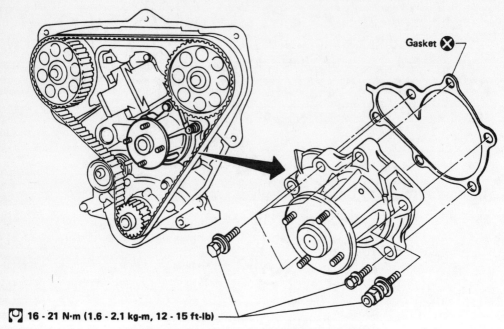

Gasket ⊗

⌂ **16 - 21 N·m (1.6 - 2.1 kg-m, 12 - 15 ft-lb)**

Exploded view of water pump installation V6 engine

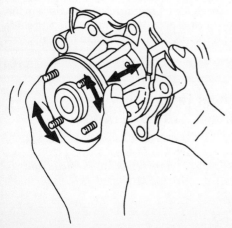

Checking water pump for excessive end play and rough operation

L18 and L20B Engines

1. Crank the engine until the No. 1 piston is TDC of the compression stroke and disconnect the negative battery cable, drain the cooling system and remove the air cleaner and attending hoses.

CAUTION: *When draining the coolant, keep in mind that cats and dogs are attracted by the ethylene glycol antifreeze, and are quite likely to drink any that is left in an uncovered container or in puddles on the ground. This will prove fatal in sufficient quantity. Always drain the coolant into a sealable container. Coolant should be reused unless it is contaminated or several years old.*

2. Remove the alternator.

3. Disconnect the carburetor throttle linkage, the fuel line and any other vacuum lines or electrical leads, and remove the carburetor.

4. Disconnect the exhaust pipe from the exhaust manifold.

5. Remove the fan and fan pulley.

6. Remove the spark plugs to protect them from damage. Lay the spark plugs aside and out of the way.

7. Remove the rocker cover.

8. Remove the water pump.

9. Remove the fuel pump.

10. Remove the fuel pump drive cam.

11. Mark the relationship of the camshaft sprocket to the timing chain with paint or chalk. If this is done, it will not be necessary to locate the factory timing marks. Before removing the camshaft sprocket, it will be necessary to wedge the chain in place so that it will not fall down into the front cover. The factory procedure is to wedge the timing chain in place with the wooden wedge shown here. The problem with this procedure is that it may allow the chain tensioner to move out far enough to cock itself against the chain. If this happens, you'll find that the chain won't go back over the sprocket after you've put the sprocket back on. In this case, you'll have to remove the front cover and push the tensioner back. After you've wedged the chain, unbolt the camshaft sprocket and remove it.

12. Loosen and remove the cylinder head bolts. You will need a 10mm Allen wrench to re-

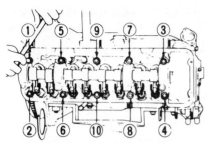

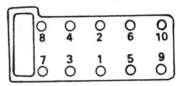

L-series four cylinder cylinder head torque sequence

Cylinder head bolt loosening sequence, L18 and L20 4-cylinder engines

move the head bolts. Keep the bolts in order since they are different sizes. Lift the cylinder head assembly from the engine. Remove the intake and exhaust manifolds as necessary.

13. Thoroughly clean the cylinder block and head mating surfaces and install a new cylinder head gasket. Check for head and block warpage; see Cleaning and Inspection and Resurfacing below. Do not use sealer on the cylinder head gasket.

14. With the crankshaft turned so that the No. 1 piston is at TDC of the compression stroke (if not already done so as mentioned in Step 1), make sure that the camshaft sprocket timing mark and the oblong groove in the plate are aligned.

15. Place the cylinder head in position on the cylinder block, being careful not to allow any of the valves to come in contact with any of the

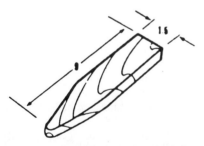

Wooden wedge dimensions (9 in. x 1.5 in.) used to hold cam chain in place

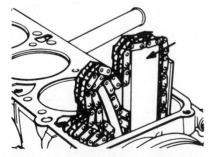

Wedge the chain with a wooden block (arrow). If you don't you'll be fishing for the chain in the crankcase (overhead cam engines)

pistons. Do not rotate the crankshaft or camshaft separately because of possible damage which might occur to the valves.

16. Temporarily tighten the two center right and left cylinder head bolts to 14.5 ft. lbs.

17. Install the camshaft sprocket together with the timing chain to the camshaft. Make sure the marks you made earlier line up with each other. If you get into trouble, see Timing Chain Removal and Installation for timing procedures.

18. Install the cylinder head bolts. Note that there are two sizes of bolts used; the longer bolts are installed on the driver's side of the engine with a smaller bolt in the center position. The remaining small bolts are installed on the opposite side of the cylinder head.

19. Tighten the cylinder head bolts in three stages: first to 29 ft. lbs., second to 43 ft. lbs., and lastly to 62 ft. lbs. Tighten the cylinder head bolts on all models in the proper sequence.

20. Install the fuel pump assembly, water pump and rocker cover.

21. Clean and regap the spark plugs then install plugs into the cylinder head. DO NOT OVER TORQUE THE SPARK PLUGS.

22. Install the fan pulley and cooling fan. Connect the exhaust pipe to the exhaust manifold.

23. Install the carburetor and connect the carburetor throttle linkage, the fuel line and any other vacuum lines or electrical leads.

24. Install the alternator, electrical connections to the alternator and drive belt.

25. Adjust the valves. Fill the cooling system start the engine and run it until normal operating temperature is reached. Retorque the cylinder head bolts to specifications, the readjust the valves. Retorque the head bolts again after 600 miles, and readjust the valves at that time.

L24 and LD28 Engines

1. Crank the engine until the No. 1 piston is at TDC of the compression stroke, disconnect the battery, and drain the cooling system.
NOTE: *To set the No. 1 piston at TDC of the compression stroke on the LD28 engine, remove the blind plug from the rear plate. Rotate the crankshaft until the marks on the flywheel and rear plate are in alignment. The No. 1 piston should now be at TDC.*

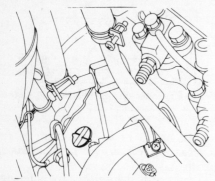

Remove the plug in the rear plate to set the No. 1 piston at TDC—diesel

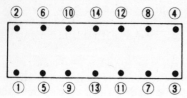

L24 series and LD28 cylinder head loosening sequence

2. Remove the radiator hoses and the heater hoses. Unbolt the alternator mounting bracket and move the alternator to one side, if necessary.

CAUTION: *When draining the coolant, keep in mind that cats and dogs are attracted by the ethylene glycol antifreeze, and are quite likely to drink any that is left in an uncovered container or in puddles on the ground. This will prove fatal in sufficient quantity. Always drain the coolant into a sealable container. Coolant should be reused unless it is contaminated or several years old.*

3. If the car is equipped with air conditioning, unbolt the compressor and place it to one side. Do not disconnect the compressor lines. Severe injury could result.

4. Remove the power steering pump.

5. Remove the spark plug leads and spark plugs (gasoline engine only).

6. Remove the cold start valve and the fuel pipe as an assembly. Remove the throttle linkage.

7. Remove all lines and hoses from the intake manifold. Mark them first so you will know where they go.

8. Unbolt the exhaust manifold from the exhaust pipe. The cylinder head can be removed with both the intake and exhaust manifolds in place.

9. Remove the camshaft cover.

10. Mark the relationship of the camshaft sprocket to the timing chain with paint. There are timing marks on the chain and the sprocket

which should be visible when the No. 1 piston is at TDC, but the marks are quite small and not particularly useful.

11. Before removing the camshaft sprocket, it will be necessary to wedge the chain in place so that it will not fall down into the front cover. The factory procedure is to wedge the timing chain in place with the wooden wedge as detailed in the previous procedure. The problem with this procedure is that it may allow the chain tensioner to move out far enough to cock itself against the chain. If this happens, you'll find that the chain won't go back over the sprocket after you've put the sprocket back on. In this case, you'll have to remove the front cover and push the tensioner back. After you've wedged the chain, unbolt the camshaft sprocket and remove it.

12. Remove the cylinder head bolts. They require an Allen wrench type socket adapter. Keep the bolts in order as two different sizes are used.

13. Lift off the cylinder head. You may have to tap it lightly with a rubber hammer.

14. Install a new head gasket and place the head in position on the block.

15. Install the head bolts in their original locations.

16. Torque the head bolts in three stages: first to 29 ft. lbs., then to 43 ft. lbs., then to 61 ft. lbs.

17. Reinstall the camshaft sprocket in its original location. The chain is installed at the same time as the sprocket. Make sure the marks you made earlier line up. If the chain has slipped, or the engine has been disturbed, correct the timing as described under Timing Chain Removal and Installation.

18. Install the camshaft cover and exhaust pipe to the exhaust manifold.

19. Reconnect all lines and hoses to the intake manifold.

20. Install the throttle linkage, cold start valve and fuel pipe assembly.

21. Clean and regap the spark plugs if so equipped. Install the the spark plugs in the cylinder head. DO NOT OVER TORQUE THE SPARK PLUGS.

22. Install the power steering pump and correctly adjust the drive belt.

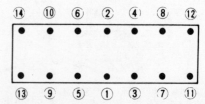

L24 series and LD28 cylinder head torque sequence

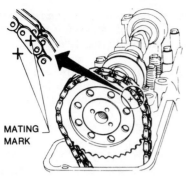

MATING MARK

Matchmark the timing chain to the camshaft sprocket

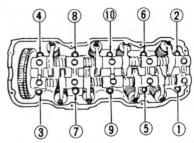

Z-series engine cylinder head bolt loosening sequence

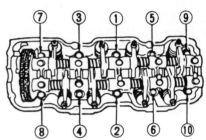

Z-series engine cylinder head bolt torque sequence

23. Install the air conditioning compressor and correctly adjust the drive belt.

24. Install the alternator mounting bracket, alternator, electrical connections to the alternator and adjust the drive belt.

25. Reconnect the heater and radiator hoses.

26. Refill the cooling system. Adjust the valves.

27. Start engine, run engine to normal operating temperature, check for the correct coolant level.

28. Check for leaks and roadtest vehicle for proper operation.

NOTE: *After 600 miles of driving, retorque the head bolts and readjust the valves.*

Z20E, Z20S and Z22 Engines

1. Complete Steps 1-5 under L24. Observe the following note for Step 5.

NOTE: *The spark plug leads should be marked; however, it would be wise to mark them yourself, especially on the dual spark plug models.*

2. Disconnect the throttle linkage, the air cleaner or its intake hose assembly (fuel injection). Disconnect the fuel line, the return fuel line and any other vacuum lines or electrical leads. On the Z20S, remove the carburetor to avoid damaging it while removing the head.

NOTE: *A good rule of thumb when disconnecting the rather complex engine wiring of today's automobiles is to put a piece of masking tape on the wire or hose and one the connection you removed the wire or hose from, then mark both pieces of tape 1, 2, 3, etc. When replacing wiring, simply match the pieces of tape.*

3. Remove the E.G.R. tube from around the rear of the engine.

4. Remove the exhaust air induction tubes from around the front of the engine on Z20S engines and from the exhaust manifold on Z20E engines.

5. Unbolt the exhaust manifold from the exhaust pipe. On the Z20S, remove the fuel pump.

6. On the Z20E, remove the intake manifold supports from under the manifold. Remove the P.C.V. valve from around the rear of the engine if necessary.

7. Remove the spark plugs to protect them from damage. Remove the valve cover.

8. Mark the relationship of the camshaft sprocket to the timing chain with paint or chalk. If this is done, it will not be necessary to locate the factory timing marks. Before removing the camshaft sprocket, it will be necessary to wedge the chain in place so that it will not fall down into the front cover. The factory procedure is to wedge the timing chain in place with the wooden wedge as detailed in the previous procedure. The problem with this procedure is that it may allow the chain tensioner to move out far enough to cock itself against the chain. If this happens, you'll find that the chain won't go back over the sprocket after you've put the sprocket back on. In this case, you'll have to remove the front cover and push the tensioner back. After you've wedged the chain, unbolt the camshaft sprocket and remove it.

9. Working from both ends in, loosen the cylinder head bolts and remove them. Remove the bolts securing the cylinder head to the front cover assembly.

10. Lift the cylinder head off the engine block. It may be necessary to tap the head lightly with a rubber mallet to loosen it.

11. Thoroughly clean the cylinder block and head surfaces and check both for warpage.

12. Fit the new head gasket. Don't use sealant. Make sure that no open valves are in the

way of raised pistons, and do not rotate the crankshaft or camshaft separately because of possible damage which might occur to the valves.

13. Temporarily tighten the two center right and left cylinder head bolts to 14 ft. lbs.

14. Install the camshaft sprocket together with the timing chain to the camshaft. Make sure the marks you made earlier line up with each other. If you get into trouble, see Timing Chain Removal and Installation for timing procedures.

15. Install the cylinder head bolts and torque them to 20 ft. lbs., then 40 ft. lbs., then 58 ft. lbs. in the order shown in the illustration.

16. Clean and regap the spark plugs then install them in the cylinder head. DO NOT OVER TORQUE THE SPARK PLUGS.

17. Install the valve cover with a new gasket.

18. On the Z20E, install the intake manifold supports from under the manifold. Install the P.C.V. valve if it was removed.

19. Connect the exhaust pipe to exhaust manifold. On the Z20S, install the fuel pump.

20. Install the exhaust air induction tubes to the front of the engine on Z20S engines and to the exhaust manifold on Z20E engines.

21. Install the E.G.R. tube from around the rear of the engine.

22. On the Z20S, install the carburetor. Connect the throttle linkage, the air cleaner or its intake hose assembly (fuel injection). Reconnect the fuel line, the return fuel line and any other vacuum lines or electrical leads.

23. Install the power steering pump if so equipped and correctly adjust the drive belt.

24. Install the air conditioning compressor and correctly adjust the drive belt.

25. Install the alternator mounting bracket, alternator, electrical connections to the alternator and adjust the drive belt.

26. Reconnect the heater and radiator hoses.

27. Refill the cooling system. Adjust the valves.

28. Start engine, run engine to normal operating temperature, check for the correct coolant level.

29. Check for leaks and roadtest vehicle for proper operation.

NOTE: *It is always wise to drain the crankcase oil after the cylinder head has been installed to avoid coolant contamination.*

V6 Engine

NOTE: *To remove or install the cylinder head, you'll need a special hex head wrench ST10120000 (J24239-01) or equivalent. The collector assembly and intake manifold have special bolt sequence for removal and installation. The distributor assembly is located in the left cylinder head mark and remove it if necessary. See note at VG30E Camshaft Removal And Installation before starting this procedure.*

1. Release the fuel pressure. See the procedure in this chapter for timing belt removal. Set the engine to Top Dead Center and then remove the timing belt.

NOTE: *Do not rotate either the crankshaft or camshaft from this point onward, or the valves could be bent by hitting the pistons.*

2. Drain the coolant from the engine. Then, disconnect all the vacuum hoses and water hoses connected to the intake collector.

CAUTION: *When draining the coolant, keep in mind that cats and dogs are attracted by the ethylene glycol antifreeze, and are quite likely to drink any that is left in an uncovered container or in puddles on the ground. This will prove fatal in sufficient quantity. Always drain the coolant into a sealable container. Coolant should be reused unless it is contaminated or several years old.*

3. Remove the collector cover and the collector. Refer to the section Intake Manifold Removal And Installation for correct bolt removal sequence.

4. Remove the intake manifold and fuel tube assembly.

5. Remove the exhaust collector bracket. Remove the exhaust manifold covers. Disconnect the exhaust manifold when it connects to the exhaust pipe (three bolts).

6. Remove the camshaft pulleys and the rear timing cover securing bolts.

7. Loosen the bolts a little at a time in numerical order.

8. Remove the cylinder head with the exhaust manifold attached. If you need to remove the exhaust manifold, refer to the procedure in this section.

9. Check the positions of the timing marks and camshaft sprockets to make sure they have not shifted.

10. Install the head with a new gasket. Apply

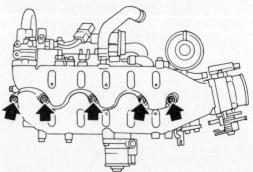

To remove the collector (V6 engines), loosen the arrowed bolts

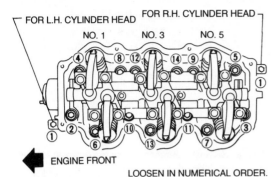

To remove the V6 cylinder head, loosen the bolts in numerical order

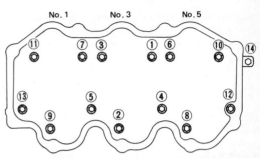

Torquing pattern for the right side V6 cylinder head

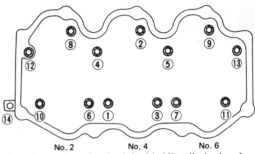

Torquing pattern for the left side V6 cylinder head

clean engine oil to the threads and seats of the bolts and install the bolts with washers in the correct position. Note that bolts 4, 5, 12, and 13 are 127mm long. The other bolts are 106mm long.

11. Torque the bolts according to the pattern for the cylinder head on each side in the following stages:

    a. Torque all bolts, in order, to 22 ft. lbs.

    b. Torque all bolts, in order, to 43 ft. lbs.

    c. Loosen all bolts completely.

    d. Torque all bolts, in order, to 22 ft. lbs.

    e. Torque all bolts, in order, to 40-47 ft. lbs. If you have a special wrench available that torques bolts to a certain angle, torque them 60-65° tighter rather than going to 40-47 ft. lbs.

12. Install the rear timing cover bolts. Install the camshaft pulleys. Make sure the pulley marked R3 goes on the right and that marked L3 goes on the left.

13. Align the timing marks if necessary and then install the timing belt and adjust the belt tension.

14. Install the front upper and lower belt covers.

15. Make sure that the rocker cover bolts, trays and washers are free of oil. Then, install the rocker covers.

16. Install the intake manifold and fuel tube. Torque NUTS as follows:

    a. Torque in numbered order to 26-43 in. lbs.

    b. Torque in numbered order to 17-20 ft. lbs.

17. Torque the BOLTS on the intake manifold as follows:

    a. Torque in numbered order to 26-43 in. lbs.

    b. Torque in numbered order to 12-14 ft. lbs.

18. Install the exhaust manifold if removed from the cylinder head.

19. Connect the exhaust manifold to the exhaust pipe connection. Install the exhaust collector bracket.

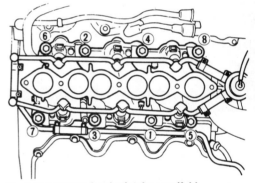

Torquing pattern for the intake manifold

20. Install the collector and collector cover. Refer to the section for Intake Manifold Removal And Installation for the correct torque pattern.

21. Connect all the vacuum hoses and water hoses to the intake collector.

22. Refill the cooling system. Start the engine check the engine timing. After the engine reaches the normal operating temperture check for the correct coolant level.

23. Roadtest the vehicle for proper operation.

CA20E and CA18ET Engines

1. Drain the cooling system.

CAUTION: *When draining the coolant, keep in mind that cats and dogs are attracted by the ethylene glycol antifreeze, and are quite likely to drink any that is left in an uncovered container or in puddles on the ground. This will prove fatal in sufficient quantity. Always drain the coolant into a sealable container. Coolant should be reused unless it is contaminated or several years old.*

2. Turn the crankshaft so that the No. 1 cylinder is at TDC on the compression stroke.

3. Remove the drive belts.

4. Remove the water pump pulley and crankshaft pulley.

5. On CA18ET engines, remove the air intake pipe.

6. Remove the timing belt.

7. Remove the distributor-to-canister vacuum tube.

8. Remove the alternator adjusting bracket.

NOTE: *After removing the timing belt, do*

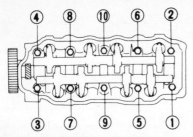

CA20E/CA18ET cylinder head bolt loosening sequence

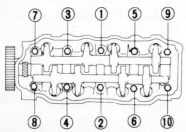

CA20E/CA18ET cylinder head bolt torque sequence. Bolt No. 8 is the longest

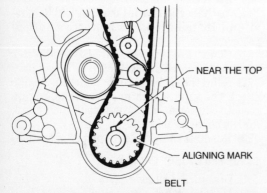

Set the CA20E and CA18ET No. 1 cylinder at TDC on the compression stroke. The keyway on the crankshaft sprocket will be almost at 12:00.

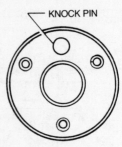

CA20E, CA18ET camshaft knock pin position for cylinder head assembly

not rotate the crankshaft and camshaft separately, as there is now no timing and the valves will hit the piston heads.

9. Loosen the cylinder head bolts in two or three stages in the sequence shown.

10. With the cylinder head removed, see the Cleaning and Inspection and Resurfacing procedures below for cylinder head service.

11. To install the head and timing belt, first set the No. 1 cylinder to TDC on the compression stroke. Make sure the crankshaft keyway is near the 12:00 position as shown in the accompanying illustration.

12. Set the camshaft pin on the top as shown.

13. Install the cylinder head on the clean top of the cylinder block, using a new head gasket.

14. Make sure all cylinder head bolts have washers. Tighten all bolts in the order shown, using the following procedure:

    a. Torque all bolts to 22 ft. lbs.

    b. Torque all bolts to 58 ft. lbs.

    c. Loosen all bolts completely.

    d. Torque all bolts to 22 ft. lbs.

    e. Torque all bolts to 54-61 ft. lbs., or if you are using an angle wrench, turn all bolts 90-95° clockwise.

15. Install the timing belt.

16. Install the alternator adjusting bracket, distributor-to-canister vacuum tube.

17. Install the air intake pipe on the CA18ET engines.

18. Install the water pump and crankshaft pulley. Install and adjust the drive belts.

19. Refill the cooling system. Start the engine check the engine timing. After the engine reaches the normal operating temperture check for the correct coolant level.

20. Roadtest the vehicle for proper operation.

KA24E Engine

NOTE: *After finishing this procedure allow the rocker cover to cylinder head rubber plugs to dry for 30 minutes before starting the engine. This will allow the liquid gasket sealer used to seal these plugs to dry completely.*

1. Drain coolant from the radiator and remove drain plug from the cylinder block.

CAUTION: *When draining the coolant, keep in mind that cats and dogs are attracted by the ethylene glycol antifreeze, and are quite likely to drink any that is left in an uncovered container or in puddles on the ground. This will prove fatal in sufficient quantity. Always drain the coolant into a sealable container. Coolant should be reused unless it is contaminated or several years old.*

2. Remove the power steering drive belt, power steering pump, idler pulley and power steering brackets.

3. Mark and disconnect all the vacuum hoses, spark plug wires and electrical connections to gain access to cylinder head. Remove the air induction hose from the collector assembly.

4. Disconnect the accelerator bracket. If necessary mark the position and remove the accelerator cable wire end from the throttle drum.

5. Remove the bolts that hold intake manifold collector to the intake manifold. Remove and position the collector assembly to the side.

6. Remove the bolts that hold intake manifold to the cylinder. Remove the intake manifold. Unplug the exhaust gas sensor and remove the exhaust cover and exhaust pipe at exhaust manifold connection. Remove the exhaust manifold from the cylinder head.

7. Remove the rocker cover. If cover sticks to the cylinder head, tap it with a rubber hammer.

NOTE: *After removing the rocker cover matchmark the timing chain with the camshaft sprocket with paint or equivalent. This step is very important for the correct installation of the timing chain to sprocket.*

8. Set No.1 cylinder piston at T.D.C. on its compression stroke. Remove the No.1 spark plug and make sure that the piston is UP.

9. Loosen the camshaft sprocket bolt. Do not turn engine when removing the bolt.

10. Support the timing chain with a block of wood as illustrated.

11. Remove the camshaft sprocket.

12. Remove the front cover to cylinder head retaining bolts.

NOTE:

The cylinder head bolts should be loosened in two or three steps in the correct order to prevent head warpage or cracking.

13. Remove the cylinder head bolts in the correct order.

14. Confirm that the No. 1 is at T.D.C. on its compression stroke as follows:

  a. Align timing mark with 0^0 mark on the crankshaft pulley.

  b. Make sure the distributor rotor head is set at No. 1 on the distributor cap.

  c. Confirm that the knock pin on the camshaft is set at the top position.

15. Install the cylinder head with a new gas-

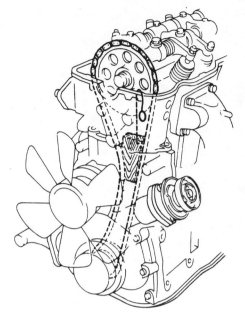

Support timing chain with block of wood

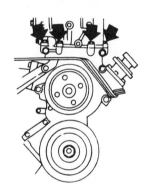

Remove front cover-cylinder head retaining bolts

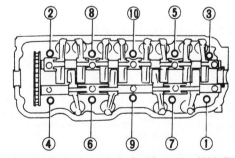

Loosen cylinder head bolts in this order—KA24E engine

ket and torque the head bolts in numerical order in 5 steps (a, b, c, d, e). Do not rotate crankshaft and camshaft separately, or valves will hit the piston heads.

  a. Torque all bolts to 22 ft. lbs.

  b. Torque all bolts to 58 ft. lbs.

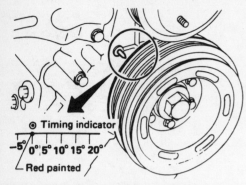

Align timing mark with 0 on timing scale

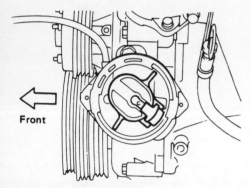

Front

Rotor at No. 1 cylinder location

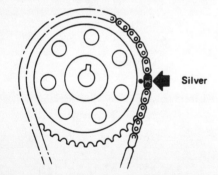

Matchmark timing chain with camshaft sprocket

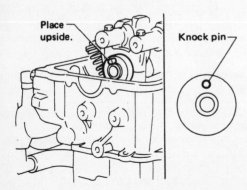

Confirm knock pin on camshaft is set at top

c. Loosen all bolts completely.

d. Torque all bolts to 22 ft. lbs.

e. Torque all bolts to 54-61 ft. lbs., or if you are using an angle wrench, turn all bolts 80-85° clockwise.

16. Remove the block of wood holding timing chain in the correct location. Position the timing chain on the camshaft sprocket by aligning each matchmark. Install the camshaft sprocket to the camshaft.

17. Tighten the camshaft sprocket bolt and the front cover to cylinder head retaining bolts.

18. Install the intake manifold and collector assembly with new gaskets. Refer to the Intake Manifold Removal and Installation procedures.

19. Install the exhaust manifold with new gaskets. Refer to the Exhaust Manifold Removal and Installation procedures.

20. Apply liquid gasket to the rubber plugs and install the rubber plugs in the correct location in the cylinder head.

21. Install the rocker cover with new gasket

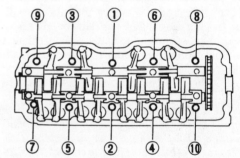

Tighten cylinder head bolts in this order—KA24E engine

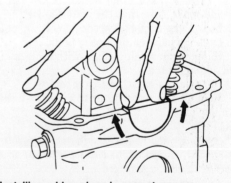

Installing rubber plugs in correct manner

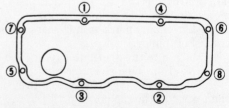

Correct rocker cover bolt torque sequence

in place. Tighten the retaining bolts in the correct order.

22. Reconnect the accelerator bracket and cable if removed.

23. Connect all the vacuum hoses, and electrical connections that were removed to gain access to cylinder head. Reconnect the air induction hose to collector assembly.

24. Clean and regap the spark plugs if necessary. Install the spark plugs and spark plug wires in the correct location. DO NOT OVERTIGHTEN!

25. Install the power steering brackets, idler pulley, and power steering pump. Install the drive belt and adjust the belt.

26. Install the drain plug in the cylinder block. Refill the cooling system.

27. Start the engine, after the engine reaches the normal operating temperture check for the correct coolant level.

28. Roadtest the vehicle for proper operation.

CLEANING AND INSPECTION

All Cylinder Heads

1. With the valves installed to protect the valve seats, remove deposits from the combustion chambers and valve heads with a scraper and a wire brush. Be careful not to damage the cylinder head gasket surface. After the valves are removed, clean the valve guide bores with a valve guide cleaning tool. Using cleaning solvent to remove dirt, grease and other deposits,

MEASURING POINTS

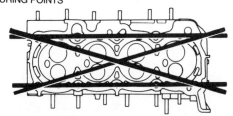

Use a straightedge to measure cylinder head flatness at these points

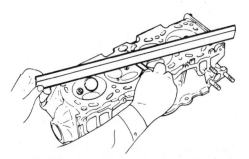

Check cylinder head flatness and warpage with a straightedge and feeler gauge. Warpage should not exceed 0.004 in.

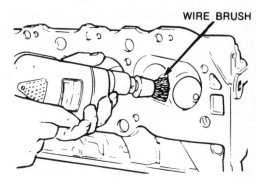
WIRE BRUSH

Clean the combustion chambers with a wire brush. Make sure you remove the deposits and do not scratch the head

clean all bolt holes; be sure the oil passages are clean.

2. Remove all deposits from the valves with a fine wire brush or buffing wheel.

3. Inspect the cylinder head for cracks or excessively burned areas in the exhaust outlet ports.

4. Check the cylinder head for cracks and inspect the gasket surface for burrs and nicks. Replace the head if it is cracked.

5. On cylinder heads that incorporate valve seat inserts, check the inserts for excessive wear, cracks or looseness.

RESURFACING

Cylinder Head Flatness

When a cylinder head is removed, check the flatness of the cylinder head gasket surface.

1. Place a straight edge across the gasket surface of the cylinder head. Using feeler gauges, determine the clearance at the center of the straightedge.

2. If warpage exceeds 0.10mm over the total length, the cylinder head must be resurfaced. Cylinder head height after resurfacing must not exceed specifications.

3. If necessary to refinish the cylinder head gasket surface, do not plane or grind off more than 0.2mm from the original gasket surface.

NOTE: *Cylinder head resurfacing should be done only by a competent machine shop.*

Valves

REMOVAL AND INSTALLATION

All Engines

The cylinder head must be removed on all engines before the valves can be removed.

A valve spring compressor is needed to remove the valves and springs; these are available at most auto parts and auto tool shops. A small magnet is very helpful for removing the keepers and spring seats.

Set the head on its side on the bench. Install the spring compressor so that the fixed side of the tool is flat against the valve head in the combustion chamber, and the screw side is against the retainer. Slowly turn the screw in towards the head, compressing the spring. As the spring compresses, the keepers will be revealed; pick them off of the valve stem with the magnet as they are easily fumbled and lost. When the keepers are removed, slowly back the screw out and remove the retainers and springs. Remove the compressor and pull the valves out of the head from the other side. Remove the valve seals by hand and remove the spring seats with the magnet.

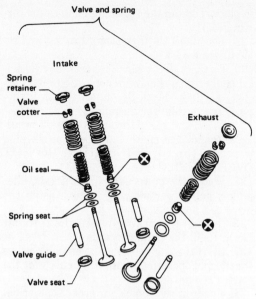

Exploded view of valves—KA24E engine—always replace oil seals after each disassembly

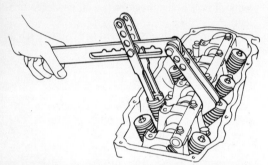

Compressing the valve springs using a valve spring compressor

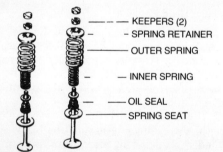

Typical valve components. Not all engines have double valve springs

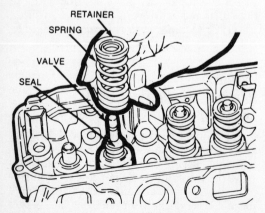

Always install new valve stem seals

Since it is very important that each valve and its spring, retainer, spring seat and keepers is reassembled in its original location, you must keep these parts in order. The best way to do this is to cut either eight (four cylinder) or twelve (six cylinder) holes in a piece of heavy cardboard or wood. Label each hole with the cylinder number and either IN or EX, corresponding to the location of each valve in the head. As you remove each valve, insert it into the holder, and assemble the seats, springs, keepers and retainers to the stem on the labeled side of the holder. This way each valve and its attending parts are kept together, and can be put back into the head in their proper locations.

After lapping each valve into its seat (see Valve Lapping below), oil each valve stem, and install each valve into the cylinder head in the reverse order of removal, so that all parts except the keepers are assembled on the stem. Always use new valve stem seals. Install the spring compressor, and compress the retainer and spring until the keeper groove on the valve stem is fully revealed. Coat the groove with a wipe of grease (to hold the keepers until the retainer is released) and install both keepers, wide end up. Slowly back the screw of the compressor out until the spring retainer covers the keepers. Remove the tool. Lightly tap the end of each valve stem with a rubber hammer to ensure proper fit of the retainers and keepers. Adjust the valves.

NOTE: *On the 1989 240SX the KA24E engine is a 4-cylinder, 12-valve engine. This engine has 2 intake valves and 1 exhaust valve for each cylinder.*

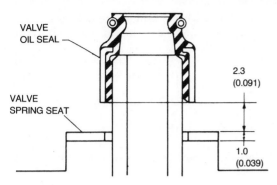

VALVE OIL SEAL

2.3 (0.091)

VALVE SPRING SEAT

1.0 (0.039)

UNIT: MM (IN)

Proper valve stem seal installation, CA20E and CA18ET

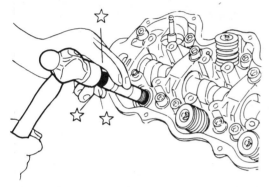

Valve spring seat installation, CA20E and CA18ET engines. Others similar

INSPECTION

Before the valves can be properly inspected, the stem, lower end of the stem and the entire valve face and head must be cleaned. An old valve works well for clipping carbon from the valve head, and a wire brush, gasket scraper or putty knife can be used for cleaning the valve face and the area between the face and lower stem. Do not scratch the valve face during cleaning. Clean the entire stem with a rag soaked in thinners to remove all varnish and gum.

Thorough inspection of the valves requires the use of a micrometer, and a dial indicator is needed to measure the inside diameter of the valve guides. If these instruments are not available to you, the valves and head can be taken to a reputable machine shop for inspection. Refer to the Valve Specifications chart for valve stem and stem-to-guide specifications.

If the above instruments are at your disposal, measure the diameter of each valve stem at the locations illustrated. Jot these measurements down. Using the dial indicator, measure the inside diameter of the valve guides at their bottom, top and midpoint 90° apart. Jot these mea-

Measuring valve stem diameter on the center of stem

Use an inside dial indicator to measure valve guide inner diameter (I.D.)

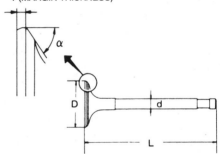

T (MARGIN THICKNESS)

Critical valve dimensions. When the valve head has been worn down to 0.020 in. in margin thickness (T), replace the valve. Grinding allowance for the valve stem tip is 0.008 in. or less.

surements down also. Subtract the valve stem measurement from the valve guide inside measurement; if the clearance exceeds that listed in the specifications chart under Stem-to-Guide Clearance, replace the valve(s). Stem-to-guide clearance can also be checked at a machine shop, where a dial indicator would be used.

Check the top of each valve stem for pitting and unusual wear due to improper rocker adjustment, etc. The stem tip can be ground flat if it is worn, but no more than 0.5mm can be removed; if this limit must be exceeded to make the tip flat and square, then the valve must be replaced. If the valve stem tips are ground, make sure you fix the valve securely into a jig

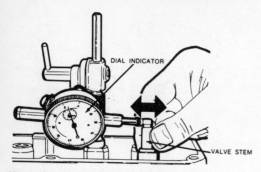

Measuring stem-to-guide clearance

designed for this purpose, so the tip contacts the grinding wheel squarely at exactly 90°. Most machine shops that handle automotive work are equipped for this job.

STEM-TO-GUIDE CLEARANCE

Valve stem-to-guide clearance should be checked upon assembling the cylinder head, and is especially necessary if the valve guides have been reamed or knurled, or if oversize valves have been installed. Excessive oil consumption often is a result of too much clearance between the valve guide and valve stem.

1. Clean the valve stem with lacquer thinner or a similar solvent to remove all gum and varnish. Clean the valve guides using solvent and an expanding wire-type valve guide cleaner (a rifle cleaning brush works well here).

2. Mount a dial indicator so that the stem is at 90° to the valve stem and as close to the valve guide as possible.

3. Move the valve off its seat, and measure the valve guide-to-stem clearance by rocking the stem back and forth to actuate the dial indicator. Measure the valve stems using a micrometer and compare to specifications, to determine whether stem or guide wear is responsible for excessive clearance.

Valve Guide
INSPECTION

Valve guides should be cleaned as outlined earlier, and checked when valve stem diameter and stem-to-guide clearance is checked. Generally, if the engine is using oil through the guides (assuming the valve seals are OK) and the valve stem diameter is within specification, it is the guides that are worn and need replacing.

REMOVAL AND INSTALLATION

The valve guides in all engines covered in this guide may be replaced. To remove the guide(s), heat the cylinder head to 302-320°F (150-160°C). Drive out the guides using a 2 ton press (many machine shops have this equipment) or a

hammer and brass drift which has been modified with washers as in the accompanying illustration.

NOTE: *Some valve guides are retained by snaprings, which must be removed prior to guide removal.*

With the guide(s) removed, the cylinder head valve guide holes should be reamed to accept the new guides. The head should then be heated again and the new guides pressed or driven into place. On engines which utilize valve guide snaprings, install the snapring to the guide first, then install the guide into the head. Ream the new valve guide bores to 8.00-8.01mm (all engines except CA20E/CA18ET; or 7.00-7.01mm (CA20E/CA18ET). On the KA24E engine reamed valve guide finished sizes are 7.00-7.01mm INTAKE VALVE and 8.00-8.01mm EXHAUST VALVE.

KNURLING

Valve guides which are not excessively worn or distorted may, in some cases, be knurled rather than reamed. Knurling is a process in

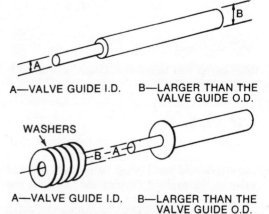

A—VALVE GUIDE I.D. B—LARGER THAN THE VALVE GUIDE O.D.

A brass drift can be modified for valve guide removal

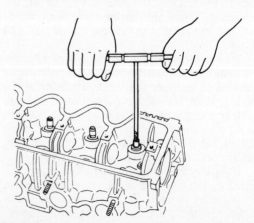

Always use two hands on the reamer handle when reaming valve guides

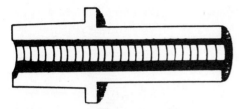

Cross-section of a knurled valve guide

which metal inside the valve guide bore is displaced and raised (forming a very fine cross-hatch pattern), thereby reducing clearance. Knurling also provides for excellent oil control. The possibility of knurling rather than reaming the guides should be discussed with a machinist.

REFACING

Valve refacing should only be handled by a reputable machine shop, as the experience and equipment needed to do the job are beyond that of the average owner/mechanic. During the course of a normal valve job, refacing is necessary when simply lapping the valves into their seats will not correct the seat and face wear. When the valves are reground (resurfaced), the valve seats must also be recut, again requiring special equipment and experience.

VALVE LAPPING

The valves must be lapped into their seats after resurfacing, to ensure proper sealing. Even if the values have not been refaced, they should be lapped into the head before reassembly.

Set the cylinder head on the workbench, combustion chamber side up. Rest the head on wooden blocks on either end, so there are 50-75mm between the tops of the valve guides and the bench.

1. Lightly lube the valve stem with clean en-

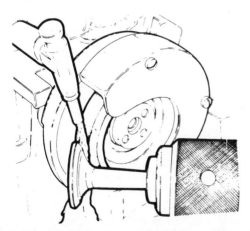

Valve refacing should be handled by an engine specialist or machinist

Lapping the valves

gine oil. Coat the valve seat completely with valve grinding compound. Use just enough compound that the full width and circumference of the seat are covered.

2. Install the valve in its proper location in the head. Attach the suction cup end of the valve lapping tool to the valve head. It usually helps to put a small amount of saliva into the suction cup to aid it sticking to the valve.

3. Rotate the tool between the palms, changing position and lifting the tool often to prevent grooving. Lap the valve in until a smooth, evenly polished seat and valve face are evident.

4. Remove the valve from the head. Wipe away all traces of grinding compound from the valve face and seat. Wipe out the port with a solvent soaked rag, and swab out the valve guide with a piece of solvent soaked rag to make sure there are no traces of compound grit inside the guide. This cleaning is very important, as the engine will ingest any grit remaining when started.

5. Proceed through the remaining valves, one at a time. Make sure the valve faces, seats, cylinder ports and valve guides are clean before reassembling the valve train.

Valve Seats
REPLACEMENT

Check the valve seat inserts for any evidence of pitting or excessive wear at the valve contact surface. The valve seats in all engines covered here can be replaced. Because the cylinder head must be machined to accept the new seat inserts, consult an engine specialist or machinist about this work.

NOTE: *When repairing a valve seat, first check the valve and guide; if wear is evident here, replace the valve and/or guide, then correct the valve seat.*

Valve Springs
REMOVAL AND INSTALLATION
Z20, Z22, CA20E, CA18ET
VG30E and KA24E Engines

The valve springs in these engines can be removed without removing the camshaft, while the cylinder head is in place. Follow the Valves Removal and Installation procedure if the head has already been removed.

1. Remove the rocker cover. Set the cylinder on which you will be working to TDC on the compression stroke.

2. Remove the rocker shaft assembly.

3. Remove one spark plug on whichever cylinder you are working.

4. Install an air hose adaptor into the spark plug hole and apply about 71 psi of pressure into the cylinder. This will hole the valves in place, preventing them from droppng into the cylinder when the springs are removed.

5. Install a valve spring compressing tool similar to the one illustrated and remove the valve spring and valve steam seal. Use care not to lose the keepers.

NOTE: *Always install new oil seals during reassembly.*

6. Reassemble the valve and components. Making sure the air pressure in the cylinder is at 71 psi while the springs are being installed.

7. Remove air adapator and install the spark plug.

8. Install the rocker shaft and rocker cover with a new gasket.

L18, L20, L24, LD28 Engines

The camshafts in these engines must be removed in order to remove the valve springs. Follow the Camshaft Removal and Installation procedure, then follow the valve spring removal procedure listed above for the Z-series and CA-series engines. If you are removing the valve springs with the cylinder head already removed

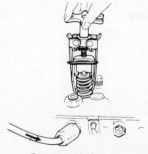

Compressed air

Use 71 psi of air pressure to keep the valve from dropping into the cylinder. Note the valve spring compressor

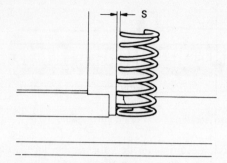

Measuring spring height and squareness. Make sure the closed coils face downward

Have the valve spring pressure tested

from the engine, follow the procedure under Valves Removal and Installation.

HEIGHT AND PRESSURE CHECK

1. Place the valve spring on a flat, clean surface next to a square.

2. Measure the height of the spring, and rotate it against the edge of the square to measure distortion (out-of-roundness). If spring height varies between springs by more than 1.5mm or if the distortion exceeds 1.5mm, replace the spring(s) in question. Outer valve spring squareness should not exceed 2.2mm; inner spring squareness should not exceed 1.9mm.

A valve spring tester is needed to test spring test pressure, so the valve springs usually must be taken to a machinist or engine specialist for this test. Compare the tested pressure with the pressures listed in the Valve Specifications chart in this chapter.

Oil Pan
REMOVAL AND INSTALLATION
All Engines Except V6

To remove the oil pan it will be necessary to unbolt the motor mounts and jack up the engine to gain clearance. Drain the oil, remove the attaching screws, and remove the oil pan and gasket.

CAUTION: *The EPA warns that prolonged contact with used engine oil may cause a number of skin disorders, including cancer!*

You should make every effort to minimize your exposure to used engine oil. Protective gloves should be worn when changing the oil. Wash your hands and any other exposed skin areas as soon as possible after exposure to used engine oil. Soap and water, or waterless hand cleaner should be used.

Do not insert a screwdriver into the oil pan to remove it, because this may bend or deform the oil pan flange. Install the oil pan with a new gasket and sealant at the points indicated, tightening the screws to 48-84 in. lbs.

Wait at least 30 minutes before refilling engine oil. Overtightening will distort the pan lip, causing leakage. Do not use a liquid gasket for the oil pan if original equipment was a rubber gasket.

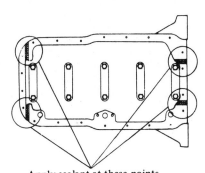

Apply sealant at these points
Z-series oil pan sealant points

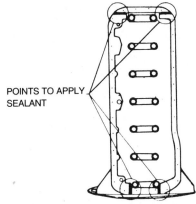

POINTS TO APPLY SEALANT

Apply sealant here when installing the oil pan on L24 and LD28 engines

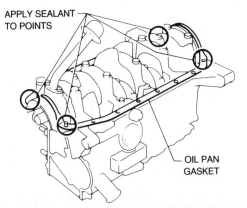

APPLY SEALANT TO POINTS

OIL PAN GASKET

Apply sealant to the CA20E and CA18ET engine oil pan mating surfaces here; also to the corresponding points on the oil pan

V6

1. Remove the front hood, connect a lifting sling to the engine, and apply upward pressure. Drain the oil pan.

CAUTION: *The EPA warns that prolonged contact with used engine oil may cause a number of skin disorders, including cancer! You should make every effort to minimize your exposure to used engine oil. Protective gloves should be worn when changing the oil. Wash your hands and any other exposed skin areas as soon as possible after exposure to used engine oil. Soap and water, or waterless hand cleaner should be used.*

2. Remove the covers from under the engine. Then, remove the engine mount insulator nuts and bolts.

3. Remove the five engine mounting bolts and remove the center crossmember assembly.

4. Remove the exhaust pipe connecting nuts. Unbolt and remove the oil pan.

5. Clean all the sealing surfaces. Apply sealant to the four joints on the lower surface of the block. Apply sealant to the corresponding areas of the oil pan gasket on both upper and lower surfaces.

6. Install the pan and gasket. Torque the pan bolts in the order shown in the illustration to 43-61 in. lbs. and then lower engine assembly.

7. Install the exhaust pipe connection.

8. Install the center crossmember assembly and engine mount bolts.

9. Install the under covers to the engine and refill the oil pan with the specified quantity of clean oil. Operate the engine and check for leaks.

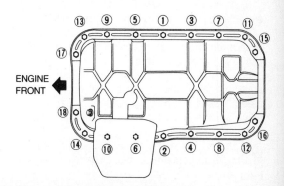

ENGINE FRONT

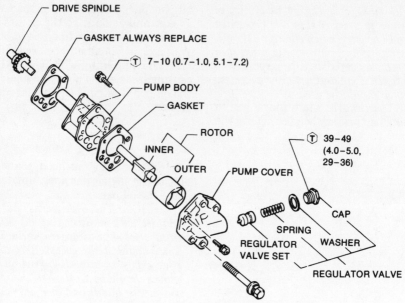

Exploded view of the diesel engine oil pump

Oil Pump

REMOVAL AND INSTALLATION

1973-79

1. Remove the distributor on the L18, L20B and L24 engines.
2. Drain the engine oil.

CAUTION: *The EPA warns that prolonged contact with used engine oil may cause a number of skin disorders, including cancer! You should make every effort to minimize your exposure to used engine oil. Protective gloves should be worn when changing the oil. Wash your hands and any other exposed skin areas as soon as possible after exposure to used engine oil. Soap and water, or waterless hand cleaner should be used.*

3. Remove the front stabilizer bar if it is in the way of removing the oil pump.
4. Remove the splash shield.
5. Remove the oil pump body with the drive spindle assembly.
6. Turn the crankshaft so that the No. 1 piston is at TDC of the compression stroke.
7. Fill the pump housing with engine oil, then align the punch mark on the spindle with the hole in the oil pump.
8. With a new gasket placed over the drive spindle, install the oil pump and drive spindle assembly so that the projection on the top of the drive spindle is located in the 11:25 o'clock position.
9. Install the distributor with the metal tip of the rotor pointing toward the No. 1 spark plug tower of the distributor cap.

Removing Z-series, L-series oil pump

1. Oil pump body
2. Inner rotor and shaft
3. Outer rotor
4. Oil pump cover
5. Regulator valve
6. Regulator spring
7. Washer
8. Regulator cap
9. Cover gasket

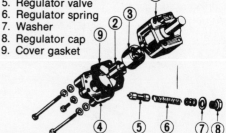

Exploded view of the Z-series, and gasoline engine L-series oil pump

10. Install the splash shield and front stabilizer bar if it was removed.
11. Refill the engine oil. Start the engine, check ignition timing and check for oil leaks.

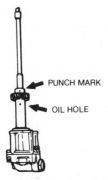

Z-series, L-series (gasoline) oil pump alignment

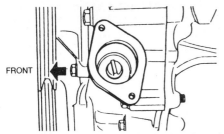

Position of the distributor drive spindle—L-series gasoline engines

1980-84

EXCEPT CA20E, CA18ET

CAUTION: *Before attempting to remove the oil pump on 1980 models, you must perform the following procedures:*

a. Drain the oil from the oil pan.

CAUTION: *The EPA warns that prolonged contact with used engine oil may cause a number of skin disorders, including cancer! You should make every effort to minimize your exposure to used engine oil. Protective gloves should be worn when changing the oil. Wash your hands and any other exposed skin areas as soon as possible after exposure to used engine oil. Soap and water, or waterless hand cleaner should be used.*

b. Turn the crankshaft so that No. 1 piston is at TDC on its compression stroke.

c. Remove the distributor cap and mark the position of the distributor rotor in relation to the distributor base with a piece of chalk (gasoline engine only).

1. Remove the front stabilizer bar, if so equipped.

2. Remove the splash shield.

3. Remove the oil pump body with the drive spindle assembly.

4. To install, fill the pump housing with engine oil, align the punch mark on the spindle with the hole in the pump. No. 1 piston should be at TDC on its compression stroke.

5. With a new gasket placed over the drive spindle, install the oil pump and drive spindle assembly. On gasoline engines make sure the tip of the drive spindle fits into the distributor shaft notch securely. The distributor rotor should be pointing to the matchmark you made earlier.

NOTE: *Great care must be taken not to disturb the distributor rotor while installing the oil pump, or the ignition timing will be wrong.*

6. Install the splash shield and front stabilizer bar if it was removed.

7. Install the distributor cap.

8. Refill the engine oil. Start the engine, check ignition timing and check for oil leaks.

NOTE: *On the KA24E engine used in the 240SX follow the above procedure for Oil Pump Removal And Installation.*

CA20E, CA18ET
VG30 Engines

1. Remove all accessory drive belts and the alternator.

2. Remove the timing (cam) belt covers and remove the timing belt.

3. Unbolt the engine from its mounts and lift or jack the engine up from the unibody.

4. Remove the oil pan.

5. Remove the oil pump assembly along with the oil strainer.

6. If installing a new or rebuilt oil pump, first pack the pump full of petroleum jelly to prevent the pump from cavitating when the engine is started. Install the pump, torquing the mounting bolts to 9-12 ft. lbs.

NOTE: *Always use a new O-ring when installing the strainer to the pump body.*

7. Install the oil pan.

8. Install the timing belt and covers.

9 Install the alternator and all drive belts. Reconnect the negative battery cable.

11. Start engine, check ignition timing and check for oil leaks.

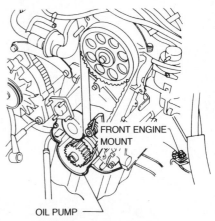

CA20E, CA18ET oil pump location

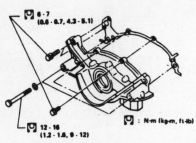

Oil pump installation—V6

Timing Chain Cover
REMOVAL AND INSTALLATION

All Gasoline Engines
Except CA20E, CA18ET and VG30E

NOTE: *It may be necessary to remove additional components to perform this operation if you cannot cut the gasket cleanly as described in Step 10. The CA20E, CA18ET and VG30E are belt driven engines there is no timing chain cover refer to Timing Belt Removal and Installation.*

1. Disconnect the negative battery cable from the battery, drain the cooling system, and remove the radiator together with the upper and lower radiator hoses.

CAUTION: *When draining the coolant, keep in mind that cats and dogs are attracted by the ethylene glycol antifreeze, and are quite likely to drink any that is left in an uncovered container or in puddles on the ground. This will prove fatal in sufficient quantity. Always drain the coolant into a sealable container. Coolant should be reused unless it is contaminated or several years old.*

2. Loosen the alternator drive belt adjusting screw and remove the drive belt. Remove the bolts, which attach the alternator bracket to the engine and set the alternator aside out of the way.

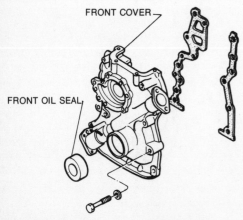

FRONT COVER

FRONT OIL SEAL

Timing chain front cover—gasoline engine

3. Mark and remove the distributor. Refer to Distributor Removal And Installation if necessary.

4. Remove the oil pump attaching screws, and take out the pump and its drive spindle.

5. Remove the cooling fan and the fan pulley together with the drive belt.

6. Remove the water pump.

7. Remove the crankshaft pulley bolt and remove the crankshaft pulley.

8. Remove the bolts holding the front cover to the front of the cylinder block, the four bolts which retain the front of the oil pan to the bottom of the front cover, and the two bolts which are screwed down through the front of the cylinder head and into the top of the front cover.

9. Carefully pry the front cover off the front of the engine.

10. Cut the exposed front section of the oil pan gasket away from the oil pan. Do the same to the gasket at the top of the front cover. Remove the two side gaskets and clean all of the mating surfaces.

11. Cut the portions needed from a new oil pan gasket and top front cover gasket.

12. Apply sealer to all of the gaskets and position them on the engine in their proper places.

13. Apply a light coating of grease to the crankshaft oil seal and carefully mount the front cover to the front of the engine and install all of the mounting bolts.

Tighten the 8mm bolts to 7-12 ft. lbs. and the 6mm bolts to 36-72 in. lbs. Tighten the oil pan attaching bolts to 48-84 in. lbs.

14. Before installing the oil pump, place the gasket over the shaft and make sure that the mark on the drive spindle faces (aligned) with the oil pump hole.

15. Install the oil pump after priming it with oil. For oil pump installation procedures, see Oil Pump Removal and Installation in this chapter.

16. Install the crankshaft pulley and bolt.

17. Install the water pump with a new gasket. Install the fan pulley and cooling fan. Install the drive belt and adjust the belt to the correct tension.

18. Install the distributor in the correct position. Reconnect the alternator bracket and alternator if it was removed. Install the drive belt and adjust the belt to the correct tension.

19. Reconnect the upper and lower radiator hoses and refill the cooling system.

20. Reconnect the negative battery cable. Start the engine, check ignition timing and check for leaks.

NOTE: *On the KA24E engine used in the 1989 240SX model follow the procedure above and remove all the drive belts and the rocker cover. Remove the oil pan if necessary.*

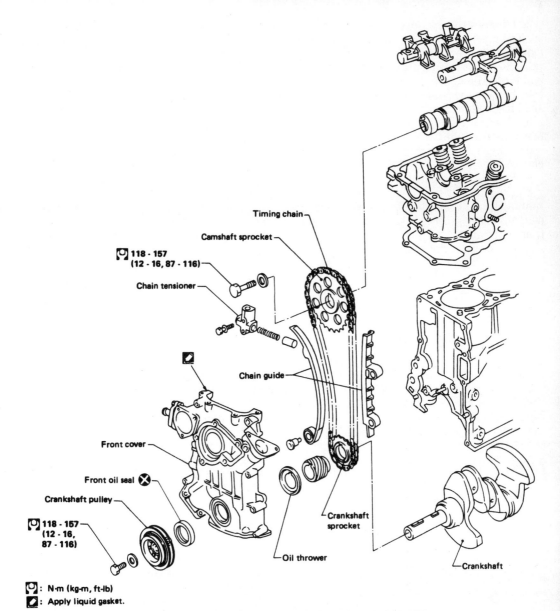

Timing chain

Camshaft sprocket

118 - 157
(12 - 16, 87 - 116)

Chain tensioner

Chain guide

Front cover

Front oil seal

Crankshaft pulley

118 - 157
(12 - 16,
87 - 116)

Crankshaft
sprocket

Oil thrower

Crankshaft

: N·m (kg-m, ft-lb)
: Apply liquid gasket.

Timing chain cover assembly—KA24E engine—1989 240SX

Diesel Engine

NOTE: *It may be necessary to remove additional components to perform this operation if you cannot cut the gasket cleanly as described in Step 18. This procedure requires the removal and subsequent installation of the fuel injection pump. It is a good idea to read through the Diesel Fuel Injection section in Chapter 4 before you continue with this procedure. You may decide that the job is better left to a qualified service technician.*

1. Disconnect the negative battery cable. Drain the cooling system and then remove the radiator together with the upper and lower radiator hoses.

CAUTION: *When draining the coolant, keep in mind that cats and dogs are attracted by the ethylene glycol antifreeze, and are quite likely to drink any that is left in an uncovered container or in puddles on the ground. This will prove fatal in sufficient quantity. Always drain the coolant into a sealable container. Coolant should be reused unless it is contaminated or several years old.*

2. Remove the fan, fan coupling and fan pulley.

3. Unscrew the retaining bolts on the crankshaft damper pulley. Use a plastic mallet and lightly tap around the outer edges of the pulley; this should loosen it enough so that you can pull it off. If not, use a two armed gear puller.

4. Remove the power steering pump, bracket and idler pulley (if so equipped).

5. Unscrew the five mounting bolts and remove the front dust cover.

6. Remove the thermostat housing and the bottom bypass inlet with the hose.

7. Remove the engine slinger.

8. Tag and disconnect all hoses and lines running from the injection pump. Make sure to plug any hoses or lines to prevent dust or dirt from entering.

9. Drain the engine oil.

CAUTION: *The EPA warns that prolonged contact with used engine oil may cause a number of skin disorders, including cancer! You should make every effort to minimize your exposure to used engine oil. Protective gloves should be worn when changing the oil. Wash your hands and any other exposed skin areas as soon as possible after exposure to used engine oil. Soap and water, or waterless hand cleaner should be used.*

10. Remove the oil cooler and coolant hose together with the oil filter.

11. Remove the water inlet, the oil dipstick and the right side engine mounting bracket.

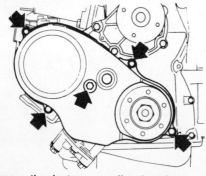

Remove the dust cover—diesel engine

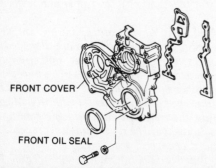

FRONT COVER

FRONT OIL SEAL

Front cover—Diesel Engine

12. Remove the oil pump.

13. Remove the injection pump as detailed in Chapter 4.

14. Remove the water pump.

15. Loosen the mounting bolt and remove the injection pump drive crank pulley. You will need a two armed gear puller.

16. Remove the bolts holding the front cover to the front of the cylinder block, the four bolts which retain the front of the oil pan to the bottom of the front cover, and the two bolts which are screwed down through the front of the cylinder head and into the top of the front cover.

17. Carefully pry the front cover off the front of the engine.

18. Cut the exposed front section of the oil pan gasket away from the oil pan. Do the same to the gasket at the top of the front cover. Remove the two side gaskets and clean all of the mating surfaces.

19. Cut the portions needed from a new oil pan gasket and top front cover gasket.

20. Apply sealer to all of the gaskets and position them on the engine in their proper places.

21. Apply a light coating of grease to the crankshaft oil seal and carefully mount the front cover to the front of the engine and install all of the mounting bolts.

22. Tighten the 8mm bolts to 7-12 ft. lbs. and the 6mm bolts to 36-72 in. lbs. Tighten the oil pan attaching bolts to 48-84 in. lbs.

23. Before installing the oil pump, place the gasket over the shaft and make sure that the mark on the drive spindle faces (aligned) with the oil pump hole.

24. Install the oil pump after priming it with oil. For oil pump installation procedures, see Oil Pump Removal and Installation in this chapter.

25. Install the injection drive crank pulley and mounting bolt.

26. Install the water pump with a new gasket.

27. Install the injection pump. Refer to Injection Pump Removal And Installation.

28. Reconnect the right side engine bracket, oil dipstick and the water outlet. Install the oil cooler, filter and necessary hoses.

29. Reconnect all lines and hoses to the injection pump. Install the engine slinger.

30. Install the thermostat housing and bypass inlet with the hose.

31. Install the front dust cover and install the idler pulley, power steering bracket and power steering pump.

32. Install the crankshaft damper pulley, cooling fan pulley, fan coupling and cooling fan.

33. Install all the drive belts that were removed and adjust the belts to the proper tension.

34. Connect the upper and lower radiator hos-

es and refill the cooling system. Reconnect the negative battery cable.

35. Check the injection pump timing and check for leaks.

Timing Chain, Gears and Tensioner
REMOVAL AND INSTALLATION

All Gasoline Engines Except
CA20E, CA18ET and VG30E Engines

NOTE: *The CA20E, CA18ET and VG30E engines use a timing belt.*

1. Before beginning any disassembly procedures, position the No. 1 piston at TDC on the compression stroke.

2. Remove the front cover as previously outlined. Remove the camshaft cover and remove the fuel pump if it runs off a cam lobe in front of the camshaft sprocket.

3. With the No. 1 piston at TDC, the timing marks in the camshaft sprocket and the timing chain should be visible. Mark both of them with paint. Also mark the relationship of the camshaft sprocket to the camshaft. At this point you will notice that there are three sets of timing marks and locating holes in the sprocket. They are for making adjustments to compensate for timing chain stretch. See the following Timing Chain Adjustment for more details.

4. With the timing marks on the cam sprocket clearly marked, locate and mark the timing marks on the crankshaft sprocket. Also mark

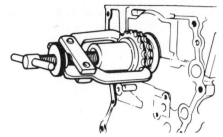

Crankshaft sprocket removal

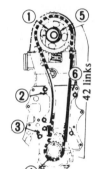

1. Fuel pump drive cam
2. Chain guide
3. Chain tensioner
4. Crank sprocket
5. Cam sprocket
6. Chain guide

Timing chain and sprocket alignment—L-series engine

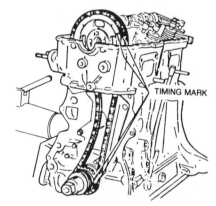

Timing chain and sprocket alignments—Z20 engines

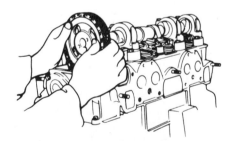

Removing the camshaft sprocket

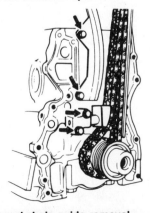

Tensioner and chain guide removal

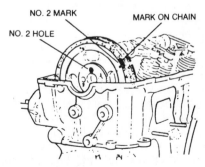

Use the No. 2 mark and hole to align camshaft—Z20 engines

the chain timing mark. Of course, if the chain is not to be re-used, marking it is useless.

5. Unbolt the camshaft sprocket and remove the sprocket along with the chain. As you remove the chain, hold it where the chain tensioner contacts it. When the chain is removed, the tensioner is going to come apart. Hold on to it and you won't lose any of the parts. There is no need to remove the chain guide unless it is being replaced.

6. Using a two armed gear puller, remove the crankshaft sprocket assembly.

7. Install the timing chain and the camshaft sprocket together after first positioning the chain over the crankshaft sprocket. Position the sprocket so that the marks made earlier line up. This is assuming that the engine has not been disturbed. The camshaft and crankshaft keys should both be pointed upward. If a new chain and/or gear is being installed, position the sprocket so that the timing marks on the chain align with the marks on the crankshaft sprocket and the camshaft sprocket (with both keys pointing up). The marks are on the right hand side of the sprockets as you face the engine. The L18 has 42 pins between the mating marks of the chain and sprockets when the chain is installed correctly. The L20B has 44 pins. The 1977-78 L24 engine used in the 810 has 42 pins between timing marks. The L24 (1979-84), Z20E and Z20S engines do not use the pin counting method for finding correct valve timing. Instead, position the key in the crankshaft sprocket so that it is pointing upward and install the camshaft sprocket on the camshaft with its dowel pin at the top using the No. 2 (No. 1 on the L24) mounting hole and timing mark. The painted links of the chain should be on the right hand side of the sprockets as you face the engine. See the illustration.

NOTE: *The factory manual refers to the pins you are to count in the L-series engines as links, but in America, this is not correct. Count the pins. There are two pins per link. This is an important step. If you do not get the exact number of pins between the timing marks, valve timing will be incorrect and the engine will either not run at all, in which case you may stand the chance of bending the valves, or the engine will run very bad.*

8. Install the chain tensioner and the front cover assembly.

If timing chain assembly uses chain guides these guides do not have to be removed to replace the timing chain. Check the timing chain for cracks and excessive wear. On the KA24E engine used in the 240SX model there are 2 oil seals in the left side mounting holes of the block were the timing chain cover will be mounted always replace these seals.

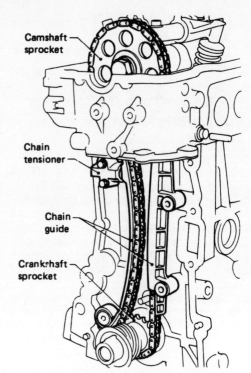

Timing chain components—KA24E engine

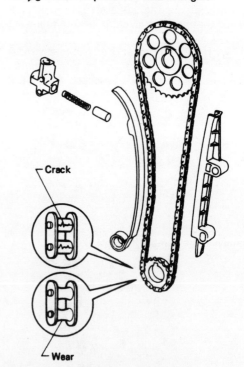

Timing chain assembly—KA24E engine

Diesel Engine

1. Follow Steps 1-6 of the preceding Gasoline Engine procedure. You need not remove the fuel pump as detailed in Step 2.

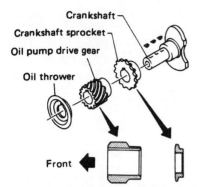

Set timing chain by aligning its mating marks with those of crankshaft sprocket and camshaft sprocket—KA24E engine

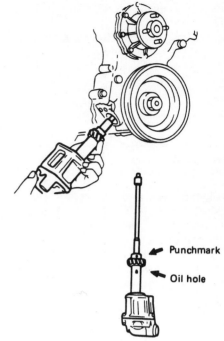

Installing oil pump—KA24E engine

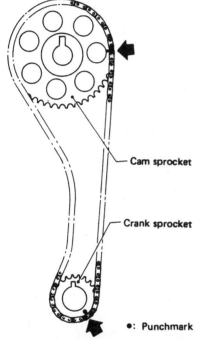

Correct installation of crankshaft sprocket, oil pump drive gear, oil thrower—KA24E engine

•: Punchmark

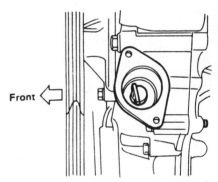

Drive spindle for oil pump in correct location—KA24E engine

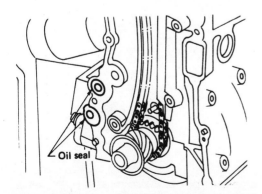

Oil seals in left side of engine block—KA24E engine

2. Install the crankshaft sprocket. Make sure that the mating marks on the sprocket face the front of the car.

3. Install the timing chain and the camshaft sprocket together after first positioning the chain over the crankshaft sprocket. Position the cam sprocket so that the marks made earlier line up. This is assuming that the engine has not been disturbed. The camshaft and crankshaft keys should be pointing upward. If a new chain and/or gear is being installed, position the sprocket so that the timing marks on the chain align with the marks on the crankshaft and camshaft sprockets (with both keys pointing up). The marks are on the right hand side of the

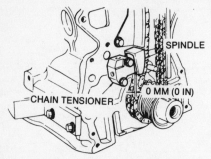

Chain tensioner mounting—1979 and later 810 and Maxima, gasoline and diesel engines

sprockets as you face the engine. Insert the camshaft dowel pin into the No. 1 hole in the camshaft sprocket. Install and tighten the camshaft sprocket bolt.

4. Install the chain guide (if removed) and the chain tensioner. Tighten the slack side (left side when facing the engine) chain guide mounting bolt so that the protrusion of the chain tensioner spindle is 0.

5. Install the front cover assembly.

TIMING CHAIN ADJUSTMENT

When the timing chain stretches excessively, the valve timing will be adversely affected. There are three sets of holes and timing marks on the camshaft sprocket.

If the stretch of the chain roller links is excessive, adjust the camshaft sprocket location by transferring the set position of the camshaft sprocket from the factory position of No. 1 or No. 2 to one of the other positions as follows:

1. Turn the crankshaft until the No. 1 piston is at TDC on the compression stroke. Examine whether the camshaft sprocket location notch is to the left of the oblong groove on the camshaft retaining plate. If the notch in the sprock-

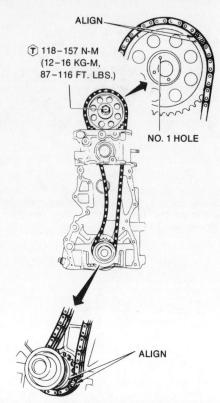

Timing chain and sprocket alignment—1979 and later 810 and Maxima, gasoline and diesel engines

et is to the left of the groove in the retaining plate, then the chain is stretched and needs adjusting.

2. Remove the camshaft sprocket together with the chain and reinstall the sprocket and chain with the locating dowel on the camshaft inserted into either the No. 2 or 3 hole of the sprocket. The timing mark on the timing chain must be aligned with the mark on the sprocket.

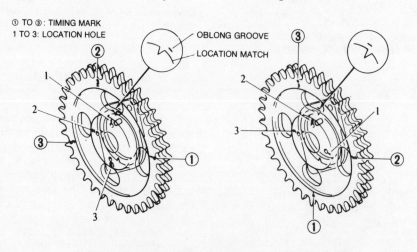

BEFORE ADJUSTMENT　　　　AFTER ADJUSTMENT
Timing chain adjustment

The amount of modification is 4° of crankshaft rotation for each mark.

3. Recheck the valve timing as outlined in Step 1. The notch in the sprocket should be to the right of the groove in the camshaft retaining plate.

4. If and when the notch cannot be brought to the right of the groove, the timing chain is worn beyond repair and must be replaced.

Timing Belt

REMOVAL AND INSTALLATION

4-Cylinder Engines

1. Remove the battery ground cable.
2. On the CA20E engine, remove the air intake ducts.
3. Remove the cooling fan.
4. Remove the power steering, alternator, and air conditioner compressor belts if so equipped.
5. Set the No. 1 cylinder at TDC on the compression stroke. The accompanying illustration shows the timing mark alignment for TDC.

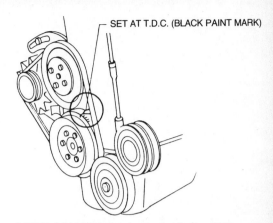

SET AT T.D.C. (BLACK PAINT MARK)

CA20E, CA18ET timing marks for finding TDC

6. Remove the front upper and lower timing belt covers.
7. Loosen the timing belt tensioner and return spring, then remove the timing belt.
8. Carefully inspect the condition of the timing belt. There should be no breaks or cracks anywhere on the belt. Especially check around the bottoms of the teeth, where they intersect

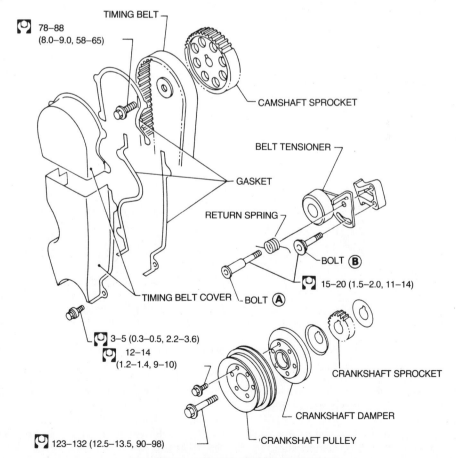

Timing belt assembly—CA20E and CA18LT

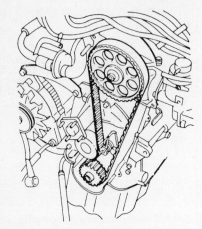

Timing belt with covers removed

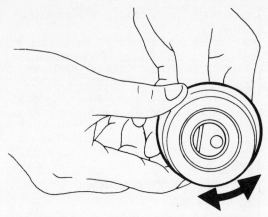

Spin the tensioner pulley to make sure it works smoothly

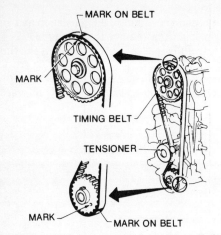

CA20E, CA18ET timing marks for belt installation

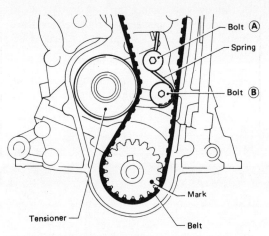

Set the tensioner spring by first hooking one end to the side of bolt "B", then the other end on the tensioner pawl bracket

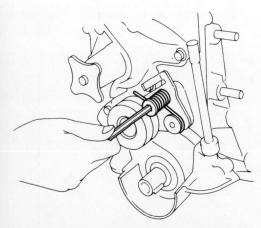

Installing the belt tensioner and return spring

the belt; cracks often show up here. Evidence of any wear or damage on the belt means the belt should be replaced.

9. To install the belt, first make sure that No. 1 cylinder is set at TDC on compression. Install the belt tensioner and return spring.

NOTE: *If the coarse stud has been removed, apply Loctite® or another locking thread sealer to the stud threads before installing.*

10. Make sure the tensioner bolts are not securely tightened before the drive belt is installed. Make sure the tensioner pulley can be rotated smoothly.

11. Make sure the timing belt is in good condition and clean. Do not bend it. Place the belt in position, aligning the white lines on the timing belt with the punch mark on the camshaft pulleys and the crankshaft pulley. Make sure the arrow on the belt is pointing toward the front belt covers.

12. Tighten the belt tensioner and assemble the spring. To set the spring, first hook one end on bolt B side, then hook the other end on the tensioner bracket pawl. Rotate the crankshaft two turns clockwise, then tighten bolt B then bolt A. At this point, belt tension will automatically be at the specified value.

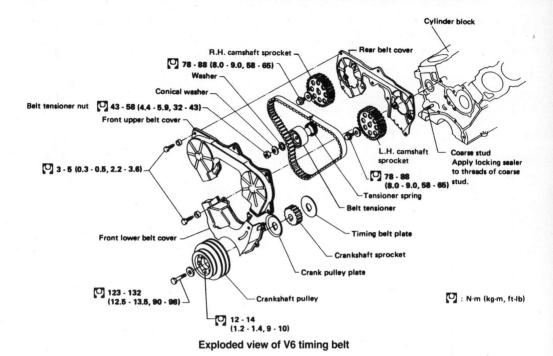

Exploded view of V6 timing belt

13. Install the upper and lower timing belt covers.

14. Install and adjust all the drive belts.

15. Install the cooling fan and reconnect the air intake ducts on the CA20E engine.

16. Connect the battery cable, start engine and check the ignition timing.

VG30E Engine (1985-87)

NOTE: *After removing timing belt, do not rotate crankshaft and camshaft separately, because valves will hit piston heads. Review the complete procedure*
before starting this repair.

1. Raise vehicle and safely support.

2. Remove the engine under covers and drain engine coolant from the radiator. Be careful not to allow coolant to contact drive belts.

CAUTION: *When draining the coolant, keep in mind that cats and dogs are attracted by the ethylene glycol antifreeze, and are quite likely to drink any that is left in an uncovered container or in puddles on the ground. This will prove fatal in sufficient quantity. Always drain the coolant into a sealable container. Coolant should be reused unless it is contaminated or several years old.*

3. Remove the front right side wheel and tire assembly. Remove the engine side cover.

4. Remove the engine coolant reservoir tank and radiator hoses.

5. Remove the A.S.C.D. (speed control device) actuator.

6. Remove all the drive belts from the engine. When removing the power steering drive belt, loosen the idler pulley from the right side wheel housing.

7. Remove the idler bracket of the compressor drive belt and crankshaft pulley.

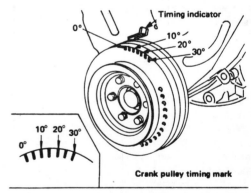

Crank pulley timing mark

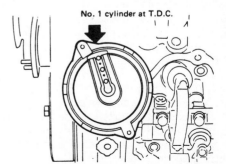

Distributor rotor position

Set No. 1 cylinder at T.D.C. on compression stroke

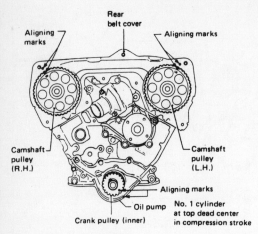

Timing marks—V6 engine

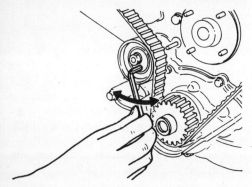

Set tensioner after timing belt installation 1985–87 V6 engine

8. Remove the timing belt covers. Rotate the engine with a socket wrench on the crankshaft pulley bolt to align the two sets of timing marks. The marks are on the camshaft pulleys and rear belt covers.

9. Remove the rocker covers. Loosen the rocker shaft securing bolts so that rockers will no longer bear on the cam lobes. Remove all spark plugs.

10. Use a hexagon wrench to turn the belt tensioner clockwise and tighten the tensioner locknut just enough to hold the tensioner in position. This is done to remove tension. Then, remove the old belt.

NOTE: *Be careful not to bend the new belt installing it. Timing belts are designed to flex only the way they turn around the pulleys.*

11. Make sure that all pulleys and the belt are free of oil and water. Install the new belt, aligning the arrow on the timing belt forward. Align the white lines on the timing belt with the punchmarks on all three pulleys.

12. Loosen the tensioner locknut to allow spring tension to tension the belt. Then, using the hexagon wrench, turn the tensioner first clockwise, then counterclockwise in three cycles. This will seat the belt. Now, torque the tensioner locknut to 32-43 ft. lbs.

13. Tighten rocker shaft bolts alternately in three stages. Before tightening each pair of bolts, turn the engine over so the affected rocker will not touch its cam lobe. Final torque is 13-16 ft. lbs. Install the rocker covers with new gaskets.

14. Install lower and upper timing belt covers.

15. Install crankshaft pulley and idler bracket of the compressor drive belt. Tighten the crankshaft pulley bolt to 90-98 ft. lbs.

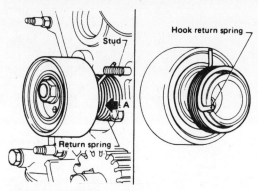

Tensioner assembly

R.H. rocker shafts

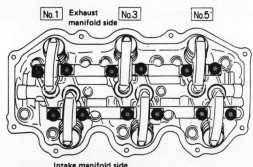

Bolt location right side rocker shafts

L.H. rocker shafts

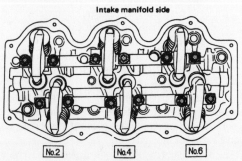

Bolt location left side rocker shafts

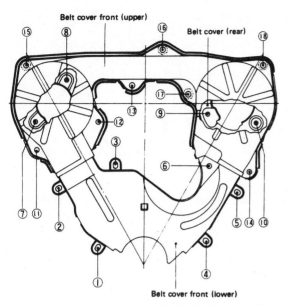

Timing belt cover bolt locations—V6 engine

Tightened parts	Section	Parts tightened with bolts
Bolt A (6 pcs.) Rubber washer Belt cover front (lower)	①, ②, ③, ④, ⑤, ⑭	①, ②, ③, ④: Cylinder block ⑤, ⑭: Compressor bracket
Bolt B (1 pc.) Rubber washer Belt cover front (lower) Water pump mounting bolt	⑥	Water pump mounting bolt
Bolt C (4 pcs.) Belt cover (rear)	⑦, ⑧, ⑨, ⑩	Cylinder head
Bolt A (7 pcs.) Rubber washer Belt cover front (upper) Belt cover (rear) Welded nut (4 pcs.)	15, 16, 17, 18 ⑪, ⑫ ⑬	15, 16, 17, 18: Welded nuts ⑪, ⑫: Cylinder head ⑬: Water outlet

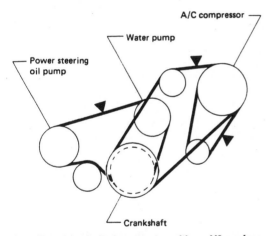

Installing drive belts in correct position—V6 engine

16. Install the drive belts. Clean and regap the spark plugs if necessary then install in the cylinder head.

17. Install the coolant reservoir tank, radiator hoses, A.S.C.D. actutator.

18. Install the right front wheel. Install engine under cover and side covers.

19. Refill the cooling system. Check ignition timing and roadtest for proper operation.

VG30E Engine (1988-89)

On these model years timing belt removal and installation is the same. Use the above procedure with the exception that the rocker covers and rocker shafts bolts are not removed, but the spark plugs are still removed. The timing belt is installed and adjusted as follows:

1. Confirm that No. 1 cylinder is at T.D.C. on its compression stroke. Install tensioner and tensioner spring. If stud is removed apply locking sealant to threads before installing.

2. Swing tensioner fully clockwise with hexagon wrench and temporarily tighten locknut.

3. Set timing belt, align the arrow on the

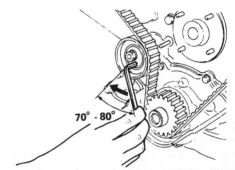

Set tensioner after timing belt installation 1987–89 V6 engine

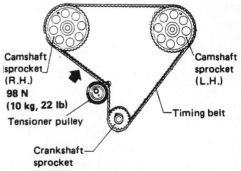

Apply force at marked position then loosen tensioner

timing belt forward. Align the white lines on the timing belt with the punchmarks on all three pulleys.

NOTE: *There are 133 total timing belt teeth. If timing belt is installed correctly there will be 40 teeth between lefthand and righthand camshaft sprocket timing marks. There will be 43 teeth betwwen lefthand camshaft sprocket and crankshaft sprocket timing marks.*

4. Loosen tensioner locknut, keeping tensioner steady with a hexagon wrench.

5. Swing tensioner 70-80° clockwise with hexagon wrench and temporarily tighten locknut.

6. Install all the spark plugs. Turn crankshaft clockwise 2 or 3 times, then slowly set No. 1 cylinder at T.D.C. on its compression stroke.

7. Push middle of timing belt between righthand camshaft sprocket and tensioner pulley with a force of 22 ft. lbs.

8. Loosen tensioner locknut, keeping tensioner steady with a hexagon wrench.

9. Using a feeler gauge or equivalent as shown in the illustration which is 0.35mm thick and 13mm wide, set gauge at the bottom of tensioner pulley and timing belt. Turn crankshaft clockwise and position gauge completely betwwen tensioner pulley and timing belt. The timing belt will move about 2.5 teeth.

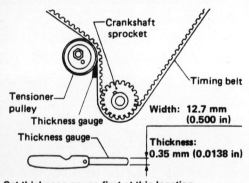

Set thickness gauge first at this location

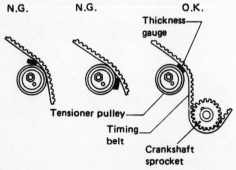

Thickness gauge in correct position for proper adjustment

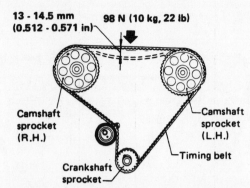

13 - 14.5 mm (0.512 - 0.571 in)   98 N (10 kg, 22 lb)

Camshaft sprocket (R.H.)   Camshaft sprocket (L.H.)

Crankshaft sprocket   Timing belt

Check timing belt deflection on 1988–89 V6 engine

10. Tighten tensioner locknut, keeping tensioner steady with a hexagon wrench.

11. Turn crankshaft clockwise or counterclockwise and remove the gauge.

12. Rotate the engine 3 times, then set No. 1 at T.D.C. on its compression stroke.

13. Check timing belt deflection on 1988 model year only. Timing belt deflection is 13.0-14.5mm at 22 lbs. of pressure. If it is out of specified range, readjust the timing belt.

Camshaft Sprocket
REMOVAL AND INSTALLATION

1. Refer to the "Timing Belt/Chain, Removal and Installation" procedures, in this section and remove the timing chain/belt.

2. Remove the sprocket retaining bolt and remove the sprocket from the camshaft. On engines with a timing chain the chain and sprocket are removed at the same time.

3. To install reverse the removal procedures. On V6 engines the right hand and left hand camshaft sprockets are different parts. Install them in the correct location. The right hand sprocket has an R3 identification and the left hand pulley has L3 identification.

NOTE: *On the belt driven engines make sure to install the crank pulley plate in the correct position. On chain driven engines make sure oil thrower, oil pump drive gear are installed in the correct position.*

Camshaft
REMOVAL AND INSTALLATION
L18, L20B, and L24 Engines

NOTE: *Removal of the cylinder head from the engine is optional. The camshaft cover and rocker cover are one and the same. Mark and keep all parts in order for correct installation.*

1. Remove the camshaft sprocket from the camshaft together with the timing chain. Refer to the Timing Chain procedures if necessary.

2. Loosen the valve rocker pivot locknut and remove the rocker arm by pressing down on the valve spring.

3. Remove the two retaining nuts on the camshaft retainer plate at the front of the cylinder head and carefuliy slide the camshaft out (towards the front of the vehicle) of the camshaft carrier.

4. Check camshaft runout, endplay, wear and journal clearance as described in this chapter.

5. Lightly coat the camshaft bearings with clean motor oil and carefully slide the camshaft into place in the camshaft carrier.

6. Install the camshaft retainer plate with the oblong groove in the face of the plate facing toward the front of the engine.

7. Check the valve timing as outlined under Timing Chain Removal and Installation and in-

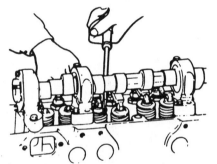
Remove the rocker arm by pressing down on the valve spring

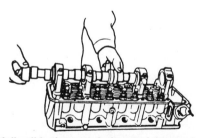
Carefully slide the camshaft out of the carrier

When installing the retaining plate, make sure the oblong groove is facing the front of the engine

stall the timing sprocket on the camshaft, tightening the bolt together with the fuel pump cam (gasoline engines only) to 86-116 ft. lbs.

8. Install the rocker arms by pressing down the valve springs with a screwdriver and install the valve rocker springs.

9. Install the cylinder head, if it was removed, and assemble the rest of the engine.

10. Start and run engine to normal operating temperature. Remove rocker cover, check and adjust valves if necessary. Install rocker cover with new gasket and check for oil leaks.

Z20E, Z20S, Z22 Engines

NOTE: *Removal of the cylinder head from the engine is optional. Mark and keep all parts in order for correct installation.*

1. Remove the camshaft sprocket from the camshaft together with the timing chain, after setting the No. 1 piston at TDC on its compression stroke. Refer to the Timing Chain Removal and Installation procedures.

2. Loosen the bolts holding the rocker shaft assembly in place and remove the six center bolts. Do not pull the four end bolts out of the rocker assembly because they hold the unit together.

NOTE: *When loosening the bolts, work from the ends in and loosen all of the bolts a little at a time so that you do not strain the camshaft or the rocker assembly. Remember, the camshaft is under pressure from the valve springs.*

3. After removing the rocker assembly, remove the camshaft. Slide the camshaft carefully out of the front of the vehicle.

NOTE: *Mark and keep the disassembled parts in order.*

If you disassembled the rocker unit, assemble as follows.

4. Install the mounting brackets, valve rockers and springs observing the following considerations:

a. The two rocker shafts are different. Both have punch marks in the ends that face the front of the engine. The rocker shaft that

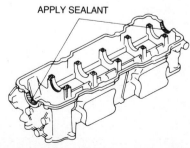
Apply sealant to these points on the Z-series cylinder head just before installing the camshaft

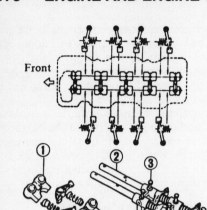

1. Rocker bracket
2. Rocker shaft
3. Bolt
4. Spring
5. Rocker arm

Rocker shaft assembly—Z20 engines

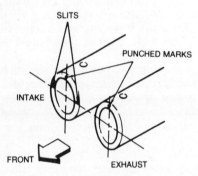

Note the difference in rocker shafts—Z20 engines

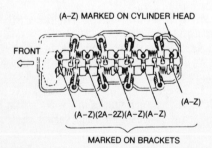

Rocker shaft mounting brackets are assembled in this order—Z20 engines

goes on the side of the intake manifold has two slits in its end just below the punch mark. The exhaust side rocker shaft does not have slits.

b. The rocker arms for the intake and exhaust valves are interchangeable between cylinders one and three and are identified by the mark 1. Similarly, the rockers for cylinders two and four are interchangeable and are identified by the mark 2.

c. The rocker shaft mounting brackets are also coded for correct placement with either an A or a Z plus a number code. See the illustration for proper placement.

5. Check camshaft runout, endplay wear and journal clearance as described in this chapter.

6. Apply sealant to the end camshaft saddles as shown in the accompanying illustration. Place the camshaft on the head with its dowel pin pointing up.

7. Fit the rocker assembly on the head, making sure you mount it on its knock pin.

8. Torque the bolts to 11-18 ft. lbs., in several stages working from the middle bolts and moving outwards on both sides.

NOTE: *Make sure the engine is on TDC of the compression stroke for No. 1 piston or you may damage some valves.*

9. Adjust the valves. Refer to the Valve Adjustment procedure.

KA24E Engine

NOTE: *Removal of the cylinder head from the engine is optional. Hydraulic valve lifters are installed in each rocker arm after removal always set rocker arm straight up to prevent possibility of air entering it. Mark and keep all parts in order for correct installation.*

1. Remove the camshaft sprocket from the camshaft together with the timing chain, after setting the No. 1 piston at TDC on its compression stroke. Refer to the Timing Chain Removal and Installation procedures.

2. Remove the rocker shaft assembly retaining bolts and remove the shaft assembly and (mark the retainer positions) retainers from the engine.

NOTE: *When loosening the bolts, work from the ends in and loosen all of the bolts a little at a time so that you do not strain the camshaft or the rocker assembly.*

3. Remove the camshaft brackets. Remove the camshaft carefully out of the front of the vehicle.

4. Mount the camshaft on the cylinder head, placing knock pin at the front end top position.

5. Install the camshaft brackets. The punch mark on the front of the brackets MUST be positioned towards the front of the engine, see illustration.

6. Install the rocker shaft assembly with retainer in the correct position.

7. Torque the rocker shaft assembly in stages and in the correct order. Torque specification for the rocker shaft assembly is 27-30 ft. lbs.

8. Install the camshaft sprocket and timing chain.

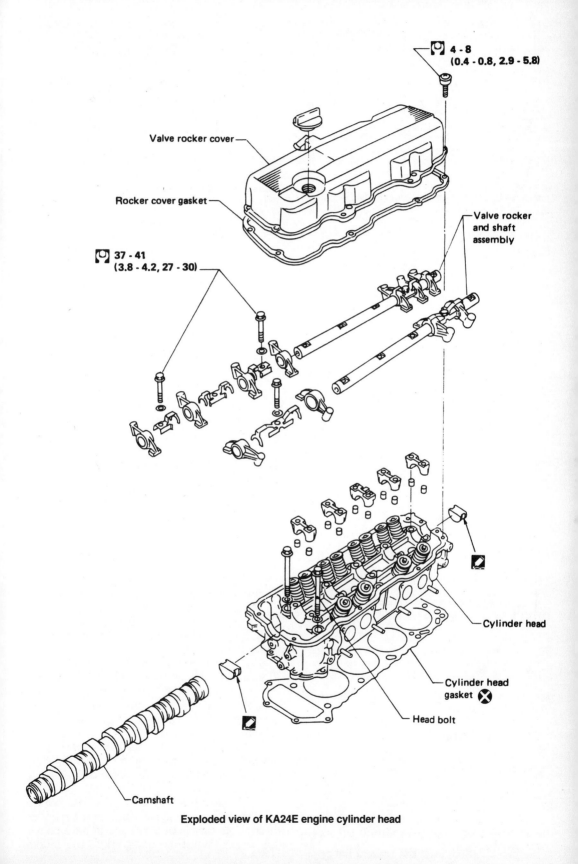

Exploded view of KA24E engine cylinder head

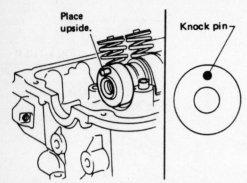

Install camshaft in correct position KA24E engine

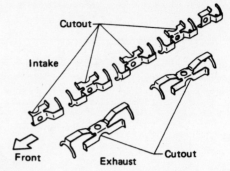

Correct position of rocker shaft retainers—KA24E engine

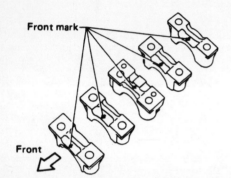

Install camshaft brackets this way—KA24E engine

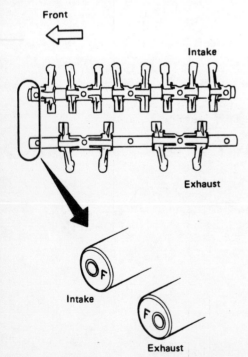

Install rocker shafts with marks towards front of engine—KA24E engine

Torque sequence for rocker shaft assembly—KA24E engine

9. After complete installation, start engine and check for any leaks. Roadtest the vehicle for proper operation.

CA20E, CA18ET Engines

1. Remove the timing belt assembly, after setting the No. 1 cylinder to TDC on the compression stroke.

2. Remove the valve rocker cover.

3. Fully loosen all rocker arm adjusting screws (the valve adjustment screws). Loosen the rocker shaft securing bolts in two or three stages, and remove the rocker shafts with the rocker arms and securing bolts. Keep all parts in order for correct reassembly.

4. Using a tool designed to hold the camshaft pulley, remove the camshaft pulley bolt and remove the pulley.

5. Carefully pry the camshaft oil seal out of the front of the cylinder head. Slowly remove the camshaft out the front of the head.

6. Check camshaft runout, endplay, wear and journal clearance as described in this chapter.

7. To install the camshaft, first lubricate it liberally with clean engine oil. Carefully slide the camshaft into position. Lube the camshaft front end and install a new oil seal.

8. Lightly lubricate the rocker shafts and install them, with their rockers, into the cylinder head. Note that both of the shafts have punch marks on their front ends, while the intake

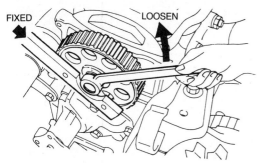

Use a sprocket holding tool when loosening the CA20E and CA18ET cam sprocket

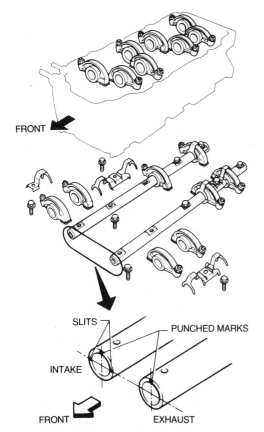

CA20E, CA18ET rocker shaft assembly. Note locating marks on the end of the shafts, slits on the intake shaft

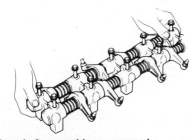

Rocker shaft assembly as removed

shaft is also marked with two slits on its front end. All components must be assembled in the correct order.

NOTE: *To prevent the rocker shaft springs from slipping out of the shaft, insert the bracket bolts into the shaft.*

9. Tighten the rocker shaft bolts gradually in two or three passes.

10. Install the camshaft pulley. Install the timing belt assembly.

11. Adjust the valve clearances. Install the rocker arm cover.

VG30E Engine

NOTE: *On the Maxima VG30E (1985-89) engine Nissan recommends that the cylinder heads be removed from the engine, with the engine mounted in the vehicle, and then remove the camshafts. On the 1987 200SX with VG30E engine Nissan recommends that the engine assembly be removed from the vehicle, then the cylinder heads disassembled. On the 1988 200SX with VG30E engine Nissan recommends that the the cylinder heads be removed from the engine, with the engine mounted in the vehicle, and then remove the camshafts. This procedure is for removing the camshafts with the engine in the vehicle.*

1. Remove the timing belt. Refer to the Timing Belt Removal and Installation procedure.

2. Drain the coolant by removing drain plug on the cylinder block.

CAUTION: *When draining the coolant, keep in mind that cats and dogs are attracted by the ethylene glycol antifreeze, and are quite likely to drink any that is left in an uncovered container or in puddles on the ground. This will prove fatal in sufficient quantity. Always drain the coolant into a sealable container. Coolant should be reused unless it is contaminated or several years old.*

3. Remove the collector assembly and intake manifold. Refer to Intake Manifold Removal and Installation procedure.

4. Remove the cylinder head fom the engine. Refer to Cylinder Head Removal and Installation.

5. With cylinder head mounted on a suitable workbench, remove the rocker shafts with rocker arms. Bolts should be loosened in two or three steps.

6. Remove hydraulic valve lifters and lifter guide.

7. Hold hydraulic valve lifters with wire so that they will not drop from lifter guide.

8. Remove the camshaft front oil seal and slide camshaft out the front of the cylinder head assembly.

9. Install camshaft, locate plate, cylinder head rear cover and front oil seal. Set camshaft

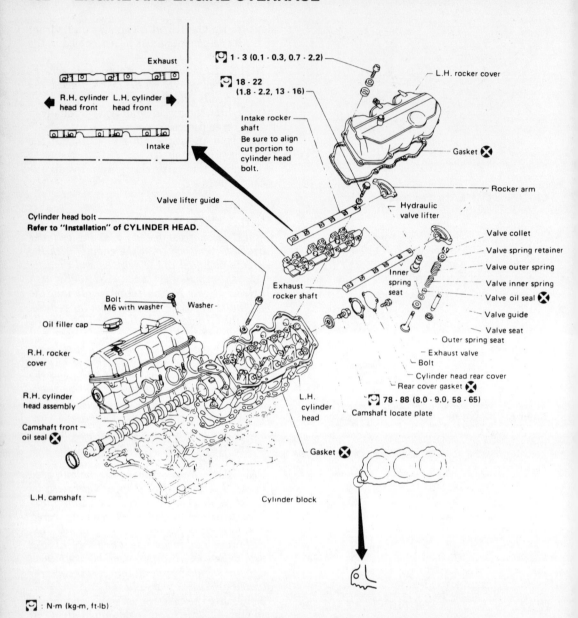

Exhaust

R.H. cylinder head front   L.H. cylinder head front

Intake

1 - 3 (0.1 - 0.3, 0.7 - 2.2)

18 - 22 (1.8 - 2.2, 13 - 16)

L.H. rocker cover

Intake rocker shaft
Be sure to align cut portion to cylinder head bolt.

Gasket ⊗

Valve lifter guide

Cylinder head bolt
Refer to "Installation" of CYLINDER HEAD.

Rocker arm

Hydraulic valve lifter

Exhaust rocker shaft

Inner spring seat

Valve collet
Valve spring retainer
Valve outer spring
Valve inner spring
Valve oil seal ⊗
Valve guide
Valve seat
Outer spring seat
Exhaust valve
Bolt
Cylinder head rear cover
Rear cover gasket ⊗
78 - 88 (8.0 - 9.0, 58 - 65)
Camshaft locate plate

Bolt M6 with washer   Washer

Oil filler cap

R.H. rocker cover

R.H. cylinder head assembly

Camshaft front oil seal ⊗

L.H. camshaft

L.H. cylinder head

Gasket ⊗

Cylinder block

⊡ : N·m (kg-m, ft-lb)

Exploded view of VG30E engine—parts marked with X are always replaced

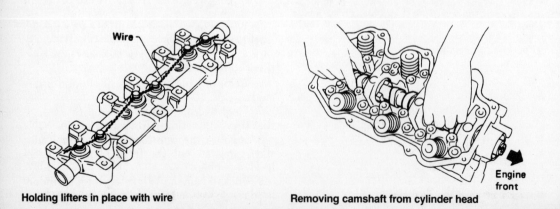

Wire

Holding lifters in place with wire

Engine front

Removing camshaft from cylinder head

Install knock pin on camshaft in correction position

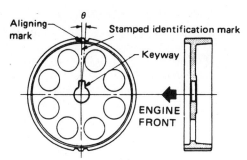

Camshaft sprocket

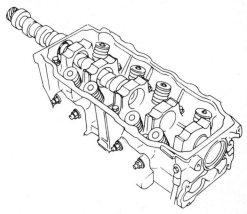

Carefully slide the camshaft into the camshaft saddles on the cylinder head

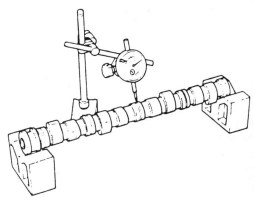

Check camshaft run-out with a dial indicator

knock pin at 12:00 o'clock position. Install cylinder head with new gasket to engine. Refer to the Cylinder Head Removal and Installation procedure.

10. Install valve lifter guide assembly. Assemble valve lifters in their original position. After installing them in the correct location remove the wire holding them in lifter guide.

11. Install rocker shafts in correct position with rocker arms. Tighten bolts in two or three stages to 13-16 ft. lbs. Before tightening, be sure to set camshaft lobe at the position where lobe is not lifted or the valve closed. You can set each cylinder one at a time or follow the procedure below (timing belt must be installed in the correct position):

    a. Set No. 1 piston at T.D.C. on its compression stroke and tighten rocker shaft bolts for No.2, No.4 and No.6 cylinders.

    b. Set No. 4 piston at T.D.C. on its compression stroke and tighten rocker shaft bolts for No.1, No.3 and No.5 cylinders.

    c. Torque specification for the rocker shaft retaining bolts is 13-16 ft. lbs.

12. Install the intake manifold and collector assembly. Refer to Intake Manifold Removal and Installation procedure.

13. Install rear timing belt cover and camshaft sprocket. The left and right camshaft sprockets are different parts. Install the correct sprocket in the correct position.

14. Install the timing belt. Refer to the Timing Belt Removal and Installation procedure.

CHECKING CAMSHAFT RUNOUT

Camshaft runout should be checked when the camshaft has been removed from the cylinder head. An accurate dial indicator is needed for this procedure; engine specialists and most machine shops have this equipment. If you have access to a dial indicator, or can take your cam to someone who does, measure cam bearing journal runout. The maximum (limit) runout on the L18, L20, L24, LD28, CA20E, CA18ET and KA24E camshafts is 0.02mm. The runout limit on the Z20 and Z22 series camshafts is 0.20mm. The maximum (limit) runout on the VG30E camshaft is 0.01mm. If the runout exceeds the limit replace the camshaft.

CHECKING CAMSHAFT LOBE HEIGHT

Use a micrometer to check cam (lobe) height, making sure the anvil and the spindle of the micrometer are positioned directly on the heel and tip of the cam lobe as shown in the accompanying illustration. Use the specifications in the following chart to determine the lobe wear.

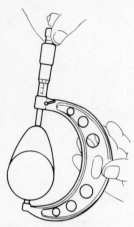

Use a micrometer to check camshaft cam lobe height

Engine Series	Lobe	Lobe Height (in.)	Wear Limit (in.)
L18	Int. and Exh.	1.5728 to 1.3748	0.0098
L20	Int. and Exh.	1.5866 to 1.5886	0.0098
L24, LD28	Intake	1.5728 to 1.5748	0.0059
	Exhaust	1.5866 to 1.5886	0.0059
Z20, Z22	Int. and Exh.	1.5148 to 1.5168	0.0098
CA18ET	Intake	1.5055 to 1.5075	0.008
	Exhaust	1.5289 to 1.5309	
CA20E	Int. and Exh.	1.5289 to 1.5309	0.008
KA24E	Int. and Exh.	1.7653–1.7728	0.008
VG30E	Int. and Exh.	1.5566–1.5641	0.0059

CHECKING CAMSHAFT JOURNALS AND CAMSHAFT BEARING SADDLES

While the camshaft is still removed from the cylinder head, the camshaft bearing journals should be measured with a micrometer. Compare the measurements with those listed in the Camshaft Specifications chart in this chapter. If the measurements are less than the limits listed in the chart, the camshaft will have to be replaced, since the camshafts in all of the engines covered in this guide run directly on the cylinder head surface; no actual bearings or bushings are used, so no oversize bearings or bushings are available.

Using an inside dial gauge or inside micrometer, measure the inside diameter of the camshaft saddles (the camshaft mounts that are either integrally cast as part of the cylinder head, or are a bolted on, one piece unit. The Z-series engines use a saddle-and-cap arrangement. The inside diameter of the saddles on all engines except the CA20E/CA18ET is 48.00-48.01mm. The CA20E/CA18ET measurement is 46.00-46.01mm. The inside diameter on the KA24E

with the camshaft bracket and rocker shaft torque to specifications is 31.5-33.00mm. On the VG30E engine contact a Nissan dealer or local machine shop for that specification. The camshaft journal oil clearances are listed in the Camshaft Specifications chart in this chapter. If the saddle inside diameters exceed those listed above, the cylinder head must be replaced (again, because oversize bearings or bushings are not available).

CHECKING CAMSHAFT ENDPLAY

After the camshaft has been installed, endplay should be checked. The camshaft sprocket should not be installed on the cam. Use a dial gauge to check the endplay, by moving the camshaft forward and backward in the cylinder head. Endplay specifications for the CA20E, CA18ET, Z20/22 series and KA24E engines should not exceed 0.20mm. L18, L20, L24 and LD28 camshaft endplay should not exceed 0.38mm. On the VG30E engine the camshaft endplay should be between 0.03-0.06mm.

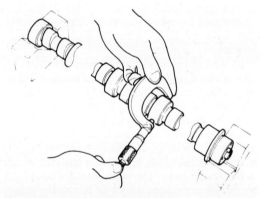

Measuring camshaft journal diameter

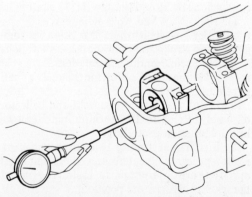

Use an inside micrometer or dial gauge to measure camshaft bearing saddle diameters

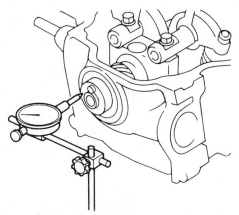

Checking camshaft end play with a dial gauge. Move the camshaft forward and backward

Pistons and Connecting Rods

REMOVAL AND INSTALLATION

All Engines

1. Remove the cylinder head.
2. Remove the oil pan.
3. Remove any carbon buildup from the cylinder wall at the top end of the piston travel with a ridge reamer tool.
4. Position the piston to be removed at the bottom of its stroke so that the connecting rod bearing cap can be reached easily from under the engine.
5. Unscrew the connecting rod bearing cap nuts and remove the cap and lower half of the bearing. Cover the rod bolts with lengths of rubber tubing or hose to protect the cylinder walls when the rod and piston assembly is driven out.
6. Push the piston and connecting rod up and out of the cylinder block with a length of wood. Use care not to scratch the cylinder wall with the connecting rod or the wooden tool.
7. Keep all of the components from each cylinder together and install them in the cylinder from which they were removed.
8. Coat the bearing face of the connecting rod and the outer face of the pistons with engine oil.
9. See the illustrations, the correct placement of the piston rings for your model and engine size.
10. Turn the crankshaft until the rod journal of the particular cylinder you are working on is brought to the TDC position.
11. With the piston and rings clamped in a ring compressor, the notched mark on the head of the piston toward the front of the engine, and the oil hole side of the connecting rod toward the fuel pump side of the engine, push the piston and connecting rod assembly into the cylin-

der bore until the big bearing end of the connecting rod contacts and is seated on the rod journal of the crankshaft. Use care not to scratch the cylinder wall with the connecting rod.

NOTE: *See LD28 Diesel below for piston installation details on that engine.*

12. Push down farther on the piston and turn

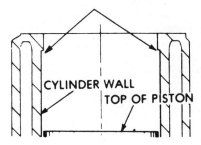

CYLINDER WALL

TOP OF PISTON

Ridge caused by cylinder wear

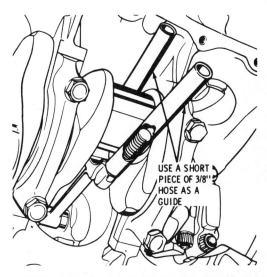

USE A SHORT PIECE OF 3/8'' HOSE AS A GUIDE

Install lengths of rubber tubing on the rod bolts before removing the piston assemblies. This will protect the cylinder walls from damage.

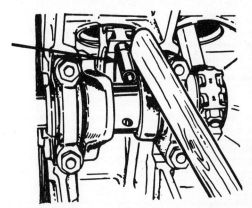

Tap out the piston assemblies with a wooden hammer handle. Note tubing covering rod bolts (arrow)

RING COMPRESSOR

Tap the piston assemblies down into the bores with a wooden hammer handle. Make sure the pistons and bores are well-lubed

the crankshaft while the connecting rod rides around on the crankshaft rod journal. Turn the crankshaft until the crankshaft rod journal is at BDC (bottom dead center).

13. Align the mark on the connecting rod bearing cap with that on the connecting rod and tighten the bearing cap bolts to the specified torque.

14. Install all of the piston/connecting rod assemblies in the manner outlined above.

15. Install the oil strainer, pickup tube and oil pan.

16. Install the cylinder head.

17. Install engine assembly in vehicle.

18. Check all fluid levels and road test.

LD28 Diesel

When replacing pistons in the LD28 diesel engine, the amount of projection of each piston crown above the deck of the block must be measured.

1. Clean the deck of the cylinder block completely.

2. Set a dial gauge, as shown on the cylinder block surface in the illustration, to zero.

3. For every cylinder, measure the piston projection and record the length.

NOTE: *Be sure to measure the length of piston projection at at least three points for every cylinder.*

4. Determine the maximum length of piston projection and select the suitable head gasket according to the chart below.

Piston Projection mm (in)	Cylinder Head Gasket Thickness mm (in)	No. of Cutouts in Cylinder Head Gasket
Below 0.487 (0.0192)	1.12 (0.0441)	1
0.487–0.573 (0.0192–0.0226)	1.2 (0.047)	2
Above 0.573 (0.0226)	1.28 (0.0504)	3

NOTE: *The head gaskets have cutout(s) in them for identification purposes. When a head gasket needs to be replaced, always install a gasket of the same thickness.*

IDENTIFICATION AND POSITIONING

The pistons are marked with a number or **F** in the piston head. When installed in the engine the number or **F** markings are to be facing toward the front of the engine.

The connecting rods are installed in the engine with the oil hole facing toward the fuel pump side (right) of the engine.

NOTE: *It is advisable to number the pistons, connecting rods, and bearing caps in some manner so that they can be reinstalled in the same cylinder, facing in the same direction from which they are removed. The CA-series rod and cap assemblies are factory-numbered.*

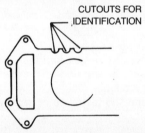

CUTOUTS FOR IDENTIFICATION

LD28 cylinder head gaskets have cutouts in them for identification purposes; when determining piston projection and selecting the suitable head gasket thickness

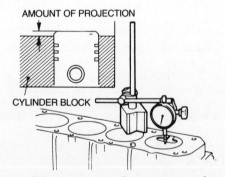

AMOUNT OF PROJECTION

CYLINDER BLOCK

Set the dial gauge at zero, then measure and record the length of each piston projection in the LD28.

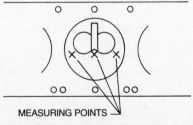

MEASURING POINTS

LD28 piston projection measuring points

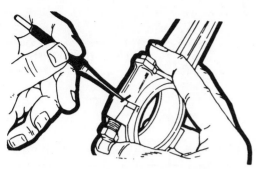

Matchmark each rod cap to its connecting rod

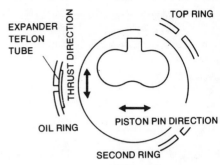

Piston ring placement—LD28 engine

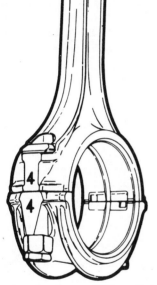

Number each rod and cap with its cylinder number for correct assembly

Piston ring placement—L20B, Z-series, CA20E, CA18ET and 1977–80 L24

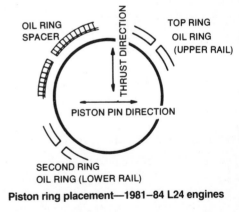

Piston ring placement—1981–84 L24 engines

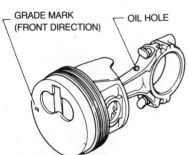

LD28 piston-to-rod relationship

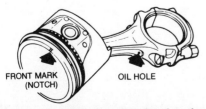

Piston and rod positioning—Z-series, L-series (except LD28) and CA20E, CA18ET engines

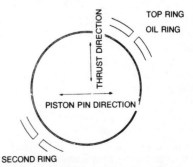

Piston ring placement—L16, L18 engines

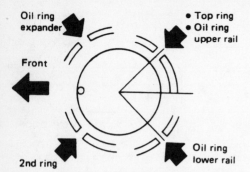

Piston ring placement—KA24E and VG30E engines

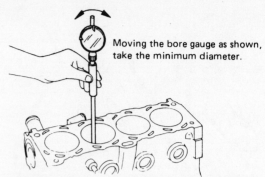

Checking cylinder bore diameter with a telescope gauge

CLEANING AND INSPECTION

Clean the piston after removing the rings (See Piston Ring and Wrist Pin Removal and Installation below), by first scraping any carbon from the piston top. Do not scratch the piston in any way during cleaning. Use a broken piston ring or ring cleaning tool to clean out the ring grooves. Clean the entire piston with solvent and a brush (NOT a wire brush).

Once the piston is thoroughly cleaned, insert the side of a good piston ring (both No. 1 and No. 2 compression on each piston) into its respective groove. Using a feeler gauge, measure the clearance between the ring and its groove. (See Piston Ring Side Clearance Check for more details). If clearance is greater than the maximum listed under Ring Side Clearance in the Piston and Ring chart, replace the ring(s) and if necessary, the piston.

To check ring endgap, insert a compression ring into the cylinder. Lightly oil the cylinder bore and push the ring down into the cylinder with a piston, to the bottom of its travel. Measure the ring endgap with a feeler gauge. If the gap is not within specification, replace the ring; DO NOT file the ring ends.

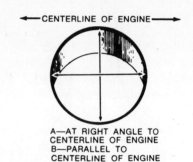

Cylinder bore measuring points

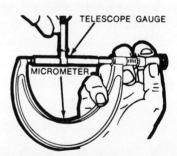

Measure the telescope gauge with a micrometer to determine cylinder bore diameter

CYLINDER BORE INSPECTION

Place a rag over the crankshaft journals. Wipe out each cylinder with a clean, solvent soaked rag. Visually inspect the cylinder bores for roughness, scoring or scuffing; also check the bores by feel. Measure the cylinder bore diameter with an inside micrometer, or a telescope gauge and micrometer. Measure the bore at points parallel and perpendicular to the engine centerline at the top (below the ridge) and bottom of the bore. Subtract the bottom measurements from the top to determine cylinder taper.

Measure the piston diameter with a micrometer; since this micrometer may not be part of your tool kit as it is necessarily large, you may have to have the pistons miked at a machine shop. Take the measurements at right angles to

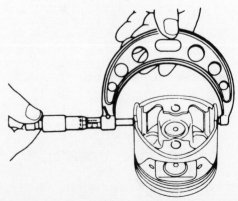

Measuring piston diameter. Check diameter on the wrist pin axis, and 90° away from the axis

the wrist pin center line, about an inch down the piston skirt from the top.

Compare this measurement to the bore diameter of each cylinder. The difference is the piston clearance. If the clearance is greater than that specified in the Piston and Ring Specifications chart, have the cylinders honed or rebored and replace the pistons with an oversize set. Piston clearance can also be checked by inverting a piston into an oiled cylinder, and sliding in a feeler gauge between the two.

NOTE: *When any one cylinder needs boring, all cylinders must be bored.*

Piston Ring and Wrist Pin

REMOVAL

A piston ring expander is necessary for removing piston rings without damaging them; any other method (screwdriver blades, pliers, etc.) usually results in the rings being bent, scratched or distorted, or the piston itself being damaged. When the rings are removed, clean the ring grooves using an appropriate ring groove cleaning tool, using care not to cut too deeply. Thoroughly clean all carbon and varnish from the piston with solvent.

All the Datsun/Nissan pistons covered in this guide have a pressed in wrist pin, requiring a special press for removal. Take the piston and

Remove the piston rings with a ring expander

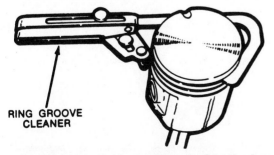

RING GROOVE
CLEANER

Use a ring groove cleaner to properly clean the ring groove

Wrist pin clips are removed with needle-nose or snap-ring pliers

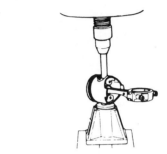

Wrist pins must be pressed in and out with a special press

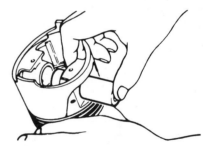

Wrist pin-to-piston fit should be such that the pin can be slid in smoothly by hand at room temperature

connecting rod assemblies to an engine specialist or machinist for wrist pin removal. The pins must also be pressed in during assembly.

PISTON RING END GAP

Piston ring end gap should be checked while the rings are removed from the pistons. Incorrect end gap indicates that the wrong size rings are being used; ring breakage could occur.

Compress the piston rings to be used in a cylinder, one at a time, into that cylinder. Squirt clean oil into the cylinder, so that the rings and the top 50mm of cylinder wall are coated. Using an inverted piston, press the rings approximately 25mm below the deck of the block. Measure the ring end gap with a feeler gauge, and compare to the Ring Gap chart in this chapter. Replace the ring if necessary.

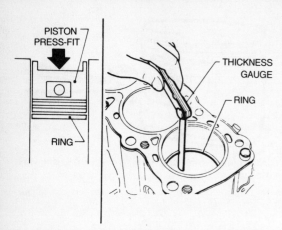

Checking ring end gap and piston-to-bore clearance

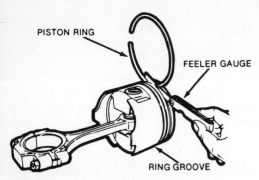

Measuring piston ring side clearance

PISTON RING SIDE CLEARANCE CHECK AND INSTALLATION

Check the pistons to see that the ring grooves and oil return holes have been properly cleaned. Slide a piston ring into its groove, and check the side clearance with a feeler gauge. On gasoline engines, make sure you insert the gauge between the ring and its lower land (lower edge of the groove), because any wear that occurs forms a step at the inner portion of the lower land. If the piston grooves have worn to the extent that relatively high steps exist on the lower land, the piston should be replaced, because these will interfere with the operation of the new rings and ring clearances will be excessive. Piston rings are not furnished in oversize widths to compensate for ring groove wear.

Install the rings on the piston, lowest ring first, using a piston ring expander. There is a high risk of breaking or distorting the rings, or scratching the piston, if the rings are installed by hand or other means.

Position the rings on the piston as illustrated; spacing of the various piston ring gaps is crucial to proper oil retention and even cylinder wear. When installing new rings, refer to the installation diagram furnished with the new parts.

Connecting Rod

INSPECTION AND BEARING REPLACEMENT

Connecting rod side clearance and big end bearing inspection and replacement should be performed while the rods are still installed in the engine. Determine the clearance between the connecting rod sides and the crankshaft using a feeler gauge. If clearance is below the minimum tolerance, check with a machinist about machining the rod to provide adequate clearance. If clearance is excessive, substitute an unworn rod and recheck; if clearance is still outside specifications, the crankshaft must be welded and reground, or replaced.

1. To check connecting rod big end bearing clearances, remove the rod bearing caps one at a time. Using a clean, dry shop rag, thoroughly clean all oil from the crank journal and bearing insert in the cap.

NOTE: *The Plastigage® gauging material you will be using to check clearances with is soluble in oil; therefore any oil on the journal or bearing could result in an incorrect reading.*

2. Lay a strip of Plastigage® along the full length of the bearing insert (along the crank journal if the engine is out of the car and inverted). Reinstall the cap and torque to specifications listed in the Torque Specifications chart.

3. Remove the rod cap and determine bearing clearance by comparing the width of the now flattened Plastigage® to the scale on the Plastigage® envelope. Journal taper is determined by comparing the width of the Plastigage® strip near its ends. Rotate the crankshaft 90° and retest, to determine journal eccentricity.

NOTE: *Do not rotate the crankshaft with the Plastigage® installed.*

4. If the bearing insert and crank journal appear intact and are within tolerances, no further service is required and the bearing caps can be reinstalled (remove Plastigage® before installation). If clearances are not within toler-

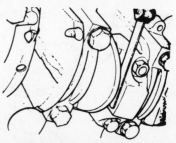

Checking connecting rod side clearance. Make sure the feeler gauge is between the shoulder of the crank journal and the side of the rod

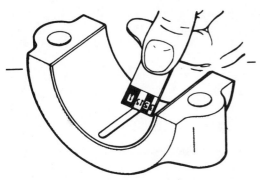

Check connecting rod bearing clearance with Plastigage

ances, the bearing inserts in both the connecting rod and rod cap must be replaced with undersize inserts, and/or the crankshaft must be reground. To install the bearing insert halves, press them into the bearing caps and connecting rods. Make sure the tab in each insert fits into the notch in each rod and cap. Lube the face of each insert with engine oil prior to installing each rod into the engine.

5. The connecting rods can be further inspected when they are removed from the engine and separated from their pistons. Rod alignment (straightness and squareness) must be checked by a machinist, as the rod must be set in a special fixture. Many machine shops also perform a Magnafluxing service, which is a process that shows up any tiny cracks that you may be unable to see.

Rear Main Oil Seal

REPLACEMENT

All Engines Except CA20E, CA18ET and V6

In order to replace the rear main oil seal, the rear main bearing cap must be removed. Removal of the rear main bearing cap requires the use of a special rear main bearing cap puller. Also, the oil seal is installed with a special crankshaft rear oil seal drift. Unless these or similar tools are available to you, it is recommended that the oil seal be replaced by a Nissan/Datsun service center or an independent shop that has the proper equipment.

1. Remove the engine and transmission assembly from the vehicle.
2. Remove the transmission from the engine. Remove the oil pan.
3. Remove the clutch from the flywheel.
4. Remove the flywheel from the crankshaft.
5. Remove the rear main bearing cap together with the bearing cap side seals.
6. Remove the rear main oil seal from around the crankshaft.
7. Apply lithium grease around the sealing lip of the oil seal and install the seal around the crankshaft using a suitable tool.

8. Apply sealer to the rear main bearing cap as indicated, install the rear main bearing cap, and tighten the cap bolts to 33-40 ft. lbs.
9. Apply sealant to the rear main bearing cap side seals and install the side seals, driving the seals into place with a suitable drift.
10. Install the oil pan with a new gasket.
11. Install the flywheel and clutch assembly.
12. Install the transmission to the engine and install the engine/transmission assembly in the vehicle. Refer to the Engine Removal and Installation procedure.
13. Check all fluid levels, start the engine and check for any leaks. Roadtest the vehicle for proper operation.

CA20E and CA18ET Engines

1. Remove the transmission.
2. Remove the flywheel.
3. Remove the rear oil seal retainer.
4. Using a pair of pliers, remove the oil seal from the retainer.
5. Liberally apply clean engine oil to the new oil seal and carefully install it into the retainer.
6. Install the rear oil seal retainer into the engine, along with a new gasket. Torque the bolts to 35-52 in. lbs. Install the flywheel and transmission in the vehicle.
7. Roadtest the vehicle for proper operation.

VG30E Engine

1. Remove the transaxle. Refer to Chapter 7 for procedure.
2. Remove the flywheel.
3. Remove the rear oil seal retainer.
4. Using a pair of pliers, remove the oil seal from the retainer.
5. Liberally apply clean engine oil to the new oil seal and carefully install it into the retainer.
6. Install the rear oil seal retainer into the engine, along with a new gasket. Torque the bolts to 48-63 in. lbs. Install the flywheel and

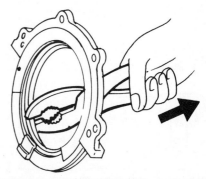

Removing the CA20E and CA18ET rear oil seal from the retainer

transaxle in the vehicle. Torque the flywheel mounting bolts to 72-80 ft. lbs.

Crankshaft and Main Bearings

REMOVAL AND INSTALLATION

NOTE: *Before removing the crankshaft, check main bearing clearances as described under Main Bearing Clearance Check below.*

1. Remove the piston and connecting rod assemblies following the procedure in this chapter.

2. Check crankshaft thrust clearance (end play) before removing the crank from the block. Using a pry bar, pry the crankshaft the extent of its travel forward, and measure thrust clearance at the center main bearing (No. 4 bearing on 6-cylinder engines, No. 3 on 4-cylinder engines) with a feeler gauge. Pry the crankshaft the extent of its rearward travel, and measure the other side of the bearing. If clearance is greater than specified, the thrust washers must be replaced (see Main Bearing Replacement, below).

3. Using a punch, mark the corresponding man bearing caps and saddles according to position. One punch on the front main cap and saddle, two on the second, three on the third, etc. This ensures correct reassembly.

4. Remove the main bearing caps after they have been marked.

5. Remove the crankshaft from the block.

6. Follow the crankshaft inspection, main bearing clearance checking and replacement procedures below before reinstalling the crankshaft.

INSPECTION

Crankshaft inspection and servicing should be handled exclusively by a reputable machinist, as most of the necessary procedures require a dial indicator and fixing jig, a large micrometer, and machine tools such as a crankshaft grinder. While at the machine shop, the crankshaft should be thoroughly cleaned (especially the oil passages),; magnafluxed (to check for minute cracks) and the following checks made:

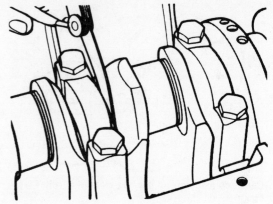

Check crankshaft end play with a feeler gauge

Main journal diameter, crank pin (connecting rod journal) diameter, taper and out-of-round, and runout. Wear, beyond specification limits, in any of these areas means the crankshaft must be reground or replaced.

MAIN BEARING CLEARANCE CHECK

Checking man bearing clearances is done in the same manner as checking connecting rod big end clearances.

1. With the crankshaft installed, remove the main bearing cap. Clean all oil from the bearing insert in the cap and from the crankshaft journal, as the Plastigage® material is oil soluble.

2. Lay a strip of Plastigage® along the full width of the bearing cap (or along the width of the crank journal if the engine is out of the car and inverted).

3. Install the bearing cap and torque to specification. Tighten bearing caps gradually in two or three stages.

NOTE: *Do not rotate the crankshaft with the Plastigage® installed.*

4. Remove the bearing cap and determine bearing clearance by comparing the width of the now flattened Plastigage® with the scale on the Plastigage® envelope. Journal taper is determined by comparing the width of the Plastigage® strip near its ends. Rotate the

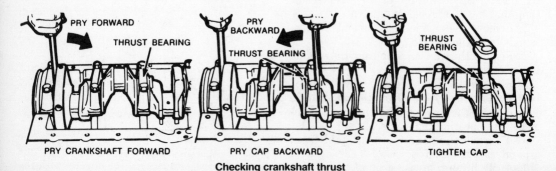

PRY CRANKSHAFT FORWARD   PRY CAP BACKWARD   TIGHTEN CAP

Checking crankshaft thrust

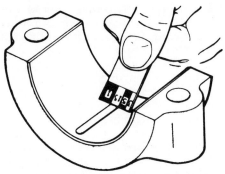

Checking main bearing clearance with Plastigage®

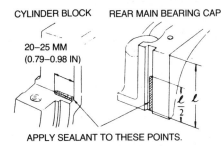

CYLINDER BLOCK   REAR MAIN BEARING CAP

20–25 MM
(0.79–0.98 IN)

$\frac{\ell}{2}$ ℓ

APPLY SEALANT TO THESE POINTS.

On all L-series 4 and 6 cylinder engine main bearing caps, apply sealant here

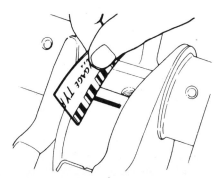

Check main bearing clearance on the crank journal as well as on the bearing cap. Use Plastigage® or equivalent

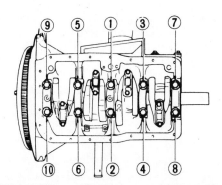

L18/L20 series main bearing cap bolt torque sequence

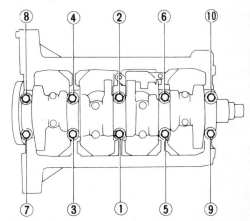

CA20E/CA18ET main bearing cap bolt torque sequence

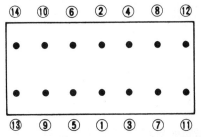

L24 and LD28 main bearing cap bolt torque sequence. Torque gradually in two or three stages, after installing the caps with the marks facing forward. Apply sealant as shown in the accompanying diagram

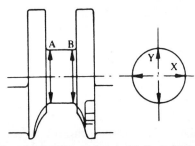

Check crankshaft journal eccentricity and taper with a micrometer at these points

crankshaft 90° and retest, to determine journal eccentricity.

5. Repeat the above for the remaining bearings. If the bearing journal and insert appear in good shape (with no unusual wear visible) and are within tolerances, no further main bearing service is required. If unusual wear is evident and/or the clearances are outside specifications, the bearings must be replaced and the cause of their wear found.

MAIN BEARING REPLACEMENT

Main bearings can be replaced with the crankshaft both in the engine (with the engine still in the car) and out of the engine (with the

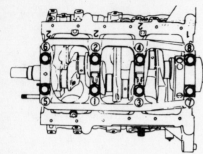

VG30E main bearing cap bolt torque sequence

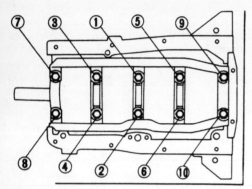

KA24E main bearing cap bolt torque sequence

engine on a workstand or bench). Both procedures are covered here. The main bearings must be replaced if the crankshaft has been reground; the replacement bearings being available in various undersize increments from most auto parts jobbers or your local Datsun/Nissan dealer.

Engine Out of Car

1. Remove the crankshaft from the engine block.
2. Remove the main bearing inserts from the bearing caps and from the main bearing saddles. Remove the thrust washers from the No. 3 (4-cylinder) or No. 4 (6-cylinder) crank journal.
3. Thoroughly clean the saddles, bearing caps, and crankshaft.
4. Make sure the crankshaft has been fully checked and is ready for reassembly. Place the upper main bearings in the block saddles so that the oil grooves and/or oil holes are correctly aligned with their corresponding grooves or holes in the saddles.
5. Install the thrust washers on the center main bearing, with the oil grooves facing out.
6. Lubricate the faces of all bearings with clean engine oil, and place the crankshaft in the block.
7. Install the main bearing caps in numbered order with the arrows or any other orientation

marks facing forward. Torque all bolts except the center cap bolts in sequence in two or three passes to the specified torque. Rotate the crankshaft after each pass to ensure even tightness.

8. Align the thrust bearing by prying the crankshaft the extent of its axial travel several times with a pry bar. On last movement hold the crankshaft toward the front of the engine and torque the thrust bearing cap to specifications. Measure the crankshaft thrust clearance (end play) as previously described in this chapter. If clearance is outside specifications (too sloppy), install a new set of oversize thrust washers and check clearance again.

Engine and Crankshaft Installed

1. Remove the main bearing caps and keep them in order.
2. Make a bearing rollout pin from a cotter pin as shown.
3. Carefully roll out the old inserts from the upper side of the crankshaft journal, noting the positions of the oil grooves and/or oil holes so the new inserts can be correctly installed.
4. Roll each new insert into its saddle after lightly oiling the crankshaft side face of each. Make sure the notches and/or oil holes are correctly positioned.
5. Replace the bearing inserts in the caps with new inserts. Oil the face of each, and install the caps in numbered order with the arrows or other orientation marks facing forward. Torque the bolts to the specified torque in two or three passes in the sequence shown.

Cylinder Block

Most inspection and service work on the cylinder block should be handled by a machinist or professional engine rebuilding shop. Included in this work are bearing alignment checks, line boring, deck resurfacing, hot-tanking and cylinder honing or boring. A block that has been checked and properly serviced will last much longer than one which has not had the proper attention when the opportunity was there for it.

Cylinder deglazing (honing) can, however, be performed by the owner/mechanic who is careful and takes his or her time. The cylinder bores

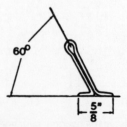

Make a bearing roll-out pin from a cotter pin

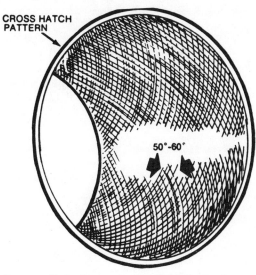

CROSS HATCH PATTERN

50°-60°

Proper cylinder bore cross-hatching after honing

become glazed during normal operation as the rings continually ride up and down against them. This shiny glaze must be removed in order for a new set of piston rings to be able to properly seat themselves.

Cylinder hones are available at most auto tool stores and parts jobbers. With the piston and rod assemblies removed from the block, cover the crankshaft completely with a rag or cover to keep grit from the hone and cylinder material off of it. Chuck a hone into a variable speed power drill (preferable here to a constant speed drill), and insert it into the cylinder.

NOTE: *Make sure the drill and hone are kept square to the cylinder bore throughout the entire honing operation.*

Start the hone and move it up and down in the cylinder at a rate which will produce approximately a 60° crosshatch pattern. DO NOT extend the hone below the cylinder bore! After developing the pattern, remove the hone and

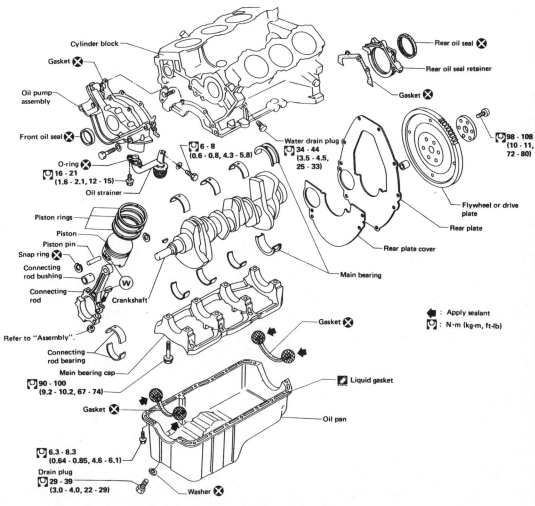

Cylinder block

Gasket ⊗

Oil pump assembly

Front oil seal ⊗

O-ring ⊗
🔧 16 - 21
(1.6 - 2.1, 12 - 15)

Oil strainer

🔧 6 - 8
(0.6 - 0.8, 4.3 - 5.8)

Water drain plug
🔧 34 - 44
(3.5 - 4.5, 25 - 33)

Rear oil seal ⊗

Rear oil seal retainer

Gasket ⊗

🔧 98 - 108
(10 - 11, 72 - 80)

Flywheel or drive plate

Rear plate

Rear plate cover

Main bearing

Piston rings

Piston

Piston pin

Snap ring ⊗

Connecting rod bushing

Connecting rod

Crankshaft

ⓦ

Refer to "Assembly".

Connecting rod bearing

Main bearing cap

🔧 90 - 100
(9.2 - 10.2, 67 - 74)

Gasket ⊗

Gasket ⊗

◀ : Apply sealant
🔧 : N·m (kg-m, ft-lb)

Liquid gasket

Oil pan

🔧 6.3 - 8.3
(0.64 - 0.85, 4.6 - 6.1)

Drain plug
🔧 29 - 39
(3.0 - 4.0, 22 - 29)

Washer ⊗

VG30E engine

recheck piston fit. Wash the cylinders with a detergent and water solution to remove the hone and cylinder grit. Wipe the bores out several times with a clean rag soaked in clean engine oil. Remove the cover from the crankshaft, and check closely to see that no grit has found its way onto the crankshaft.

Flywheel and Ring Gear
REMOVAL AND INSTALLATION
All models except Maxima 1985-89

NOTE: *The clutch cover and the pressure plate are balanced as an assembly; if replace-*

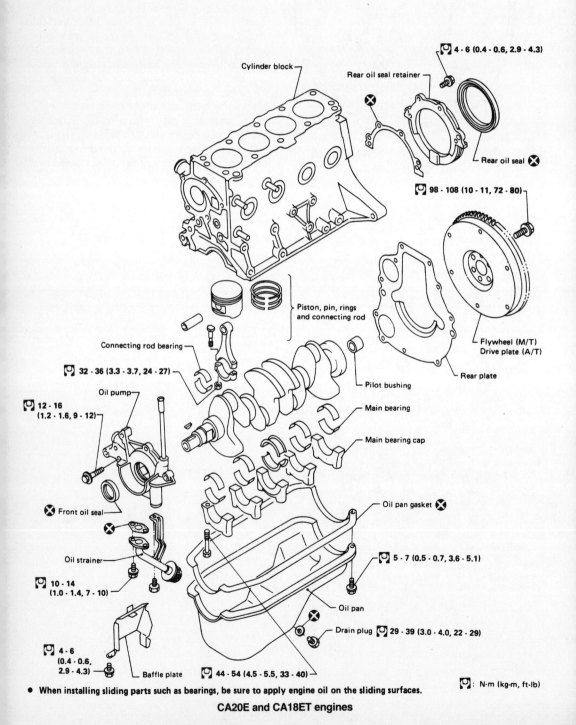

● When installing sliding parts such as bearings, be sure to apply engine oil on the sliding surfaces.

CA20E and CA18ET engines

ment of either part becomes necessary, replace both parts as an assembly. If vehicle is equipped with a automatic transmission use this procedure as a guide. See exploded view of engine assembly for flywheel/drive plate installation and quick torque reference.

1. Refer to the Clutch Removal and Installation procedures in Chapter 7 and remove the clutch assembly.

2. Remove the flywheel-to-crankshaft bolts and the flywheel.

NOTE: *If necessary the clutch disc should be inspected and/or replaced at this time; the clutch lining wear limit is 0.30mm above the rivet heads.*

3. To install, reverse the removal procedures. Torque the flywheel-to-crankshaft bolts to specifications, the clutch cover-to-flywheel

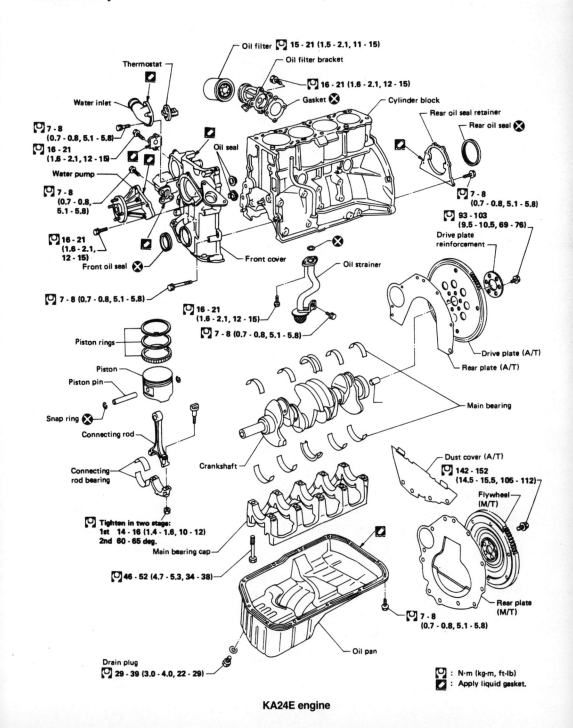

KA24E engine

bolts and the bearing housing-to-clutch housing bolts to specifications. Refer to the Torque Specification Chart or Chapter 7.

Maxima 1985-89

1. If equipped with a manual transaxle, refer to the Clutch Removal and Installation procedures in Chapter 7, then remove the transaxle and the clutch assembly. If equipped with an automatic transaxle, refer to the Automatic Transaxle Removal and Installation procedures in Chapter 7, then remove the transaxle and the torque converter.

2. For manual transaxles, remove the flywheel-to-crankshaft bolts and the flywheel. For automatic transaxles, remove the drive plate-to-crankshaft bolts and the drive plate.

3. To install, reverse the removal procedures. Torque all bolts to specifications. Refer to the Torque Specification Chart or Chapter 7.

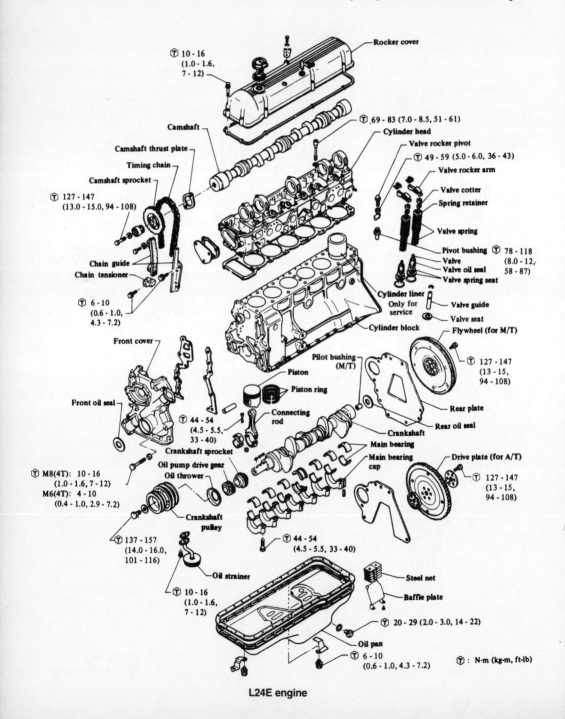

L24E engine

EXHAUST SYSTEM
Safety Precautions

For a number of reasons, exhaust system work can be dangerous. Always observe the following precautions:

1. Support the vehicle securely by using jackstands or equivalent under the frame of the vehicle.

2. Wear safety goggles to protect your eyes from metal chips that may fly free while working on the exhaust system.

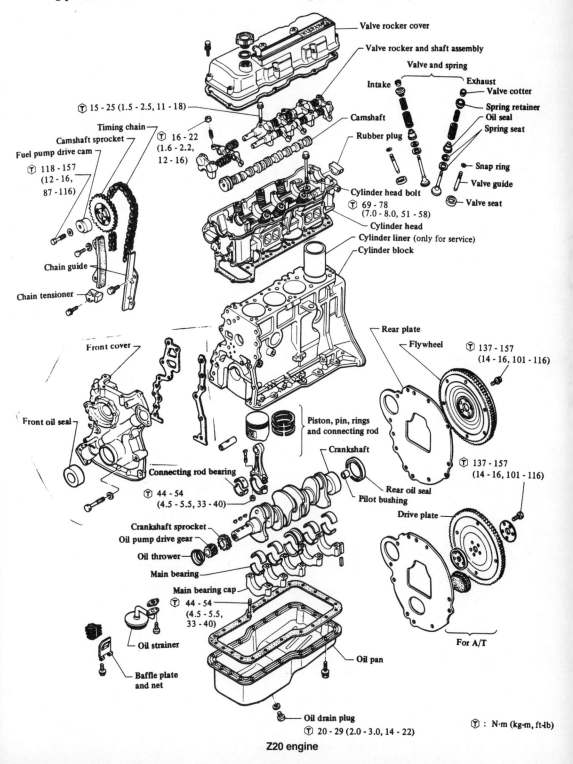

Valve rocker cover

Valve rocker and shaft assembly

Valve and spring

Intake — Exhaust

Valve cotter

Spring retainer

Oil seal

Spring seat

Ⓣ 15 - 25 (1.5 - 2.5, 11 - 18)

Timing chain

Camshaft sprocket

Fuel pump drive cam

Ⓣ 118 - 157
(12 - 16,
87 - 116)

Ⓣ 16 - 22
(1.6 - 2.2,
12 - 16)

Camshaft

Rubber plug

Snap ring

Valve guide

Valve seat

Cylinder head bolt

Ⓣ 69 - 78
(7.0 - 8.0, 51 - 58)

Cylinder head

Cylinder liner (only for service)

Cylinder block

Chain guide

Chain tensioner

Front cover

Rear plate

Flywheel

Ⓣ 137 - 157
(14 - 16, 101 - 116)

Front oil seal

Piston, pin, rings
and connecting rod

Crankshaft

Ⓣ 137 - 157
(14 - 16, 101 - 116)

Connecting rod bearing

Rear oil seal

Pilot bushing

Drive plate

Ⓣ 44 - 54
(4.5 - 5.5, 33 - 40)

Crankshaft sprocket

Oil pump drive gear

Oil thrower

Main bearing

Main bearing cap

Ⓣ 44 - 54
(4.5 - 5.5,
33 - 40)

Oil strainer

Baffle plate
and net

Oil pan

For A/T

Oil drain plug

Ⓣ 20 - 29 (2.0 - 3.0, 14 - 22)

Ⓣ : N·m (kg-m, ft-lb)

Z20 engine

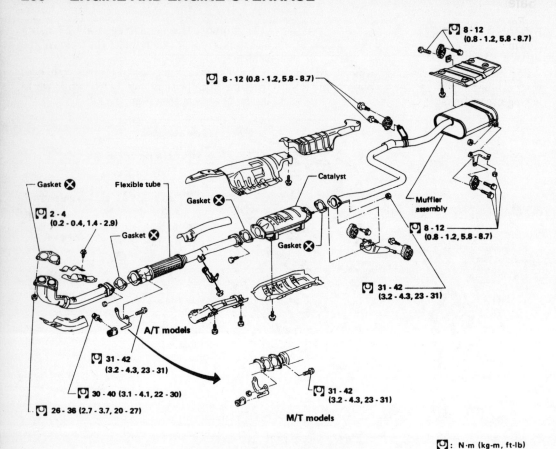

Exploded view Maxima exhaust system

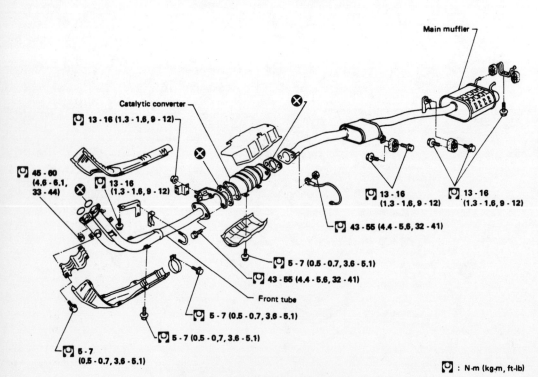

Exploded view 240SX exhaust system

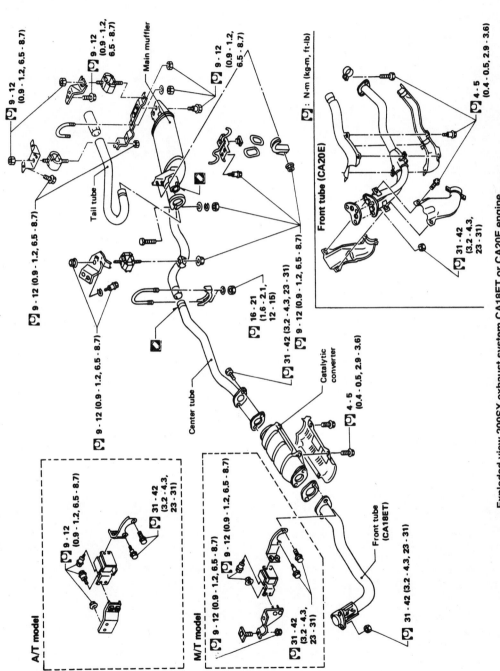

9 - 12 (0.9 - 1.2, 6.5 - 8.7)

9 - 12 (0.9 - 1.2, 6.5 - 8.7)

Main muffler

9 - 12 (0.9 - 1.2, 6.5 - 8.7)

9 - 12 (0.9 - 1.2, 6.5 - 8.7)

Tail tube

9 - 12 (0.9 - 1.2, 6.5 - 8.7)

9 - 12 (0.9 - 1.2, 6.5 - 8.7)

16 - 21 (1.6 - 2.1, 12 - 15)

31 - 42 (3.2 - 4.3, 23 - 31)

9 - 12 (0.9 - 1.2, 6.5 - 8.7)

Catalytic converter

Center tube

4 - 5 (0.4 - 0.5, 2.9 - 3.6)

4 - 5 (0.4 - 0.5, 2.9 - 3.6)

: N·m (kg-m, ft-lb)

Front tube (CA20E)

31 - 42 (3.2 - 4.3, 23 - 31)

A/T model

9 - 12 (0.9 - 1.2, 6.5 - 8.7)

31 - 42 (3.2 - 4.3, 23 - 31)

M/T model

9 - 12 (0.9 - 1.2, 6.5 - 8.7)

9 - 12 (0.9 - 1.2, 6.5 - 8.7)

31 - 42 (3.2 - 4.3, 23 - 31)

Front tube (CA18ET)

31 - 42 (3.2 - 4.3, 23 - 31)

Exploded view 200SX exhaust system CA18ET or CA20E engine

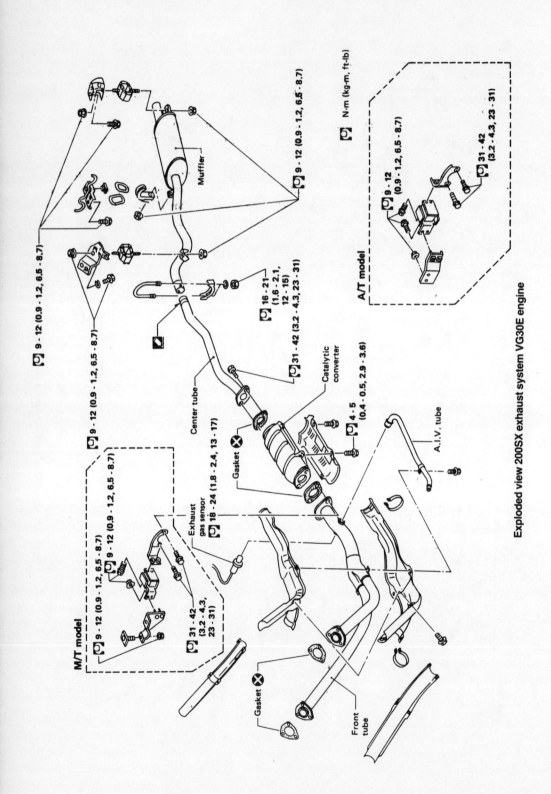

Muffler

9 - 12 (0.9 - 1.2, 6.5 - 8.7)

9 - 12 (0.9 - 1.2, 6.5 - 8.7)

9 - 12 (0.9 - 1.2, 6.5 - 8.7)

16 - 21 (1.6 - 2.1, 12 - 15)

31 - 42 (3.2 - 4.3, 23 - 31)

Catalytic converter

Center tube

4 - 5 (0.4 - 0.5, 2.9 - 3.6)

A.I.V. tube

Gasket

18 - 24 (1.8 - 2.4, 13 - 17)

Exhaust gas sensor

31 - 42 (3.2 - 4.3, 23 - 31)

9 - 12 (0.9 - 1.2, 6.5 - 8.7)

9 - 12 (0.9 - 1.2, 6.5 - 8.7)

M/T model

Gasket

Front tube

N·m (kg-m, ft-lb)

9 - 12 (0.9 - 1.2, 6.5 - 8.7)

31 - 42 (3.2 - 4.3, 23 - 31)

9 - 12 (0.9 - 1.2, 6.5 - 8.7)

A/T model

Exploded view 200SX exhaust system VG30E engine

3. If you are using a torch be careful not to come close to any fuel lines.

4. Always use the proper tool for the job.

Special Tools

A number of special exhaust tools can be rented or bought from a local auto parts store. It may also be quite helpful to use solvents designed to loosen rusted nuts or bolts. Remember that these products are often flammable, apply only to parts after they are cool.

Front Pipe

REMOVAL AND INSTALLATION

1. Support the vehicle securely by using jackstands or equivalent under the frame of the vehicle.

2. Remove the exhaust pipe clamps and any front exhaust pipe shield.

3. Soak the exhaust manifold front pipe mounting studs with penetrating oil. Remove attaching nuts and gasket from the manifold.

NOTE: *If these studs snap off, while removing the front pipe the manifold will have to be removed and the stud will have to be drill out and the hole tapped.*

4. Remove any exhaust pipe mounting hanger or bracket.

5. Remove front pipe from the catalytic connverter.

6. Install the front pipe on the manifold with seal if so equipped.

7. Install the pipe on the catalytic connverter. Assemble all parts loosely and position pipe to insure proper clearance from body of vehicle.

8. Tighten mounting studs, bracket bolts on exhaust clamps.

9. Install exhaust pipe shield.

10. Start engine and check for exhaust leaks.

Catalytic Converter

REMOVAL AND INSTALLATION

1. Remove the converter lower shield.

2. Disconnect converter from front pipe.

3. Disconnect converter from center pipe.

NOTE: *Assemble all parts loosely and position converter before tightening the exhaust clamps.*

4. Remove catalytic converter.

5. To install reverse the removal procedures. Always use new clamps and exhaust seals, start engine and check for leaks.

Tailpipe And Muffler

REMOVAL AND INSTALLATION

1. Remove tailpipe conection at center pipe.

2. Remove all brackets and exhaust clamps.

3. Remove tailpipe from muffler. On some models the tailpipe and muffler are one piece.

4. To install reverse the removal procedures. Always use new clamps and exhaust seals, start engine and check for leaks.

Emission Controls

EMISSION CONTROLS

There are three sources of automotive pollutants: Crankcase fumes, exhaust gases and gasoline evaporation. The pollutants formed from these substances fall into three categories: unburnt hydrocarbons (HC), carbon monoxide (CO) and oxides of nitrogen (NOx). The equipment that is used to limit these pollutants is commonly called emission control equipment.

Crankcase Emission Controls

The crankcase emission control equipment consists of a positive crankcase ventilation valve (PCV), a closed or open oil filler cap and hoses to connect this equipment.

NOTE: *The crankcase emission control system on the diesel engine is basically the same as that which is on the gasoline engine. Its major difference is the crankcase emission control valve. Although its function is the same as the gasoline engine's PCV valve, it's shape and location are different.*

When the engine is running, a small portion of the gases which are formed in the combustion chamber during combustion leak by the piston rings and enter the crankcase. Since these gases are under pressure they tend to escape from the crankcase and enter into the atmosphere. If these gases were allowed to remain in the crankcase for any length of time, they would contaminate the engine oil and cause sludge to build up. If the gases are allowed to escape into the atmosphere, they would pollute the air, as they contain unburned hydrocarbons. The crankcase emission control equipment recycles these gases back into the engine combustion chamber where they are burned.

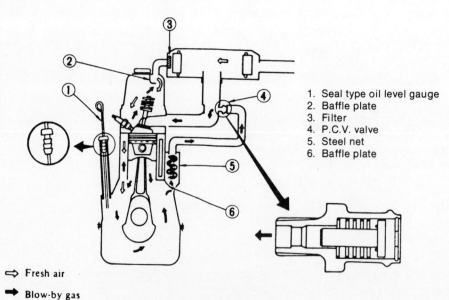

1. Seal type oil level gauge
2. Baffle plate
3. Filter
4. P.C.V. valve
5. Steel net
6. Baffle plate

⇨ Fresh air

➡ Blow-by gas

PCV system—L20B

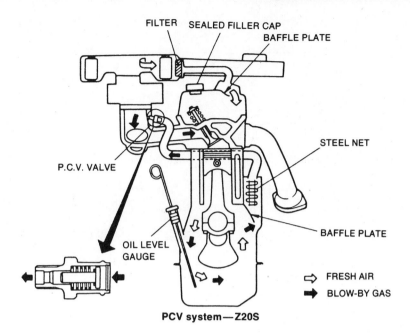

FILTER   SEALED FILLER CAP

BAFFLE PLATE

STEEL NET

P.C.V. VALVE

BAFFLE PLATE

OIL LEVEL
GAUGE

FRESH AIR

BLOW-BY GAS

PCV system—Z20S

Crankcase gases are recycled in the following manner: while the engine is running, clean filtered air is drawn into the crankcase through the air filter and then through a hose leading to the rocker cover. As the air passes through the crankcase it picks up the combustion gases and carries them out of the crankcase, up through the PCV valve and into the intake manifold. After they enter the intake manifold they are drawn into the combustion chamber and burned.

The most critical component in the system is the PCV valve. This vacuum controlled valve regulates the amount of gases which are recycled into the combustion changer. At low engine speeds the valve is partially closed, limiting the flow of gases into the intake manifold. As engine speed increases, the valve opens to admit greater quantities of the gases into the intake manifold. If the valve should become blocked or plugged, the gases will be prevented from escaping from the crankcase by the normal route. Since these gases are under pressure, they will find their own way out of the

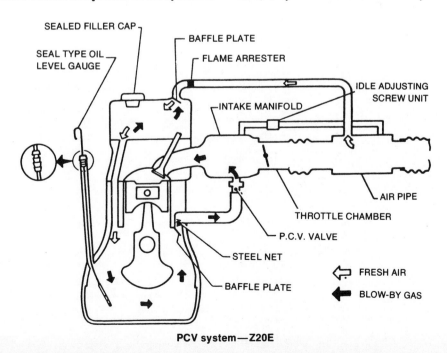

SEALED FILLER CAP

SEAL TYPE OIL
LEVEL GAUGE

BAFFLE PLATE

FLAME ARRESTER

IDLE ADJUSTING
SCREW UNIT

INTAKE MANIFOLD

AIR PIPE

THROTTLE CHAMBER

P.C.V. VALVE

STEEL NET

BAFFLE PLATE

FRESH AIR

BLOW-BY GAS

PCV system—Z20E

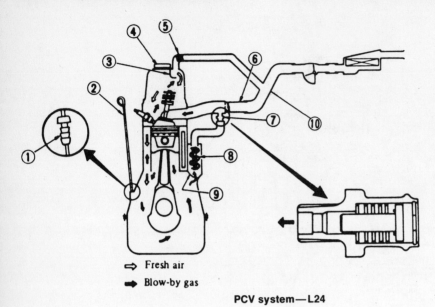

1. Seal rubber
2. Oil level gauge
3. Baffle plate
4. Oil filler cap
5. Flame arrester
6. Throttle chamber
7. P.C.V. valve
8. Steel net
9. Baffle plate
10. Air duct

⇨ Fresh air

➡ Blow-by gas

PCV system—L24

crankcase. This alternate route is usually a weak oil seal or gasket in the engine. As the gas escapes by the gasket it also creates an oil leak. Besides causing oil leaks, a clogged PCV valve also allows these gases to remain in the crankcase for an extended period of time, promoting the formation of sludge in the engine.

The above explanation and the troubleshooting procedure which follows applies to all engines with PCV systems.

TESTING

Check the PCV system hoses and connections, to see that there are no leaks. Then replace or tighten, as necessary.

Gasoline Engine

To check the valve, remove it and blow through both of its ends. When blowing from the side which goes toward the intake manifold,

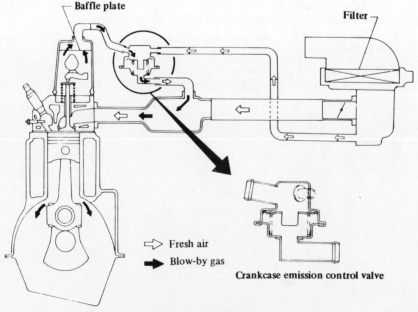

Baffle plate

Filter

⇨ Fresh air

➡ Blow-by gas

Crankcase emission control valve

PCV system—LD28

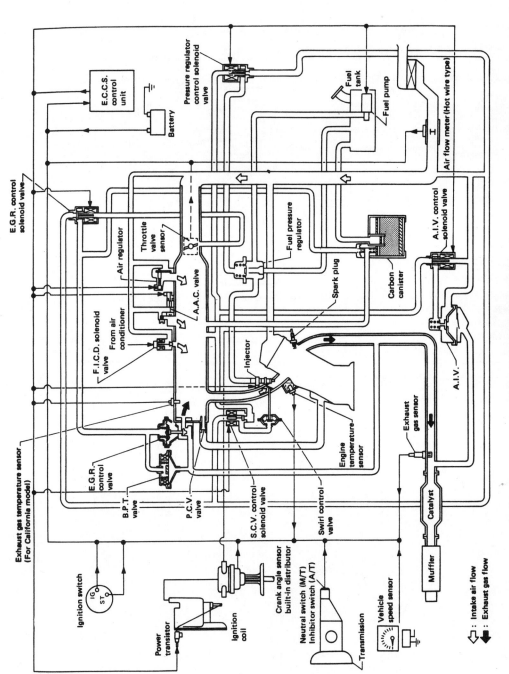

Emission control system diagram—KA24E engine

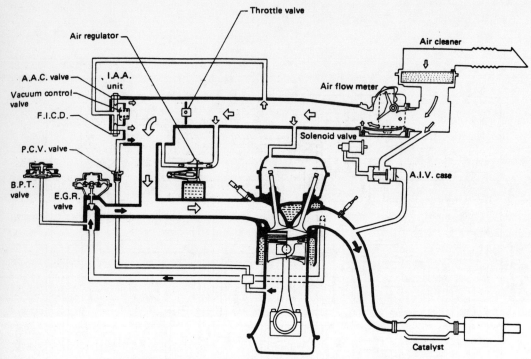

Emission control system diagram—CA20E engine— CA18ET similar

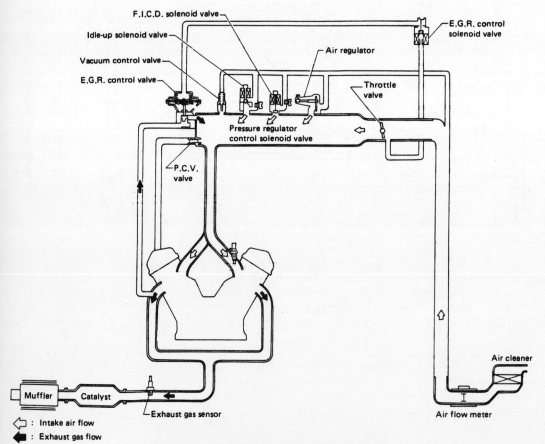

◁ : Intake air flow

◀ : Exhaust gas flow

Emission control system diagram VG30E engine

very little air should pass through it. When blowing from the crankcase (valve cover) side, air should pass through freely.

Replace the valve with a new one, if the valve fails to function as outlined.

NOTE: *Do not attempt to clean or adjust the valve. Replace it with a new one. The CA20E, CA18ET, KA24E and VG30E engines PCV valve locations and diagrams are also in Chapter 1.*

Diesel Engine

Remove the crankcase emission control valve and suck on the pipe that leads to the intake manifold. Air should flow freely. You should be able to hear the diaphragm in the valve click open while you are sucking. If the valve fails to function as detailed, replace it with a new one.

REMOVAL AND INSTALLATION

To remove the PCV valve, simply loosen the hose clamp and remove the valve from the manifold-to-crankcase hose and intake manifold. Install the PCV valve in the reverse order of removal.

Removal and installation procedures for the diesel crankcase emission control valve are detailed in Chapter 1.

Evaporative Emission Control System

When raw fuel evaporates, the vapors contain hydrocarbons. To prevent these fumes from escaping into the atmosphere, the fuel evaporative emission control system was developed.

There are two different evaporative emission control systems used on Datsun/Nissan. The system used through 1974 consists of a sealed fuel tank, a vapor/liquid separator, a flow guide

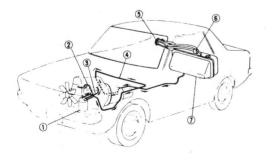

1. Carbon canister
2. Vacuum signal line
3. Canister vent line
4. Vapor vent line
5. Fuel filler cap with vacuum relief valve
6. Fuel check valve
7. Fuel tank

Evaporative emission control system schematic

(check) valve, and all of the hoses connecting these components, in the above order, leading from the fuel tank to the PCV hose, which connects the crankcase to the PCV valve.

In operation, the vapor formed in the fuel tank passes through the vapor separator, onto the flow guide valve and the crankcase. When the engine is not running, if the fuel vapor pressure in the vapor separator goes about 0.4 in. Hg, the flow guide valve opens and allows the vapor to enter the engine crankcase. Otherwise the flow guide valve is closed to the vapor separator while the engine is not running. When the engine is running, and a vacuum is developed in the fuel tank or in the engine crankcase and the difference of pressure between the relief side and the fuel tank or crankcase becomes 2 in. Hg, the relief valve opens and allows ambient air from the air cleaner into the fuel tank or the engine crankcase. This ambient air replaces the vapor within the fuel tank or crankcase, bring the fuel tank or crankcase back into a neutral or positive pressure range.

The system used on 1975 and later models consists of a sealed fuel tank, a vapor/liquid separator (certain models only), a vapor vent line, a carbon canister, a vacuum signal line and a canister purge line.

In operation, fuel vapors and/or liquid are routed to the liquid/vapor separator or check valve where liquid fuel is directed back into the fuel tank as fuel vapors flow into the charcoal filled canister. The charcoal absorbs and stores the fuel vapors when the engine is not running or is at idle. When the throttle valves in the carburetor (or air intakes for fuel injection) are opened, vacuum from above the throttle valves is routed through a vacuum signal line to the purge control valve on the canister. The control valve opens and allows the fuel vapors to be drawn from the canister through a purge line and into the intake manifold and the combustion chambers.

INSPECTION AND SERVICE

Check the hoses for proper connections and damage. Replace as necessary. Check the vapor separator tank for fuel leaks, distortion and dents, and replace as necessary.

Flow Guide Valve
Through 1974

Remove the flow guide valve and inspect it for leakage by blowing air into the ports in the valve. When air is applied from the fuel tank side, the flow guide valve is normal if the air passes into the check side (crankcase side), but not into the relief side (air cleaner side). When air is applied from the check side, the valve is normal if the passage of air is restricted. When

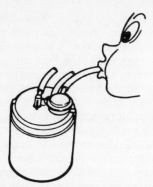

When checking the purge control valve, apply vacuum (inhale) to the hose

air is applied from the relief side (air cleaner side), the valve is normal if air passes into the fuel tank side or into the check side.

1975 and Later
Carbon Canister and Purge Control Valve

To check the operation of the carbon canister purge control valve, disconnect the rubber hose between the canister control valve and the T-fitting, at the T-fitting. Apply vacuum to the hose leading to the control valve. The vacuum condition should be maintained indefinitely. If the control valve leaks, remove the top cover of the valve and check for a dislocated or cracked diaphragm. If the diaphragm is damaged, a repair kit containing a new diaphragm, retainer,

and spring is available and should be installed.

The carbon canister has an air filter in the bottom of the canister. The filter element should be checked once a year or every 12,000 miles; more frequently if the car is operated in dusty areas. Replace the filter by pulling it out of the bottom of the canister and installing a new one.

REMOVAL AND INSTALLATION

Removal and installation of the various evaporative emission control system components consists of disconnecting the hoses, loosening retaining screws, and remove the part which is to be replaced or checked. Install in the reverse order. When replacing hose, make sure that it is fuel and vapor resistant.

Spark Timing Control System
Dual Point Distributor

The 1973 610 is equipped with this system. The dual point distributor has two sets of breaker points which operate independently of each other and are positioned with a relative phase angle of 7° apart. This makes one set the advanced points and the other set the retarded points.

The two sets of points, which mechanically operate continuously, are connected in parallel to the primary side of the ignition circuit. One

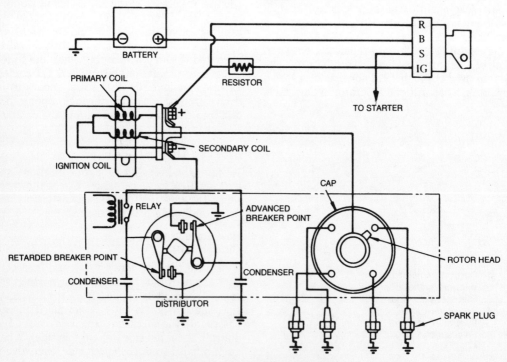

Dual point ignition system schematic

set of points controls the firing of the spark plugs and hence, the ignition timing, depending on whether or not the retarded set of points is energized.

When both sets of points are electrically energized, the first set to open (the advanced set, 7° sooner) has no control over breaking the ignition coil primary circuit because the retarded set is still closed and maintaining a complete circuit to ground. When the retarded set of points opens, the advanced set is still open, and the primary circuit is broken causing the electromagnetic field in the coil to collapse and the ignition spark is produced.

When the retarded set of points is removed from the primary ignition circuit through the operation of a distributor relay inserted into the retraded points circuit, the advanced set of points controls the primary circuit. The retarded set of points is activated as follows:

The retarded set of points is activated only while the throttle is partially open, the temperature is above 50°F (10°C) and the transmission is any gear but Fourth gear.

NOTE: *When the ambient temperature is below 30°F (– 1°C), the retarded set of points is removed from the ignition circuit no matter what switch is ON.*

In the case of an automatic transmission, the retarded set of points is activated at all times except under heavy acceleration and high speed cruising (wide open throttle) with the ambient temperature about 50°F (10°C).

There are three switches which control the operation of the distributor relay. All of the switches must be ON in order to energize the distributor relay, thus energizing the retarded set of points.

The switches and their operation are as follows:

A transmission switch located in the transmission closes an electrical circuit when the transmission is all gears except Fourth gear.

A throttle switch located on the throttle linkage at the carburetor is ON when the throttle valve is removed within a 45° angle.

The temperature sensing switch is located near the hood release level inside the passenger compartment. The temperature sensing switch comes on between 41°F (5°C) and 55°F (13°C) and rising and goes OFF above 34°F (1°C) when the temperature falls.

The distributor vacuum advance mechanism produced a spark advance based on the amount of vacuum in the intake manifold. With a high vacuum, less air/fuel mixture enters the engine cylinders and the mixture is therefore less highly compressed. Consequently, this mixture burns more slowly and the advance mechanism gives it more time to burn. This longer burning time results in higher combustion temperatures at peak pressure and hence, more time for nitrogen to react with oxygen and form nitrogen oxides (NOx). At the same time, this advanced timing results in less complete combustion due to the greater area of cylinder wall (quench area) exposed at the instant of ignition. This cooled fuel will not burn as readily and hence, results in higher unburned hydrocarbons (HC). The production of NOx and HC resulting from the vacuum advance is highest during the moderate acceleration in lower gears.

Retardation of the ignition timing is necessary to reduce NOx and HC emissions. Various ways of retarding the ignition spark have been used in autombles, all of which remove vacuum to the distributor vacuum advance mechanism at different times under certain conditions. Another way of accomplishing the same goal is the dual point distributor system.

Transmission Switch

Disconnect the electrical leads at the switch and connect a self powered test light to the electrical leads. The switch should conduct electricity only when the gearshift is moved to Fourth gear.

If the switch fails to perform in the above manner, replace it with a new one.

Throttle Switch

The throttle switch located on the throttle linkage at the carburetor is checked with a self powered test light. Disconnect the electrical leads of the switch and connect the test light. The switch should not conduct current when the throttle valve is closed or opened, up to 45°. When the throttle is fully opened, the switch should conduct current.

Temperature Sensing Switch

The temperature sensing switch mounted in the passenger compartment near the hood release lever should not conduct current when the temperature is above 55°F (13°C) when connected to a self powered test light as previously outlined for the throttle switch.

Dual Spark Plug Ignition System
Z20E, Z20S, CA20E, CA18ET

The 1980 California model and all 1981-83 Z-series and CA-series engines have two spark plugs per cylinder. This arrangement allows the engine to burn large amounts of recirculated exhaust gases without affecting performance. In fact, the system works so well it improves gas mileage under most circumstances.

Both spark plugs fire simultaneously, which substantially shortens the time required to burn the air/fuel mixture when exhaust gases (EGR) are not being recirculated. When gases are being recirculated, the dual spark plug system brings the ignition level up to that of a single plug system which is not recirculating exhaust gases.

ADJUSTMENT

The only adjustments necessary are the tune-up and maintenance procedures outlined in Chapters One and Two.

Spark Timing Control System
GASOLINE ENGINE ONLY

The spark timing control system has been used in different forms on Nissan/ Datsuns since 1972. The first system, Transnmission Controlled Spark System (TCS) was used on most Nissan/Datsuns through 1979. This system consists of a thermal vacuum valve, a vacuum switching valve, a high gear detecting switch, and a number of vacuum hoses. Basically, the system is designed to retard full spark advance except when the car is in high gear and the engine is at normal operating temperature. At all other times, the spark advance is retarded to one degree or another.

The 1980 and later Spark Timing Control System replaces the TCS system. The major difference is that it works solely from engine water temperature changes rather than a transmission mounted switch. The system includes a thermal vacuum valve, a vacuum delay valve, and attendant hoses. It performs the same function as the earlier TCS system. To retard full spark advance at times when high levels of pollutants would otherwise be given off.

INSPECTION AND ADJUSTMENTS

Normally the TCS and Spark Timing Control systems should be trouble-free. However, if you suspect a problem in the system, first check to make sure all wiring (if so equipped) and hoses are connected and free from dirt. Also check to make sure the distributor vacuum advance is working properly. If everything appears all right, connect a timing light to the engine and make sure the initial timing is correct. On vehicles with the TCS system, run the engine until it reaches normal operating temperature, and then have an assistant sit in the car and shift the transmission through all the gears slowly. If the system is functioning properly, the timing will be 10-15° advanced in high gear (compared to the other gear positions). If the system is still not operating correctly, you will have to check for continuity at all the connections with a test light.

To test the Spark Timing Control System, connect a timing light and check the ignition timing while the temperature gauge is in the cold position. Write down the reading. Allow the engine to run with the timing light attached until the temperature needle reaches the center of the gauge. As the engine is warming up, check with the timing light to make sure the ignition timing retards. When the temperature needle is in the middle of the gauge, the ignition timing should advance from its previous position. If the ignition timing does not change, replace the thermal vacuum valve.

Spark Plug Switching Control System

This system, used only on the 1982 200SX, is designed to change the ignition system from 2-plug ignition to 1-plug ignition during heavy load driving conditions in order to reduce engine noise. The system also functions to ad-

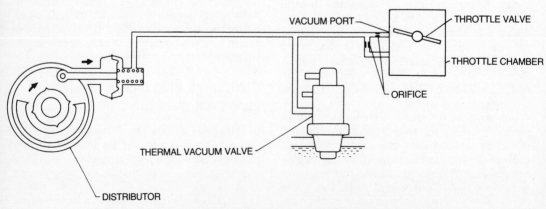

1980 and later Spark Timing Control System, CA20E engine system shown

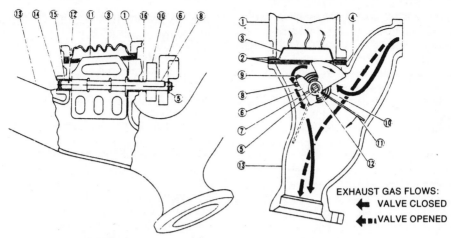

1. Intake manifold
2. Stove gasket
3. Manifold stove
4. Heat shield plate
5. Snap ring
6. Counterweight
7. Key
8. Stopper pin
9. Screw
10. Thermostat spring
11. Heat control valve
12. Control valve shaft
13. Exhaust manifold
14. Cap
15. Bushing
16. Coil spring

Typical EFE system

vance ignition timing by the proper amount during 1-plug ignition.

Early Fuel Evaporation System
GASOLINE ENGINES ONLY

The Early Fuel Evaporation System is used on some L-series engines. The system's purpose is to heat the air/fuel mixture when the engine is below normal operating temperature. The L-series engines use a system much similar to the old style exhaust manifold heat riser. The only adjustment necessary is to occasionally lubricate the counterweight. Other than that, the system should be trouble-free.

The 1980 and later carbureted engines use coolant water heat instead of exhaust gas heat to prewarm the fuel mixture. This system should be trouble-free.

Boost Control Deceleration Device (BCDD)
GASOLINE ENGINES ONLY

The Boost Control Deceleration Device (BCDD) used on the L-series engines to reduce hydrocarbon emissions during coasting conditions.

High manifold vacuum during coasting prevents the complete combustion of the air/fuel mixture because of the reduced amount of air. This condition will result in a large amount of HC emission. Enriching the air/fuel mixture for a short time (during the high vacuum condition) will reduce the emission of the HC.

However, enriching the air/fuel mixture with only the mixture adjusting screw will cause poor engine idle or invite an increase in the carbon monoxide (CO) content of the exhaust gases. The BCDD consists of an independent system that kicks in when the engine is coasting and enriches the air/fuel mixture, which reduces the hydrocarbon content of the exhaust gases. This is accomplished without adversely affecting engine idle and the carbon monoxide content of the exhaust gases.

ADJUSTMENT

Normally, the BCDD does not need adjustment. However, if the need should arise because of suspected malfunction of the system, proceed as follows:

1. Connect the tachometer to the engine.
2. Connect a quick response vacuum gauge to the intake manifold.
3. Disconnect the solenoid valve electrical leads.

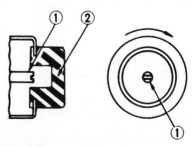

(1) BCDD adjusting screw (2) cover

4. Start and warm up the engine until it reaches normal operating temperature.

5. Adjust the idle speed to the proper specification.

6. Raise the engine speed to 3,000-3,500 rpm under no-load (transmission in Neutral or Park), then allow the throttle to close quickly. Take notice as to whether or not the engine rpm returns to idle speed and if it does, how long the fall in rpm is interrupted before it reaches idle speed.

At the moment the throttle is snapped closed at high engine rpm and the vacuum in the intake manifold reaches between −23 in.Hg and −27.7 in.Hg and then gradually falls to about −16.5 in. Hg at idle speed. The process of the fall of the intake manifold vacuum and the engine rpm will take one of the following three forms:

a. When the operating pressure of the BCDD is too high, the system remains inoperative, and the vacuum in the intake manifold decreases without interruption just like that of an engine without a BCDD.

b. When the operating pressure is lower than that of the case given above, but still higher than the proper set pressure, the fall of vacuum in the intake manifold is interrupted and kept constant at a certain level (operating pressure) for about one second and then gradually falls down to the normal vacuum at idle speed.

c. When the set of operating pressure of the BCDD is lower than the intake manifold vacuum when the throttle is suddenly released, the engine speed will not lower to idle speed.

To adjust the set operating pressure of the BCDD, remove the adjusting screw cover from the BCDD mechanism mounted on the side of the carburetor. On 810 models, the BCDD system is installed under the throttle chamber.

The adjusting screw is a left hand threaded screw. Late models may have an adjusting nut instead of a screw. Turning the screw ⅛ of a turn in either direction will change the operation pressure about 0.8 in. Hg. Turning the screw counterclockwise will increase the amount of vacuum needed to operate the mechanism. Turning the screw clockwise will decrease the amount of vacuum needed to operate the mechanism.

The operating pressure for the BCDD on most models should be between −19.9 to −22.05 in. Hg. The decrease in intake manifold vacuum should be interrupted at these levels for about one second when the BCDD is operating correctly.

Don't forget to install the adjusting screw cover after the system is adjusted.

Intake Manifold Vacuum Control System

This system, used in 1980-81 510s, is designed to reduce the engine's oil consumption when the intake manifold vacuum increases to an extremely high level during deceleration. The system consists of two units. A boost control unit as the vacuum sensor, and a by-pass air control unit as an actuator. The boost control unit senses the manifold vacuum. When the level of the manifold vacuum increases above the predetermined value, the boost control valve opens and transmits the manifold vacuum to the by-pass air control unit. The manifold vacuum then pulls the diaphragm in and opens the by-pass air control valve, thereby causing the air to be bypassed to the intake manifold. After completion of the air by-pass, the manifold vacuum is lowered. This results in the closing of the boost control valve and then the closing of the air control valve. This system operates in a tightly controlled circuit so that the manifold vacuum can be kept very close to the predetermined value during deceleration.

Aside from a routine check of the hoses and their connections, no service or adjustments should ever be necessary on this system. If at some time you feel that an adjustment is required, it is suggested that you take the car to a Nissan/Datsun dealer or an authorized service representative.

Automatic Temperature Controlled Air Cleaner

This system is used on all Datsun models covered in this guide except the 810 and the 200SX.

The rate at which fuel is drawn into the airstream in a carburetor varies with the temperature of the air that the fuel is being mixed with. The air/fuel ratio cannot be held constant for efficient fuel combustion with a wide range of air temperatures. Cold air being drawn into the engine causes a richer air/fuel mixture, and thus, more hydrocarbons in the exhaust gas. Hot air being drawn into the engine causes a leaner air/fuel mixture and more efficient combustion for less hydrocarbons in the exhaust gases.

The automatic temperature controlled air cleaner is designed so that the temperature of the ambient air being drawn into the engine is automatically controlled, to hold the temperature of the air and, consequently, the fuel/air ratio at a constant rate for efficient fuel combustion.

A temperature sensing vacuum switch controls vacuum applied to a vacuum motor oper-

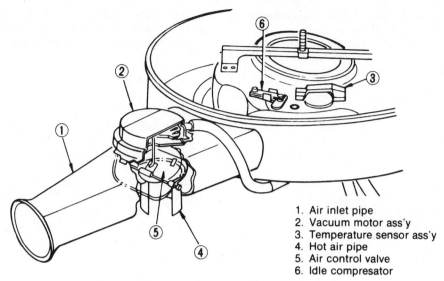

1. Air inlet pipe
2. Vacuum motor ass'y
3. Temperature sensor ass'y
4. Hot air pipe
5. Air control valve
6. Idle compresator

Automatic temperature controlled air cleaner

ating a valve in the intake snorkle of the air cleaner. When the engine is cold or the air being drawn into the engine is cold, the vacuum motor opens the valve, allowing air heated by the exhaust manifold to be drawn into the engine. As the engine warms up, the temperature sensing unit shuts off the vacuum applied to the vacuum motor which allows the valve to close, shutting off the heated air and allowing cooler, outside (under hood) air to be drawn into the engine.

TESTING

When the air around the temperature sensor of the unit mounted inside the air cleaner housing reaches 100°F (38°C), the sensor should allow vacuum to pass onto the air valve vacuum motor thus blocking off the air cleaner snorkle to under hood (unheated) air.

When the temperature around the sensor is above 188°F (87°C), the air control valve should be completely open to under hood air.

If the air cleaner fails to operate correctly, check for loose or broken vacuum hoses. If the hoses are not the cause, replace the vacuum motor in the air cleaner.

Exhaust Gas Recirculation (EGR)
GASOLINE ENGINES

This system is used on all 1974 and later models. Exhaust gas recirculation is used to reduce combustion temperatures in the engine, thereby reducing the oxides of nitrogen emissions.

An EGR valve is mounted on the center of the intake manifold. The recycled exhaust gas is drawn into the bottom of the intake manifold

riser portion through the exhaust manifold heat stove and EGR valve. A vacuum diaphragm is connected to a timed signal port at the carburetor flange.

As the throttle valve is opened, vacuum is applied to the EGR valve vacuum diaphragm. When the vacuum reaches about 2 in. Hg, the diaphragm moves against string pressure and is in a fully up position at 8 in. Hg of vacuum. As the diaphragm moves up, it opens the exhaust gas metering valve which allows exhaust gas to be pulled into the engine intake manifold. The system does not operate when the engine is

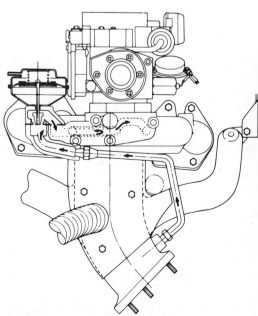

EGR system—carbureted models

idling because the exhaust gas recirculation would cause a rough idle.

On 1975 and later models, a thermal vacuum valve inserted in the engine thermostat housing controls the application of the vacuum to the EGR valve. When the engine coolant reaches a predetermined temperature, the thermal vacuum valve opens and allows vacuum to be routed to the EGR valve. Below the predetermined temperature, the thermal vacuum valve closes and blocks vacuum to the EGR valve.

All 1978-79 models, the 1980 810 and the 1980-81 510 (Canadian), 200SX (Canadian) and 1983 and later 200SX have a B.P.T. valve installed between the EGR valve and the thermal vacuum valve. The B.P.T. valve has a diaphragm which is raised or lowered by exhaust back pressure. The diaphragm opens or closes an air bleed, which is connected into the EGR vacuum line. High pressure results in higher levels of EGR, because the diaphragm is raised, closing off the air bleed, which allows more vacuum to reach and open the EGR valve. Thus the amount of recirculated exhaust gas varies with exhaust pressure.

All 1980 200SX (USA) models and all 1980-81 510 (USA) models use a V.V.T. valve (venturi vacuum transducer valve) instead of the B.P.T. valve. The V.V.T. valve monitors exhaust pressure and carburetor vacuum in order to activate the diaphragm which controls the throttle vacuum applied to the EGR control valve. This system expands the operating range of the EGR flow rate as compared to the B.P.T. unit.

NOTE: *1981 510s built for California are equipped with two EGR valves. The second one is directly below the normal one.*

Many 1975 and later Datsuns are equipped with an EGR warning system which signals via a light in the dashboard that the EGR system may need service. The EGR warning light should come on every time the starter is engaged as a test to make sure the bulb is not blown. The system uses a counter which works in conjunction with the odometer, and lights the warning signal after the vehicle has traveled a predetermined number of miles.

To reset the counter, which is mounted in the engine compartment, remove the grommet installed in the side of the counter and insert the tip of a small screwdriver into the hole. Press down on the knob inside the hole. Reinstall the grommet.

TESTING

1974

Check the operation of the EGR system as follows:

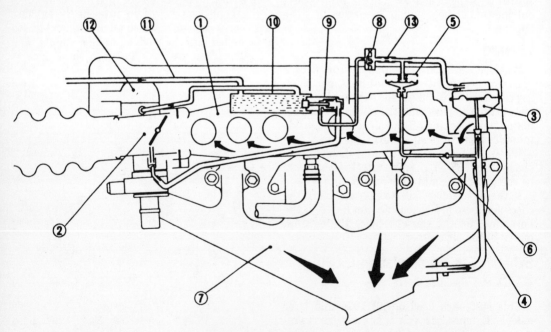

1. Intake manifold
2. Throttle chamber
3. E.G.R. control valve
4. E.G.R. tube
5. B.P.T. valve
6. B.P.T. valve control tube
7. Exhaust manifold
8. Vacuum delay valve
   (California automatic
   transmission models only)
9. Thermal vacuum vlave
10. Heater housing
11. Water return tube
12. Thermostat housing
13. Vacuum orifice

810 EGR system schematic

1. Visually inspect the entire EGR control system. Clean the mechanism free of oil and dirt. Replace any rubber hoses found to be cracked or broken.

2. Make sure that the EGR solenoid valve is properly wired.

3. Increase the engine speed from idling to 2,000-3,500 rpm. The plate of the EGR control valve diaphragm and the valve shaft should move upward as the engine speed is increased.

4. Disconnect the EGR solenoid valve electrical leads and connect them directly to the vehicle's 12v electrical supply (battery). Race the engine again with the EGR solenoid valve connected to a 12v power source. The EGR control valve should remain stationary.

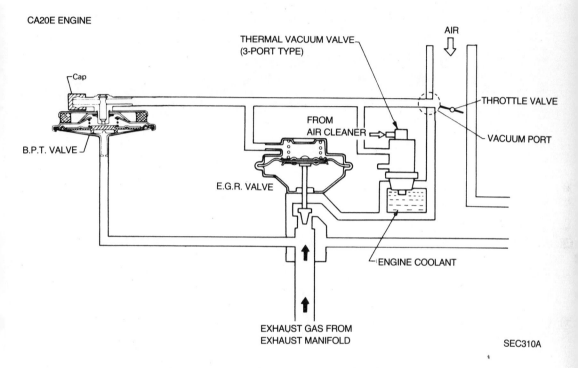

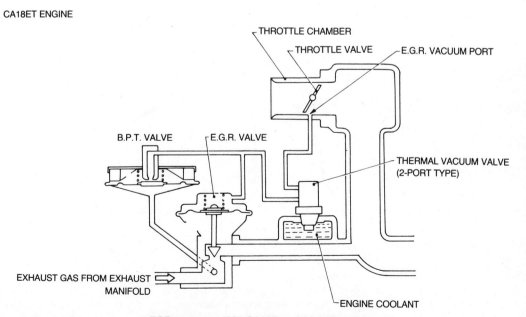

EGR systems, 1984 CA20E and CA18ET engines

5. With the engine running at idle, push up on the EGR control valve diaphragm with your finger. When this is done, the engine idle should become rough and uneven.

Inspect the two components of the EGR system as necessary in the following manner:

a. Remove the EGR control valve from the intake manifold.

b. Apply 4.7-5.1 in. Hg of vacuum to the EGR control valve by sucking on a tube attached to the outlet on top of the valve. The valve should move to the full up position. The valve should remain open for more than 30 seconds after the application of vacuum is discontinued and the vacuum hose is blocked.

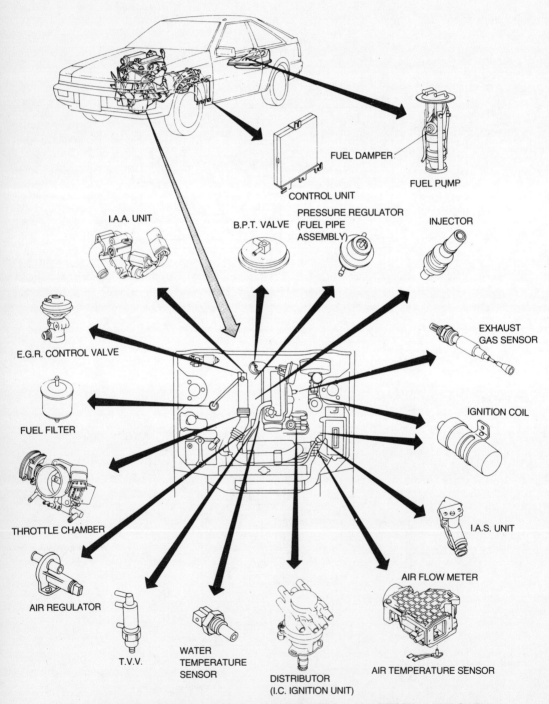

FUEL DAMPER

FUEL PUMP

CONTROL UNIT

I.A.A. UNIT

B.P.T. VALVE

PRESSURE REGULATOR (FUEL PIPE ASSEMBLY)

INJECTOR

E.G.R. CONTROL VALVE

EXHAUST GAS SENSOR

FUEL FILTER

IGNITION COIL

THROTTLE CHAMBER

I.A.S. UNIT

AIR REGULATOR

AIR FLOW METER

T.V.V.

WATER TEMPERATURE SENSOR

DISTRIBUTOR (I.C. IGNITION UNIT)

AIR TEMPERATURE SENSOR

Various emissions and injection component locations, 1984 and later 200SX and 200 SX Turbo

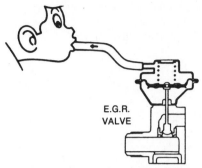

You can apply vacuum to the EGR valve by sucking on the air tube which is connected to it

c. Inspect the EGR valve for any signs of warpage or damage.

d. Clean the EGR valve seat with a brush and compressed air to prevent clogging.

e. Connect the EGR solenoid valve to a 12v DC power source and notice if the valve clicks when intermittently electrified. If the valve clicks, it is considered to be working properly.

f. Check the EGR temperature sensing switch by removing it from the engine and placing it in a container of water together with a thermometer. Connect a self powered test light to the two electrical leads of the switch.

g. Heat the container of water.

h. The switch should conduct current when the water temperature is below 77°F (25°C) and stop conducting current when the water reaches a temperature somewhere between 88-106°F (31-41°C). Replace the switch if it functions otherwise.

1975 And Later

1. Remove the EGR valve and apply enough vacuum to the diaphragm to open the valve.

2. The valve should remain open for over 30 seconds after the vacuum is removed.

3. Check the valve for damage, such as warpage, cracks, and excessive wear around the valve and seat.

4. Clean the seat with a brush and compressed air and remove any deposits from around the valve and port (seat).

5. To check the operation of the thermal vacuum valve, remove the valve from the engine and apply vacuum to the ports of the valve. The valve should not allow vacuum to pass.

6. Place the valve in a container of water with a thermometer and heat the water. When the temperature of the water reaches 134-145°F (57-63°C), remove the valve and apply vacuum to the ports. The valve should allow vacuum to pass through it.

Clean the seat of the EGR valve with a stiff brush

7. To test the B.P.T. valve installed on 1978 and later models, disconnect the two vacuum hoses from the valve. Plug one of the ports. While applying pressure to the bottom of the valve, apply vacuum to the unplugged port and check for leakage. If any exists, replace the valve.

8. To test the check valve installed in some 1978 and later models, remove the valve and blow into the side which connects the EGR valve. Air should flow. When air is supplied to the other side, air flow resistance should be greater. If not, replace the valve.

9. To check the V.V.T. valve which replaces the B.P.T. valve on some 1980 and later models, disconnect the top and bottom center hoses and apply a vacuum to the top hose. Check for leaks. If a leak is present, replace the valve.

REMOVAL AND INSTALLATION

EGR Control Valve

1. Remove the nuts which attach the EGR tube and/or the BP tube to the EGR valve (if so equipped).

2. Unscrew the mounting bolts and remove the heat shield plate from the EGR control valve (if so equipped).

3. Tag and disconnect the EGR vacuum hose(s).

4. Unscrew the mounting bolts and remove the EGR control valve.

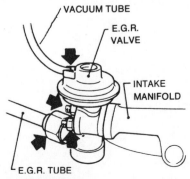

Removing the EGR valve

5. Install the EGR valve assembly with mounting bolts to intake manifold location.

6. Connect all vacuum hoses and install the heat shield if so equipped.

7. Connect EGR tube or BP tube to the EGR valve if so equipped.

NOTE: *Always be sure that the new valve is identical to the old one.*

DIESEL ENGINES

This system is designed to control the formation of NOx emissions by recirculating the exhaust gas into the intake manifold passage through the control valve.

The EGR flow rate is controlled in three stages in accordance with the engine speed and load. The first stage, High EGR, is obtained through the combination of a closed throttle valve and an open EGR valve. The second stage, Low EGR, is obtained through the opening of the throttle valve. The third stage, Zero EGR, is obtained closing the EGR valve.

The engine load signal is picked up by the potentiometer installed on the injection pump control lever. The engine speed signal is transmitted by an electromagnetic revolution sensor attached to the front cover. The throttle diaphragm and the EGR valve are both actuated by vacuum generated at the vacuum pump. Solenoids are used to convert the electrical signal from the control unit into the vacuum signal.

The EGR system is deactivated under extremely high or low coolant temperatures in order to assure good driveability.

TESTING

1. Visually check the entire EGR system as detailed in the previous Gasoline Engine section.

2. With the engine off, check the EGR control valve and throttle body for an indication of binding or sticking by moving the diaphragm/rod upward with your finger.

3. Start the engine and place your finger on

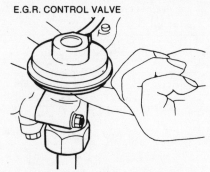

Place your finger on the EGR diaphragm

the underside of the EGR valve. You should feel the diaphragm.

CAUTION: *Be careful that your finger doesn't get caught between the diaphragm and the body of the valve.*

4. When the temperature of the engine is at or below 86°F (30°C), make sure that the EGR valve does not operate and the throttle valve is open when the engine is revved.

5. If the EGR valve operates or the throttle valve is closed, check the water temperature sensor. If the sensor appears normal, replace the EGR control unit.

6. When the temperature of the engine is high, above 86°F (30°C), make sure that the EGR valve operates and the throttle valve is closed when the engine is idling.

7. Increase the engine speed gradually and make sure that the throttle valve opens and the EGR valve closes in this order.

8. If the EGR valve and/or the throttle valve do not operate properly in this step, check them as follows:

a. Run the engine at idle and disconnect the harness connector at the solenoid valve. Apply battery voltage to the connector and check that the EGR valve and the throttle valve operate normally.

b. If they do not, check the EGR valve and the throttle diaphragm independently. If

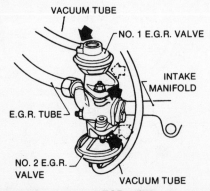

Some models have two EGR valves

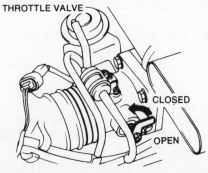

The position of this lever will tell you whether the throttle valve is open or closed

they operate normally, check the rev sensor, the potentiometer and all electrical circuits. If they appear normal, replace the EGR control unit.

REMOVAL AND INSTALLATION

Follow the procedures given in the Gasoline Engine section.

Air Injection Reactor System
GASOLINE ENGINES ONLY

This system is used on 1974-79 models. In gasoline engines, it is difficult to completely burn the air/fuel mixture through normal combustion in the combustion chambers. Under certain operating conditions, unburned fuel is exhausted into the atmosphere.

The air injection reactor system is designed so that ambient air, pressurized by the air pump, is injected through the injection nozzles into the exhaust ports near each exhaust valve. The exhaust gases are at high temperatures and ignite when brought into contact with the oxygen. Unburned fuel is then burned in the exhaust ports and manifold.

In 1976 California models utilized a secondary system consisting of an air control valve which limits injection of secondary air and an emergency relief valve which controls the supply of secondary air. This system protects the catalytic converter from overheating. In 1977 the function of these two valves was taken by a single combined air control (C.A.C.) valve.

All engines with the air pump system have a series of minor alterations to accommodate the system. These are:

1. Special close tolerance carburetor. Most engines, except the L16, require a slightly rich idle mixture adjustment.

2. Distributor with special advance curve. Ignition timing is retarded about 10° at idle in most cases.

3. Cooling system changes such as larger fan, higher fan speed, and thermostatic fan clutch. This is required to offset the increase in temperature caused by retarded timing at idle.

4. Faster idle speed.

5. Heated air intake on some engines.

The only periodic maintenance required on the air pump system is replacement of the drive belt.

TESTING

Air Pump

If the air pump makes an abnormal noise and cannot be corrected without removing the pump from the vehicle, check the following in sequence:

1. Turn the pulley ¾ of a turn in the clockwise direction and ¼ of a turn in the counterclockwise direction. If the pulley is binding and if rotation is not smooth, a defective bearing is indicated.

2. Check the inner wall of the pump body, vanes and rotor for wear. If the rotor has abnormal wear, replace the air pump.

3. Check the needle roller bearing for wear and damage. If the bearings are defective, the air pump should be replaced.

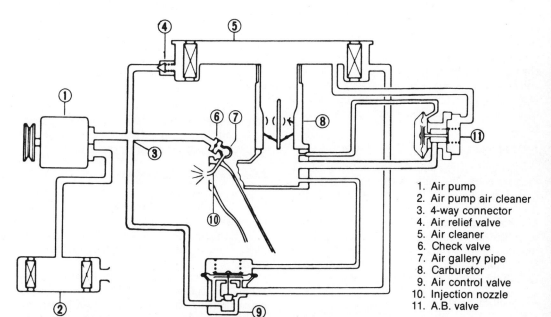

1. Air pump
2. Air pump air cleaner
3. 4-way connector
4. Air relief valve
5. Air cleaner
6. Check valve
7. Air gallery pipe
8. Carburetor
9. Air control valve
10. Injection nozzle
11. A.B. valve

Air injection system schematic—typical

Air pump (arrow)

4. Check and replace the rear side seal if abnormal wear or damage is noticed.

5. Check and replace the carbon shoes holding the vanes if they are found to be worn or damaged.

6. A deposit of carbon particles on the inner wall of the pump body and vanes is normal, but should be removed with compressed air before reassembling the air pump.

Check Valve

Remove the check valve from the air pump discharge line. Test it for leakage by blowing air into the valve from the air pump side and from the air manifold side. Air should only pass through the valve from the air pump side if the valve is functioning normally. A small amount of air leakage from the manifold side can be overlooked. Replace the check valve if it is found to be defective.

Anti-Backfire Valve

Disconnect the rubber hose connecting the mixture control valve with the intake manifold and plug the hose. If the mixture control valve is operating correctly, air will continue to blow out the mixture control valve for a few seconds after the accelerator pedal is fully depressed (engine running) and released quickly. If air continues to blow out for more than five seconds, replace the mixture control valve.

Air Pump Relief Valve

Disconnect the air pump discharge hose leading to the exhaust manifold. With the engine running, restrict the air flow coming from the pump. The air pump relief valve should vent the pressurized air to the atmosphere if it is working properly.

NOTE: *When performing this test do not completely block the discharge line of the air pump as damage may result if the relief valve fails to function properly.*

Air Injection Nozzles

Check around the air manifold for air leakage with the engine running at 2,000 rpm. If air is leaking from the eye joint bolt, retighten or replace the gasket. Check the air nozzles for restrictions by blowing air into the nozzles.

Hoses

Check and replace hoses if they are found to be weakened or cracked. Check all hose connections and clips. Be sure that the hoses are not in contact with other parts of the engine.

Emergency Air Relief Valve

1. Warm up the engine.

2. Check all hoses for leaks, kinks, improper connections, etc.

3. Run the engine up to 2000 rpm under no load. No air should be discharged from the valve.

4. Disconnect the vacuum hose from the valve. This is the hose which runs to the intake manifold. Run the engine up to 2000 rpm. Air should be discharged from the valve. If not, replace it.

Combined Air Control (CAC) Valve

1. Check all hoses for leaks, kinks, and improper connections.

2. Thoroughly warm up the engine.

3. With the engine idling, check for air discharge from the relief opening in the air cleaner case.

4. Disconnect and plug the vacuum hose from the valve. Air should be discharged from the valve with the engine idling. If the disconnect vacuum hose is not plugged, the engine will stumble.

5. Connect a hand operated vacuum pump to the vacuum fitting on the valve and apply 7.8-9.8 in. Hg of vacuum. Run the engine speed up to 3000 rpm. No air should be discharged from the valve.

6. Disconnect and plug the air hose at the check valve, with the conditions as in the preceding step. This should cause the valve to discharge air. If not, or if any of the conditions in this procedure are not met, replace the valve.

Air Induction System
GASOLINE ENGINES ONLY

Models using this system include the 1980-81 510, the 1980 200SX and the 49 state version of the 1980 810. The air induction system is used to send fresh, secondary air to the exhaust manifold by utilizing vacuum created by the exhaust pulsation in the manifold.

The exhaust pressure usually pulsates in response to the opening and closing of the exhaust valve and it periodically decreases below atmospheric pressure. If a secondary air intake pipe is opened to the atmosphere under a vacuum condition, secondary air can then be drawn into the exhaust manifold in proportion of the vacuum. Because of this, the air induction system is able to reduce the CO and HC content in the exhaust gases. The system consists of two air induction valves, a filter, hoses and E.A.I. tubes.

The only periodic maintenance required is replacement of the air induction filter as detailed in Chapter 1.

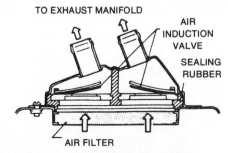

TO EXHAUST MANIFOLD

AIR INDUCTION VALVE

SEALING RUBBER

AIR FILTER

Cross section of the air induction valve

Fuel Shut-Off System

This system, used only in the 1980-81 510, is designed to reduce HC emissions and also to improve fuel economy during deceleration.

The system is operated by an anti-dieseling solenoid valve in the carburetor which is controlled by a vacuum switch. When the intake manifold vacuum increases to an extremely high level (which it does during deceleration), the fuel flow of the slow system is shut off by the anti-dieseling solenoid valve. When the intake manifold vacuum drops to a low level again, the fuel flow the the slow system is resupplied.

The fuel shut-off system is further controlled by the clutch switch and gear position switches such as the neutral switch (manual transmission) and the inhibitor switch (automatic transmission) to ensure that fuel cannot be shut off even if the manifold vacuum is high enough to trigger the normal fuel shut-off operation.

Injection Timing Advance System
DIESEL ENGINE ONLY

This system is designed to control the formation of HC emissions. It controls the amount of recirculating fuel in the fuel injection pump in order to control the injection timing.

The injection timing advance system is composed of an injection timing control solenoid valve, a potentiometer, and EGR control unit and a revolution sensor. This system is also called a Partial Load Advancer (PLA). The system operates along much the same lines as the EGR system and shares many of the same components.

High Altitude Emission Control System
DIESEL ENGINES ONLY

The high altitude emission control system is designed to control the formation of HC and CO emissions and to improve the driveability of the car in high altitude areas. In order to ensure decreased exhaust emissions, the injection timing and EGR tube have to be changed/replaced.

There is an altitude compensator located on top of the injection pump. The altitude shaft is in contact with a pin which is connected to the control lever which is in contact with the governor lever. The higher the altitude, the lower the atmospheric pressure. Due to this fact, the pressure inside the aneroid is higher than that of the atmosphere at high altitudes, which causes the aneroid to expand like a balloon. When this happens, the aneroid shaft is pushed

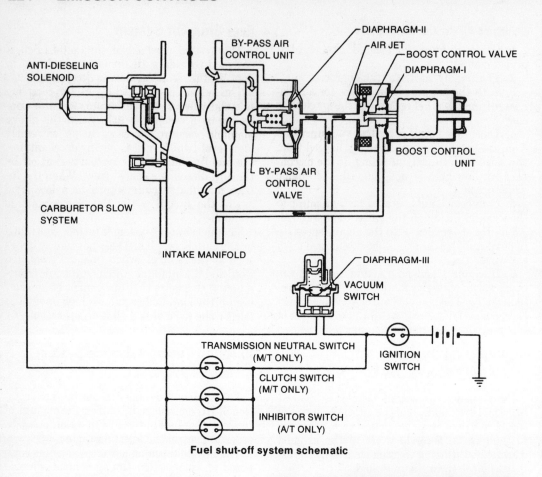

Fuel shut-off system schematic

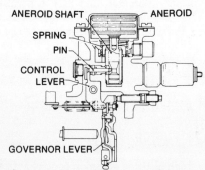

Cross-section of the altitude compensator

Electric choke (arrow)

down, changing the contact surface with the pin, thus decreasing the fuel. Hence, the system controls the amount of fuel supplied in direct proportion to the altitude.

Electric Choke

The purpose of the electric choke, used on all models, except the 810, and Z20E (200XS) covered in this guide is to shorten the time the choke is in operation after the engine is started, thus shortening the time of high HC output.

An electric heater warms the bimetal spring which controls the opening and closing of the choke valve. The heater starts to heat as soon as the engine starts.

Catalytic Converter
GASOLINE ENGINES ONLY

The catalytic converter is a muffler like container built into the exhaust system to aid in the reduction of exhaust emissions. The catalyst element consists of individual pellets or a honeycomb monolithic substrate coated with a noble metal such as platinum, palladium, rhodium or a combination. When the exhaust gases come into contact with the catalyst, a chemical reaction occurs which will reduce the pollutants into harmless substances like water and carbon dioxide.

There are essentially two types of catalytic converters: an oxidizing type is used on all 1975-79 models built for California, all 1980 200SX models, the 49 state version of the 1980 810, and 1980-81 510s. It requires the addition of oxygen to spur the catalyst into reducing the engine's HC and CO emissions into H_2O and CO_2. Because of this need for oxygen, the Air Injection system is used with all these models.

The oxidizing catalytic converter, while effectively reducing HC and CO emissions, does little, if anything in the way of reducing NOx emissions. Thus, the three way catalytic converter.

The three way converter, unlike the oxidizing type, is capable of reducing HC, CO and NOx emissions; all at the same time. In theory, it seems impossible to reduce all three pollutants in one system since the reduction of HC and CO requires the addition of oxygen, while the reduction of NOx calls for the removal of oxygen. In actuality, the three way system really can reduce all three pollutants, but only if the amount of oxygen in the exhaust system is precisely controlled. Due to this precise oxygen control requirement, the three way converter system is used only in cars equipped with an oxygen sensor system: the 1980 810 (Calif.), the 1981-82 810 (all), the 1981 and later 200SX (all), the 1985-89 Maxima and the 1989 240SX models.

1975-78 models (all California models) have a floor temperature warning system, consisting of a temperature sensor installed onto the floor of the car above the converter, a relay, located under the passenger seat, and a light, installed on the instrument panel. The lamp illuminates when floor temperatures become abnormally high, due to converter or engine malfunction. The light also comes on when the ignition switch is turned to Start, to check its operation. 1979 and later models do not have the warning system.

All models with the three way converter have an oxygen sensor warning light on the dashboard, which illuminates at the first 30,000 mile interval, signaling the need for oxygen sensor replacement. The oxygen sensor is part of the Mixture Ratio Feedback System, described in this section. The Feedback System uses the three way converter as one of its major components.

No regular maintenance is required for the catalytic converter system, except for periodic replacement of the Air Induction System filter (if so equipped). The Air Induction System is described earlier in this chapter. Filter replacement procedures are in Chapter 1. The Air Induction System is used to supply the catalytic converter with fresh air. Oxygen present in the air is used in the oxidation process.

PRECAUTIONS

1. Use only unleaded fuel.
2. Avoid prolonged idling. The engine should run on longer than 20 min. at curb idle and no longer than 10 min. at fast idle.
3. Do not disconnect any of the spark plug leads while the engine is running.
4. Make engine compression checks as quickly as possible.

TESTING

At the present time there is no known way to reliably test catalytic converter operation in the field. The only reliable test is a 12 hour and 40 min. soak test (CVS) which must be done in a laboratory.

An infrared HC/CO tester is not sensitive enough to measure the higher tailpipe emissions from a failing converter. Thus, a bad converter may allow enough emissions to escape so that the car is no longer in compliance with Federal or state stands, but will still not cause the needle on a tester to move off zero.

The chemical reactions which occur inside a catalytic converter generate a great deal of heat. Most converter problems can be traced to fuel or ignition system problems which cause unusually high emissions. As a result of the increased intensity of the chemical reactions, the converter literally burns itself up.

A completely failed converter might cause a tester to show a slight reading. as a result, it is occasionally possible to detect one of these.

As long as you avoid severe overheating and the use of leaded fuels it is reasonably safe to assume that the converter is working properly. If you are in doubt, take the car to a diagnostic center that has a tester.

NOTE: *If the catalytic converter becomes blocked the engine will not run. The converter has 5 year or 50,000 mile warranty contact your local Datsun/Nissan dealer for more information.*

Mixture Ratio Feedback System
GASOLINE ENGINES ONLY

The need for better fuel economy coupled to increasingly strict emission control regulations dictates a more exact control of the engine air/

fuel mixture. Datsun/Nissan has developed a Mixture Ratio Feedback System in response to these needs. The system is installed on all 1980 810s sold in California and all 1981 and later 810, Maxima, 200SX and 240SX models.

The principle of the system is to control the air/fuel mixture exactly, so that more complete combustion can occur in the engine, and more thorough oxidation and reduction of the exhaust gases can occur in the catalytic converter. The object is to maintain a stoichiometric air/fuel mixture, which is chemically correct for theoretically complete combustion. The stoichiometric ratio is 14.7:1 (air to fuel). At that point, the converter's efficiency is greatest in oxidizing and reducing HC, CO, and NOx into CO_2, H_2O, O_2, and N_2.

Components used in the system include an oxygen sensor, installed in the exhaust manifold upstream of the converter, a three way oxidation reduction catalytic converter, an electronic control unit, and the fuel injection system itself.

The oxygen sensor reads the oxygen content of the exhaust gases. It generates an electric signal which is sent to the control unit. The control unit then decides how to adjust the mixture to keep it at the correct air/fuel ratio. For example, if the mixture is too lean, the control unit increases the fuel metering to the injectors. The monitoring process is a continual one, so that fine mixture adjustments are going on at all times.

The system has two modes of operation: open loop and closed loop. Open loop operation takes place when the engine is still cold. In this mode, the control unit ignores signals from the oxygen sensor and provides a fixed signal to the fuel injection unit. Closed loop operation takes place when the engine and catalytic converter have warmed to normal operating temperature. In closed loop operation, the control unit uses the oxygen sensor signals to adjust the mixture. The burned mixture's oxygen content is read by the oxygen sensor, which continues to signal the control unit, and so on. Thus, the closed loop mode is an interdependent system of information feedback.

Mixture is, of course, not readily adjustable in this system. All system adjustments require the use of a CO meter. Thus, they should be entrusted to a qualified dealer with access to the equipment and special training in the system's repair. The only regularly scheduled maintenance is replacement of the oxygen sensor at 30,000 mile intervals. This procedure is covered in the following section.

It should be noted that proper operation of the system is entirely dependent on the oxygen sensor. Thus, if the sensor is not replaced at the correct interval, or if the sensor fails during normal operation, the engine fuel mixture will be incorrect, resulting in poor fuel economy, starting problems, or stumbling and stalling of the engine when warm.

Oxygen Sensor
Inspection and Replacement

An exhaust gas sensor warning light will illuminate on the instrument panel when the car has reached 30,000 miles This is a signal that the oxygen sensor must be replaced. It is important to replace the oxygen sensor every 30,000 miles, to ensure proper monitoring and control of the engine air/fuel mixture. Refer to "Maintenance Reminder Lights" section.

The oxygen sensor can be inspected using the following procedure:

1. Start the engine and allow it to reach normal operating temperature.

2. Run the engine at approximately 2,000 rpm under no load. Block the front wheels and set the parking brake.

3. An inspection lamp has been provided on the bottom of the control unit, which is located in the passenger compartment on the driver's side kick panel, next to the clutch or brake pedal. If the oxygen sensor is operating correctly, the inspection lamp will go on and off more than 5 times in 10 seconds (9 times in 10 seconds on 1984 and later 200SX). The inspection lamp can be more easily seen with the aid of a mirror.

4. If the lamp does not go on and off as specified, the system is not operating correctly. Check the battery, ignition system, engine oil and coolant levels, all fuses, the fuel injection wiring harness connectors, all vacuum hoses, the oil filler cap and dipstick for proper seating, and the valve clearance and engine compression. If all of these parts are in good order, and the inspection lamp still does not go on and off at least 5 times in 10 seconds (9 times in 10 seconds on 1984 and later 200SX), the oxygen sen-

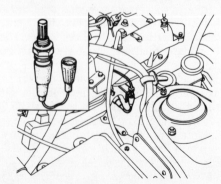

Oxygen sensor location—810 and Maxima

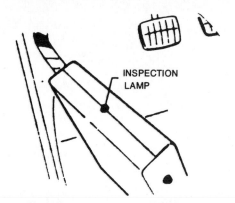

Check the inspection lamp on the bottom of the control panel

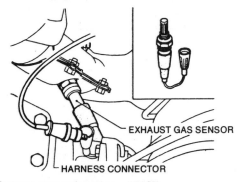

Oxygen sensor location—200SX

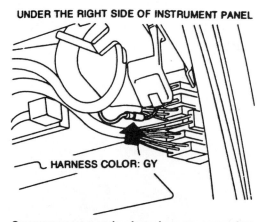

Oxygen sensor warning lamp harness connector—1981–83 200SX

sor is probably faulty. However, the possibility exists that the malfunction could be in the fuel injection control unit. The system should be tested by a qualified dealer with specific training in the Mixture Ratio Feedback System.

To replace the oxygen sensor:

1. Disconnect the negative battery cable and the sensor electrical lead. Unscrew the sensor from the exhaust manifold.

2. Coat the threads of the replacement sensor with a nickel base anti-seize compound. Do not use other types of compounds, since they may electrically insulate the sensor. Do not get compound on sensor housing. Install the sensor into the manifold. Installation torque for the sensor is about 18-25 ft. lbs. on 1988 and later models torque is 30-37 ft. lbs. Connect the electrical lead. Be careful handling the electrical lead. It is easily damaged.

3. Reconnect the battery cable.

The oxygen sensor is installed in the exhaust manifold and is removed in the same manner as a spark plug. Exercise care when handling the sensor do not drop or handle the sensor roughly. Care should be used not to get compound on the sensor itself.

Maintenance Reminder Lights
RESETTING
U.S.A. Models

On models with a sensor relay, reset the relay by pushing or inserting a small screwdriver into the reset hole. Reset relay at 30,000 and 60,000 miles. At 90,000 miles, locate and disconnect warning light wire connector.

On models without sensor light relay and Canada models locate and disconnect the single warning light harness connector. The reminder light will no longer function.

WARNING LIGHT CONNECTOR LOCATIONS

After 30,000 miles on Datsun/Nissan (1981-1983) 200SX Model disconnect a green/green and white stripe wire under the right side of the instrument panel. On (1984) 200SX models disconnect white connector under the right side of the instrument panel. On 810/Maxima models 1982-85 disconnect warning lamp harness connector at the left of the brake pedal.

On 1985-88 200SX vehicles disconnect the warning lamp harness connnector behind the fuse box after 90,000 miles. The sensor relay is located is located to the right of the center console.

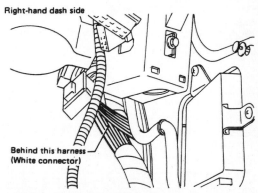

Oxygen sensor warning lamp harness connector 1984 200SX

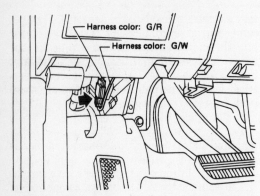

Oxygen sensor warning lamp harness connector
1982–85 810/Maxima

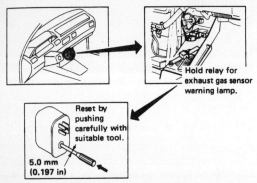

Sensor relay location—1985–88 200SX

Behind fuse box

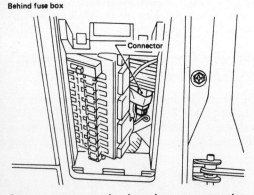

Oxygen sensor warning lamp harness connector—
1985–88 200SX

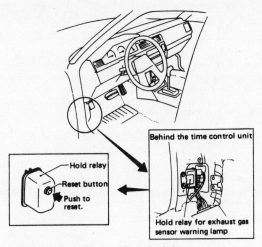

Sensor relay location—1986 Maxima

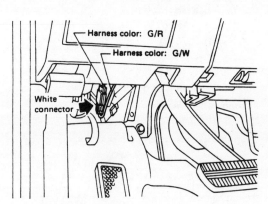

Oxygen sensor warning lamp harness connector—
1986–89 Maxima

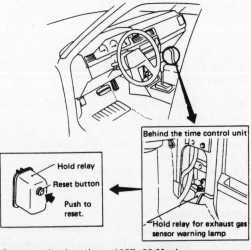

Sensor relay location—1987–89 Maxima

On 1986 Maxima vehicle disconnect the warning lamp harness connnector at the left of the brake pedal, after 90,000 miles. The sensor relay is located is located at the lower left side of the instrument panel.

On 1987-89 Maxima vehicles disconnect the warning lamp harness connnector at the left of the brake pedal, after 90,000 miles. The sensor relay is located at the lower right side of the instrument panel.

Fuel System

5

CARBURETED FUEL SYSTEMS

Mechanical Fuel Pump

REMOVAL AND INSTALLATION

CAUTION: *Never smoke when working around gasoline! Avoid all sources of sparks or ignition. Gasoline vapors are EXTREMELY volatile!*

1. Disconnect the two fuel lines from the fuel pump. Be sure to keep the line leading from the fuel tank up high to prevent the excess loss of fuel.

2. Remove the two fuel pump mounting nuts and remove the fuel pump assembly from the side of the engine.

3. Install the fuel pump in the reverse order of removal, using a new gasket and sealer on the mating surface.

TESTING

CAUTION: *Never smoke when working around gasoline! Avoid all sources of sparks or ignition. Gasoline vapors are EXTREMELY volatile!*

Troubleshooting Basic Fuel System Problems

Problem	Cause	Solution
Engine cranks, but won't start (or is hard to start) when cold	• Empty fuel tank • Incorrect starting procedure • Defective fuel pump • No fuel in carburetor • Clogged fuel filter • Engine flooded • Defective choke	• Check for fuel in tank • Follow correct procedure • Check pump output • Check for fuel in the carburetor • Replace fuel filter • Wait 15 minutes; try again • Check choke plate
Engine cranks, but is hard to start (or does not start) when hot— (presence of fuel is assumed)	• Defective choke	• Check choke plate
Rough idle or engine runs rough	• Dirt or moisture in fuel • Clogged air filter • Faulty fuel pump	• Replace fuel filter • Replace air filter • Check fuel pump output
Engine stalls or hesitates on acceleration	• Dirt or moisture in the fuel • Dirty carburetor • Defective fuel pump • Incorrect float level, defective accelerator pump	• Replace fuel filter • Clean the carburetor • Check fuel pump output • Check carburetor
Poor gas mileage	• Clogged air filter • Dirty carburetor • Defective choke, faulty carburetor adjustment	• Replace air filter • Clean carburetor • Check carburetor
Engine is flooded (won't start accompanied by smell of raw fuel)	• Improperly adjusted choke or carburetor	• Wait 15 minutes and try again, without pumping gas pedal • If it won't start, check carburetor

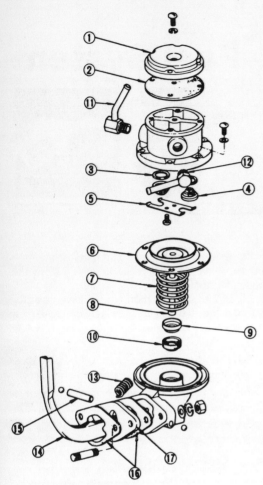

1. Fuel pump cap
2. Cap gasket
3. Valve packing assembly
4. Fuel pump valve assembly
5. Valve retainer
6. Diaphragm assembly
7. Diaphragm spring
8. Pull rod
9. Lower body seal washer
10. Lower body seal
11. Inlet connector
12. Outlet connector
13. Rocker arm spring
14. Rocker arm
15. Rocker arm side pin
16. Fuel pump packing
17. Spacer-fuel pump to cylinder block

Exploded view of the fuel pump—L-series engines

The fuel pump is a mechanically operated, diaphragm type driven by the fuel pump eccentric on the camshaft. Design of the fuel pump permits disassembly, cleaning, and repair or replacement of defective parts. The fuel pump is mounted on the right side of the cylinder block, near the front.

1. Disconnect the line between the carburetor and the pump at the carburetor.

2. Connect a fuel pump pressure gauge on the line.

3. Start the engine. The pressure should be between 3.0 and 3.9 psi. There is usually enough gas in the float bowl to perform this test.

4. If the pressure is ok, perform a capacity test. Remove the gauge from the line. Use a graduated container to catch the gas from the fuel line. Fill the carburetor float bowl with gas. Run the engine for one minute at about 1,000 rpm. The pump should deliver 1,000cc in a minute or less.

Carburetor

The carburetor used is a 2-barrel downdraft type with a low speed (primary) side and a high speed (secondary) side.

All models have an electrically operated anti-dieseling solenoid. As the ignition switch is turned off, the valve is energized and shuts off the supply of fuel to the idle circuit of the carburetor.

ADJUSTMENTS

Throttle Linkage

On all models, make sure the throttle is wide open when the accelerator pedal is floored. Some models have an adjustable accelerator pedal stop to prevent strain on the linkage.

Dashpot

A dashpot is used on carburetor of all cars with automatic transmissions and many late model manual transmission models. The dashpot slowly closes the throttle on automatic transmissions to prevent stalling and serves as an emission control device on all late model vehicles.

The dashpot should be adjusted to contact the throttle lever on deceleration at approximately 1,900-2,100 rpm for automatic transmissions or 1,600-1,800 rpm for automatic transmissions with the L-series engines. The Z20S engine's dashpot contact point should be

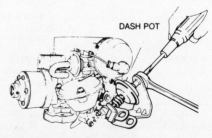

DASH POT

L-series dashpot adjustment

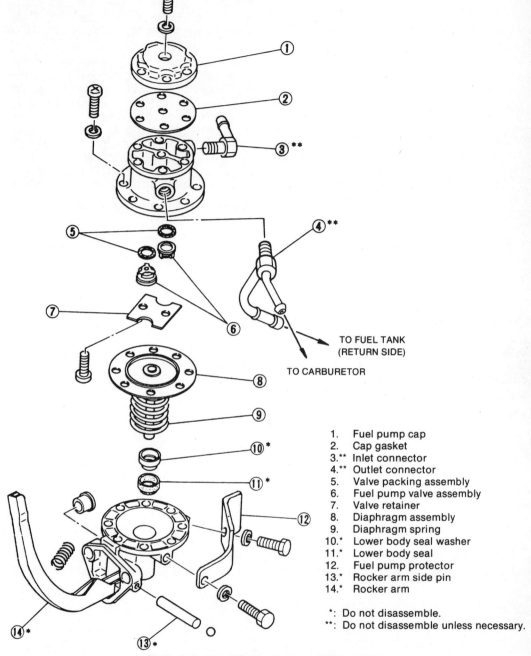

1.   Fuel pump cap
2.   Cap gasket
3.** Inlet connector
4.** Outlet connector
5.   Valve packing assembly
6.   Fuel pump valve assembly
7.   Valve retainer
8.   Diaphragm assembly
9.   Diaphragm spring
10.* Lower body seal washer
11.* Lower body seal
12.   Fuel pump protector
13.* Rocker arm side pin
14.* Rocker arm

*: Do not disassemble.
**: Do not disassemble unless necessary.

TO FUEL TANK
(RETURN SIDE)

TO CARBURETOR

Exploded view of the fuel pump—Z20S engines

between 1,400-1,600 rpm for automatic transmissions.

NOTE: *Before attempting to adjust the dashpot, make sure the idle speed, timing and mixture adjustments are correct.*

Secondary Throttle Linkage

All Datsun/Nissan carburetors discussed in this book are two stage type carburetors. On this type of carburetor, the engine runs on the primary barrel most of the time, with the secondary barrel being used for acceleration purposes. When the throttle valve on the primary side opens to an angle of approximately 50° from its fully closed position, the secondary throttle valve is pulled open by the connecting linkage. The 50° angle of throttle valve opening works out to a clearance measurement of somewhere between 6.5-8.0mm between the throttle valve and the carburetor body. The easiest way

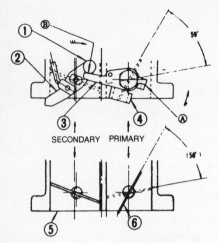

1. Roller
2. Connecting lever
3. Return plate
4. Adjust plate
5. Throttle chamber
6. Throttle valve

Secondary throttle linkage adjustment

to measure this is to use a drill bit. Drill bits from size H to size P (standard letter size drill bits) should fit. Check the appendix in the back of the book for the exact size of the various drill bits. If an adjustment is necessary, bend the connecting link between the two linkage assemblies.

Float Level

The fuel level is normal if it is within the lines on the window glass of the float chamber (or the sight glass) when the vehicle is resting on level ground and the engine is off.

If the fuel level is outside the lines, remove the float housing cover. Have an absorbent cloth under the cover to catch the fuel from the fuel bowl. Adjust the float level by bending the needle seat on the float.

The needle valve should have an effective stroke of about 1.5mm. When necessary, the

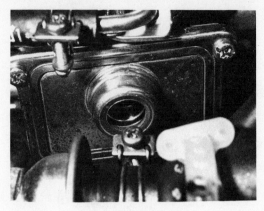

Close-up of float level sight window

needle valve stroke can be adjusted by bending the float stopper.

NOTE: *Be careful not to bend the needle valve rod when installing the float and baffle plate, if removed.*

Fast Idle

1. With the carburetor removed from the vehicle, place the upper side of the fast idle screw on the second step (first step for 1977-81 L and Z engines) of the fast idle cam and measure the clearance between the throttle valve and the wall of the throttle valve chamber at the center of the throttle valve. Check it against the following specifications:

1973-74 610, 1974 710:
- 0.90-1.00mm manual transmission
- 1.10-1.20mm automatic transmission

1975-76 610, 710:
- 1.00-1.20mm manual transmission
- 1.25-1.33mm automatic transmission

1977 710, 1978-79 510, 200SX:
- 0.95-1.15mm manual transmission
- 1.15-1.40mm automatic transmission

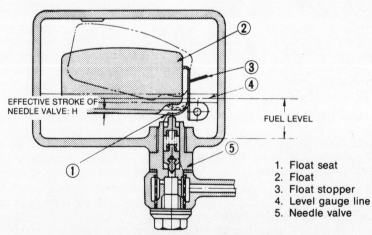

1. Float seat
2. Float
3. Float stopper
4. Level gauge line
5. Needle valve

Z20S, and L-series float level adjustment

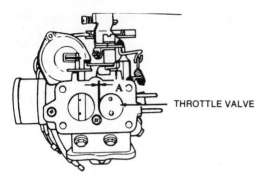

THROTTLE VALVE

FAST IDLE CAM STEPS

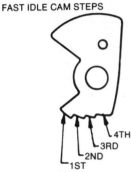

4TH
3RD
2ND
1ST

Fast idle adjustment

1980-81 510:
- 0.75-0.90mm manual transmission
- 0.95-1.10mm automatic transmission

NOTE: *The first step of the fast idle adjustment procedure is not absolutely necessary.*

2. Install the carburetor on the engine.
3. Start the engine and measure the fast idle rpm with the engine at operating temperature. The cam should be at the 2nd step.

1974-76 710, 610:
- MT 1,900-2,100 rpm
- AT 2,300-2,500 rpm

1977 710, 1978-79 510, 200SX:
- manual transmission 1,900-2,800 rpm
- automatic transmission 2,200-3,200 rpm

4. To adjust the fast idle speed, turn the fast idle adjusting screw counterclockwise to increase the fast idle speed and clockwise to decrease the fast idle speed.

Automatic Choke

1. With the engine cold, make sure the choke is fully closed (press the gas pedal all the way to the floor and release).
2. Check the choke linkage for binding. The choke plate should be easily opened and closed with your finger. If the choke sticks or binds, it can usually be freed with a liberal application of a carburetor cleaner made for the purpose. If not, the carburetor will have to be disassembled for repairs.
3. The choke is correctly adjusted when the

index mark on the choke housing (notch) aligns with the center mark on the carburetor body. If the setting is incorrect, loosen the three screws clamping the choke body in place and rotate the choke cover left or right until the marks align. Tighten the screws carefully to avoid cracking the housing.

Choke Unloader

1. Close the choke valve completely.
2. Hold the choke valve closed by stretching a rubber band between the choke piston lever and a stationary part of the carburetor.
3. Open the throttle lever fully.
4. Adjust the gap between the choke plate and the carburetor body to:

L-series engines, 1980-81 Z20S engine:
- 1973-74: 4.4mm
- 1975-77:
    Exc. 710: 2.4mm
    710: 2.05-2.85mm
- 1978-80: 2.05-2.85mm

REMOVAL AND INSTALLATION

1. Remove the air cleaner.
2. Disconnect the electrical connector(s) if so equipped, the fuel and the vacuum hoses from the carburetor.
3. Remove the throttle lever.
4. Remove the four nuts and washers retaining the carburetor to the manifold.
5. Lift the carburetor from the manifold.
6. Remove and discard the gasket used between the carburetor and the manifold.
7. Install carburetor on the manifold, use a new base gasket and torque the carburetor mounting nuts to 9-13 ft. lbs.
8. Install the throttle lever.
9. Connect the electrical connector(s) if so equipped, the fuel and the vacuum hoses to the carburetor.
10. Install the air cleaner.
11. Start engine, warm engine and adjust as necessary.

OVERHAUL

CAUTION: *Never smoke when working around gasoline! Avoid all sources of sparks or ignition. Gasoline vapors are EXTREMELY volatile!*

Efficient carburetion depends greatly on careful cleaning and inspection during overhaul, since dirt, gum, water, or varnish in or on the carburetor parts are often responsible for poor performance.

Overhaul your carburetor in a clean, dustfree area. Carefully disassemble the carburetor, referring often to the exploded views. Keep all similar and look-alike parts segregated during disassembly and cleaning to avoid accidental interchange during assembly. Make a note of all jet sizes.

When the carburetor is disassembled, wash all parts (except diaphragms, electric choke units, pump plunger, and any other plastic, leather, fiber, or rubber parts) in clean carburetor solvent. Do not leave parts in the solvent any longer than is necessary to sufficiently loosen the deposits. Excessive cleaning may remove the special finish from the float bowl and choke valve bodies, leaving these parts unfit for service. Rinse all parts in clean solvent and blow them dry with compressed air to allow them to air dry. Wipe clean all cork, plastic, leather, and fiber parts with a clean, lint-free cloth.

Blow out all passages and jets with compressed air and be sure that there are no restrictions or blockages. Never use wire or similar tools to clean jets, fuel passages, or air

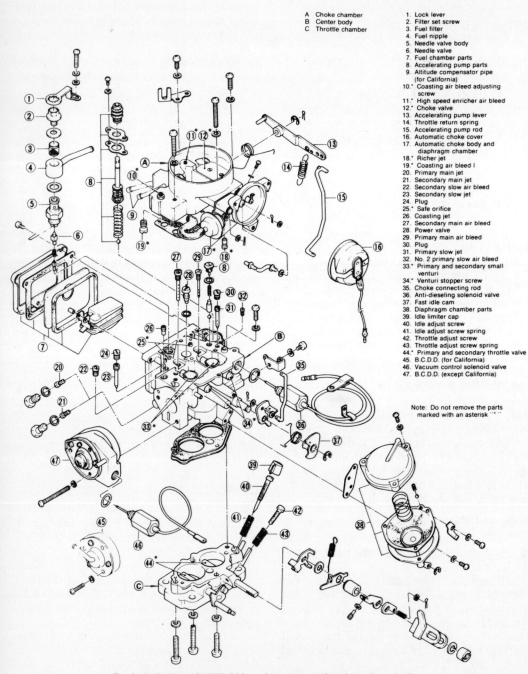

A   Choke chamber
B   Center body
C   Throttle chamber

1. Lock lever
2. Filter set screw
3. Fuel filter
4. Fuel nipple
5. Needle valve body
6. Needle valve
7. Fuel chamber parts
8. Accelerating pump parts
9. Altitude compensator pipe
    (for California)
10.* Coasting air bleed adjusting
    screw
11.* High speed enricher air bleed
12.* Choke valve
13. Accelerating pump lever
14. Throttle return spring
15. Accelerating pump rod
16. Automatic choke cover
17. Automatic choke body and
    diaphragm chamber
18.* Richer jet
19.* Coasting air bleed l
20. Primary main jet
21. Secondary main jet
22. Secondary slow air bleed
23. Secondary slow jet
24. Plug
25.* Safe orifice
26. Coasting jet
27. Secondary main air bleed
28. Power valve
29. Primary main air bleed
30. Plug
31. Primary slow jet
32. No. 2 primary slow air bleed
33.* Primary and secondary small
    venturi
34.* Venturi stopper screw
35. Choke connecting rod
36. Anti-dieseling solenoid valve
37. Fast idle cam
38. Diaphragm chamber parts
39. Idle limiter cap
40. Idle adjust screw
41. Idle adjust screw spring
42. Throttle adjust screw
43. Throttle adjust screw spring
44.* Primary and secondary throttle valve
45. B.C.D.D. (for California)
46. Vacuum control solenoid valve
47. B.C.D.D. (except California)

Note: Do not remove the parts
       marked with an asterisk "* "

Exploded view of 1975 710 carburetor—other L-series similar

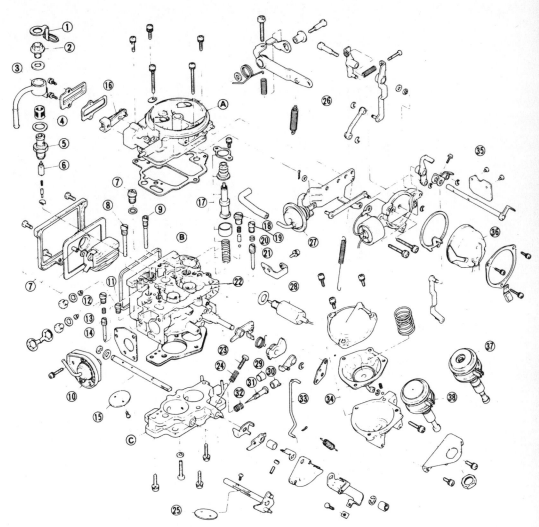

1. Lock lever
2. Filter set screw
3. Fuel nipple
4. Fuel filter
5. Needle valve body
6. Needle valve
7. Power valve
8. Secondary main air bleed
9. Primary main air bleed
10. B.C.D.D.
11. Secondary slow air bleed
12. Secondary main jet
13. Plug
14. Secondary slow jet
15. Primary throttle valve
16. Idle compensator
17. Accelerating pump parts
18. Plug for accelerating mechanism
19. Plug
20. Spring
21. Primary slow jet
22. Primary and secondary small venturi
23. Throttle adjusting screw
24. Throttle adjusting screw spring
25. Secondary throttle valve
26. Accelerating pump lever
27. Vacuum break diaphragm
28. Anti-dieseling solenoid valve
29. Blind plug (California)
30. Idle limiter cap (Except California)
31. Idle adjusting screw
32. Idle adjusting screw spring
33. Choke connecting rod
34. Diaphragm chamber parts
35. Choke valve
36. Automatic choke cover
37. F.I. pot (A/T)
38. F.I.C.D. actuator (M/T air conditioner equipped models only)

Exploded view of 1980 510 (Z20S) engine carburetor

Carburetor Specifications

Year	Engine	Vehicle Model	Carb Model	Main Jet #		Main Air Bleed #		Slow Jet #		Float Level (in.)	Power Jet #
				Primary	Secondary	Primary	Secondary	Primary	Secondary		
1973	L18	610	DCH340-2 ① DCH340-1 ②	97.5	170	65	60	48 ③	90 ③	0.906	53
1974	L18	710	DCH340-10 ① DCH340-11 ②	100	170	60	60	45 ③	90 ③	0.906	41
	L20B	610	DCH340-15 ① DCH340-14 ②	102	170	60	60	46 ③	160 ③	0.906	50
1975	L20B (California)	710	DCH340-41 ① DCH340-42 ②	99	160	70	60	48	80	0.906	43
	L20B (Federal)	710	DCH340-43 ① DCH340-44 ②	97	160	70	60	48	100	0.906	48
1976	L20B (California)	710, 610	DCH340-41A ① DCH340-42B ②	101	160	70	60	48	80	0.906	40
	L20B (Federal)	710, 610	DCH340-43A ① DCH340-44A ②	99	160	70	60	48	100	0.906	43
1977	L20B (California)	710	DCH340-41B ① DCH340-42C ②	101	160	70	60	48	80	0.91	40
	L20B (Federal)	710	DCH340-51A ① DCH340-52A ②	105	165	60	60	48	100	0.91	43
	L20B (California)	200SX	DCH340-49A ① DCH340-50A ②	101	160	70	60	48	80	0.91	43
	L20B (Federal)	200SX	DCH340-53B ① DCH340-54B ②	105	165	60	60	48	100	0.91	43

Year	Model		Carburetor								
1978	L20B (California)	200SX	DCH340-91A ① DCH340-92A ②	102	158	70	60	48	70	0.91	40
	L20B (Federal)	200SX	DCH340-93A ① DCH340-94A ②	104	160	60	60	48	70	0.91	43
	L20B (California)	510	DCH340-99 ① DCH340-92A ②	103 102	158	70	60	48	70	0.91	35 40
	L20B (Federal)	510	DCH340-93A ① DCH340-94A ②	104	160	60	60	48	70	0.91	43
1979	L20B (California)	200SX	DCH340-91C ① DCH340-92C ②	102	158	70	60	48	70	0.91	40
	L20B (Federal)	200SX	DCH340-69 ① DCH340-94B ②	104	160	60	60	48	70	0.91	35 43
	L20B (California)	510	DCH340-99C ① DCH340-92C ②	103 102	158	70	60	48	70	0.91	35 40
	L20B (Fedral)	510	DCH340-69 ① DCH340-94B ②	104	160	60	60	48	70	0.91	35 43
1980	Z20S (California)	510	All	107	170	110	60	47	100	0.91	35
	Z20S (Federal)	510	All	99	166	90	60	47	100	0.91	40
1981	Z20S (California)	510	All	112	155	90	60	47	100	0.91	35 ④
	Z20S (Federal)	510	All	112	155	90	60	47	100	0.91	35

① Manual Transmission
② Automatic Transmission
③ Slow jet air bleed: Primary #145, Secondary #100
④ Models with A/T: #45

bleeds. Clean all jets and valves separately to avoid accidental interchange.

Check all parts for wear or damage. If wear or damage is found, replace the defective parts. Especially check the following:

1. Check the float needle and seat for wear. If wear is found, replace the complete assembly.

2. Check the float hinge pin for wear and the float(s) for dents or distortion. Replace the float if fuel has leaked into it.

3. Check the throttle and choke shaft bores for wear or an out-of-round condition. Damage or wear to the throttle arm, shaft, or shaft bore will often require replacement of the throttle body. These parts require a close tolerance of fit. Wear may allow air leakage, which could affect starting and idling.

NOTE: *Throttle shafts and bushings are not included in overhaul kits. They can be purchased separately.*

4. Inspect the idle mixture adjusting needles for burrs or grooves. Any such condition requires replacement of the needle, since you will not be able to obtain a satisfactory idle.

5. Text the accelerator pump check valves. They should pass air one way but not the other. Test for proper seating by blowing and sucking on the valve. Replace the valve if necessary. If the valve is satisfactory, wash the valve again to remove breath moisture.

6. Check the bowl cover for warped surfaces with a straightedge.

7. Closely inspect the valves and seats for wear and damage, replacing as necessary.

8. After the carburetor is assembled, check the choke valve for freedom of operation.

Carburetor overhaul kits are recommended for each overhaul. These kits contain all gaskets and new parts to replace those that deteriorate most rapidly. Failure to replace all parts supplied with the kit (especially gaskets) can result in poor performance later.

Some carburetor manufacturers supply overhaul kits of three basic types: minor repair, major repair, and gasket kits. Basically, they contain the following:

Minor Repair Kits:
- All gaskets
- Float needle valve
- Volume control screw
- All diaphragms
- Spring for the pump diaphragm

Major Repair Kits:
- All jets and gaskets
- All diaphragms
- Float needle valve
- Volume control screw
- Pump ball valve
- Main jet carrier
- Float

Gasket Kits:
- All gaskets

After cleaning and checking all components, reassemble the carburetor, using new parts and referring to the exploded view. When reassembling, make sure that all screws and jets are tight in their seats, but do not overtighten as the tips will be distorted. Tighten all screws gradually in rotation. Do not tighten needle valves into their seats; uneven jetting will result. Always use new gaskets. Be sure to adjust the float level when reassembling.

GASOLINE FUEL INJECTION SYSTEM

NOTE: *This book contains basic testing and service procedures for your car's fuel injection system. More comprehensive testing and diagnosis procedures may be found in CHILTON'S GUIDE TO FUEL INJECTION AND FEEDBACK CARBURETORS, book No. 7488, available at your local retailer.*

The electronic fuel injection (EFI) system uses various types of sensors to convert engine operating conditions into electronic signals. This generated information is fed to a control unit, where it is analyzed, then calculated electrical signals are then sent to various equipment, to control idle speed, timing and amount of fuel being injected into the engine.

For the most part, diagnosing and testing the system is a very difficult job requiring specialized training and equipment. It should be left to a highly qualified professional.

Electric Fuel Pump
REMOVAL AND INSTALLATION
External Mount Electric Pump

1. Before disconnecting the fuel lines or any of the fuel system components, refer to Fuel Pressure Release procedures and release the fuel pressure. Reducing the fuel pressure to zero is a very important step for correct removal of the electric fuel pump. See Fuel Pressure Release procedures in this section.

2. Disconnect the electrical harness connector at the pump. The 810/Maxima (rear wheel drive) pump is located near the fuel tank. The 200SX pump is located near the center of the car, except on 1984 200SX, on which the pump is located on the fuel tank.

3. Clamp the hose between the fuel tank and the pump to prevent gas from spewing out from the tank.

4. Remove the inlet and outlet hoses at the

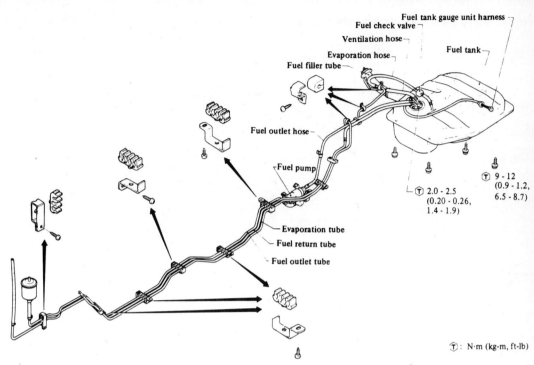

Typical external mounted fuel pump

pump. Unclamp the inlet hose and allow the fuel lines to drain into a suitable container.

5. Unbolt and remove the pump. The 200SX pump and fuel damper can be removed at the same time.

6. Install the fuel pump in the correct position. Reconnect all hoses. Use new clamps and be sure all hoses are properly seated on the fuel pump body.

7. Reconnect the electrical harness connec-

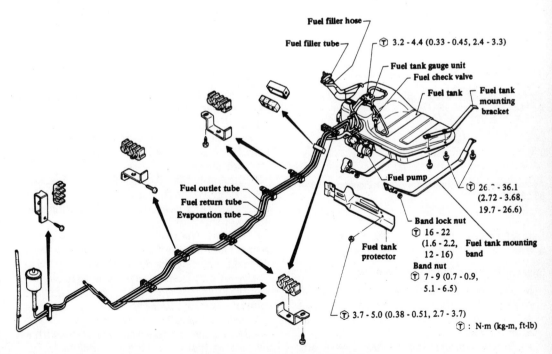

Typical external mounted fuel pump

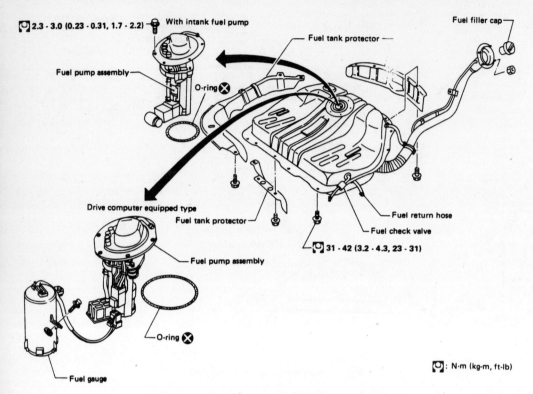

2.3 - 3.0 (0.23 - 0.31, 1.7 - 2.2)   With intank fuel pump

Fuel filler cap

Fuel pump assembly

Fuel tank protector

O-ring ✖

Drive computer equipped type
Fuel tank protector

Fuel pump assembly

Fuel return hose

Fuel check valve

31 - 42 (3.2 - 4.3, 23 - 31)

Fuel gauge

O-ring ✖

: N·m (kg-m, ft-lb)

Late model Maxima/in-tank fuel pump assembly

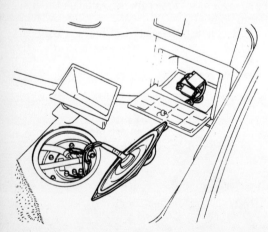

Access plate and electrical connector location—1984–88 200SX

tor at the pump. Start engine and check for fuel leaks.

Internal Mount (In-Tank) Electric Pump

NOTE: *On Maxima (front wheel drive) models 1985-89, 200SX models 1984-88 and 240SX 1989 models the fuel pump is mounted in the fuel tank.*

1. Before disconnecting the fuel lines or any of the fuel system components, refer to Fuel

Pressure Release procedures and release the fuel pressure. Reducing the fuel pressure to zero is a very important step for correct removal of the electric fuel pump. See Fuel Pressure Release procedures in this section.

2. Disconnect the negative battery cable. Open the trunk lid, disconnect the fuel gauge electrical connector and remove the fuel tank inspection cover.

NOTE: *If vehicle has no fuel tank inspection cover the fuel tank must be lowered or removed to gain access to the in-tank fuel pump. See illustration of access plate and electrical connector location for the 200SX model.*

3. Disconnect the fuel outlet and the return hoses. Remove the fuel tank if necessary. Refer to the Fuel Tank Removal And Installation procedure in this section.

4. Remove the ring retaining bolts and the O-ring, then lift the fuel pump assembly from the fuel tank. Plug the opening with a clean rag to prevent dirt from entering the system.

NOTE: *When removing or installing the fuel pump assembly, be careful not to damage or deform it. Install a new O-ring.*

5. Install fuel pump assembly in tank with a new O-ring. Install the ring retaining bolts. Install the fuel tank if removed, refer to the Fuel

Tank Removal And Installation procedure in this section.

6. Reconnect the fuel lines and the electrical connection.

7. Install the fuel tank inspection cover.

8. Connect battery cable, start engine and check for fuel leaks.

NOTE: *On some late models the "Check Engine Light" will stay on after installation is completed. The memory code in the control unit must be erased. To erase the code disconnect the battery cable for 10 seconds then reconnect after installation of fuel pump.*

TESTING

1. Release the fuel pressure. Connect a fuel pressure gauge between the fuel filter outlet and fuel feed pipe.

2. Start the engine and read the pressure. All models except the 240SX, it should be 30 psi at

idle, and 37 psi at the moment the accelerator pedal is fully depressed. On the 240SX model the pressure should be 33 psi at idle.

NOTE: *Make sure that the fuel filter is not blocked before replacing any fuel system components.*

3. If pressure is not as specified, replace the pressure regulator and repeat the test. If the pressure is still incorrect, check for clogged or deformed fuel lines, then replace the fuel pump.

FUEL PRESSURE RELEASE PROCEDURE

CAUTION: *Never smoke when working around gasoline! Avoid all sources of sparks or ignition. Gasoline vapors are EXTREMELY volatile!*

Any time the fuel system is being worked on always keep a dry chemical (Class B) fire extinguisher near the work area.

1. Remove the fuel pump fuse from the fuse

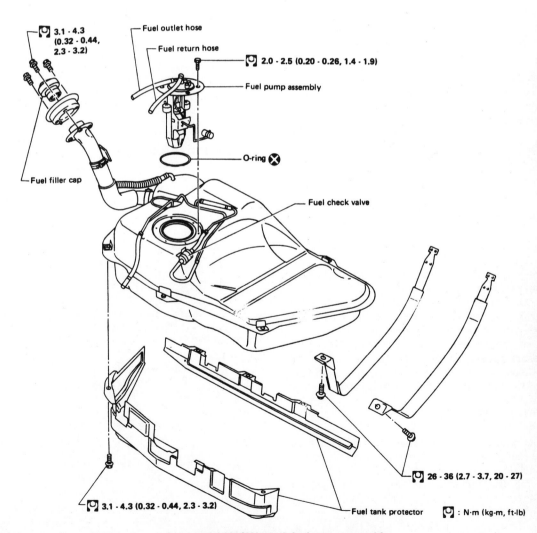

Late model 200SX/in-tank fuel pump assembly

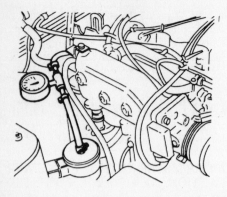

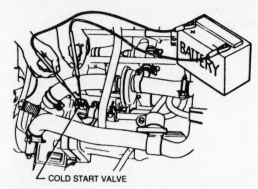

Releasing pressure at the cold start valve—810 and Maxima

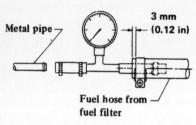

Typical installation of fuel pressure test gauge

TOOL BOX (REAR RIGHT-HAND SIDE)

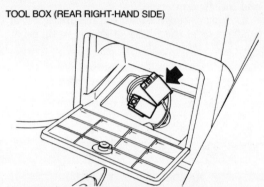

Unplug the connectors before releasing fuel pressure on the 1984 and later 200SX

block, fuel pump relay or disconnect the harness connector at the tank while engine is running.

2. It should run and then stall when the fuel in the lines is exhausted. When the engine stops, crank the starter for about 5 seconds to make sure all pressure in the fuel lines is released.

3. Install the fuel pump fuse, relay or harness connector after repair is made.

4. On some late models the "Check Engine Light" will stay on after test has been completed. The memory code in the control unit must be erased. To erase the code disconnect the battery cable for 10 seconds then reconnect.

On 1977-79 810, disconnect the ground cable from the battery. Disconnect the cold start valve wiring harness at the connector. Connect two jumper wires to the terminals of the cold start valve. Touch the other ends of the jumpers to the positive and negative terminals of the battery for a few seconds to release the pressure.

For 1980-84 810, Maxima and 200SX start the engine, disconnect the harness connector of fuel pump relay 2 except on 1984-89 200SX on these models, disconnect the connector in the tool box in the rear right hand side of the car) while the engine is running. On the 1985-89 Maxima and 1989 240SX remove the fuel pump fuse. After the engine stalls, crank it over two or three times to make sure all of the fuel pressure is released.

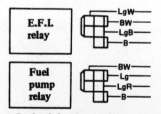

Both of the above relays are green, but can be distinguished by the color of harness.

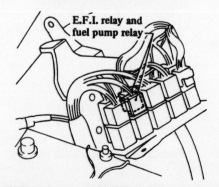

Fuel pump relay—1984 Maxima

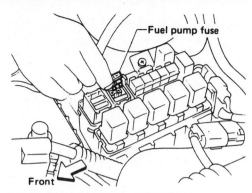

Fuel pump fuse location—1989 240SX

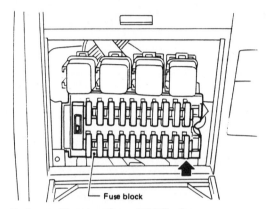

Fuel pump fuse location—1986 Maxima

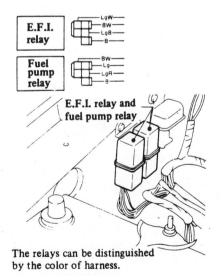

The relays can be distinguished by the color of harness.

Fuel pump relay—1982 200SX—others similar

Throttle Body/Chamber

REMOVAL AND INSTALLATION

CAUTION: *Never smoke when working around gasoline! Avoid all sources of sparks or ignition. Gasoline vapors are EXTREMELY volatile!*

1. Disconnect the negative battery cable and remove the intake duct from the throttle chamber.

2. Disconnect the vacuum hoses and the electrical harness connector from the throttle chamber. Disconnect the accelerator cable from the throttle chamber.

3. Remove the mounting bolts and the throttle chamber from the intake manifold.

4. To install, use a new gasket and reverse the removal procedures. Torque the throttle chamber bolts to 13-16 ft. lbs. Adjust the throttle cable if necessary.

Check the throttle for smooth operation and make sure the by-pass port is free from obstacles and is clean. Check to make sure the idle speed adjusting screw moves smoothly.

Do not touch the EGR vacuum port screw or, on some later models, the throttle valve stopper screw, as they are factory adjusted.

Because of the sensitivity of the air flow meter, there cannot be any air leaks in the fuel system. Even the smallest leak could unbalance the system and affect the performance of the automobile.

During every check pay attention to hose connections, dipstick and oil filler cap for evidence of air leaks. Should you encounter any, take steps to correct the problem.

Fuel Injectors

REMOVAL AND INSTALLATION

Z-Series 4-Cylinder Engines

NOTE: *Review the entire procedure before starting this repair.*

1. Release fuel pressure by following the correct procedure. Refer to Fuel Pressure Release Procedure.

2. Disconnect the negative battery cable and the accelerator cable.

3. Disconnect the injector harness connector.

4. Tag and disconnect the vacuum hose at the fuel pipe connection end. Disconnect the air regulator and its harness connector, and tag and disconnect any other hoses that may hinder removal of the injection assembly.

5. Disconnect the fuel feed hose and fuel return hose from the fuel pipe.

NOTE: *Place a rag under the fuel pipe to prevent splashing of the fuel.*

6. Remove the vacuum hose connecting the pressure regulator to the intake manifold.

7. Remove the bolts securing the fuel pipe and pressure regulator.

8. Remove the screws securing the fuel injectors. Remove the fuel pipe assembly, by pulling

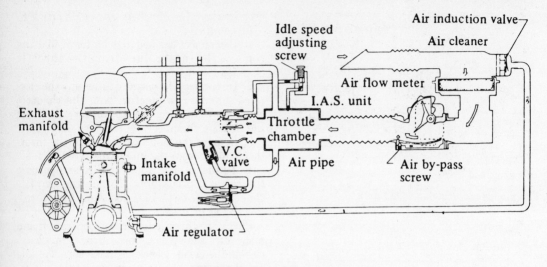

1980 200SX fuel injection system

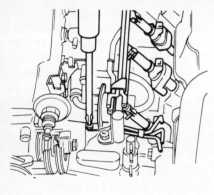

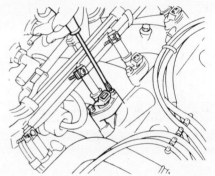

Removing the injector securing screws, all models similar

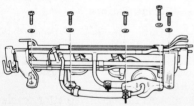

Top: Removing the Z-series fuel pressure regulator-to-fuel pipe screws. Bottom: Fuel pipe assembly securing screws

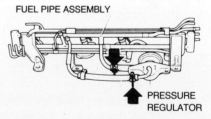

FUEL PIPE ASSEMBLY

PRESSURE REGULATOR

Fuel pressure regulator location and connections, all models similar

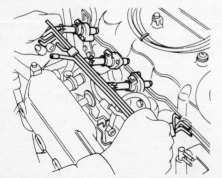

Removing the fuel pipe and injector assembly, Z-series engines

out the fuel pipe, injectors and pressure regulator as an assembly.

9. Unfasten the hose clamp on the injectors and remove the injectors from the fuel pipe.

10. Install the fuel injectors in the fuel pipe with new hose clamps.

11. Install the fuel pipe assembly, injectors with new O-rings and pressure regulator as an assembly.

12. Connect the fuel feed hose and fuel return hose to the fuel pipe. Use new hose clamps on

all connections. Reconnect all vacuum hoses and electrical connections.

13. Reconnect the accelerator cable and battery cable. Note the following:

a. When installing the injectors, check that there are no scratches or abrasion at the lower rubber insulator, and securely install it, making sure it is air-tight.

b. When installing the fuel hose, make sure the hose end is inserted onto the metal pipe until the end contacts the unit, as far as it will go. Push the end of the injector rubber hose onto the fuel pipe until it is 25mm from the end of the pipe.

c. Never reuse hose clamps on the injection system. Always renew the clamps. When tightening clamps, make sure the screw does not come in contact with adjacent parts.

14. Start the engine and check for fuel leaks.

L-Series 6-Cylinder Engines

1. Release fuel pressure by following the correct procedure. Refer to Fuel Pressure Release Procedure. Disconnect the negative battery cable.

2. Disconnect the electric connector from the injector and cold start valve.

3. Disengage the harness from the fuel pipe wire clamp.

4. Disconnect the blow-by hose at the side of the rocker cover.

5. Disconnect the vacuum tube, which connects the pressure regulator to the intake manifold, from the pressure regulator.

6. Remove the air regulator pipe.

7. Disconnect the fuel feed hose and fuel return hose from the fuel pipe.

NOTE: *Place a rag underneath the fuel pipe to catch fuel spillage.*

8. Remove the bolts securing the fuel pipe and cold start valve. Remove the screws securing the fuel injectors.

9. Remove the fuel pipe assembly by pulling out the fuel pipe, injectors, pressure regulator and cold start valve as an assembly.

10. Unfasten the hose clamp on the injectors and remove the injectors from the fuel pipe.

11. Install the fuel injectors in the fuel pipe with a new hose clamps.

12. Install the fuel pipe assembly, injectors with new O-rings, pressure regulator and cold start valve as an assembly.

13. Connect the fuel feed hose and fuel return hose to the fuel pipe. Always use new hose clamps.

14. Install the air regulator pipe.

15. Reconnect the vacuum tube to the pressure regulator. The vacuum tube connects the pressure regulator to the intake manifold.

16. Connect the blow-by hose to the side of the rocker cover. Reconnect all vacuum hoses if removed and all electrical connections.

17. Reconnect the battery cable. Start the engine and check for fuel leaks.

CA-series 4-Cylinder Engines

1. Release fuel pressure by following the correct procedure. Refer to Fuel Pressure Release Procedure. Disconnect the negative battery cable.

2. On the CA20E engine, drain the engine coolant. Disconnect the fuel injection wiring harness, the ignition wires, and remove the collector with the throttle chamber. Tag and disconnect all related hoses.

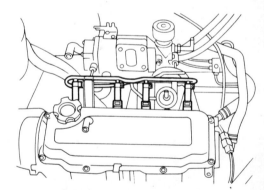

CA20E/CA18ET injector assembly location

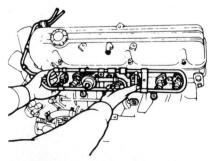

Removing the injector/fuel pipe assembly from the L24 six cylinder

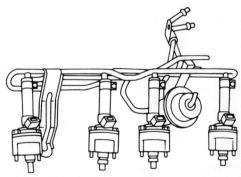

CA20E, CA18ET injector assembly including fuel pressure regulator

3. On the CA18ET engine, disconnect the air intake pipe, the fuel injection wiring harness, the ignition wires and accelerator cable. Remove the throttle chamber.

4. On all engines, disconnect the fuel hoses and pressure regulator vacuum hoses.

5. Remove the fuel injectors with the fuel rail assembly.

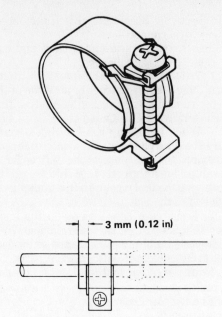

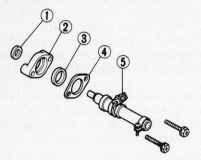

Typical fuel injector and related mounting hardware. When replacing injector, always replace the lower rubber insulator (1) and the upper rubber insulator (3)

— 3 mm (0.12 in)

Always renew the hose clamps. Note proper installation

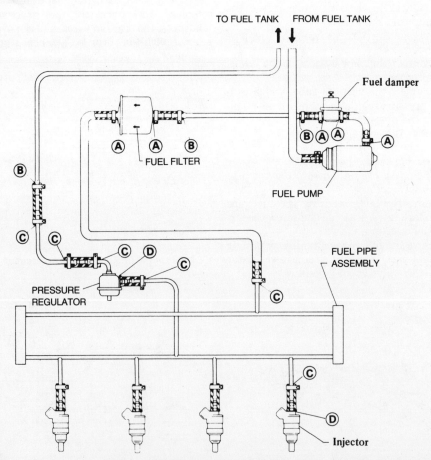

Typical fuel injection hose connections. Note proper hose installation. L24E engines similar except have six injectors

6. Remove the fuel injector hose-to-fuel rail clamp(s), then pull the injector from the fuel rail.

7. To remove the fuel hose from the injector, use a hot soldering iron, then cut (melt) a line in the fuel hose (to the braided reinforcement), starting at the injector socket to ¾" long. Remove the hose from the injector, by hand.

NOTE: *DO NOT allow the soldering iron to cut all the way through the hose, nor touch the injector seat or damage the plastic socket connector.*

8. To install a new fuel hose, clean the injector tail section, wet the inside of the new hose with fuel, push the hose into the fuel injector hose socket (as far as it will go) retain it with a new hose clamp if necessary. Assemble the injector(s) onto the fuel rail.

9. Install the injectors with new O-rings and fuel rail as an assembly.

10. Connect the fuel hoses and pressure regulator vacuum hoses.

11. On the CA18ET engine, connect the air intake pipe, the fuel injection wiring harness, the ignition wires and accelerator cable. Install the throttle chamber.

12. On the CA20E engine, reconnect the fuel injection wiring harness, the ignition wires, and install the collector with the throttle chamber.

Reconnect all related hoses and refill the cooling system.

13. Reconnect the battery cable. Start the engine and check for fuel leaks.

VG30 Engine

1. Release fuel pressure by following the correct procedure. Refer to Fuel Pressure Release Procedure. Disconnect the negative battery cable.

2. Disconnect these items at the intake collector: the air inatke duct; accelerator linkage; PCV hose; air regulator pressure hose; B.C.D.D. hose; fuel hoses; E.G.R tube; wiring harness clamps; wiring harness connectors; intake collector cover. Then, drain some coolant out of the cooling system and disconnect the coolant hoses connecting into the collector.

3. Remove the intake collector assembly.

4. Remove the bolts securing the fuel tube.

5. Remove the bolts securing the injectors and remove the injectors, fuel tubes, and pressure regulator as an assembly.

6. To remove the fuel hoses, heat a sharp knife until it is hot. Cut into the braided reinforcement from the mark on the hose to the end of the fuel tube connection.

NOTE: *Make sure the knife does not cut all*

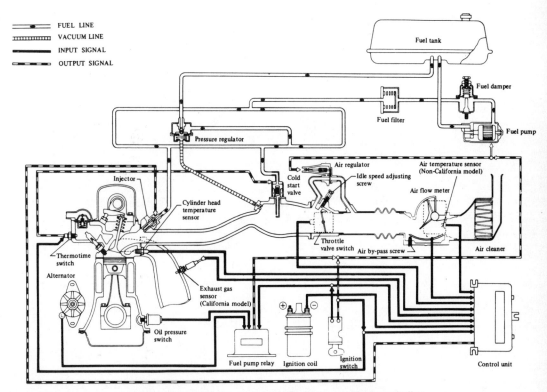

1980 810 fuel injection system. Later 810s and Maxima similar

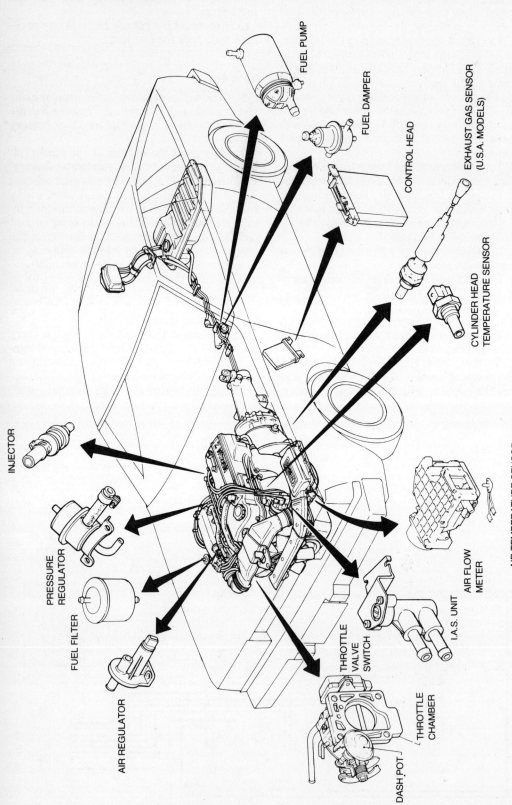

INJECTOR

FUEL PUMP

FUEL DAMPER

CONTROL HEAD

EXHAUST GAS SENSOR
(U.S.A. MODELS)

CYLINDER HEAD
TEMPERATURE SENSOR

PRESSURE
REGULATOR

FUEL FILTER

AIR REGULATOR

THROTTLE
VALVE
SWITCH

THROTTLE
CHAMBER

DASH POT

I.A.S. UNIT

AIR FLOW
METER

AIR TEMPERATURE SENSOR

1983 200SX fuel system component locations

the way through the hose and nick the injector tail piece or connector fitting.

7. Pull the hose off of the injectors. DO NOT install the injectors in a vise to hold them as you pull off the hoses.

8. To install new hose, clean the exterior of the injector tail piece and the end of the fuel tube with a safe solvent. Then, wet the inside diameter of the new hose with fuel. Push the ends of the hoses and fittings onto the injector

tail piece and the end of the fuel tube as far as they will go by hand, retain it with a new hose clamp if necessary

9. Assemble the injector(s) onto the fuel rail. Install the injectors with new O-rings and fuel rail as an assembly.

10. Install the intake collector assembly.

11. Connect the air intake duct; accelerator linkage; PCV hose; air regulator pressure hose; B.C.D.D. hose; fuel hoses; E.G.R tube; wiring

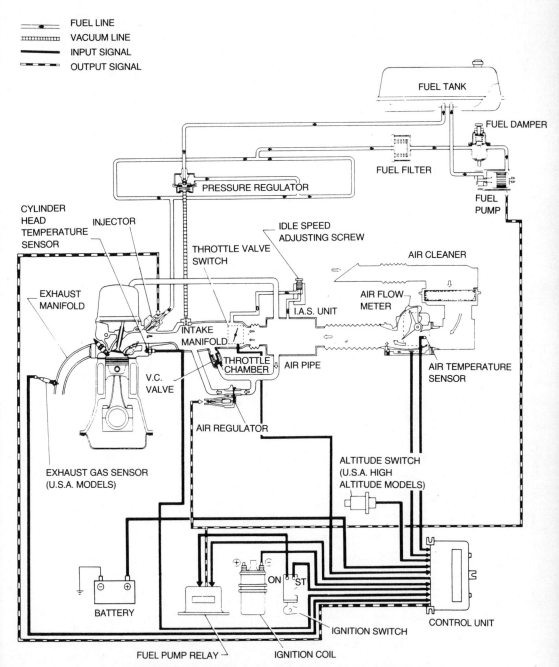

Z22 series fuel, air flow and ignition schematic, 1983 200SX shown

CA20E fuel and vacuum schematic

CHILTON'S
FUEL ECONOMY
& TUNE-UP TIPS

55 WAYS TO IMPROVE FUEL ECONOMY

Tune-up • Spark Plug Diagnosis • Emission Controls

Fuel System • Cooling System • Tires and Wheels

General Maintenance

CHILTON'S FUEL ECONOMY & TUNE-UP TIPS

Fuel economy is important to everyone, no matter what kind of vehicle you drive. The maintenance-minded motorist can save both money and fuel using these tips and the periodic maintenance and tune-up procedures in this Repair and Tune-Up Guide.

There are more than 130,000,000 cars and trucks registered for private use in the United States. Each travels an average of 10-12,000 miles per year, and, and in total they consume close to 70 billion gallons of fuel each year. This represents nearly ⅔ of the oil imported by the United States each year. The Federal government's goal is to reduce consumption 10% by 1985. A variety of methods are either already in use or under serious consideration, and they all affect you driving and the cars you will drive. In addition to "down-sizing", the auto industry is using or investigating the use of electronic fuel delivery, electronic engine controls and alternative engines for use in smaller and lighter vehicles, among other alternatives to meet the federally mandated Corporate Average Fuel Economy (CAFE) of 27.5 mpg by 1985. The government, for its part, is considering rationing, mandatory driving curtailments and tax increases on motor vehicle fuel in an effort to reduce consumption. The government's goal of a 10% reduction could be realized — and further government regulation avoided — if every private vehicle could use just 1 less gallon of fuel per week.

How Much Can You Save?

Tests have proven that almost anyone can make at least a 10% reduction in fuel consumption through regular maintenance and tune-ups. When a major manufacturer of spark plugs sur-

TUNE-UP

1. Check the cylinder compression to be sure the engine will really benefit from a tune-up and that it is capable of producing good fuel economy. A tune-up will be wasted on an engine in poor mechanical condition.

2. Replace spark plugs regularly. New spark plugs alone can increase fuel economy 3%.

3. Be sure the spark plugs are the correct type (heat range) for your vehicle. See the Tune-Up Specifications.

Heat range refers to the spark plug's ability to conduct heat away from the firing end. It must conduct the heat away in an even pattern to avoid becoming a source of pre-ignition, yet it must also operate hot enough to burn off conductive deposits that could cause misfiring.

The heat range is usually indicated by a number on the spark plug, part of the manufacturer's designation for each individual spark plug. The numbers in bold-face indicate the heat range in each manufacturer's identification system.

Manufacturer	Typical Designation
AC	R **45** TS
Bosch (old)	WA **145** T30
Bosch (new)	HR **8** Y
Champion	RBL **15** Y
Fram/Autolite	**415**
Mopar	P-**62** PR
Motorcraft	BRF-**42**
NGK	BP **5** ES-15
Nippondenso	W **16** EP
Prestolite	14GR **5** 2A

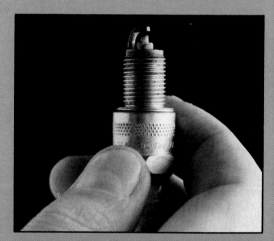

Periodically, check the spark plugs to be sure they are firing efficiently. They are excellent indicators of the internal condition of your engine.

On AC, Bosch (new), Champion, Fram/Autolite, Mopar, Motorcraft and Prestolite, a higher number indicates a hotter plug. On Bosch (old), NGK and Nippondenso, a higher number indicates a colder plug.

4. Make sure the spark plugs are properly gapped. See the Tune-Up Specifications in this book.

5. Be sure the spark plugs are firing efficiently. The illustrations on the next 2 pages show you how to "read" the firing end of the spark plug.

6. Check the ignition timing and set it to specifications. Tests show that almost all cars have incorrect ignition timing by more than 2°.

veyed over 6,000 cars nationwide, they found that a tune-up, on cars that needed one, increased fuel economy over 11%. Replacing worn plugs alone, accounted for a 3% increase. The same test also revealed that 8 out of every 10 vehicles will have some maintenance deficiency that will directly affect fuel economy, emissions or performance. Most of this mileage-robbing neglect could be prevented with regular maintenance.

Modern engines require that all of the functioning systems operate properly for maximum efficiency. A malfunction anywhere wastes fuel. You can keep your vehicle running as efficiently and economically as possible, by being aware of your vehicle's operating and performance characteristics. If your vehicle suddenly develops performance or fuel economy problems it could be due to one or more of the following:

PROBLEM	POSSIBLE CAUSE
Engine Idles Rough	Ignition timing, idle mixture, vacuum leak or something amiss in the emission control system.
Hesitates on Acceleration	Dirty carburetor or fuel filter, improper accelerator pump setting, ignition timing or fouled spark plugs.
Starts Hard or Fails to Start	Worn spark plugs, improperly set automatic choke, ice (or water) in fuel system.
Stalls Frequently	Automatic choke improperly adjusted and possible dirty air filter or fuel filter.
Performs Sluggishly	Worn spark plugs, dirty fuel or air filter, ignition timing or automatic choke out of adjustment.

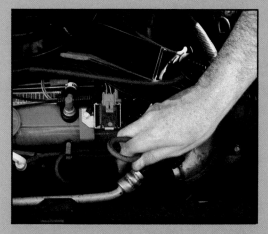

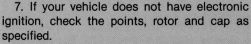

Check spark plug wires on conventional point type ignition for cracks by bending them in a loop around your finger.

Be sure that spark plug wires leading to adjacent cylinders do not run too close together. (Photo courtesy Champion Spark Plug Co.)

7. If your vehicle does not have electronic ignition, check the points, rotor and cap as specified.

8. Check the spark plug wires (used with conventional point-type ignitions) for cracks and burned or broken insulation by bending them in a loop around your finger. Cracked wires decrease fuel efficiency by failing to deliver full voltage to the spark plugs. One misfiring spark plug can cost you as much as 2 mpg.

9. Check the routing of the plug wires. Misfiring can be the result of spark plug leads to adjacent cylinders running parallel to each other and too close together. One wire tends to pick up voltage from the other causing it to fire "out of time".

10. Check all electrical and ignition circuits for voltage drop and resistance.

11. Check the distributor mechanical and/or vacuum advance mechanisms for proper functioning. The vacuum advance can be checked by twisting the distributor plate in the opposite direction of rotation. It should spring back when released.

12. Check and adjust the valve clearance on engines with mechanical lifters. The clearance should be slightly loose rather than too tight.

SPARK PLUG DIAGNOSIS

Normal

APPEARANCE: This plug is typical of one operating normally. The insulator nose varies from a light tan to grayish color with slight electrode wear. The presence of slight deposits is normal on used plugs and will have no adverse effect on engine performance. The spark plug heat range is correct for the engine and the engine is running normally.

CAUSE: Properly running engine.

RECOMMENDATION: Before reinstalling this plug, the electrodes should be cleaned and filed square. Set the gap to specifications. If the plug has been in service for more than 10-12,000 miles, the entire set should probably be replaced with a fresh set of the same heat range.

Oil Deposits

APPEARANCE: The firing end of the plug is covered with a wet, oily coating.

CAUSE: The problem is poor oil control. On high mileage engines, oil is leaking past the rings or valve guides into the combustion chamber. A common cause is also a plugged PCV valve, and a ruptured fuel pump diaphragm can also cause this condition. Oil fouled plugs such as these are often found in new or recently overhauled engines, before normal oil control is achieved, and can be cleaned and reinstalled.

RECOMMENDATION: A hotter spark plug may temporarily relieve the problem, but the engine is probably in need of work.

Incorrect Heat Range

APPEARANCE: The effects of high temperature on a spark plug are indicated by clean white, often blistered insulator. This can also be accompanied by excessive wear of the electrode, and the absence of deposits.

CAUSE: Check for the correct spark plug heat range. A plug which is too hot for the engine can result in overheating. A car operated mostly at high speeds can require a colder plug. Also check ignition timing, cooling system level, fuel mixture and leaking intake manifold.

RECOMMENDATION: If all ignition and engine adjustments are known to be correct, and no other malfunction exists, install spark plugs one heat range colder.

Photos Courtesy Fram Corporation

Carbon Deposits

APPEARANCE: Carbon fouling is easily identified by the presence of dry, soft, black, sooty deposits.

CAUSE: Changing the heat range can often lead to carbon fouling, as can prolonged slow, stop-and-start driving. If the heat range is correct, carbon fouling can be attributed to a rich fuel mixture, sticking choke, clogged air cleaner, worn breaker points, retarded timing or low compression. If only one or two plugs are carbon fouled, check for corroded or cracked wires on the affected plugs. Also look for cracks in the distributor cap between the towers of affected cylinders.

RECOMMENDATION: After the problem is corrected, these plugs can be cleaned and reinstalled if not worn severely.

MMT Fouled

APPEARANCE: Spark plugs fouled by MMT (Methycyclopentadienyl Maganese Tricarbonyl) have reddish, rusty appearance on the insulator and side electrode.

CAUSE: MMT is an anti-knock additive in gasoline used to replace lead. During the combustion process, the MMT leaves a reddish deposit on the insulator and side electrode.

RECOMMENDATION: No engine malfunction is indicated and the deposits will not affect plug performance any more than lead deposits (see Ash Deposits). MMT fouled plugs can be cleaned, regapped and reinstalled.

High Speed Glazing

APPEARANCE: Glazing appears as shiny coating on the plug, either yellow or tan in color.

CAUSE: During hard, fast acceleration, plug temperatures rise suddenly. Deposits from normal combustion have no chance to fluff-off; instead, they melt on the insulator forming an electrically conductive coating which causes misfiring.

RECOMMENDATION: Glazed plugs are not easily cleaned. They should be replaced with a fresh set of plugs of the correct heat range. If the condition recurs, using plugs with a heat range one step colder may cure the problem.

Ash (Lead) Deposits

APPEARANCE: Ash deposits are characterized by light brown or white colored deposits crusted on the side or center electrodes. In some cases it may give the plug a rusty appearance.

CAUSE: Ash deposits are normally derived from oil or fuel additives burned during normal combustion. Normally they are harmless, though excessive amounts can cause misfiring. If deposits are excessive in short mileage, the valve guides may be worn.

RECOMMENDATION: Ash-fouled plugs can be cleaned, gapped and reinstalled.

Detonation

APPEARANCE: Detonation is usually characterized by a broken plug insulator.

CAUSE: A portion of the fuel charge will begin to burn spontaneously, from the increased heat following ignition. The explosion that results applies extreme pressure to engine components, frequently damaging spark plugs and pistons.

Detonation can result by over-advanced ignition timing, inferior gasoline (low octane) lean air/fuel mixture, poor carburetion, engine lugging or an increase in compression ratio due to combustion chamber deposits or engine modification.

RECOMMENDATION: Replace the plugs after correcting the problem.

Photos Courtesy Champion Spark Plug Co.

EMISSION CONTROLS

13. Be aware of the general condition of the emission control system. It contributes to reduced pollution and should be serviced regularly to maintain efficient engine operation.

14. Check all vacuum lines for dried, cracked or brittle conditions. Something as simple as a leaking vacuum hose can cause poor performance and loss of economy.

15. Avoid tampering with the emission control system. Attempting to improve fuel econ-

FUEL SYSTEM

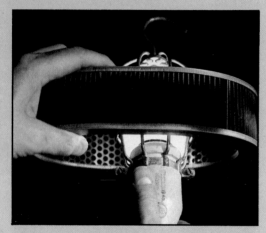

Check the air filter with a light behind it. If you can see light through the filter it can be reused.

Extremely clogged filters should be discarded and replaced with a new one.

18. Replace the air filter regularly. A dirty air filter richens the air/fuel mixture and can increase fuel consumption as much as 10%. Tests show that ⅓ of all vehicles have air filters in need of replacement.

19. Replace the fuel filter at least as often as recommended.

20. Set the idle speed and carburetor mixture to specifications.

21. Check the automatic choke. A sticking or malfunctioning choke wastes gas.

22. During the summer months, adjust the automatic choke for a leaner mixture which will produce faster engine warm-ups.

COOLING SYSTEM

29. Be sure all accessory drive belts are in good condition. Check for cracks or wear.

30. Adjust all accessory drive belts to proper tension.

31. Check all hoses for swollen areas, worn spots, or loose clamps.

32. Check coolant level in the radiator or expansion tank.

33. Be sure the thermostat is operating properly. A stuck thermostat delays engine warm-up and a cold engine uses nearly twice as much fuel as a warm engine.

34. Drain and replace the engine coolant at least as often as recommended. Rust and scale

TIRES & WHEELS

38. Check the tire pressure often with a pencil type gauge. Tests by a major tire manufacturer show that 90% of all vehicles have at least 1 tire improperly inflated. Better mileage can be achieved by over-inflating tires, but never exceed the maximum inflation pressure on the side of the tire.

39. If possible, install radial tires. Radial tires deliver as much as ½ mpg more than bias belted tires.

40. Avoid installing super-wide tires. They only create extra rolling resistance and decrease fuel mileage. Stick to the manufacturer's recommendations.

41. Have the wheels properly balanced.

omy by tampering with emission controls is more likely to worsen fuel economy than improve it. Emission control changes on modern engines are not readily reversible.

16. Clean (or replace) the EGR valve and lines as recommended.

17. Be sure that all vacuum lines and hoses are reconnected properly after working under the hood. An unconnected or misrouted vacuum line can wreak havoc with engine performance.

23. Check for fuel leaks at the carburetor, fuel pump, fuel lines and fuel tank. Be sure all lines and connections are tight.

24. Periodically check the tightness of the carburetor and intake manifold attaching nuts and bolts. These are a common place for vacuum leaks to occur.

25. Clean the carburetor periodically and lubricate the linkage.

26. The condition of the tailpipe can be an excellent indicator of proper engine combustion. After a long drive at highway speeds, the inside of the tailpipe should be a light grey in color. Black or soot on the insides indicates an overly rich mixture.

27. Check the fuel pump pressure. The fuel pump may be supplying more fuel than the engine needs.

28. Use the proper grade of gasoline for your engine. Don't try to compensate for knocking or "pinging" by advancing the ignition timing. This practice will only increase plug temperature and the chances of detonation or pre-ignition with relatively little performance gain.

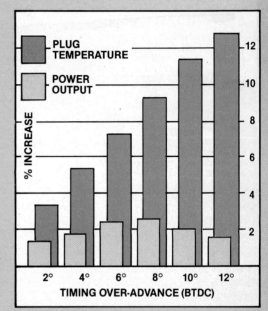

Increasing ignition timing past the specified setting results in a drastic increase in spark plug temperature with increased chance of detonation or preignition. Performance increase is considerably less. (Photo courtesy Champion Spark Plug Co.)

that form in the engine should be flushed out to allow the engine to operate at peak efficiency.

35. Clean the radiator of debris that can decrease cooling efficiency.

36. Install a flex-type or electric cooling fan, if you don't have a clutch type fan. Flex fans use curved plastic blades to push more air at low speeds when more cooling is needed; at high speeds the blades flatten out for less resistance. Electric fans only run when the engine temperature reaches a predetermined level.

37. Check the radiator cap for a worn or cracked gasket. If the cap does not seal properly, the cooling system will not function properly.

42. Be sure the front end is correctly aligned. A misaligned front end actually has wheels going in differed directions. The increased drag can reduce fuel economy by .3 mpg.

43. Correctly adjust the wheel bearings. Wheel bearings that are adjusted too tight increase rolling resistance.

Check tire pressures regularly with a reliable pocket type gauge. Be sure to check the pressure on a cold tire.

GENERAL MAINTENANCE

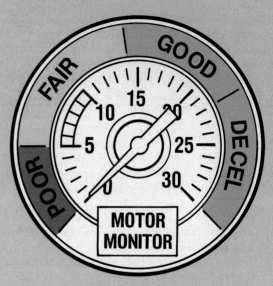

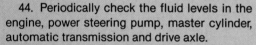

Check the fluid levels (particularly engine oil) on a regular basis. Be sure to check the oil for grit, water or other contamination.

A vacuum gauge is another excellent indicator of internal engine condition and can also be installed in the dash as a mileage indicator.

44. Periodically check the fluid levels in the engine, power steering pump, master cylinder, automatic transmission and drive axle.

45. Change the oil at the recommended interval and change the filter at every oil change. Dirty oil is thick and causes extra friction between moving parts, cutting efficiency and increasing wear. A worn engine requires more frequent tune-ups and gets progressively worse fuel economy. In general, use the lightest viscosity oil for the driving conditions you will encounter.

46. Use the recommended viscosity fluids in the transmission and axle.

47. Be sure the battery is fully charged for fast starts. A slow starting engine wastes fuel.

48. Be sure battery terminals are clean and tight.

49. Check the battery electrolyte level and add distilled water if necessary.

50. Check the exhaust system for crushed pipes, blockages and leaks.

51. Adjust the brakes. Dragging brakes or brakes that are not releasing create increased drag on the engine.

52. Install a vacuum gauge or miles-per-gallon gauge. These gauges visually indicate engine vacuum in the intake manifold. High vacuum = good mileage and low vacuum = poorer mileage. The gauge can also be an excellent indicator of internal engine conditions.

53. Be sure the clutch is properly adjusted. A slipping clutch wastes fuel.

54. Check and periodically lubricate the heat control valve in the exhaust manifold. A sticking or inoperative valve prevents engine warm-up and wastes gas.

55. Keep accurate records to check fuel economy over a period of time. A sudden drop in fuel economy may signal a need for tune-up or other maintenance.

© 1980 Chilton Book Company, Radnor, PA 19089

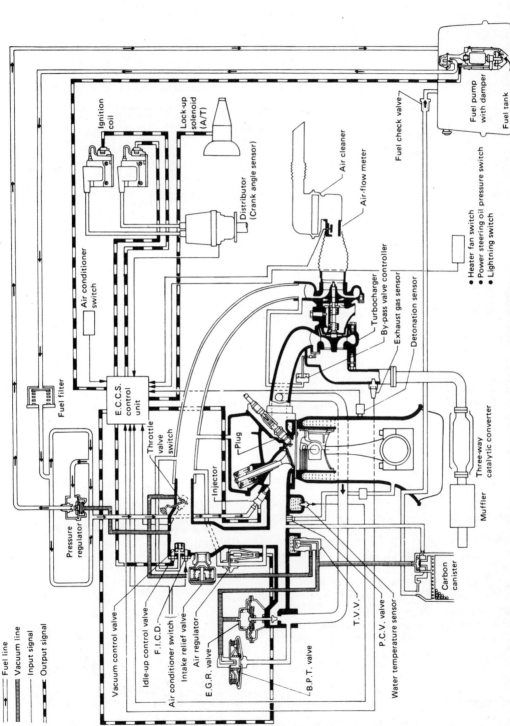

CA18ET Turbo fuel and vacuum schematic

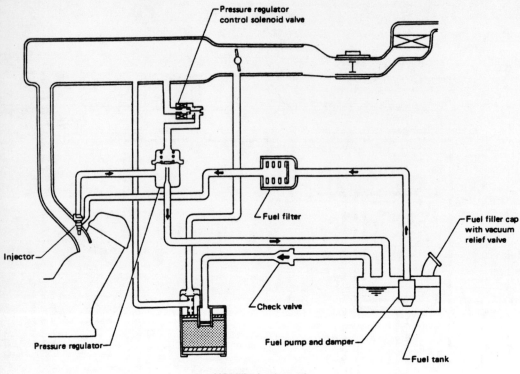

VG30 fuel schematic

harness clamps; wiring harness connectors and intake collector cover to the collector assembly.

12. Connect the coolant hoses to the collector and refill the cooling system to the proper level.

13. Reconnect the battery cable. Start the engine and check for fuel leaks.

DIESEL FUEL SYSTEM

Injectors

REMOVAL AND INSTALLATION

1. Remove the injection tubes at the injector and then remove the spill tube assembly.

2. Unscrew the two mounting bolts and pull out the injectors and their washers.

3. Installation is in the reverse order of removal. Tighten the injector mounting nuts to 12-15 ft. lbs. (16-21 Nm). Tighten the injection tube-to-injector nut to 16-18 ft. lbs. (22-25 Nm). Always use a new injector small washer.

Injection Pump

NOTE: *The diesel injection pump is located at the right front side of the engine. In case of pump failure or damage, the pump must be replaced as an assembly, except for certain simple parts on the outside of the pump.*

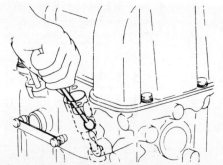

Use tweezers to remove and install injector small washer

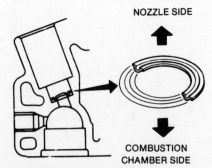

NOZZLE SIDE

COMBUSTION CHAMBER SIDE

Proper positioning of the small washer

REMOVAL AND INSTALLATION

1. Disconnect the negative battery cable.
2. Remove the air cleaner duct. Remove the engine under cover.
3. Drain the engine coolant and then remove the radiator and its shroud.
4. Loosen the fan pulley nuts and then remove the drive belts (air conditioning, alternator and power steering pump).
5. Disconnect the power steering oil pump and position it out of the way.
6. Tag and disconnect the accelerator wire, the overflow hose (on the spill tube side), the fuel cut solenoid connector and the fuel return hose.
7. Tag and disconnect the potentiometer, the injection timing control solenoid valve wire, the cold start device water hoses (at the 4-way connector side) and the vacuum hoses for the vacuum modulator (automatic transmission models only).
8. Remove the crank damper pulley. Use a plastic mallet and tap lightly around the sides. If this does not loosen the pulley you will need a two armed gear puller.
9. Remove the pulley bracket and the idler pulley (if so equipped) and then remove the front dust cover.
10. Loosen the spring set pin, set the tensioner pulley to the free tension position and then tighten them.
11. Slide the injection pump drive belt off its pulleys.
12. Loosen the retaining nut and remove the injection pump drive gear. You may need a two armed gear puller.
13. Disconnect the injection tubes at the injection nozzle side.
14. Unscrew the injection pump fixing nuts and the bracket bolt.
15. Remove the injection pump assembly with the injection tubes attached.
   NOTE: *If you plan to measure plunger lift, remove the injection tubes before removing the pump.*
16. Install the injection pump assembly and bracket in the correct position. Observe the following:

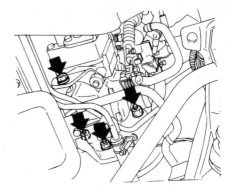

Injection pump mounting nuts and bolt

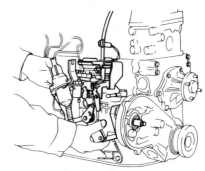

Removing the injection pump

   a. Set the No. 1 cylinder at TDC of the compression stroke. Make sure that the grooves in the rear plate and the flywheel align and that the No. 1 cam lobe on the camshaft is in the position shown.
   b. Install the injection pump and temporarily tighten the mounting bolts.
   c. Use the alignment marks as shown in the illustration and install the injection pump drive gear. Tighten the nut to 43-51 ft. lbs. (59-69 Nm).
NOTE: *The injection pump drive shaft is tapered.*
If the drive gear is difficult to install, use a plastic mallet and drive it into place.
17. Make sure that the tensioner pulley is still

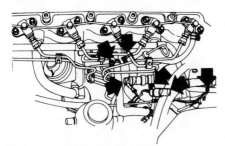

Remove these hoses and wires

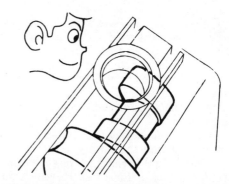

Make sure the No. 1 cam lobe is in this position

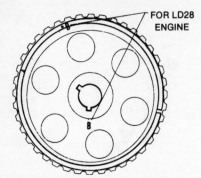

FOR LD28
ENGINE

B

Injection pump drive gear alignment marks

in the free position and slide the injection drive belt over the pulleys.

18. The drive belt should have two timing marks on it. Align one with the mark on the crank pulley and the other with the mark on the drive gear. If the timing marks on the drive belt are not clear enough to read, set the marks on the drive gear and the crank pulley so that there are 20 cogs of the drive belt between them when it is installed.

19. Loosen the spring set pin and the tensioner so that the belt is automatically set to the tension position.

20. Adjust the injection timing as detailed in this chapter.

21. Tighten the injection pump nuts to 12-15 ft. lbs. (16-21 Nm) and the bracket bolt to 22-26 ft. lbs. (30-35 Nm).

22. Reconnect the injection tubes. Connect them to the cylinders in this order: 4, 2, 6, 1, 5, 3.

23. Bleed the air from the fuel system as detailed in this chapter.

24. Install the idler pulley and bracket if so equipped. Install the crank damper pulley.

25. Reconnect the potentiometer, the injection timing control solenoid valve wire, the cold start device water hoses (at the 4-way connector side) and the vacuum hoses to the vacuum modulator (automatic transmission models only).

26. Connect the accelerator wire, the overflow hose (on the spill tube side), the fuel cut solenoid connector and the fuel return hose.

27. Install the power steering oil pump and all drive belts. Adjust all drive belts to the correct tension.

28. Install the radiator and shroud, refill the cooling system.

29. Install the air cleaner duct and engine undercover. Reconnect the battery cable.

30. Check all fluid levels, start the engine and inspect for any leaks. Road test the vehicle for proper operation.

INJECTION PUMP TIMING

1. Remove the under cover and drain the coolant.

2. Remove the coolant hoses that are connected to the cold start device.

3. Remove the power steering pump.

4. Set the No. 1 cylinder at TDC of its compression stroke. Make sure that the grooves in the rear plate and the drive plate are aligned with each other. Make sure that the No. 1 camshaft lobe is in the position shown in the illustration.

5. Using two wrenches, remove the fuel injection tubes.

6. Loosen the fork retaining screw on the cold start device. Turn the fork 90° and then set the cold start device in the free position.

NOTE: *Never remove the screw on the cold start device wire. If it should be removed accidentally, the pump assembly should be readjusted at a service shop specified by the manufacturer.*

7. Remove the plug bolt from the rear side of the injection pump and, in its place, attach a dial indicator.

8. Loosen the injection pump mounting nuts and bracket bolt.

9. Turn the crankshaft counterclockwise 15-20° from the No. 1 cylinder TDC position.

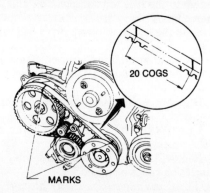

20 COGS

MARKS

Timing mark alignment on the injection pump drive belt

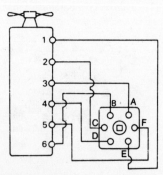

1
2
3
4
5
6

B A
C F
D
E

Injection tube routing

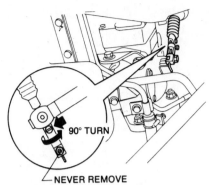

Loosen the fork retaining screw on the cold start device

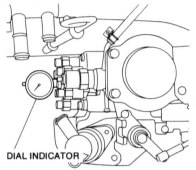

Remove the plug bolt and attach a dial indicator

10. Find the dial indicator needle rest point and set the gauge to zero.

11. Turn the crankshaft clockwise two complete revolutions in order to remove the play in the camshaft mechanism. Loosen the tensioner and then retighten it.

12. Turn the crankshaft clockwise until the No. 1 cylinder is again at TDC and then read the dial indicator.

	Plunger Lift mm (in) For Low Altitudes
M/T	0.85±0.03 (0.0335±0.0012)
A/T	0.81−0.03 (0.0319±0.0012)

	For High Altitudes (Non-California Model Only)
M/T	0.90±0.03 (0.0354±0.0012)
A/T	0.85±0.03 (0.0335±0.0012)

13. If the dial indicator is not within the above range, turn the injection pump counterclockwise to increase the reading and clockwise to decrease it.

14. Tighten the injection pump mounting nuts and bracket bolt (torque figures are given in the preceding section).

15. Remove the dial indicator and reinstall the plug bolt with a new washer. Tighten the plug bolt to 10-14 ft. lbs. (14-20 Nm).

16. Set the fork at the cold start device in its original position by pulling on the cold start device wire and then tighten the fork screw.

17. Connect the injection tubes.

18. Install the power steering pump, connect the cold start device water hoses, refill with coolant and install the under cover.

BLEED THE FUEL SYSTEM

NOTE: *Air should be bled from the fuel system whenever the injection pump is removed or the fuel system is repaired.*

1. Loosen the priming pump vent screw and pump a few times. Make sure that the fuel overflows at the vent screw.

2. Tighten the vent screw.

3. Disconnect the fuel return hose and install a suitable hose over the overflow connector. Place a small pan under the overflow hose.

4. Prime the priming pump to make sure that the fuel overflows at the open end of the hose.

5. Remove the pan and the overflow hose and then install the return hose.

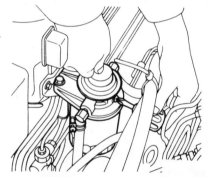

Loosen the priming pump vent screw on the fuel filter

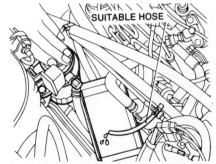

Install a suitable hose over the overflow connector

Glow plugs

REMOVAL AND INSTALLATION

1. Disconnect the glow plug electrical leads. Remove the glow plug connecting plate.

2. Remove the glow plug by unscrewing them from the cylinder head.

3. Inspect the tips of the plugs for any evidence of melting. If even one glow plug tip looks bad, all the glow plugs must be replaced. This a general rule-of-thumb which applies to all diesel engines.

4. Install the glow plugs in the cylinder head. Torque the glow plugs to 14-18 ft. lbs.

5. Install the glow plug connecting plates.

6. Reconnect the glow plug electrical leads.

FUEL TANK

REMOVAL AND INSTALLATION

610 and 710 Station Wagon

1. Disconnect the battery ground cable.

2. Remove the inspection plate from the rear floor. Disconnect the gauge wiring.

3. Remove the spare tire.

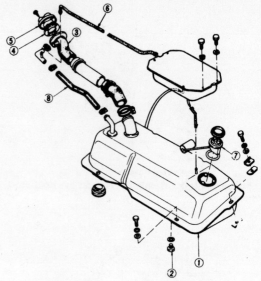

1. Fuel tank	5. Filler cap
2. Drain plug	6. Breather tube
3. Filler hose	7. Fuel gauge unit
4. Filler neck	8. Ventilation hose

710 fuel tank

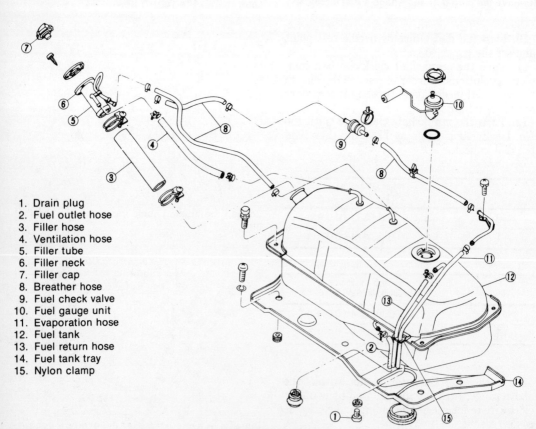

1. Drain plug
2. Fuel outlet hose
3. Filler hose
4. Ventilation hose
5. Filler tube
6. Filler neck
7. Filler cap
8. Breather hose
9. Fuel check valve
10. Fuel gauge unit
11. Evaporation hose
12. Fuel tank
13. Fuel return hose
14. Fuel tank tray
15. Nylon clamp

1978 200SX fuel tank

4. Place a pan under the drain plug and remove the plug.

5. Disconnect the filler hose, ventilation lines, and the fuel line from the tank.

6. Remove the retaining bolts and remove the tank.

7. Install the tank with retaining bolts to vehicle.

8. Reconnect all fuel lines, filler hose, ventilation hoses and the electrical connection.

9. Install the spare tire and inspection plate. Connect the battery ground cable.

1977-79 200SX

1. Disconnect the battery ground cable.

2. Remove the rubber plug located on the floor panel above the left side rear axle.

3. Remove the drain plug and drain the tank.

4. Detach the rear set cushion, seat back, and rear seat backboard.

5. Disconnect the fuel hose.

6. Remove the two bolts which secure the fuel tank in the front.

7. Open the trunk, remove the trim in front of the tank if necessary, and remove all the hoses and lines.

8. Remove the two bolts which hold the fuel tank in the back and remove the tank.

9. Install the fuel tank with retaining bolts to vehicle.

10. Reconnect all fuel hoses and lines and install trim if removed.

11. Reconnect the rear seat assembly. Install the drain plug and rubber access plug.

12. Connect the battery ground cable.

810 and Maxima (Rear Wheel Drive) Sedan

1. Disconnect the battery ground cable.

2. Remove the mat and the spare tire from the trunk.

3. Place a suitable container under the fuel tank and drain the tank. There is a drain plug in the bottom of the tank.

4. Disconnect the filler hose, the vent tube, and the outlet hose.

5. Disconnect the wires from the sending unit.

6. Remove the four bolts securing the fuel tank and remove the tank.

7. Install the fuel tank with retaining bolts to vehicle.

8. Reconnect all fuel lines, filler hose, outlet hose, vent tube and the electrical connection.

9. Install the spare tire and mat. Connect the battery ground cable.

810 and Maxima (Rear Wheel Drive) Station Wagon

1. Disconnect the battery ground cable.

2. Loosen the tire hanger and take out the spare tire.

3. Loosen the drain plug and drain the tank.

4. Disconnect the filler hose, ventilation hose, evaporation hose, and outlet hose.

5. Remove the tire stopper. Disconnect the wiring from the gauge.

6. Remove the four bolts securing the fuel tank and remove the tank.

7. Install the fuel tank with retaining bolts to vehicle.

8. Install the tire stopper.

9. Connect the filler hose, ventilation hose, evaporation hose, and outlet hose.

10. Install the spare tire in the correct manner. Connect the battery ground cable.

1978-81 510 Sedan

1. Disconnect the battery ground cable.

2. Remove the back seat trim in the luggage compartment.

3. Drain the fuel in the fuel tank.

4. Remove the bolts securing the tank and remove the tank.

5. Installation is in the reverse order of removal.

1978-81 510 Hatchback

1. Disconnect the battery ground cable. Drain the fuel from the tank, then disconnect the fuel hose.

2. Remove the luggage carpet, luggage board, and fuel filler hose protector.

3. Disconnect all the hoses and wires to the tank and unbolt the fuel tank and remove it.

4. Installation is in the reverse order of removal.

1978-81 510 Station Wagon

1. Disconnect the battery ground cable.

2. Drain the fuel from the tank. Disconnect all the hoses and lines.

3. Remove the spare tire and fuel tank support.

4. Unbolt and remove the tank.

5. Installation is in the reverse order of removal.

1980-83 200SX

1. Remove the battery ground cable.

2. Drain the fuel from the fuel tank.

3. Remove the protector from the luggage compartment, and then remove the following parts:

   a. Harness connector for the fuel tank gauge unit.

   b. Ventilation hose.

   c. Evaporation hoses

   d. Fuel filler hose (Hatchback)

4. Remove the following parts from beneath the floor:

SEDAN

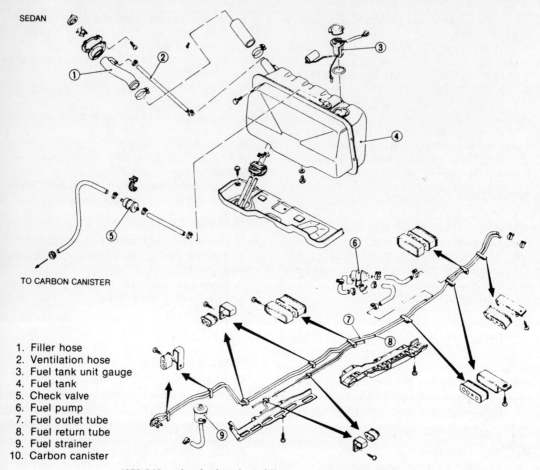

TO CARBON CANISTER

1. Filler hose
2. Ventilation hose
3. Fuel tank unit gauge
4. Fuel tank
5. Check valve
6. Fuel pump
7. Fuel outlet tube
8. Fuel return tube
9. Fuel strainer
10. Carbon canister

1978 810 sedan fuel tank and lines—most models similar

STATION WAGON

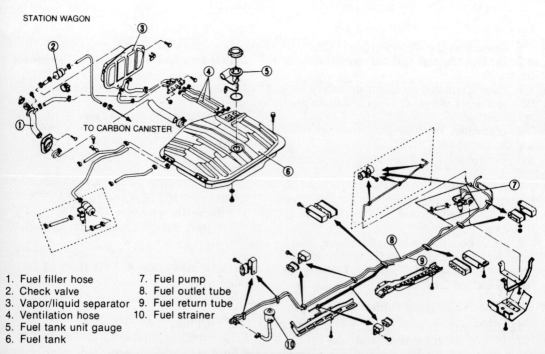

TO CARBON CANISTER

1. Fuel filler hose
2. Check valve
3. Vapor/liquid separator
4. Ventilation hose
5. Fuel tank unit gauge
6. Fuel tank
7. Fuel pump
8. Fuel outlet tube
9. Fuel return tube
10. Fuel strainer

1978 810 station wagon fuel tank and lines—most models similar

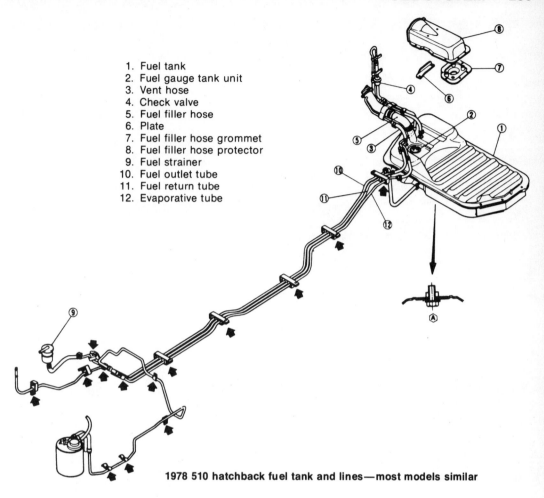

1. Fuel tank
2. Fuel gauge tank unit
3. Vent hose
4. Check valve
5. Fuel filler hose
6. Plate
7. Fuel filler hose grommet
8. Fuel filler hose protector
9. Fuel strainer
10. Fuel outlet tube
11. Fuel return tube
12. Evaporative tube

1978 510 hatchback fuel tank and lines—most models similar

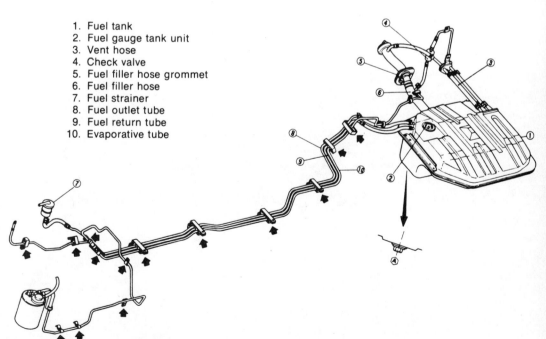

1. Fuel tank
2. Fuel gauge tank unit
3. Vent hose
4. Check valve
5. Fuel filler hose grommet
6. Fuel filler hose
7. Fuel strainer
8. Fuel outlet tube
9. Fuel return tube
10. Evaporative tube

1978 510 station wagon fuel tank and lines—most models similar

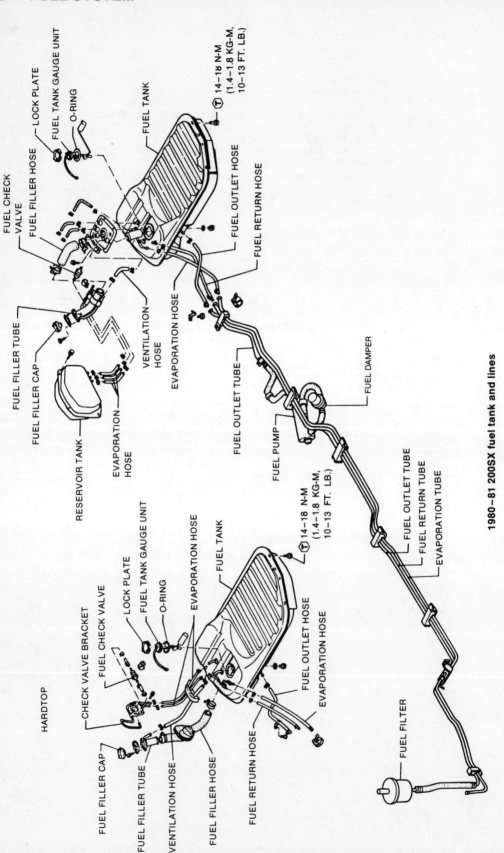

HATCHBACK

FUEL CHECK VALVE

FUEL FILLER HOSE — LOCK PLATE

FUEL TANK GAUGE UNIT

O-RING

FUEL TANK

⊤ 14–18 N-M
(1.4–1.8 KG-M,
10–13 FT. LB.)

FUEL FILLER HOSE

FUEL OUTLET HOSE

FUEL RETURN HOSE

FUEL FILLER TUBE

FUEL FILLER CAP

RESERVOIR TANK

EVAPORATION HOSE

VENTILATION HOSE

EVAPORATION HOSE

FUEL OUTLET TUBE

FUEL DAMPER

FUEL PUMP

FUEL OUTLET TUBE

FUEL RETURN TUBE

EVAPORATION TUBE

HARDTOP

CHECK VALVE BRACKET

FUEL CHECK VALVE

LOCK PLATE

FUEL TANK GAUGE UNIT

O-RING

EVAPORATION HOSE

FUEL TANK

⊤ 14–18 N-M
(1.4–1.8 KG-M,
10–13 FT. LB.)

FUEL OUTLET HOSE

EVAPORATION HOSE

FUEL FILLER CAP

FUEL FILLER TUBE

VENTILATION HOSE

FUEL FILLER HOSE

FUEL RETURN HOSE

FUEL FILTER

1980–81 200SX fuel tank and lines

a. Fuel outlet hose
b. Fuel return hose
c. Evaporation hose
d. Fuel filler hose (Hardtop)

5. Remove the bolts which secure the fuel tank and remove the tank.

To remove the Reservoir tank from the Hatchback:

6. Remove the battery cable.

7. Remove the protector from the luggage compartment. Also remove the right hand speaker and side lower finisher.

8. Remove the evaporation hoses and then remove the reservoir tank.

9. Install the reservoir tank in place and fuel tank assembly in the correct position.

10. Reconnect all lines, hoses and the electrical connection.

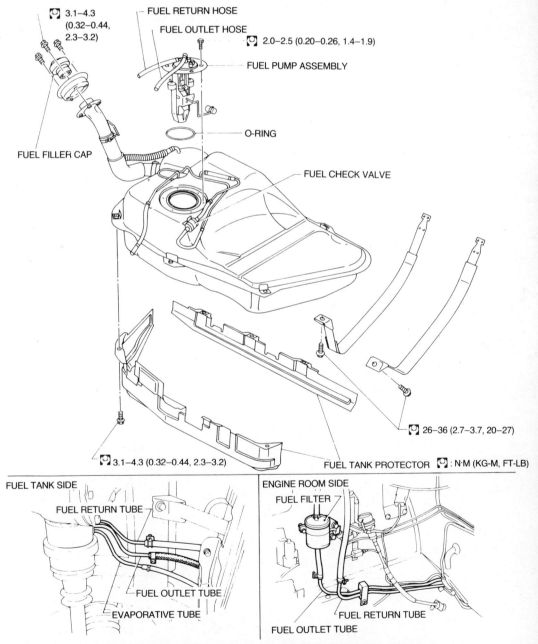

1984 and later 200SX fuel tank assembly showing fuel line connections

11. Install the protector in the the luggage compartment. Connect the battery ground cable.

1984-88 200SX
1989 240SX

1. Remove the battery ground cable.
2. Drain the fuel from the fuel tank.
3. Remove the access plate from the trunk area. Disconnect the hoses, evaporative (vent)

tube line if so equipped and fuel pump electrical connection.

4. Raise the rear of vehicle and safely support it with the proper jackstands.
5. Remove the fuel tank protector assembly.
6. Disconnect the fuel filler hose at the gas tank.
7. Remove the gas tank strap retaining bolts and slowly lower the tank assembly down from the vehicle.

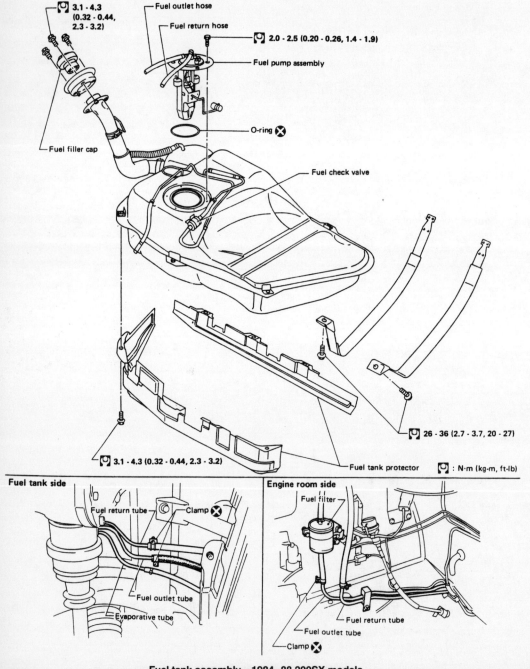

Fuel tank assembly—1984–88 200SX models

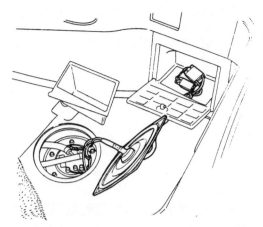

Access plate location in trunk area—1984–88 200SX

13. Refill the gas tank. Reconnect the battery ground cable.

1985-89 Maxima

NOTE: *Replace any fuel hose before installing gas tank assembly.*

1. Remove the battery ground cable and drain the fuel from the fuel tank.

2. Raise the rear of vehicle and safely support it with proper jackstands.

3. Remove the fuel tank protector assembly.

4. Disconnect all hoses, lines and the electrical connection from the gas tank assembly.

5. Disconnect the fuel filler hose at the gas tank.

6. Remove the gas tank strap retaining bolts and slowly lower the tank assembly down from the vehicle.

7. Install the tank in the correct position.

8. While supporting the tank in place torque the gas tank strap retaining bolts to 20-26 ft. lbs. On some models, the gas tank is hold in by retaining bolts instead of gas tank straps torque these retaining bolts to 23-31 ft. lbs.

9. Reconnect the fuel filler hose at the gas tank with a new hose clamp.

10. Connect all hoses, lines and the electrical connection to the gas tank assembly. Always use new hose clamps to prevent leaks.

11. Install the fuel tank protector assembly.

12. Refill the gas tank. Reconnect the battery ground cable.

8. Install the tank in the correct position.

9. While supporting the tank in place torque the gas tank strap retaining bolts to 20-27 ft. lbs.

10. Reconnect the fuel filler hose at the gas tank using a new clamp.

11. Install the fuel tank protector assembly and connect the evaporative (vent) tube line if so equipped.

12. Lower the vehicle, connect all hoses with new clamps and the electrical connection. Install the access plate.

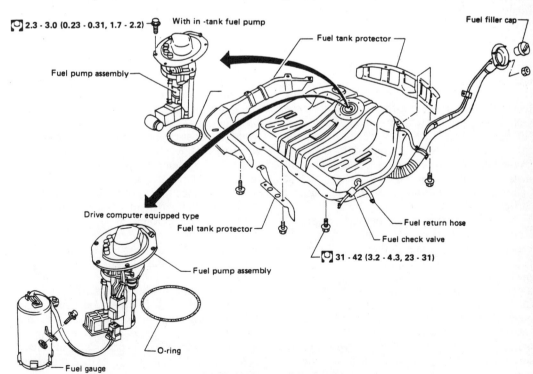

Fuel assembly—1986 Maxima

Chassis Electrical

6

UNDERSTANDING AND TROUBLESHOOTING ELECTRICAL SYSTEMS

At the rate which both import and domestic manufacturers are incorporating electronic control systems into their production lines, it won't be long before every new vehicle is equipped with one or more on-board computer. These electronic components (with no moving parts) should theoretically last the life of the vehicle, provided nothing external happens to damage the circuits or memory chips.

While it is true that electronic components should never wear out, in the real world malfunctions do occur. It is also true that any computer-based system is extremely sensitive to electrical voltages and cannot tolerate careless or haphazard testing or service procedures. An inexperienced individual can literally do major damage looking for a minor problem by using the wrong kind of test equipment or connecting test leads or connectors with the ignition switch **ON**. When selecting test equipment, make sure the manufacturers instructions state that the tester is compatible with whatever type of electronic control system is being serviced. Read all instructions carefully and double check all test points before installing probes or making any test connections.

The following section outlines basic diagnosis techniques for dealing with computerized automotive control systems. Along with a general explanation of the various types of test equipment available to aid in servicing modern electronic automotive systems, basic repair techniques for wiring harnesses and connectors is given. Read the basic information before attempting any repairs or testing on any computerized system, to provide the background of information necessary to avoid the most common and obvious mistakes that can cost both time and money. Although the replacement and test-ing procedures are simple in themselves, the systems are not, and unless one has a thorough understanding of all components and their function within a particular computerized control system, the logical test sequence these systems demand cannot be followed. Minor malfunctions can make a big difference, so it is important to know how each component affects the operation of the overall electronic system to find the ultimate cause of a problem without replacing good components unnecessarily. It is not enough to use the correct test equipment; the test equipment must be used correctly.

Safety Precautions

CAUTION: *Whenever working on or around any computer based microprocessor control system, always observe these general precautions to prevent the possibility of personal injury or damage to electronic components.*

• Never install or remove battery cables with the key ON or the engine running. Jumper cables should be connected with the key OFF to avoid power surges that can damage electronic control units. Engines equipped with computer controlled systems should avoid both giving and getting jump starts due to the possibility of serious damage to components from arcing in the engine compartment when connections are made with the ignition ON.

• Always remove the battery cables before charging the battery. Never use a high output charger on an installed battery or attempt to use any type of "hot shot" (24 volt) starting aid.

• Exercise care when inserting test probes into connectors to insure good connections without damaging the connector or spreading the pins. Always probe connectors from the rear (wire) side, NOT the pin side, to avoid accidental shorting of terminals during test procedures.

• Never remove or attach wiring harness

connectors with the ignition switch ON, especially to an electronic control unit.

• Do not drop any components during service procedures and never apply 12 volts directly to any component (like a solenoid or relay) unless instructed specifically to do so. Some component electrical windings are designed to safely handle only 4 or 5 volts and can be destroyed in seconds if 12 volts are applied directly to the connector.

• Remove the electronic control unit if the vehicle is to be placed in an environment where temperatures exceed approximately 176°F (80°C), such as a paint spray booth or when arc or gas welding near the control unit location in the car.

ORGANIZED TROUBLESHOOTING

When diagnosing a specific problem, organized troubleshooting is a must. The complexity of a modern automobile demands that you approach any problem in a logical, organized manner. There are certain troubleshooting techniques that are standard:

1. Establish when the problem occurs. Does the problem appear only under certain conditions? Were there any noises, odors, or other unusual symptoms?

2. Isolate the problem area. To do this, make some simple tests and observations; then eliminate the systems that are working properly. Check for obvious problems such as broken wires, dirty connections or split or disconnected vacuum hoses. Always check the obvious before assuming something complicated is the cause.

3. Test for problems systematically to determine the cause once the problem area is isolated. Are all the components functioning properly? Is there power going to electrical switches and motors? Is there vacuum at vacuum switches and/or actuators? Is there a mechanical problem such as bent linkage or loose mounting screws? Doing careful, systematic checks will often turn up most causes on the first inspection without wasting time checking components that have little or no relationship to the problem.

4. Test all repairs after the work is done to make sure that the problem is fixed. Some causes can be traced to more than one component, so a careful verification of repair work is important to pick up additional malfunctions that may cause a problem to reappear or a different problem to arise. A blown fuse, for example, is a simple problem that may require more than another fuse to repair. If you don't look for a problem that caused a fuse to blow, for example, a shorted wire may go undetected.

TEST EQUIPMENT

Jumper Wires

Jumper wires are simple, yet extremely valuable, pieces of test equipment. Jumper wires are merely wires that are used to bypass sections of a circuit. The simplest type of jumper wire is merely a length of multistrand wire with an alligator clip at each end. Jumper wires are usually fabricated from lengths of standard automotive wire and whatever type of connector (alligator clip, spade connector or pin connector) that is required for the particular vehicle being tested. The well equipped tool box will have several different styles of jumper wires in several different lengths. Some jumper wires are made with three or more terminals coming from a common splice for special purpose testing. In cramped, hard-to-reach areas it is advisable to have insulated boots over the jumper wire terminals in order to prevent accidental grounding, sparks, and possible fire, especially when testing fuel system components.

Jumper wires are used primarily to locate open electrical circuits, on either the ground (−) side of the circuit or on the hot (+) side. If an electrical component fails to operate, connect the jumper wire between the component and a good ground. If the component operates only with the jumper installed, the ground circuit is open. If the ground circuit is good, but the component does not operate, the circuit between the power feed and component is open. You can sometimes connect the jumper wire directly from the battery to the hot terminal of the component, but first make sure the component uses 12 volts in operation. Some electrical components, such as fuel injectors, are designed to operate on about 4 volts and running 12 volts directly to the injector terminals can burn out the wiring. By inserting an inline fuseholder between a set of test leads, a fused jumper wire can be used for bypassing open circuits. Use a 5 amp fuse to provide protection against voltage spikes. When in doubt, use a voltmeter to check the voltage input to the component and measure how much voltage is being applied normally. By moving the jumper wire successively back from the lamp toward the power source, you can isolate the area of the circuit where the open is located. When the component stops functioning, or the power is cut off, the open is in the segment of wire between the jumper and the point previously tested.

NOTE: *Never use jumpers made from wire that is of lighter gauge than used in the circuit under test. If the jumper wire is of too small gauge, it may overheat and possibly melt. Never use jumpers to bypass high resistance loads (such as motors) in a circuit. By-*

passing resistances, in effect, creates a short circuit which may, in turn, cause damage and fire. Never use a jumper for anything other than temporary bypassing of components in a circuit.

12 Volt Test Light

The 12 volt test light is used to check circuits and components while electrical current is flowing through them. It is used for voltage and ground tests. Twelve volt test lights come in different styles but all have three main parts; a ground clip, a probe, and a light. The most commonly used 12 volt test lights have pick-type probes. To use a 12 volt test light, connect the ground clip to a good ground and probe wherever necessary with the pick. The pick should be sharp so that it can penetrate wire insulation to make contact with the wire, without making a large hole in the insulation. The wrap-around light is handy in hard to reach areas or where it is difficult to support a wire to push a probe pick into it. To use the wrap around light, hook the wire to probed with the hook and pull the trigger. A small pick will be forced through the wire insulation into the wire core.

NOTE: *Do not use a test light to probe electronic ignition spark plug or coil wires. Never use a pick-type test light to probe wiring on computer controlled systems unless specifically instructed to do so. Any wire insulation that is pierced by the test light probe should be taped and sealed with silicone after testing.*

Like the jumper wire, the 12 volt test light is used to isolate opens in circuits. But, whereas the jumper wire is used to bypass the open to operate the load, the 12 volt test light is used to locate the presence of voltage in a circuit. If the test light glows, you know that there is power up to that point; if the 12 volt test light does not glow when its probe is inserted into the wire or connector, you know that there is an open circuit (no power). Move the test light in successive steps back toward the power source until the light in the handle does glow. When it does glow, the open is between the probe and point previously probed.

NOTE: *The test light does not detect that 12 volts (or any particular amount of voltage) is present; it only detects that some voltage is present. It is advisable before using the test light to touch its terminals across the battery posts to make sure the light is operating properly.*

Self-Powered Test Light

The self-powered test light usually contains a 1.5 volt penlight battery. One type of self-powered test light is similar in design to the 12 volt test light. This type has both the battery and the light in the handle and pick-type probe tip. The second type has the light toward the open tip, so that the light illuminates the contact point. The self-powered test light is dual purpose piece of test equipment. It can be used to test for either open or short circuits when power is isolated from the circuit (continuity test). A powered test light should not be used on any computer controlled system or component unless specifically instructed to do so. Many engine sensors can be destroyed by even this small amount of voltage applied directly to the terminals.

Open Circuit Testing

To use the self-powered test light to check for open circuits, first isolate the circuit from the vehicle's 12 volt power source by disconnecting the battery or wiring harness connector. Connect the test light ground clip to a good ground and probe sections of the circuit sequentially with the test light. (start from either end of the circuit). If the light is out, the open is between the probe and the circuit ground. If the light is on, the open is between the probe and end of the circuit toward the power source.

Short Circuit Testing

By isolating the circuit both from power and from ground, and using a self-powered test light, you can check for shorts to ground in the circuit. Isolate the circuit from power and ground. Connect the test light ground clip to a good ground and probe any easy-to-reach test point in the circuit. If the light comes on, there is a short somewhere in the circuit. To isolate the short, probe a test point at either end of the isolated circuit (the light should be on). Leave the test light probe connected and open connectors, switches, remove parts, etc., sequentially, until the light goes out. When the light goes out, the short is between the last circuit component opened and the previous circuit opened.

NOTE: *The 1.5 volt battery in the test light does not provide much current. A weak battery may not provide enough power to illuminate the test light even when a complete circuit is made (especially if there are high resistances in the circuit). Always make sure that the test battery is strong. To check the battery, briefly touch the ground clip to the probe; if the light glows brightly the battery is strong enough for testing. Never use a self-powered test light to perform checks for opens or shorts when power is applied to the electrical system under test. The 12 volt vehicle power will quickly burn out the 1.5 volt light bulb in the test light.*

Voltmeter

A voltmeter is used to measure voltage at any point in a circuit, or to measure the voltage drop across any part of a circuit. It can also be used to check continuity in a wire or circuit by indicating current flow from one end to the other. Voltmeters usually have various scales on the meter dial and a selector switch to allow the selection of different voltages. The voltmeter has a positive and a negative lead. To avoid damage to the meter, always connect the negative lead to the negative (−) side of circuit (to ground or nearest the ground side of the circuit) and connect the positive lead to the positive (+) side of the circuit (to the power source or the nearest power source). Note that the negative voltmeter lead will always be black and that the positive voltmeter will always be some color other than black (usually red). Depending on how the voltmeter is connected into the circuit, it has several uses.

A voltmeter can be connected either in parallel or in series with a circuit and it has a very high resistance to current flow. When connected in parallel, only a small amount of current will flow through the voltmeter current path; the rest will flow through the normal circuit current path and the circuit will work normally. When the voltmeter is connected in series with a circuit, only a small amount of current can flow through the circuit. The circuit will not work properly, but the voltmeter reading will show if the circuit is complete or not.

Available Voltage Measurement

Set the voltmeter selector switch to the 20V position and connect the meter negative lead to the negative post of the battery. Connect the positive meter lead to the positive post of the battery and turn the ignition switch ON to provide a load. Read the voltage on the meter or digital display. A well charged battery should register over 12 volts. If the meter reads below 11.5 volts, the battery power may be insufficient to operate the electrical system properly. This test determines voltage available from the battery and should be the first step in any electrical trouble diagnosis procedure. Many electrical problems, especially on computer controlled systems, can be caused by a low state of charge in the battery. Excessive corrosion at the battery cable terminals can cause a poor contact that will prevent proper charging and full battery current flow.

Normal battery voltage is 12 volts when fully charged. When the battery is supplying current to one or more circuits it is said to be "under load". When everything is off the electrical system is under a "no-load" condition. A fully charged battery may show about 12.5 volts at no load; will drop to 12 volts under medium load; and will drop even lower under heavy load. If the battery is partially discharged the voltage decrease under heavy load may be excessive, even though the battery shows 12 volts or more at no load. When allowed to discharge further, the battery's available voltage under load will decrease more severely. For this reason, it is important that the battery be fully charged during all testing procedures to avoid errors in diagnosis and incorrect test results.

Voltage Drop

When current flows through a resistance, the voltage beyond the resistance is reduced (the larger the current, the greater the reduction in voltage). When no current is flowing, there is no voltage drop because there is no current flow. All points in the circuit which are connected to the power source are at the same voltage as the power source. The total voltage drop always equals the total source voltage. In a long circuit with many connectors, a series of small, unwanted voltage drops due to corrosion at the connectors can add up to a total loss of voltage which impairs the operation of the normal loads in the circuit.

INDIRECT COMPUTATION OF VOLTAGE DROPS

1. Set the voltmeter selector switch to the 20 volt position.
2. Connect the meter negative lead to a good ground.
3. Probe all resistances in the circuit with the positive meter lead.
4. Operate the circuit in all modes and observe the voltage readings.

DIRECT MEASUREMENT OF VOLTAGE DROPS

1. Set the voltmeter switch to the 20 volt position.
2. Connect the voltmeter negative lead to the ground side of the resistance load to be measured.
3. Connect the positive lead to the positive side of the resistance or load to be measured.
4. Read the voltage drop directly on the 20 volt scale.

Too high a voltage indicates too high a resistance. If, for example, a blower motor runs too slowly, you can determine if there is too high a resistance in the resistor pack. By taking voltage drop readings in all parts of the circuit, you can isolate the problem. Too low a voltage drop indicates too low a resistance. If, for example, a blower motor runs too fast in the MED and/or LOW position, the problem can be isolated in the resistor pack by taking voltage drop readings in all parts of the circuit to locate a possibly shorted resistor. The maximum allowable voltage drop under load is critical, especially if there is more than one high resistance problem in a circuit because all voltage drops are cumulative. A small drop is normal due to the resistance of the conductors.

HIGH RESISTANCE TESTING

1. Set the voltmeter selector switch to the 4 volt position.

2. Connect the voltmeter positive lead to the positive post of the battery.

3. Turn on the headlights and heater blower to provide a load.

4. Probe various points in the circuit with the negative voltmeter lead.

5. Read the voltage drop on the 4 volt scale. Some average maximum allowable voltage drops are:

FUSE PANEL — 7 volts
IGNITION SWITCH — 5volts
HEADLIGHT SWITCH — 7 volts
IGNITION COIL (+) — 5 volts
ANY OTHER LOAD — 1.3 volts

NOTE: *Voltage drops are all measured while a load is operating; without current flow, there will be no voltage drop.*

Ohmmeter

The ohmmeter is designed to read resistance (ohms) in a circuit or component. Although there are several different styles of ohmmeters, all will usually have a selector switch which permits the measurement of different ranges of resistance (usually the selector switch allows the multiplication of the meter reading by 10, 100, 1,000, and 10,000). A calibration knob allows the meter to be set at zero for accurate measurement. Since all ohmmeters are powered by an internal battery (usually 9 volts), the ohmmeter can be used as a self-powered test light. When the ohmmeter is connected, current from the ohmmeter flows through the circuit or component being tested. Since the ohmmeter's internal resistance and voltage are known values, the amount of current flow through the meter depends on the resistance of the circuit or component being tested.

The ohmmeter can be used to perform continuity test for opens or shorts (either by observation of the meter needle or as a self-powered test light), and to read actual resistance in a circuit. It should be noted that the ohmmeter is used to check the resistance of a component or wire while there is no voltage applied to the circuit. Current flow from an outside voltage source (such as the vehicle battery) can damage the ohmmeter, so the circuit or component should be isolated from the vehicle electrical system before any testing is done. Since the

ohmmeter uses its own voltage source, either lead can be connected to any test point.

NOTE: *When checking diodes or other solid state components, the ohmmeter leads can only be connected one way in order to measure current flow in a single direction. Make sure the positive (+) and negative (−) terminal connections are as described in the test procedures to verify the one-way diode operation.*

In using the meter for making continuity checks, do not be concerned with the actual resistance readings. Zero resistance, or any resistance readings, indicate continuity in the circuit. Infinite resistance indicates an open in the circuit. A high resistance reading where there should be none indicates a problem in the circuit. Checks for short circuits are made in the same manner as checks for open circuits except that the circuit must be isolated from both power and normal ground. Infinite resistance indicates no continuity to ground, while zero resistance indicates a dead short to ground.

RESISTANCE MEASUREMENT

The batteries in an ohmmeter will weaken with age and temperature, so the ohmmeter must be calibrated or "zeroed" before taking measurements. To zero the meter, place the selector switch in its lowest range and touch the two ohmmeter leads together. Turn the calibration knob until the meter needle is exactly on zero.

NOTE: *All analog (needle) type ohmmeters must be zeroed before use, but some digital ohmmeter models are automatically calibrated when the switch is turned on. Self-calibrating digital ohmmeters do not have an adjusting knob, but its a good idea to check for a zero readout before use by touching the leads together. All computer controlled systems require the use of a digital ohmmeter with at least 10 meagohms impedance for testing. Before any test procedures are attempted, make sure the ohmmeter used is compatible with the electrical system or damage to the onboard computer could result.*

To measure resistance, first isolate the circuit from the vehicle power source by disconnecting the battery cables or the harness connector. Make sure the key is OFF when disconnecting any components or the battery. Where necessary, also isolate at least one side of the circuit to be checked to avoid reading parallel resistances. Parallel circuit resistances will always give a lower reading than the actual resistance of either of the branches. When measuring the resistance of parallel circuits, the total resistance will always be lower than the smallest resistance in the circuit. Connect the meter leads to both sides of the circuit (wire or component) and read the actual measured ohms on the meter scale. Make sure the selector switch is set to the proper ohm scale for the circuit being tested to avoid misreading the ohmmeter test value.

NOTE: *Never use an ohmmeter with power applied to the circuit. Like the self-powered test light, the ohmmeter is designed to operate on its own power supply. The normal 12 volt automotive electrical system current could damage the meter!*

Ammeters

An ammeter measures the amount of current flowing through a circuit in units called amperes or amps. Amperes are units of electron flow which indicate how fast the electrons are flowing through the circuit. Since Ohms Law dictates that current flow in a circuit is equal to the circuit voltage divided by the total circuit resistance, increasing voltage also increases the current level (amps). Likewise, any decrease in resistance will increase the amount of amps in a circuit. At normal operating voltage, most circuits have a characteristic amount of amperes, called "current draw" which can be measured using an ammeter. By referring to a specified current draw rating, measuring the amperes, and comparing the two values, one can determine what is happening within the circuit to aid in diagnosis. An open circuit, for example, will not allow any current to flow so the ammeter reading will be zero. More current flows through a heavily loaded circuit or when the charging system is operating.

An ammeter is always connected in series with the circuit being tested. All of the current that normally flows through the circuit must also flow through the ammeter; if there is any other path for the current to follow, the ammeter reading will not be accurate. The ammeter itself has very little resistance to current flow and therefore will not affect the circuit, but it will measure current draw only when the circuit is closed and electricity is flowing. Excessive current draw can blow fuses and drain the battery, while a reduced current draw can cause motors to run slowly, lights to dim and other components to not operate properly. The ammeter can help diagnose these conditions by locating the cause of the high or low reading.

Multimeters

Different combinations of test meters can be built into a single unit designed for specific tests. Some of the more common combination test devices are known as Volt/Amp testers, Tach/Dwell meters, or Digital Multimeters. The Volt/Amp tester is used for charging system, starting system or battery tests and consists of a voltmeter, an ammeter and a variable resistance carbon pile. The voltmeter will usually have at least two ranges for use with 6, 12 and 24 volt systems. The ammeter also has more than one range for testing various levels of battery loads and starter current draw and the carbon pile can be adjusted to offer different amounts of resistance. The Volt/Amp tester has heavy leads to carry large amounts of current and many later models have an inductive ammeter pickup that clamps around the wire to simplify test connections. On some models, the ammeter also has a zero-center scale to allow testing of charging and starting systems without switching leads or polarity. A digital multimeter is a voltmeter, ammeter and ohmmeter combined in an instrument which gives a digital readout. These are often used when testing solid state circuits because of their high input impedance (usually 10 megohms or more).

The tach/dwell meter combines a tachometer and a dwell (cam angle) meter and is a specialized kind of voltmeter. The tachometer scale is marked to show engine speed in rpm and the dwell scale is marked to show degrees of distributor shaft rotation. In most electronic ignition systems, dwell is determined by the control unit, but the dwell meter can also be used to check the duty cycle (operation) of some electronic engine control systems. Some tach/dwell meters are powered by an internal battery, while others take their power from the car battery in use. The battery powered testers usually require calibration much like an ohmmeter before testing.

Special Test Equipment

A variety of diagnostic tools are available to help troubleshoot and repair computerized engine control systems. The most sophisticated of these devices are the console type engine analyzers that usually occupy a garage service bay, but there are several types of aftermarket electronic testers available that will allow quick circuit tests of the engine control system by plugging directly into a special connector located in the engine compartment or under the dashboard. Several tool and equipment manufacturers offer simple, hand held testers that measure various circuit voltage levels on command to check all system components for proper operation. Although these testers usually cost about $300-500, consider that the average computer control unit (or ECM) can cost just as much and the money saved by not replacing perfectly good sensors or components in an attempt to correct a problem could justify the purchase price of a special diagnostic tester the first time it's used.

These computerized testers can allow quick and easy test measurements while the engine is operating or while the car is being driven. In addition, the on-board computer memory can be read to access any stored trouble codes; in effect allowing the computer to tell you where it hurts and aid trouble diagnosis by pinpointing exactly which circuit or component is malfunctioning. In the same manner, repairs can be tested to make sure the problem has been corrected. The biggest advantage these special testers have is their relatively easy hookups that minimize or eliminate the chances of making the wrong connections and getting false voltage readings or damaging the computer accidentally.

NOTE: *It should be remembered that these testers check voltage levels in circuits; they don't detect mechanical problems or failed components if the circuit voltage falls within the preprogrammed limits stored in the tester PROM unit. Also, most of the hand held testes are designed to work only on one or two systems made by a specific manufacturer.*

A variety of aftermarket testers are available to help diagnose different computerized control systems. Owatonna Tool Company (OTC), for example, markets a device called the OTC Monitor which plugs directly into the assembly line diagnostic link (ALDL). The OTC tester makes diagnosis a simple matter of pressing the correct buttons and, by changing the internal PROM or inserting a different diagnosis cartridge, it will work on any model from full size to subcompact, over a wide range of years. An adapter is supplied with the tester to allow connection to all types of ALDL links, regardless of the number of pin terminals used. By inserting an updated PROM into the OTC tester, it can be easily updated to diagnose any new modifications of computerized control systems.

Wiring Harnesses

The average automobile contains about ½ mile of wiring, with hundreds of individual connections. To protect the many wires from damage and to keep them from becoming a confusing tangle, they are organized into bundles, enclosed in plastic or taped together and called wire harnesses. Different wiring harnesses serve different parts of the vehicle. Individual wires are color coded to help trace them through a harness where sections are hidden from view.

A loose or corroded connection or a replacement wire that is too small for the circuit will add extra resistance and an additional voltage drop to the circuit. A ten percent voltage drop can result in slow or erratic motor operation, for example, even though the circuit is complete. Automotive wiring or circuit conductors can be in any one of three forms:

1. Single strand wire
2. Multistrand wire
3. Printed circuitry

Single strand wire has a solid metal core and is usually used inside such components as alternators, motors, relays and other devices. Multistrand wire has a core made of many small strands of wire twisted together into a single conductor. Most of the wiring in an automotive electrical system is made up of multistrand wire, either as a single conductor or grouped together in a harness. All wiring is color coded on the insulator, either as a solid color or as a colored wire with an identification stripe. A printed circuit is a thin film of copper or other conductor that is printed on an insulator backing. Occasionally, a printed circuit is sandwiched between two sheets of plastic for more protection and flexibility. A complete printed circuit, consisting of conductors, insulating material and connectors for lamps or other components is called a printed circuit board. Printed circuitry is used in place of individual wires or harnesses in places where space is limited, such as behind instrument panels.

Wire Gauge

Since computer controlled automotive electrical systems are very sensitive to changes in resistance, the selection of properly sized wires is critical when systems are repaired. The wire gauge number is an expression of the cross section area of the conductor. The most common system for expressing wire size is the American Wire Gauge (AWG) system.

Wire cross section area is measured in circular mils. A mil is $\frac{1}{1000}''$ (0.001"); a circular mil is the area of a circle one mil in diameter. For example, a conductor ¼" in diameter is 0.250 in. or 250 mils. The circular mil cross section area of the wire is 250 squared (250^2) or 62,500 circular mils. Imported car models usually use metric wire gauge designations, which is simply the cross section area of the conductor in square millimeters (mm^2).

Gauge numbers are assigned to conductors of various cross section areas. As gauge number increases, area decreases and the conductor becomes smaller. A 5 gauge conductor is smaller than a 1 gauge conductor and a 10 gauge is smaller than a 5 gauge. As the cross section area of a conductor decreases, resistance increases and so does the gauge number. A conductor with a higher gauge number will carry less current than a conductor with a lower gauge number.

NOTE: *Gauge wire size refers to the size of the conductor, not the size of the complete wire. It is possible to have two wires of the same gauge with different diameters because one may have thicker insulation than the other.*

12 volt automotive electrical systems generally use 10, 12, 14, 16 and 18 gauge wire. Main power distribution circuits and larger accessories usually use 10 and 12 gauge wire. Battery cables are usually 4 or 6 gauge, although 1 and 2 gauge wires are occasionally used. Wire length must also be considered when making repairs to a circuit. As conductor length increases, so does resistance. An 18 gauge wire, for example, can carry a 10 amp load for 10 feet without excessive voltage drop; however if a 15 foot wire is required for the same 10 amp load, it must be a 16 gauge wire.

An electrical schematic shows the electrical current paths when a circuit is operating properly. It is essential to understand how a circuit works before trying to figure out why it doesn't. Schematics break the entire electrical system down into individual circuits and show only one particular circuit. In a schematic, no attempt is made to represent wiring and components as they physically appear on the vehicle; switches and other components are shown as simply as possible. Face views of harness connectors show the cavity or terminal locations in all multi-pin connectors to help locate test points.

If you need to backprobe a connector while it is on the component, the order of the terminals must be mentally reversed. The wire color code can help in this situation, as well as a keyway, lock tab or other reference mark.

NOTE: *Wiring diagrams are not included in this book. As trucks have become more complex and available with longer option lists, wiring diagrams have grown in size and complexity. It has become almost impossible to provide a readable reproduction of a wiring diagram in a book this size. Information on ordering wiring diagrams from the vehicle manufacturer can be found in the owner's manual.*

WIRING REPAIR

Soldering is a quick, efficient method of joining metals permanently. Everyone who has the occasion to make wiring repairs should know how to solder. Electrical connections that are soldered are far less likely to come apart and will conduct electricity much better than connections that are only "pig-tailed" together. The most popular (and preferred) method of soldering is with an electrical soldering gun. Soldering irons are available in many sizes and wattage ratings. Irons with higher wattage ratings deliver higher temperatures and recover lost heat faster. A small soldering iron rated for no more than 50 watts is recommended, especially on electrical systems where excess heat can damage the components being soldered.

There are three ingredients necessary for successful soldering; proper flux, good solder and sufficient heat. A soldering flux is necessary to clean the metal of tarnish, prepare it for soldering and to enable the solder to spread into tiny crevices. When soldering, always use a resin flux or resin core solder which is non-corrosive and will not attract moisture once the job is finished. Other types of flux (acid core) will leave a residue that will attract moisture and cause the wires to corrode. Tin is a unique metal with a low melting point. In a molten state, it dissolves and alloys easily with many metals. Solder is made by mixing tin with lead. The most common proportions are 40/60, 50/50 and 60/40, with the percentage of tin listed first. Low priced solders usually contain less tin, making them very difficult for a beginner to use because more heat is required to melt the solder. A common solder is 40/60 which is well suited for all-around general use, but 60/40 melts easier, has more tin for a better joint and is preferred for electrical work.

Soldering Techniques

Successful soldering requires that the metals to be joined be heated to a temperature that will melt the solder – usually 360-460°F (182-238°C). Contrary to popular belief, the purpose of the soldering iron is not to melt the solder itself, but to heat the parts being soldered to a temperature high enough to melt the solder when it is touched to the work. Melting flux-cored solder on the soldering iron will usually destroy the effectiveness of the flux.

NOTE: *Soldering tips are made of copper for good heat conductivity, but must be "tinned" regularly for quick transference of heat to the project and to prevent the solder from sticking to the iron. To "tin" the iron, simply heat it and touch the flux-cored solder to the tip; the solder will flow over the hot tip. Wipe the excess off with a clean rag, but be careful as the iron will be hot.*

After some use, the tip may become pitted. If so, simply dress the tip smooth with a smooth file and "tin" the tip again. An old saying holds that "metals well cleaned are half soldered." Flux-cored solder will remove oxides but rust, bits of insulation and oil or grease must be removed with a wire brush or emery cloth. For maximum strength in soldered parts, the joint must start off clean and tight. Weak joints will result in gaps too wide for the solder to bridge.

If a separate soldering flux is used, it should be brushed or swabbed on only those areas that are to be soldered. Most solders contain a core of flux and separate fluxing is unnecessary. Hold the work to be soldered firmly. It is best to solder on a wooden board, because a metal vise will only rob the piece to be soldered of heat and make it difficult to melt the solder. Hold the soldering tip with the broadest face against the work to be soldered. Apply solder under the tip close to the work, using enough solder to give a heavy film between the iron and the piece being soldered, while moving slowly and making sure the solder melts properly. Keep the work level or the solder will run to the lowest part and favor the thicker parts, because these require more heat to melt the solder. If the soldering tip overheats (the solder coating on the face of the tip burns up), it should be retinned. Once the soldering is completed, let the soldered joint stand until cool. Tape and seal all soldered wire splices after the repair has cooled.

Wire Harness and Connectors

The on-board computer (ECM) wire harness electrically connects the control unit to the various solenoids, switches and sensors used by the control system. Most connectors in the engine compartment or otherwise exposed to the elements are protected against moisture and dirt which could create oxidation and deposits on the terminals. This protection is important because of the very low voltage and current levels used by the computer and sensors. All connectors have a lock which secures the male and female terminals together, with a secondary lock holding the seal and terminal into the connector. Both terminal locks must be released when disconnecting ECM connectors.

These special connectors are weather-proof and all repairs require the use of a special terminal and the tool required to service it. This tool is used to remove the pin and sleeve terminals. If removal is attempted with an ordinary pick, there is a good chance that the terminal will be bent or deformed. Unlike standard blade type terminals, these terminals cannot be straightened once they are bent. Make certain that the connectors are properly seated and all of the sealing rings in place when connecting leads. On some models, a hinge-type flap provides a backup or secondary locking feature for the terminals. Most secondary locks are used to improve the connector reliability by retaining the terminals if the small terminal lock tangs are not positioned properly.

Molded-on connectors require complete replacement of the connection. This means splicing a new connector assembly into the harness. All splices in on-board computer systems should be soldered to insure proper contact. Use care when probing the connections or replacing terminals in them as it is possible to short between opposite terminals. If this happens to the wrong terminal pair, it is possible to damage certain components. Always use jumper wires between connectors for circuit checking and never probe through weatherproof seals.

Open circuits are often difficult to locate by sight because corrosion or terminal misalignment are hidden by the connectors. Merely wiggling a connector on a sensor or in the wiring harness may correct the open circuit condition. This should always be considered when an open circuit or a failed sensor is indicated. Intermittent problems may also be caused by oxidized or loose connections. When using a circuit tester for diagnosis, always probe connections from the wire side. Be careful not to damage sealed connectors with test probes.

All wiring harnesses should be replaced with identical parts, using the same gauge wire and connectors. When signal wires are spliced into a harness, use wire with high temperature insulation only. With the low voltage and current levels found in the system, it is important that the best possible connection at all wire splices be made by soldering the splices together. It is seldom necessary to replace a complete harness. If replacement is necessary, pay close attention to insure proper harness routing. Secure the harness with suitable plastic wire clamps to prevent vibrations from causing the harness to wear in spots or contact any hot components.

NOTE: *Weatherproof connectors cannot be replaced with standard connectors. Instructions are provided with replacement connector and terminal packages. Some wire harnesses have mounting indicators (usually pieces of colored tape) to mark where the harness is to be secured.*

In making wiring repairs, it's important that you always replace damaged wires with wires that are the same gauge as the wire being replaced. The heavier the wire, the smaller the gauge number. Wires are color-coded to aid in identification and whenever possible the same color coded wire should be used for replacement. A wire stripping and crimping tool is necessary to install solderless terminal connectors. Test all crimps by pulling on the wires; it should not be possible to pull the wires out of a good crimp.

Wires which are open, exposed or otherwise damaged are repaired by simple splicing. Where possible, if the wiring harness is accessible and the damaged place in the wire can be located, it is best to open the harness and check for all possible damage. In an inaccessible harness, the wire must be bypassed with a new insert, usually taped to the outside of the old harness.

When replacing fusible links, be sure to use

fusible link wire, NOT ordinary automotive wire. Make sure the fusible segment is of the same gauge and construction as the one being replaced and double the stripped end when crimping the terminal connector for a good contact. The melted (open) fusible link segment of the wiring harness should be cut off as close to the harness as possible, then a new segment spliced in as described. In the case of a damaged fusible link that feeds two harness wires, the harness connections should be replaced with two fusible link wires so that each circuit will have its own separate protection.

NOTE: *Most of the problems caused in the wiring harness are due to bad ground connections. Always check all vehicle ground connections for corrosion or looseness before performing any power feed checks to eliminate the chance of a bad ground affecting the circuit.*

Repairing Hard Shell Connectors

Unlike molded connectors, the terminal contacts in hard shell connectors can be replaced. Weatherproof hard-shell connectors with the leads molded into the shell have non-replaceable terminal ends. Replacement usually involves the use of a special terminal removal tool that depress the locking tangs (barbs) on the connector terminal and allow the connector to be removed from the rear of the shell. The connector shell should be replaced if it shows any evidence of burning, melting, cracks, or breaks. Replace individual terminals that are burnt, corroded, distorted or loose.

NOTE: *The insulation crimp must be tight to prevent the insulation from sliding back on the wire when the wire is pulled. The insulation must be visibly compressed under the crimp tabs, and the ends of the crimp should be turned in for a firm grip on the insulation.*

The wire crimp must be made with all wire strands inside the crimp. The terminal must be fully compressed on the wire strands with the ends of the crimp tabs turned in to make a firm grip on the wire. Check all connections with an ohmmeter to insure a good contact. There should be no measurable resistance between the wire and the terminal when connected.

Mechanical Test Equipment

Vacuum Gauge

Most gauges are graduated in inches of mercury (in.Hg), although a device called a manometer reads vacuum in inches of water (in. H_2O). The normal vacuum reading usually varies between 18 and 22 in.Hg at sea level. To test engine vacuum, the vacuum gauge must be connected to a source of manifold vacuum. Many

engines have a plug in the intake manifold which can be removed and replaced with an adapter fitting. Connect the vacuum gauge to the fitting with a suitable rubber hose or, if no manifold plug is available, connect the vacuum gauge to any device using manifold vacuum, such as EGR valves, etc. The vacuum gauge can be used to determine if enough vacuum is reaching a component to allow its actuation.

Hand Vacuum Pump

Small, hand-held vacuum pumps come in a variety of designs. Most have a built-in vacuum gauge and allow the component to be tested without removing it from the vehicle. Operate the pump lever or plunger to apply the correct amount of vacuum required for the test specified in the diagnosis routines. The level of vacuum in inches of Mercury (in.Hg) is indicated on the pump gauge. For some testing, an additional vacuum gauge may be necessary.

Intake manifold vacuum is used to operate various systems and devices on late model vehicles. To correctly diagnose and solve problems in vacuum control systems, a vacuum source is necessary for testing. In some cases, vacuum can be taken from the intake manifold when the engine is running, but vacuum is normally provided by a hand vacuum pump. These hand vacuum pumps have a built-in vacuum gauge that allow testing while the device is still attached to the component. For some tests, an additional vacuum gauge may be necessary.

HEATING AND AIR CONDITIONING

Refer to Chapter 1 for discharging, charging of the air conditioning system.

Heater Assembly
REMOVAL AND INSTALLATION
610, 710

1. Disconnect the battery ground cable.
2. Drain the coolant.

CAUTION: *When draining the coolant, keep in mind that cats and dogs are attracted by the ethylene glycol antifreeze, and are quite likely to drink any that is left in an uncovered container or in puddles on the ground. This will prove fatal in sufficient quantity. Always drain the coolant into a sealable container. Coolant should be reused unless it is contaminated or several years old.*

3. Detach the coolant inlet and outlet hoses.
4. On the 610, remove the center ventilator grille from the bottom of the instrument panel.
5. Remove the heater duct hose from both

sides of the heater unit. Remove the defroster hose or hoses on the 610. On the 710, remove the intake duct and defroster duct from both sides of the heater unit. Remove the console box on the 710 if so equipped.

6. Disconnect the electrical wires of the heater unit (and air conditioner, if so equipped) at their connections.

7. Disconnect and remove the heater control cables.

8. On 710 and 1974-76 610, remove the two bolts on each side of the unit and one on the top. For 1973 610s, remove one attaching bolt from each side and one from the top center of the unit.

9. Remove the unit.

10. Install the unit in the vehicle with retaining bolts. Connect the heater control cables and the electrical wires of the heater unit (and air conditioner, if so equipped) at their connections.

11. Install the heater duct hose to both sides of the heater unit. Install the defroster hose or hoses on the 610. On the 710, install the intake duct and defroster duct to both sides of the heater unit. Install the console box on the 710 if so equipped.

12. On the 610, install the center ventilator grille to the bottom of the instrument panel.

13. Reconnect the two heater hoses with new hose clamps. Connect the battery ground cable and refill the cooling system.

14. Run the engine for a few minutes with the heater on to make sure the coolant level is correct. Check for any coolant leaks.

15. Check the heater system for proper operation.

1977-79 200SX

1. Disconnect the battery cable.

2. Drain the engine coolant and remove the heater hoses from the engine side.

CAUTION: *When draining the coolant, keep in mind that cats and dogs are attracted by the ethylene glycol antifreeze, and are quite likely to drink any that is left in an uncovered container or in puddles on the ground. This will prove fatal in sufficient quantity. Always drain the coolant into a sealable container. Coolant should be reused unless it is contaminated or several years old.*

3. Inside the passenger compartment, disconnect the lead wires from the heater unit to the instrument harness.

4. At this point, the instrument panel must be removed in order to remove the heater assembly. To remove the panel proceed as follows:

5. Remove the steering wheel cover.

6. Disconnect the speedometer cable and the radio antenna cable.

7. After noting their position, disconnect the following connectors: instrument harness to body, harness to engine room, transistor ignition unit, and the wiring to the console.

8. Remove the bolts securing the column clamp and lower the steering column.

9. Remove the package tray.

10. Remove the bolts which attach the instrument panel to the mounting bracket on the left and right hand sides.

11. Remove the trim on the right side windshield pillar, and remove the bolt attaching instrument panel to the pillar.

12. Remove the trim on the top of the instrument panel.

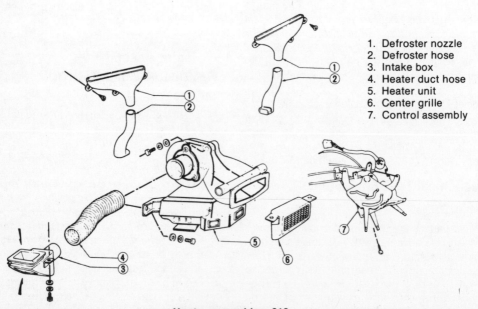

1. Defroster nozzle
2. Defroster hose
3. Intake box
4. Heater duct hose
5. Heater unit
6. Center grille
7. Control assembly

Heater assembly—610

13. Remove the bolts attaching the instrument panel.

14. Move the instrument panel to the right to remove it.

15. Remove the defroster hoses on both sides of the heater unit.

16. Disconnect the wires to the air conditioner if so equipped. Disconnect the heater control cables.

17. Remove the three heater retaining bolts and remove the heater assembly.

18. Install the heater assembly with retaining bolts in the vehicle.

19. Reconnect the wires to the air conditioner if so equipeed. Reconnect the heater control cables.

20. Connect the defroster hoses on both sides of the heater unit.

21. Install the instrument panel and all necessary components that were removed to gain access to the instrument panel retaining bolts.

22. Inside the passenger compartment, connect the lead wires to the heater unit from the instrument harness.

23. Reconnect the two heater hoses with new hose clamps. Connect the battery ground cable and refill the cooling system.

24. Run the engine for a few minutes with the heater on to make sure the coolant level is correct. Check for any coolant leaks and the heater system for proper operation.

1980 and Later 200SX
1989 240SX

NOTE: *On the 1984-88 200SX and 1989 240SX models no factory removal and installation procedures are given use this procedure as a guide. Refer to the exploded view of each heater system.*

1. Set the TEMP lever to the HOT position and drain the coolant.

CAUTION: *When draining the coolant, keep in mind that cats and dogs are attracted by the ethylene glycol antifreeze, and are quite likely to drink any that is left in an uncovered container or in puddles on the ground. This will prove fatal in sufficient quantity. Always drain the coolant into a sealable container. Coolant should be reused unless it is contaminated or several years old.*

2. Disconnect the heater hoses from the driver's side of the heater unit.

3. At this point the manufacturer suggests you remove the front seats. To do this, remove the plastic covers over the ends of the seat runners, both front and back, to expose the seat mounting bolts. Remove the bolts and remove the seats.

4. Remove the console box and the floor carpets.

5. Remove the instrument panel lower covers from both the driver's and passenger's sides of the car. Remove the lower cluster lids.

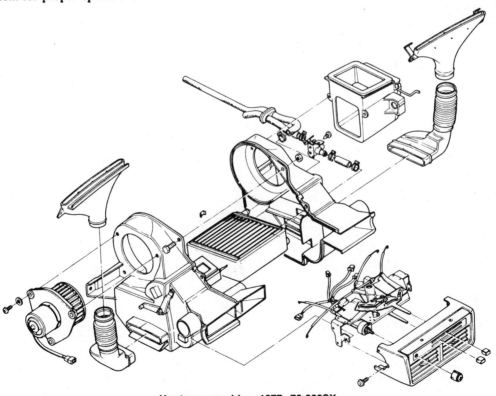

Heater assembly—1977–79 200SX

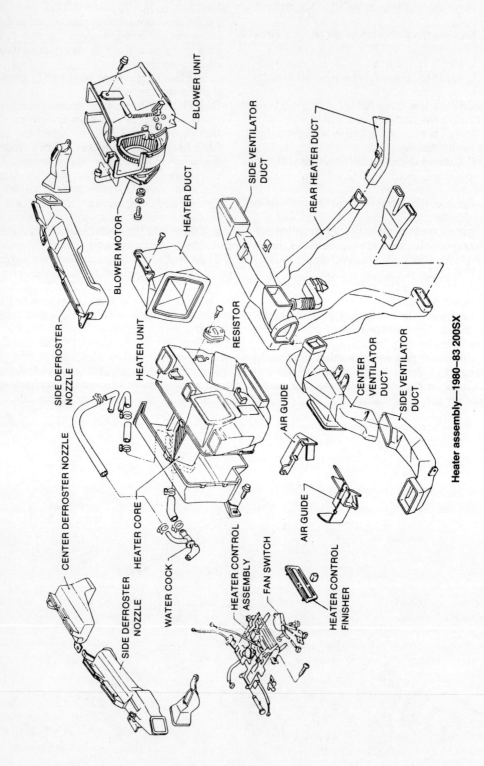

BLOWER UNIT

SIDE VENTILATOR DUCT

REAR HEATER DUCT

BLOWER MOTOR

HEATER DUCT

RESISTOR

CENTER VENTILATOR DUCT

SIDE VENTILATOR DUCT

SIDE DEFROSTER NOZZLE

HEATER UNIT

AIR GUIDE

CENTER DEFROSTER NOZZLE

HEATER CORE

WATER COCK

HEATER CONTROL ASSEMBLY

FAN SWITCH

AIR GUIDE

SIDE DEFROSTER NOZZLE

HEATER CONTROL FINISHER

Heater assembly—1980–83 200SX

6. Remove the left hand side ventilator duct.

7. Remove the radio, sound balancer and stereo cassette deck if so equipped.

8. Remove the instrument panel-to-transmission tunnel stay.

9. Remove the rear heater duct from the floor of the vehicle.

10. Remove the center ventilator duct.

11. Remove the left and right hand side air guides from the lower heater outlets.

12. Disconnect the wire harness connections.

13. Remove the two screws at the bottom sides of the heater unit and the one screw and the top of the unit and remove the unit together with the heater control assembly.

NOTE: *On late models the heater control cables and control assembly may have to be removed before the heater unit is removed. Always mark control cables before removing them to ensure correct adjustment and proper operation.*

14. Install the heater assembly with retaining bolts in the vehicle. Reconnect all electrical and heater control cable connections if removed.

15. Install the left and right hand side air guides to the lower heater outlets.

16. Install the center ventilator duct.

17. Install the rear heater duct to the floor of the vehicle and all components that were removed to gain access to the rear heater duct retaining bolts.

18. Install the instrument panel lower covers, floor carpets, console box and seats if removed.

19. Reconnect the two heater hoses with new hose clamps. Connect the battery ground cable and refill the cooling system.

20. Run the engine for a few minutes with the heater on to make sure the coolant level is correct. Check for any coolant leaks and the heater system for proper operation.

NOTE: *You may be able to skip several of the above steps if only certain components of the heater unit need service.*

1977-80 810

1. Disconnect the battery ground cable.
2. Drain the engine coolant.

CAUTION: *When draining the coolant, keep in mind that cats and dogs are attracted by the ethylene glycol antifreeze, and are quite likely to drink any that is left in an uncovered container or in puddles on the ground. This will prove fatal in sufficient quantity. Always drain the coolant into a sealable container. Coolant should be reused unless it is contaminated or several years old.*

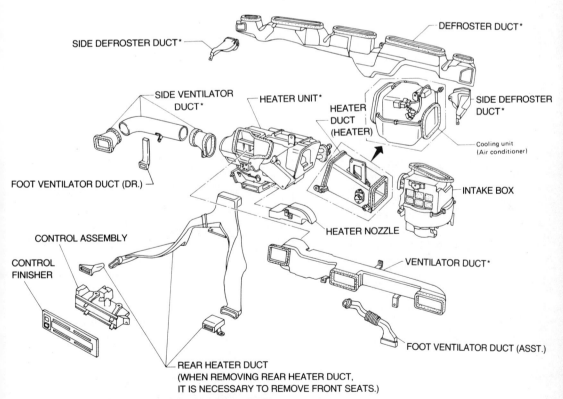

*For removal, it is necessary to remove instrument assembly.

Heater assembly—1984–86½ 200SX

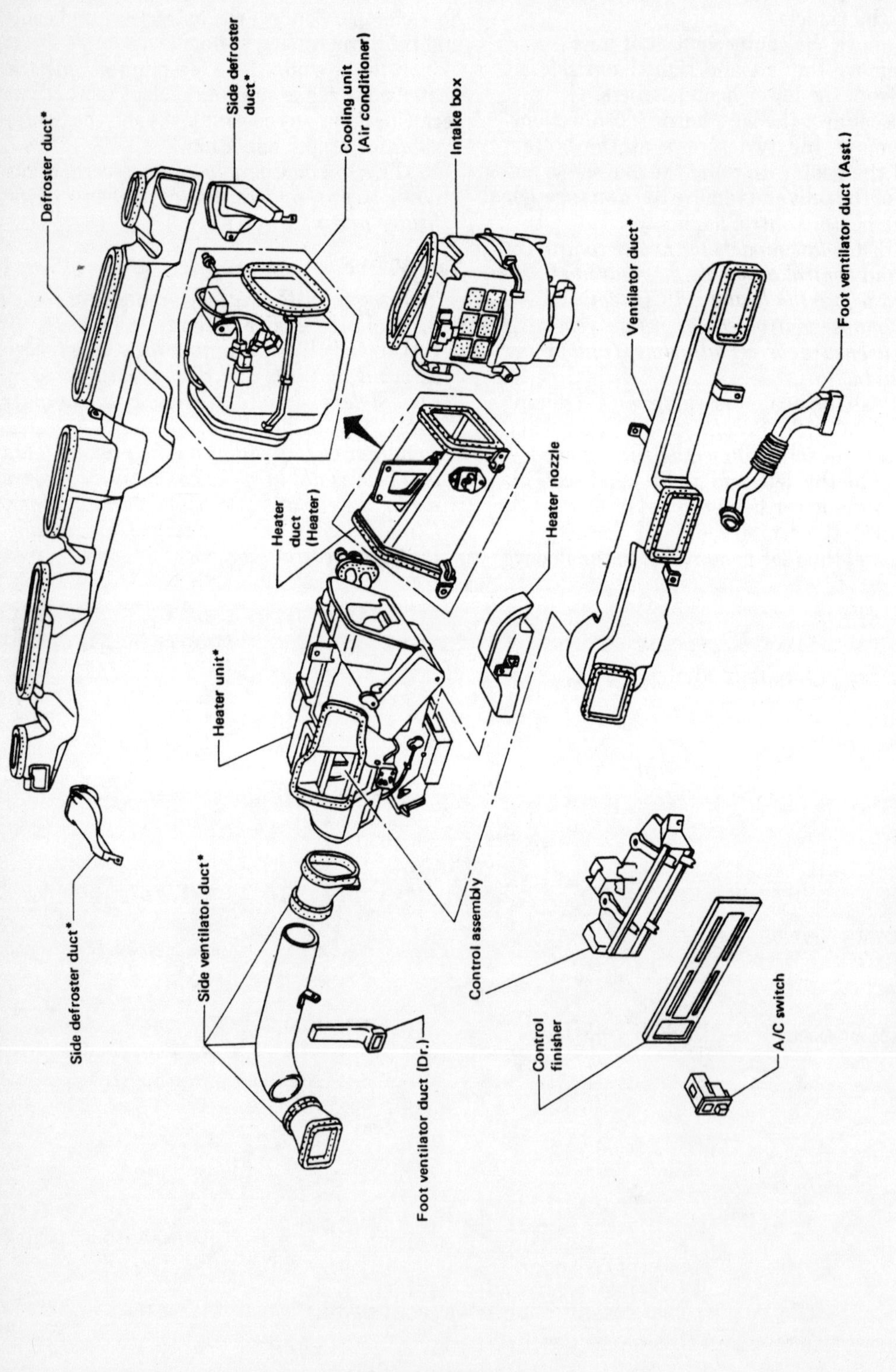

Defroster duct*

Side defroster duct*

Cooling unit (Air conditioner)

Intake box

Ventilator duct*

Foot ventilator duct (Asst.)

Side defroster duct*

Heater duct (Heater)

Heater unit*

Heater nozzle

Side ventilator duct*

Control assembly

Foot ventilator duct (Dr.)

Control finisher

A/C switch

*For removal, it is necessary to remove instrument assembly.

Heater assembly—1986½–88 200SX

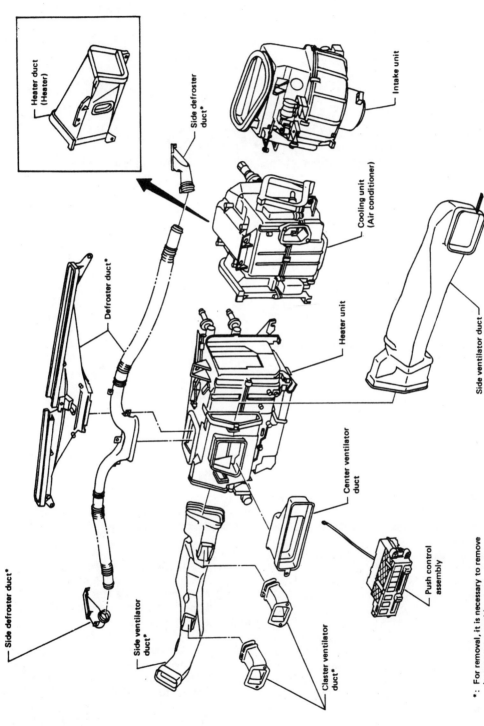

Heater duct
(Heater)

Side defroster
duct*

Intake unit

Cooling unit
(Air conditioner)

Defroster duct*

Heater unit

Side ventilator duct

Side defroster duct*

Side ventilator
duct*

Claster ventilator
duct*

Center ventilator
duct

Push control
assembly

Heater assembly—1989 240SX

*: For removal, it is necessary to remove
instrument assembly.

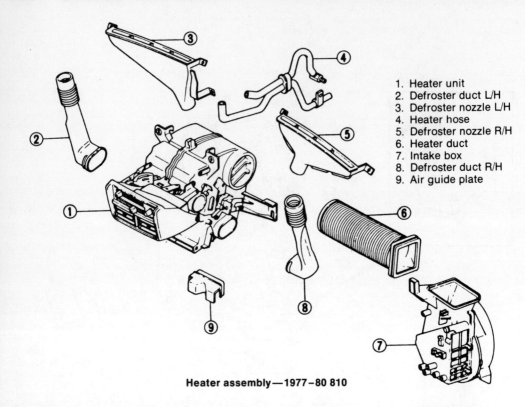

1. Heater unit
2. Defroster duct L/H
3. Defroster nozzle L/H
4. Heater hose
5. Defroster nozzle R/H
6. Heater duct
7. Intake box
8. Defroster duct R/H
9. Air guide plate

Heater assembly—1977–80 810

3. Remove the console box and the console box bracket. Remove the front floor mat.

4. Loosen the screws and remove the rear heater duct.

5. Remove the hose clamps and remove the inlet and outlet hoses.

6. Remove the heater duct and remove the defroster hoses from the assembly.

7. Remove the air intake door control cable.

8. Disconnect the wiring harness to the heater.

9. Remove the retaining bolts and remove the heater unit.

10. Install the heater unit with retaining bolts in the vehicle.

11. Connect the wiring harness and heater control cables to the heater unit.

12. Reconnect the heater hoses with new hose clamps. Install the rear heater duct.

13. Install the console box assembly and floor mat.

14. Connect the battery ground cable and re-fill the cooling system. Run the engine for a few minutes with the heater on to make sure the coolant level is correct. Check for any coolant leaks and the heater system for proper operation.

1981 and Later 810 and Maxima

NOTE: *On the 1985-89 Maxima models no factory removal and installation procedures are given use this procedure as a guide. Refer*

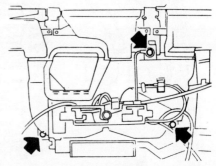

The heater vent on the 1981 and later 810 and Maxima has three mounting bolts

to the exploded view of each heater system. You may be able to skip several of the following steps if only certain components of the heater assembly need service.

1. Set the TEMP lever to the HOT position and drain the coolant.

CAUTION: *When draining the coolant, keep in mind that cats and dogs are attracted by the ethylene glycol antifreeze, and are quite likely to drink any that is left in an uncovered container or in puddles on the ground. This will prove fatal in sufficient quantity. Always drain the coolant into a sealable container. Coolant should be reused unless it is contaminated or several years old.*

2. Disconnect the heater hoses from the driver's side of the heater unit.

3. At this point the manufacturer suggests that you remove the front seats. To do this, remove the plastic covers over the ends of the seat runners, front and back, to expose the seat mounting bolts. Remove the bolts and lift out the seats.

4. Remove the front floor carpets.

5. Remove the instrument panel lower covers from both the driver's and passenger's sides of the car.

6. Remove the left side ventilator duct.

7. Remove the instrument panel assembly.

8. Remove the rear heater duct from the floor of the car.

9. Tag and disconnect the wire harness connectors.

10. Remove the two screws at the bottom sides of the heater unit and the one screw from the top of the unit. Lift out the heater together with the heater control assembly.

NOTE: *On late models the heater control cables and control assembly may have to be removed before the heater unit is removed. Always mark control cables before removing them to ensure correct adjustment and proper operation.*

11. Install the heater assembly with retaining bolts in the vehicle. Reconnect all electrical and heater control cable connections if removed.

12. Install the rear heater duct to the floor of the vehicle and all components that were removed to gain access to the rear heater duct retaining bolts.

13. Install the instrument panel assembly and the left side ventilator duct.

14. Install the instrument panel lower covers, floor carpets and seats if removed.

15. Reconnect the two heater hoses with new hose clamps. Connect the battery ground cable and refill the cooling system.

16. Run the engine for a few minutes with the heater on to make sure the coolant level is correct.

17. Check for any coolant leaks and the heater system for proper operation.

1978-80 510

1. Disconnect the ground cable at the battery. Drain the coolant.

CAUTION: *When draining the coolant, keep in mind that cats and dogs are attracted by the ethylene glycol antifreeze, and are quite likely to drink any that is left in an uncovered container or in puddles on the ground. This*

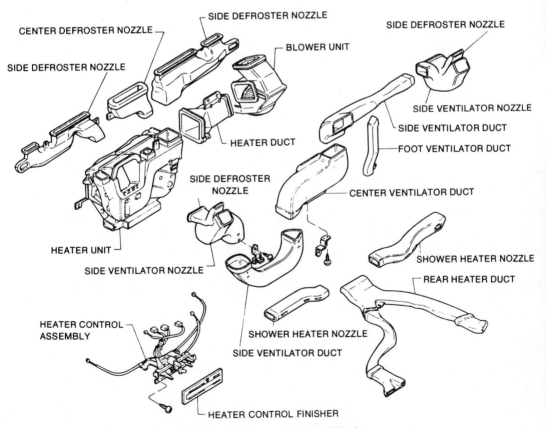

Heater assembly—1981–84 810/Maxima

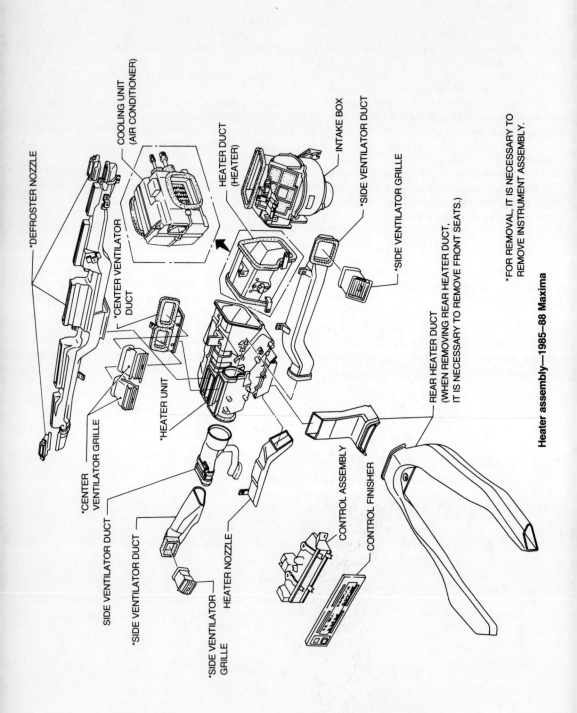

*DEFROSTER NOZZLE

COOLING UNIT
(AIR CONDITIONER)

HEATER DUCT
(HEATER)

INTAKE BOX

*CENTER VENTILATOR
DUCT

*SIDE VENTILATOR DUCT

*SIDE VENTILATOR GRILLE

*SIDE VENTILATOR GRILLE

*HEATER UNIT

*CENTER
VENTILATOR GRILLE

SIDE VENTILATOR DUCT

*SIDE VENTILATOR DUCT

*SIDE VENTILATOR
GRILLE

HEATER NOZZLE

CONTROL ASSEMBLY

CONTROL FINISHER

REAR HEATER DUCT
(WHEN REMOVING REAR HEATER DUCT,
IT IS NECESSARY TO REMOVE FRONT SEATS.)

*FOR REMOVAL, IT IS NECESSARY TO
REMOVE INSTRUMENT ASSEMBLY.

Heater assembly—1985–88 Maxima

will prove fatal in sufficient quantity. Always drain the coolant into a sealable container. Coolant should be reused unless it is contaminated or several years old.

2. Remove the console box.

3. Remove the driver's side of the instrument panel.

4. Remove the heater control assembly: remove the defroster ducts, vent door cables at the doors and harness connector.

5. Remove the radio.

6. Disconnect the heater ducts, side defrosters and the center vent duct.

7. Remove the screws attaching the defroster nozzle to the unit. Disconnect the blower wiring harness and the heater hoses.

8. Remove the retaining bolts and the heater unit.

9. Install the heater unit with retaining bolts in the vehicle.

10. Connect the blower wiring harness electrical connection and heater hoses with new hose clamps.

11. Install the defroster nozzle to the heater unit, the heater ducts, side defrosters and the center vent duct.

12. Install the radio and heater control assembly. Install the defroster ducts, vent door cables at the doors and harness electrical connector.

13. Install the driver's side of the instrument panel and console box.

14. Connect the battery ground cable and refill the cooling system.

15. Run the engine for a few minutes with the heater on to make sure the coolant level is cor-

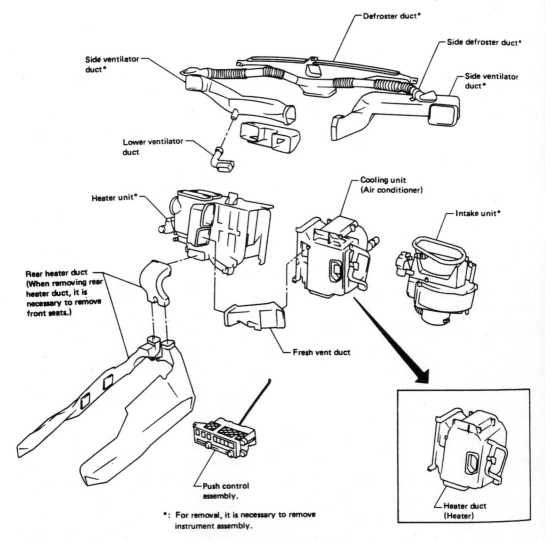

Heater assembly—1989 Maxima

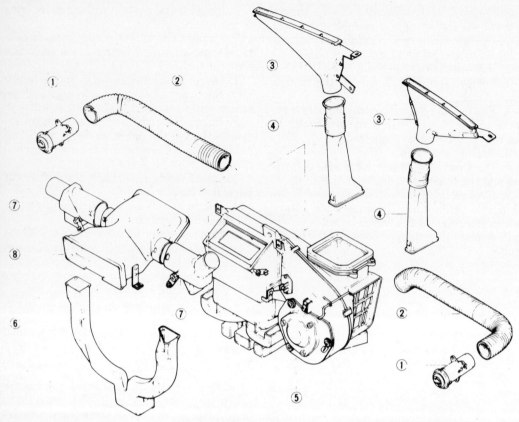

1. Side outlet
2. Cooler duct
3. Defroster nozzle
4. Defroster duct
5. Heater unit
6. Side defroster center duct
7. Side defroster connector
8. Center ventilation duct

Heater assembly—510

rect. Check for any coolant leaks and the heater system for proper operation.

Heater Blower

REMOVAL AND INSTALLATION

610, 710, and 1977-79 200SX

1. Remove the heater unit from the vehicle. NOTE: *You may be able to remove the blower on some models without removing the heater unit from the vehicle.*

2. Remove the three or four screws holding the blower motor in the case and remove the motor with the fan attached.

3. Installation is the reverse of removal. Refer to the exploded view of the heater assembly.

1980 and Later 200SX

NOTE: *On all 1984-88 200SX models the blower motor is located behind the glove box, facing the floor. Use this procedure as a guide and refer to the exploded view of the heater assembly.*

1. Disconnect the battery ground cable. Re-

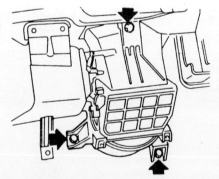

Remove the three bolts and remove the blower—1980–82 200SX

move the instrument panel lower cover and cluster lid on the right hand side.

2. Disconnect the control cable and harness connector from the blower unit.

3. Remove the three bolts and remove the blower unit.

4. Remove the three screws holding the blower motor in the case, unplug the hose run-

ning from the rear of the motor into the case and pull the motor together with the fan cage out of the case.

5. Installation is the reverse of removal. Make sure the electrical connection is installed in the correct position.

810 and Maxima

NOTE: *It may be necessary to remove the glove box assembly to gain clearance for heater blower removal and installation. The blower motor is located behind the glove box, facing the floor. Use this procedure as a guide on 1985-89 Maxima models and refer to the exploded view of the heater assembly.*

1. Disconnect the negative battery cable. Remove the heater duct running from the blower case to the heater unit.

2. Disconnect the control cable from the blower case and the harness connector.

3. Remove the screws holding the blower case in place and remove the blower case.

4. Remove the three bolts holding the blower motor in place and remove the blower motor.

5. Installation is the reverse of removal. Make sure the electrical connection is installed in the correct position.

1978-81 510

1. Disconnect the battery ground cable and the blower motor harness connector.

2. Remove the blower motor by removing the three outer retaining screws and pulling the motor with the fan out of the case.

NOTE: *Make sure you remove the three outer screws and not the three screws holding the motor to the backing plate.*

3. Installation is the reverse of removal. Make sure the electrical connection is installed in the correct position.

Heater Core

REMOVAL AND INSTALLATION

610 and 710

The heater unit need not be removed to remove the heater core. It must be removed to remove the blower motor.

1. Drain the coolant and remove the coolant hoses.

CAUTION: *When draining the coolant, keep in mind that cats and dogs are attracted by the ethylene glycol antifreeze, and are quite likely to drink any that is left in an uncovered container or in puddles on the ground. This will prove fatal in sufficient quantity. Always drain the coolant into a sealable container. Coolant should be reused unless it is contaminated or several years old.*

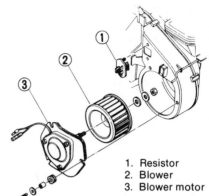

1. Resistor
2. Blower
3. Blower motor

Removing the blower—510

2. Disconnect the control cables on the sides of the heater unit.

3. Remove the clips and the cover from the front of the heater unit. Pull out the core.

4. Reverse the procedure for installation. Run the engine with the heater on for a few minutes to make sure that the system fills with coolant. Always use new heater hose clamps.

1977-79 200SX

1. Remove the heater assembly from the vehicle.

2. Remove the control lever assembly. Remove the knobs, disconnect the lamp wire, remove the center vent (4 screws), disconnect the fan wires, remove the clips and cables, remove the retaining screws and the unit.

3. Disconnect the hose from the heater cock.

4. Remove the connection rod (with bracket) from the air door.

5. Remove the clips on each side of the box, split the box, and remove the core.

6. Install the heater core in the correct location. Reconnect the heater box with the retaining clips.

7. Install the connection rod (with bracket) to the air door.

8. Connect the hose to the heater cock.

9. Install the control lever assembly with attaching parts.

10. Install the heater assembly in the vehicle.

1980 and Later 200SX

1. Remove the heater unit and the heater core hoses.

2. Remove the heater core from the heater unit box.

3. Installation is the reverse of removal.

810 and Maxima

1. Remove the heater assembly. Loosen the clips and screws and remove the center ventilation cover and heater control assembly.

2. Remove the screws securing the door shafts.

3. Remove the clips securing the left and right heater cases, and then separate the cases. Remove the heater core.

4. Installation is in the reverse order of removal.

1978-81 510

1. Remove the heater unit. Loosen the hose clamps and disconnect the inlet and outlet hoses.

2. Remove the clips securing the case halves and separate the cases.

3. Remove the heater core.

4. Installation is in the reverse order of removal.

Evaporator Core/Cooling Unit
REMOVAL AND INSTALLATION
510, 610, 710 Models

NOTE: *On some models an air filter is installed between the evaporator housing and the air intake housing. This filter should be cleaned once a year. The evaporator housing and cooling unit are the same part.*

1. Disconnect battery ground cable.

2. Discharge air conditioning system, refer to Chapter 1 for more details.

3. Loosen flare nuts at each connection of inlet and outlet pipes of evaporator.

NOTE: *Be sure to use two wrenches when removing or connecting pipe joints. Always plug pipe openings immediately after pipe disconnection.*

4. Remove the instrument cluster lid cover. On 610 models remove the center console box.

5. Disconnect all electrical connections and control cables from cooling unit.

6. Remove the upper and lower attaching bolts and remove the cooling unit.

7. Remove all attaching parts from cooling unit.

8. Remove screws or clips securing upper case to lower case.

9. Separated case and remove the evaporator.

10. Install evaporator core in cooling unit case.

11. Install the attaching parts on the cooling unit.

12. Install the cooling unit with retaining bolts in the vehicle.

13. Connect all electrical connections and control cables. Reconnect the pressure pipes with new O-rings. Install the instrument cluster lid cover.

14. On 610 models, install the center console box.

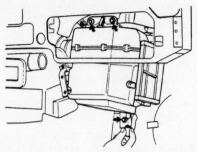

Removing evaporator housing retaining bolts—610 models

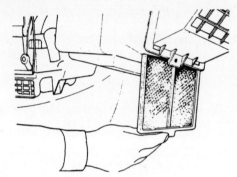

Removing air filter for evaporator

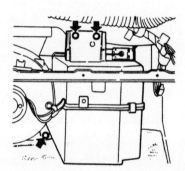

Removing cooling unit retaining bolts—510 model

Coat seat surfaces with compressor oil and then tighten.

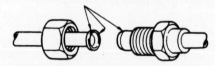

Typical A/C fittings—always use new O-rings

15. Connect battery cable and charge the air conditioning system. Refer to Chapter 1 if necessary.

16. Check system for proper operation.

810 and Maxima (Rear Wheel Drive) 1977-83 200SX

1. Disconnect battery ground cable.

2. Remove the instrument lower cover and cluster lid cover.

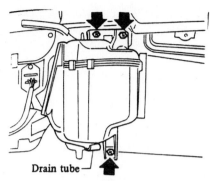

Removing cooling unit retaining bolts—1983 200SX models

Drain tube

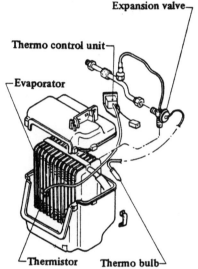

Expansion valve

Thermo control unit

Evaporator

Thermistor   Thermo bulb

Evaporator housing or cooling unit assembly—1983 200SX

3. Discharge air conditioning system, refer to Chapter 1 for more details.

4. Disconnect refrigerant lines and electrical harness from the cooling unit.

NOTE: *Be sure to use two wrenches when removing or connecting pipe joints. Always plug pipe openings immediately after pipe disconnection.*

5. Remove the cooling unit with drain tube.

6. Remove the clips fixing the upper case to lower case.

7. Remove the evaporator core from the cooling unit.

8. Install the evaporator core in the cooling unit. Connect lower and upper case with retaining clips.

9. Install the cooling unit with retaining bolts in the vehicle.

10. Connect all electrical connections. Reconnect the pressure pipes with new O-rings. In-

stall the instrument lower cover and cluster lid cover.

11. Connect battery cable and charge the air conditioning system. Refer to Chapter 1 if necessary.

12. Check system for proper operation.

1985-89 Maxima (Front Wheel Drive)
1984-88 200SX
1989 240SX

On these vehicles there is no removal and installation procedure for evaporator core or cooling unit given by Datsun/Nissan. Use the early model procedures as a guide refer to the exploded view of the heater assembly if necessary.

RADIO

REMOVAL AND INSTALLATION

610 and 710

1. Disconnect the negative battery cable. Remove the instrument cluster. Disconnect all electrical connections, antenna and the speaker connections.

2. Remove the radio knobs and retaining nuts.

3. Remove the rear support bracket and remove the radio.

4. Reverse the procedure for installation.

1977-79 200SX

1. Disconnect the negative battery cable. The instrument panel must be removed in order to remove the radio. The instrument panel is referred to as the cluster lid in the illustrations.

2. Pull out the radio switch knobs.

3. In order to remove the instrument panel, first remove the steering wheel and cover.

4. Remove the control knobs on the instrument panel by pushing in on them and turning them counterclockwise. Once the knobs are removed, remove the nuts.

5. Remove the instrument panel screws. See the illustration for their location.

6. Disconnect the switch wires (after noting their location) and remove the panel.

7. Loosen the screws and remove the radio from its bracket. Disconnect the wires and pull the radio free.

8. Install the radio in the radio bracket and connect all electrical connections, speaker wires and antenna.

9. Connect all electrical connections and install the instrument panel and all knobs.

10. Install the steering wheel in the correct position.

11. Reconnect the battery cable. Start the engine and check all components on the the instrument panel for proper operation.

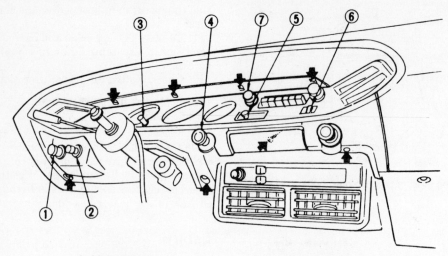

1. Light switch
2. Illumination control knob
3. Trip meter knob
4. Windshield wiper and washer switch knob
5. Hazard switch
6. Rear defogger switch
7. Radio knob

Instrument panel removal points—1977–79 200SX

1980-83 200SX

1. Disconnect the battery. Before removing the radio (audio assembly), you must remove the center instrument cluster which holds the heater controls, etc. Remove the two side screws in the cluster. Remove the heater control and the control panel. Remove the two bolts behind the heater control panel and the two bolts at the case of the cluster. Pull the cluster out of the way after disconnecting the lighter wiring and any other control cables.

2. Remove the radio knobs and fronting panel.

3. Remove the five screws holding the radio assembly in place.

4. Remove the radio after unplugging all connections.

5. Installation is the reverse of removal.

810 and Maxima (Rear Wheel Drive)

1. Disconnect the battery ground cable. Remove the knobs and nuts on the radio and the choke control wire. Remove the ash tray.

2. Remove the steering column cover, and disconnect the main harness connectors.

3. Remove the retaining screws and remove the instrument panel cover.

4. Disconnect the wires from the radio and remove the radio from the bracket.

5. Installation is in the reverse order of removal.

1978-81 510

NOTE: *Refer to 1978 510 instrument panel removal points illustration.*

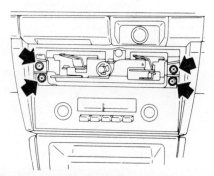

Radio securing screws, Maxima

1. Disconnect the battery ground cable.

2. Remove the steering column covers and disconnect the hazard warning switch connector.

3. Loosen the wiper switch attaching screws and remove the wiper switch.

4. Pull out the ash tray and the heater control knobs.

5. Remove the heater control finisher. Insert a screwdriver into the FAN lever slit to remove the finisher. Remove finisher A.

6. Remove the radio knobs, nuts and washers.

7. Remove the manual choke knob and the defroster control knob.

8. Disconnect the following connectors:
   a. center illumination light
   b. cigarette lighter
   c. clock
   d. turn signal switch.

9. Remove the screws from the instrument

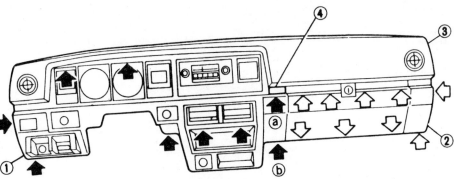

1. Cluster lid A
2. Cluster lid B
3. Instrument panel
4. Finisher A

◀ Cluster lid A securing screw positions

◁ Cluster lid B securing screw positions

1978 510 instrument panel removal points

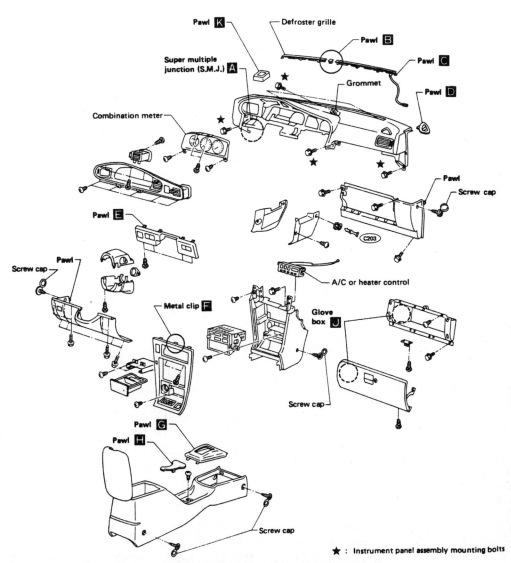

Pawl **K**

Defroster grille

Pawl **B**

Super multiple junction (S.M.J.) **A**

Pawl **C**

Grommet

Pawl **D**

Combination meter

Pawl **E**

Pawl

Screw cap

C203

A/C or heater control

Screw cap

Pawl

Metal clip **F**

Glove box **J**

Pawl

Screw cap

Pawl **G**

Pawl **H**

Screw cap

★ : Instrument panel assembly mounting bolts

Instrument panel assembly—1989 Maxima

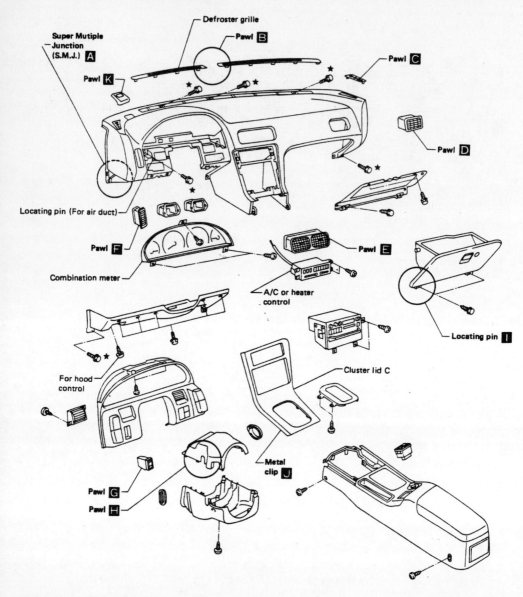

Defroster grille

Super Mutiple Junction (S.M.J.) **A**

Pawl **B**

Pawl **C**

Pawl **K**

Pawl **D**

Locating pin (For air duct)

Pawl **F**

Combination meter

Pawl **E**

A/C or heater control

Locating pin **I**

For hood control

Cluster lid C

Metal clip **J**

Pawl **G**

Pawl **H**

★ : Instrument panel assembly mounting bolts

Instrument panel assembly—1989 240SX

panel (referred to as cluster lid A in the illustration). The black arrows mark the screws locations.

10. Remove the instrument panel cover. Remove the connections from the radio and remove the radio from its bracket.

11. Install the radio in the radio bracket and connect all electrical connections, speaker wires and antenna.

12. Connect all electrical connections and install the instrument panel and cover.

13. Install the ashtray assembly, all knobs, heater control finisher and any other electrical connection if necessary..

14. Install the wiper switch assembly. Connect the hazard warning switch connector. Install the steering column covers.

15 Reconnect the battery cable. Start the engine check all components on the the instrument panel for proper operation.

1984-88 200SX
1989 240SX
1985-89 Maxima (Front Wheel Drive)

On these vehicles there is no removal and installation procedure for the radio given by Datsun/Nissan. Use the early model procedures as

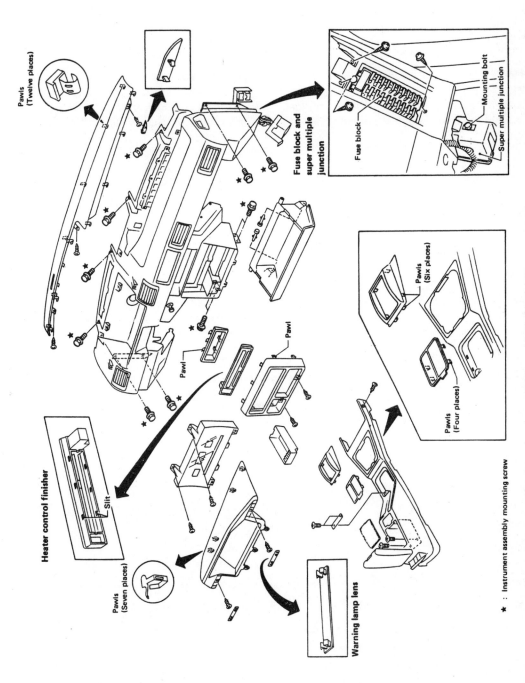

Pawls (Twelve places)

Fuse block and super multiple junction

Mounting bolt

Super multiple junction

Fuse block

Heater control finisher

Slit

Pawl

Pawl

Pawls (Seven places)

Warning lamp lens

Pawls (Six places)

Pawls (Four places)

Instrument panel assembly—1988 200SX—other years similar

★ : Instrument assembly mounting screw

a guide refer to the exploded view of the instrument panel assembly if necessary.

WINDSHIELD WIPER

Blade and Arm

REMOVAL AND INSTALLATION

All Models

NOTE: *On some new models a wiper arm lock is used to keep the wiper arm off the glass surface when washing the glass or replacing*

the blade. On 1984-88 200SX models the wiper arms are a different length. They have an identifying mark and care must be taken to install them properly.

1. Pull the wiper arm up.
2. Push the lock pin, then remove the wiper blade.
3. Insert the new wiper blade to the wiper arm until a click sounds.
4. Make sure the wiper blade contacts the glass. Otherwise, the arm may be damaged.
5. To remove the arm assembly lift the end of the wiper arm, which is spring loaded, at the base and remove the attaching nut. On early

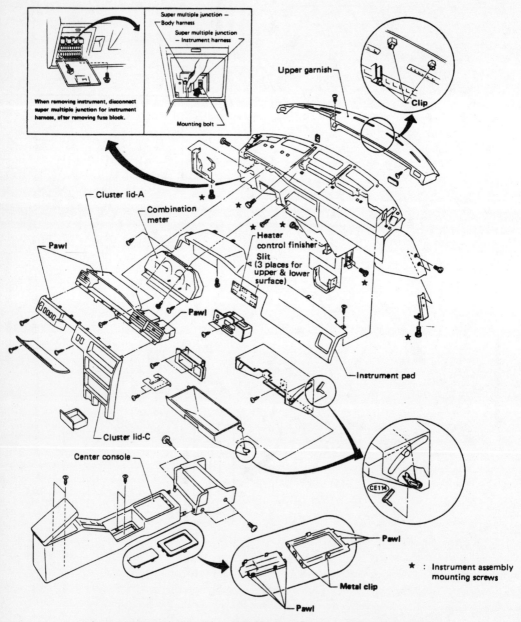

Instrument panel assembly—1988 Maxima (Canada)—other years similar

models just remove the attaching nut at the base of the wiper arm.

Motor and Linkage

REMOVAL AND INSTALLATION

610, 710, 810, Maxima 1977-79 200SX

1. Disconnect the battery ground cable. The wiper motor and linkage are accessible from un-der the hood. Raise the wiper blade from the windshield and remove the retaining nut. Re-move the wiper blades and arms.

2. Remove the nuts holding the wiper pivots to the body. Remove the screws holding the wiper motor to the firewall.

3. Disconnect the wiper motor wiring con-nector and remove the cowl air intake grille.

4. Disconnect the wiper motor from the link-

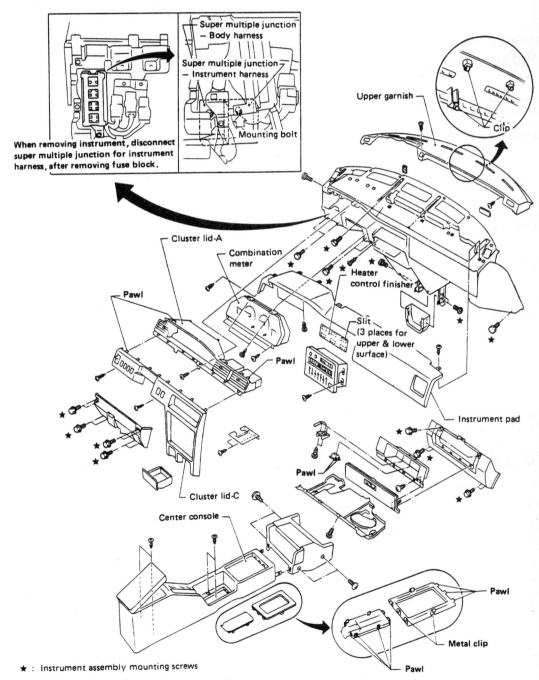

When removing instrument, disconnect super multiple junction for instrument harness, after removing fuse block.

★ : Instrument assembly mounting screws

Instrument panel assembly—1988 Maxima (USA)—other years similar

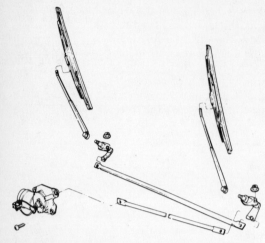

Windshield wiper motor and linkage—710. 810 and Maxima similar

age and remove the linkage assembly through the cowl top.

5. Installation is the reverse of removal.

NOTE: *If the wipers do not park correctly, adjust the position of the automatic stop cover of the wiper motor, if so equipped.*

1978-81 510

1. Disconnect the battery ground cable. Remove the wiper motor.

2. Remove the wiper link inspection cover under the hood.

3. Remove the wiper arms from the pivot shafts by lifting the arms then removing the attaching nuts.

4. Loosen and remove the large nuts securing the pivot shafts to the body. Remove the linkage through the inspection hole.

5. Installation is the reverse of removal.

NOTE: *Make sure you install the wiper arms in the correct positions by running the system without the arms on, stopping it, then attaching the arms.*

1980-88 200SX

1. Disconnect the battery ground cable.

2. Open the hood and disconnect the motor wiring connection.

3. Unbolt the motor from the body.

4. Disconnect the wiper linkage from the motor and remove the motor.

5. Installation is the reverse of removal.

1989 240SX

1. Remove the wiper arm.

2. Remove the cowl cover. Remove the wiper motor so that the wiper motor link comes out of hole in the front cowl top panel.

3. Disconnect the ball joint which connects

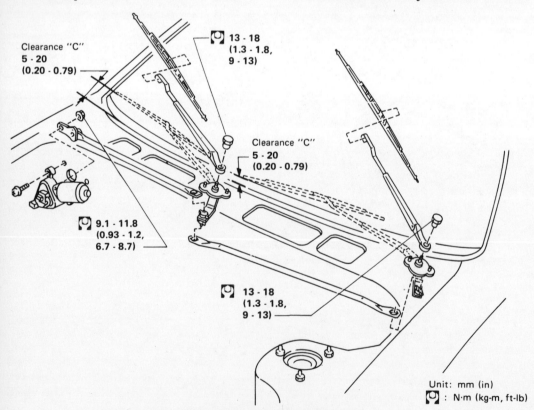

Clearance ''C''
5 - 20
(0.20 - 0.79)

13 - 18
(1.3 - 1.8,
9 - 13)

Clearance ''C''
5 - 20
(0.20 - 0.79)

9.1 - 11.8
(0.93 - 1.2,
6.7 - 8.7)

13 - 18
(1.3 - 1.8,
9 - 13)

Unit: mm (in)
: N·m (kg-m, ft-lb)

1984 and later 200SX wiper linkage

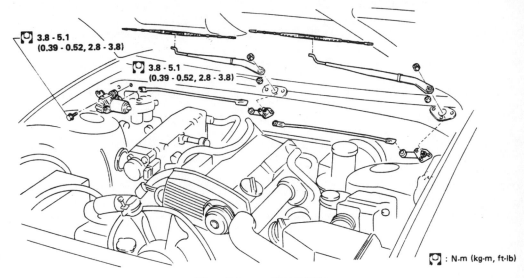

3.8 - 5.1
(0.39 - 0.52, 2.8 - 3.8)

3.8 - 5.1
(0.39 - 0.52, 2.8 - 3.8)

: N.m (kg-m, ft-lb)

Wiper linkage—1989 240SX

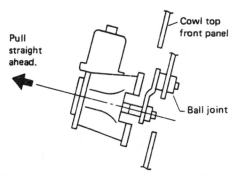

Pull
straight
ahead.

Cowl top
front panel

Ball joint

Remove wiper motor to gain access to ball joint

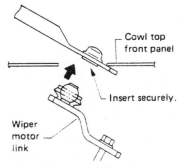

Cowl top
front panel

Insert securely.

Wiper
motor
link

Install ball joint to wiper linkage securely

motor link and wiper link. Remove the wiper
motor from the vehicle.

4. Remove wiper link pivot blocks on driver
and passenger sides. Remove the wiper link and
pivot blocks as an assembly from the oblong
hole on the left side of cowl top.

5. To install reverse the removal procedures.

Apply a small amount of grease to bal joints before installation. Refer to the illustrations.

INSTRUMENTS AND SWITCHES

Instrument Cluster

REMOVAL AND INSTALLATION

610 and 710

NOTE: *It may be necessary to drop the steering column to aid removal. Refer to the exploded view of the 710 instrument cluster removal illustration. Tag all wiring for correct
installation.*

1. Disconnect the battery ground cable.
2. Remove the four screws and the steering
column cover.
3. Remove the screws which attach the cluster face. Two are just above the steering column, and there is one inside each of the outer
instrument recesses.
4. Pull the cluster lid forward.
5. Disconnect the multiple connector.
6. Disconnect the speedometer cable.
7. Disconnect any other wiring.
8. Remove the cluster face.
9. Remove the odometer knob if so equipped.
10. Remove the six screws and the cluster.
11. Instruments may now be readily replaced.
12. Reconnect all electrical connections and
speedometer cable to the instrument cluster.
Install the cluster in position with retaining
screws.
13. Install the odometer knob if so equipped.

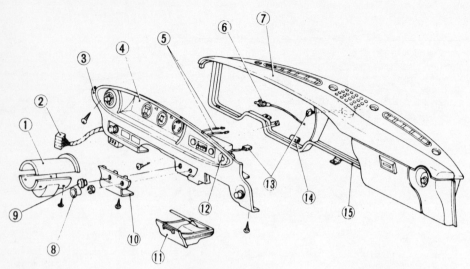

1. Steering column covers
2. Instrument harness
3. Cluster cover
4. Gauges
5. Light monitor
6. Speedometer cable
7. Upper instrument pad
8. Wiper/washer switch knob
9. Light control switch
10. Cluster cover
11. Ash tray
12. Clock
13. Speaker harness
14. Illumination bulb
15. Instrument panel

710 instrument cluster removal

14. Install the the cluster face and the steering column cover.

15. Reconnect the battery ground cable.

1977-80 810

1. Disconnect the battery ground cable. Remove the knobs and nuts on the radio and the knob on the choke control wire. Remove the ash tray.

2. Remove the steering column covers.

3. Disconnect the harness connectors after noting their location and marking them.

4. Remove the retaining screws and remove the instrument panel.

5. Installation is in the reverse order of removal.

1981 and Later 810 and Maxima (Rear Wheel Drive)

NOTE: *On the 1985-89 (front wheel drive) Maxima there is no removal and installation procedure given by Datsun/Nissan. Use the early model procedures as a guide refer to the exploded view of the instrument panel assembly if necessary.*

1. Disconnect the negative battery cable. Remove the instrument lower cover.

2. Remove the steering wheel.

3. Disconnect the speedometer cable. Remove the six mounting screws and lift out the cluster lid.

4. Unscrew the mounting bolts and lift off the left side instrument pad (this is the hooded part of the dashboard that the instrument cluster sits in).

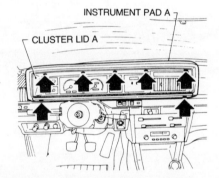

Maxima instrument panel/cluster screws

5. Loosen the instrument cluster mounting screws, pull it out slightly and disconnect all wiring. Remove the cluster.

6. Reconnect all electrical connections and speedometer cable to the instrument cluster. Install the cluster in position with retaining screws.

7. Install the steering wheel and the instrument lower cover. Reconnect the negative battery cable.

1977-79 200SX

NOTE: *This procedure is for instrument panel and cluster. Refer to the the exploded view of 1977-79 200SX instrument panel illustration.*

1. Disconnect the battery ground cable.

2. Remove the steering column covers.

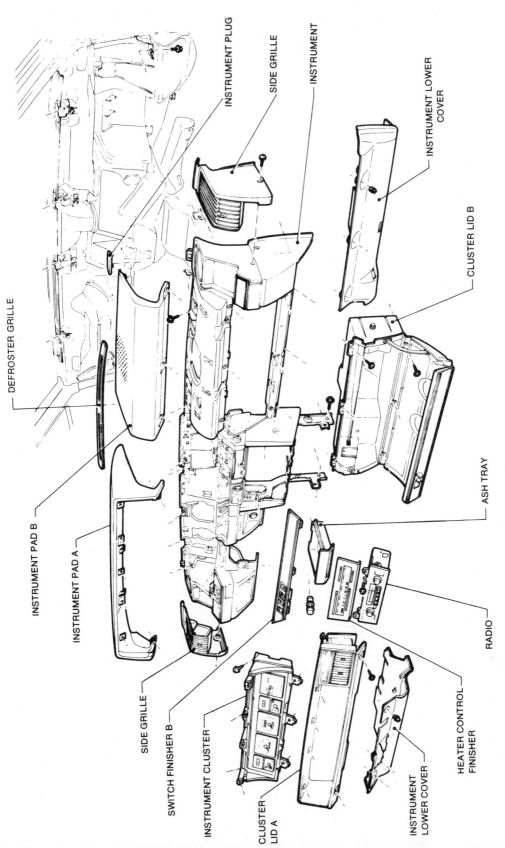

INSTRUMENT PLUG

SIDE GRILLE

INSTRUMENT

INSTRUMENT LOWER COVER

DEFROSTER GRILLE

CLUSTER LID B

INSTRUMENT PAD B

INSTRUMENT PAD A

ASH TRAY

SIDE GRILLE

SWITCH FINISHER B

INSTRUMENT CLUSTER

CLUSTER LID A

INSTRUMENT LOWER COVER

HEATER CONTROL FINISHER

RADIO

1981 and later 810 and Maxima instrument panel

3. Disconnect the speedometer cable and the radio antenna.

4. Disconnect all the wires from the back of the panel after noting their location and marking them.

5. Remove the bolts which secure the steering column clamp. Remove the package tray.

6. Unbolt the panel from the brackets on the left and right hand sides.

7. Remove the right side windshield pillar trim and remove the bolt which attaches the panel to the pillar.

8. Remove the instrument garnish.

9. Remove the retaining bolts and remove the panel.

10. Install the panel with retaining bolts in the correct position. Install the instrument garnish.

11. Reconnect all the wires to the back of the panel in the correct location.

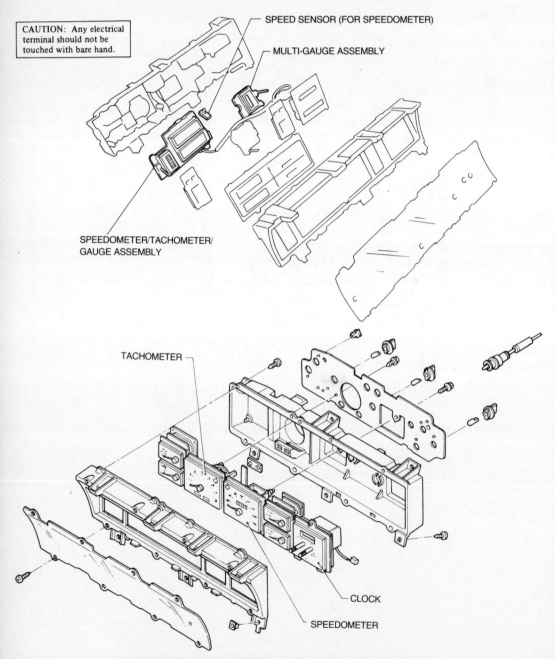

CAUTION: Any electrical terminal should not be touched with bare hand.

SPEED SENSOR (FOR SPEEDOMETER)

MULTI-GAUGE ASSEMBLY

SPEEDOMETER/TACHOMETER/ GAUGE ASSEMBLY

TACHOMETER

CLOCK

SPEEDOMETER

1984 Maxima instrument cluster, electronic cluster (optional) at top

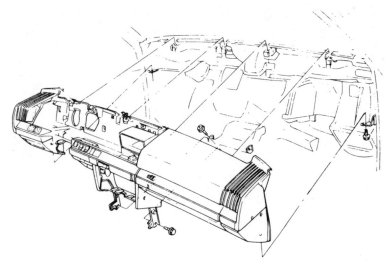

Removing the 1984 Maxima instrument panel

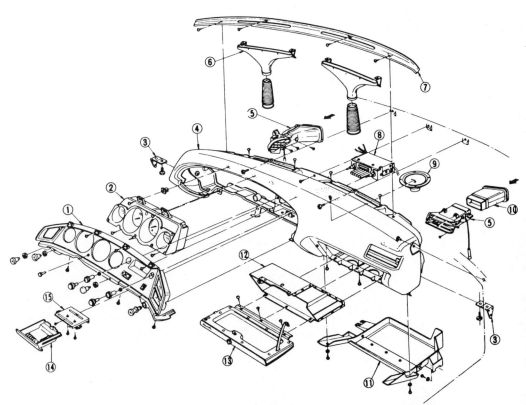

1. Cluster lid	6. Defroster nozzle	11. Package tray
2. Meter assembly	7. Instrument garnish	12. Glove box
3. Instrument mounting lower bracket	8. Radio	13. Glove box lid
4. Instrument pad	9. Speaker	14. Ash tray
5. Ventilation grille	10. Ventilation duct	15. Outer case

1977–79 200SX instrument panel

12. Connect the speedometer cable, radio antenna and steering column covers.

13. Install the right side windshield pillar trim, steering column clamp and package tray.

14. Reconnect the battery ground cable.

1980 and Later 200SX
1989 240SX

NOTE: *On the 1984-88 200SX and 1989 240SX there is no removal and installation procedure given by Datsun/Nissan. Use the early model procedures as a guide refer to the exploded view of the instrument panel assembly if necessary.*

1. Disconnect the battery ground terminal. It may be necessary to remove the steering wheel and covers to remove the instrument cluster.

2. Remove the five bolts holding the cluster in place and pull the cluster out, then remove all connections from its back. Make sure you mark the wiring to avoid confusion during reassembly.

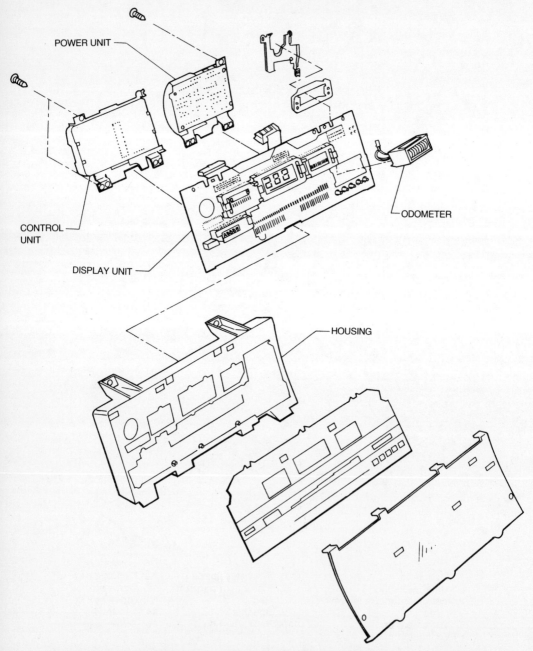

POWER UNIT

CONTROL UNIT

DISPLAY UNIT

ODOMETER

HOUSING

1984 200SX electronic digital instrument cluster. No user-serviceable equipment is found here

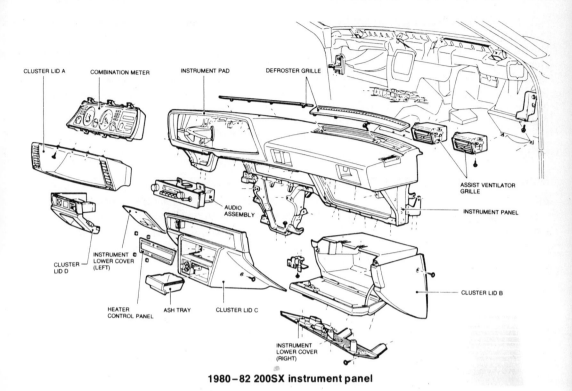

CLUSTER LID A   COMBINATION METER   INSTRUMENT PAD   DEFROSTER GRILLE

ASSIST VENTILATOR GRILLE

INSTRUMENT PANEL

CLUSTER LID B

CLUSTER LID D

INSTRUMENT LOWER COVER (LEFT)

AUDIO ASSEMBLY

HEATER CONTROL PANEL   ASH TRAY   CLUSTER LID C

INSTRUMENT LOWER COVER (RIGHT)

1980–82 200SX instrument panel

3. Remove the instrument cluster.

4. Installation is the reverse of removal.

1978 and Later 510

NOTE: *Refer to 1978 510 instrument panel removal points illustration.*

1. Disconnect the battery ground cable.

2. Remove the steering column covers. Disconnect the hazard warning switch connector.

3. Remove the wiper switch. Pull out the ash tray, remove the heater, control knobs, and remove the heater control plate by inserting a screwdriver into the fan lever slit and levering the plate out.

4. Remove the finish plate to the left of the glove compartment.

5. Pull off the radio knobs and remove the nuts and washers.

6. Remove the choke and side defroster knobs.

7. Remove the cluster lid screws.

8. Disconnect the electrical connectors.

9. Remove the cluster lid.

10. Remove the instrument cluster retaining screws. Disconnect the speedometer cable by pushing and turning counterclockwise.

11. Disconnect the instrument cluster wire connectors and remove the cluster.

12. Reconnect all electrical connections and speedometer cable to the instrument cluster. Install the cluster in position with retaining screws.

13. Install the cluster lid and all knobs.

14. Install the finish plate to the left of the glove compartment.

15. Install the wiper switch, ash tray, heater control knobs and heater control plate.

16. Connect the electrical connection for the hazard warning switch and install the steering column covers.

17. Reconnect the battery ground cable.

Ignition Switch

Ignition switch removal and installation procedures are covered in Chapter 8, Suspension and Steering.

Speedometer Cable

REMOVAL AND INSTALLATION

1. Remove any lower dash covers that may be in the way and disconnect the speedometer cable from the back of the speedometer.

NOTE: *On some models it may be easier to remove the instrument cluster to gain access to the cable.*

2. Remove the cable from the cable housing. On late models, press the tab at the top of the connector behind the speedometer to release it. If the cable is broken, the other half of the cable will have to be removed from the transmission end. Unscrew the retaining knob at the transmission and remove the cable from the transmission extension housing.

3. Lubricate the cable with graphite power (sold as speedometer cable lubricant) and feed the cable into the housing. It is best to start at the speedometer end and feed the cable down towards the transmission. It is also usually necessary to unscrew the transmission connection and install the cable end to the gear, then reconnect the housing to the transmission. Slip the cable end into the speedometer and reconnect the cable housing.

Seat Belt Warning Buzzer and Light

610

Beginning in 1971, all cars are required to have a warning system which operates a buzzer and warning system light if either of the front seat belts are not fastened when the seats are occupied and the car is in a forward gear. A light with the words Seat Belts, or Fasten Seat Belts is located on the dash board while a buzzer is located under the dash. They are controlled by pressure sensitive switches hidden in the front bench or bucket seats. A switch in each of the front seat belt retractors turns off the warning system only when the belt or belts are pulled a specified distance out of their retractors.

Two different types of switches are used to control the system, depending upon the type of transmission used.

On manual transmission equipped cars, the transmission neutral switch is used to activate the seat belt warning circuit.

Automatic transmissions use the inhibitor switch to activate the seat belt warning circuit.

When removing the seats, be sure to unplug the pressure sensitive switches at their connections.

Seat Belt/Starter Interlock System

1974-75

As required by law, all 1974 and most 1975 Datsun passenger cars cannot be started until the front seat occupants are seated and have fastened their seat belts. If the proper sequence is not followed, e.g., the occupants fasten the seat belts and then sit on them, the engine cannot be started.

The shoulder harness and lap belt are permanently fastened together, so that they both must be worn. The shoulder harness uses an inertia lock reel to allow freedom of movement under normal driving conditions.

NOTE: *This type of reel locks up when the car decelerates rapidly, as during a crash.*

The switches for the interlock system have been removed from the lap belt retractors and placed in the belt buckles. The seat sensors remain the same as those used in 1973.

For ease of service, the car may be started from outside, by reaching in and turning the key, but without depressing the seat sensors.

In case of system failure, an override switch is located under the hood. This is a one start switch and it must be reset each time it is used.

LIGHTING

Headlights

REMOVAL AND INSTALLATION

All Except 1984 and later 200SX and Non-Sealed Beam Halogen Headlamps

NOTE: *Many Datsuns have radiator grilles which are unit constructed to also serve as headlight frames. In this case, it will be necessary to remove the grille to gain access to the headlights.*

1. Remove the grille, if necessary.
2. Remove the headlight retaining ring screws. These are the three or four short screws in the assembly. There are also two longer screws at the top and side of the headlight

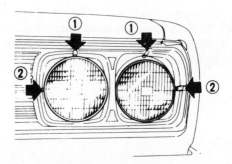

1. Vertical adjustment
2. Horizontal adjustment

Headlight adjusting screws—most models similar

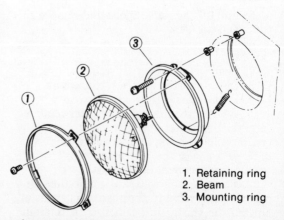

1. Retaining ring
2. Beam
3. Mounting ring

Exploded view of standard headlight

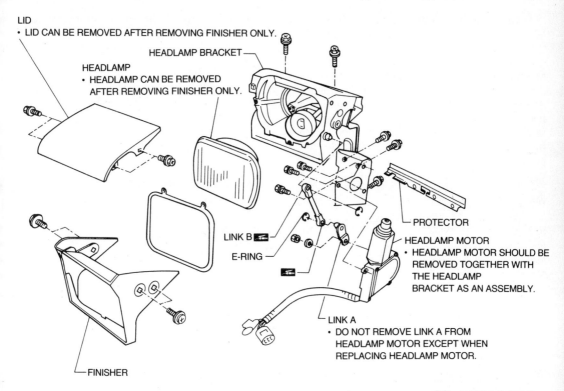

LID
• LID CAN BE REMOVED AFTER REMOVING FINISHER ONLY.

HEADLAMP BRACKET

HEADLAMP
• HEADLAMP CAN BE REMOVED
   AFTER REMOVING FINISHER ONLY.

LINK B

E-RING

PROTECTOR

HEADLAMP MOTOR
• HEADLAMP MOTOR SHOULD BE
   REMOVED TOGETHER WITH
   THE HEADLAMP
   BRACKET AS AN ASSEMBLY.

LINK A
• DO NOT REMOVE LINK A FROM
   HEADLAMP MOTOR EXCEPT WHEN
   REPLACING HEADLAMP MOTOR.

FINISHER

: GREASING POINT

1984 and later 200SX headlamp assembly

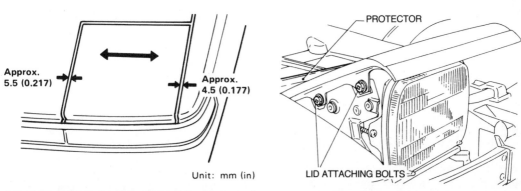

Approx.
5.5 (0.217)

Approx.
4.5 (0.177)

Unit: mm (in)

PROTECTOR

LID ATTACHING BOLTS

Adjust the lid to these dimensions at the joints, and so it is flush with the hood and fenders

1984 and later 200SX headlight lid adjustment

which are used to aim the headlight. Do not tamper with these or the headlight will have to be reaimed.

3. Remove the ring on round headlights by turning it clockwise.

4. Pull the headlight bulb from its socket and disconnect the electrical plug.

5. Connect the plug to the new bulb.

6. Position the headlight in the shell. Make sure that the word TOP is, indeed, at the top and that the knobs in the headlight lens engage the slots in the mounting shell.

7. Place the retaining ring over the bulb and install the screws.

8. Install the grille, if removed.

1984-88 200SX
1989 240SX

NOTE: *If headlamps do not open on these models, first check the fusible link for the headlight motor. Also check the retract switch. If headlamps do not retract, check the retract control relay. Refer to the Manual Operation Of Headlight Doors procedure.*

1. Open the headlamp.
2. Unbolt and remove the finisher.
3. Remove the headlamp lid.
4. Remove the bulb retaining ring. Unplug and remove the headlamp bulb.
5. Reverse the removal procedure to install. Adjust the headlamp lid so it is flush with the hood and fender, and so the lid joint is as shown in the accompanying illustration. This is done by adjusting the lid mounting screws while open and close the headlamp by operating the manual knob on the headlamp motor. Make sure the lid not interfering with the protector. Adjust the headlights.

MANUAL OPERATION OF HEADLIGHTS DOORS

1. Turn OFF both headlight switch and retractable headlight switch.
2. Disconnect the battery negative terminal.
3. Remove the motor shaft cap.
4. Turn the motor shaft counterclockwise by hand until the headlights are opened or closed.
5. Reinstall the motor shaft cap and connect the battery cable.

Non-Sealed Beam Halogen Headlamps

1985-89 MAXIMA

1. Disconnect the negative battery cable. Turn the bulb retaining ring counterclockwise until it is free of the headlight reflector, and remove it.
2. Disconnect the electrical connector at the rear of the bulb. Then, remove the bulb carefully without rotating or shaking it.
3. Install in reverse order.
CAUTION: *Do not remove a healdight bulb and leave the reflector empty. If you do this, the reflector will become contaminated by dust and smoke. Do not remove one bulb until another is available for immediate replacement.*
NOTE: *Do not touch the glass portion of the bulb. Handle it only by the plastic base!*

Manual operation of power headlight doors

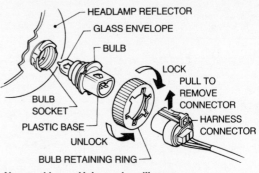

Non-seal beam Halogen headliamps

Signal And Marker Lights
REMOVAL AND INSTALLATION
Front Turn Signal And Parking Lights

1. Remove turn signal/parking light lens with retaining screws.
2. Slightly depress the bulb and turn it counterclockwise to release it.
3. To install the bulb carefully push down and turn bulb clockwise at the same time.
4. Install the turn signal/parking light lens with retaining screws.

Side Marker Lights

1. Remove side marker light lens with retaining screws.
2. Turn the bulb socket counterclockwise to release it from lens.
3. Pull bulb straight out.
4. To install bulb carefully push straight in.
5. Turn the bulb socket clockwise to install it in lens.
6. Install side marker light lens with retaining screws.

Signal and marker light bulb—removal and installation

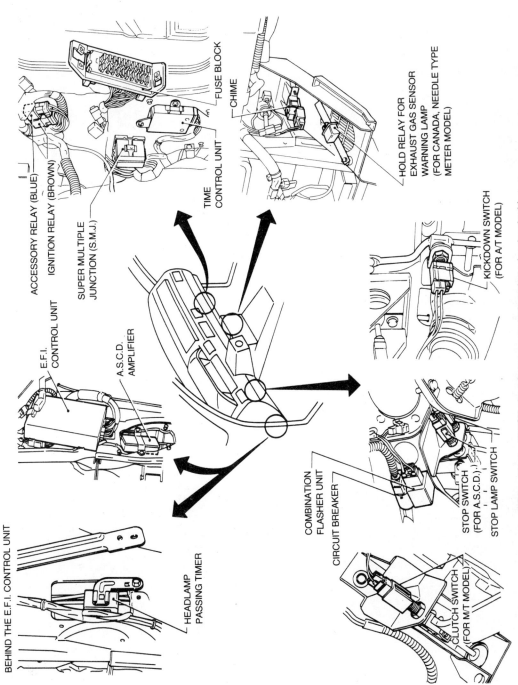

1984 and later 200SX electric component locations (under dash)

FUSE BLOCK

CHIME

TIME
CONTROL UNIT

HOLD RELAY FOR
EXHAUST GAS SENSOR
WARNING LAMP
(FOR CANADA; NEEDLE TYPE
METER MODEL)

ACCESSORY RELAY (BLUE)

IGNITION RELAY (BROWN)

SUPER MULTIPLE
JUNCTION (S.M.J.)

E.F.I.
CONTROL UNIT

A.S.C.D.
AMPLIFIER

KICKDOWN SWITCH
(FOR A/T MODEL)

COMBINATION
FLASHER UNIT

CIRCUIT BREAKER

STOP SWITCH
(FOR A.S.C.D.)

STOP LAMP SWITCH

CLUTCH SWITCH
(FOR M/T MODEL)

BEHIND THE E.F.I. CONTROL UNIT

HEADLAMP
PASSING TIMER

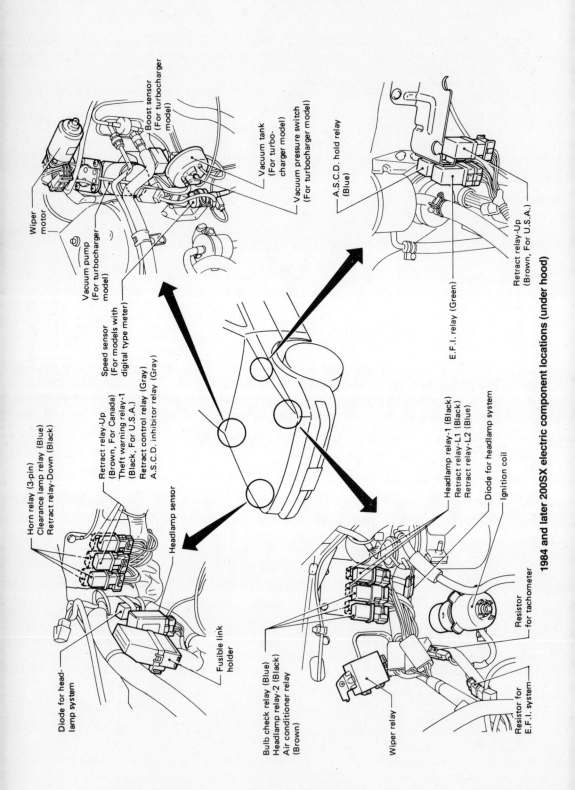

Wiper motor

Boost sensor (For turbocharger model)

Vacuum pump (For turbocharger model)

Vacuum tank (For turbo-charger model)

Vacuum pressure switch (For turbocharger model)

A.S.C.D. hold relay (Blue)

E.F.I. relay (Green)

Retract relay-Up (Brown, For U.S.A.)

Speed sensor (For models with digital type meter)

Retract control relay (Gray)
A.S.C.D. inhibitor relay (Gray)

Horn relay (3-pin)
Clearance lamp relay (Blue)
Retract relay-Down (Black)

Retract relay-Up (Brown, For Canada)
Theft warning relay-1 (Black, For U.S.A.)

Headlamp sensor

Diode for head-lamp system

Fusible link holder

Headlamp relay-1 (Black)
Retract relay-L1 (Black)
Retract relay-L2 (Blue)

Diode for headlamp system

Ignition coil

Resistor for tachometer

Resistor for E.F.I. system

Wiper relay

Bulb check relay (Blue)
Headlamp relay-2 (Black)
Air conditioner relay (Brown)

1984 and later 200SX electric component locations (under hood)

Rear Turn Signal, Brake And Parking Lights

1. Remove rear trim panel in rear of vehicle if necessary to gain access to the bulb socket.

2. Slightly depress the bulb and turn it counterclockwise to release it.

3. To install the bulb carefully push down and turn bulb clockwise at the same time.

4. Install trim panel if necessary.

CIRCUIT PROTECTION

Fuses

REMOVAL AND INSTALLATION

The fuses can be easily inspected to see if they are blown. Simply pull the fuse from the block, inspect it and replace it with a new one, if necessary.

NOTE: *When replacing a blown fuse, be certain to replace it with one of the correct amperage.*

Fusible Links

A fusible link(s) is a protective device used in an electrical circuit. When current increases beyond a certain amperage, the fusible metal wire of the link melts, thus breaking the electrical circuit and preventing further damage to the other components and wiring. Whenever a fusible link is melted because of a short circuit, correct the cause before installing a new link. All fusible links are the plug in kind. To replace them, simply unplug the bad link and insert the new one.

Circuit Breakers

Circuit breakers are also located in the fuse block. A circuit breaker is an electrical switch which breaks the circuit during an electrical overload. The circuit breaker will remain open

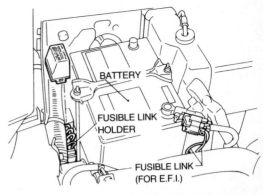

Most fusible links are found beside the battery

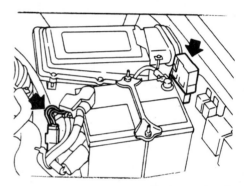

Fusible link locations—1988 Maxima—other years similar

until the short or overload condition in the circuit is corrected.

Flashers

To replace the flasher carefully pull it from the electrical connector. If necessary remove any component that restricts removal.

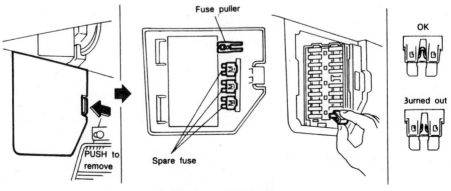

Typical late model fuse box

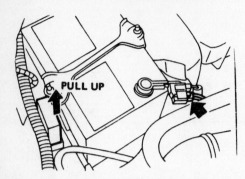

Fusible link locations—1988 200SX—other years similar

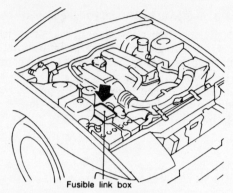

Fusible link box

Fusible link location—1989 240SX

Fusible Links

Year	Model	Number	Location
1973–74	610	2	At positive battery terminal
1976 1974–77	610 710	4	On relay bracket, front right side of engine compartment
1977–84	810/Maxima	6	On relay bracket, in engine compartment ①
1977–79	200SX	2	At positive battery terminal
1980–84	200SX	4	At positive battery terminal
1978–81	510	2	At positive battery terminal
1985–88	200SX	—	At positive battery terminal and the side of battery
1989	240SX	—	To the side of battery
1985–89	Maxima	—	At positive battery terminal and on inner finder well to the side of battery

① The fusible links for the fuel injection and the glow plugs (diesel) are located at the positive battery terminal

Fuse Box and Flasher Location

Year	Model	Fuse Box Location	Flasher Location
1973–77	610, 710	Under instrument panel	Top of pedal assembly ①
1977–80	810	Right side kick panel	Under driver's side of dashboard ①
1981–84	810/Maxima (rear wheel drive)	Underneath glove box	Under driver's side of dashboard, near steering column
1977–79	200SX	Underneath glove box	Turn signal: Behind radio Hazard: Behind glove box
1980–88	200SX	Underneath glove box	Under driver's side dashboard ① ③
1978–81	510	Under instrument panel, Next to hood release	Under driver's side dashboard ①
1985–89	Maxima (front wheel drive)	Under dash to extreme left	To left of upper steering column ② above brake pedal
1989	240SX	Under dash to extreme left	To left of upper steering column above brake pedal

① Both the turn signal and the hazard flashers are side by side
② Combination flasher unit
③ 1984–89 200SX use combination flasher unit
NOTE: The original turn signal flasher unit is pink, and larger than the original hazard flasher unit, which is gold.

Troubleshooting Basic Turn Signal and Flasher Problems

Most problems in the turn signals or flasher system, can be reduced to defective flashers or bulbs, which are easily replaced. Occasionally, problems in the turn signals are traced to the switch in the steering column, which will require professional service.

F = Front   R = Rear   ● = Lights off   ○ = Lights on

Problem		Solution
Turn signals light, but do not flash		• Replace the flasher
No turn signals light on either side		• Check the fuse. Replace if defective. • Check the flasher by substitution • Check for open circuit, short circuit or poor ground
Both turn signals on one side don't work		• Check for bad bulbs • Check for bad ground in both housings
One turn signal light on one side doesn't work		• Check and/or replace bulb • Check for corrosion in socket. Clean contacts. • Check for poor ground at socket
Turn signal flashes too fast or too slow		• Check any bulb on the side flashing too fast. A heavy-duty bulb is probably installed in place of a regular bulb. • Check the bulb flashing too slow. A standard bulb was probably installed in place of a heavy-duty bulb. • Check for loose connections or corrosion at the bulb socket
Indicator lights don't work in either direction		• Check if the turn signals are working • Check the dash indicator lights • Check the flasher by substitution

One indicator light doesn't light		• On systems with 1 dash indicator: See if the lights work on the same side. Often the filaments have been reversed in systems combining stoplights with taillights and turn signals.
		   Check the flasher by substitution
		• On systems with 2 indicators: Check the bulbs on the same side
		   Check the indicator light bulb
		   Check the flasher by substitution

Troubleshooting Basic Dash Gauge Problems

Problem	Cause	Solution
Coolant Temperature Gauge		
Gauge reads erratically or not at all	• Loose or dirty connections • Defective sending unit	• Clean/tighten connections • Bi-metal gauge: remove the wire from the sending unit. Ground the wire for an instant. If the gauge registers, replace the sending unit.
	• Defective gauge	• Magnetic gauge: disconnect the wire at the sending unit. With ignition ON gauge should register COLD. Ground the wire; gauge should register HOT.
Ammeter Gauge—Turn Headlights ON (do not start engine). Note reaction		
Ammeter shows charge Ammeter shows discharge Ammeter does not move	• Connections reversed on gauge • Ammeter is OK • Loose connections or faulty wiring • Defective gauge	• Reinstall connections • Nothing • Check/correct wiring • Replace gauge
Oil Pressure Gauge		
Gauge does not register or is inaccurate	• On mechanical gauge, Bourdon tube may be bent or kinked	• Check tube for kinks or bends preventing oil from reaching the gauge
	• Low oil pressure	• Remove sending unit. Idle the engine briefly. If no oil flows from sending unit hole, problem is in engine.
	• Defective gauge	• Remove the wire from the sending unit and ground it for an instant with the ignition ON. A good gauge will go to the top of the scale.
	• Defective wiring	• Check the wiring to the gauge. If it's OK and the gauge doesn't register when grounded, replace the gauge.
	• Defective sending unit	• If the wiring is OK and the gauge functions when grounded, replace the sending unit
All Gauges		
All gauges do not operate	• Blown fuse • Defective instrument regulator	• Replace fuse • Replace instrument voltage regulator
All gauges read low or erratically	• Defective or dirty instrument voltage regulator	• Clean contacts or replace
All gauges pegged	• Loss of ground between instrument voltage regulator and car • Defective instrument regulator	• Check ground • Replace regulator
Warning Lights		
Light(s) do not come on when ignition is ON, but engine is not started	• Defective bulb • Defective wire	• Replace bulb • Check wire from light to sending unit
	• Defective sending unit	• Disconnect the wire from the sending unit and ground it. Replace the sending unit if the light comes on with the ignition ON.
Light comes on with engine running	• Problem in individual system • Defective sending unit	• Check system • Check sending unit (see above)

Troubleshooting the Heater

Problem	Cause	Solution
Blower motor will not turn at any speed	· Blown fuse · Loose connection · Defective ground · Faulty switch · Faulty motor · Faulty resistor	· Replace fuse · Inspect and tighten · Clean and tighten · Replace switch · Replace motor · Replace resistor
Blower motor turns at one speed only	· Faulty switch · Faulty resistor	· Replace switch · Replace resistor
Blower motor turns but does not circulate air	· Intake blocked · Fan not secured to the motor shaft	· Clean intake · Tighten security
Heater will not heat	· Coolant does not reach proper temperature · Heater core blocked internally · Heater core air-bound · Blend-air door not in proper position	· Check and replace thermostat if necessary · Flush or replace core if necessary · Purge air from core · Adjust cable
Heater will not defrost	· Control cable adjustment incorrect · Defroster hose damaged	· Adjust control cable · Replace defroster hose

Troubleshooting Basic Windshield Wiper Problems

Problem	Cause	Solution
Electric Wipers		
Wipers do not operate— Wiper motor heats up or hums	· Internal motor defect · Bent or damaged linkage · Arms improperly installed on linking pivots	· Replace motor · Repair or replace linkage · Position linkage in park and reinstall wiper arms
Wipers do not operate— No current to motor	· Fuse or circuit breaker blown · Loose, open or broken wiring · Defective switch · Defective or corroded terminals · No ground circuit for motor or switch	· Replace fuse or circuit breaker · Repair wiring and connections · Replace switch · Replace or clean terminals · Repair ground circuits
Wipers do not operate— Motor runs	· Linkage disconnected or broken	· Connect wiper linkage or replace broken linkage
Vacuum Wipers		
Wipers do not operate	· Control switch or cable inoperative · Loss of engine vacuum to wiper motor (broken hoses, low engine vacuum, defective vacuum/fuel pump) · Linkage broken or disconnected · Defective wiper motor	· Repair or replace switch or cable · Check vacuum lines, engine vacuum and fuel pump · Repair linkage · Replace wiper motor
Wipers stop on engine acceleration	· Leaking vacuum hoses · Dry windshield · Oversize wiper blades · Defective vacuum/fuel pump	· Repair or replace hoses · Wet windshield with washers · Replace with proper size wiper blades · Replace pump

Troubleshooting Basic Lighting Problems

Problem	Cause	Solution
Lights		
One or more lights don't work, but others do	• Defective bulb(s) • Blown fuse(s) • Dirty fuse clips or light sockets • Poor ground circuit	• Replace bulb(s) • Replace fuse(s) • Clean connections • Run ground wire from light socket housing to car frame
Lights burn out quickly	• Incorrect voltage regulator setting or defective regulator • Poor battery/alternator connections	• Replace voltage regulator • Check battery/alternator connections
Lights go dim	• Low/discharged battery • Alternator not charging • Corroded sockets or connections • Low voltage output	• Check battery • Check drive belt tension; repair or replace alternator • Clean bulb and socket contacts and connections • Replace voltage regulator
Lights flicker	• Loose connection • Poor ground • Circuit breaker operating (short circuit)	• Tighten all connections • Run ground wire from light housing to car frame • Check connections and look for bare wires
Lights "flare"—Some flare is normal on acceleration—if excessive, see "Lights Burn Out Quickly"	• High voltage setting	• Replace voltage regulator
Lights glare—approaching drivers are blinded	• Lights adjusted too high • Rear springs or shocks sagging • Rear tires soft	• Have headlights aimed • Check rear springs/shocks • Check/correct rear tire pressure
Turn Signals		
Turn signals don't work in either direction	• Blown fuse • Defective flasher • Loose connection	• Replace fuse • Replace flasher • Check/tighten all connections
Right (or left) turn signal only won't work	• Bulb burned out • Right (or left) indicator bulb burned out • Short circuit	• Replace bulb • Check/replace indicator bulb • Check/repair wiring
Flasher rate too slow or too fast	• Incorrect wattage bulb • Incorrect flasher	• Flasher bulb • Replace flasher (use a variable load flasher if you pull a trailer)
Indicator lights do not flash (burn steadily)	• Burned out bulb • Defective flasher	• Replace bulb • Replace flasher
Indicator lights do not light at all	• Burned out indicator bulb • Defective flasher	• Replace indicator bulb • Replace flasher

Drive Train

7

UNDERSTANDING THE MANUAL TRANSMISSION

Because of the way an internal combustion engine breathes, it can produce torque, or twisting force, only within a narrow speed range. Most modern, overhead valve engines must turn at about 2,500 rpm to produce their peak torque. By 4,500 rpm they are producing so little torque that continued increases in engine speed produce no power increases.

The manual transmission and clutch are employed to vary the relationship between engine speed and the speed of the wheels so that adequate engine power can be produced under all circumstances. The clutch allows engine torque to be applied to the transmission input shaft gradually, due to mechanical slippage. The car can, consequently, be started smoothly from a full stop.

The transmission changes the ratio between the rotating speeds of the engine and the wheels by the use of gears. On trucks, three-speed or four-speed transmissions are most common. The lower gears allow full engine power to be applied to the rear wheels during acceleration at low speeds.

The transmission contains a mainshaft which passes all the way through the transmission, from the clutch to the driveshaft. This shaft is separated at one point, so that front and rear portions can turn at different speeds.

Power is transmitted by a countershaft in the lower gears and reverse. The gears of the countershaft mesh with gears on the mainshaft, allowing power to be carried from one to the other. All the countershaft gears are integral with that shaft, while several of the mainshaft gears can either rotate independently of the shaft or be locked to it. Shifting from one gear to the next causes one of the gears to be freed from rotating with the shaft and locks another to it. Gears are locked and unlocked by internal dog clutches which slide between the center of the gear and the shaft. The forward gears usually employ synchronizers; friction members which smoothly bring gear and shaft to the same speed before the toothed dog clutches are engaged.

The clutch is operating properly if:

1. It will stall the engine when released with the vehicle held stationary.

2. The shift lever can be moved freely between 1st and reverse gears when the vehicle is stationary and the clutch disengaged.

MANUAL TRANSMISSION

Identification

On all models covered in this book the manual transmission serial number is stamped on the front upper face of the transmission case.

Adjustments
LINKAGE AND SHIFTER

All models are equipped with an integral linkage system. No adjustments are either possible or necessary.

MANUAL TRANSMISSION NUMBER

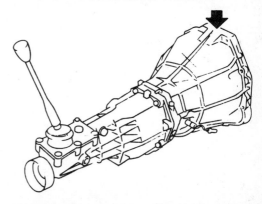

Troubleshooting the Manual Transmission and Transfer Case

Problem	Cause	Solution
Transmission shifts hard	• Clutch adjustment incorrect • Clutch linkage or cable binding • Shift rail binding	• Adjust clutch • Lubricate or repair as necessary • Check for mispositioned selector arm roll pin, loose cover bolts, worn shift rail bores, worn shift rail, distorted oil seal, or extension housing not aligned with case. Repair as necessary.
	• Internal bind in transmission caused by shift forks, selector plates, or synchronizer assemblies • Clutch housing misalignment • Incorrect lubricant • Block rings and/or cone seats worn	• Remove, dissemble and inspect transmission. Replace worn or damaged components as necessary. • Check runout at rear face of clutch housing • Drain and refill transmission • Blocking ring to gear clutch tooth face clearance must be 0.030 inch or greater. If clearance is correct it may still be necessary to inspect blocking rings and cone seats for excessive wear. Repair as necessary.
Gear clash when shifting from one gear to another	• Clutch adjustment incorrect • Clutch linkage or cable binding • Clutch housing misalignment • Lubricant level low or incorrect lubricant • Gearshift components, or synchronizer assemblies worn or damaged	• Adjust clutch • Lubricate or repair as necessary • Check runout at rear of clutch housing • Drain and refill transmission and check for lubricant leaks if level was low. Repair as necessary. • Remove, disassemble and inspect transmission. Replace worn or damaged components as necessary.
Transmission noisy	• Lubricant level low or incorrect lubricant • Clutch housing-to-engine, or transmission-to-clutch housing bolts loose • Dirt, chips, foreign material in transmission • Gearshift mechanism, transmission gears, or bearing components worn or damaged • Clutch housing misalignment	• Drain and refill transmission. If lubricant level was low, check for leaks and repair as necessary. • Check and correct bolt torque as necessary • Drain, flush, and refill transmission • Remove, disassemble and inspect transmission. Replace worn or damaged components as necessary. • Check runout at rear face of clutch housing
Jumps out of gear	• Clutch housing misalignment • Gearshift lever loose • Offset lever nylon insert worn or lever attaching nut loose • Gearshift mechanism, shift forks, selector plates, interlock plate, selector arm, shift rail, detent plugs, springs or shift cover worn or damaged • Clutch shaft or roller bearings worn or damaged	• Check runout at rear face of clutch housing • Check lever for worn fork. Tighten loose attaching bolts. • Remove gearshift lever and check for loose offset lever nut or worn insert. Repair or replace as necessary. • Remove, disassemble and inspect transmission cover assembly. Replace worn or damaged components as necessary. • Replace clutch shaft or roller bearings as necessary

Troubleshooting the Manual Transmission and Transfer Case (cont.)

Problem	Cause	Solution
Jumps out of gear (cont.)	· Gear teeth worn or tapered, synchronizer assemblies worn or damaged, excessive end play caused by worn thrust washers or output shaft gears · Pilot bushing worn	· Remove, disassemble, and inspect transmission. Replace worn or damaged components as necessary. · Replace pilot bushing
Will not shift into one gear	· Gearshift selector plates, interlock plate, or selector arm, worn, damaged, or incorrectly assembled · Shift rail detent plunger worn, spring broken, or plug loose · Gearshift lever worn or damaged · Synchronizer sleeves or hubs, damaged or worn	· Remove, disassemble, and inspect transmission cover assembly. Repair or replace components as necessary. · Tighten plug or replace worn or damaged components as necessary · Replace gearshift lever · Remove, disassemble and inspect transmission. Replace worn or damaged components.
Locked in one gear—cannot be shifted out	· Shift rail(s) worn or broken, shifter fork bent, setscrew loose, center detent plug missing or worn · Broken gear teeth on countershaft gear, clutch shaft, or reverse idler gear Gearshift lever broken or worn, shift mechanism in cover incorrectly assembled or broken, worn damaged gear train components	· Inspect and replace worn or damaged parts · Inspect and replace damaged part · Disassemble transmission. Replace damaged parts or assemble correctly.
Transfer case difficult to shift or will not shift into desired range	· Vehicle speed too great to permit shifting · If vehicle was operated for extended period in 4H mode on dry paved surface, driveline torque load may cause difficult shifting · Transfer case external shift linkage binding · Insufficient or incorrect lubricant · Internal components binding, worn, or damaged	· Stop vehicle and shift into desired range. Or reduce speed to 3–4 km/h (2–3 mph) before attempting to shift. · Stop vehicle, shift transmission to neutral, shift transfer case to 2H mode and operate vehicle in 2H on dry paved surfaces · Lubricate or repair or replace linkage, or tighten loose components as necessary · Drain and refill to edge of fill hole with SAE 85W-90 gear lubricant only · Disassemble unit and replace worn or damaged components as necessary
Transfer case noisy in all drive modes	· Insufficient or incorrect lubricant	· Drain and refill to edge of fill hole with SAE 85W-90 gear lubricant only. Check for leaks and repair if necessary. Note: If unit is still noisy after drain and refill, disassembly and inspection may be required to locate source of noise.
Noisy in—or jumps out of four wheel drive low range	· Transfer case not completely engaged in 4L position · Shift linkage loose or binding · Shift fork cracked, inserts worn, or fork is binding on shift rail	· Stop vehicle, shift transfer case in Neutral, then shift back into 4L position · Tighten, lubricate, or repair linkage as necessary · Disassemble unit and repair as necessary
Lubricant leaking from output shaft seals or from vent	· Transfer case overfilled · Vent closed or restricted	· Drain to correct level · Clear or replace vent if necessary

Troubleshooting the Manual Transmission and Transfer Case (cont.)

Problem	Cause	Solution
Lubricant leaking from output shaft seals or from vent (cont.)	• Output shaft seals damaged or installed incorrectly	• Replace seals. Be sure seal lip faces interior of case when installed. Also be sure yoke seal surfaces are not scored or nicked. Remove scores, nicks with fine sandpaper or replace yoke(s) if necessary.
Abnormal tire wear	• Extended operation on dry hard surface (paved) roads in 4H range	• Operate in 2H on hard surface (paved) roads

Back-Up Light Switch

REMOVAL AND INSTALLATION

All Models

1. Raise vehicle and support safely.
2. Disconnect the electrical connections from the switch.
3. Remove switch from transmission housing, when removing place drain pan under transmission to catch fluid.
4. To install reverse removal procedures and check the fluid level.

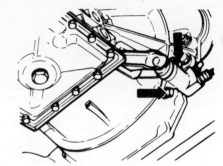

Remove the clutch slave cylinder

Transmission

REMOVAL AND INSTALLATION

1. Disconnect the negative battery cable.
2. Disconnect the accelerator linkage on the 1980-82 200SX and the 1981 and later 810 and Maxima.
3. Raise the car and support it with jackstands.
4. Disconnect the exhaust pipe from the manifold and bracket if necessary to gain clearance for transmission removal.
5. Tag and disconnect any switches that are connected to the transmission case (back-up, neutral, top gear or overdrive).
6. Disconnect the speedometer cable where it attaches to the transmission.
7. Remove the driveshaft. Don't forget to plug the opening in the rear extension so that oil won't flow out.
8. Remove the clutch slave cylinder.
9. Remove the rubber boot and console box (if so equipped). Place the shift lever in neutral, remove the E-ring (later models only) and then remove the shifter.
10. Support the engine by placing a jack under the oil pan with a wooden block used between the jack and the pan.

NOTE: *Do not place a jack directly under the drain plug with a block of wood between the jack and the transmission.*

Early models used nuts to secure the shifter

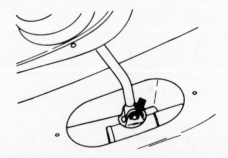

Later models used an E-ring to secure the shifter

11. Support the transmission with a transmission jack.
12. Loosen the rear engine mount securing nuts temporarily and then remove the crossmember.

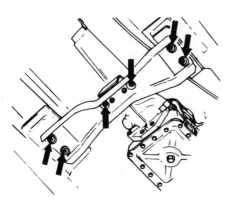

Crossmember mounting bolts—610 and 710

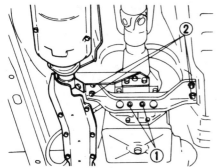

Rear engine mount nuts (1), crossmember mounting nuts (2)—510

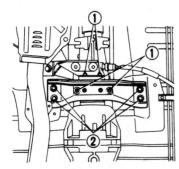

Rear engine mount nuts (1), crossmember mounting nuts (2)—200SX

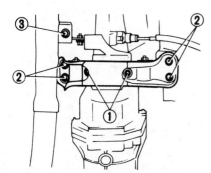

Rear engine mount nuts (1), crossmember mounting nuts (2), exhaust bracket mounting nut (3)—810

13. Lower the rear of the engine slightly to allow additional clearance.

14. Remove the starter electrical connections and the starter motor.

15. Remove the transmission-to-engine mounting bolts, lower the transmission and remove it toward the rear.

16. Install the transmission in ther correct position. Tighten all the transmission-to-engine mounting bolts.

17. Install the starter motor and electrical connections.

18. Install the crossmember assembly and tighten all retaining nuts to crossmember and rear engine mounts.

19. Install the shifter. Install the rubber boot and console box if so equipped.

20. Install the clutch slave cylinder.

21. Install the driveshaft and connect the speedometer cable.

22. Connect any switches that are connected to the transmission case (back-up, neutral, top gear or overdrive).

23. Connect the exhaust pipe to the manifold and bracket if necessary.

24. Connect the accelerator linkage on the 1980-82 200SX and the 1981 and later 810 and Maxima.

25. Connect the negative battery cable. Bleed the clutch hydraulic system if necessary. Road test the vehicle for proper shift pattern operation.

OVERHAUL

4-Speed (Model F4W71B)

DISASSEMBLY

This transmission is constructed in three sections: clutch housing, transmission housing and extension housing. There are no case cover plates. There is a cast iron adapter plate between the transmission and extension housings.

1. Remove the clutch housing dust cover. Remove the retaining spring, release bearing sleeve and lever.

2. Remove the backup light/neutral safety switch.

3. Unbolt and remove the clutch housing, rapping with a soft hammer if necessary. Remove the gasket, mainshaft bearing shim, and countershaft bearing shim.

4. Remove the speedometer pinion sleeve.

5. Remove the striker rod pin from the rod. Separate the striker rod from the shift lever bracket.

6. Unbolt and remove the rear extension. It may be necessary to rap the housing with a soft hammer.

7. Remove the mainshaft bearing snapring.

8. Remove the adapter plate and gear assembly from the transmission case.

9. Punch out the shift fork retaining pins. Remove the shift rod snaprings. Remove the detent plugs, springs and balls from the adapter plate. Remove the shift rods, being careful not to lose the interlock balls.

10. Remove the snapring, speedometer drive gear and locating ball.

11. Remove the nut, lockwasher, thrust washer, reverse hub and reverse gear.

12. Remove the snapring and countershaft reverse gear. Remove the snapring, reverse idler gear, thrust washer and needle bearing.

13. Support the gear assembly while rapping on the rear of the mainshaft with a soft hammer.

14. Remove the setscrew from the adapter plate. Remove the shaft nut, spring washer, plain washer and reverse idler shaft.

15. Remove the bearing retainer and the mainshaft rear bushing.

16. To disassemble the mainshaft (rear section), remove the front snapring, 3rd/4th synchronizer assembly, 3rd gear and needle bearing. From the rear, remove the thrust washer, locating ball, 1st gear, needle bearing, 1st gear bushing, 1st/2nd synchronizer assembly, 2nd gear, and needle bearing.

17. To disassemble the clutch shaft, remove the snapring and bearing spacer and press off the bearing.

18. To disassemble the countershaft, press off the front bearing. Press off the rear bearing, press off the gears and remove the keys.

19. Remove the retaining pin, control arm pin and shift control arm from the rear of the extension housing.

ASSEMBLY

1. Place the O-ring in the front cover. Install the front cover to the clutch housing with a press. Put in the front cover oil seal.

2. Install the rear extension oil seal.

3. Assemble the 1st/2nd and 3rd/4th synchronizer assemblies. Make sure that the ring gaps are not both on the same side of the unit.

4. On the rear end of the mainshaft, install the needle bearing, 2nd gear, baulk ring, 1st/2nd synchronizer assembly, baulk ring, 1st gear bushing, needle bearing, 1st gear, locating ball and thrust washer.

5. Drive or press on the mainshaft rear bearing.

6. Install the countershaft rear bearing to the adapter plate. Drive or press the mainshaft rear bearing into the adapter plate until the bearing snapring groove comes through the rear side of the plate. Install the snapring. If it

is not tight against the plate, press the bearing back in slightly.

7. Insert the countershaft bearing ring between the countershaft rear bearing and bearing retainer. Install the bearing retainer to the adapter plate. Stake both ends of the screws.

8. Insert the reverse idler shaft from the rear of the adapter plate. Install the spring washer and plain washer to the idler shaft.

9. Place the two keys on the countershaft and oil the shaft lightly. Press on 3rd gear and install a snapring.

10. Install the countershaft into its rear bearing.

11. From the front of the mainshaft, install the needle bearing, 3rd gear, baulk ring, 3rd/4th synchronizer assembly and snapring. snaprings are available in thicknesses from 1.4-1.6mm to adjust gear end-play.

12. Press the main drive bearing onto the clutch shaft. Install the main drive gear spacer and a snapring. Snaprings are available in thicknesses from 1.8-2.0mm to adjust gear end-play.

13. Insert a key into the countershaft drive gear with 4th gear and drive on the countershaft 4th gear with a drift. The rear end of the countershaft should be held steady while driving on the gear, to prevent rear bearing damage.

14. Install the reverse hub, reverse gear, thrust washer, and lock tab on the rear of the mainshaft. Install the shaft nut temporarily.

15. Install the needle bearing, reverse idler gear, thrust washer, and snapring.

16. Place the countershaft reverse gear and snapring on the rear of the countershaft. Snaprings are available in thicknesses from 1.0-1.5mm to adjust gear end-play.

17. Engage both 1st and 2nd gears to lock the shaft.

18. On the rear of the mainshaft, install the snapring, locating ball, speedometer drive gear, and snapring. snaprings are available in thicknesses from 1.0-1.5mm.

19. Recheck end-play and backlash of all gears.

20. Place the reverse shift fork on the reverse gear and install the reverse shift rod. Install the detent ball, spring and plug. Install the fork retaining pin. Place two interlock balls between the reverse shift rod and the 3rd/4th shift rod location. Install the 3rd/4th shift fork and rod. Install the detent ball, spring and plug. This plug is shorter than the other two. Install the fork retaining pin. Place two interlock balls between the 1st/2nd shift rod location and the 3rd/4th shift rod. Install the 1st/2nd shift fork and rod. Install the detent ball, spring and plug.

21. Install the shift rod snaprings.

22. Apply sealant sparingly to the adapter plate and transmission housing. Install the transmission housing to the adapter plate and bolt it down temporarily.

23. Drive in the countershaft front bearing with a drift. Place the snapring in the mainshaft front bearing.

24. Apply sealant sparingly to the adapter plate and extension housing. Align the shift rods in the neutral positions. Position the striker rod to the shift rods and bolt down the extension housing.

25. Insert the striker rod pin, connect the rod to the shift lever bracket and install the striker rod pin retaining ring. Replace the shift control arm.

26. To select the proper mainshaft bearing shim, first measure the amount the bearing protrudes from the front of the transmission case. Then measure the depth of the bearing recess in the rear of the clutch housing. Required shim thickness is found by subtracting, the difference is required shim size. Shims are available in thicknesses of 1.4mm and 1.6mm.

27. To select the proper countershaft front bearing shim, measure the amount that the bearing is recessed into the transmission case. Shim thickness should equal this measurement. Shims are available in thicknesses from 0.04mm to 1.0mm.

28. Apply sealant sparingly to the clutch and transmission housing mating surfaces.

29. Replace the clutch operating mechanism.

30. Install the shift lever temporarily and check shifting action.

5-Speed (Models FS5W71B and FS5W71C)

This transmission is similar to the 4-speed transmission (Model F4W71B). The overhaul can be accomplished by following the outline for the disassembly and assembly of the 4-speed.

Servo type synchromesh is used, instead of the Borg Warner type in the four speed. Shift linkage and interlock arrangements are the same, except the reverse shift rod also operates 5th gear. Most service procedures are identical to those for the four speed unit.

Those unique to the 5-speed follow:

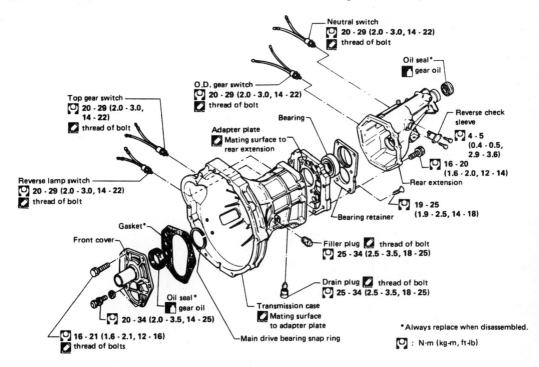

Transmission switch application

Engine	Switch			
	Reverse	Top	O.D.	Neutral
CA18ET	O	O	O	–
CA20E	O	–	–	O

Case components—FS5W71B transmission

DISASSEMBLY

To disassemble the synchronizers, remove the circlip, synchronizer ring, thrust block, brake band, and anchor block. Be careful not to mix parts of the different synchronizer assemblies.

ASSEMBLY

1. The synchronizer assemblies for 2nd, 3rd, and 4th are identical. When assembling the 1st gear synchronizer, be sure to install the 2.2mm thick brake band at the bottom.

2. When assembling the mainshaft, select a 3rd gear synchronizer hub snapring to minimize hub end-play. snaprings are available in thicknesses of 1.5-1.6mm, 1.50-1.55mm and 1.45-1.50mm. The synchronizer hub must be installed with the longer boss to the rear.

3. When reassembling the gear train, install the mainshaft, countershaft, and gears to the

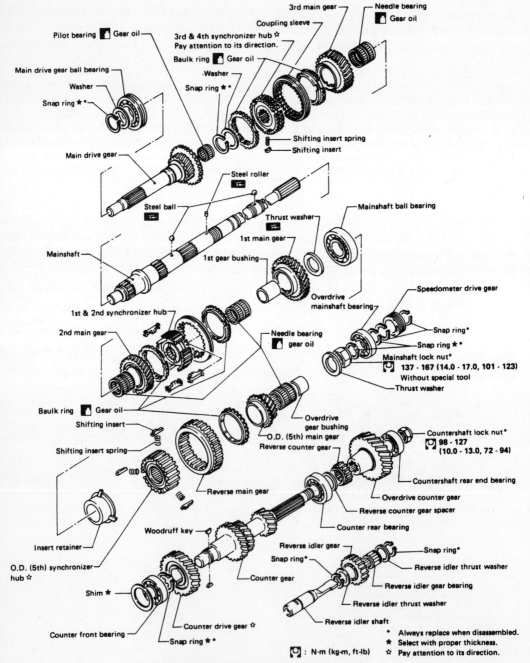

Gear components—FS5W71B transmission

adapter plate. Hold the rear nut and force the front nut against it to a torque of 217 ft. lbs. for 1979 models and 123 ft. lbs. for 1980 and later models. Select a snapring to minimize end-play of the 5th gear bearing at the rear of the mainshaft. snaprings are available in thicknesses from 1.0-1.5mm.

MANUAL TRANSAXLE

Identification

The manual transaxle serial number label is stamped on the upper part of the transaxle housing.

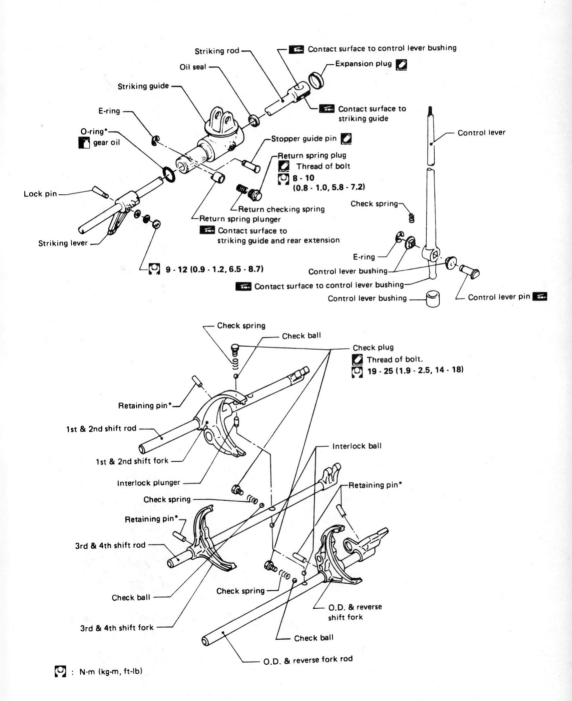

Shift control components—FS5W71B transmission

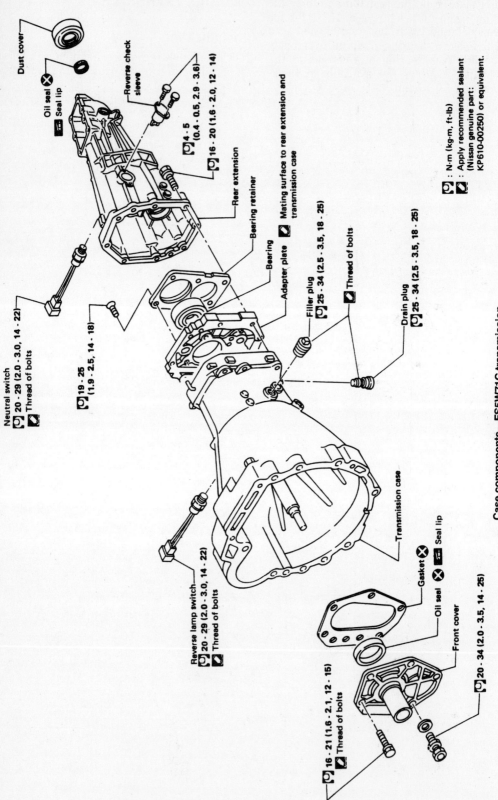

Dust cover

Oil seal
⟨◯ᴙ⟩ Seal lip

Reverse check sleeve

⟨□⟩ 4 - 5 (0.4 - 0.5, 2.9 - 3.6)
⟨□⟩ 16 - 20 (1.6 - 2.0, 12 - 14)

Rear extension

Bearing retainer

Bearing

Adapter plate

Mating surface to rear extension and transmission case

Filler plug
⟨□⟩ 25 - 34 (2.5 - 3.5, 18 - 25)

Thread of bolts

Drain plug
⟨□⟩ 25 - 34 (2.5 - 3.5, 18 - 25)

Neutral switch
⟨□⟩ 20 - 29 (2.0 - 3.0, 14 - 22)
Thread of bolts

⟨□⟩ 19 - 25 (1.9 - 2.5, 14 - 18)

Reverse lamp switch
⟨□⟩ 20 - 29 (2.0 - 3.0, 14 - 22)
Thread of bolts

Transmission case

Gasket ⟨◯ᴙ⟩

Oil seal ⟨◯ᴙ⟩ Seal lip

Front cover

⟨□⟩ 20 - 34 (2.0 - 3.5, 14 - 25)

⟨□⟩ 16 - 21 (1.6 - 2.1, 12 - 15)
Thread of bolts

⟨□⟩ : N·m (kg-m, ft-lb)
⟨◯ᴙ⟩ : Apply recommended sealant (Nissan genuine part: KP610-00250) or equivalent.

Case components—FS5W71C transmission

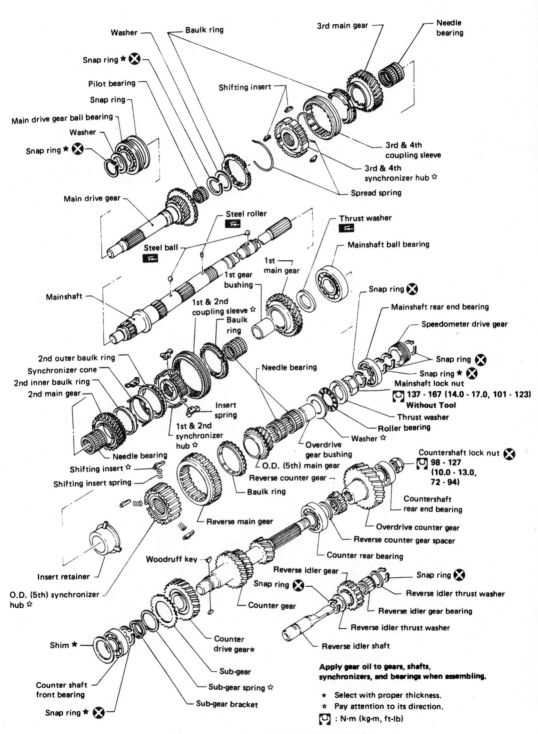

Washer

Baulk ring

3rd main gear

Needle bearing

Snap ring ★ ⊗

Pilot bearing

Snap ring

Main drive gear ball bearing

Washer

Snap ring ★ ⊗

Shifting insert

3rd & 4th coupling sleeve

3rd & 4th synchronizer hub ☆

Spread spring

Main drive gear

Steel roller

Thrust washer

Steel ball

1st main gear

Mainshaft ball bearing

1st gear bushing

Snap ring ⊗

Mainshaft

Mainshaft rear end bearing

Speedometer drive gear

1st & 2nd coupling sleeve ☆

Baulk ring

Snap ring ⊗

2nd outer baulk ring

Needle bearing

Snap ring ★ ⊗

Synchronizer cone

Mainshaft lock nut

2nd inner baulk ring

⊡ 137 - 167 (14.0 - 17.0, 101 - 123) Without Tool

2nd main gear

Insert spring

Thrust washer

1st & 2nd synchronizer hub ☆

Roller bearing

Washer ☆

Needle bearing

Overdrive gear bushing

Shifting insert ☆

O.D. (5th) main gear

Countershaft lock nut ⊗

Shifting insert spring

Reverse counter gear

⊡ 98 - 127 (10.0 - 13.0, 72 - 94)

Baulk ring

Countershaft rear end bearing

Reverse main gear

Overdrive counter gear

Woodruff key

Reverse counter gear spacer

Counter rear bearing

Insert retainer

Reverse idler gear

O.D. (5th) synchronizer hub ☆

Snap ring ⊗

Snap ring ⊗

Counter gear

Reverse idler thrust washer

Shim ★

Reverse idler gear bearing

Counter drive gear☆

Reverse idler thrust washer

Counter shaft front bearing

Sub-gear

Reverse idler shaft

Sub-gear spring ☆

Apply gear oil to gears, shafts, synchronizers, and bearings when assembling.

Snap ring ★ ⊗

Sub-gear bracket

★   Select with proper thickness.

☆   Pay attention to its direction.

⊡ : N·m (kg-m, ft-lb)

Gear components—FS5W71C transmission

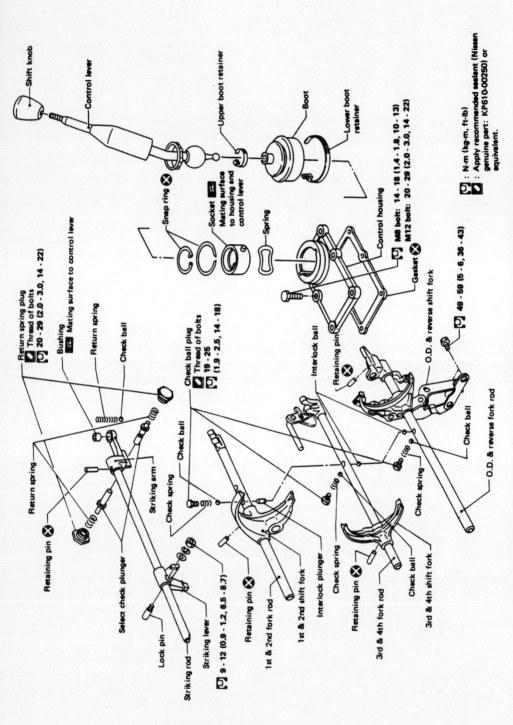

Shift control components—FS5W71C transmission (with mainshaft braking mechanism)

Shift knob

Control lever

Upper boot retainer

Boot

Lower boot retainer

Snap ring

Socket

Mating surface to housing and control lever

Spring

Control housing

M8 bolt: 14 - 18 (1.4 - 1.8, 10 - 13)
M12 bolt: 20 - 29 (2.0 - 3.0, 14 - 22)

Gasket

O.D. & reverse shift fork

Retaining pin

Interlock ball

Check ball

O.D. & reverse fork rod

Return spring plug
Thread of bolts
20 - 29 (2.0 - 3.0, 14 - 22)

Bushing
Mating surface to control lever

Return spring

Check ball

Check ball plug
Thread of bolts
19 - 25
(1.9 - 2.5, 14 - 18)

Check ball

Return spring

Retaining pin

Select check plunger

Striking arm

Check spring

49 - 59 (5 - 6, 36 - 43)

Check spring

Check ball

3rd & 4th shift fork

Lock pin

Striking rod

Striking lever

9 - 12 (0.9 - 1.2, 6.5 - 8.7)

Retaining pin

1st & 2nd fork rod

1st & 2nd shift fork

Interlock plunger

Check spring

Retaining pin

3rd & 4th fork rod

: N·m (kg-m, ft-lb)

: Apply recommended sealant (Nissan genuine part: KP610-00250) or equivalent.

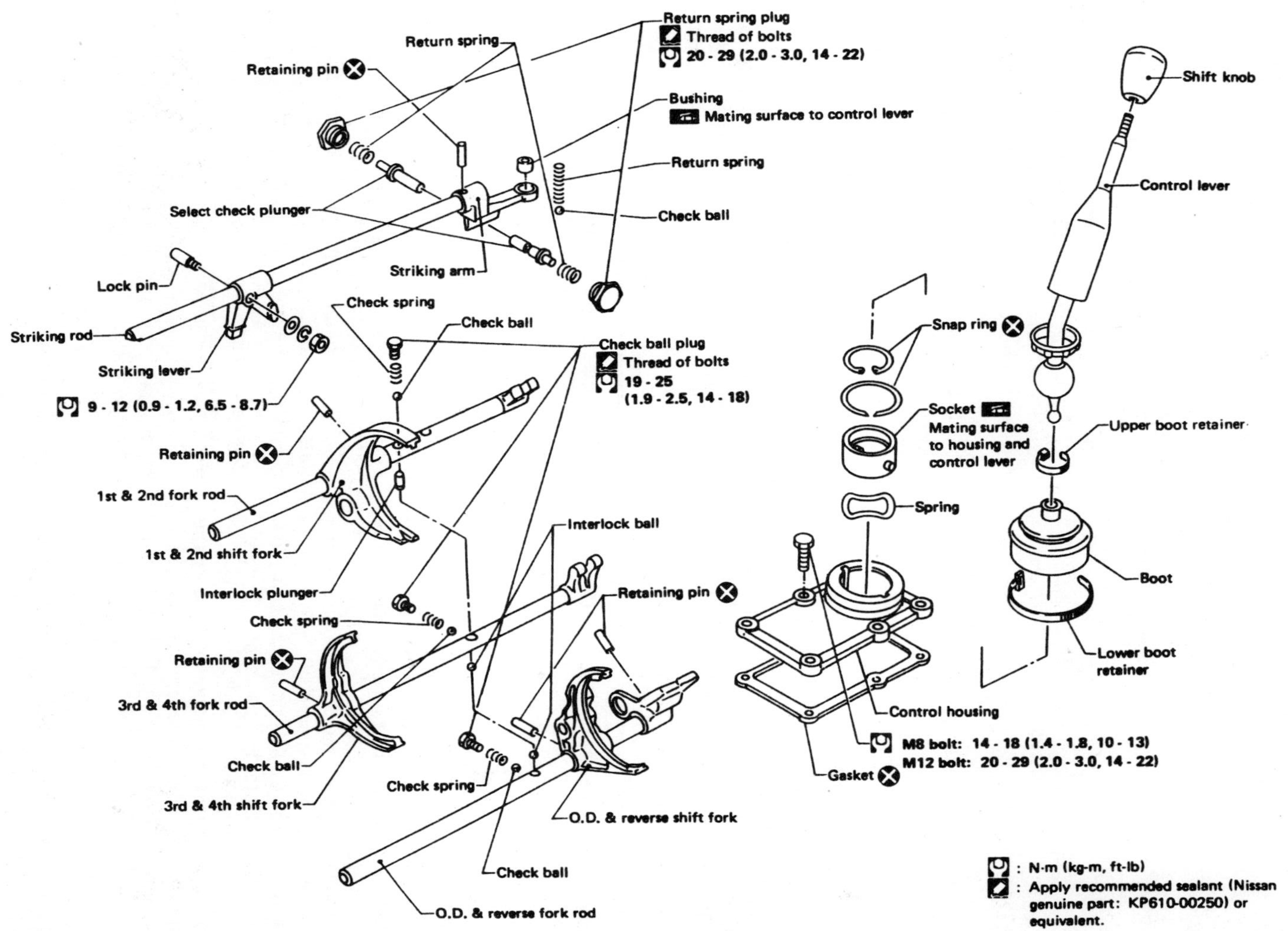

Shift knob

Control lever

Upper boot retainer

Boot

Lower boot retainer

Snap ring

Socket

Mating surface to housing and control lever

Spring

Control housing

M8 bolt: 14 - 18 (1.4 - 1.8, 10 - 13)
M12 bolt: 20 - 29 (2.0 - 3.0, 14 - 22)

Gasket

: N·m (kg-m, ft-lb)

: Apply recommended sealant (Nissan genuine part: KP610-00250) or equivalent.

Return spring plug

Thread of bolts
20 - 29 (2.0 - 3.0, 14 - 22)

Bushing

Mating surface to control lever

Return spring

Check ball

Check ball plug

Thread of bolts
19 - 25
(1.9 - 2.5, 14 - 18)

Interlock ball

Retaining pin

O.D. & reverse shift fork

Return spring

Check spring

Check ball

Check ball

Retaining pin

Striking arm

Check spring

O.D. & reverse fork rod

Retaining pin

Select check plunger

1st & 2nd fork rod

1st & 2nd shift fork

Interlock plunger

Check spring

Check ball

Check spring

Lock pin

Striking lever

9 - 12 (0.9 - 1.2, 6.5 - 8.7)

Retaining pin

3rd & 4th fork rod

3rd & 4th shift fork

Striking rod

Shift control components—FS5W71C transmission (without mainshaft braking mechanism)

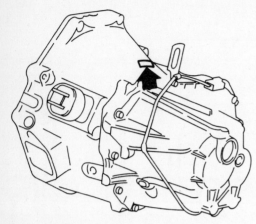

Manual transaxle serial number location

Adjustments
LINKAGE AND SHIFTER

All models are equipped with an integral linkage system. No adjustments are either possible or necessary.

Back-Up Light Switch
REMOVAL AND INSTALLATION

1. Raise vehicle and support safely.
2. Disconnect the electrical connections.
3. Remove swith from transaxle housing, when removing place drain pan under transaxle to catch fluid.
4. To install reverse removal procedures.

Transaxle
REMOVAL AND INSTALLATION

1. Raise the car and support it in a secure manner so there is clearance to remove the transaxle from underneath. Securely support the engine via the oil pan using a cushioning wooden block and a floorjack.
2. Pull both driveshafts out of the transmission as described later in this chapter. Securely support the transmission with another jack.
3. Disconnect the speedometer cable at the transmission and drain the transmission fluid.
4. Remove the vertical bolts from the transmission mount. Unbolt the transmission from the engine. Then, remove it from the car by sliding the transmission input shaft out of the clutch, lowering the rear of the transmission and then lowering the transmission out of the car.
5. Install the transmission in the correct position. Torque the transmission-to-engine bolts to 29-40 ft. lbs., and the vertical nut and bolt fastening the transaxle to its mount to 39-49 ft. lb.

6. Refill the transmission with the required amount of approved fluid and connect the speedometer cable.
NOTE: *The oil fill capacity for RS5F50A manual transaxle is 5.0 U.S. quarts.*
7. Install the driveshafts. Road test the vehicle for proper shift operation.

OVERHAUL
5-Speed (Model RS5F50A)
DISASSEMBLY OF TRANSAXLE

1. Drain the oil from the transaxle.
2. Before removing the transaxle case, remove the bolts and plugs shown in the illustration.
3. Tap on the case lightly with a rubber mallet and then lift off the transaxle case.
4. With a rubber mallet, remove the position switch from the case.
5. Mesh the 4th gear and then remove the reverse idler gear.
6. Remove the reverse arm shaft and the reverse level assembly.
7. Remove the 5th/reverse check plug, spring and ball.
8. Remove the stopper rings and retaining pins from the 5th/reverse and 3rd/4th fork rods.
9. Remove the 5th/reverse and 3rd/4th fork rods. Then remove the forks and brackets.
10. Remove both the input and mainshafts with the 1st/2nd fork and fork rod as a set.
11. Remove the final drive assembly.
12. Remove the reverse check assembly.
13. With a hammer and punch, remove the retaining pin and detach the selector.
14. To make it easier to remove the retaining pin which hods the striking lever to the striking rod, remove the drain plug.
15. With a hammer and punch remove the retaining pin and then withdraw the striking level and striking rod.

Gears and Shafts
END PLAY MEASUREMENT

Before disassembly of the input shaft or the main shaft, measure the gear endplay to insure that it is within the specified limit. If the end play is not within the specified limit, disassemble and check the parts. Replace any worn or damaged parts.

Input Shaft
NOTE: *The following removal procedures require the use of a hydraulic press and various bearing adapter.*
1. Using a press and bearing adapter, remove the input shaft rear bearing.

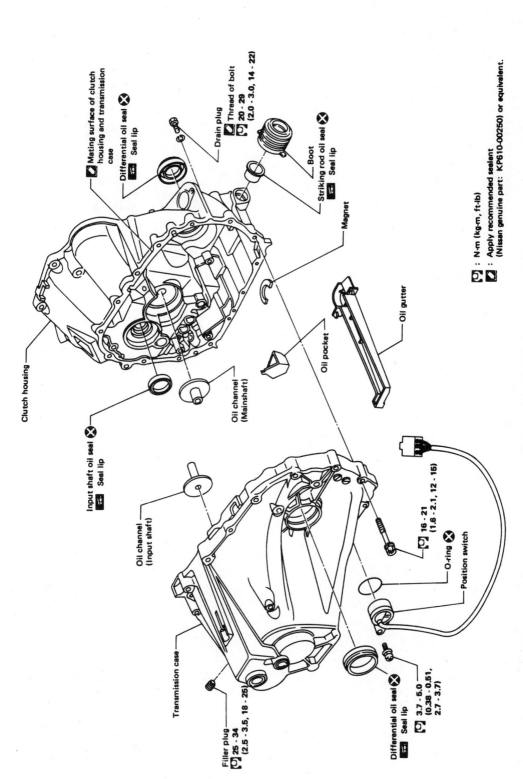

Mating surface of clutch housing and transmission case

Differential oil seal
Seal lip

Drain plug
Thread of bolt
20 - 29
(2.0 - 3.0, 14 - 22)

Boot

Striking rod oil seal
Seal lip

Magnet

Clutch housing

Input shaft oil seal
Seal lip

Oil channel
(Mainshaft)

Oil pocket

Oil gutter

Oil channel
(Input shaft)

16 - 21
(1.6 - 2.1, 12 - 15)

O-ring

Position switch

Transmission case

Filler plug
25 - 34
(2.5 - 3.5, 18 - 25)

Differential oil seal
Seal lip

3.7 - 5.0
(0.38 - 0.51,
2.7 - 3.7)

: N·m (kg-m, ft-lb)

: Apply recommended sealant
(Nissan genuine part: KP610-00250) or equivalent.

Case components—RS5F50A

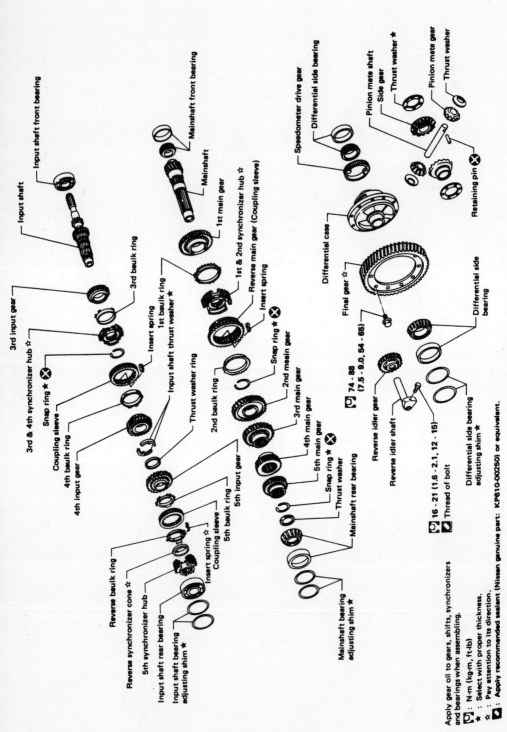

Gear components—RS5F50A

Input shaft front bearing

Input shaft

3rd baulk ring

3rd input gear

3rd & 4th synchronizer hub ☆

Snap ring ★

Coupling sleeve

4th baulk ring

4th input gear

Reverse baulk ring

5th synchronizer hub

Input shaft rear bearing

Input shaft bearing adjusting shim ★

Insert spring ☆

Coupling sleeve

5th baulk ring

5th input gear

Mainshaft front bearing

Mainshaft

1st main gear

1st & 2nd synchronizer hub ☆

Reverse main gear (Coupling sleeve)

Insert spring

Insert spring

1st baulk ring

Input shaft thrust washer ★

Thrust washer ring

2nd baulk ring

Snap ring ★

2nd main gear

3rd main gear

4th main gear

5th main gear

Snap ring ★

Thrust washer

Mainshaft rear bearing

Mainshaft bearing adjusting shim ★

Speedometer drive gear

Differential side bearing

Pinion mate shaft

Side gear

Thrust washer ★

Pinion mate gear

Thrust washer

Retaining pin ⊗

Differential case

Final gear ☆

74 - 88
(7.5 - 9.0, 54 - 65)

Reverse idler gear

Reverse idler shaft

16 - 21 (1.6 - 2.1, 12 - 15)

Thread of bolt

Differential side bearing adjusting shim ★

Differential side bearing

Apply gear oil to gears, shifts, synchronizers
and bearings when assembling.

N·m (kg-m, ft-lb)

★ : Select with proper thickness.

☆ : Pay attention to its direction.

⊗ : Apply recommended sealant (Nissan genuine part: KP810-00250) or equivalent.

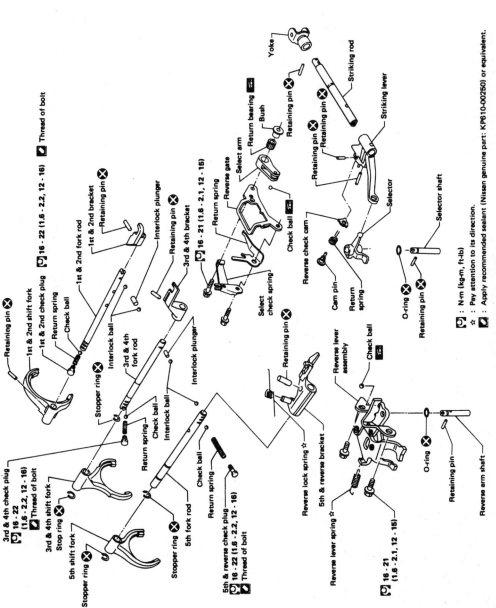

Retaining pin ⊗

1st & 2nd shift fork

1st & 2nd check plug
Return spring
Check ball

1st & 2nd fork rod

Stopper ring ⊗

Interlock ball

3rd & 4th
fork rod

Return spring

Check ball

Interlock ball

Check ball

Return spring

Check ball

Interlock plunger

⊗ 16 · 22 (1.6 · 2.2, 12 · 16)   ⊠ Thread of bolt

1st & 2nd bracket

Retaining pin ⊗

Retaining pin ⊗

3rd & 4th bracket

Interlock plunger

⊗ 16 · 21 (1.6 · 2.1, 12 · 15)

Return spring

Reverse gate

Select arm

Return bearing 🔧

Bush

Retaining pin ⊗

Retaining pin ⊗

Retaining pin ⊗

Yoke

Striking rod

Striking lever

Selector

Selector shaft

Check ball 🔧

Reverse check cam

Cam pin ⊗

Return
spring

O-ring ⊗

Retaining pin ⊗

⊗ : N·m (kg-m, ft-lb)

🔧 : Pay attention to its direction.

☆ : Apply recommended sealant (Nissan genuine part: KP610-00250) or equivalent.

Shift control components—RS5F50A

3rd & 4th check plug
⊗ 16 · 22
(1.6 · 2.2, 12 · 16)   ⊠ Thread of bolt

3rd & 4th shift fork

Stop ring

5th shift fork

Stopper ring ⊗

Stopper ring ⊗

5th fork rod

Return spring

Check ball

Check ball

5th & reverse check plug
⊗ 16 · 22 (1.6 · 2.2, 12 · 16)   ⊠ Thread of bolt

Reverse lock spring ☆

Reverse lever spring ☆

Retaining pin ⊗

Reverse lever
assembly

5th & reverse bracket

Check ball 🔧

⊗ 16 · 21
(1.6 · 2.1, 12 · 15)

O-ring ⊗

Retaining pin ⊗

Reverse arm shaft

Select
check spring

2. Using a press and bearing adapter, remove the 5th gear synchronizer and the 5th input gear.

3. Remove the thrust washer ring, thrust washers and the 4th input gear.

4. Remove the snapring and then using a press and bearing adapter, remove the 3rd/4th synchronizer and the 3rd input gear.

5. Press off the input shaft front bearing.

To assemble:

6. Place the inserts in the 3 grooves on the coupling sleeve of the 3rd/4th synchronizer and

the 5th synchronizer. Lubricate the 3rd input gear inner surface with gear oil, then install the 3rd input gear and 3rd baulk ring.

7. Press the 3rd/4th synchronizer hub together, pay attention to its direction.

8. Install the snapring of the proper thickness that will minimize the clearance of the groove in the input shaft. The allowable groove clearance should be 0-0.100mm.

9. Lubricate the 4th input gear with gear oil, then install the 4th input gear, thrust washers and thrust washer ring. The thrust washers

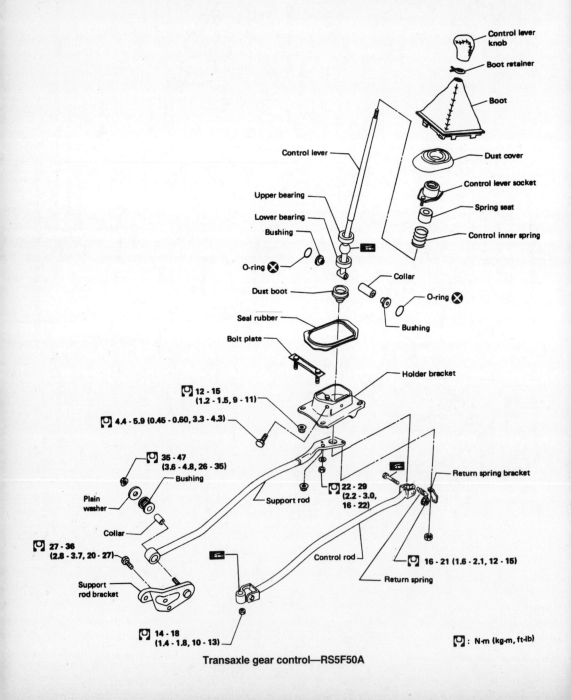

Transaxle gear control—RS5F50A

3rd and 4th input gear

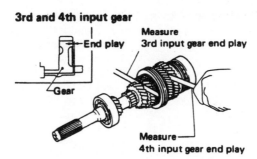

Measuring gear endplay—mainshaft

Gears	End play mm (in)
3rd input gear	0.23 - 0.43 (0.0091 - 0.0169)
4th input gear	0.25 - 0.55 (0.0098 - 0.0217)
5th input gear	0.23 - 0.48 (0.0091 - 0.0189)

should be selected to minimize clearance of the groove in the input shaft. The allowable groove clearance should be 0-0.06mm.

10. Lubricate the inner surface of 5th gear with gear oil, then install 5th gear.

11. Press on the 5th gear synchronizer.

12. Install the input shaft front and rear bearing.

13. Measure the gear endplay and correct as required.

Mainshaft

NOTE: *The following removal procedures require the use of a hydraulic press and various bearing adapters.*

1. Using a press and bearing adapter, remove the mainshaft rear bearing.

2. Remove the thrust washer and snapring.

3. Using a press and bearing adapter, remove the 5th and 4th main gears.

4. Using a press and bearing adapter, remove the 3rd and the 2nd main gears.

5. Remove the snapring and then using a press and bearing adapter, remove the 1st/2nd synchronizer and the 1st main gear.

6. Press off the mainshaft front bearing.

To Assemble:

7. Place the inserts in the 3 grooves on the coupling sleeve of the 1st/2nd synchronizer.

8. Lubricate the 1st gear inner surface with gear oil, then install the 1st gear and 1st baulk ring.

9. Press the 1st/2nd synchronizer hub together, pay attention to its direction.

10. Install the coupling sleeve with 3 inserts and the 2nd gear baulk ring.

11. Install the snapring of the proper thickness that will minimize the clearance of the groove in the mainshaft. The allowable groove clearance should be 0-0.100mm.

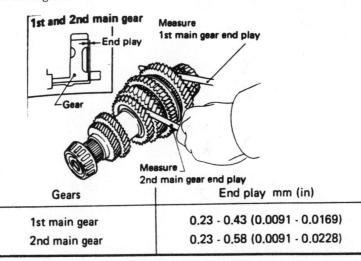

Gears	End play mm (in)
1st main gear	0.23 - 0.43 (0.0091 - 0.0169)
2nd main gear	0.23 - 0.58 (0.0091 - 0.0228)

Measuring gear endplay—input shaft

12. Lubricate the 2nd gear with gear oil, then install the 2nd gear.

13. Press on 3rd gear.

14. Press on 4th gear.

15. Press on 5th gear.

16. Install the snapring of proper thickness that will minimize clearance of the groove in the mainshaft. The allowable groove clearance should be 0-0.15mm.

ASSEMBLY OF TRANSAXLE

1. With a pin punch, install the striking lever and select lever.

2. Instal the select shifter and retaining pin.

3. Install the reverse gate assembly.

4. Install the final drive assembly.

5. Install the input shaft and the mainshaft with the 1st and 2nd shift fork assembly.

NOTE: *Be careful not to damage the input shaft oil seal during installation.*

6. Install the interlock balls and plunger.

7. Install the 3rd/4th shift fork and bracket, then install the 3rd/4th shift rod, circular clip and retaining pin.

8. Install the interlock balls.

9. Install the 5th shift fork and bracket, then install the shift rod, circular clip and retaining pin.

10. Install the 5th/reverse check plug, spring and ball.

11. Install the reverse lever assembly.

12. Install the reverse arm shaft and retaining pin.

13. Mesh 4th gear. Then install the reverse idler gear and shaft, paying attention to the direction of the tapped hole.

14. Place the U-shaped magnet on the clutch housing.

NOTE: *To aid in the installation of the transaxle case, place the shift selector in the 1st/2nd shift bracket or between the 1st/2nd bracket and the 3rd/4th bracket.*

15. Apply sealant to the mating surface of the transmission case and install it.

16. Install the position switch.

17. Apply sealant to the threads of the check plugs. Install the balls, springs and plugs.

18. After assembly, check that the transaxle can be shifted into each gear smoothly.

Halfshaft

REMOVAL AND INSTALLATION

NOTE: *Installation of the halfshafts will require a special tool for the spline alignment of the halfshaft end and the transaxle case. Do not perform this procedure without access to this tool. The Kent Moore tool Number is J-34296 and J-34297*

1. Raise the front of the vehicle and support it with jackstands.

2. Remove the wheel. Remove the brake caliper assembly. The brake hose does not need to be disconnected from the caliper. Be careful not to depress the brake pedal, or the piston will pop out. Do not twist the brake hose.

3. Pull out the cotter pin from the castellated nut on the wheel hub and then remove the wheel bearing lock nut.

NOTE: *Cover the boots with a shop towel or waste cloth so not to damage them when removing the halfshaft.*

4. Separate the halfshaft from the steering knuckle by tapping it with a block of wood and a mallet. It may be necessary to loosen (do not remove) the strut mounting bolts to gain clearance for steering knuckle removal from the halfshaft.

5. Remove the tie rod ball joint. Remove the three mounting nuts for the lower ball joint and then pull it down.

NOTE: *Always use a new nut when replacing the tie rod ball joint.*

6. On models with a manual transaxle, using a suitable tool, reach through the engine crossmember and carefully tap the right side inner CV-joint out of the transaxle case.

7. Using a block of wood on an hydraulic floor jack, support the engine under the oil pan.

8. Remove the support bearing bracket from the engine and then withdraw the right halfshaft.

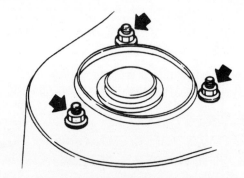

Loosen (DO NOT REMOVE) strut mounting nuts

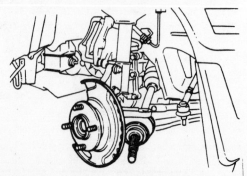

Removing halfshaft from steering knuckle

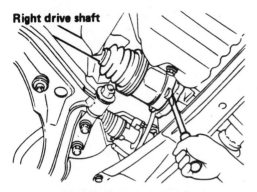

Removing right halfshaft from transaxle

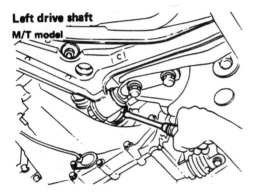

Removing left halfshaft from transaxle—manual transaxle

9. On models with manual transaxle, carefully insert a small prybar between the left CV-joint inner flange and the transaxle case mounting surface and pry the halfshaft out of the case. Withdraw the shaft from the steering knuckle and remove it.

10. On models with automatic transaxle, insert a dowel through the right side halfshaft hole (remove the right side halfshaft the same way as on manual transaxle models) and use a small mallet to tap the left halfshaft out of the transaxle case. Withdraw the shaft from the steering knuckle and remove it.

NOTE: *Be careful not to damage the pinion mating shaft and the side gear while tapping the left halfshaft out of the transaxle case.*

11. When installing the shafts into the transaxle, use a new oil seal and then install an alignment tool along the inner circumference of the oil seal.

12. Insert the halfshaft into the transaxle, align the serrations and then remove the alignment tool.

13. Push the halfshaft, then press-fit the circular clip on the shaft into the clip groove on the side gear.

NOTE: *After insertion, attempt to pull the flange out of the side joint to make sure that the circular clip is properly seated in the side gear and will not come out.*

14. Install support bearing bracket retaining bolts and insert the halfshaft in the steering knuckle. Tighten the strut mounting bolts if loosen.

15. Connect the lower ball joint and tie rod end in the correct position.

16. Install the caliper assembly and the wheel bearing locknut. Tighten the nut to 174-231 ft. lbs.

17. Install a new cotter pin on the wheel hub and install the wheel.

18. Bleed the brake system if necessary. Road test the vehicle for proper operation.

CV-JOINT OVERHAUL

Transaxle Side Joint

1. Remove boot bands.

2. Match mark slide joint housing and driveshaft and separate.

3. Match mark spider assembly and then remove snapring and spider assembly. DO NOT disassemble spider assembly.

NOTE: *Cover driveshaft serration with tape so not to damage the boot.*

4. Remove axle boot from driveshaft.

5. To install reverse the removal procedures.

NOTE: *Always use new snaprings and align all matchmarks. Pack driveshaft and boot assembly with grease.*

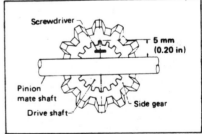

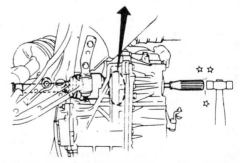

Removing left halfshaft from transaxle—automatic transaxle

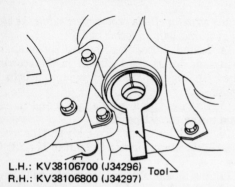

L.H.: KV38106700 (J34296) Tool
R.H.: KV38106800 (J34297)

Set special tool along the inner circumference of oil seal transaxle side

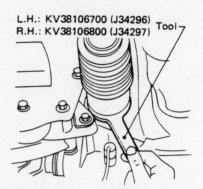

L.H.: KV38106700 (J34296) Tool
R.H.: KV38106800 (J34297)

Insert halfshaft into transaxle with special tool aligned properly

Wheel Side Joint

NOTE: *The joint on the wheel side cannot be disassembled.*

1. Match mark the driveshaft and the joint assembly.
2. Separate joint assembly with suitable tool.
3. Remove boot bands.
4. Install boot with new boot bands.
5. Align matchmarks lightly tap joint assembly onto the shaft.
6. Pack driveshaft with grease.

7. Lock both boot band clamps.
NOTE: *There are two different type (transaxle side) front axle joints used on Datsun/Nissan models.*

CLUTCH

The purpose of the clutch is to disconnect and connect engine power at the transmission. A car at rest requires a lot of engine torque to get all that weight moving. An internal combustion

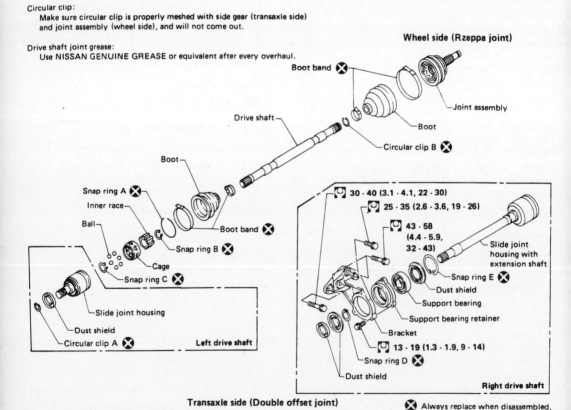

Circular clip:
   Make sure circular clip is properly meshed with side gear (transaxle side) and joint assembly (wheel side), and will not come out.

Drive shaft joint grease:
   Use NISSAN GENUINE GREASE or equivalent after every overhaul.

Wheel side (Rzeppa joint)

Boot band ✖

Drive shaft

Joint assembly

Boot

Circular clip B ✖

Boot

Snap ring A ✖
Inner race
Ball
Boot band ✖
Snap ring B ✖
Cage
Snap ring C ✖
Slide joint housing
Dust shield
Circular clip A ✖
Left drive shaft

30 - 40 (3.1 - 4.1, 22 - 30)
25 - 35 (2.6 - 3.6, 19 - 26)
43 - 58 (4.4 - 5.9, 32 - 43)
Slide joint housing with extension shaft
Snap ring E ✖
Dust shield
Support bearing
Support bearing retainer
Bracket
13 - 19 (1.3 - 1.9, 9 - 14)
Snap ring D ✖
Dust shield
Right drive shaft

Transaxle side (Double offset joint)

✖ Always replace when disassembled.
[tool] : N·m (kg-m, ft-lb)

Be careful not to damage boots. Use suitable protector or cloth during removal and installation.

Exploded view of front half shaft

engine does not develop a high starting torque (unlike steam engines), so it must be allowed to operate without any load until it builds up enough torque to move the car. Torque increases with engine rpm. The clutch allows the engine to build up torque by physically disconnecting the engine from the transmission, relieving the engine of any load or resistance. The transfer of engine power to the transmission (the load) must be smooth and gradual; if it weren't, drive line components would wear out or break quickly. This gradual power transfer is made possible by gradually releasing the clutch pedal. The clutch disc and pressure plate are the connecting link between the engine and transmission. When the clutch pedal is released, the disc and plate contact each other (clutch engagement), physically joining the engine and transmission. When the pedal is pushed in, the disc and plate separate (the clutch is disengaged), disconnecting the engine from the transmission.

The clutch assembly consists of the flywheel, the clutch disc, the clutch pressure plate, the throwout bearing and fork, the actuating linkage and the pedal. The flywheel and clutch pressure plate (driving members) are connected to the engine crankshaft and rotate with it. The clutch disc is located between the flywheel and pressure plate, and splined to the transmission shaft. A driving member is one that is attached to the engine and transfers engine power to a driven member (clutch disc) on the transmission shaft. A driving member (pressure plate) rotates (drives) a driven member (clutch disc) on contact and, in so doing, turns the transmission shaft. There is a circular diaphragm spring within the pressure plate cover (transmission side). In a relaxed state (when the clutch pedal is fully released), this spring is convex; that is, it is dished outward toward the transmission. Pushing in the clutch pedal actuates an attached linkage rod. Connected to the other end of this rod is the throwout bearing fork. The throwout bearing is attached to the fork. When the clutch pedal is depressed, the clutch linkage pushes the fork and bearing forward to contact the diaphragm spring of the pressure plate. The outer edges of the spring are secured to the pressure plate and are pivoted on rings so that when the center of the spring is compressed by the throwout bearing, the outer edges bow outward and, by so doing, pull the pressure plate in the same direction - away from the clutch disc. This action separates the disc from the plate, disengaging the clutch and allowing the transmission to be shifted into another gear. A coil type clutch return spring attached to the clutch pedal arm permits full release of the pedal. Releasing the pedal pulls the throwout bearing

away from the diaphragm spring resulting in a reversal of spring position. As bearing pressure is gradually released from the spring center, the outer edges of the spring bow outward, pushing the pressure plate into closer contact with the clutch disc. As the disc and plate move closer together, friction between the two increases and slippage is reduced until, when full spring pressure is applied (by fully releasing the pedal), The speed of the disc and plate are the same. This stops all slipping, creating a direct connection between the plate and disc which results in the transfer of power from the engine to the transmission. The clutch disc is now rotating with the pressure plate at engine speed and, because it is splined to the transmission shaft, the shaft now turns at the same engine speed. Understanding clutch operation can be rather difficult at first; if you're still confused after reading this, consider the following analogy. The action of the diaphragm spring can be compared to that of an oil can bottom. The bottom of an oil can is shaped very much like the clutch diaphragm spring and pushing in on the can bottom and then releasing it produces a similar effect. As mentioned earlier, the clutch pedal return spring permits full release of the pedal and reduces linkage slack due to wear. As the linkage wears, clutch free-pedal travel will increase and free-travel will decrease as the clutch wears. Free-travel is actually throwout bearing lash.

The diaphragm spring type clutches used are available in two different designs: flat diaphragm springs or bent spring. The bent fingers are bent back to create a centrifugal boost ensuring quick re-engagement at higher engine speeds. This design enables pressure plate load to increase as the clutch disc wears and makes low pedal effort possible even with a heavy-duty clutch. The throwout bearing used with the bent finger design is 1¼" long and is shorter than the bearing used with the flat finger design. These bearings are not interchangeable. If the longer bearing is used with the bent finger clutch, free-pedal travel will not exist. This results in clutch slippage and rapid wear.

The transmission varies the gear ratio between the engine and rear wheels. It can be shifted to change engine speed as driving conditions and loads change. The transmission allows disengaging and reversing power from the engine to the wheels.

CAUTION: *The clutch driven disc contains asbestos, which has been determined to be a cancer causing agent. Never clean clutch surface with compressed air! Avoid inhaling any dust from any clutch surface! When cleaning clutch surfaces, use a commercially available brake cleaning fluid.*

Adjustments

PEDAL HEIGHT AND FREE PLAY

Refer to the Clutch Specifications Chart for clutch pedal height above floor and pedal free play.

All models have a hydraulically operated clutch. Pedal height is usually adjusted with a stopper limiting the upward travel of the pedal. Pedal free-play is adjusted at the master cylinder pushrod. If the pushrod is nonadjustable, free-play is adjusted by placing shims between the master cylinder and the firewall.

Driven Disc And Pressure Plate

REMOVAL AND INSTALLATION

1. Remove the transmission or transaxle from the engine as detailed earlier in this chapter.
2. Insert a clutch aligning bar or similar tool all the way into the clutch disc hub. This must be done so as to support the weight of the clutch disc during removal. Mark the clutch assembly-

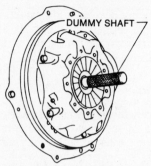

Use a dummy shaft for alignment purposes

to-flywheel relationship with paint or a center punch so that the clutch assembly can be assembled in the same position from which it is removed.

3. Loosen the bolts in sequence, a turn at a time. Remove the bolts.
4. Remove the pressure plate and clutch disc.
5. Remove the release mechanism from the transmission housing. Apply lithium based molybdenum disulfide grease to the bearing sleeve inside groove, the contact point of the with-

Troubleshooting Basic Clutch Problems

Problem	Cause
Excessive clutch noise	Throwout bearing noises are more audible at the lower end of pedal travel. The usual causes are: • Riding the clutch • Too little pedal free-play • Lack of bearing lubrication A bad clutch shaft pilot bearing will make a high pitched squeal, when the clutch is disengaged and the transmission is in gear or within the first 2″ of pedal travel. The bearing must be replaced. Noise from the clutch linkage is a clicking or snapping that can be heard or felt as the pedal is moved completely up or down. This usually requires lubrication. Transmitted engine noises are amplified by the clutch housing and heard in the passenger compartment. They are usually the result of insufficient pedal free-play and can be changed by manipulating the clutch pedal.
Clutch slips (the car does not move as it should when the clutch is engaged)	This is usually most noticeable when pulling away from a standing start. A severe test is to start the engine, apply the brakes, shift into high gear and SLOWLY release the clutch pedal. A healthy clutch will stall the engine. If it slips it may be due to: • A worn pressure plate or clutch plate • Oil soaked clutch plate • Insufficient pedal free-play
Clutch drags or fails to release	The clutch disc and some transmission gears spin briefly after clutch disengagement. Under normal conditions in average temperatures, 3 seconds is maximum spin-time. Failure to release properly can be caused by: • Too light transmission lubricant or low lubricant level • Improperly adjusted clutch linkage
Low clutch life	Low clutch life is usually a result of poor driving habits or heavy duty use. Riding the clutch, pulling heavy loads, holding the car on a grade with the clutch instead of the brakes and rapid clutch engagement all contribute to low clutch life.

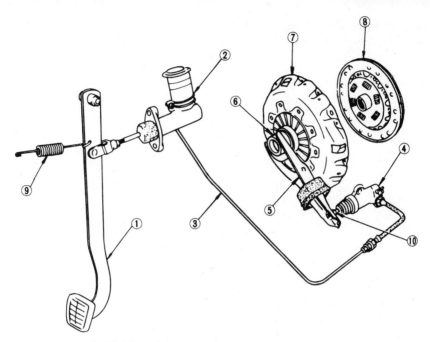

1. Clutch pedal
2. Clutch master cylinder
3. Clutch piping
4. Operating cylinder
5. Withdrawal lever
6. Release bearing
7. Clutch cover
8. Clutch disc
9. Return spring
10. Push rod

510, 610 and 710 clutch control system

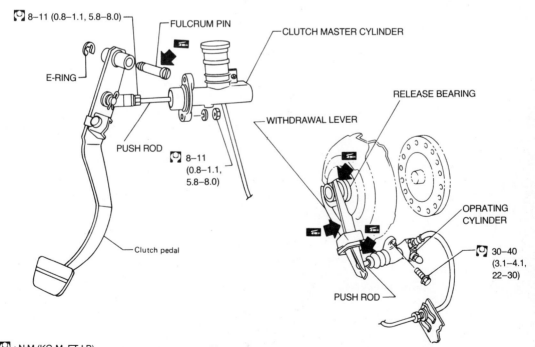

8–11 (0.8–1.1, 5.8–8.0)

FULCRUM PIN

CLUTCH MASTER CYLINDER

E-RING

PUSH ROD

8–11
(0.8–1.1,
5.8–8.0)

RELEASE BEARING

WITHDRAWAL LEVER

OPRATING
CYLINDER

30–40
(3.1–4.1,
22–30)

Clutch pedal

PUSH ROD

: N·M (KG-M, FT-LB)

1984 and later 200SX clutch operating mechanism

Clutch Specifications

Model	Pedal Height Above Floor (in.)	Pedal Free-Play (in.)
510	6.5	0.04–0.20
610	6.9	0.04–0.12
710	7.09	0.04–0.20
1977–80 810	6.9	0.04–0.20
1981–83 810, Maxima	7.25	0.04–0.20
1977–79 200SX	7.60	0.04–0.12
1980–83 200SX	6.70	0.04–0.20
1984–85 200SX	7.60–7.99	0.04–0.06
1984 Maxima	6.9	0.04–0.20
1986–88 200SX	7.44–7.83 ①	0.039–0.118
1989 240SX	7.32–7.72	0.039–0.118
1985–88 Maxima	6.73–7.13	0.04–0.12
1989 Maxima	6.50–6.89	0.039–0.118

① 7.72–8.11 on VG30E engine

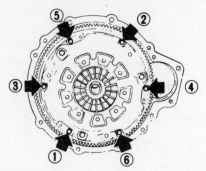

Loosen the bolts in sequence, one turn at a time

spect the release bearing and replace as necessary. Apply a small amount of grease to the transmission splines. Install the disc on the splines and slide back and forth a few times. Remove the disc and remove excess grease on hub. Be sure no grease contacts the disc or pressure plate.

drawal lever and bearing sleeve, the contact surface of the lever ball pin and lever. Replace the release mechanism.

6. Inspect the pressure plate for wear, scoring, etc., and reface or replace as necessary. In-

7. Install the disc, aligning it with a splined dummy shaft.

8. Install the pressure plate and torque the bolts to 11-16 ft. lbs. (16-22 ft. lbs. on 1984 and later 200SX, 240SX and front wheel drive Maxima).

9. Remove the dummy shaft.

10. Replace the transmission or transaxle.

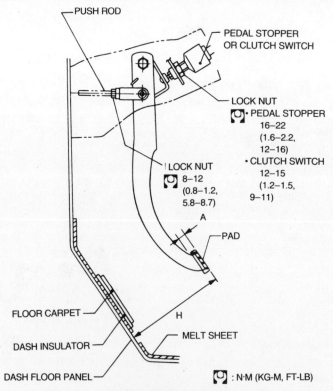

Clutch adjusting points

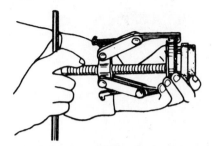
Use a universal puller and adapter to pull the release bearing out of the bearing sleeve

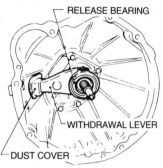
Withdrawal lever-to-release bearing relationship

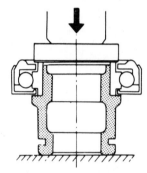
Install the release bearing on the sleeve using a press

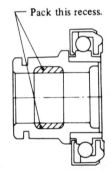
Apply grease to the release bearing here

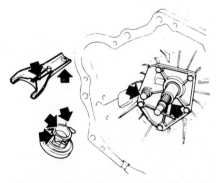
Grease these points before installing the clutch

Clutch Master Cylinder

REMOVAL AND INSTALLATION

1. Disconnect the clutch pedal arm from the pushrod.

2. Disconnect the clutch hydraulic line from the master cylinder.

NOTE: *Take precautions to keep brake fluid from coming in contact with any painted surfaces.*

3. Remove the nuts attaching the master cylinder and remove the master cylinder and pushrod toward the engine compartment side.

4. Install the master cylinder in the reverse order of removal and bleed the clutch hydraulic system.

OVERHAUL

NOTE: *Use this procedure as a guide on all late model years.*

1. Remove the master cylinder from the vehicle.

2. Drain the clutch fluid from the master cylinder reservoir.

3. Remove the boot and circlip and remove the pushrod.

4. Remove the stopper, piston, cup and return spring.

5. Clean all of the parts in clean brake fluid.

6. Check the master cylinder and piston for wear, corrosion and scores and replace the parts as necessary. Light scoring and glaze can be removed with crocus cloth soaked in brake fluid.

7. Generally, the cup seal should be replaced each time the master cylinder is disassembled. Check the cup and replace it if it is worn, fatigued, or damaged.

8. Check the clutch fluid reservoir, filler cap, dust cover and the pipe for distortion and damage and replace the parts as necessary.

9. Lubricate all new parts with clean brake fluid.

10. Reassemble the master cylinder parts in

1. Disc
2, 3. Clutch cover assembly with pressure plate
4. Bolt
5. Lockwasher
6. Withdrawal lever
7. Retainer spring
8. Bearing sleeve

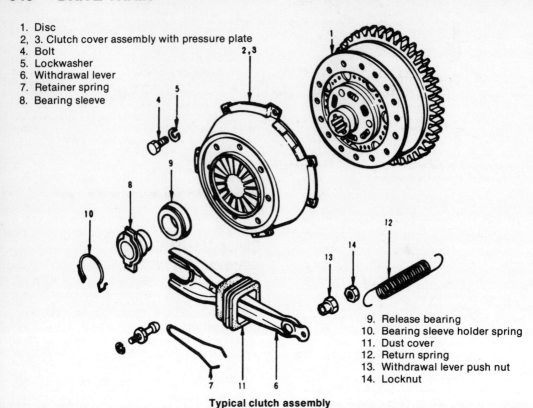

9. Release bearing
10. Bearing sleeve holder spring
11. Dust cover
12. Return spring
13. Withdrawal lever push nut
14. Locknut

Typical clutch assembly

the reverse order of disassembly, taking note of the following:

   a. Reinstall the cup seal carefully to prevent damaging the lipped portions.

   b. Adjust the height of the clutch pedal af-ter installing the master cylinder in position on the vehicle.

   c. Fill the master cylinder and clutch fluid reservoir and then bleed the clutch hydraulic system.

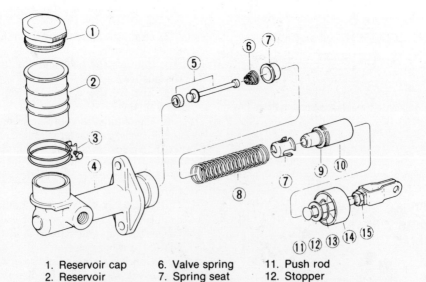

1. Reservoir cap	6. Valve spring	11. Push rod
2. Reservoir	7. Spring seat	12. Stopper
3. Reservoir band	8. Return spring	13. Stopper ring
4. Cylinder body	9. Piston cup	14. Dust cover
5. Valve assembly	10. Piston	15. Nut

Exploded view of typical master cylinder

Clutch Slave Cylinder
REMOVAL AND INSTALLATION

1. Remove the slave cylinder attaching bolts and the pushrod from the shift fork.

2. Disconnect the flexible fluid hose from the slave cylinder and remove the unit from the vehicle.

3. Install the slave cylinder in the reverse order of removal and bleed the clutch hydraulic system.

OVERHAUL

NOTE: *Use this procedure as a guide on late model years.*

1. Remove the slave cylinder from the vehicle.

2. Remove the pushrod and boot.

3. Force out the piston by blowing compressed air into the slave cylinder at the hose connection.

CAUTION: *Be careful not to apply excess air pressure to avoid possible injury.*

4. Clean all of the parts in clean brake fluid.

5. Check and replace the slave cylinder bore and piston if wear or severe scoring exists. Light scoring and glaze can be removed with crocus cloth soaked in brake fluid.

6. Normally the piston cup should be replaced when the slave cylinder is disassembled. Check the piston cup and replace it if it is found to be worn, fatigued or scored.

7. Replace the rubber boot if it is cracked or broken.

8. Lubricate all of the new parts in clean brake fluid and reassemble in the reverse order of disassembly, taking note of the following:

   a. Use care when reassembling the piston cup to prevent damaging the lipped portion of the piston cup.

   b. Fill the master cylinder with brake fluid and bleed the clutch hydraulic system.

   c. Adjust the clearance between the pushrod and the shift fork to $\frac{5}{64}$″.

BLEEDING THE CLUTCH HYDRAULIC SYSTEM

1. Check and fill the clutch fluid reservoir to the specified level as necessary. During the bleeding process, continue to check and replenish the reservoir to prevent the fluid level from getting lower than ½ the specified level.

2. Remove the dust cap from the bleeder screw on the clutch slave cylinder and connect a tube to the bleeder screw and insert the other end of the tube into a clean glass or metal container.

NOTE: *Take precautionary measures to prevent the brake fluid from getting on any painted surfaces.*

3. Pump the clutch pedal SLOWLY several

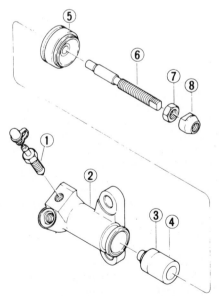

1. Bleeder screw
2. Cylinder body
3. Piston cup
4. Piston
5. Dust cover
6. Push rod
7. Lock nut
8. Push nut

Exploded view of a typical slave cylinder

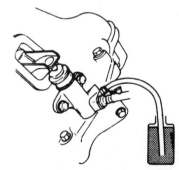

Run a hose from the bleeder screw into a clear container filled with brake fluid

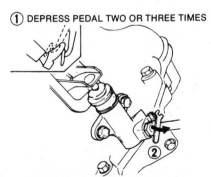

① DEPRESS PEDAL TWO OR THREE TIMES

Pump the clutch pedal several times and then open the bleeder screw

times, hold it down and loosen the bleeder screw.

4. Tighten the bleeder screw and release the clutch pedal gradually. Repeat this operation until air bubbles disappear from the brake fluid being expelled out through the bleeder screw.

5. Repeat until all evidence of air bubbles completely disappears from the brake fluid being pumped out through the tube.

6. When the air is completely removed, securely tighten the bleeder screw and replace the dust cap.

7. Check and refill the master cylinder reservoir as necessary.

8. Depress the clutch pedal several times to check the operation of the clutch and check for leaks.

AUTOMATIC TRANSMISSION

Understanding Automatic Transmissions

The automatic transmission allows engine torque and power to be transmitted to the rear wheels within a narrow range of engine operating speeds. The transmission will allow the engine to turn fast enough to produce plenty of power and torque at very low speeds, while keeping it at a sensible rpm at high vehicle speeds. The transmission performs this job entirely without driver assistance. The transmission uses a light fluid as the medium for the transmission of power. This fluid also works in the operation of various hydraulic control circuits and as a lubricant. Because the transmission fluid performs all of these three functions, trouble within the unit can easily travel from one part to another. For this reason, and because of the complexity and unusual operating principles of the transmission, a very sound understanding of the basic principles of operation will simplify troubleshooting.

THE TORQUE CONVERTER

The torque converter replaces the conventional clutch. It has three functions:

1. It allows the engine to idle with the vehicle at a standstill, even with the transmission in gear.

2. It allows the transmission to shift from range to range smoothly, without requiring that the driver close the throttle during the shift.

3. It multiplies engine torque to an increasing extent as vehicle speed drops and throttle opening is increased. This has the effect of making the transmission more responsive and reduces the amount of shifting required.

The torque converter is a metal case which is shaped lika sphere that has been flattened on opposite sides. It is bolted to the rear end of the engine's crankshaft. Generally, the entire metal case rotates at engine speed and serves as the engine's flywheel.

The case contains three sets of blades. One set is attached directly to the case. This set forms the torus or pump. Another set is directly connected to the output shaft, and forms the turbine. The third set is mounted on a hub which, in turn, is mounted on a stationary shaft through a one-way clutch. This third set is known as the stator.

A pump, which is driven by the covnerter hub at engine speed, keeps the torque converter full of transmission fluid at all times. Fluid flows continuously through the unit to provide cooling.

Under low-speed acceleration, the torque converter functions as follows:

The torus is turning faster than the turbine. It picks up fluid at the center of the converter and, through centrifugal force, slings it outward. Since the outer edge of the converter moves faster than the portions at the center, the fluid picks up speed.

The fluid then enters the outer edge of the turbine blades. It then travels back toward the center of the converter case along the turbine blades. In impinging upon the turbine blades, the fluid loses the energy picked up in the torus.

If the fluid were now to immediately be returned directly into the torus, both halves of the converter would have to turn at approximately the same speed at all times, and torque input and output would both be the same.

In flowing through the torus and turbine, the fluid picks up two types of flow, or flow in two spearate directions. It flows through the turbine blades, and it spins with the engine. The stator, whose blades are stationary when the vehicle is being accelerated at low speeds, converts one type of flow into another. Instead of allowing the fluid to flow straight back into the torus, the stator's curved blades turn the fluid almost 90 degrees toward the direction of rotation of the engine. Thus the fluid does not flow as fast toward the torus, but is already spinning when the torus picks it up. This has the effect of allowing the torus to turn much faster than the turbine. This difference in speed may be compared to the difference in speed between the smaller and larger gears in any gear train. The result is that engine power output is higher, and engine torque is multiplied.

As the speed of the turbine increases, the fluid spins faster and faster in the direction of engine rotation. As a result, the ability of the stator to redirect the fluid flow is reduced. Under

Lockup Torque Converter Service Diagnosis

Problem	Cause	Solution

No lockup	• Faulty oil pump
	• Sticking governor valve
	• Valve body malfunction
	   (a) Stuck switch valve
	   (b) Stuck lockup valve
	   (c) Stuck fail-safe valve
	• Failed locking clutch
	• Leaking turbine hub seal
	• Faulty input shaft or seal ring
		• Replace oil pump
		• Repair or replace as necessary
		• Repair or replace valve body or its internal components as necessary
		
		• Replace torque converter
		• Replace torque converter
		• Repair or replace as necessary

Will not unlock	• Sticking governor valve
	• Valve body malfunction
	   (a) Stuck switch valve
	   (b) Stuck lockup valve
	   (c) Stuck fail-safe valve
		• Repair or replace as necessary
		• Repair or replace valve body or its internal components as necessary

Stays locked up at too low a speed in direct	• Sticking governor valve
	• Valve body malfunction
	   (a) Stuck switch valve
	   (b) Stuck lockup valve
	   (c) Stuck fail-safe valve
		• Repair or replace as necessary
		• Repair or replace valve body or its internal components as necessary

Locks up or drags in low or second	• Faulty oil pump
	• Valve body malfunction
	   (a) Stuck switch valve
	   (b) Stuck fail-safe valve
		• Replace oil pump
		• Repair or replace valve body or its internal components as necessary

Sluggish or stalls in reverse	• Faulty oil pump
	• Plugged cooler, cooler lines or fittings
	• Valve body malfunction
	   (a) Stuck switch valve
	   (b) Faulty input shaft or seal ring
		• Replace oil pump as necessary
		• Flush or replace cooler and flush lines and fittings
		• Repair or replace valve body or its internal components as necessary

Loud chatter during lockup engagement (cold)	• Faulty torque converter • Failed locking clutch • Leaking turbine hub seal	• Replace torque converter • Replace torque converter • Replace torque converter
Vibration or shudder during lockup engagement	• Faulty oil pump • Valve body malfunction • Faulty torque converter • Engine needs tune-up	• Repair or replace oil pump as necessary • Repair or replace valve body or its internal components as necessary • Replace torque converter • Tune engine
Vibration after lockup engagement	• Faulty torque converter • Exhaust system strikes underbody • Engine needs tune-up • Throttle linkage misadjusted	• Replace torque converter • Align exhaust system • Tune engine • Adjust throttle linkage
Vibration when revved in neutral Overheating: oil blows out of dip stick tube or pump seal	• Torque converter out of balance • Plugged cooler, cooler lines or fittings • Stuck switch valve	• Replace torque converter • Flush or replace cooler and flush lines and fittings • Repair switch valve in valve body or replace valve body
Shudder after lockup engagement	• Faulty oil pump • Plugged cooler, cooler lines or fittings • Valve body malfunction • Faulty torque converter • Fail locking clutch • Exhaust system strikes underbody • Engine needs tune-up • Throttle linkage misadjusted	• Replace oil pump • Flush or replace cooler and flush lines and fittings • Repair or replace valve body or its internal components as necessary • Replace torque converter • Replace torque converter • Align exhaust system • Tune engine • Adjust throttle linkage

Troubleshooting Basic Automatic Transmission Problems

Problem	Cause	Solution
Fluid leakage	· Defective pan gasket	· Replace gasket or tighten pan bolts
	· Loose filler tube	· Tighten tube nut
	· Loose extension housing to transmission case	· Tighten bolts
	· Converter housing area leakage	· Have transmission checked professionally
Fluid flows out the oil filler tube	· High fluid level	· Check and correct fluid level
	· Breather vent clogged	· Open breather vent
	· Clogged oil filter or screen	· Replace filter or clean screen (change fluid also)
	· Internal fluid leakage	· Have transmission checked professionally
Transmission overheats (this is usually accompanied by a strong burned odor to the fluid)	· Low fluid level	· Check and correct fluid level
	· Fluid cooler lines clogged	· Drain and refill transmission. If this doesn't cure the problem, have cooler lines cleared or replaced.
	· Heavy pulling or hauling with insufficient cooling	· Install a transmission oil cooler
	· Faulty oil pump, internal slippage	· Have transmission checked professionally
Buzzing or whining noise	· Low fluid level	· Check and correct fluid level
	· Defective torque converter, scored gears	· Have transmission checked professionally
No forward or reverse gears or slippage in one or more gears	· Low fluid level	· Check and correct fluid level
	· Defective vacuum or linkage controls, internal clutch or band failure	· Have unit checked professionally
Delayed or erratic shift	· Low fluid level	· Check and correct fluid level
	· Broken vacuum lines	· Repair or replace lines
	· Internal malfunction	· Have transmission checked professionally

Transmission Fluid Indications

The appearance and odor of the transmission fluid can give valuable clues to the overall condition of the transmission. Always note the appearance of the fluid when you check the fluid level or change the fluid. Rub a small amount of fluid between your fingers to feel for grit and smell the fluid on the dipstick.

If the fluid appears:	It indicates:
Clear and red colored	· Normal operation
Discolored (extremely dark red or brownish) or smells burned	· Band or clutch pack failure, usually caused by an overheated transmission. Hauling very heavy loads with insufficient power or failure to change the fluid, often result in overheating. Do not confuse this appearance with newer fluids that have a darker red color and a strong odor (though not a burned odor).
Foamy or aerated (light in color and full of bubbles)	· The level is too high (gear train is churning oil) · An internal air leak (air is mixing with the fluid). Have the transmission checked professionally.
Solid residue in the fluid	· Defective bands, clutch pack or bearings. Bits of band material or metal abrasives are clinging to the dipstick. Have the transmission checked professionally.
Varnish coating on the dipstick	· The transmission fluid is overheating

cruising conditions, the stator is eventually forced to rotate on its one-way clutch in the direction of engine rotation. Under these conditions, the torque converter begins to behave almost like a solid shaft, with the torus and turbine speeds being almost equal.

THE PLANETARY GEARBOX

The ability of the torque converter to multiply engine torque is limited. Also, the unit tends to be more efficient when the turine is rotating at relatively high speeds. Therefore, a planetary gearbox is used to carry the power output of the turbine to the driveshaft.

Planetary gears function very similarly to conventional transmission gears. However, their construction is different in that three elements make up one gear system, and, in that all three elements are different from one another. The three elements are: an outer gear that is shaped like a hoop, with teeth cut into the inner surface; a sun gear, mounted on a shaft and located at the very center of the outer gear; and a set of three planet gears, held by pins in a ring-like planet carrier, meshing with both the sun gear and the outer gear. Either the outer gear or the sun gear may be held stationary, providing more than one possible torque multiplication factor for each set of gears. Also, if all three gears are forced to rotate at the same speed, the gearset forms, in effect, a solid shaft.

Most modern automatics use the planetary gears to provide either a single reduction ratio of about 1.8:1, or two reduction gears: a low of about 2.5:1, and an intermediate of about 1.5:1. Bands and clutches are used to hold various portions of the gearsets to the transmission case or to the shaft on which they are mounted. Shifting is accomplished, then, by changing the portion of each planetary gearset which is held to the tranmission case or to the shaft.

THE SERVOS AND ACCUMULATORS

The servos are hydraulic pistons and cylinders. They resemble the hydraulic actuators used on many familiar machines, such as bulldozers. Hydraulic fluid enters the cylinder, under pressure, and forces the piston to move to engage the band or clutches.

The accumulators are used to cushion the engagement of the servos. The transmission fluid must pass through the accumulator on the way to the servo. The accumulator housing contains a thin piston which is sprung away from the discharge passage of the accumulator. When fluid passes through the accumulator on the way to the servo, it must move the piston against spring pressure, and this action smooths out the action of the servo.

THE HYDRAULIC CONTROL SYSTEM

The hydraulic pressure used to operate the servos comes from the main transmission oil pump. This fluid is channeled to the various servos through the shift valves. There is generally a manual shift valve which is operated by the tranmission selector lever and an automatic shift valvee for each automatic upshift the transmission provides: i.e., two-speed automatics have a low-high shift valve, while three-speeds have a 1-2 valve, and a 2-3 vavle.

There are two pressures which effect the operation of these valves. One is the governor pressure which is affected by vehicle speed. The other is the modulator pressure which is affected by intake manifold vacuum or throttle position. Governor pressure rises with an increase in vehicle speed, and modulator pressure rises as the throttle is opened wider. By responding to these two pressures, the shift valves cause the upshift points to be delayed with increased throttle opening to make the best use of the engine's power output.

Most transmissions also make use of an auxiliary circuit for downshifting. This circuit may be actuated by the throttle linkage or the vacuum line which actuates the modulator, or by a cable or solenoid. It applies pressure to a special downshift surface on the shift valve or valves.

The transmission modulator also governs the line pressure, used to actuate the servos. In this way, the clutches and bands will be actuated with a force matching the torque output of the engine.

Identification

The automatic transmission serial number label is attached to the side of the transmission housing on all models and to the rear tailshaft section on the 240SX model.

Fluid Pan and Filter

REMOVAL AND INSTALLATION

1. Jack up the front of the car and support it safely on stands.
2. Slide a drain pan under the transmission.

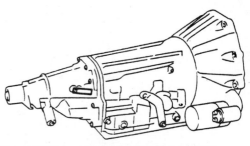

Transmission serial number location—240SX

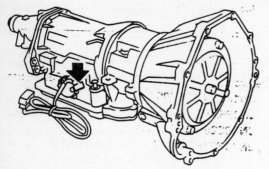

Transmission serial number location—200SX

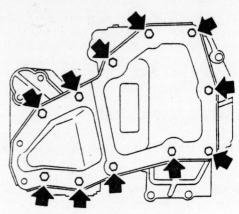

Transmission filter retaining bolt locations

Loosen the rear oil pan bolts first, to allow most of the fluid to drain off without making a mess on your garage floor.

3. Remove the remaining bolts and drop the pan. Remove the 11 transmission filter retaining bolts and remove the filter from the transmission. Install a new filter in the correct position and torque the transmission filter retaining bolts to 2-3 ft. lbs.

4. Discard the old gasket, clean the pan, and reinstall the pan with a new gasket.

5. Tighten the retaining bolts in a crisscross pattern starting at the center.

NOTE: *The transmission case is aluminum, so don't exert too much force on the bolts. Torque the bolts to 3.6-5.1 ft. lbs.*

6. Refill the transmission through the dipstick tube and check the fluid level.

Adjustments

SHIFT LINKAGE

1973-78

1. Loosen the trunnion locknuts at the lower end of the control level. Remove the selector level knob and console.

2. Put the transmission selector in N and put the transmission shift level in the Neutral position by pushing it all the way back, then moving it forward two stops.

3. Check the vertical clearance between the top of the shift level pin and transmission control bracket (A in the illustration). It should be 0.5-1.5mm. Adjust the nut at the lower end of

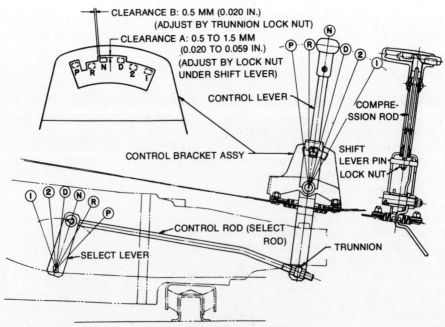

Shift linkage adjustment—1973-78

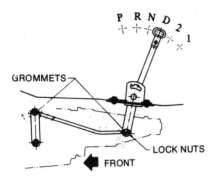

Shift linkage adjustment—1979 and later models

the selector lever compression rod, as necessary.

4. Check the horizontal clearance (B) between the shift lever pin and transmission control bracket. It should be 0.5mm. Adjust the trunnion locknuts as necessary to get this clearance.

5. Replace the console with the shift pointer correctly aligned. Install the shift knob.

1979 and Later Models

Adjustment is made at the locknuts at the base of the shifter, which control the length of the shift control rod.

1. Place the shift lever in D.

2. Loosen the locknuts and move the shift lever until it is firmly in the D range, the pointer is aligned, and the transmission is in D range.

3. Tighten the locknuts.

4. Check the adjustment. Start the car and apply the parking brake. Shift through all the ranges, starting in P. As the lever is moved from P to 1, you should be able to feel the detents in each range. If proper adjustment is not possible, the grommets are probably worn and should be replaced.

CHECKING KICK-DOWN SWITCH AND SOLENOID

1. Turn the key to the normal ON position, and depress the accelerator all the way. The so-

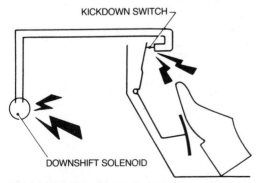

Kickdown switch and downshift solenoid

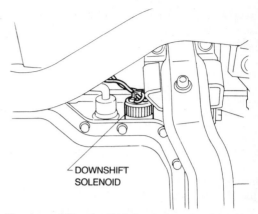

The downshift solenoid is located on the side of the transmission just above the pan

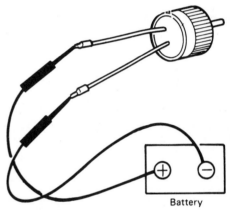

Check downshift solenoid operation by applying battery voltage

lenoid in the transmission should make an audible click.

2. If the solenoid does not work, inspect the wiring, and test it electrically to determine whether the problem is in the wiring, the kickdown switch, or the solenoid.

3. If the solenoid requires replacement, drain a little over 2 pts (1 liter) of fluid from the transmission before removing it.

Neutral Safety Switch/Inhibitor Switch

REMOVAL, INSTALLATION AND ADJUSTMENT

1973-80

The switch unit is bolted to the left side of the transmission case, behind the transmission shift lever. The switch prevents the engine from being started in any transmission position except Park or Neutral. It also controls the backup lights.

1. Apply the brakes and check to see that the starter works only in the P and N transmission

ranges. If the starter works with the transmission in gear, adjust the switch as described below.

2. Remove the transmission shift level retaining nut and the lever.

3. Remove the switch.

4. Remove the machine screw in the case under the switch.

5. Align the switch to the case by inserting a 1.5mm pin, through the hole in the switch into the screw hole. Mark the switch location.

6. Remove the pin, replace the machine screw, install the switch as marked, and replace the transmission shift lever and retaining nut.

7. Make sure while holding the brakes on, that the engine will start only in Park or Neutral. Check that the backup lights go on only in Reverse.

1981-89

The switch unit is bolted to the the transmission case, behind the transmission shift lever. The switch prevents the engine from being started in any transmission position except

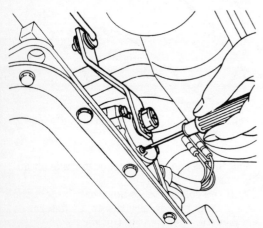
Removing screw from inhibitor switch

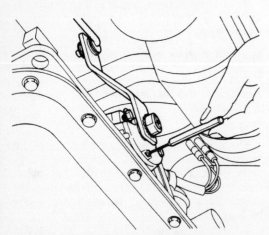
Inhibitor switch adjustment with aligning pin

Park or Neutral. It also controls the backup lights.

1. Place the transmission selector lever in the Neutral range.

2. Remove the screw from the switch (see illustration).

3. Loosen the attaching bolts. With a aligning pin (2.0mm diameter) move the switch until the pin falls into the hole in the rotor.

4. Tighten the attaching bolts equally.

5. Make sure while holding the brakes on, that the engine will start only in Park or Neutral. Check that the backup lights go on only in Reverse.

Transmission
REMOVAL AND INSTALLATION

1. Disconnect the battery cable.

NOTE: *Take care not to damage any adjacent parts when dismounting transmission.*

2. Remove the accelerator linkage.

3. Detach the shift linkage.

4. Disconnect the neutral safety switch/inhibitor and downshift solenoid wiring.

5. Drain the transmission.

6. Remove the front exhaust pipe.

7. Remove the vacuum tube and speedometer cable.

8. Disconnect the fluid cooler tubes.

9. Remove the driveshaft and starter.

10. Support the transmission with a jack under the oil pan. Support the engine also.

11. Remove the rear crossmember.

Disconnecting the torque converter bolts through the access hole

Remove the transmission gussets

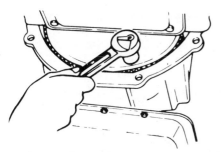

Removing the bolts securing the torque converter to the drive plate

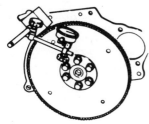

Checking drive plate (flywheel) runout with a dial gauge

Refill the torque converter before installation

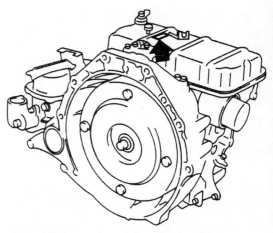

Automatic transaxle serial number location

all the linkage, electrical connections and hoses if they were removed.

17. Reconnect the battery cable. Refill the transmission and check the fluid level.

18. After the fluid level is correct and no leaks are present, roadtest the vehicle for proper operation.

AUTOMATIC TRANSAXLE

Identification

The automatic transaxle serial number label is attached to the upper portion of the automatic transaxle oil pan.

Control Valve Assembly Cover

REMOVAL AND INSTALLATION

NOTE: *To remove the transaxle oil filter or oil strainer the transaxle must be removed from the vehicle and the transaxle disassembled.*

1. Raise and support the vehicle on jackstands.

2. Place a container under the transaxle to catch the oil when the pan is removed.

3. Remove the transaxle pan bolts.

NOTE: *If the pan sticks, bump it with a soft hammer to break it loose.*

4. Using a putty knife, clean the gasket mounting surfaces.

5. To install, use a new gasket, sealant and reverse the removal procedures. Torque the oil pan bolts to 3.6-5.1 ft. lbs. Refill the transaxle to the correct level.

Adjustments

SHIFT LINKAGE

1. Release the parking brake. Raise the car and support it securely on jackstands.

12. Mark the relationship between the torque converter and the drive plate (flywheel). Remove the four bolts holding the converter to the drive plate through the hole at the front, under the engine. Unbolt the transmission from the engine.

13. Install the transmission to the engine and the crossmember in the correct position. Torque the drive plate to crankshaft bolts 101-116 ft. lbs. Torque the drive plate to torque converter and converter housing to engine bolts 29-36 ft. lbs. Torque the transmission to crossmember bolts to 23-31 ft. lbs. and the crossmember to body frame mounting bolts to 43-58 ft. lbs.

14. Connect the driveshaft and install the starter with the electrical connections.

15. Connect the fluid cooler tubes and the speedometer cable.

16. Install the exhaust system and reconnect

2. Then, working under the car, remove the nut from behind the transmission shift lever and disconnect the control cable from it. Now, pull the control cable to force the manual lever on the transmission into Park. Check that this has occurred by attempting to turn both drive-shafts. They should both be locked. If not, the cable must be pulled more forcefully.

3. Slide the bottom of the shift lever back and forth to make sure it works freely and then force it to the Park position (in the direction that would pull the control cable.

4. Loosen the two locknuts that position the control lever fitting on the cable and, when it is free, insert it into the lower control lever. Install and tighten the mounting nut.

5. Gently tighten the two locknuts so as to avoid tensioning the cable and then, when they touch the lever fitting, tighten both equally in opposite directions to lock the adjustment in place.

THROTTLE CABLE

The throttle cable is operated via a cam on the throttle shaft of the injection unit. The adjustment is located on the side of the air intake plenum (this is the lower cable located there.)

1. Loosen the two locknuts that position the cable. Open the throttle lever and hold it at the fully open position.

2. Back off both locknuts. Slide the outer cable as far as it will go away from the throttle cam.

3. Turn the nut on the side away from the throttle until it just starts to hold. Then, back it off ¾-1¼ revolutions. Tighten the nut on the throttle side to lock this position securely.

Neutral Safety Switch/Inhibitor Switch

The inhibitor switch allows the back-up lights to work when the transaxle is placed in Reverse range and acts as a Neutral switch, by allowing the current to pass to the starter when the transaxle is placed in Neutral or Park.

REMOVAL AND INSTALLATION

1. Disconnect and remove the battery.
2. Remove the air cleaner, air flow meter, air damper and solenoid valves as an assembly.
3. Remove the control cable end from the unit.
4. Disconnect the electrical harness then remove the inhibitor switch retaining bolts.
5. To install reverse the removal procedure.

ADJUSTMENT

1. Raise and support the vehicle on jackstands.

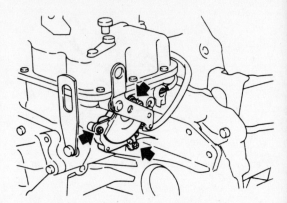

Inhibitor switch retaining screws—Maxima

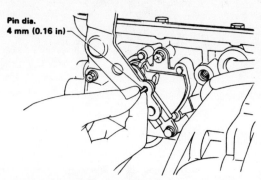

Pin dia. 4 mm (0.16 in)

Inhibitor switch adjustment—Maxima

2. Loosen the inhibitor switch adjusting screws. Place the select lever in the Neutral position.

3. Using a 4mm diameter pin, place the pin into the adjustment holes on both the inhibitor switch and the switch lever (the switch lever should be as near vertical position as possible).

4. Tighten the adjusting screws to 16-22 in. lbs.

5. Make sure while holding the brakes on, that the engine will start only in Park or Neutral. Check that the backup lights go on only in Reverse.

Transaxle

REMOVAL AND INSTALLATION

1. Drain the transmission pan. Disconnect the shift linkage and throttle cable. Refer to Chapter 3 and remove the engine and transaxle assembled.

2. Remove the transaxle-to-engine bolts and pull the transaxle straight off the rear mounting plate. Then, carefully matchmark the relationship between the torque converter and drive plate. Remove the bolts securing the converter to the drive plate and remove it.

3. Install in reverse order, lining up coverter mounting matchmarks. Apply locking sealer to

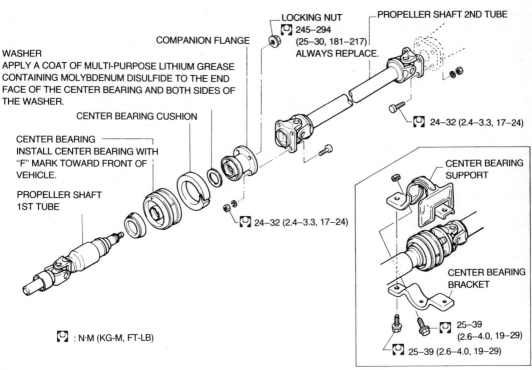

WASHER
APPLY A COAT OF MULTI-PURPOSE LITHIUM GREASE
CONTAINING MOLYBDENUM DISULFIDE TO THE END
FACE OF THE CENTER BEARING AND BOTH SIDES OF
THE WASHER.

COMPANION FLANGE

LOCKING NUT
245–294
(25–30, 181–217)
ALWAYS REPLACE.

PROPELLER SHAFT 2ND TUBE

24–32 (2.4–3.3, 17–24)

CENTER BEARING CUSHION

CENTER BEARING
INSTALL CENTER BEARING WITH
"F" MARK TOWARD FRONT OF
VEHICLE.

PROPELLER SHAFT
1ST TUBE

24–32 (2.4–3.3, 17–24)

CENTER BEARING
SUPPORT

CENTER BEARING
BRACKET

25–39
(2.6–4.0, 19–29)

25–39 (2.6–4.0, 19–29)

: N·M (KG-M, FT-LB)

Exploded view of the two-piece driveshaft (3 U-joints)

the mounting bolts before installing them. Torque to 22-36 ft. lbs. Then, rotate the crankshaft several revolutions to make sure the transmission rotates freely.

4. Adjust the neutral safety switch and throttle cable. Refill with the correct fluid to the proper level.

Halfshaft

For Removal, Installation and Overhaul procedures refer to the Manual Transaxle section in this Chapter.

DRIVELINE

Driveshaft and Universal Joints

The driveshaft transfers power from the engine and transmission to the differential and rear axles and then to the rear wheels to drive the car. All of the models covered in this book (except front wheel drive Maxima) utilize a conventional driveshaft. Except on the 610 wagon, the 810/Maxima, the 1977-79 200SX with manual transmission only and all 1980-82 200SX models, the driveshaft assembly has two uni-

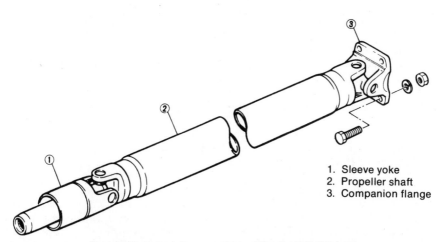

1. Sleeve yoke
2. Propeller shaft
3. Companion flange

Exploded view of the one-piece driveshaft (2 U-joints)

versal joints – one at each end – and a slip yoke at the front of the assembly which fits into the back of the transmission. The 610, 810/Maxima, and 200SX incorporate an additional universal joint at the center of the driveshaft with a support bearing.

On the front wheel drive Maxima, unequal lenght halfshafts transmit the power from the transaxle to the front wheels directly. The shorter shaft, on the driver's side, runs directly from the transaxle to the steering knuckle. The right side shaft runs directly to a center bearing and thence through a CV joint to the steering knuckle. There are CV joints at either end of

Troubleshooting Basic Driveshaft and Rear Axle Problems

When abnormal vibrations or noises are detected in the driveshaft area, this chart can be used to help diagnose possible causes. Remember that other components such as wheels, tires, rear axle and suspension can also produce similar conditions.

BASIC DRIVESHAFT PROBLEMS

Problem	Cause	Solution
Shudder as car accelerates from stop or low speed	• Loose U-joint • Defective center bearing	• Replace U-joint • Replace center bearing
Loud clunk in driveshaft when shifting gears	• Worn U-joints	• Replace U-joints
Roughness or vibration at any speed	• Out-of-balance, bent or dented driveshaft • Worn U-joints • U-joint clamp bolts loose	• Balance or replace driveshaft • Replace U-joints • Tighten U-joint clamp bolts
Squeaking noise at low speeds	• Lack of U-joint lubrication	• Lubricate U-joint; if problem persists, replace U-joint
Knock or clicking noise	• U-joint or driveshaft hitting frame tunnel • Worn CV joint	• Correct overloaded condition • Replace CV joint

BASIC REAR AXLE PROBLEMS

First, determine when the noise is most noticeable.

Drive Noise: Produced under vehicle acceleration.

Coast Noise: Produced while the car coasts with a closed throttle.

Float Noise: Occurs while maintaining constant car speed (just enough to keep speed constant) on a level road.

Road Noise

Brick or rough surfaced concrete roads produce noises that seem to come from the rear axle. Road noise is usually identical in Drive or Coast and driving on a different type of road will tell whether the road is the problem.

Tire Noise

Tire noises are often mistaken for rear axle problems. Snow treads or unevenly worn tires produce vibrations seeming to originate elsewhere. **Temporarily** inflating the tires to 40 lbs will significantly alter tire noise, but will have no effect on rear axle noises (which normally cease below about 30 mph).

Engine/Transmission Noise

Determine at what speed the noise is most pronounced, then stop the car in a quiet place. With the transmission in Neutral, run the engine through speeds corresponding to road speeds where the noise was noticed. Noises produced with the car standing still are coming from the engine or transmission.

Front Wheel Bearings

While holding the car speed steady, lightly apply the footbrake; this will often decease bearing noise, as some of the load is taken from the bearing.

Rear Axle Noises

Eliminating other possible sources can narrow the cause to the rear axle, which normally produces noise from worn gears or bearings. Gear noises tend to peak in a narrow speed range, while bearing noises will usually vary in pitch with engine speeds.

NOISE DIAGNOSIS

The Noise Is	Most Probably Produced By
• Identical under Drive or Coast	• Road surface, tires or front wheel bearings
• Different depending on road surface	• Road surface or tires
• Lower as the car speed is lowered	• Tires
• Similar with car standing or moving	• Engine or transmission
• A vibration	• Unbalanced tires, rear wheel bearing, unbalanced driveshaft or worn U-joint
• A knock or click about every 2 tire revolutions	• Rear wheel bearing
• Most pronounced on turns	• Damaged differential gears
• A steady low-pitched whirring or scraping, starting at low speeds	• Damaged or worn pinion bearing
• A chattering vibration on turns	• Wrong differential lubricant or worn clutch plates (limited slip rear axle)
• Noticed only in Drive, Coast or Float conditions	• Worn ring gear and/or pinion gear

the left side shaft and at either end of the right side shaft on the knuckle side of the center bearing.

REMOVAL AND INSTALLATION

510, 610 (Except Station Wagon), 710, 1977-79 200SX with Automatic Trans.

These driveshafts are the one piece type with a U-joint and flange at the rear, and a U-joint and a splined sleeve yoke which fits into the rear of the transmission, at the front. The U-joints must be disassembled for lubrication at 24,000 mile intervals. The splines are lubricated by transmission oil.

1. Release the handbrake and loosen the muffler (510 model) and rotate it out of the way.
2. On the 510 model, remove the handbrake rear cable adjusting nut and disconnect the left handbrake cable from the adjuster. Unbolt the rear flange.
3. Pull the driveshaft down and back and plug the transmission extension housing.
4. Reverse the procedure to install, oiling the splines. Flange bolt torque is 15-24 ft. lbs.

610 Station Wagon, 810/Maxima, and 1977-79 200SX with Manual Transmission

These models use a driveshaft with three U-joints and a center support bearing. The driveshaft is balanced as an assembly.

1. Mark the relationship of the driveshaft flange to the differential flange.
2. Unbolt the center bearing bracket.
3. Unbolt the driveshaft back under the rear axle. Plug the rear of the transmission to prevent oil or fluid loss.
5. On installation, align the marks made in Step 1. Torque the flange bolts to 15-24 ft. lbs.

U-JOINT OVERHAUL

Disassembly

1. Mark the relationship of all components for reassembly.
2. Remove the snaprings. On early units, the snaprings are seated in the yokes. On later units, the snaprings seat in the needle bearing races.
3. Tap the yoke with brass or rubber mallet

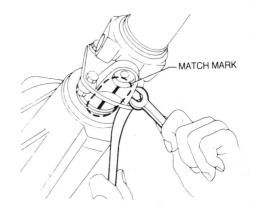

Matchmark the rear drive shaft flange to the axle flange

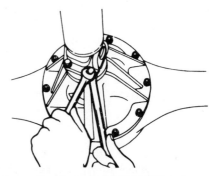

Disconnecting the rear driveshaft flange

to release one bearing cap. Be careful not to lose the needle rollers.

4. Remove the other bearing caps. Remove the U-joint spiders from the yokes.

Inspection

1. Spline backlash should not exceed 0.5mm.
2. Driveshaft runout should not exceed 0.4mm.
3. On later model with snaprings seated in the needle bearing races, different thicknesses of snaprings are available for U-joint adjustment. Play should not exceed 0.02mm.
4. U-joint spiders must be replaced if their bearing journals are worn more than 0.15mm from their original diameter.

Assembly

1. Place the needle rollers in the races and hold them in place with grease.
2. Put the spider into place in its yokes.
3. Replace all seals.
4. Tap the races into position and secure them with snaprings.

CENTER BEARING REPLACEMENT

The center bearing is a sealed unit which must be replaced as an assembly if defective.

1. Remove the driveshaft.
2. Paint a matchmark across where the flanges behind the center yoke are joined. This is for assembly purposes. If you don't paint or somehow mark the relationship between the two shafts, they may be out of balance when you put them back together.
3. Remove the bolts and separate the shafts. Make a matchmark on the front driveshaft half which lines up with the mark you made on the flange half.
4. You must devise a way to hold the driveshaft while unbolting the companion flange from the front driveshaft. Do not place the front driveshaft tube in a vise, because the

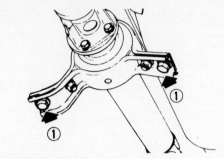

Remove the center bearing bracket

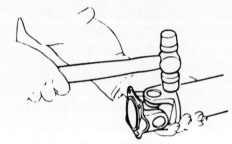

Removing the U-joint bearings

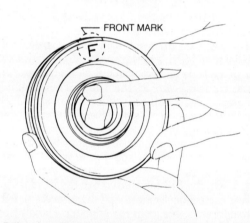

Before installing the center bearing, position the "F" mark so it is facing the front of the car

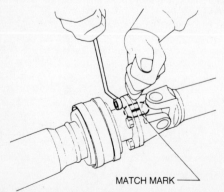

Matchmark the center bearing flange-to-driveshaft flange before unbolting

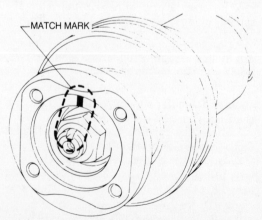

Matchmark the flange-to-shaft for later installation

Always use a new nut, and stake it after tightening

chances are it will get crushed. The best way is to grip the flange somehow while loosening the nut. It is going to require some strength to remove.

5. Press the companion flange off the front driveshaft and press the center bearing from its mount.

6. The new bearing is already lubricated. Install it into the mount, making sure that the seals and so on are facing the same way as when removed. Also make sure the F mark is facing the front of the car.

7. Slide the companion flange on to the front driveshaft, aligning the marks made during removal. Install the washer and lock nut. If the washer and locknut are separate pieces, tighten them to 145-175 ft. lbs. If they were a unit. tighten it to 180-217 ft. lbs. Check that the bearing rotates freely around the driveshaft. Stake the nut (always use a new nut).

8. Connect the companion flange to the other half of the driveshaft, aligning the marks made during removal. Tighten the bolts securely.

9. Install the driveshaft.

REAR AXLE

Identification

There are a few different types of rear axles used on the cars covered in this guide. A solid rear axle is used on 1977-84 200SX (except the 1984 Turbo model) 710, and all station wagon models. The 1978-81 510 uses a solid rear axle with either coil springs or leaf springs, depending on whether it is a sedan or a wagon. Independent rear suspension (I.R.S.) is used on the 610 sedans, 1984-88 200SX, and the 810/Maxima sedan (some models use solid rear axle) and the 1989 240SX model (different version). In this (I.R.S.) design separate axle driveshafts are used to transmit power from the differential to the wheels.

Determining Axle Ratio

The drive axle is said to have a certain axle ratio. This number (usually a whole number and a decimal fraction) is actually a comparison of the number of gear teeth on the ring gear and the pinion gear. For example, a 4.11 rear means that theoretically, there are 4.11 teeth on the ring gear and one tooth on the pinion gear or, put another way, the driveshaft must turn 4.11 times to turn the wheels once. Actually, on a 4.11 rear, there might be 37 teeth on the ring gear and 9 teeth on the pinion gear. By dividing the number of teeth on the pinion gear into the number of teeth on the ring gear, the numerical axle ratio (4.11) is obtained. This also provides a good method of ascertaining exactly what axle ratio one is dealing with.

Another method of determining gear ratio is to jack up and support the car so that both rear wheels are off the ground. Make a chalk mark on the rear wheel and the driveshaft. Put the transmission in neutral. Turn the rear wheel one complete turn and count the number of turns that the driveshaft makes. The number of turns that the driveshaft makes in one complete revolution of the rear wheel is an approximation of the rear axle ratio.

Axle Shaft (Solid Rear Axle)
REMOVAL AND INSTALLATION

NOTE: *Bearings must be pressed on and off the shaft with an arbor press. Unless you have access to one, it is inadvisable to attempt any repair work on the axle shaft and bearing assemblies.*

1. Remove the hub cap or wheel cover. Loosen the lug nuts.

2. Raise the rear of the car and support it safely on stands.

3. Remove the rear wheel. Remove the four brake backing plate retaining nuts. Detach the parking brake linkage from the brake backing plate.

4. Attach a slide hammer to the axle shaft and remove it. Use a slide hammer and a two pronged puller to remove the oil seal from the housing.

NOTE: *If a slide hammer is not available, the axle can sometimes be pried out using pry bars on opposing sides of the hub.*

If endplay is found to be excessive, the bearing should be replaced. Shimming the bearing is not recommended as this ignores end play of the bearing itself and could result in improper seating of the bearing.

5. Using a chisel, carefully nick the bearing retainer in three or four places. The retainer does not have to be cut, only collapsed enough

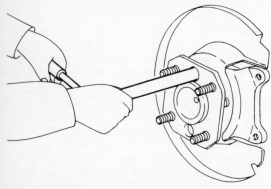

Removing the brake backing plate nuts

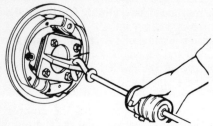

Use a slide hammer to remove the axle shaft—solid rear axle models

to allow the bearing retainer to be slid off the shaft.

6. Pull or press the old bearing off and install the new one by pressing it into position.

7. Install the outer bearing retainer with its raised surface facing the wheel hub, and then install the bearing and the inner bearing retainer in that order on the axle shaft.

8. With the smaller chamfered side of the inner bearing retainer facing the bearing, press on the retainer. The edge of the retainer should fully touch the bearing.

9. Clean the oil seal seat in the rear axle housing. Apply a thin coat of chassis grease.

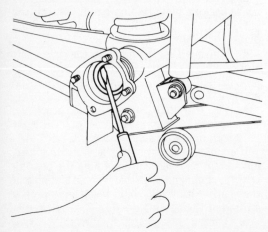

Carefully remove the oil seal. Replace the seal before axle shaft installation

Use a chisel to cut the bearing retainer

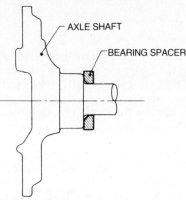

AXLE SHAFT

BEARING SPACER

Install the bearing spacer with the chamfer side facing the axle shaft flange

10. Using a seal installation tool, drive the oil seal into the rear axle housing. Wipe a thin coat of bearing grease on the lips of the seal.

11. Determine the number of retainer gaskets which will give the correct bearing-to-outer retainer clearance of 0.25mm.

12. Insert the axle shaft assembly into the axle housing, being careful not to damage the seal. Ensure that the shaft splines engage those of the differential pinion. Align the vent holes of the gasket and the outer bearing retainer. Install the retaining bolts.

13. Install the nuts on the bolts and tighten them evenly, and in a criss-cross pattern, to 20 ft. lbs.

Halfshaft (Independent Rear Suspension)

REMOVAL AND INSTALLATION

All Except 1982 and Later 810/Maxima, 1984 and Later 200SX, 200SX Turbo and 240SX

1. Raise and support the car.

2. Remove the U-joint yoke flange bolts at the outside. Remove the U-joint center bolt at the differential.

3. Remove the axle shaft.

4. Installation is the reverse. Torque the outside flange bolts to 36-43 ft. lbs. Tighten the four differential side flange bolts to 36-43 ft.

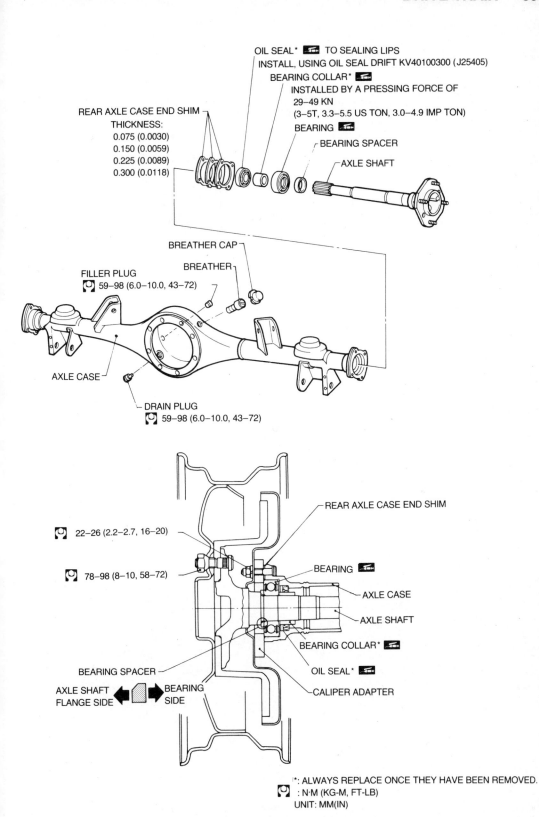

OIL SEAL* ◤▦ TO SEALING LIPS
INSTALL, USING OIL SEAL DRIFT KV40100300 (J25405)
BEARING COLLAR* ◤▦
INSTALLED BY A PRESSING FORCE OF
29–49 KN
(3–5T, 3.3–5.5 US TON, 3.0–4.9 IMP TON)
BEARING ◤▦
BEARING SPACER
AXLE SHAFT

REAR AXLE CASE END SHIM
THICKNESS:
0.075 (0.0030)
0.150 (0.0059)
0.225 (0.0089)
0.300 (0.0118)

BREATHER CAP
BREATHER
FILLER PLUG
◉ 59–98 (6.0–10.0, 43–72)

AXLE CASE

DRAIN PLUG
◉ 59–98 (6.0–10.0, 43–72)

REAR AXLE CASE END SHIM

◉ 22–26 (2.2–2.7, 16–20)

◉ 78–98 (8–10, 58–72)

BEARING ◤▦
AXLE CASE
AXLE SHAFT
BEARING COLLAR* ◤▦
OIL SEAL* ◤▦
CALIPER ADAPTER

BEARING SPACER
AXLE SHAFT
FLANGE SIDE ◀▨▶ BEARING
SIDE

*: ALWAYS REPLACE ONCE THEY HAVE BEEN REMOVED.
◉ : N·M (KG-M, FT-LB)
UNIT: MM(IN)

Solid rear axle assembly

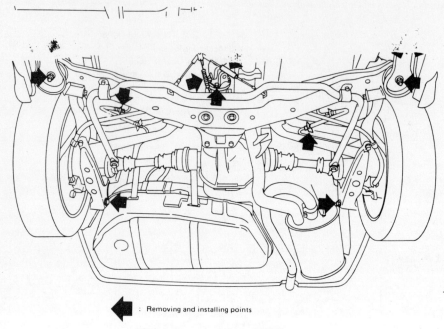

◀ : Removing and installing points

I.R.S. type suspension—200SX

Wheel alignment
● Camber cannot be adjusted.
● Vehicle requires only toe-in adjustment.
  −2 to 0 mm (−0.08 to 0 in), (−12' to 0)
  Refer to section MA for checking wheel alignment.

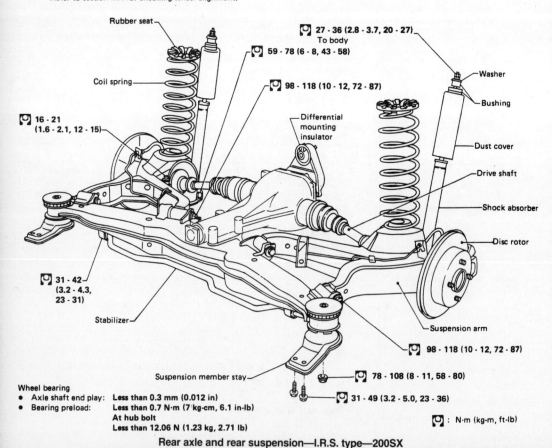

Rubber seat

Coil spring

27 - 36 (2.8 - 3.7, 20 - 27)
To body

59 - 78 (6 - 8, 43 - 58)

98 - 118 (10 - 12, 72 - 87)

Differential mounting insulator

16 - 21
(1.6 - 2.1, 12 - 15)

Washer

Bushing

Dust cover

Drive shaft

Shock absorber

Disc rotor

Suspension arm

31 - 42
(3.2 - 4.3, 23 - 31)

98 - 118 (10 - 12, 72 - 87)

Stabilizer

Suspension member stay

78 - 108 (8 - 11, 58 - 80)

31 - 49 (3.2 - 5.0, 23 - 36)

: N·m (kg-m, ft-lb)

Wheel bearing
● Axle shaft end play: **Less than 0.3 mm (0.012 in)**
● Bearing preload: **Less than 0.7 N·m (7 kg-cm, 6.1 in-lb)**
  At hub bolt
  Less than 12.06 N (1.23 kg, 2.71 lb)

Rear axle and rear suspension—I.R.S. type—200SX

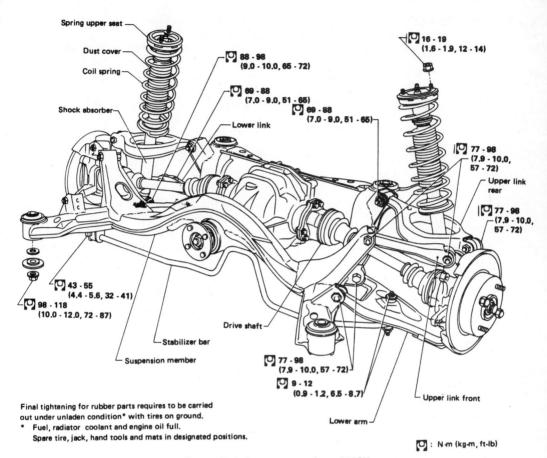

Spring upper seat

Dust cover

Coil spring

Shock absorber

88 - 98
(9.0 - 10.0, 65 - 72)

69 - 88
(7.0 - 9.0, 51 - 65)

69 - 88
(7.0 - 9.0, 51 - 65)

Lower link

16 - 19
(1.6 - 1.9, 12 - 14)

77 - 98
(7.9 - 10.0, 57 - 72)

Upper link rear

77 - 98
(7.9 - 10.0, 57 - 72)

43 - 55
(4.4 - 5.6, 32 - 41)

98 - 118
(10.0 - 12.0, 72 - 87)

Drive shaft

Stabilizer bar

Suspension member

77 - 98
(7.9 - 10.0, 57 - 72)

9 - 12
(0.9 - 1.2, 6.5 - 8.7)

Lower arm

Upper link front

Final tightening for rubber parts requires to be carried out under unladen condition* with tires on ground.
* Fuel, radiator coolant and engine oil full.
  Spare tire, jack, hand tools and mats in designated positions.

: N·m (kg-m, ft-lb)

Rear axle and rear suspension—240SX

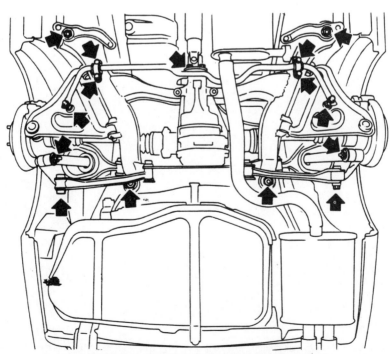

Removal points of rear suspension assembly—240SX

lbs. On axle shafts retained to the differential with a single center bolt, tighten the bolt to 17-23 ft. lbs., 1973-77, or 23-31 ft. lbs., 1978-81.

1982 and Later 810 and Maxima Rear Wheel Drive, 1984 and Later 200SX, 200SX Turbo and 240SX

NOTE: *Use this procedure as a guide for the 1989 240SX model.*
1. Raise and support the rear of the car.
2. Disconnect the halfshaft on the wheel side by removing the four flange bolts.
3. Grasp the halfshaft at the center and ex-

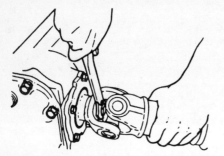

Removing the yoke flange center bolt at the differential

tract it from the differential carrier by prying it with a suitable pry bar.
4. Installation is in the reverse order of removal. Install the differential end first and then the wheel end. Tighten the four flange bolts to 20-27 ft. lbs.
NOTE: *Take care not to damage the oil seal or either end of the halfshaft during installation.*

INSPECTION

All Except 1982 and Later 810/Maxima, 1984 and Later 200SX, 200SX Turbo and 240SX

Before disassembling the axle shaft, inspect it as follows:
1. Check the parts for wear or damage. Replace the shaft as an assembly if defects are found.
2. Extend and compress the axle shaft (full stroke). Check the action for smoothness.
3. Check the play in the axle shaft. Fully compress the shaft and check the play with a dial indicator. If play exceeds 0.1mm through 1978, or 0.2mm, 1979-80, the shaft must be replaced. The sleeve yoke, balls, spacers and outer shaft are not available as service parts.

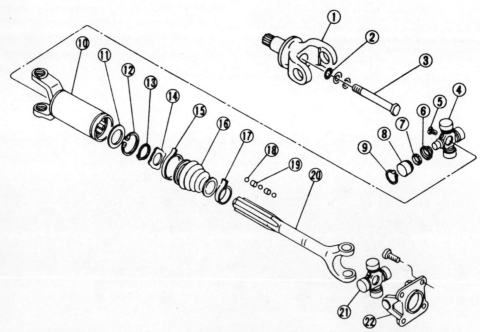

1. Side yoke	9. Bearing race snap ring	17. Boot band (short)
2. O-ring	10. Sleeve yoke	18. Ball
3. Side yoke bolt	11. Sleeve yoke stopper	19. Ball spacer
4. Spider journal	12. Snap ring	20. Driveshaft
5. Filler plug	13. Drive shaft snap ring	21. Spider assembly
6. Dust cover	14. Drive shaft stopper	22. Flange yoke
7. Oil seal	15. Boot band (long)	
8. Bearing race assembly	16. Rubber boot	

Exploded view of the halfshaft—all except the 1982 and later 810 and Maxima, and the 1984 and later 200SX Turbo

Measuring the play in the half shaft

4. Check the U-joints for smoothness. If movement is notchy or loose, overhaul the U-joints.

5. Check the U-joint axial play. If it exceeds 0.02mm, overhaul the U-joints.

OVERHAUL

All Except 1982 and Later 810/Maxima, and 1984 and Later 200SX, 200SX Turbo and 240SX

NOTE: *You will need a pair of snapring pliers for this job.*

1. Matchmark the parts across the U-joint journals, and across the sliding yoke (outer shaft to sleeve yoke). The axle shaft was balanced as a unit and must be rebuilt as originally assembled.

2. Remove the snap spring from the U-joints and disassemble them as outlined in the U-joint Overhaul procedure in this chapter.

3. Cut the boot band and remove the boot from the sleeve yoke.

4. Remove the snapring from the sleeve yoke at the boot end.

5. Remove the outer shaft carefully. Do not lose any of the balls or spacers.

6. It is not necessary to remove the snapring and sleeve yoke plug at the differential end of the sleeve yoke, because the parts are not available for service. If any damage is present, the entire axle shaft must be replaced.

7. Clean the spacers, balls, and sleeve yoke and outer shaft grooves in solvent. Check the parts for wear, distortion, cracks, straightness, etc. If there is any question as to the integrity of the part, replace the axle shaft.

8. Check the snapring, grease seal, and dust seal for wear or damage. These parts are available for service and should be replaced as necessary.

9. Apply a fairly generous amount of grease to the yoke and shaft grooves. Install the balls and spacers onto the shaft. The grease will retain them. Be sure they are in the correct sequence.

10. Before assembling the shaft and sleeve

yoke, apply a large glob of grease to the inner end of the sleeve yoke. You can put a blob of grease on the end of the shaft, too.

11. Align the parts according to the matchmarks made in Step 1. Slide the shaft into the sleeve yoke, making sure none of the balls or spacers is displaced.

12. Compress the shaft and check the play again. Refer to the inspections procedure. Replace the shaft if necessary.

13. Install the boot onto the sleeve yoke and retain with a new boot band.

14. Clean, repack, and assemble the U-joints. Select snaprings which will yield 0.02mm of axial play. Be certain to use the same thickness snapring on opposite sides of the journals to retain driveline balance, and to keep the stresses evenly distributed.

15. Install the axle shaft.

1982 and Later 810 and Maxima Rear Wheel Drive, 1984 and Later 200SX, 200SX Turbo and 240SX

1. Clamp the halfshaft in a vise using soft jaws.

2. Using pliers, pry the plug from the wheel side of the halfshaft.

3. Remove the plug seal, spring, spring cap and the boot bands.

NOTE: *Never reuse boot bands once they have been removed.*

4. Scribe a matchmark on the spider assembly and the halfshaft.

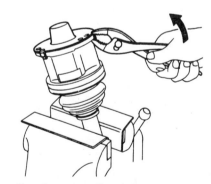

Use pliers to remove the plug

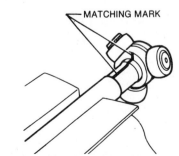

Matchmark the spider assembly to the half shaft

5. Remove the spider assembly with a press. Do not attempt to touch the contact surface of the halfshaft end at the spring cap or housing subassembly. Always support the halfshaft with your hand while you are removing the spider assembly.

6. Draw out the slide joint boot and the boot bands.

7. Loosen the vise and turn the halfshaft around so that the differential end is up.

8. Using a hacksaw, cut off the hold joint boot assembly and then remove the housing subassembly.

NOTE: *When cutting the hold joint boot assembly, make sure that the halfshaft is pushed into the housing subassembly in order to prevent the spider assembly from being scratched. Never reuse the boot assembly after it has been removed.*

9. Remove and discard the boot band and then remove the spider assembly as detailed in Steps 4-5.

10. Cut off the remaining part of the hold joint boot assembly and remove it from the housing subassembly. Be careful not to scratch the housing ring or assembly.

11. Remove and discard the housing cover and the O-ring.

12. Remove the housing ring.

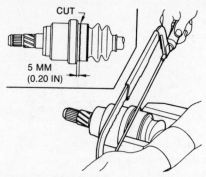

Cutting the hold joint boot

13. Remove all remaining parts of the hold joint boot assembly and the boot band from the halfshaft.

14. Attach a housing ring, an O-ring, a housing subassembly and a housing cover to a new hold joint boot assembly. Place the assembled unit flange in a vise. Don't forget to grease the O-ring.

15. Place a board on a housing cover to prevent it from being scratched. Use a mallet and bend the edge over along the entire circumference.

16. Withdraw the housing subassembly, install a new boot band and then hold the joint boot assembly on the halfshaft.

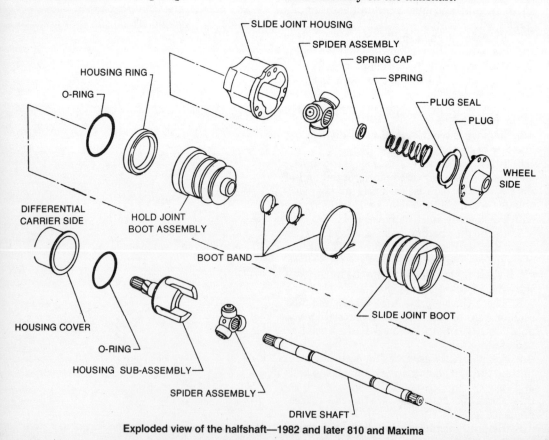

Exploded view of the halfshaft—1982 and later 810 and Maxima

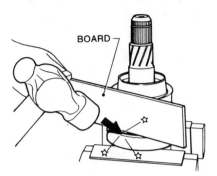

Bending the housing cover

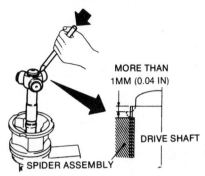

You must stake the serrated sides of the spider assembly upon installation

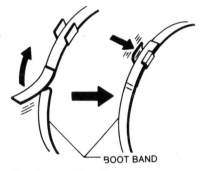

Installing the boot bands

17. Install the spider assembly securely, making sure that the matchmarks are aligned. Make sure that when press fitting the assembly, the serration chamfer faces the shaft.

18. Stake the serration sides evenly at three places, avoiding areas that have been previously staked. Always stake two or three teeth in an area where the staked gap is more than 0.1mm.

19. Pack with grease.

20. Install the greased O-ring to the housing assembly and then place the hold joint boot assembly so that its flange is in the vise. Be sure that no other part of the assembly is in the vise.

21. Insert the housing subassembly into place and then bend the edge as detailed in Step 2 for the housing cover.

22. Apply sealant. Set the boot and install the boot bands.

23. Turn the halfshaft in the vise so that the wheel side is up.

24. Install the new boot bands, slide joint boot and slide joint housing on the halfshaft. Be careful not to scratch the boot with the end of the shaft.

25. Install the spider assembly as previously detailed.

26. Install the large diameter boot band and then pack with grease.

27. Install the spring cap, spring and plug seal. Install the plug and secure with dummy

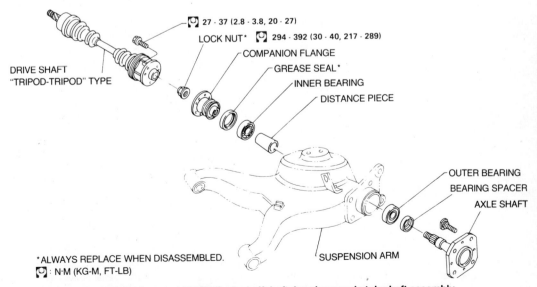

810, Maxima and 200SX Turbo halfshaft, bearings and stub shaft assembly

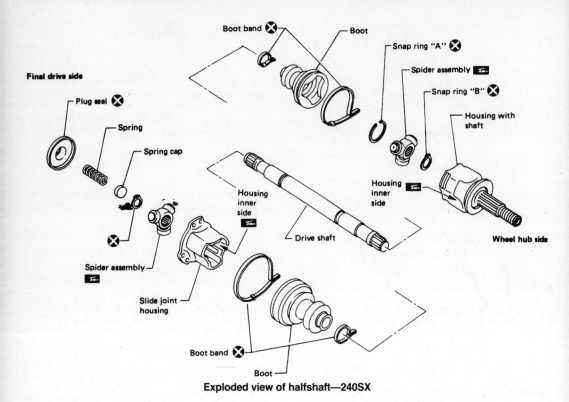

Exploded view of halfshaft—240SX

bolts. Lock the plug by bending it and then remove the dummy bolts.

28. Install the small diameter boot band and replace the halfshaft.

Stub Axle and Rear Wheel Bearings Independent Rear Suspension Models

REMOVAL AND INSTALLATION

1. Block the front wheels. Loosen the wheel nuts, raise and support the car, and remove the wheel.

2. Remove the halfshaft.

3. On cars with rear disc brakes, unbolt the caliper and move it aside. Do not allow the caliper to hang by the hose. Support the caliper with a length of wire or rest it on a suspension member.

4. Remove the brake disc on models with rear disc brakes. Remove the brake drum on cars with drum brakes.

5. Remove the stub axle nut. You will have to hold the sub axle at the outside while removing the nut from the axle shaft side. The nut will require a good deal of force to remove, so be sure to hold the stub axle firmly.

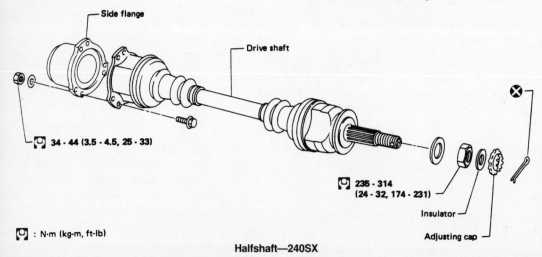

34 - 44 (3.5 - 4.5, 25 - 33)

235 - 314
(24 - 32, 174 - 231)

Insulator

Adjusting cap

: N·m (kg-m, ft-lb)

Halfshaft—240SX

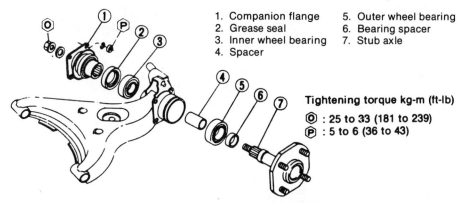

1. Companion flange
2. Grease seal
3. Inner wheel bearing
4. Spacer
5. Outer wheel bearing
6. Bearing spacer
7. Stub axle

Tightening torque kg-m (ft-lb)

◎ : 25 to 33 (181 to 239)
℗ : 5 to 6 (36 to 43)

Stub axle and rear wheel bearings—all models similar

Hold the stub axle while removing the nut from the half shaft side

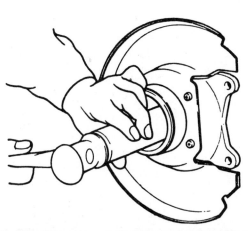

Remove the grease seal and inner bearing with a drift or driver

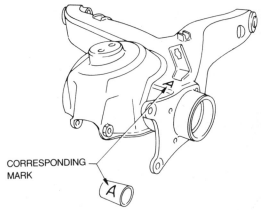

CORRESPONDING MARK

Make sure you install a spacer which is marked the same as the mark on the bearing housing

6. Remove the stub axle with a slide hammer and an adapter. The outer wheel bearing will come off with the stub axle.

7. Remove the companion flange from the lower arm.

8. Remove and discard the grease seal and inner bearing from the lower arm using a drift made for the purpose or a length of pipe of the proper diameter. The outer bearing can be removed from the stub axle with a puller. If the grease seal or the bearings are removed, new parts must be used on assembly.

9. Clean all the parts to be reused in solvent.

10. Sealed type bearings are used. When the new bearings are installed, the sealed side must face out. Install the sealed side of the outer bearing facing the wheel, and the sealed side of the inner bearing facing the differential.

11. Press the outer bearing onto the stub axle. NOTE: *When a spacer is reused, make sure that both ends are not collapsed or deformed. When installing, make sure that the larger side faces the axle shaft flange.*

12. The bearing housing is stamped with a

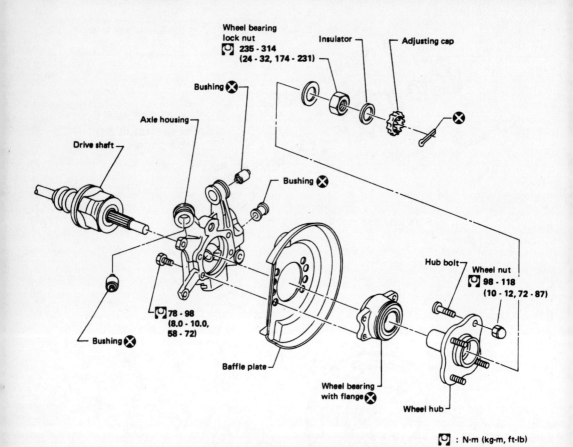

Wheel bearing lock nut
235 - 314
(24 - 32, 174 - 231)

Insulator

Adjusting cap

Bushing

Axle housing

Drive shaft

Bushing

Hub bolt

Wheel nut
98 - 118
(10 - 12, 72 - 87)

78 - 98
(8.0 - 10.0,
58 - 72)

Bushing

Baffle plate

Wheel bearing
with flange

Wheel hub

: N·m (kg-m, ft-lb)

Rear axle hub assembly—240SX

letter. Select a spacer with the same marking. Install the spacer on the stub axle.

13. Install the stub axle into the lower arm.

14. Install the new inner bearing into the lower arm with the stub axle in place. Install a new grease seal.

15. Install the companion flange onto the stub axle.

16. Install the sub axle nut. Tighten to 181-239 ft. lbs. On 1984-87 200SX models the torque specification is 217-289 ft. lbs. for the axle stub nut. On the 1988 200SX model the torque specification is 152-210 ft. lbs. for the axle stub nut.

17. Install the brake disc or drum, and the caliper if removed.

18. Install the halfshaft. Install the wheel and lower the car.

Suspension and Steering

8 🎯

FRONT SUSPENSION

Front MacPherson Strut

REMOVAL AND INSTALLATION

Rear Wheel Drive Vehicles

All strut assemblies for front and rear wheel drive vehicles are precision parts and retain the springs under tremendous pressure even when removed from the car. For these reasons, several expensive special tools and substantial specialized knowledge are required to safely and effectively work on these parts. We recommend that if spring or shock absorber repair work is required, you remove the strut or struts involved and take them to a repair facility which is fully equipped and familiar with the car.

1. Jack up the car and support it safely. Remove the wheel.

2. Remove the brake caliper. Remove the disc and hub assembly.

3. Disconnect the tension rod and stabilizer bar from the transverse link.

4. Unbolt the steering arm. Pry the control arm down to detach it from the strut.

5. Place a jack under the bottom of the strut.

6. Open the hood and remove the nuts holding the top of the strut.

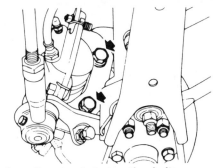

Brake caliper-to-strut mounting bolts

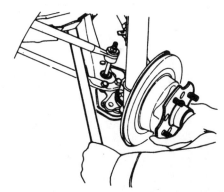

Pry the control arm down to separate the strut from the knuckle

7. Lower the jack slowly and cautiously until the strut assembly can be removed.

8. Install the strut assembly on the vehicle and torque the strut-to-knuckle arm to 53-72 ft. lbs. Torque the tension rod to transverse link to 33-40 ft. lbs. and the strut to hoodledge bolts to 23-31 ft. lbs.

NOTE: *The self-locking nuts holding the top of the strut must always be replaced when removed.*

9. Bleed the brakes.

10. Install the wheel.

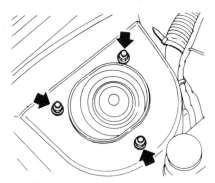

Remove the top strut nuts

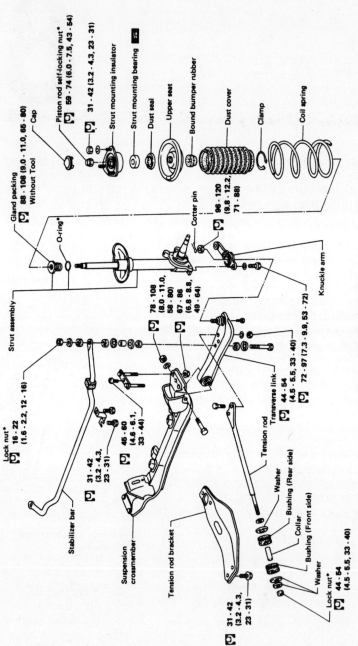

When removing each suspension part, check wheel alignment and adjust if necessary.

When installing a bushing, do not allow it to project beyond the surface area of the washer.

Do not allow the bushings and washers to come in contact with grease, oil, soapy water, etc.

*: Always replace whenever disassembled.

• Final tightening should be carried out under unladen condition**
   with tires on ground when installing each bushing.
** Fuel, radiator coolant and engine oil are filled up.
   Spare tire, jack, hand tools and mats are in designed position.

Gland packing
88 - 108 (9.0 - 11.0, 65 - 80)
Without Tool

Cap

Piston rod self-locking nut*
59 - 74 (6.0 - 7.5, 43 - 54)

31 - 42 (3.2 - 4.3, 23 - 31)

Strut mounting insulator

Strut mounting bearing

Dust seal

Upper seat

Bound bumper rubber

Dust cover

Clamp

Coil spring

O-ring*

Cotter pin

96 - 120
(9.8 - 12.2,
71 - 88)

Strut assembly

Knuckle arm

78 - 108
(8.0 - 11.0,
58 - 80)
67 - 86
(6.8 - 8.8,
49 - 64)

72 - 97 (7.3 - 9.9, 53 - 72)

Transverse link

Tension rod

44 - 54
(4.5 - 5.5, 33 - 40)

Lock nut*
16 - 22
(1.6 - 2.2, 12 - 16)

31 - 42
(3.2 - 4.3,
23 - 31)

Stabilizer bar

45 - 60
(4.6 - 6.1,
33 - 44)

Washer

Bushing (Rear side)

Collar

Bushing (Front side)

Washer

Lock nut*
44 - 54
(4.5 - 5.5, 33 - 40)

Suspension
crossmember

Tension rod bracket

31 - 42
(3.2 - 4.3,
23 - 31)

Front suspension—rear wheel drive

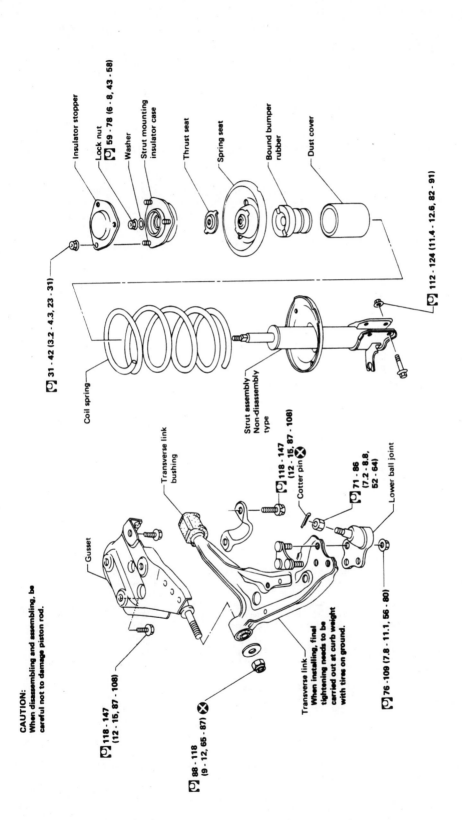

Front suspension—front wheel drive

CAUTION:
When disassembling and assembling, be careful not to damage piston rod.

⊗ : Always replace when disassembled.
🔧 : N·m (kg-m, ft-lb)

Insulator stopper
Lock nut 59 - 78 (6 - 8, 43 - 58)
Washer
Strut mounting insulator case
Thrust seat
Spring seat
Bound bumper rubber
Dust cover
112 - 124 (11.4 - 12.6, 82 - 91)

31 - 42 (3.2 - 4.3, 23 - 31)
Coil spring
Strut assembly Non-disassembly type

Transverse link bushing
118 - 147 (12 - 15, 87 - 108)
Cotter pin ⊗
71 - 86 (7.2 - 8.8, 52 - 64)
Lower ball joint
Gusset
118 - 147 (12 - 15, 87 - 108)
Transverse link
When installing, final tightening needs to be carried out at curb weight with tires on ground.
76 - 109 (7.8 - 11.1, 56 - 80)
88 - 118 (9 - 12, 65 - 87) ⊗

Front Wheel Drive Vehicles

NOTE: *If your Maxima is equipped with adjustable shocks follow this procedure an disconnect the sub-harness connector at the strut tower.*

1. Raise and support the vehicle on jackstands.
2. Remove the wheel.
3. Detach the brake tube from the strut.
4. Support the transverse link with a jackstand.
5. Detach the steering knuckle from the strut.
6. Support the strut and remove the three upper attaching nuts. Remove the strut from the vehicle.
7. Install the strut assembly on the vehicle and torque the strut-to-body nuts to 23-31 ft. lbs and the strut-to-knuckle bolts to 82-91 ft. lbs.
8. If brake line was removed bleed brakes and install the wheel.

OVERHAUL
STRUT CARTRIDGE REPLACEMENT

CAUTION: *The coil springs are under considerable tension, and can exert enough force to cause serious injury. Disassemble the struts only using the proper tools, and use extreme caution.*

Coil springs on all models must be removed with the aid of a coil spring compressor. If you don't have one, don't try to improvise by using something else: you could risk injury. The Datsun/Nissan coil spring compressor is Special Tool ST3565S001 or variations of that number. Basically, they are all the same tool, except for the 1980 and later 200SX and the 1981 and later 810 and Maxima spring compressor, Special Tool HT71730000, which is a totally different unit. These are the recommended compressors, although they are probably not the only spring compressors which will work. Always follow manufacturer's instructions when operating a spring compressor. You can now buy cartridge

Troubleshooting Basic Steering and Suspension Problems

Problem	Cause	Solution
Hard steering (steering wheel is hard to turn)	• Low or uneven tire pressure • Loose power steering pump drive belt • Low or incorrect power steering fluid • Incorrect front end alignment • Defective power steering pump • Bent or poorly lubricated front end parts	• Inflate tires to correct pressure • Adjust belt • Add fluid as necessary • Have front end alignment checked/adjusted • Check pump • Lubricate and/or replace defective parts
Loose steering (too much play in the steering wheel)	• Loose wheel bearings • Loose or worn steering linkage • Faulty shocks • Worn ball joints	• Adjust wheel bearings • Replace worn parts • Replace shocks • Replace ball joints
Car veers or wanders (car pulls to one side with hands off the steering wheel)	• Incorrect tire pressure • Improper front end alignment • Loose wheel bearings • Loose or bent front end components • Faulty shocks	• Inflate tires to correct pressure • Have front end alignment checked/adjusted • Adjust wheel bearings • Replace worn components • Replace shocks
Wheel oscillation or vibration transmitted through steering wheel	• Improper tire pressures • Tires out of balance • Loose wheel bearings • Improper front end alignment • Worn or bent front end components	• Inflate tires to correct pressure • Have tires balanced • Adjust wheel bearings • Have front end alignment checked/adjusted • Replace worn parts
Uneven tire wear	• Incorrect tire pressure • Front end out of alignment • Tires out of balance	• Inflate tires to correct pressure • Have front end alignment checked/adjusted • Have tires balanced

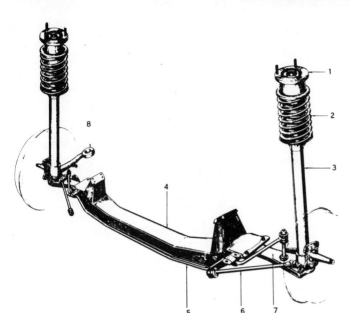

1. Strut mounting insulator
2. Coil spring
3. Strut assembly
4. Suspension cross member
5. Stabilizer
6. Tension rod
7. Transverse link
8. Steering knuckle arm

Front suspension—610 and 710

1. Strut mounting insulator
2. Coil spring
3. Strut assembly
4. Stabilizer
5. Suspension crossmember
6. Tension rod bracket
7. Tension rod
8. Transverse link
9. Lower ball joint

Front suspension—200SX; 510, 810 and Maxima similar

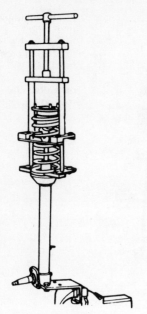

Spring compressor installed on the coil spring for removal

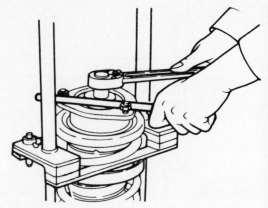

Hold the upper mount with a rod to unscrew the piston rod nut

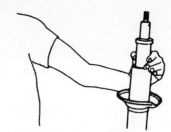

Removing the shock absorber from the gland tube

O-RING

Removing the O-ring

type shock absorbers for many Datsun/Nissan: installation procedures are not the same as those given here. In this case, follow the instructions that come with the shock absorbers.

To remove the coil spring, you must first remove the strut assembly from the vehicle. See above for procedures.

1. Secure the strut assembly in a vise.

2. Attach the spring compressor to the spring, leaving the top few coils free.

3. Remove the dust cap from the top of the strut to expose the center nut, if a dust cap is provided.

4. Compress the spring just far enough to permit the strut insulator to be turned by hand. Remove the self locking center nut.

5. Take out the strut insulator, strut bearing, oil seal, upper spring seat and bound bumper rubber from the top of the strut. Note their sequence of removal and be sure to assemble them in the same order.

6. Remove the spring with the spring compressor still attached.

7. Reassembly the strut assembly and observe the following:

   a. Make sure you assemble the unit with the shock absorber piston rod fully extended.

   b. When assembling, take care that the rubber spring seats, both top and bottom, and the spring are positioned in their grooves before releasing the spring.

8. To remove the shock absorber: Remove the dust cap, if so equipped, and push the piston rod down until it bottoms. With the piston in this position, loosen and remove the gland

packing shock absorber retainer. This calls for Datsun/ Nissan Special Tool ST35500001, but you should be able to loosen it either with a pipe wrench or by tapping it around with a drift.

NOTE: *If the gland tube is dirty, clean it before removing it to prevent dirt from contaminating the fluid inside the strut tube.*

9. Remove the O-ring from the top of the piston rod guide and lift out the piston rod together with the cylinder. Drain all of the fluid from the strut and shock components into a suitable container. Clean all parts.

NOTE: *The piston rod, piston rod guide and cylinder are a matched set: single parts of this shock assembly should not be exchanged with parts of other assemblies.*

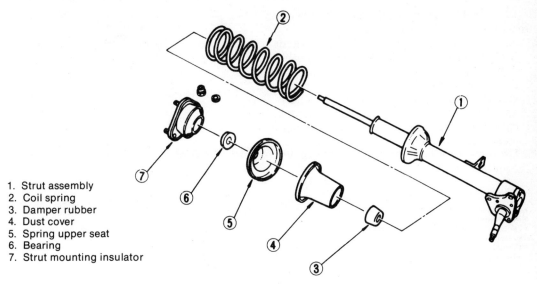

1. Strut assembly
2. Coil spring
3. Damper rubber
4. Dust cover
5. Spring upper seat
6. Bearing
7. Strut mounting insulator

Exploded view of the typical strut assembly

CAUTION:
When disassembling and assembling, be careful not to damage piston rod.

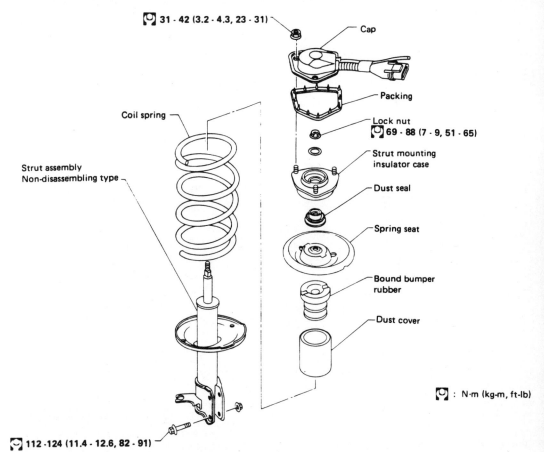

31 - 42 (3.2 - 4.3, 23 - 31)

Cap

Packing

Lock nut
69 - 88 (7 - 9, 51 - 65)

Strut mounting insulator case

Dust seal

Spring seat

Bound bumper rubber

Dust cover

Coil spring

Strut assembly
Non-disassembling type

: N·m (kg-m, ft-lb)

112 -124 (11.4 - 12.6, 82 - 91)

Adjustable front shock absorber—FWD Maxima

10. Assembly the shock absorber into the assembly with the following notes:

a. After installing the cylinder and piston rod assembly (the shock absorber kit) in the outer casing, remove the piston rod guide, if so equipped, from the cylinder and pour the correct amount of new fluid into the cylinder and strut outer casing. To find this amount consult the instructions with your shock absorber kit. The amount of oil should be listed. Use only Nissan Genuine Strut Oil or its equivalent.

Filling the shock assembly with oil

• Axial end play: 0.05 mm (0.0020 in) or less
Wheel alignment
• Camber, caster and kingpin inclination cannot be adjusted.
• The vehicle requires only toe-in adjustments.
    Toe-in   : 1 - 3 mm (0.04 - 0.12 in)
    (Total toe-in): 6' - 16'

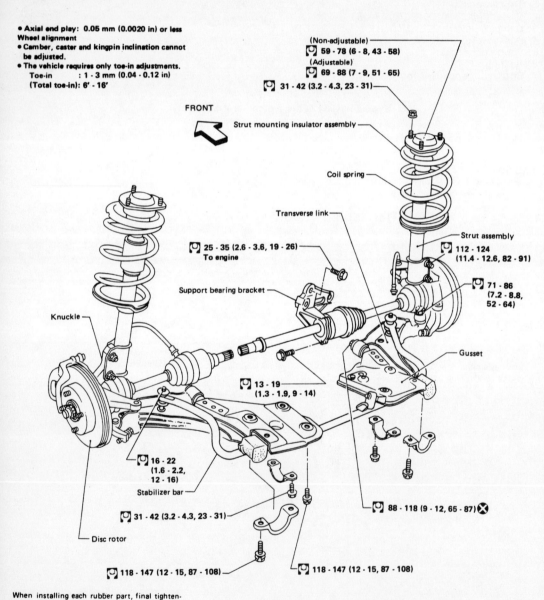

(Non-adjustable)
59 - 78 (6 - 8, 43 - 58)
(Adjustable)
69 - 88 (7 - 9, 51 - 65)
31 - 42 (3.2 - 4.3, 23 - 31)

FRONT

Strut mounting insulator assembly

Coil spring

Transverse link

25 - 35 (2.6 - 3.6, 19 - 26)
To engine

Strut assembly

112 - 124 (11.4 - 12.6, 82 - 91)

Support bearing bracket

71 - 86 (7.2 - 8.8, 52 - 64)

Knuckle

Gusset

13 - 19 (1.3 - 1.9, 9 - 14)

16 - 22 (1.6 - 2.2, 12 - 16)

Stabilizer bar

88 - 118 (9 - 12, 65 - 87) ⊗

31 - 42 (3.2 - 4.3, 23 - 31)

Disc rotor

118 - 147 (12 - 15, 87 - 108)

118 - 147 (12 - 15, 87 - 108)

When installing each rubber part, final tightening must be carried out under unladen condition* with tires on ground.
* Fuel, radiator coolant and engine oil full. Spare tire, jack, hand tools and mats in designated position.

⊗ : Always replace when disassembled.
[T] : N·m (kg-m, ft-lb)

Front axle and front suspension—1985–89 Maxima

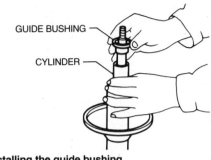

Installing the guide bushing

Bleeding air from the assembled strut

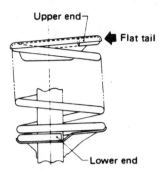

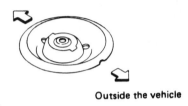

Correct coil spring and strut assembly—FWD Maxima

hold the strut with its bottom end facing down. Pull the piston rod out as far as it will go. Turn the strut upside down and push the piston in as far as it will go. Repeat this procedure several times until an equal pressure is felt on both the pull out and the push in strokes of the piston rods. The remaining assembly is the reverse of disassembly.

Ball Joint
INSPECTION

The lower ball joint should be replaced when play becomes excessive. Nissan/Datsun does not publish specifications on just what constitutes excessive play, relying instead on a method of determining the force (in inch pounds) required to keep the ball joint turning. This method is not very helpful to the backyard mechanic since it involves removing the ball joint, which is what we are trying to avoid in the first place. An effective way to determine ball joint play is to jack up the car until the wheel is just a couple of inches off the ground and the ball joint is unloaded (meaning you can't jack directly underneath the ball joint). Place a long bar under the tire and move the wheel and tire assembly up and down. Keep one hand on top of the tire while you are doing this. If there is over ¼″ of play at the top of the tire, the ball joint is proba-

NOTE: *It is important that the correct amount of fluid be poured into the strut to assure correct shock absorber damping force.*

b. Install the O-ring, fluid and any other cylinder components. Fit the gland packing and tighten it after greasing the gland packing-to-piston rod mating surfaces. Note that on the Maxima with front wheel drive, you must install the spring as shown in the illustration. Also, make sure on this model that the spring seat is positioned with the notch toward the outside of the car.

NOTE: *When tightening the gland packing, extend the piston rod about 3 to 5 inches from the end of the outer casing to expel most of the air from the strut.*

c. After the kit is installed, bleed the air from the system in the following manner:

bly bad. This is assuming that the wheel bearings are in good shape and properly adjusted. As a double check on this, have someone watch the ball joint while you move the tire up and down with the bar. If you can see considerably play, besides feeling play at the top of the wheel, the ball joint needs replacing.

REMOVAL AND INSTALLATION

Except 1981 and Later and Front Wheel Drive Maxima

The ball joint should be greased every 30,000 miles. There is a plugged hole in the bottom for the joint for the installation of a grease fitting.

1. Raise and support the car so that the wheels hang free. Remove the wheel.
2. Unbolt the tension rod and stabilizer bar from transverse link.
3. Unbolt the strut from the steering arm.
4. Remove the cotter pin and ball joint stud nut. Separate the ball joint and steering arm.

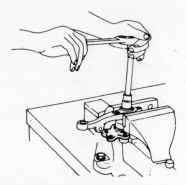

Removing the ball joint, all models except 1981 and later 810, Maxima and 200SX

5. Unbolt the ball joint from the transverse link.
6. Install the ball joint to the transverse link. Grease the joint after installation.
7. Reconnect the steering arm and the ball joint. Install a new cotter pin and ball joint stud nut.
8. Connect the strut to the steering arm.
9. Bolt the tension rod and stabilizer bar to the transverse link. Install the wheel.

1981 and Later Models except Front Wheel Drive Maxima

The ball joints on these models are a press fit into the knuckle arm. Follow the Lower Control Arm removal and installation procedure below. After Step 8 is completed, the knuckle arm ball joint must be pressed out of the knuckle arm using a special press. Most suspension specialists have this equipment.

Front Wheel Drive Maxima

1. Raise and support the car on jackstands. Remove the driveshaft from the front hub as described in the previous chapter.

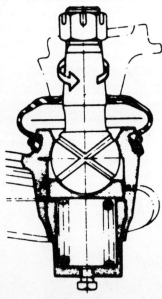

Cross section of a ball joint. Note the plug at the bottom for a grease nipple. Make sure the rubber boot is in good condition; if not, replace it

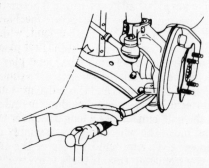

Separate the ball joint from the knuckle

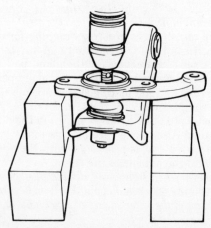

The 1981 and later ball joints must be pressed out of the knuckle

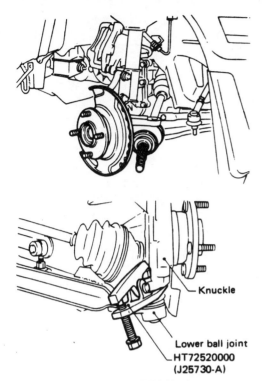

Removing lower ball joint—FWD Maxima

Knuckle

Lower ball joint
HT72520000
(J25730-A)

verse link (control arm) on the steering gear side, separate the gear arm from the sector shaft and lower steering linkage. To remove the transverse link on the idler arm side, detach the idler arm assembly from the body frame and lower steering linkage.

8. Remove the lower control arm (transverse link) with the suspension ball joint and knuckle arm still attached.

9. Install the the lower control arm (transverse link) with the ball joint and knuckle arm attached.

NOTE: *When installing the control arm, temporarily tighten the nuts and/or bolts securing the control arm to the suspension crossmember. Tighten them fully only after the car is sitting on its wheels.*

10. Install the nuts or bolts connecting the lower control arm (transverse link) to the suspension crossmember.

11. Connect the steering knuckle arm to the MacPherson strut.

12. Install the tension rod and stabilizer bar to the lower arm.

13. Install the (steering arm) ball joint to the side rod and torque the lock nut to 58-72 ft. lbs. Install the castle nut with a new cotter pin.

14. Install the wheel and lower the vehicle al-

2. Remove the nuts fastening the ball joint to the control arm. Remove the cotter pin and nut and press the ball joint out of the steering knuckle.

3. Reverse the procedure to install. Torque the ball joint-to-knuckle nut to 52-64 ft. lbs. and the nuts securing the joint to the control arm to 56-80 ft. lbs.

Lower Control Arm (Transverse Link) and Ball Joint

REMOVAL AND INSTALLATION

Except Front Wheel Drive Maxima

You'll need a ball joint remover for this operation.

1. Jack up the vehicle and support it with jack stands. Remove the wheel.

2. Remove the splash board, if so equipped.

3. Remove the cotter pin and castle nut from the tie rod (steering arm) ball joint and separate the ball joint from the side rod. You'll need either a fork type or puller type joint remover.

4. Separate the steering knuckle arm from the MacPherson strut.

5. Remove the tension rod and stabilizer bar from the lower arm.

6. Remove the nuts or bolts connecting the lower control arm (transverse link) to the suspension crossmember on all models.

7. On the 810/Maxima, to remove the trans-

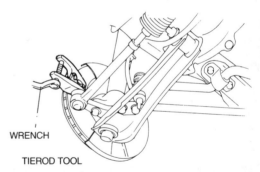

WRENCH

TIEROD TOOL

Separating the knuckle from the tie-rod using a tie-rod removal tool

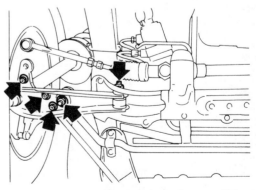

Removing the knuckle arm from the strut (left arrows) and the control arm (transverse link) from the car

ways tighten all bolts and nuts to correct specifications. Tighten the lower control arm to the suspension crossmember bolts to 58-80 ft. lbs. Tighten the tension rod to transverse link to 33-40 ft. lbs. and the stabilizer bar to transverse link to 12-16 ft. lbs. Tighten the knuckle arm to knuckle spindle to 53-72 ft. lbs.

15. Install the splash board if so equipped. Lubricate the ball joints after the complete installation.

Lower Control Arm

REMOVAL AND INSTALLATION

Front Wheel Drive Maxima

1. Raise the vehicle and support it securely on jackstands. Remove the nut fastening the link between the stabilizer bar and the control arm to the control arm.

2. Remove the three nuts fastening the ball joint to the lower control arm. Then, remove the two bolts attaching the front and rear hinge joints of the control arm to the body, and remove the control arm.

3. Install in reverse order. Tighten all bolts and nuts until they are snug enough to support the weight of the vehicle, but not quite fully tightenened. Then, lower the car to the ground.

4. Torque the forward bolts attaching the hinge joint to the body to 65-87 ft. lbs.. The rearward hinge joint mounting bolts to 87-108 ft. lbs., and the balljoint mounting nuts to 56-80 ft. lbs.

Front Axle Hub, Knuckle And Bearing

REMOVAL AND INSTALLATION

Front Wheel Drive Maxima

NOTE: *Refer to the exploded views of the Front Axle and the Front Suspension for front wheel drive vehicles for torque specifications and hub components assembly.*

1. Raise and support the front of the vehicle safely and remove the wheels.

Removing wheel bearing locknut—FWD Maxima

2. Remove wheel bearing lock nut.
3. Remove brake caliper assembly. Make sure not to twist the brake hose.
4. Remove tie rod ball joint.

NOTE: *Cover axle boots with waste cloth or equivalent so as not to damage them when removing driveshaft. Make a matching mark on strut housing and ajusting pin before removing them.*

5. Separate halfshaft from the knuckle by slightly tapping it.
6. Mark and remove the strut mounting bolts.
7. Remove lower ball joint from knuckle.
8. Remove knuckle from lower control arm.

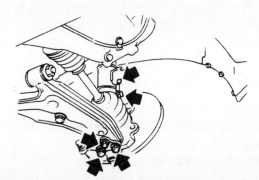

Removal points front axle hub, knuckle and bearing—FWD Maxima

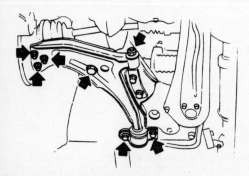

Removing transverse link—FWD Maxima

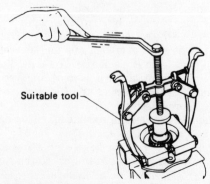

Suitable tool

Typical wheel bearing press

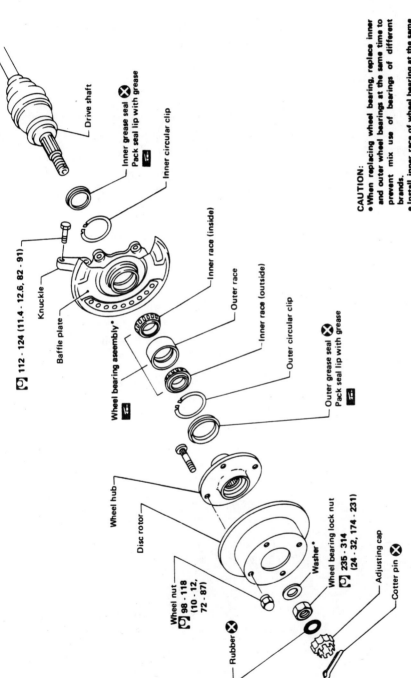

Drive shaft

Inner grease seal ⊗
Pack seal lip with grease

Inner circular clip

☒ 112 - 124 (11.4 - 12.6, 82 - 91)

Knuckle

Baffle plate

Wheel bearing asembly*

Inner race (inside)

Outer race

Inner race (outside)

Outer circular clip

Outer grease seal ⊗
Pack seal lip with grease

Wheel hub

Disc rotor

Wheel nut
☒ 98 - 118
(10 - 12,
72 - 87)

Rubber ⊗

Washer*

Wheel bearing lock nut
☒ 235 - 314
(24 - 32, 174 - 231)

Adjusting cap

Cotter pin ⊗

CAUTION:
- When replacing wheel bearing, replace inner and outer wheel bearings at the same time to prevent mix use of bearings of different brands.
- Install inner race of wheel bearing at the same position as they were installed before disassembly.
- Install washer with chamfer side facing wheel bearing lock nut.

⊗ : Always replace when disassembled.
☒ : N·m (kg-m, ft-lb)

Front axle hub—FWD Maxima

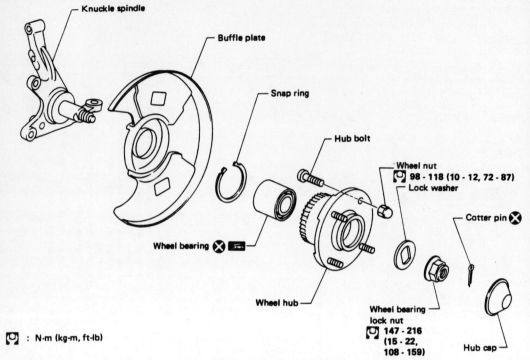

- Knuckle spindle
- Buffle plate
- Snap ring
- Hub bolt
- Wheel nut
  - 98 - 118 (10 - 12, 72 - 87)
- Lock washer
- Cotter pin ⊗
- Wheel bearing ⊗
- Wheel hub
- Wheel bearing lock nut
  - 147 - 216 (15 - 22, 108 - 159)
- Hub cap

⌷ : N·m (kg-m, ft-lb)

Front axle hub assembly—240SX

NOTE: *To replace the wheel bearings and races they must be pressed in and out of the knuckle assembly. To pack the wheel bearings they will have to be removed from the knuckle assembly.*

9. Install the knuckle to the lower control arm and connect the ball joint.
10. Connect the knuckle to the strut and to the halfshaft.
11. Install the tie rod ball joint.

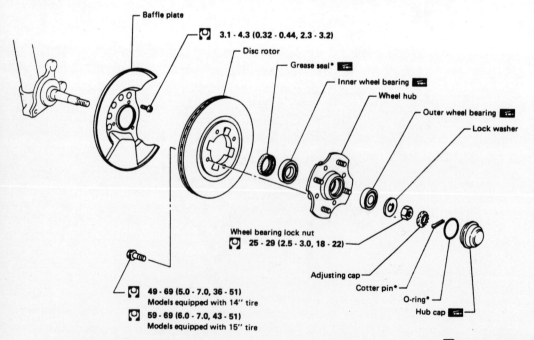

- Baffle plate
  - 3.1 - 4.3 (0.32 - 0.44, 2.3 - 3.2)
- Disc rotor
- Grease seal*
- Inner wheel bearing
- Wheel hub
- Outer wheel bearing
- Lock washer
- Wheel bearing lock nut
  - 25 - 29 (2.5 - 3.0, 18 - 22)
- Adjusting cap
- Cotter pin*
- O-ring*
- Hub cap

- 49 - 69 (5.0 - 7.0, 36 - 51)
  Models equipped with 14" tire
- 59 - 69 (6.0 - 7.0, 43 - 51)
  Models equipped with 15" tire

*: Always replace once they have been removed.

⌷ : N·m (kg-m, ft-lb)

Front axle hub assembly—200SX

12. Install the brake caliper assembly.

13. Install the wheel bearing lock nut and torque hub nut to 174-231 ft. lbs.

14. Install the front wheels.

Front Wheel Bearings

REMOVAL AND INSTALLATION

Rear Wheel Drive

NOTE: *After the wheel bearings have been removed or replaced or the front axle has been reassembled be sure to adjust wheel bearing preload. Refer to the Adjustment procedure below. On the 1989 240SX there is just one wheel bearing, pressed into the hub and no adjusting cap. Refer to the exploded view of the Front Axle Hub Assembly.*

1. Raise and support the vehicle safely.

2. Remove the front wheels and the brake caliper assemblies.

NOTE: *Brake hoses do not need to be disconnected from the brake caliper assemblies. Make sure the brake hoses are secure and do not let cailper assemblies hang unsupported from the vehicle.*

3. Work off center hub cap by using thin tool. If necessary tap around it with a soft hammer while removing.

4. Pry off cotter pin and take out adjusting cap and wheel bearing lock nut.

5. Remove wheel hub with disc brake rotor from spindle with bearings installed. Remove the outer bearing from the hub.

6. Remove inner bearing and grease seal from hub using long brass drift pin or equivalent.

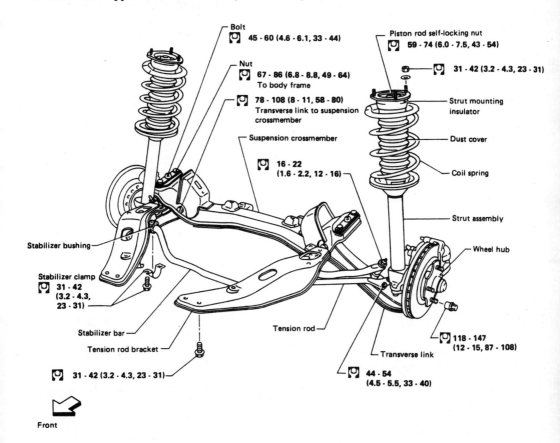

Bolt
45 - 60 (4.6 - 6.1, 33 - 44)

Piston rod self-locking nut
59 - 74 (6.0 - 7.5, 43 - 54)

Nut
67 - 86 (6.8 - 8.8, 49 - 64)
To body frame

31 - 42 (3.2 - 4.3, 23 - 31)

78 - 108 (8 - 11, 58 - 80)
Transverse link to suspension crossmember

Strut mounting insulator

Suspension crossmember

Dust cover

16 - 22
(1.6 - 2.2, 12 - 16)

Coil spring

Strut assembly

Stabilizer bushing

Wheel hub

Stabilizer clamp
31 - 42
(3.2 - 4.3,
23 - 31)

Stabilizer bar

Tension rod

Tension rod bracket

118 - 147
(12 - 15, 87 - 108)

31 - 42 (3.2 - 4.3, 23 - 31)

Transverse link

44 - 54
(4.5 - 5.5, 33 - 40)

Front

Wheel bearing
- Do not overtighten wheel bearing nut, as this can cause wheel bearing seizure.
- Axial play: 0 mm (0 in)
- Tightening torque   25 - 29 N·m (2.5 - 3.0 kg-m, 18 - 22 ft-lb)
- Return angle   60°
- Rotation starting torque
  with new grease seal   0.39 - 0.83 N·m (4.0 - 8.5 kg-cm, 3.5 - 7.4 in-lb)
  with used grease seal   0.10 - 0.44 N·m (1.0 - 4.5 kg-cm, 0.87 - 3.9 in-lb)
  As measured at wheel hub bolt
  with new grease seal   6.9 - 14.7 N (0.7 - 1.5 kg, 1.5 - 3.3 lb)
  with used grease seal   2.0 - 7.8 N (0.2 - 0.8 kg, 0.4 - 1.8 lb)
- When measuring starting torque, do not include "dragging" resistance with brake pads.

: N·m (kg-m, ft-lb)

Front axle and front suspension—200SX

7. If it is necessary to replace the bearing outer races, drive them out of the hub with a brass drift pin and mallet.

8. Install the outer bearing race with a tool (KV401021S0 special tool number) until it seats in the hub flush.

NOTE: *Place a large glob of grease into the palm of one hand and push the bearing through it with a sliding motion. The grease must be forced through the side of the bearing and in between each roller. Continue until the grease begins to ooze out the other side through the gaps between the rollers. The bearing must be completely packed with grease.*

9. Pack each wheel bearing with high temperature wheel bearing grease. Pack hub and hub cap with the recommended wheel bearing grease up to shaded portions. Refer to the illustration.

10. Install the inner bearing and grease seal in the proper position in the hub.

11. Install the wheel hub with disc brake rotor to the spindle.

12. Install the outer wheel bearing, lock washer, wheel bearing lock nut, adjusting cap,

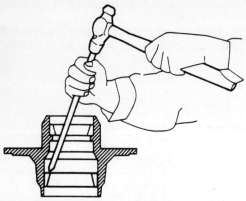

Removing inner front wheel bearing—RWD model

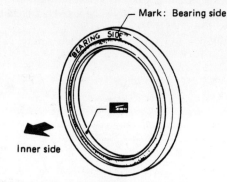

Installing grease seal—RWD model

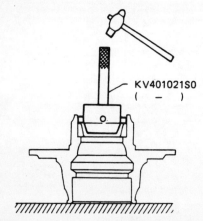

Installing race in hub with special tool—RWD model

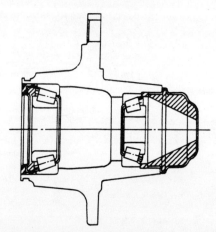

Pack shaded portions with wheel bearing grease—RWD model

Packing front wheel bearings—RWD model

Spread cotter pin after wheel bearing installation—RWD model

cotter pin (always use a new cotter pin and O-ring for installation), spread cotter pin then install the O-ring and dust cap.

13. Install the brake caliper assemblies and bleed brakes if necessary. Install the front wheels.

ADJUSTMENT

Rear Wheel Drive

NOTE: *Before adjustment clean all parts. Apply wheel bearing grease sparingly to the threaded portion of spindle and contact surface between lock washer and outer wheel bearing.*

1. Raise and support the vehicle safely, remove the front wheels and the brake caliper assemblies.

2. Torque wheel bearing lock nut to 18-22 ft. lbs.

NOTE: *On the 1989 240SX model, the wheel bearing lock nut torque is 108-159 ft. lbs. On this model make sure that the wheel bearing is properly seated and then just torque it to the specification. There is just one wheel bearing and no adjusting cap on this model just use a new cotter pin after the torque spsecification is reached.*

3. Turn the wheel hub several times in both directions to seat wheel bearing correctly.

4. Again tighten wheel bearing nut to specification 18-22 ft. lbs.

5. Loosen lock nut approximately 60°. Install adjusting cap and align groove of nut with hole in spindle. If alignment cannot be obtained, change position of adjusting cap. Also, if alignment cannot be obtained, loosen lock nut slightly but not more than 15°.

NOTE: *If possible measure the wheel bearing preload and axial play. Repeat above procedures until correct starting torque is obtained. Refer to the illustration.*

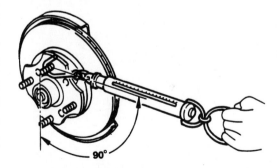

Axial play: 0 mm (0 in)
When bearing preload (As measured at wheel hub bolt):
   With new parts   6.9 - 14.7 N (0.7 - 1.5 kg, 1.5 - 3.3 lb)
   With used parts   2.0 - 7.8 N (0.2 - 0.8 kg, 0.4 - 1.8 lb)

Measure wheel bearing preload and axial play—RWD model

6. Spread the cotter pin and install hub cap with a new O-ring.

7. Install cailper assemblies and front wheels.

Front End Alignment
CASTER AND CAMBER

Caster is the forward or rearward tilt of the upper end of the kingpin, or the upper ball joint, which results in a slight tilt of the steering axis forward or backward. Rearward tilt is referred to as a positive caster, while forward tilt is referred to as negative caster.

Camber is the inward or outward tilt from the vertical, measured in degrees of the front wheels at the top. An outward tilt gives the wheel positive camber. Proper camber is critical to assure even tire wear.

Since caster and camber are adjusted traditionally by adding or subtracting shims behind the upper control arms, and the Datsun/Nissans covered in this guide have replaced the upper control arm with the MacPherson strut, the only way to adjust caster and camber is to replace bent or worn parts of the front suspension.

TOE

Toe is the amount, measured in a fraction of an inch, that the wheels are closer together at one end than the other. Toe-in means that the front wheels are closer together at the front than the rear. Toe-out means the rears are closer than the front. Datsun/Nissans are adjusted to have a slight amount of toe-in. Toe-in is adjusted by turning the tie rod, which has a right hand thread on one end and a left hand thread on the other.

You can check your vehicle's toe-in yourself without special equipment if you make careful measurements. The wheels must be straight ahead.

1. Toe-in can be determined by measuring the distance between the center of the tire

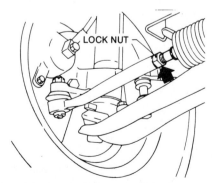

Toe adjustment is made at the tie-rod

Wheel Alignment Specifications

Year	Model	Caster Range (deg)	Caster Preferred Setting (deg)	Camber Range (deg)	Camber Preferred Setting (deg)	Toe-In (in.)	Steering Axis Inclination (deg)	Wheel Pivot Ratio (deg) Inner Wheel	Wheel Pivot Ratio (deg) Outer Wheel
1973	610	1¼–2¾	2	1½–2¾	2	½	6$^{21}/_{32}$	32½+	30½
	610 Station Wagon	1¼–2¾	2	1½–3	2¼	½	6$^{21}/_{32}$	32½+	30½
1974	610	1¼–2¾	2	1¼–2¾	2	½	6$^{21}/_{32}$	32½+	30½
	610 Station Wagon	1¼–2¾	2	1½–3	2¼	½	6$^{21}/_{32}$	32½+	30½
	710	1$^3/_{16}$–2$^{11}/_{16}$	1$^{15}/_{16}$	1$^7/_{16}$–2$^{15}/_{16}$	1⅛	⅝	6$^{13}/_{32}$	37½+	31$^{27}/_{32}$
1975	610 (Front)	1¼–2¾	2	1¼–2¾	2	½	6$^{21}/_{32}$	32½+	30½
	610 (Rear)	—	—	¾–2¼	1½	$^5/_{16}$	—	—	—
	610 Station Wagon	1¼–2¾	2	1½–3	2¼	½	6$^{21}/_{32}$	32½+	30½
	710	1$^3/_{16}$–2$^{11}/_{16}$	1$^{15}/_{16}$	2$^{15}/_{16}$	2$^{15}/_{16}$	⅜	6$^{13}/_{32}$	32½+	30½
1976–77	610, 710 (Bias Tires)	—	—	—	—	¼	7	32½+	30½
	610, 710 (Radials)	1$^1/_{16}$–2$^9/_{16}$	1$^{13}/_{16}$	1¼–2¾	2	$^7/_{32}$	7	32½+	30½
1977	200SX	1$^1/_{32}$–2¼	1$^{21}/_{32}$	½–1½	1	⅛	7$^{13}/_{16}$	35	30
1977–80	810 (Front)	1$^3/_{16}$–2$^{11}/_{16}$	2¼	0–1½	¾	⅛	7$^{29}/_{32}$	20	18$^{20}/_{32}$
	810 (Rear)	—	—	—	—	$^3/_{16}$	—	—	—

1978–79	200SX	$1\frac{1}{16}$–$2\frac{9}{16}$	$1\frac{13}{16}$	$\frac{5}{16}$–$1\frac{13}{16}$	$\frac{17}{16}$	$\frac{1}{8}$	$7\frac{13}{16}$	35	30
1978–81	510 Station Wagon	$\frac{15}{16}$–$2\frac{7}{16}$	$1\frac{9}{16}$	$\frac{1}{16}$–$1\frac{9}{16}$	$\frac{3}{4}$	$\frac{1}{16}$	$8\frac{5}{32}$	20	$19\frac{1}{2}$
1979–81	510	$1\frac{1}{16}$–$2\frac{9}{16}$	$1\frac{13}{16}$	$-\frac{1}{4}$–$1\frac{1}{4}$	$\frac{1}{2}$	$\frac{1}{16}$	$8\frac{27}{32}$	20	$19\frac{1}{2}$
1981–83	810 (Front)	$1\frac{15}{16}$–$4\frac{7}{16}$	$3\frac{11}{16}$	$-\frac{5}{16}$–$1\frac{3}{16}$	$\frac{7}{16}$	$\frac{1}{32}$	$12\frac{1}{8}$	20	$18\frac{11}{16}$
	810 (Rear)	—	—	$\frac{15}{16}$–$2\frac{7}{16}$	$1\frac{11}{16}$	$\frac{7}{32}$	—	—	—
1980–83	200SX	$1\frac{3}{4}$–$3\frac{1}{4}$	$2\frac{1}{2}$	$-\frac{11}{16}$–$1\frac{3}{16}$	$\frac{1}{16}$	$\frac{3}{64}$	$8\frac{5}{32}$	20	$18\frac{45}{64}$
1984	Maxima (Front)	$2\frac{15}{16}$–$4\frac{7}{16}$	$3\frac{11}{16}$	$-1\frac{5}{16}$–$1\frac{3}{16}$	$\frac{7}{16}$	$\frac{1}{32}$	$12\frac{1}{8}$	20	$18\frac{11}{16}$
	Maxima (Rear)	—	—	$1\frac{1}{4}$–$2\frac{3}{4}$	2	$\frac{5}{32}$	—	—	—
1984	200SX	$2\frac{3}{4}$–$4\frac{1}{4}$	$3\frac{1}{2}$	$-\frac{3}{8}$–$1\frac{1}{16}$	$1\frac{7}{8}$	$\frac{3}{64}$	$11\frac{11}{16}$	20	$18\frac{11}{16}$
1985–86	200SX	$2\frac{3}{4}$–$4\frac{1}{4}$	$3\frac{1}{2}$	$-\frac{1}{4}$–$1\frac{1}{20}$	$\frac{1}{3}$	$\frac{3}{8}$	$12\frac{5}{8}$	36	30
	Maxima	$2\frac{3}{4}$–$4\frac{1}{4}$	$3\frac{1}{2}$	$-\frac{1}{4}$–$1\frac{1}{20}$	$\frac{1}{3}$	$\frac{1}{16}$	$14\frac{1}{2}$	36	29
1987–88	200SX (Front)	$2\frac{3}{4}P$–$4\frac{1}{4}P$	$3\frac{1}{2}P$	$\frac{7}{16}N$–$1\frac{1}{16}P$	$\frac{1}{4}P$	$\frac{1}{32}N$–$\frac{1}{32}P$	$12\frac{3}{4}$	36–39	30–33
	200SX (Rear)	—	—	$1\frac{1}{4}N$–$1\frac{1}{4}P$	$\frac{1}{2}N$	$\frac{5}{64}N$–0	—	—	—
1987–89	Maxima (Front)	$1\frac{1}{4}P$–$2\frac{3}{4}P$	$2P$	$\frac{7}{16}N$–$1\frac{1}{16}P$	$\frac{5}{16}P$	$\frac{1}{16}P$–$\frac{1}{4}P$	$14\frac{1}{2}$	34–38	27–31
	Maxima (rear)	—	—	$1\frac{3}{16}N$–$\frac{5}{16}P$	$\frac{7}{16}N$	$\frac{3}{32}P$–$\frac{1}{4}P$	—	—	—
1989	240SX (Front)	$6P$–$7P$	$6\frac{1}{2}P$	$1N$–0	$\frac{1}{2}N$	0	—	39–43	33
	240SX (Rear)	—	—	$1N$–0	$\frac{1}{2}N$	0	—	—	—

treads, at the front of the tire and at the rear. If the tread pattern of your car's tires makes this impossible, you can measure between the edges of the wheel rims, but make sure to move the car forward and measure in a couple of places to avoid errors caused by bent rims or wheel runout.

2. If the measurement is not within specifications, loosen the locknuts at both ends of the tie rod (the driver's side locknut is left hand threaded).

3. Turn the top of the tie rod toward the front of the car to reduce toe-in, or toward the rear to increase it. When the correct dimension is reached, tighten the locknuts and check the adjustment.

NOTE: *The length of the tie rods must always be equal to each other.*

REAR SUSPENSION

Springs

REMOVAL AND INSTALLATION

Leaf Spring Type-Rear Wheel Drive

610 STATION WAGON
ALL 710
1977-79 200SX MODELS

1. Raise the rear axle until the wheels hang free. Support the car on stands. Support the rear axle with a floor jack.

2. Remove the spare tire.

3. Unbolt the bottom end of the shock absorber.

4. Unbolt the axle from the spring leaves.

5. Unbolt the front spring bracket from the body. Lower the spring end and bracket to the floor.

6. Unbolt and remove the rear shackle.

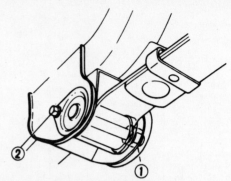

Remove the spring pin by removing the nuts (1) and (2)—all leaf spring rear suspension cars

7. Unbolt the bracket from the spring.

8. Before reinstallation, coat the front bracket pin and bushing, and the shackle pin and bushing with a soap solution.

9. Install the spring and shackle in the correct position to the vehicle. Connect the axle housing to the spring leaves. The front pin nut and the shock absorber mounting should be tightened after the vehicle is lowered to the floor. Make sure that the elongated flange of the rubber bumper is to the rear.

10. Remove the floor jack and install the spare tire.

510 AND 810 STATION WAGON MODELS

1. Raise the rear of the car and support it with jackstands.

2. Remove the wheels and tires.

3. Disconnect the lower end of the shock absorber and remove the U-bolt nuts.

4. Place a jack under the rear axle.

5. Disconnect the spring shackle bolts at the front and rear of the spring.

6. Lower the jack slowly and remove the spring.

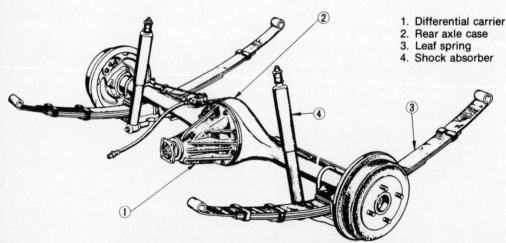

1. Differential carrier
2. Rear axle case
3. Leaf spring
4. Shock absorber

Rear suspension—710 sedans; all station wagons similar

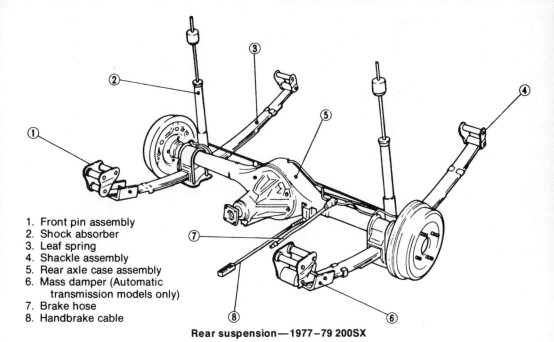

1. Front pin assembly
2. Shock absorber
3. Leaf spring
4. Shackle assembly
5. Rear axle case assembly
6. Mass damper (Automatic transmission models only)
7. Brake hose
8. Handbrake cable

Rear suspension—1977–79 200SX

7. Installation is in the reverse order of removal.

Coil Spring Type
Rear Wheel Drive

610 SEDAN MODEL

1. Raise the rear of the vehicle and support it on stands.

2. Remove the wheels.

3. Disconnect the handbrake linkage and return spring.

4. Unbolt the axle driveshaft flange at the wheel end.

5. Unbolt the rubber bumper inside the bottom of the coil spring.

6. Jack up the suspension arm and unbolt the shock absorber lower mounting.

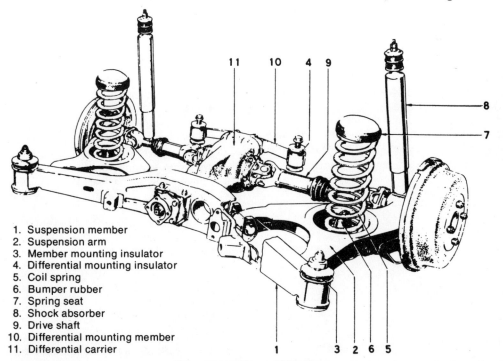

1. Suspension member
2. Suspension arm
3. Member mounting insulator
4. Differential mounting insulator
5. Coil spring
6. Bumper rubber
7. Spring seat
8. Shock absorber
9. Drive shaft
10. Differential mounting member
11. Differential carrier

Rear suspension—610 sedan

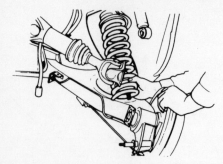

Coil spring removal, all independent rear suspension cars except 810 and Maxima

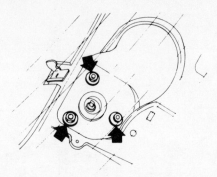

Disconnect the rear strut top bolts from inside the trunk

7. Lower the jack slowly and cautiously. Remove the coil spring, spring seat, and rubber bumper.

8. Install the spring assembly in the correct position, making sure that the flat face of the spring is at the top.

9. Jack up the suspension arm and bolt the shock absorber to the lower mounting.

10. Bolt the rubber bumper inside the bottom of the coil spring and connect the axle driveshaft flange at the wheel end.

11. Connect the handbrake linkage and return spring and install the wheels.

Rear MacPherson Strut
Rear Wheel Drive

810/MAXIMA SEDAN
1989 240SX MODELS

These models utilizes MacPherson struts in the rear suspension. The struts and spring are removed as a unit. Disassembly of the strut requires a spring compressor. For strut disassembly, follow the procedure given for front suspension MacPherson struts. On the 240SX refer to the exploded view of the Rear Suspension.

1. Raise the car and safely support the rear end with jackstands and a floor jack.

2. Open the trunk and remove the three nuts which secure the top of the strut to the body.

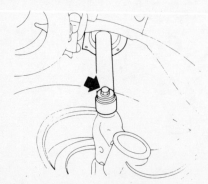

Disconnect the lower end of the strut

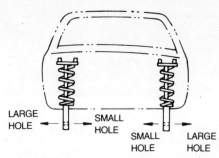

Install the rear struts so that the larger hole on the lower end faces out

3. Disconnect the strut at the bottom by removing the bolt at the suspension arm.

4. Service the strut as detailed under Front Suspension.

5. Installation is the reverse of removal. Install the strut so that the larger hole on the lower end faces out.

Coil Spring
Rear Wheel Drive

510 SEDAN AND HATCHBACK
1980-84 200SX MODELS

1. Raise the car and support it with jackstands.

2. Support the center of the differential with a jack or other suitable tool.

3. Remove the rear wheels.

4. Remove the bolts securing the lower ends of the shock absorbers.

5. Lower the jack under the differential slowly and carefully and remove the coil springs after they are fully extended.

6. Installation is in the reverse order of removal.

Coil Spring (I.R.S.)
Rear Wheel Drive

1984-88 200SX

1. Set a suitable spring compressor on the coil spring.

2. Jack up the rear end of the car.

3. Compress the coil spring until it is of sufficient length to be removed. Remove the spring.

4. When installing the spring, be sure the upper and lower spring seat rubbers are not twisted and have not slipped off when installing the coil spring.

**Rear MacPherson Strut
Front Wheel Drive**

1985-89 MAXIMA

NOTE: *These models utilizes MacPherson struts in the rear suspension. The struts and spring are removed as a unit. Do not jack the*

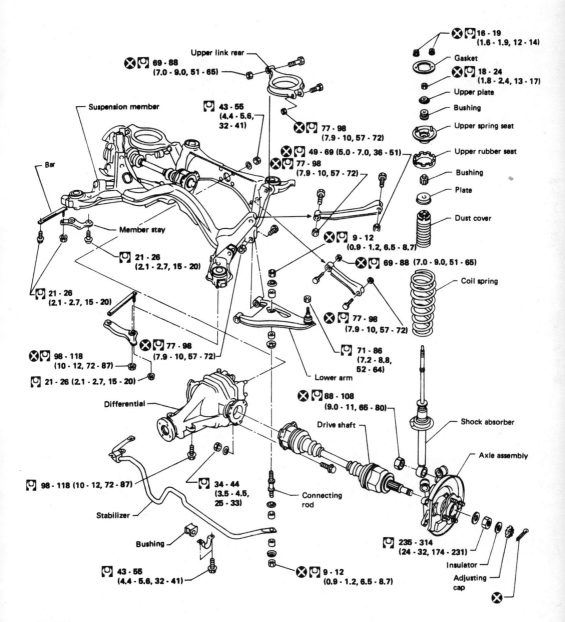

Upper link rear

69 · 88
(7.0 · 9.0, 51 · 65)

Suspension member

43 · 55
(4.4 · 5.6, 32 · 41)

Bar

Member stay

21 · 26
(2.1 · 2.7, 15 · 20)

21 · 26
(2.1 · 2.7, 15 · 20)

98 · 118
(10 · 12, 72 · 87)

21 · 26 (2.1 · 2.7, 15 · 20)

77 · 98
(7.9 · 10, 57 · 72)

Differential

98 · 118 (10 · 12, 72 · 87)

Stabilizer

Bushing

43 · 55
(4.4 · 5.6, 32 · 41)

16 · 19
(1.6 · 1.9, 12 · 14)

Gasket

18 · 24
(1.8 · 2.4, 13 · 17)

Upper plate

Bushing

Upper spring seat

77 · 98
(7.9 · 10, 57 · 72)

49 · 69 (5.0 · 7.0, 36 · 51)

77 · 98
(7.9 · 10, 57 · 72)

Upper rubber seat

Bushing

Plate

Dust cover

9 · 12
(0.9 · 1.2, 6.5 · 8.7)

69 · 88 (7.0 · 9.0, 51 · 65)

Coil spring

77 · 98
(7.9 · 10, 57 · 72)

71 · 86
(7.2 · 8.8, 52 · 64)

Lower arm

88 · 108
(9.0 · 11, 65 · 80)

Drive shaft

Shock absorber

Axle assembly

34 · 44
(3.5 · 4.5, 25 · 33)

Connecting rod

235 · 314
(24 · 32, 174 · 231)

Insulator

Adjusting cap

9 · 12
(0.9 · 1.2, 6.5 · 8.7)

CAUTION:
Do not jack up at lower arm.
When installing each rubber part, final tightening must be carried out under unladen condition* with tires on ground.
* Fuel, radiator coolant and engine oil full. Spare tire, jack, hand tools and mats in designated positions.

: N·m (kg-m, ft-lb)

Rear suspension—1989 240SX

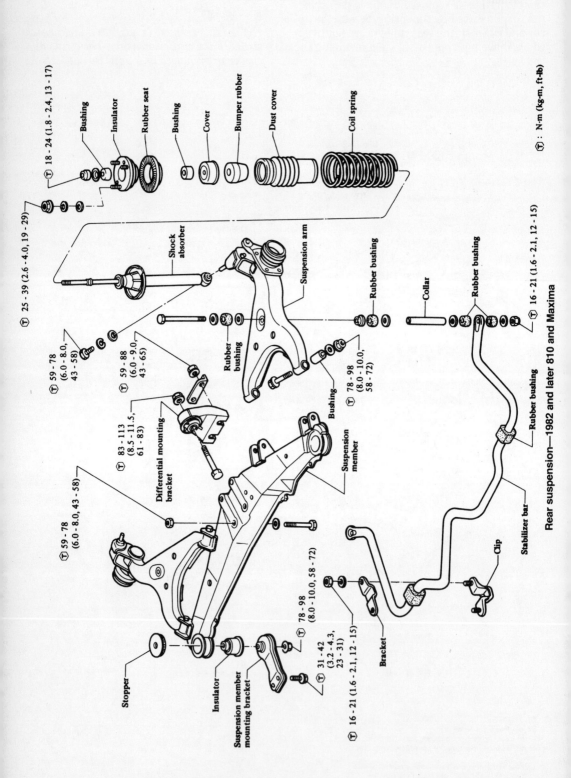

Bushing

Insulator

Rubber seat

Bushing

Cover

Bumper rubber

Dust cover

Coil spring

Ⓣ 18 - 24 (1.8 - 2.4, 13 - 17)

Ⓣ : N·m (kg·m, ft·lb)

Ⓣ 25 - 39 (2.6 - 4.0, 19 - 29)

Shock absorber

Suspension arm

Rubber bushing

Collar

Rubber bushing

Ⓣ 16 - 21 (1.6 - 2.1, 12 - 15)

Rubber bushing

Ⓣ 59 - 78 (6.0 - 8.0, 43 - 58)

Ⓣ 59 - 88 (6.0 - 9.0, 43 - 65)

Bushing

Ⓣ 78 - 98 (8.0 - 10.0, 58 - 72)

Ⓣ 83 - 113 (8.5 - 11.5, 61 - 83)

Differential mounting bracket

Suspension member

Rubber bushing

Stabilizer bar

Rear suspension—1982 and later 810 and Maxima

Ⓣ 59 - 78 (6.0 - 8.0, 43 - 58)

Clip

Stopper

Insulator

Suspension member mounting bracket

Ⓣ 78 - 98 (8.0 - 10.0, 58 - 72)

Ⓣ 31 - 42 (3.2 - 4.3, 23 - 31)

Bracket

Ⓣ 16 - 21 (1.6 - 2.1, 12 - 15)

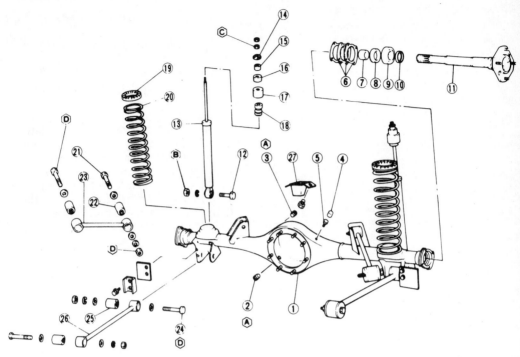

1. Rear axle case	12. Shock absorber lower end bolt
2. Drain plug	13. Shock absorber assembly
3. Filler plug	14. Special washer
4. Breather cap	15. Shock absorber mounting bushing A
5. Breather	16. Shock absorber mounting bushing B
6. Rear axle case end shim	17. Bound bumper cover
7. Bearing collar	18. Bound bumper rubber
8. Oil seal	19. Shock absorber mounting insulator
9. Rear axle bearing	20. Coil spring
10. Bearing spacer	21. Upper link bushing bolt
11. Rear axle shaft	22. Upper link bushing

Rear suspension—510 sedan; 1980 and later 200SX (non-Turbo) similar

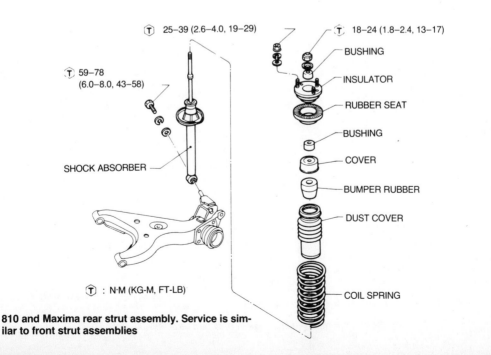

810 and Maxima rear strut assembly. Service is similar to front strut assemblies

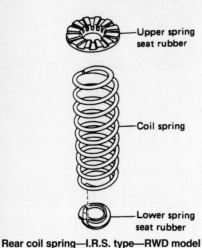

Upper spring seat rubber

Coil spring

Lower spring seat rubber

Rear coil spring—I.R.S. type—RWD model

vehicle up at the parallel links or radius links.

1. Unclip the rear brake hydraulic line at the strut. Then, unbolt and remove the brake assembly, wheel bearings, and backing plate. Suspend the brake caliper so the hydraulic line will not be stressed.

2. Remove the radius rod mounting bolt, radius rod bracket mounting bolt and the two parallel link mounting bolts.

3. Remove the rear seat and parcel shelf. Then, support the strut from underneath. Remove the three nuts attaching the strut to the body. Lower the strut and remove it.

4. Install in reverse order. Tighten all bolts sufficiently to safely support the vehicle. Then, lower the car to the ground. Final torque the at-

WHEEL ALIGNMENT
- CAMBER CANNOT BE ADJUSTED.
- VEHICLE REQUIRES ONLY TOE-IN ADJUSTMENT.
  −2 TO 0 MM (−0.08 TO 0 IN), (−12′ TO 0)

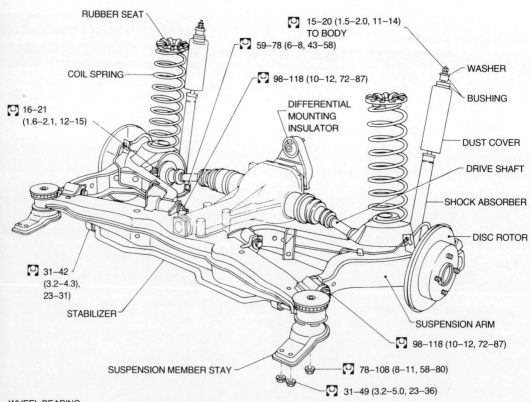

RUBBER SEAT

COIL SPRING

16–21 (1.6–2.1, 12–15)

15–20 (1.5–2.0, 11–14) TO BODY

59–78 (6–8, 43–58)

98–118 (10–12, 72–87)

DIFFERENTIAL MOUNTING INSULATOR

WASHER

BUSHING

DUST COVER

DRIVE SHAFT

SHOCK ABSORBER

DISC ROTOR

31–42 (3.2–4.3, 23–31)

STABILIZER

SUSPENSION ARM

98–118 (10–12, 72–87)

SUSPENSION MEMBER STAY

78–108 (8–11, 58–80)

31–49 (3.2–5.0, 23–36)

WHEEL BEARING
- AXLE SHAFT END PLAY: LESS THAN 0.3 MM (0.012 IN)
- BEARING PRELOAD: LESS THAN 0.7 N·M (7 KG-CM, 6.1 IN-LB)
  AT HUB BOLT
  LESS THAN 12.06 N (1.23 KG, 2.71 LB)

: N·M (KG-M, FT-LB)

Rear suspension—I.R.S. type—1984 and later 200SX

taching nuts and bolts as follows: Upper strut mounts to 23-31 ft. lbs.; radius rod bracket bolts to 43-58 ft. lbs.; parallel link mounting bolts to 65-87 ft. lbs.

Shock Absorber

REMOVAL AND INSTALLATION

200SX and 510, 610, 710 Sedans

1. Open the trunk and remove the cover panel if necessary to expose the shock mounts. Pry off the mount covers, if so equipped. On leaf spring models, jack up the rear of the vehicle and support the rear axle on stands.

2. Remove the two nuts holding the top of the shock absorber (one nut on 1984 and later

200SX). Unbolt the bottom of the shock absorber.

3. Remove the shock absorber.

4. Installation is the reverse of removal.

510, 610, 710, 810 Station Wagons

1. Jack up the rear of the car and support the axle on stands.

2. Remove the lower retaining nut on the shock absorber.

3. Remove the upper retaining bolt(s).

4. Remove the shock from under the car. On the 610, remove the retaining strap from the old shock and install it on the replacement shock.

5. Installation is the reverse of removal.

CAUTION:
Do not jack up at the parallel links or radius rods.

Wheel alignment
- Camber cannot be adjusted.
  −1° 10′ to 0° 20′
- Vehicle requires only toe-out adjustment.
  2 - 6 mm (0.08 - 0.24 in)

Wheel bearing
- Axial end play: 0 mm (0 in)
- Bearing preload: Refer to PRELOAD ADJUSTMENT of Rear Wheel Bearing in REAR AXLE.

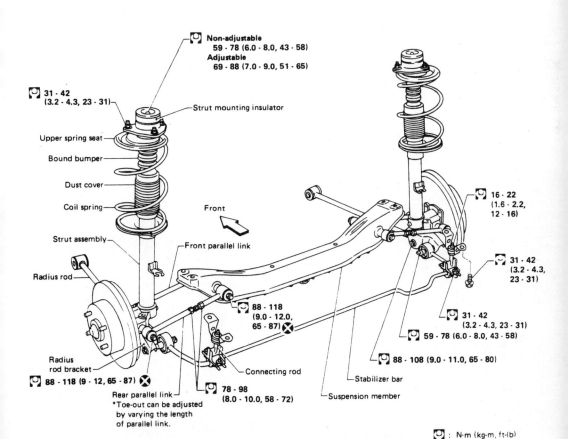

Non-adjustable
59 - 78 (6.0 - 8.0, 43 - 58)
Adjustable
69 - 88 (7.0 - 9.0, 51 - 65)

31 - 42
(3.2 - 4.3, 23 - 31)

Strut mounting insulator

Upper spring seat

Bound bumper

Dust cover

Coil spring

Front

16 - 22
(1.6 - 2.2, 12 - 16)

Strut assembly

Front parallel link

Radius rod

31 - 42
(3.2 - 4.3, 23 - 31)

88 - 118
(9.0 - 12.0, 65 - 87)

31 - 42
(3.2 - 4.3, 23 - 31)

59 - 78 (6.0 - 8.0, 43 - 58)

88 - 108 (9.0 - 11.0, 65 - 80)

Radius rod bracket
88 - 118 (9 - 12, 65 - 87)

Rear parallel link
*Toe-out can be adjusted by varying the length of parallel link.

Connecting rod

78 - 98
(8.0 - 10.0, 58 - 72)

Stabilizer bar

Suspension member

: N·m (kg-m, ft-lb)

Rear axle and rear suspension—FWD Maxima

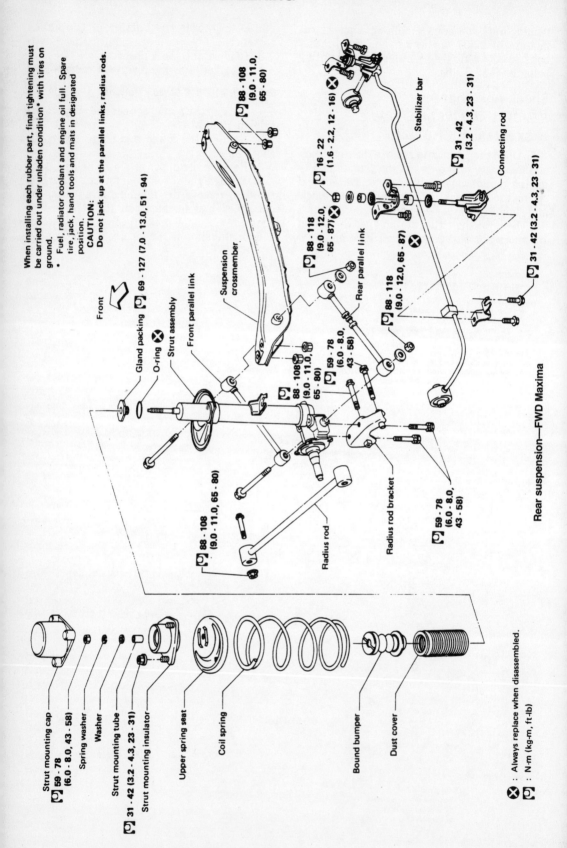

When installing each rubber part, final tightening must be carried out under unladen condition* with tires on ground.
* Fuel, radiator coolant and engine oil full. Spare tire, jack, hand tools and mats in designated position.

CAUTION:
Do not jack up at the parallel links, radius rods.

Front

Gland packing — 🔧 69 - 127 (7.0 - 13.0, 51 - 94)

O-ring — ❌

Strut assembly

Front parallel link

Suspension crossmember

🔧 88 - 108 (9.0 - 11.0, 65 - 80)

🔧 16 - 22 (1.6 - 2.2, 12 - 16)

🔧 88 - 118 (9.0 - 12.0, 65 - 87) ❌

Rear parallel link

🔧 88 - 118 (9.0 - 12.0, 65 - 87) ❌

🔧 88 - 108 (9.0 - 11.0, 65 - 80)

🔧 59 - 78 (6.0 - 8.0, 43 - 58)

Stabilizer bar

🔧 31 - 42 (3.2 - 4.3, 23 - 31)

Connecting rod

🔧 31 - 42 (3.2 - 4.3, 23 - 31)

🔧 88 - 108 (9.0 - 11.0, 65 - 80)

Radius rod

🔧 59 - 78 (6.0 - 8.0, 43 - 58)

Radius rod bracket

🔧 59 - 78 (6.0 - 8.0, 43 - 58)

Rear suspension—FWD Maxima

Strut mounting cap
🔧 59 - 78 (6.0 - 8.0, 43 - 58)

Spring washer

Washer

Strut mounting tube

🔧 31 - 42 (3.2 - 4.3, 23 - 31)

Strut mounting insulator

Upper spring seat

Coil spring

Bound bumper

Dust cover

❌ : Always replace when disassembled.

🔧 : N·m (kg-m, ft-lb)

❌ 🔧

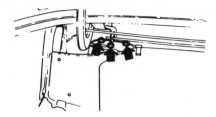

On some models, the upper shock mounting nuts are in the trunk

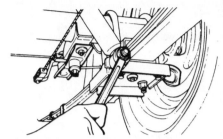

Removing the lower shock mounting nut

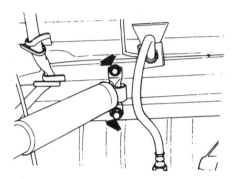

On other models, the upper shock mounting nuts are under the car

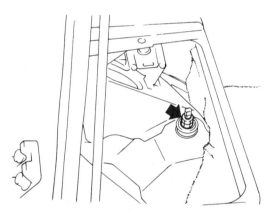

1984 and later 200SX top rear shock nut

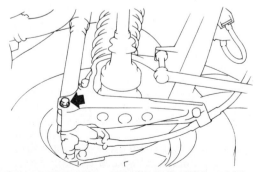

Rear shock bottom mounting bolt, 1984 and later 200SX

Rear MacPherson Strut

REMOVAL AND INSTALLATION

810 Sedans
1984-89 Maxima
1989 240SX

The shock absorber is actually a MacPherson strut on these models. See Spring Removal in this chapter. Disassembly of the rear strut assembly is similar to the front strut procedure.

OVERHAUL

NOTE: *It is necessary throughout strut work to keep all parts absolutely clean. This procedure is for when a shock absorber kit-cartridge is not used. On the 240SX the shock absorber must be replaced.*

1. Matchmark the strut mounting insulator for reassembly at the same angle.

2. Install a spring compressor and compress the spring until the spring insulator can be turned by hand.

3. Remove the rebound stop locknut so the threads on the piston rod will not be damaged. Use a tool such as ST35490000 (J26083) or equivalent to remove the packing. Then, force the piston rod downward until it bottoms.

4. Withdraw the piston rod and guide from the strut cylinder.

5. Pour the correct amount of an approved strut fluid into the strut. Use 11.2 fl. oz. for non-adjustable struts and 11.0 fl. oz. for adjustable struts.

6. Then, lubricate the sealing lip of the gland packing. Tape over the strut rod threads and then install the gland packing. Tighten it with the special wrench. Torque to 65-80 ft. lbs.

7. Pump the strut rod up and down several times with it in its normal vertical position and upside down to remove air bubbles.

8. Install the upper spring seat and mounting insulator. Make sure the matchmark on the insulator corresponds with the location hole on the upper spring seat.

9. Position the spring so its end rests against the stop on the lower seat. Install the remaining spring retaining parts including the piston rod self locking nut (torque to 43-58 ft. lbs.) and

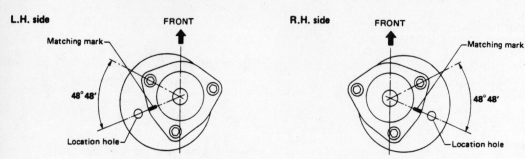

Correct position for upper spring seat—rear strut assembly—FWD Maxima

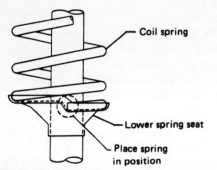

Correct position for spring—rear strut assembly—FWD Maxima

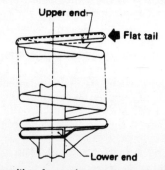

Correct position for spring—rear strut assembly—240SX

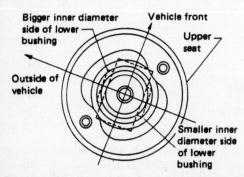

Correct position for upper spring seat—rear strut assembly—240SX

the upper nut that retains the flexible washer (torque to 26-35 ft. lbs.).

Rear Wheel Bearings
REMOVAL AND INSTALLATION
1985-88 Maxima

NOTE: *After the rear wheel bearings have been removed or replaced or the rear axle has been reassembled be sure to adjust wheel bearing preload. Refer to the Adjustment procedure below. The 1989 Maxima rear wheel hub bearing is different than in previous years. It requires no adjustment or maintenance.*

1. Raise and support the vehicle safely.
2. Remove the rear wheels and the brake caliper assemblies.

NOTE: *Brake hoses do not need to be disconnected from the brake caliper assemblies. Make sure the brake hoses are secure and do not let cailper assemblies hang unsupported from the vehicle. DO NOT DEPRESS BRAKE PEDAL OR PISTON WILL POP OUT.*

3. Work off center hub cap by using thin tool. If necessary tap around it with a soft hammer while removing.
4. Pry out cotter pin and take off adjusting cap and wheel bearing lock nut.
5. Remove wheel hub/disc brake rotor from spindle with bearings installed. Remove the outer bearing from the hub/disc brake rotor.
6. Remove inner bearing and grease seal from hub/disc brake rotor using long brass drift pin or equivalent.
7. If it is necessary to replace the bearing outer races, drive them out of the hub/disc brake rotor with a brass drift pin and mallet.
8. Install the outer bearing race with a tool until it seats in the hub/disc brake rotor flush. The Datsun/Nissan special tool number for this tool is KV401021S0.
9. Pack each wheel bearing with high tem-

CAUTION:
When disassembling and assembling, be
careful not to damage piston rod.

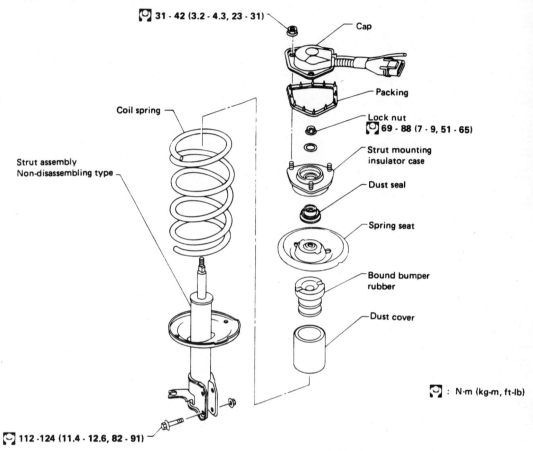

🔧 31 - 42 (3.2 - 4.3, 23 - 31)

Cap

Packing

Lock nut
🔧 69 - 88 (7 - 9, 51 - 65)

Strut mounting
insulator case

Dust seal

Coil spring

Strut assembly
Non-disassembling type

Spring seat

Bound bumper
rubber

Dust cover

🔧 : N·m (kg-m, ft-lb)

🔧 112 -124 (11.4 - 12.6, 82 - 91)

Adjustable rear shock absorber—FWD Maxima

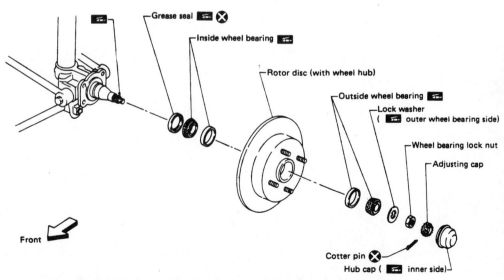

Grease seal ⊗

Inside wheel bearing

Rotor disc (with wheel hub)

Outside wheel bearing

Lock washer
(outer wheel bearing side)

Wheel bearing lock nut

Adjusting cap

Front

Cotter pin ⊗

Hub cap (inner side)

⊗ : Always replace when disassembled.

Rear axle assembly—1985–88 Maxima

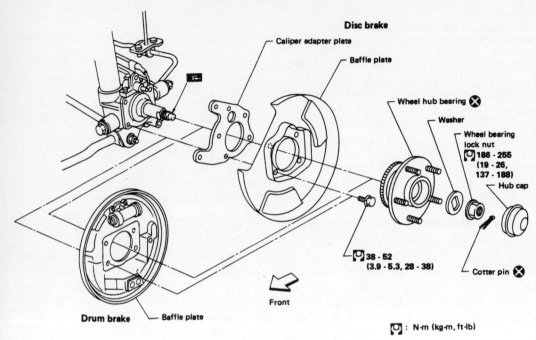

Rear axle assembly—1989 Maxima

perature wheel bearing grease. Pack hub cap with the recommended wheel bearing grease up to shaded portions. Refer to the illustration.

10. Install the inner bearing and grease seal (make sure that the white nylon guide faces the spindle) in the proper position in the hub/disc brake rotor.

11. Install the wheel hub/disc brake rotor to the spindle.

12. Install the outer wheel bearing, lock washer, wheel bearing lock nut, adjusting cap, cotter pin (always use a new cotter pin for installation), spread cotter pin then install the dust cap.

13. Install the brake caliper assemblies and bleed brakes if necessary. Install the rear wheels.

WHEEL BEARING PRELOAD ADJUSTMENT

NOTE: *Before adjustment, thoroughly clean all parts to prevent dirt entry. Remove the brake caliper.*

1. Apply multi-purpose grease to the following parts:

    a. threaded portion of the wheel spindle.

    b. mating surfaces of the lock washer and outer wheel bearing.

    c. inner hub cap.

    d. grease seal lip.

2. Tighten the wheel bearing nut to 18-25 ft. lbs.

3. Turn the wheel hub several times in both directions to seat the bearing correctly.

4. Loosen the wheel bearing lock nut until there is no preload and then tighten it to 6.5-8.7 ft. lbs. Turn the wheel hub several times again and then retighten it to 6.5-8.7 ft. lbs.

5. Install the adjusting cap and align any of its slots with the hole in the spindle.

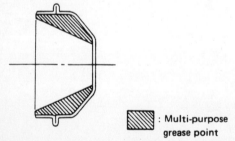

: Multi-purpose grease point

Pack hub cap with wheel bearing grease in shaded areas

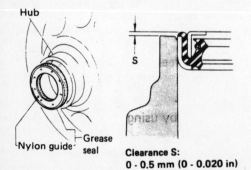

Clearance S:
0 - 0.5 mm (0 - 0.020 in)

Rear wheel bearing grease seal installation—1985–88 Maxima

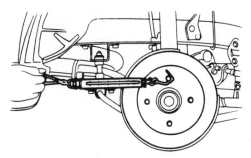

Measure wheel bearing preload and axial play—1985–88 Maxima

Spread cotter pin position—rear wheel bearing

NOTE: *If necessary, loosening the lock nut as much as 15" in order to align the spindle hole with one in the adjusting cap.*

6. Rotate the hub in both directions several times while measuring its starting torque and axial play. They should be as follows:
- Axial play: 0
- Wheel bearing preload (new grease seal) when measured at wheel hub bolt: 3.1 lbs.
- Wheel bearing preload (used grease seal) when measured at wheel hub bolt: 2.4 lbs.

7. Correctly measure the rotation from the starting force toward the tangential direction against the hub bolt. The above figures do not allow for any "dragging" resistance. When measuring starting torque, confirm that no "dragging" exists. No wheel bearing axial play can exist at all.

8. Spread the cotter pin and install the inner hub cap.

Rear End Alignment

1985-89 MAXIMA

The rear camber is preset at the factory and cannot be adjusted; if the rear camber alignment is not within specifications, check the associated parts, then repair or replace them. The only adjustments that can be performed is rear toe-out.

1989 240SX

The rear camber and rear toe-in can be adjust on this model.

1984-88 200SX

The rear camber is preset at the factory and cannot be adjusted. The vehicle requires only rear toe-in adjustment.

STEERING

Steering Wheel

REMOVAL AND INSTALLATION

1. Position the wheels in the straight ahead direction. The steering wheel should be right side up and level.

2. Disconnect the battery ground cable.

3. Look at the back of your steering wheel. If there are countersunk screws in the back of the spokes, remove the screws and pull of the horn pad. Some models have a horn wire running from the pad to the steering wheel. Disconnect it. There are three other types of horn buttons

610 horn pad removal

Horn pads on later models pull right off

Use a puller to remove the steering wheel

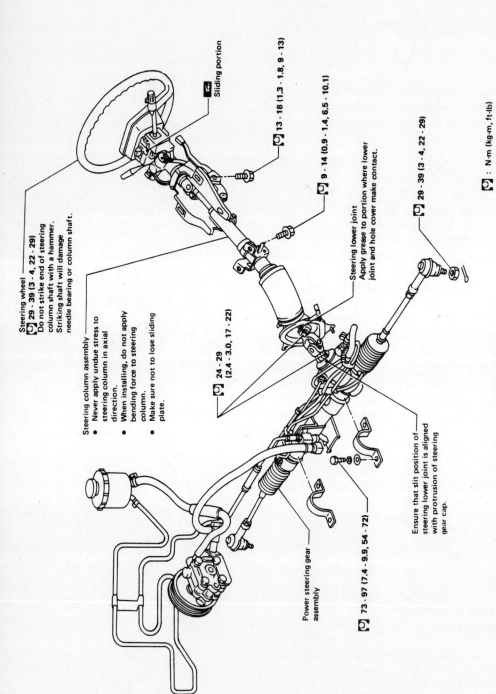

Steering wheel

29 - 39 (3 - 4, 22 - 29)

Do not strike end of steering column shaft with a hammer. Striking shaft will damage needle bearing or column shaft.

Sliding portion

13 - 18 (1.3 - 1.8, 9 - 13)

9 - 14 (0.9 - 1.4, 6.5 - 10.1)

Steering column assembly
- Never apply undue stress to steering column in axial direction.
- When installing, do not apply bending force to steering column.
- Make sure not to lose sliding plate.

24 - 29 (2.4 - 3.0, 17 - 22)

Steering lower joint
Apply grease to portion where lower joint and hole cover make contact.

29 - 39 (3 - 4, 22 - 29)

: N·m (kg-m, ft-lb)

Power steering gear assembly

Ensure that slit position of steering lower joint is aligned with protrusion of steering gear cap.

73 - 97 (7.4 - 9.9, 54 - 72)

Steering system—1988 200SX—others similar

Troubleshooting the Steering Column

Problem	Cause	Solution
Will not lock	• Lockbolt spring broken or defective	• Replace lock bolt spring
High effort (required to turn ignition key and lock cylinder)	• Lock cylinder defective • Ignition switch defective • Rack preload spring broken or deformed • Burr on lock sector, lock rack, housing, support or remote rod coupling • Bent sector shaft • Defective lock rack • Remote rod bent, deformed • Ignition switch mounting bracket bent • Distorted coupling slot in lock rack (tilt column)	• Replace lock cylinder • Replace ignition switch • Replace preload spring • Remove burr • Replace shaft • Replace lock rack • Replace rod • Straighten or replace • Replace lock rack
Will stick in "start"	• Remote rod deformed • Ignition switch mounting bracket bent	• Straighten or replace • Straighten or replace
Key cannot be removed in "off-lock"	• Ignition switch is not adjusted correctly • Defective lock cylinder	• Adjust switch • Replace lock cylinder
Lock cylinder can be removed without depressing retainer	• Lock cylinder with defective retainer • Burr over retainer slot in housing cover or on cylinder retainer	• Replace lock cylinder • Remove burr
High effort on lock cylinder between "off" and "off-lock"	• Distorted lock rack • Burr on tang of shift gate (automatic column) • Gearshift linkage not adjusted	• Replace lock rack • Remove burr • Adjust linkage
Noise in column	• One click when in "off-lock" position and the steering wheel is moved (all except automatic column) • Coupling bolts not tightened • Lack of grease on bearings or bearing surfaces • Upper shaft bearing worn or broken • Lower shaft bearing worn or broken • Column not correctly aligned • Coupling pulled apart • Broken coupling lower joint • Steering shaft snap ring not seated • Shroud loose on shift bowl. Housing loose on jacket—will be noticed with ignition in "off-lock" and when torque is applied to steering wheel.	• Normal—lock bolt is seating • Tighten pinch bolts • Lubricate with chassis grease • Replace bearing assembly • Replace bearing. Check shaft and replace if scored. • Align column • Replace coupling • Repair or replace joint and align column • Replace ring. Check for proper seating in groove. • Position shroud over lugs on shift bowl. Tighten mounting screws.
High steering shaft effort	• Column misaligned • Defective upper or lower bearing • Tight steering shaft universal joint • Flash on I.D. of shift tube at plastic joint (tilt column only) • Upper or lower bearing seized	• Align column • Replace as required • Repair or replace • Replace shift tube • Replace bearings
Lash in mounted column assembly	• Column mounting bracket bolts loose • Broken weld nuts on column jacket • Column capsule bracket sheared	• Tighten bolts • Replace column jacket • Replace bracket assembly

Troubleshooting the Steering Column (cont.)

Problem	Cause	Solution
Lash in mounted column assembly (cont.)	• Column bracket to column jacket mounting bolts loose	• Tighten to specified torque
	• Loose lock shoes in housing (tilt column only)	• Replace shoes
	• Loose pivot pins (tilt column only)	• Replace pivot pins and support
	• Loose lock shoe pin (tilt column only)	• Replace pin and housing
	• Loose support screws (tilt column only)	• Tighten screws
Housing loose (tilt column only)	• Excessive clearance between holes in support or housing and pivot pin diameters	• Replace pivot pins and support
	• Housing support-screws loose	• Tighten screws
Steering wheel loose—every other tilt position (tilt column only)	• Loose fit between lock shoe and lock shoe pivot pin	• Replace lock shoes and pivot pin
Steering column not locking in any tilt position (tilt column only)	• Lock shoe seized on pivot pin	• Replace lock shoes and pin
	• Lock shoe grooves have burrs or are filled with foreign material	• Clean or replace lock shoes
	• Lock shoe springs weak or broken	• Replace springs
Noise when tilting column (tilt column only)	• Upper tilt bumpers worn	• Replace tilt bumper
	• Tilt spring rubbing in housing	• Lubricate with chassis grease
One click when in "off-lock" position and the steering wheel is moved	• Seating of lock bolt	• None. Click is normal characteristic sound produced by lock bolt as it seats.
High shift effort (automatic and tilt column only)	• Column not correctly aligned	• Align column
	• Lower bearing not aligned correctly	• Assemble correctly
	• Lack of grease on seal or lower bearing areas	• Lubricate with chassis grease
Improper transmission shifting— automatic and tilt column only	• Sheared shift tube joint	• Replace shift tube
	• Improper transmission gearshift linkage adjustment	• Adjust linkage
	• Loose lower shift lever	• Replace shift tube

Troubleshooting the Ignition Switch

Problem	Cause	Solution
Ignition switch electrically inoperative	• Loose or defective switch connector	• Tighten or replace connector
	• Feed wire open (fusible link)	• Repair or replace
	• Defective ignition switch	• Replace ignition switch
Engine will not crank	• Ignition switch not adjusted properly	• Adjust switch
Ignition switch wil not actuate mechanically	• Defective ignition switch	• Replace switch
	• Defective lock sector	• Replace lock sector
	• Defective remote rod	• Replace remote rod
Ignition switch cannot be adjusted correctly	• Remote rod deformed	• Repair, straighten or replace

Troubleshooting the Turn Signal Switch

Problem	Cause	Solution
Turn signal will not cancel	• Loose switch mounting screws • Switch or anchor bosses broken • Broken, missing or out of position detent, or cancelling spring	• Tighten screws • Replace switch • Reposition springs or replace switch as required
Turn signal difficult to operate	• Turn signal lever loose • Switch yoke broken or distorted • Loose or misplaced springs • Foreign parts and/or materials in switch • Switch mounted loosely	• Tighten mounting screws • Replace switch • Reposition springs or replace switch • Remove foreign parts and/or material • Tighten mounting screws
Turn signal will not indicate lane change	• Broken lane change pressure pad or spring hanger • Broken, missing or misplaced lane change spring • Jammed wires	• Replace switch • Replace or reposition as required • Loosen mounting screws, reposition wires and retighten screws
Turn signal will not stay in turn position	• Foreign material or loose parts impeding movement of switch yoke • Defective switch	• Remove material and/or parts • Replace switch
Hazard switch cannot be pulled out	• Foreign material between hazard support cancelling leg and yoke	• Remove foreign material. No foreign material impeding function of hazard switch—replace turn signal switch.
No turn signal lights	• Inoperative turn signal flasher • Defective or blown fuse • Loose chassis to column harness connector • Disconnect column to chassis connector. Connect new switch to chassis and operate switch by hand. If vehicle lights now operate normally, signal switch is inoperative • If vehicle lights do not operate, check chassis wiring for opens, grounds, etc.	• Replace turn signal flasher • Replace fuse • Connect securely • Replace signal switch • Repair chassis wiring as required
Instrument panel turn indicator lights on but not flashing	• Burned out or damaged front or rear turn signal bulb • If vehicle lights do not operate, check light sockets for high resistance connections, the chassis wiring for opens, grounds, etc. • Inoperative flasher • Loose chassis to column harness connection • Inoperative turn signal switch • To determine if turn signal switch is defective, substitute new switch into circuit and operate switch by hand. If the vehicle's lights operate normally, signal switch is inoperative.	• Replace bulb • Repair chassis wiring as required • Replace flasher • Connect securely • Replace turn signal switch • Replace turn signal switch
Stop light not on when turn indicated	• Loose column to chassis connection • Disconnect column to chassis connector. Connect new switch into system without removing old.	• Connect securely • Replace signal switch

Troubleshooting the Turn Signal Switch (cont.)

Problem	Cause	Solution
Stop light not on when turn indicated (cont.)	Operate switch by hand. If brake lights work with switch in the turn position, signal switch is defective.	
	• If brake lights do not work, check connector to stop light sockets for grounds, opens, etc.	• Repair connector to stop light circuits using service manual as guide
Turn indicator panel lights not flashing	• Burned out bulbs • High resistance to ground at bulb socket	• Replace bulbs • Replace socket
	• Opens, ground in wiring harness from front turn signal bulb socket to indicator lights	• Locate and repair as required
Turn signal lights flash very slowly	• High resistance ground at light sockets	• Repair high resistance grounds at light sockets
	• Incorrect capacity turn signal flasher or bulb	• Replace turn signal flasher or bulb
	• If flashing rate is still extremely slow, check chassis wiring harness from the connector to light sockets for high resistance	• Locate and repair as required
	• Loose chassis to column harness connection	• Connect securely
	• Disconnect column to chassis connector. Connect new switch into system without removing old. Operate switch by hand. If flashing occurs at normal rate, the signal switch is defective.	• Replace turn signal switch
Hazard signal lights will not flash—turn signal functions normally	• Blow fuse • Inoperative hazard warning flasher	• Replace fuse • Replace hazard warning flasher in fuse panel
	• Loose chassis-to-column harness connection	• Conect securely
	• Disconnect column to chassis connector. Connect new switch into system without removing old. Depress the hazard warning lights. If they now work normally, turn signal switch is defective.	• Replace turn signal switch
	• If lights do not flash, check wiring harness "K" lead for open between hazard flasher and connector. If open, fuse block is defective	• Repair or replace brown wire or connector as required

Troubleshooting the Manual Steering Gear

Problem	Cause	Solution
Hard or erratic steering	• Incorrect tire pressure	• Inflate tires to recommended pressures
	• Insufficient or incorrect lubrication	• Lubricate as required (refer to Maintenance Section)
	• Suspension, or steering linkage parts damaged or misaligned	• Repair or replace parts as necessary
	• Improper front wheel alignment	• Adjust incorrect wheel alignment angles
	• Incorrect steering gear adjustment	• Adjust steering gear
	• Sagging springs	• Replace springs

Troubleshooting the Manual Steering Gear (cont.)

Problem	Cause	Solution
Play or looseness in steering	• Steering wheel loose	• Inspect shaft spines and repair as necessary. Tighten attaching nut and stake in place.
	• Steering linkage or attaching parts loose or worn	• Tighten, adjust, or replace faulty components
	• Pitman arm loose	• Inspect shaft splines and repair as necessary. Tighten attaching nut and stake in place
	• Steering gear attaching bolts loose	• Tighten bolts
	• Loose or worn wheel bearings	• Adjust or replace bearings
	• Steering gear adjustment incorrect or parts badly worn	• Adjust gear or replace defective parts
Wheel shimmy or tramp	• Improper tire pressure	• Inflate tires to recommended pressures
	• Wheels, tires, or brake rotors out-of-balance or out-of-round	• Inspect and replace or balance parts
	• Inoperative, worn, or loose shock absorbers or mounting parts	• Repair or replace shocks or mountings
	• Loose or worn steering or suspension parts	• Tighten or replace as necessary
	• Loose or worn wheel bearings	• Adjust or replace bearings
	• Incorrect steering gear adjustments	• Adjust steering gear
	• Incorrect front wheel alignment	• Correct front wheel alignment
Tire wear	• Improper tire pressure	• Inflate tires to recommended pressures
	• Failure to rotate tires	• Rotate tires
	• Brakes grabbing	• Adjust or repair brakes
	• Incorrect front wheel alignment	• Align incorrect angles
	• Broken or damaged steering and suspension parts	• Repair or replace defective parts
	• Wheel runout	• Replace faulty wheel
	• Excessive speed on turns	• Make driver aware of conditions
Vehicle leads to one side	• Improper tire pressures	• Inflate tires to recommended pressures
	• Front tires with uneven tread depth, wear pattern, or different cord design (i.e., one bias ply and one belted or radial tire on front wheels)	• Install tires of same cord construction and reasonably even tread depth, design, and wear pattern
	• Incorrect front wheel alignment	• Align incorrect angles
	• Brakes dragging	• Adjust or repair brakes
	• Pulling due to uneven tire construction	• Replace faulty tire

Troubleshooting the Power Steering Gear

Problem	Cause	Solution
Hissing noise in steering gear	• There is some noise in all power steering systems. One of the most common is a hissing sound most evident at standstill parking. There is no relationship between this noise and performance of the steering. Hiss may be expected when steering wheel is at end of travel or when slowly turning at standstill.	• Slight hiss is normal and in no way affects steering. Do not replace valve unless hiss is extremely objectionable. A replacement valve will also exhibit slight noise and is not always a cure. Investigate clearance around flexible coupling rivets. Be sure steering shaft and gear are aligned so flexible coupling rotates in a flat plane and is not distorted as

Troubleshooting the Power Steering Gear (cont.)

Problem	Cause	Solution
		shaft rotates. Any metal-to-metal contacts through flexible coupling will transmit valve hiss into passenger compartment through the steering column.
Rattle or chuckle noise in steering gear	• Gear loose on frame	• Check gear-to-frame mounting screws. Tighten screws to 88 N·m (65 foot pounds) torque.
	• Steering linkage looseness	• Check linkage pivot points for wear. Replace if necessary.
	• Pressure hose touching other parts of car	• Adjust hose position. Do not bend tubing by hand.
	• Loose pitman shaft over center adjustment	• Adjust to specifications
	NOTE: A slight rattle may occur on turns because of increased clearance off the "high point." This is normal and clearance must not be reduced below specified limits to eliminate this slight rattle.	
	• Loose pitman arm	• Tighten pitman arm nut to specifications
Squawk noise in steering gear when turning or recovering from a turn	• Damper O-ring on valve spool cut	• Replace damper O-ring
Poor return of steering wheel to center	• Tires not properly inflated	• Inflate to specified pressure
	• Lack of lubrication in linkage and ball joints	• Lube linkage and ball joints
	• Lower coupling flange rubbing against steering gear adjuster plug	• Loosen pinch bolt and assemble properly
	• Steering gear to column misalignment	• Align steering column
	• Improper front wheel alignment	• Check and adjust as necessary
	• Steering linkage binding	• Replace pivots
	• Ball joints binding	• Replace ball joints
	• Steering wheel rubbing against housing	• Align housing
	• Tight or frozen steering shaft bearings	• Replace bearings
	• Sticking or plugged valve spool	• Remove and clean or replace valve
	• Steering gear adjustments over specifications	• Check adjustment with gear out of car. Adjust as required.
	• Kink in return hose	• Replace hose
Car leads to one side or the other (keep in mind road condition and wind. Test car in both directions on flat road)	• Front end misaligned	• Adjust to specifications
	• Unbalanced steering gear valve	• Replace valve
	NOTE: If this is cause, steering effort will be very light in direction of lead and normal or heavier in opposite direction.	
Momentary increase in effort when turning wheel fast to right or left	• Low oil level	• Add power steering fluid as required
	• Pump belt slipping	• Tighten or replace belt
	• High internal leakage	• Check pump pressure. (See pressure test)

Troubleshooting the Power Steering Gear (cont.)

Problem	Cause	Solution
Steering wheel surges or jerks when turning with engine running especially during parking	• Low oil level • Loose pump belt • Steering linkage hitting engine oil pan at full turn • Insufficient pump pressure • Pump flow control valve sticking	• Fill as required • Adjust tension to specification • Correct clearance • Check pump pressure. (See pressure test). Replace relief valve if defective. • Inspect for varnish or damage, replace if necessary
Excessive wheel kickback or loose steering	• Air in system • Steering gear loose on frame • Steering linkage joints worn enough to be loose • Worn poppet valve • Loose thrust bearing preload adjustment • Excessive overcenter lash	• Add oil to pump reservoir and bleed by operating steering. Check hose connectors for proper torque and adjust as required. • Tighten attaching screws to specified torque • Replace loose pivots • Replace poppet valve • Adjust to specification with gear out of vehicle • Adjust to specification with gear out of car
Hard steering or lack of assist	• Loose pump belt • Low oil level **NOTE:** Low oil level will also result in excessive pump noise • Steering gear to column misalignment • Lower coupling flange rubbing against steering gear adjuster plug • Tires not properly inflated	• Adjust belt tension to specification • Fill to proper level. If excessively low, check all lines and joints for evidence of external leakage. Tighten loose connectors. • Align steering column • Loosen pinch bolt and assemble properly • Inflate to recommended pressure
Foamy milky power steering fluid, low fluid level and possible low pressure	• Air in the fluid, and loss of fluid due to internal pump leakage causing overflow	• Check for leak and correct. Bleed system. Extremely cold temperatures will cause system aeriation should the oil level be low. If oil level is correct and pump still foams, remove pump from vehicle and separate reservoir from housing. Check welsh plug and housing for cracks. If plug is loose or housing is cracked, replace housing.
Low pressure due to steering pump	• Flow control valve stuck or inoperative • Pressure plate not flat against cam ring	• Remove burrs or dirt or replace. Flush system. • Correct
Low pressure due to steering gear	• Pressure loss in cylinder due to worn piston ring or badly worn housing bore • Leakage at valve rings, valve body-to-worm seal	• Remove gear from car for disassembly and inspection of ring and housing bore • Remove gear from car for disassembly and replace seals

Troubleshooting the Power Steering Pump

Problem	Cause	Solution
Chirp noise in steering pump	• Loose belt	• Adjust belt tension to specification
Belt squeal (particularly noticeable at full wheel travel and stand still parking)	• Loose belt	• Adjust belt tension to specification
Growl noise in steering pump	• Excessive back pressure in hoses or steering gear caused by restriction	• Locate restriction and correct. Replace part if necessary.
Growl noise in steering pump (particularly noticeable at stand still parking)	• Scored pressure plates, thrust plate or rotor • Extreme wear of cam ring	• Replace parts and flush system • Replace parts
Groan noise in steering pump	• Low oil level • Air in the oil. Poor pressure hose connection.	• Fill reservoir to proper level • Tighten connector to specified torque. Bleed system by operating steering from right to left—full turn.
Rattle noise in steering pump	• Vanes not installed properly • Vanes sticking in rotor slots	• Install properly • Free up by removing burrs, varnish, or dirt
Swish noise in steering pump	• Defective flow control valve	• Replace part
Whine noise in steering pump	• Pump shaft bearing scored	• Replace housing and shaft. Flush system.
Hard steering or lack of assist	• Loose pump belt • Low oil level in reservoir **NOTE:** Low oil level will also result in excessive pump noise • Steering gear to column misalignment • Lower coupling flange rubbing against steering gear adjuster plug • Tires not properly inflated	• Adjust belt tension to specification • Fill to proper level. If excessively low, check all lines and joints for evidence of external leakage. Tighten loose connectors. • Align steering column • Loosen pinch bolt and assemble properly • Inflate to recommended pressure
Foaming milky power steering fluid, low fluid level and possible low pressure	• Air in the fluid, and loss of fluid due to internal pump leakage causing overflow	• Check for leaks and correct. Bleed system. Extremely cold temperatures will cause system aeration should the oil level be low. If oil level is correct and pump still foams, remove pump from vehicle and separate reservoir from body. Check welsh plug and body for cracks. If plug is loose or body is cracked, replace body.
Low pump pressure	• Flow control valve stuck or inoperative • Pressure plate not flat against cam ring	• Remove burrs or dirt or replace. Flush system. • Correct
Momentary increase in effort when turning wheel fast to right or left	• Low oil level in pump • Pump belt slipping • High internal leakage	• Add power steering fluid as required • Tighten or replace belt • Check pump pressure. (See pressure test)
Steering wheel surges or jerks when turning with engine running especially during parking	• Low oil level • Loose pump belt • Steering linkage hitting engine oil pan at full turn • Insufficient pump pressure	• Fill as required • Adjust tension to specification • Correct clearance • Check pump pressure. (See pressure test). Replace flow control valve if defective.

Troubleshooting the Power Steering Pump (cont.)

Problem	Cause	Solution
Steering wheel surges or jerks when turning with engine running especially during parking (cont.)	• Sticking flow control valve	• Inspect for varnish or damage, replace if necessary
Excessive wheel kickback or loose steering	• Air in system	• Add oil to pump reservoir and bleed by operating steering. Check hose connectors for proper torque and adjust as required.
Low pump pressure	• Extreme wear of cam ring	• Replace parts. Flush system.
	• Scored pressure plate, thrust plate, or rotor	• Replace parts. Flush system.
	• Vanes not installed properly	• Install properly
	• Vanes sticking in rotor slots	• Freeup by removing burrs, varnish, or dirt
	• Cracked or broken thrust or pressure plate	• Replace part

or rings on Datsuns. The first simply pulls off. The second, which is usually a large, semitriangular pad, must be pushed up, then pulled off. The third must be pushed in and turned clockwise.

4. Remove the rest of the horn switching mechanism, noting the relative location of the parts. Remove the mechanism only if it hinders subsequent wheel removal procedures.

5. Matchmark the top of the steering column shaft and the steering wheel flange.

6. Remove the attaching nut and remove the steering wheel with a puller.

NOTE: *Do not strike the shaft with a hammer, which may cause the column to collapse.*

7. Install the steering wheel in the reverse order of removal, aligning the punch marks. On 1985-89 Maxima, 1987-88 200SX and 1989 240SX models coat the entire surface of the turn signal canceling pin and the horn contact slip ring with multipurpose grease. Do not drive or hammer the wheel into place, or you may cause the collapsible steering column to collapse, in which case you'll have to buy a whole new steering column unit.

8. Tighten the steering wheel nut to 22-25 ft. lbs. on the 1977-79 200SX and front wheel drive Maximas. Tighten all other steering wheel nuts to 28-36 ft. lbs. except the 1984-88 200SX and 1989 240SX wheel nut, which is tightened to 22-29 ft. lbs.

9. Reinstall the horn button, pad, or ring.

Turn Signal/Combination Switch
REMOVAL AND INSTALLATION

On some models, the turn signal switch is part of a combination switch. The whole unit is removed together.

1. Disconnect the battery ground cable.

2. Remove the steering wheel as previously outlined. Observe the caution on the collapsible steering column.

3. Remove the steering column covers.

4. Disconnect the electrical plugs from the switch.

NOTE: *On some late model vehicles the control (lighting, wiper and washer, hazzard and cruise control set) switches can be replaced without removing the combination base. Refer to the illustration of Combination Switch.*

5. Remove the retaining screws and remove the switch.

6. Install the switch in the proper position. Many models have turn signal switches that have a tab which must fit into a hole in the steering shaft in order for the system to return the switch to the neutral position after the turn has been made. Be sure to align the tab and the hole when installing.

7. Install the steering column covers and steering wheel.

8. Reconnect the battery cable. Turn key to the ON position and check system for proper

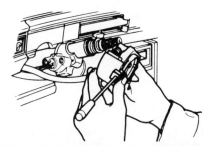

Removing the turn signal switch—610 shown

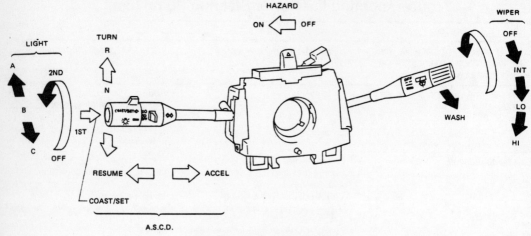

Combination switch operation

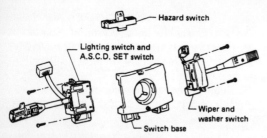

Late model combination switch

operation. Make sure that the turn signals will cancel after the vehicle has made a turn.

NOTE: *On many models, the individual stalk assemblies can be removed without removing the combination switch base assembly. Simply disconnect the electrical lead and remove the 2 stalk-to-base mounting screws.*

Steering Lock
REMOVAL AND INSTALLATION

The steering lock/ignition switch/warning buzzer assembly is attached to the steering col-

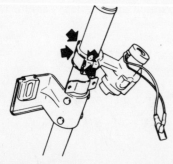

Steering lock securing screws—1977–79 200SX, others similar

umn by special screws whose heads shear off on installation. The screws must be drilled out to remove the assembly. The ignition switch or warning switch can be replaced without removing the assembly. The ignition switch is on the back of the assembly, and the warning switch on the side. The warning buzzer, which sounds when the driver's door is opened with the steering unlocked, is located behind the instrument panel. Install shear type screws and then cut off the screw heads.

Tie Rod Ends (Steering Side Rods)
REMOVAL AND INSTALLATION

You will need a ball joint remover for this operation.

1. Jack up the front of the vehicle and support it on jack stands.

2. Locate the faulty tie rod end. It will have a lot of play in it and the dust cover will probably be ripped.

3. Remove the cotter key and nut from the tie rod stud. Note the position of the tie rod end in relation to the rest of the steering linkage.

4. Loosen the locknut holding the tie rod to the rest of the steering linkage.

5. Free the tie rod ball joint from either the relay rod or steering knuckle by using a ball joint remover.

6. Unscrew and remove the tie rod end, counting the number of turns it takes to completely free it.

7. Install the new tie rod end, turning it in exactly as far as you screwed out the old one. Make sure it is correctly positioned in relation to the rest of the steering linkage.

8. Fit the ball joint and nut, tighten them

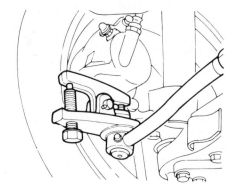

Tie-rod puller

and install a new cotter pin. Before finally tightening the tie rod lock nut or clamp, adjust the toe-in of the vehicle.

Manual Steering Gear

REMOVAL AND INSTALLATION

NOTE: *The 1985-89 Maxima and 1987-88 200SX are available with power steering only.*

1977-86 200SX

1. Disconnect the exhaust pipe from the exhaust manifold, if necessary, and remove the bolt securing the exhaust pipe to the transmission mounting insulator.

2. Remove the bolt holding the worm shaft to the rubber coupling.

NOTE: *On 1984 and later models, rack and pinion steering system is used. Remove the tie rod ball studs from the knuckle arms using a ball joint removal tool or the equivalent, and disconnect the steering column lower joint. Remove the rack and pinion gear attaching bolts and then remove the rack and pinion from the vehicle.*

3. Remove the nut holding the pitman arm to the sector shaft and remove the pitman arm.

4. Remove the steering gear attaching bolts and then remove the steering gear from the vehicle.

5. Install the steering gear with attaching bolts to the vehicle.

6. Install the pitman arm assembly to the selector shaft.

7. Connect the worm shaft to the rubber coupling.

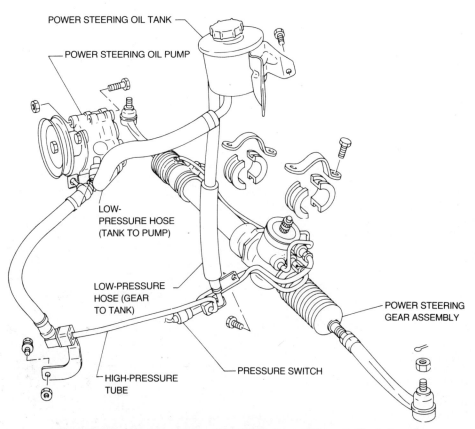

Typical power steering system, 1984 200SX shown. Others similar in layout

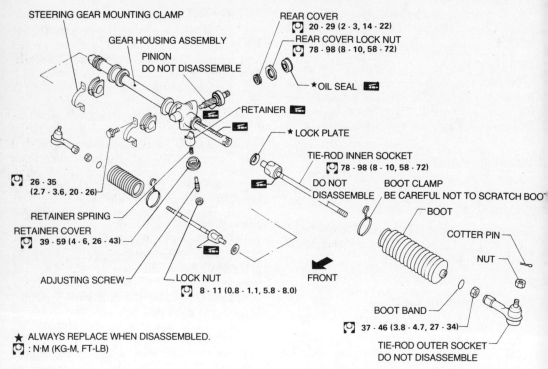

STEERING GEAR MOUNTING CLAMP

GEAR HOUSING ASSEMBLY

PINION
DO NOT DISASSEMBLE

REAR COVER
20 - 29 (2 - 3, 14 - 22)

REAR COVER LOCK NUT
78 - 98 (8 - 10, 58 - 72)

★OIL SEAL

RETAINER

★LOCK PLATE

TIE-ROD INNER SOCKET
78 - 98 (8 - 10, 58 - 72)

DO NOT
DISASSEMBLE

BOOT CLAMP
BE CAREFUL NOT TO SCRATCH BOOT

BOOT

COTTER PIN

NUT

26 - 35
(2.7 - 3.6, 20 - 26)

RETAINER SPRING

RETAINER COVER
39 - 59 (4 - 6, 26 - 43)

ADJUSTING SCREW

LOCK NUT
8 - 11 (0.8 - 1.1, 5.8 - 8.0)

FRONT

BOOT BAND

37 - 46 (3.8 - 4.7, 27 - 34)

TIE-ROD OUTER SOCKET
DO NOT DISASSEMBLE

★ ALWAYS REPLACE WHEN DISASSEMBLED.

: N·M (KG-M, FT-LB)

200SX rack and pinion system showing tie rod ends. Other models' rack and pinion systems similar

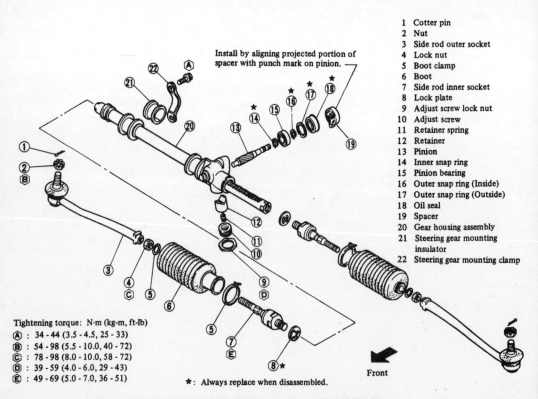

Install by aligning projected portion of
spacer with punch mark on pinion.

1 Cotter pin
2 Nut
3 Side rod outer socket
4 Lock nut
5 Boot clamp
6 Boot
7 Side rod inner socket
8 Lock plate
9 Adjust screw lock nut
10 Adjust screw
11 Retainer spring
12 Retainer
13 Pinion
14 Inner snap ring
15 Pinion bearing
16 Outer snap ring (Inside)
17 Outer snap ring (Outside)
18 Oil seal
19 Spacer
20 Gear housing assembly
21 Steering gear mounting
      insulator
22 Steering gear mounting clamp

Tightening torque: N·m (kg-m, ft-lb)
Ⓐ : 34 - 44 (3.5 - 4.5, 25 - 33)
Ⓑ : 54 - 98 (5.5 - 10.0, 40 - 72)
Ⓒ : 78 - 98 (8.0 - 10.0, 58 - 72)
Ⓓ : 39 - 59 (4.0 - 6.0, 29 - 43)
Ⓔ : 49 - 69 (5.0 - 7.0, 36 - 51)

★ : Always replace when disassembled.

Front

Manual steering gear assembly—1982 810/Maxima

8. Reconnect the exhaust system if necessary. Check the wheel alignment after installation.

1977-81 810 Model

Refer to the procedure above as a guide for Removal and Installation of the manual steering gear. The front steering (non rack and pinion) gear used in these vehicles is very similar as the above.

1982-84 810/Maxima

NOTE: *These vehicles use a rack and pinion steering gear type.*

1. Raise and support the front of the vehicle safely and remove the front wheels.
2. Remove the lower joint from the steering column at the rubber coupling.
3. Remove the lower joint assembly from the pinion.
4. Remove the side rod studs from the steering knuckles.

5. Remove the gear housing-to-crossmember bolts and then remove the steering gear from the vehicle.
6. Installation is the reverse order of the removal procedure.

Power Steering Gear
REMOVAL AND ADJUSTMENT
1980-83 200SX

1. Remove the air cleaner and remove the bolt securing the U-joint to the worm shaft.
2. Disconnect and plug the hoses from the power steering gear.
3. Remove the pitman arm from the sector shaft, using a suitable puller.
4. Remove the steering gear securing bolts and remove the steering gear from the vehicle.
5. Installation is the reverse order of the removal procedure.

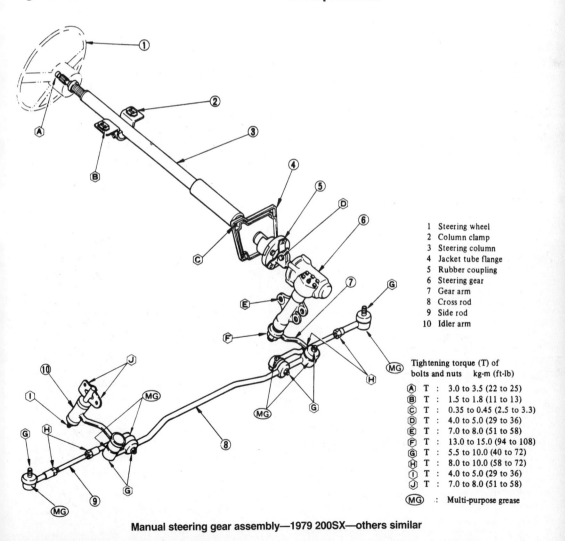

1   Steering wheel
2   Column clamp
3   Steering column
4   Jacket tube flange
5   Rubber coupling
6   Steering gear
7   Gear arm
8   Cross rod
9   Side rod
10 Idler arm

Tightening torque (T) of
bolts and nuts   kg-m (ft-lb)

Ⓐ T : 3.0 to 3.5 (22 to 25)
Ⓑ T : 1.5 to 1.8 (11 to 13)
Ⓒ T : 0.35 to 0.45 (2.5 to 3.3)
Ⓓ T : 4.0 to 5.0 (29 to 36)
Ⓔ T : 7.0 to 8.0 (51 to 58)
Ⓕ T : 13.0 to 15.0 (94 to 108)
Ⓖ T : 5.5 to 10.0 (40 to 72)
Ⓗ T : 8.0 to 10.0 (58 to 72)
Ⓘ T : 4.0 to 5.0 (29 to 36)
Ⓙ T : 7.0 to 8.0 (51 to 58)

ⓂⒼ : Multi-purpose grease

Manual steering gear assembly—1979 200SX—others similar

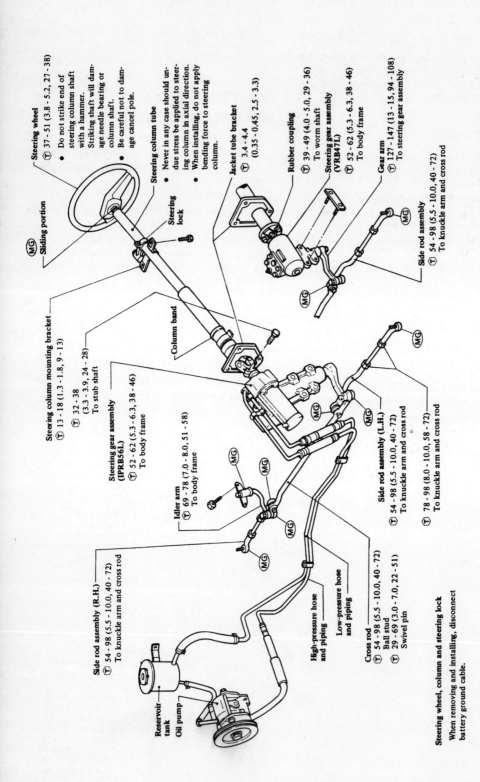

Power steering gear—1983 200SX

Steering wheel
- ⓣ 37 - 51 (3.8 - 5.2, 27 - 38)
- Do not strike end of steering column shaft with a hammer. Striking shaft will damage needle bearing or column shaft.
- Be careful not to damage cancel pole.

Steering column tube
- Never in any case should under stress be applied to steering column in axial direction. When installing, do not apply bending force to steering column.

Jacket tube bracket
- ⓣ 3.4 - 4.4 (0.35 - 0.45, 2.5 - 3.3)

Rubber coupling
- ⓣ 39 - 49 (4.0 - 5.0, 29 - 36) To worm shaft

Steering gear assembly (VRB47L)
- ⓣ 52 - 62 (5.3 - 6.3, 38 - 46) To body frame

Gear arm
- ⓣ 127 - 147 (13 - 15, 94 - 108) To steering gear assembly

Side rod assembly
- ⓣ 54 - 98 (5.5 - 10.0, 40 - 72) To knuckle arm and cross rod

ⓣ : N·m (kg-m, ft-lb)
ⓜⓖ : Multi-purpose greasing points

MG Sliding portion

Steering lock

Steering column mounting bracket
- ⓣ 13 - 18 (1.3 - 1.8, 9 - 13)

Column band

ⓣ 32 - 38 (3.3 - 3.9, 24 - 28) To stub shaft

Steering gear assembly (IPRB56L)
- ⓣ 52 - 62 (5.3 - 6.3, 38 - 46) To body frame

Idler arm
- ⓣ 69 - 78 (7.0 - 8.0, 51 - 58) To body frame

Side rod assembly (L.H.)
- ⓣ 54 - 98 (5.5 - 10.0, 40 - 72) To knuckle arm and cross rod

ⓣ 78 - 98 (8.0 - 10.0, 58 - 72) To knuckle arm and cross rod

Side rod assembly (R.H.)
- ⓣ 54 - 98 (5.5 - 10.0, 40 - 72) To knuckle arm and cross rod

High-pressure hose and piping

Low-pressure hose and piping

Cross rod
- ⓣ 54 - 98 (5.5 - 10.0, 40 - 72) Ball stud
- ⓣ 29 - 69 (3.0 - 7.0, 22 - 51) Swivel pin

Reservoir tank
Oil pump

Steering wheel, column and steering lock
When removing and installing, disconnect battery ground cable.

Each dust cover
When removing and installing, be careful not to damage dust cover.

1984-88 200SX

NOTE: *These vehicles use a rack and pinion type power steering gear.*

1. Remove the bolt securing the lower shaft to power steering gear assembly.

2. Disconnect the hoses from the power steering gear and plug the hoses to prevent leakage.

3. Remove the power steering gear mounting bolts.

4. Remove the exhaust pipe mounting nut.

5. Disconnect the control cable or linkage for the transmission and position it out of the way.

6. Remove the steering gear from the vehicle.

7. Install the steering gear to the vehicle. Torque the clamp retaining bolts to 29-36 ft.lbs.

8. Connect the control cable or linkage to the transmission and install the exhaust system.

9. Reconnect the hoses to the power steering gear. Install the bolt securing the lower shaft to power steering gear assembly.

10. Check the fluid level. Start the engine check for leaks and for proper operation of the system.

1982-84 810/Maxima

The procedure for these models, is very similar to the 1984-88 200SX rack and pinion type power steering gear. Refer to the procedure above as a guide.

1985-89 Maxima
1989 240SX

1. Raise and support the front of the vehicle safely and remove the wheels.

2. Disconnect the power steering hose from the power steering gear and plug all hoses to prevent leakage.

3. Disconnect the side rod studs from the steering knuckles.

4. Remove the lower joint assembly from the steering gear pinion.

5. Remove the steering gear and linkage assembly from the vehicle.

6. Installation is the reverse order of the removal procedure.

Power Steering Pump
REMOVAL AND INSTALLATION

1. Remove the hoses at the pump and plug the openings shut to prevent contamination. Position the disconnected lines in a raised attitude to prevent leakage.

2. Remove the pump belt.

3. Loosen the retaining bolts and any braces, and remove the pump.

4. Installation is the reverse of removal. Adjust the belt tension by referring to the Belts section in Chapter one, General Information and Maintenance. Bleed the system.

BLEEDING THE POWER STEERING SYSTEM

1. Fill the pump reservoir and allow to remain undisturbed for a few minutes.

2. Raise the car until the front wheels are clear of the ground.

3. With the engine off, quickly turn the wheels right and left several times, lightly contacting the stops.

4. Add fluid if necessary.

5. Start the engine and let it idle.

6. Repeat Steps 3 and 4 with the engine idling.

7. Stop the engine, lower the car until the wheels just touch the ground. Start the engine, allow it to idle, and turn the wheels back and forth several times. Check the fluid level and refill if necessary.

Brakes

BRAKE SYSTEM

CAUTION: *Brake shoes contain asbestos, which has been determined to be a cancer causing agent. Never clean the brake surfaces with compressed air! Avoid inhaling any dust from any brake surface! When cleaning brake surfaces, use a commercially available brake cleaning fluid.*

Adjustment

Front disc brakes are used on all Datsun/Nissans covered in this manual. All models are equipped with independent front and rear hydraulic systems with a warning light to indicate loss of pressure in either system. Most early models have rear drum brakes. All 1985–89 Maxima models have rear disc brakes. Rear disc brakes are available on certain other late models.

The 1980–82 200SX is equipped with rear disc brakes with the parking brake system activating the main brake pads via a mechanical lever assembly. All models have a vacuum booster system to lessen the required pedal pressure. The parking brake on all models operates the rear brakes through a cable system.

NOTE: *Only certain types of drum brakes require adjustment. Some drum brakes are automatically adjusted when the parking brake is applied. No disc brakes need adjustment. They are self adjusting.*

To adjust the brakes, raise the wheels, disconnect the parking brake linkage from the rear wheels, apply the brakes hard a few times to center the drums, and proceed as follows:

BOLT TYPE ADJUSTER

Turn the adjuster bolt on the backing plate until the wheel can no longer be turned, then back off until the wheel is free of drag. Repeat the procedure on the other adjuster bolt on the

710 rear brake adjuster

same wheel. Some models may have only one adjuster bolt per wheel.

Some models incorporate a click arrangement with the bolt adjuster. The adjustment proceeds in clicks or notches. The wheel will often be locked temporarily as the adjuster passes over the center for each click. Thus, the adjuster is alternately hard and easy to turn. When the wheel is fully locked, back off 1–3 clicks.

TOOTHED ADJUSTING NUT

Remove the rubber cover from the backing plate. Align the hole in the brake backing plate with the adjusting nut. To spread the brake shoes, turn the toothed adjusting nut with a tool. Stop turning when a considerable drag is felt. Back off the nut a few notches so that the correct clearance is reached between the brake drum and the brake shoes. Make sure that the wheel rotates freely.

AUTOMATIC ADJUSTERS

No manual adjustment is necessary. The self adjuster operates whenever the hand or foot brake brakes (on some models) are used.

After Adjustment – All Models

After adjusting the brakes, reconnect the handbrake linkage. Make sure that there is no

Troubleshooting the Brake System

Problem	Cause	Solution
Low brake pedal (excessive pedal travel required for braking action.)	• Excessive clearance between rear linings and drums caused by inoperative automatic adjusters	• Make 10 to 15 alternate forward and reverse brake stops to adjust brakes. If brake pedal does not come up, repair or replace adjuster parts as necessary.
	• Worn rear brakelining	• Inspect and replace lining if worn beyond minimum thickness specification
	• Bent, distorted brakeshoes, front or rear	• Replace brakeshoes in axle sets
	• Air in hydraulic system	• Remove air from system. Refer to Brake Bleeding.
Low brake pedal (pedal may go to floor with steady pressure applied.)	• Fluid leak in hydraulic system	• Fill master cylinder to fill line; have helper apply brakes and check calipers, wheel cylinders, differential valve tubes, hoses and fittings for leaks. Repair or replace as necessary.
	• Air in hydraulic system	• Remove air from system. Refer to Brake Bleeding.
	• Incorrect or non-recommended brake fluid (fluid evaporates at below normal temp).	• Flush hydraulic system with clean brake fluid. Refill with correct-type fluid.
	• Master cylinder piston seals worn, or master cylinder bore is scored, worn or corroded	• Repair or replace master cylinder
Low brake pedal (pedal goes to floor on first application—o.k. on subsequent applications.)	• Disc brake pads sticking on abutment surfaces of anchor plate. Caused by a build-up of dirt, rust, or corrosion on abutment surfaces	• Clean abutment surfaces
Fading brake pedal (pedal height decreases with steady pressure applied.)	• Fluid leak in hydraulic system	• Fill master cylinder reservoirs to fill mark, have helper apply brakes, check calipers, wheel cylinders, differential valve, tubes, hoses, and fittings for fluid leaks. Repair or replace parts as necessary.
	• Master cylinder piston seals worn, or master cylinder bore is scored, worn or corroded	• Repair or replace master cylinder
Decreasing brake pedal travel (pedal travel required for braking action decreases and may be accompanied by a hard pedal.)	• Caliper or wheel cylinder pistons sticking or seized	• Repair or replace the calipers, or wheel cylinders
	• Master cylinder compensator ports blocked (preventing fluid return to reservoirs) or pistons sticking or seized in master cylinder bore	• Repair or replace the master cylinder
	• Power brake unit binding internally	• Test unit according to the following procedure: (a) Shift transmission into neutral and start engine (b) Increase engine speed to 1500 rpm, close throttle and fully depress brake pedal (c) Slow release brake pedal and stop engine (d) Have helper remove vacuum check valve and hose from power unit. Observe for backward movement of brake pedal. (e) If the pedal moves backward, the power unit has an internal bind—replace power unit

Troubleshooting the Brake System (cont.)

Problem	Cause	Solution
Spongy brake pedal (pedal has abnormally soft, springy, spongy feel when depressed.)	• Air in hydraulic system • Brakeshoes bent or distorted • Brakelining not yet seated with drums and rotors • Rear drum brakes not properly adjusted	• Remove air from system. Refer to Brake Bleeding. • Replace brakeshoes • Burnish brakes • Adjust brakes

Hard brake pedal (excessive pedal pressure required to stop vehicle. May be accompanied by brake fade.)	• Loose or leaking power brake unit vacuum hose
	• Incorrect or poor quality brakelining
	• Bent, broken, distorted brakeshoes
	• Calipers binding or dragging on mounting pins. Rear brakeshoes dragging on support plate.
	
	• Caliper, wheel cylinder, or master cylinder pistons sticking or seized
	• Power brake unit vacuum check valve malfunction
	
	• Power brake unit has internal bind
		• Tighten connections or replace leaking hose
		• Replace with lining in axle sets
		
		• Replace brakeshoes
		• Replace mounting pins and bushings. Clean rust or burrs from rear brake support plate ledges and lubricate ledges with molydisulfide grease.
		NOTE: If ledges are deeply grooved or scored, do not attempt to sand or grind them smooth—replace support plate.
		• Repair or replace parts as necessary
		
		• Test valve according to the following procedure:
		  (a) Start engine, increase engine speed to 1500 rpm, close throttle and immediately stop engine
		  (b) Wait at least 90 seconds then depress brake pedal
		  (c) If brakes are not vacuum assisted for 2 or more applications, check valve is faulty
		• Test unit according to the following procedure:
		  (a) With engine stopped, apply brakes several times to exhaust all vacuum in system
		  (b) Shift transmission into neutral, depress brake pedal and start engine
		  (c) If pedal height decreases with foot pressure and less pressure is required to hold pedal in applied position, power unit vacuum system is operating normally. Test power unit. If power unit exhibits a bind condition, replace the power unit.

	• Master cylinder compensator ports (at bottom of reservoirs) blocked by dirt, scale, rust, or have small burrs (blocked ports prevent fluid return to reservoirs). • Brake hoses, tubes, fittings clogged or restricted • Brake fluid contaminated with improper fluids (motor oil, transmission fluid, causing rubber components to swell and stick in bores • Low engine vacuum	• Repair or replace master cylinder **CAUTION:** Do not attempt to clean blocked ports with wire, pencils, or similar implements. Use compressed air only. • Use compressed air to check or unclog parts. Replace any damaged parts. • Replace all rubber components, combination valve and hoses. Flush entire brake system with DOT 3 brake fluid or equivalent. • Adjust or repair engine

Troubleshooting the Brake System (cont.)

Problem	Cause	Solution
Grabbing brakes (severe reaction to brake pedal pressure.)	• Brakelining(s) contaminated by grease or brake fluid	• Determine and correct cause of contamination and replace brakeshoes in axle sets
	• Parking brake cables incorrectly adjusted or seized	• Adjust cables. Replace seized cables.
	• Incorrect brakelining or lining loose on brakeshoes	• Replace brakeshoes in axle sets
	• Caliper anchor plate bolts loose	• Tighten bolts
	• Rear brakeshoes binding on support plate ledges	• Clean and lubricate ledges. Replace support plate(s) if ledges are deeply grooved. Do not attempt to smooth ledges by grinding.
	• Incorrect or missing power brake reaction disc	• Install correct disc
	• Rear brake support plates loose	• Tighten mounting bolts
Dragging brakes (slow or incomplete release of brakes)	• Brake pedal binding at pivot	• Loosen and lubricate
	• Power brake unit has internal bind	• Inspect for internal bind. Replace unit if internal bind exists.
	• Parking brake cables incorrrectly adjusted or seized	• Adjust cables. Replace seized cables.
	• Rear brakeshoe return springs weak or broken	• Replace return springs. Replace brakeshoe if necessary in axle sets.
	• Automatic adjusters malfunctioning	• Repair or replace adjuster parts as required
	• Caliper, wheel cylinder or master cylinder pistons sticking or seized	• Repair or replace parts as necessary
	• Master cylinder compensating ports blocked (fluid does not return to reservoirs).	• Use compressed air to clear ports. Do not use wire, pencils, or similar objects to open blocked ports.
Vehicle moves to one side when brakes are applied	• Incorrect front tire pressure	• Inflate to recommended cold (reduced load) inflation pressure
	• Worn or damaged wheel bearings	• Replace worn or damaged bearings
	• Brakelining on one side contaminated	• Determine and correct cause of contamination and replace brakelining in axle sets
	• Brakeshoes on one side bent, distorted, or lining loose on shoe	• Replace brakeshoes in axle sets
	• Support plate bent or loose on one side	• Tighten or replace support plate
	• Brakelining not yet seated with drums or rotors	• Burnish brakelining
	• Caliper anchor plate loose on one side	• Tighten anchor plate bolts
	• Caliper piston sticking or seized	• Repair or replace caliper
	• Brakelinings water soaked	• Drive vehicle with brakes lightly applied to dry linings
	• Loose suspension component attaching or mounting bolts	• Tighten suspension bolts. Replace worn suspension components.
	• Brake combination valve failure	• Replace combination valve
Chatter or shudder when brakes are applied (pedal pulsation and roughness may also occur.)	• Brakeshoes distorted, bent, contaminated, or worn	• Replace brakeshoes in axle sets
	• Caliper anchor plate or support plate loose	• Tighten mounting bolts
	• Excessive thickness variation of rotor(s)	• Refinish or replace rotors in axle sets
Noisy brakes (squealing, clicking, scraping sound when brakes are applied.)	• Bent, broken, distorted brakeshoes	• Replace brakeshoes in axle sets
	• Excessive rust on outer edge of rotor braking surface	• Remove rust

Troubleshooting the Brake System (cont.)

Problem	Cause	Solution
Noisy brakes (squealing, clicking, scraping sound when brakes are applied.) (cont.)	• Brakelining worn out—shoes contacting drum of rotor	• Replace brakeshoes and lining in axle sets. Refinish or replace drums or rotors.
	• Broken or loose holdown or return springs	• Replace parts as necessary
	• Rough or dry drum brake support plate ledges	• Lubricate support plate ledges
	• Cracked, grooved, or scored rotor(s) or drum(s)	• Replace rotor(s) or drum(s). Replace brakeshoes and lining in axle sets if necessary.
	• Incorrect brakelining and/or shoes (front or rear).	• Install specified shoe and lining assemblies
Pulsating brake pedal	• Out of round drums or excessive lateral runout in disc brake rotor(s)	• Refinish or replace drums, re-index rotors or replace

rear wheel drag with the handbrake released. Loosen the handbrake adjustment if necessary.

BRAKE PEDAL ADJUSTMENT

Before adjusting the pedal, make sure that the wheelbrakes are correctly adjusted. Adjust the pedal free play by means of the adjustable pushrod or by replacing shims between the master cylinder and the brake booster or firewall. Free play should be approximately 1-5mm on all models through 1984. On all models from 1985 to 1989 the pedal free play should be 1-3mm.

Adjust the pedal height by means of the ad-

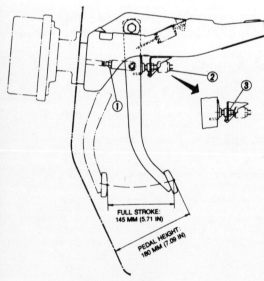

FULL STROKE:
145 MM (5.71 IN)

PEDAL HEIGHT
180 MM (7.09 IN)

1. Push rod lock nut
2. Brake lamp switch
3. Brake lamp switch lock nut

Brake pedal adjustment—all models similar

justable pedal arm stop pad in the driver's compartment on models through 1984. On later models, adjust the brake booster input rod by loosening the locknut and turning the rod.

The pedal height (floorboard-to-pedal pad) should be approximately 152mm for all 510s and the 1980–81 200SX and 178mm for 1982–83 200SX model.

Pedal height should be about 165mm for the 1981–84 810/Maxima; 178mm for all 1977–79 200SX, 610s, 710s and the 1977–80 810.

On the 1985–88 Maxima, the pedal free height should be 184-194mm; on the 1989 Maxima, 159-169mm (manual transaxle) and 169-179mm (automatic transaxle).

On the 1984–86½ 200SX, it should be 189-199mm on cars with a (manual transmission) and 191-201mm on cars with (automatic transmission).

On the 1986½–88 200SX, it should be 185-195mm on cars with a (manual transmission) and 187-197mm on cars with (automatic transmission).

The brake pedal free height for the 1989 240SX model is 177-187mm for (manual transmission) and 186-196mm for (automatic transmission).

Brake Light Switch
REMOVAL AND INSTALLATION

1. Disconnect the negative battery cable.
2. Disconnect the wiring connector at the switch.
3. Remove the switch lock nut.
4. Remove the switch.
5. Install the switch and adjust it so the brake lights are not on unless the brake pedal is depressed.

Master Cylinder

REMOVAL AND INSTALLATION

1. Clean the outside of the master cylinder thoroughly, particularly around the cap and fluid lines. Disconnect the fluid lines and cap them to exclude dirt.

2. If equipped with a fluid level sensor, disconnect the wiring harness from the master cylinder.

3. Disconnect the brake fluid tubes, then plug the openings to prevent dirt from entering the system.

4. Remove the mounting bolts at the firewall or the brake booster (if equipped) and remove the master cylinder from the vehicle.

5. Install the master cylinder to the vehicle. Connect all brake lines and fluid level sensor wiring is so equipped. Refill the reservoir with brake fluid and bleed the system.

NOTE: *Ordinary brake fluid will boil and cause brake failure under the high temperatures developed in disc brake systems; use DOT 3 brake fluid in the brake systems. The adjustable pushrod is used to adjust brake pedal free-play. If the pushrod is not adjustable, there will be shims between the cylinder and the mount. These shims, or the adjustable pushrod, are used to adjust brake pedal free play.*

OVERHAUL

NOTE: *Master cylinders are supplied to Datsun/Nissan by two manufacturers: Nabco and Tokico. Parts between these manufacturers are not interchangeable. Be sure you obtain the correct rebuilding kit for your master cylinder.*

The master cylinder can be disassembled using the illustrations as a guide. Clean all parts in clean brake fluid. Replace the cylinder or piston as necessary if clearance between the two exceed 0.15mm. Lubricate all parts with clean brake fluid on assembly. Master cylinder rebuilding kits, containing all the wearing parts, are available to simplify overhaul.

Power Booster

REMOVAL AND INSTALLATION

NOTE: *Make sure all vacuum lines and connectors are in good condition. A small vacuum leak will cause a big problem in the power brake system.*

1. Remove the master cylinder mounting nuts and pull the master cylinder assembly (brake lines connected) away from the power booster.

2. Detach the vacuum lines from the booster.

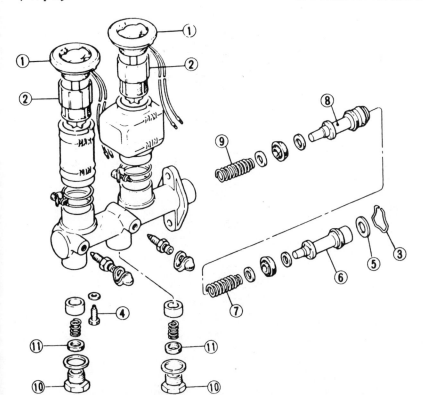

1. Reservoir cap
2. Strainer
3. Stopper ring
4. Stopper screw
5. Stopper
6. Primary piston
7. Spring
8. Secondary piston
9. Spring
10. Plug
11. Check valve

Exploded view of the 1973–80 master cylinder—all models similar

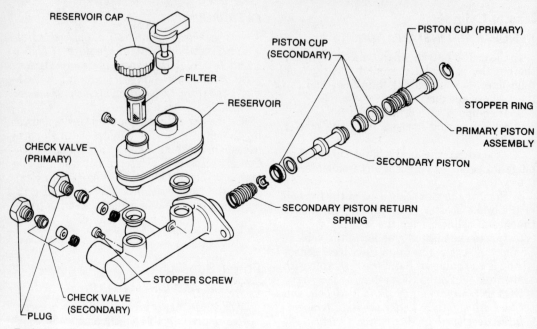

Exploded view of the 1981 and later master cylinder, all models similar except 1984 and later 200SX, 1985–89 Maxima and 1989 240SX

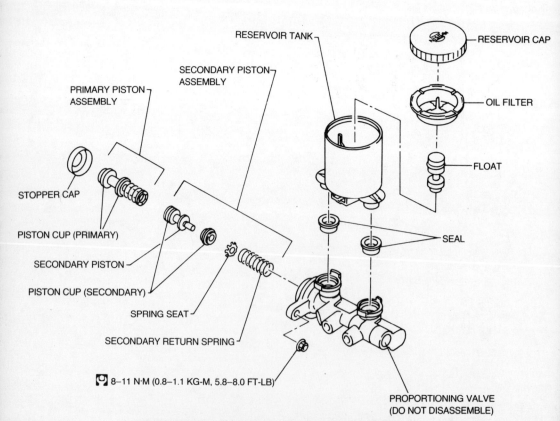

8–11 N·M (0.8–1.1 KG-M, 5.8–8.0 FT-LB)

1984 and later 200SX master cylinder and 1985–89 Maxima

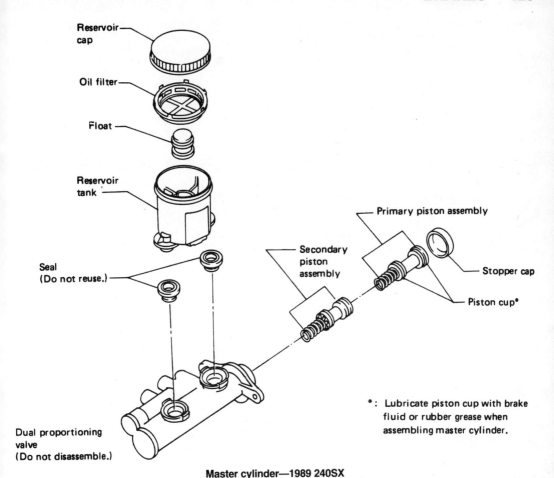

Reservoir cap

Oil filter

Float

Reservoir tank

Seal (Do not reuse.)

Dual proportioning valve (Do not disassemble.)

Secondary piston assembly

Primary piston assembly

Stopper cap

Piston cup*

*: Lubricate piston cup with brake fluid or rubber grease when assembling master cylinder.

Master cylinder—1989 240SX

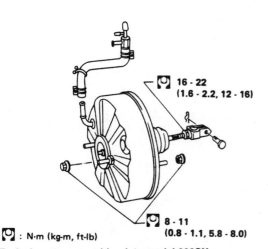

16 - 22 (1.6 - 2.2, 12 - 16)

8 - 11 (0.8 - 1.1, 5.8 - 8.0)

: N·m (kg-m, ft-lb)

Brake booster assembly—late model 200SX

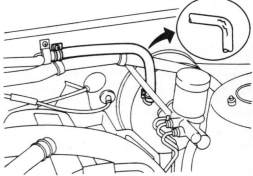

Check condition of vacuum hose on power brake booster

3. Detach the booster pushrod at the pedal clevis.

4. Unbolt the booster from under the dash and lift it out of the engine compartment.

5. Install the brake booster assembly to the vehicle. Torque the master cylinder-to-booster nuts to 72-96 in. lbs.; the booster-to-firewall nuts to 72-96 in. lbs.

6. Connect the booster pushrod to the pedal clevis. Connect the vacuum lines to brake booster.

7. Start the engine and check brake operation.

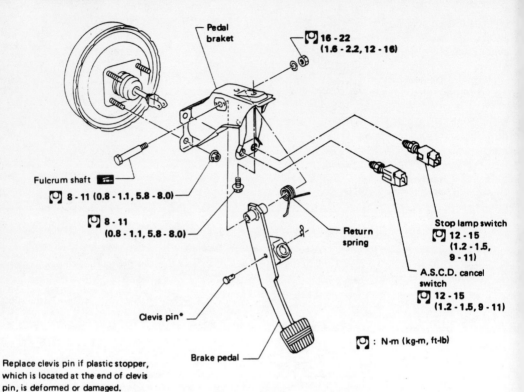

Pedal braket

🔧 16 - 22
(1.6 - 2.2, 12 - 16)

Fulcrum shaft 🔧
🔧 8 - 11 (0.8 - 1.1, 5.8 - 8.0)

🔧 8 - 11
(0.8 - 1.1, 5.8 - 8.0)

Return spring

Stop lamp switch
🔧 12 - 15
(1.2 - 1.5,
9 - 11)

A.S.C.D. cancel switch
🔧 12 - 15
(1.2 - 1.5, 9 - 11)

Clevis pin*

🔧 : N·m (kg-m, ft-lb)

Brake pedal

* Replace clevis pin if plastic stopper,
which is located at the end of clevis
pin, is deformed or damaged.

Brake booster and pedal assembly—1989 240SX

Brake Proportioning Valve

All Datsun/Nissans covered in this guide are equipped with brake proportioning valves of several different types. The valves all do the same job, which is to separate the front and rear brake lines, allowing them to function independently, and preventing the rear brakes from locking before the front brakes. Damage, such as brake line leakage, in either the front or rear brake system will not affect the normal operation of the unaffected system. If, in the event of a panic stop, the rear brakes lock up before the front brakes, it could mean the proportioning valve is defective. In that case, replace the entire proportioning valve.

REMOVAL AND INSTALLATION

NOTE: *Models built in 1985 and later years do not use a separate proportioning valve.*
1. Disconnect and plug the brake lines at the valve.
2. Unscrew the mounting bolt(s) and remove the valve.
NOTE: *Do not disassemble the valve.*
3. Installation is in the reverse order of removal. Bleed the system.

Bleeding

The purpose of bleeding the brakes is to expel air trapped in the hydraulic system. The system must be bled whenever the pedal feels spongy,

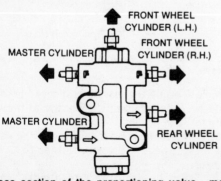

FRONT WHEEL CYLINDER (L.H.)
FRONT WHEEL CYLINDER (R.H.)
MASTER CYLINDER
MASTER CYLINDER
REAR WHEEL CYLINDER

Cross section of the proportioning valve—most models similar

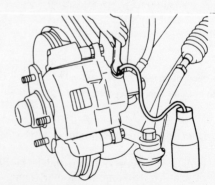

Bleeding the brakes

indicating that air, which is compressible, has entered the system. It must also be bled whenever the system has been opened or repaired. You will need a helper for this job.

Never reuse brake fluid which has been bled from the system.

The sequence for bleeding is right rear, left rear, right front, left front. The usual procedure is to bleed at the points farthest from the master cylinder first.

1. Clean all dirt from around the master cylinder reservoir caps. Remove the caps and fill the master cylinder to the proper level with clean, fresh brake fluid meeting DOT 3 specifications.

NOTE: *Brake fluid picks up moisture from the air, which reduces its effectiveness and causes brake line corrosion. Don't leave the master cylinder or the fluid container open any longer than necessary. Be careful not to spill brake fluid on painted surfaces. Wipe up any spilled fluid immediately and rinse the area with clear water.*

2. Clean all the bleeder screws. You may want to give each one a shot of penetrating solvent to loosen it up. Seizure is a common problem with bleeder screws, which then break off, sometimes requiring replacement of the part to which they are attached.

3. Attach a length of clear vinyl tubing to the bleeder screw on the wheel cylinder. Insert the other end of the tube into a clear, clean jar half filled with brake fluid.

4. Have your helper slowly depress the brake pedal. As this is done, open the bleeder screw ⅓–½ of a turn, and allow the fluid to run through the tube. Close the bleeder screw before the pedal reaches the end of its travel. Have your assistant slowly release the pedal. Repeat this process until no air bubbles appear in the expelled fluid.

NOTE: *Some front drum brakes have two hydraulic cylinders and two bleeder screws. Both cylinders must be bled.*

5. Repeat the procedure on the other three brakes, checking the fluid level in the master cylinder reservoirs often. Do not allow the reservoirs to run dry, or the bleeding process will have to be repeated.

FRONT DISC BRAKES

CAUTION: *Brake shoes contain asbestos, which has been determined to be a cancer causing agent. Never clean the brake surfaces with compressed air! Avoid inhaling any dust from any brake surface! When cleaning brake surfaces, use a commercially available brake cleaning fluid.*

Brake Pads
INSPECTION

You should be able to check the pad lining thickness without removing the pads. Check the Brake Specifications chart at the end of this chapter to find the manufacturer's pad wear limit. However, this measurement may disagree with your state inspection laws. When replacing pads, always check the surface of the rotors for scoring or wear. The rotors should be removed for resurfacing if badly scored.

REMOVAL AND INSTALLATION

NOTE: *All four front brake pads MUST ALWAYS be replaced as a set. If vehicle is equipped with Anti-Lock Brake System it is recommended to return to the dealer for any kind of brake service.*

Types N20, N22, N22A, N32, N34L

1. Raise and support the front of the car or truck. Remove the wheels.
2. Remove the retaining clip from the outboard pad.
3. Remove the pad pins retaining the anti-squeal springs.
4. Remove the pads.
5. To install, open the bleeder screw slightly and push the outer piston into the cylinder until the dust seal groove aligns with the end of the seal retaining ring, then close the bleed screw. Be careful because the piston can be pushed too far, requiring disassembly of the caliper to repair. Install the inner pad.
6. Pull the yoke to push the inner piston into place. Install the outer pad.
7. Lightly coat the areas where the pins touch the pads, and where the pads touch the caliper (at the top) with grease. Do not allow grease to get on the pad friction surfaces.
8. Install the anti-squeal springs and pad pins. Install the clip.
9. Apply the brakes a few times to seat the pads. Check the master cylinder level. Add fluid if necessary. Bleed the brakes if necessary.

Annette Type

1. Raise and support the front of the car. Remove the wheels.
2. Remove the clip, pull out the pins, and remove the pad springs.
3. Remove the pads by pulling them out with pliers.
4. To install, first lightly coat the yoke groove and end surface of the piston with grease. Do not allow grease to contact the pads or rotor.
5. Open the bleeder screw slightly and push the outer piston into the cylinder until its end

aligns with the end of the boot retaining ring. Do not push too far, which will require caliper disassembly to correct. Install the inner pad.

6. Pull the yoke toward the outside of the car to push the inner piston into place. Install the outer pad.

7. Apply the brakes a few times to seat the pads. Check the master cylinder and add fluid if necessary. Bleed the brakes if necessary.

SC Type

1. Raise and support the front of the car. Remove the wheels.

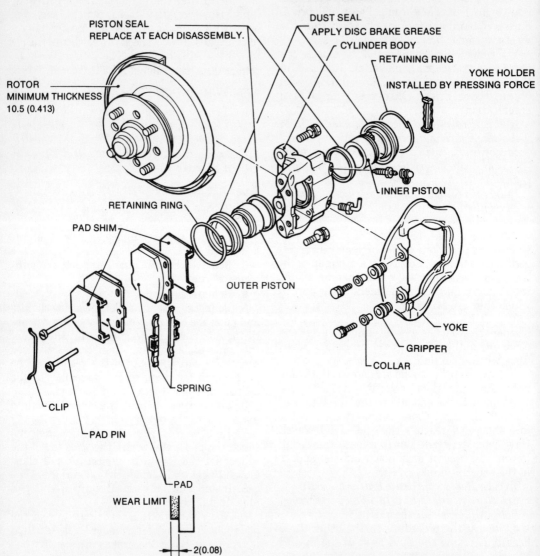

Exploded view of the N22 disc brake assembly—N20, N22A, N32 and N34L similar

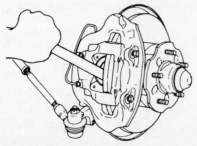

Pushing the inner piston in to install new brake pads (all calipers)

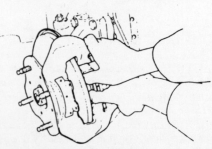

Don't push the piston in too far

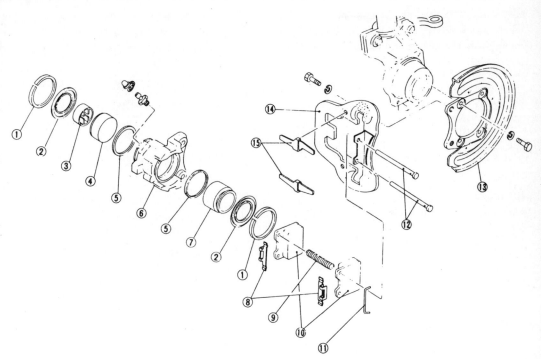

1. Retaining ring
2. Boot
3. Bias ring
4. Piston A (inner piston)
5. Piston seal

6. Cylinder body
7. Piston B (outer piston)
8. Hanger spring
9. Spring
10. Pad

11. Clip
12. Clevis pin
13. Buffle plate
14. Yoke
15. Yoke spring

Exploded view of the Annette disc brake assembly

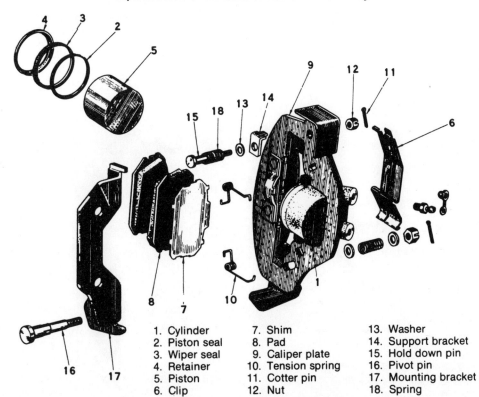

1. Cylinder
2. Piston seal
3. Wiper seal
4. Retainer
5. Piston
6. Clip

7. Shim
8. Pad
9. Caliper plate
10. Tension spring
11. Cotter pin
12. Nut

13. Washer
14. Support bracket
15. Hold down pin
16. Pivot pin
17. Mounting bracket
18. Spring

Exploded view of the SC disc brake assembly

2. Push up on the clip to remove.

3. Insert a small prybar into the back of the pad opposite the piston and move the caliper all the way out.

4. Remove the pads.

5. Open the bleeder screw slightly and press the piston into the caliper.

6. Install the pads, shims, and clips.

7. Apply the brakes a few times to seat the pads. Check the master cylinder level and add fluid if necessary. Bleed the brakes as required.

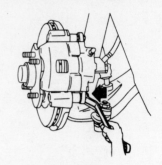

Remove the lower pin bolt

Type CL22V

1. Raise the front of the car and support it with safety stands.

2. Unscrew and remove the lower pin bolt (sub pin).

3. Swing the cylinder body upward and then remove the pad retainer, the inner and outer shims and the pads themselves.

NOTE: *Do not depress the brake pedal when the cylinder body is in the raised position or the piston will pop out.*

4. Clean the piston end of the cylinder body and the pin bolt holes. Be careful not to get oil on the rotor.

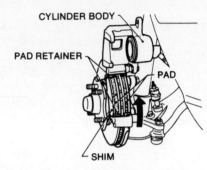

Raise the cylinder body to remove the pads

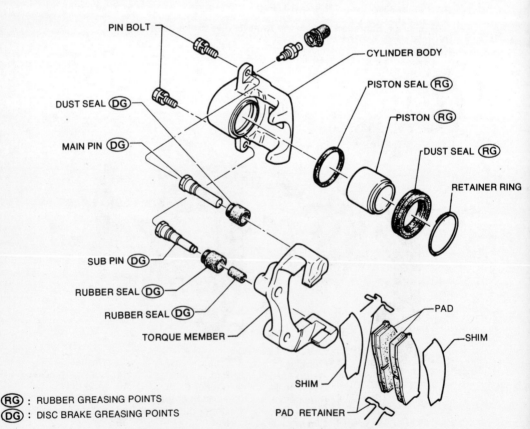

(RG) : RUBBER GREASING POINTS
(DG) : DISC BRAKE GREASING POINTS

Exploded view of the CL22V disc brake assembly

5. Pull the cylinder body to the outer side and install the inner pad.

6. Install the outer pad, the shim and the pad retainer.

7. Reposition the cylinder body and then tighten the pin bolt to 12–15 ft. lbs. (16–21 Nm).

8. Apply the brakes a few times to seat the new pads. Check the fluid level and bleed the brakes as required.

Type AD22V

1. Remove the road wheel.

2. Remove the lower caliper guide pin. See the accompanying illustration.

3. Rotate the brake caliper body upward.

4. Remove the brake pad retainer and the inner and outer pad shims.

5. Remove the brake pads.

NOTE: *Do not depress the brake pedal when*

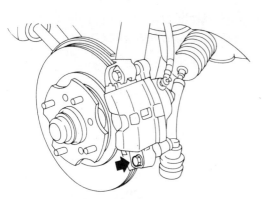

Remove the AD22V guide pin . . .

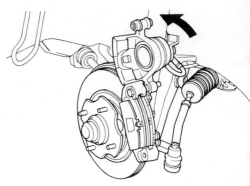

. . . and rotate the caliper up and away from the rotor. Do not apply the brakes with the caliper in this position!

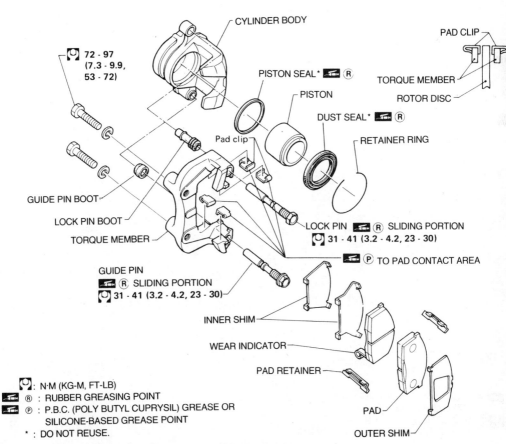

AD22V brake caliper

the caliper body is raised. The brake piston will be forced out of the caliper.

6. Clean the piston end of the caliper body and the pin bolt holes. Be careful not to get oil on the brake rotor.

7. Pull the caliper body to the outer side and install the inner brake pad. Make sure both new pads are kept clean!

8. Install the outer pad, shim and pad retainer.

9. Reposition the caliper body and then tighten the guide pin bolt to 23–30 ft. lbs.

10. Apply the brakes a few times to seat the pads before driving out on the road.

Types CL28VB, CL22VB and CL25VB

1. Raise the vehicle and support it securely. Remove the front wheel. Remove the pin (lower) bolt from the caliper.

2. Swing the caliper body upward on the upper bolt. Remove the pad retainers and inner and outer shims.

NOTE: *Do not depress the brake pedal when the cylinder body is in the raised position or the piston will pop out. Avoid damaging the piston seal when removing/installing the pads and retainers.*

3. Check the level of fluid in the master cyl-inder. If the fluid is near the maximum level, use a clean syringe to remove fluid until the level is down well below the lip of the reservoir. Then, use a large C-clamp to press the caliper piston back into the caliper, to allow room for the installation of the thicker new pads.

4. Install the new pads, utilizing new shims, in reverse order. Torque the lower retaining bolt to 16–23 ft. lbs. Make sure you pump the brakes and get a hard pedal before driving the car!

Brake Calipers

REMOVAL AND INSTALLATION

Refer to Brake Pads Removal and Installation procedure in this Chapter. Remove both guide pins, torque member fixing bolts and brake hose connector. The brake system must be bled refer to the necessary procedure.

OVERHAUL

Types N20, N22, N22A, N32, N34L

1. With the vehicle supported safely and the front wheels off, remove the brake fluid tube from the caliper assembly.

2. Remove the caliper from the knuckle as-

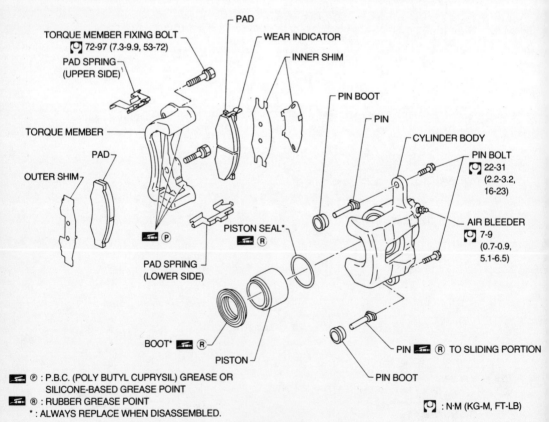

CL28VB caliper

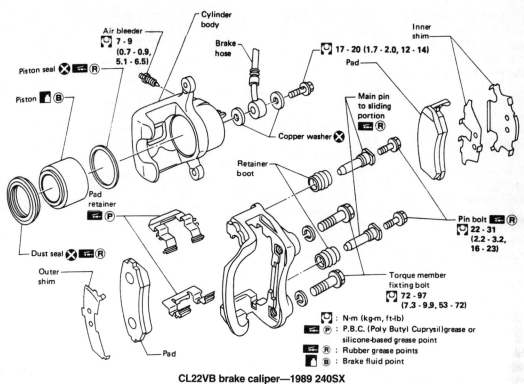

CL22VB brake caliper—1989 240SX

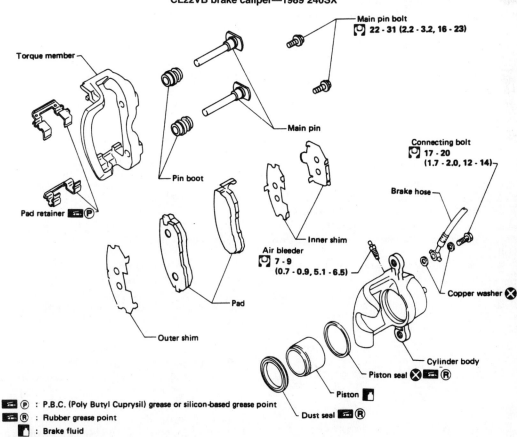

CL25VB brake caliper—1989 Maxima

sembly by removing the mounting bolts, located at the rear of the caliper, and lifting the caliper from the rotor.

3. Remove the pads from the caliper (refer to the pad removal procedure).

4. Remove the gripper pin attaching nuts and separate the yoke from the cylinder body.

5. Remove the yoke holder from the piston and remove the retaining rings and dust seals from the ends of both pistons.

6. Apply air pressure gradually into the fluid chamber of the caliper, to force the pistons from the cylinders.

7. Remove the piston seals.

8. Inspect the components for damage or excessive wear. Replace or repair as needed.

9. To assemble, install the piston seals in the cylinder bore. Lubricate seals and pistons.

10. Slide the A piston into the cylinder, followed by the B piston so that its yoke groove coincides with the yoke groove of the cylinder.

11. Install the dust seal and clamp tightly with the retaining ring.

12. Install the yoke holder on the A piston and install the gripper to yoke.

NOTE: *The use of soapy water will aid in the installation of the gripper pins.*

13. Support the end of B piston and press the yoke into the yoke holder.

14. Install the pads, anti squeal springs, pad pins and retain with the clip.

15. Tighten the gripper pin attaching nuts to 12–15 ft. lbs. and install the caliper on the spindle knuckle. Torque the caliper mounting bolts to 53–72 ft. lbs.

16. Bleed the system, check the fluid level, install the wheels and lower the vehicle.

Annette Type

1. Remove the pads.

2. Disconnect the brake tube.

3. Remove the two bottom strut assembly installation bolts to provide clearance.

4. Remove the caliper assembly mounting bolts.

5. Loosen the bleeder screw and press the pistons into their bores.

6. Clamp the yoke in a vise and tap the yoke

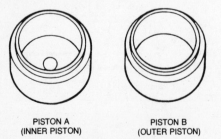

PISTON A
(INNER PISTON)

PISTON B
(OUTER PISTON)

Piston comparison (inner and outer)

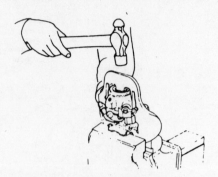

Tapping the yoke head with a hammer

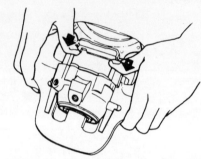

Assembling the yoke and cylinder (Annette type)

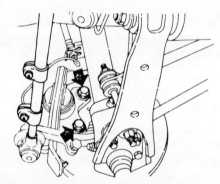

Caliper removal

head with a hammer to loosen the cylinder. Be careful that the primary piston does not fall out.

7. Remove the bias ring from the primary piston. Remove the retaining rings and boots from both pistons. Depress and remove the pistons from the cylinder. Remove the piston seal from the cylinder carefully with the fingers so as not to mar the cylinder wall.

8. Remove the yoke springs from the yoke.

9. Wash all parts with clean brake fluid.

10. If the piston or cylinder is badly worn or scored, replace both. The piston surface is plated and must not be polished with emery paper. Replace all seals. The rotor can be removed and machined if scored, but final thickness must be at least 8.5mm. Runout must not exceed 0.025mm.

11. Lubricate the cylinder bore with clean brake fluid and install the piston seal.

12. Insert the bias ring into primary piston so that the rounded ring portion comes to the bottom of the piston. Primary piston has a small depression inside, while secondary does not.

13. Lubricate the pistons with clean brake fluid and insert into the cylinder. Install the boot and retaining ring. The yoke groove of the bias ring of primary piston must align with the yoke groove of the cylinder.

14. Install the yoke springs to the yoke so the projecting portion faces to the disc (rotor).

15. Lubricate the sliding portion of the cylinder and yoke. Assemble the cylinder and yoke by tapping the yoke lightly.

16. Replace the caliper assembly and pads. Torque the mounting bolts to 33–41 ft. lbs. Rotor bolt torque is 20–27 ft. lbs. Strut bolt torque is 33–44 ft. lbs. Bleed the system of air.

SC Type

1. Remove the brake pads.

2. Disconnect the brake hose.

3. Remove the cotter pins from the hold down and pivot pins. Remove the retaining nuts.

4. Remove the caliper plate from its mounting bracket.

5. Remove the torsion spring and remove the cylinder assembly from the caliper plate.

6. Apply air into the fluid chamber of the caliper and force the piston from the cylinder.

7. Remove the wiper seal and piston seal retainer.

8. Inspect the components for abnormal wear or damage. Repair or replace as necessary.

9. Fit the seal into its groove in the cylinder. Lubricate the seal and piston. Install the piston into the cylinder.

10. Place the caliper plate over the cylinder assembly and install the torsion spring.

11. Install the caliper plate on the mounting bracket and install the nuts and cotter pins.

12. Bled the system and check the reservoir level.

Types CL22V and AD2V

1. Disconnect and plug the brake line.

2. Unscrew the two mounting bolts and remove the caliper.

3. Remove the main pin and the sub pin and then separate the cylinder body from the torque member.

4. Remove the piston dust cover.

5. Apply compressed air gradually to the fluid chamber until the piston pops out.

6. Carefully pry out the piston seal.

7. Inspect the components for damage or excessive wear. Replace or repair as necessary.

8. Install the piston seal in the cylinder bore. Lubricate the seals and pistons.

9. Fit the dust seal onto the piston, insert the dust seal into the groove on the cylinder body and then install the piston.

10. Place the cylinder body and torque member together, grease the main and sub pins, install the pins and tighten them to 12–15 ft. lbs. (16–21 Nm) on the CL22V, and 23–30 ft. lbs. on the AD22V.

11. Install the caliper and tighten the mounting bolts to 36–51 ft. lbs. (49–69 Nm) on the CL22V, and 53–72 ft. lbs. on the AD22V. Reconnect the brake line and install the wheels.

12. Bleed the system, check the fluid level and lower the vehicle.

Types CL28VB, CL22VB and CL25VB

1. Remove the brake pads as described above. Disconnect the brake hose and plug the open end of the hose. Remove the two caliper mounting bolts and remove the caliper.

2. Place a wooden block between the caliper piston and the pad retainer opposite it. Then, gently apply compressed air to the brake hose connection. This will remove the piston and dust seal. Note the direction in which the piston seal is installed.

3. Clean all parts in clean brake fluid. Inspect the inner cylinder bore for rust, scoring, or mechanical wear. Remove minor imperfections with emery paper. Replace the caliper body if these imperfections cannot be removed. Inspect the piston for such imperfections. If they exist, it must be replaced, as the surface is polished!

4. Inspect the lockpins, bolts, piston seal, bushings, and pin seals for damage and replace all parts as necessary.

5. Insert the piston seal into the groove on the caliper body. Install the inner edge of the rubber boot into the piston groove and then install the piston. Work the edge of the rubber boot into the groove in the caliper body.

6. Perform the remaining procedures in the reverse of removal. Torque the caliper mounting pins to 53–72 ft. lbs. Refill the system with clean brake fluid and bleed it thoroughly. Make sure you pump the brakes and get a hard pedal before operating the car.

Brake Disc (Rotor)
REMOVAL AND INSTALLATION

NOTE: *On front wheel drive vehicles just remove the brake caliper assembly.*

1. Raise and support the front of the vehicle safely and remove the wheels.

2. Remove brake caliper assembly and wheel hub assembly. Refer to the necessary proce-

dures in Chapter 8. Make sure not to twist the brake hose.

3. Remove the brake disc/wheel hub from the vehicle.

4. Installation is the reverse of removal. Adjust the wheel bearings.

INSPECTION

Check the brake rotor for roughness, cracks or chips. The rotor can be machined on a brake lathe most auto parts stores have complete machine shop service. The rotors should be machined or replaced during every front disc brake pad replacement.

REAR DISC BRAKES

CAUTION: *Brake shoes contain asbestos, which has been determined to be a cancer causing agent. Never clean the brake surfaces with compressed air! Avoid inhaling any dust from any brake surface! When cleaning brake surfaces, use a commercially available brake cleaning fluid.*

Brake Pads

REMOVAL AND INSTALLATION

Type AN12H

1. Raise and support the rear of the car. Remove the wheels.

2. Remove the clip at the outside of the pad pins.

3. Remove the pad pins. Hold the anti-squeal springs in place with your finger.

4. Remove the pads.

5. To install, first clean the end of the piston with clean brake fluid.

6. Lightly coat the caliper-to-pad, the yoke-to-pad, retaining pin-to-pad, and retaining pin-to-bracket surfaces with grease. Do not allow grease to get on the rotor or pad surfaces.

7. Push the piston into place with a screwdriver by pushing in on the piston while at the same time turning it clockwise into the bore. Then, with a lever between the rotor and yoke, push the yoke over until the clearance to install the pads is equal.

8. Install the shims and pads, anti-squeal springs and pins. Install the clip. Note that the inner pad has a tab which must fit into the piston notch. Therefore, be sure that the piston notch is centered to allow proper pad installation.

9. Apply the brake a few times to center the pads. Check the master cylinder fluid level and add if necessary.

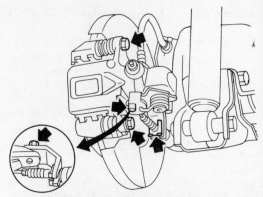

On the 200SX, remove the parking brake cable stay fixing bolt, pin bolts and lock spring before removing the pads and shims. 1984 model shown

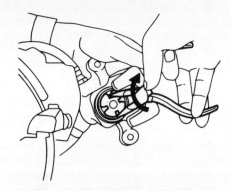

Use needle-nosed pliers to retract the piston

Types CL11H and CL9H

1. Raise the rear of the car and support it with safety stands. Remove the brake pads.

2. Remove the pin bolts and lift off the caliper body.

3. Pull out the pad springs and then remove the pads and their shims.

4. Clean the piston end of the caliper body and the area around the pin holes. Be careful not to get oil on the rotor.

5. Using a pair of needle nosed pliers, carefully turn the piston clockwise back into the caliper body. Take care not to damage the piston boot.

6. Coat the pad contact area on the mounting support with a silicone based grease.

7. Install the pads, shims and the pad springs.

Remove the parking brake cable mounting brace bolt (CL11H caliper)

1. Yoke
2. Yoke spring
3. Clip
4. Pad pin
5. Anti-squeal spring
6. Pad
7. Retaining ring
8. Dust seal
9. Outer piston
10. Oil seal
11. Adjusting nut
12. Bearing
13. Spacer
14. Wave washer
15. Snap ring B
16. Piston seal
17. Cylinder body
18. Retainer
19. Snap ring A
20. Spring cover
21. Spring
22. Spring seat
23. Snap ring C
24. Key plate
25. Push rod
26. O-ring
27. Strut
28. Inner piston
29. Cam
30. Toggle lever
31. Spring
32. Washer
33. Nut

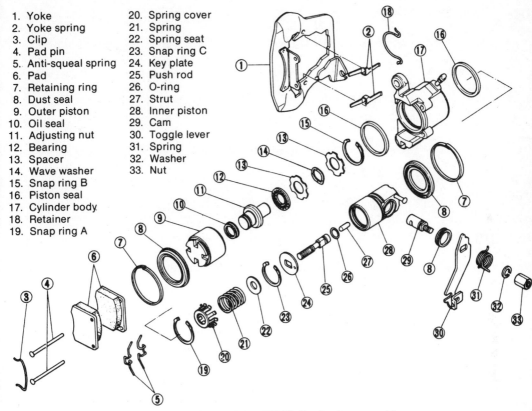

Exploded view of the AN12H disc brake assembly

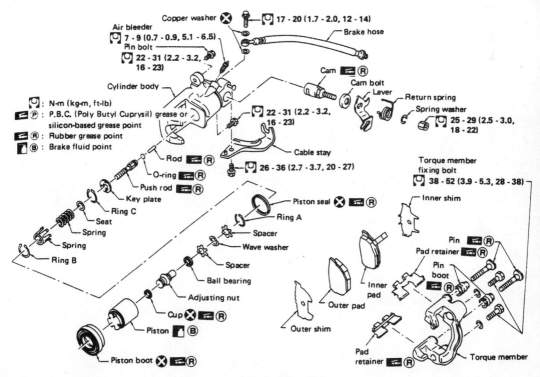

CL11HB brake caliper

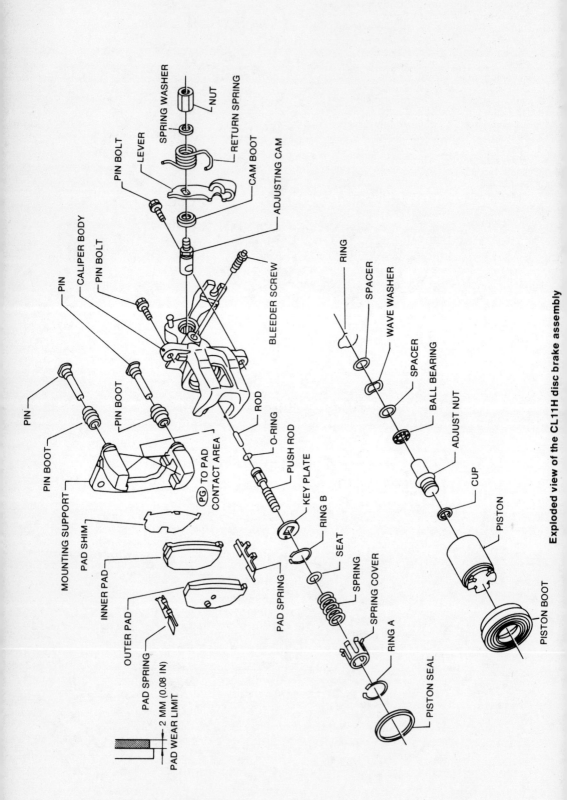

SPRING WASHER

NUT

RETURN SPRING

PIN BOLT

LEVER

CAM BOOT

ADJUSTING CAM

CALIPER BODY

PIN BOLT

PIN

BLEEDER SCREW

PIN

RING

SPACER

WAVE WASHER

PIN BOOT

SPACER

PIN

BALL BEARING

PIN BOOT

ROD

ADJUST NUT

O-RING

MOUNTING SUPPORT

PUSH ROD

(PG) TO PAD
CONTACT AREA

CUP

PAD SHIM

KEY PLATE

INNER PAD

RING B

PISTON

SEAT

SPRING

OUTER PAD

PAD SPRING

SPRING COVER

PISTON BOOT

PAD SPRING

RING A

2 MM (0.08 IN)

PAD WEAR LIMIT

PISTON SEAL

Exploded view of the CL11H disc brake assembly

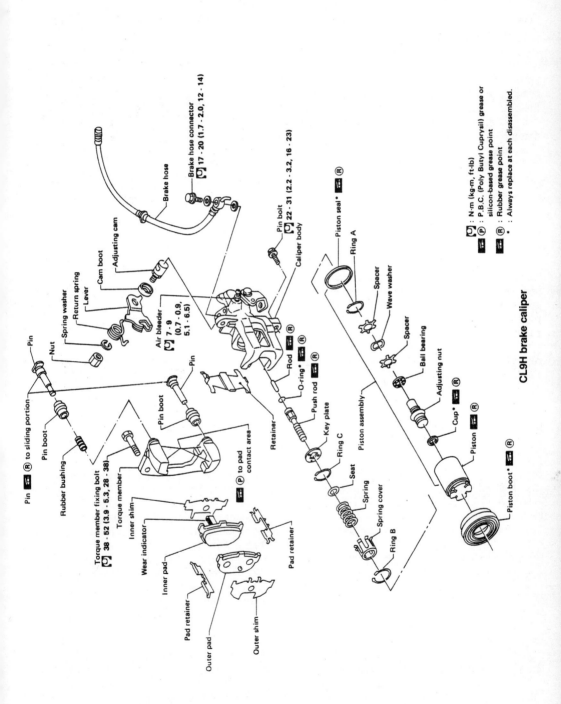

CL9H brake caliper

Pin [R] to sliding portion

Pin

Nut

Pin boot

Rubber bushing

Torque member fixing bolt
[T] 38 - 52 (3.9 - 5.3, 28 - 38)

Torque member

Inner shim

Wear indicator

Inner pad

Pad retainer

Outer pad

Outer shim

Pad retainer

Pin boot

Pin

Spring washer

Return spring

Lever

Cam boot

Adjusting cam

Nut

Brake hose

Brake hose connector
[T] 17 - 20 (1.7 - 2.0, 12 - 14)

Pin bolt

[P] to pad contact area

Air bleeder
[T] 7 - 9
(0.7 - 0.9,
5.1 - 6.5)

Rod [R]

O-ring* [R]

Push rod

Key plate

Retainer

Ring C

Seat

Spring

Spring cover

Ring B

Caliper body

[T] 22 - 31 (2.2 - 3.2, 16 - 23)

Piston seal* [R]

Ring A

Spacer

Wave washer

Spacer

Ball bearing

Adjusting nut

Piston assembly

Cup* [R]

Piston

Piston boot* [R]

[T] : N·m (kg-m, ft-lb)
[P] : P.B.C. (Poly Butyl Cuprysil) grease or
silicon-based grease point
[R] : Rubber grease point
* : Always replace at each disassembled.

NOTE: *Always use new shims.*

8. Position the caliper body in the mounting support and tighten the pin bolts to 16–23 ft. lbs. (22–31 Nm.).

9. Replace the wheel, lower the car and bleed the system.

Types CL11HB and CL14B

1. Raise the vehicle and support it securely. Remove the rear wheel.

2. Remove the two pin bolts and the lock spring. Remove the caliper, suspending it above the disc so as to avoid putting any strain on the hose.

3. Remove the pad retainers, pads, and shims.

NOTE: *Do not depress the brake pedal when the cylinder body is in the raised position or the piston will pop out. Avoid damaging the piston seal when removing/installing the pads and retainers.*

4. Check the level of fluid in the master cylinder. If the fluid is near the maximum level, use a clean syringe to remove fluid until the level is down well below the lip of the reservoir. Then, press the caliper piston back into the caliper by turning it clockwise (it has a helical groove on the outer diameter). This will allow room for the installation of the thicker new pads.

5. Install the new pads using new shims in reverse order of the removal procedure. Torque the caliper pin bolts to 16–23 ft. lbs. Make sure you pump the brakes and get a hard pedal before driving the car!

Brake Caliper

REMOVAL INSTALLATION AND OVERHAUL

Type AN12H

1. Disconnect the brake hose from the caliper. Plug the hose and caliper to prevent fluid loss.

2. Disconnect the parking brake cable.

3. Remove the mounting bolts and remove the caliper from the suspension arm.

4. Remove the pads.

5. Stand the caliper assembly on end, large end down, and push on the caliper to separate it from the yoke.

6. Remove the retaining rings and dust seals from both pistons.

7. Push in on the outer piston to force out the piston assembly. Remove the piston seals.

8. Remove the yoke spring from the yoke.

9. Disengage the piston assembly by turning the outer piston counterclockwise.

10. Disassemble the outer piston by removing the snap ring.

11. Disassemble the inner piston by removing

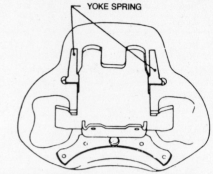

Yoke showing the yoke springs—AN12H

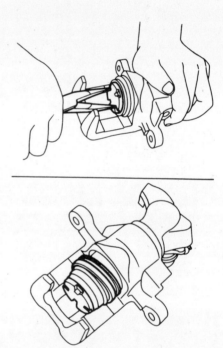

Turn the piston counterclockwise to remove it from the caliper body

the snap ring. This will allow the spring cover, spring, and spring seat to come out. Remove the inner snap ring to remove the key plate, push rod, and strut.

12. To install, assemble the pistons in reverse order of disassembly. Apply a thin coat of grease to the groove in the push rod, its O-ring, the strut ends, oil seal, piston seal, and the inside of the dust seal.

13. Install the piston seals. Apply a thin coat of grease to the sliding surfaces of the piston and caliper bore. Install the pistons into the caliper. Install the retainers onto the dust seals.

14. Install the yoke springs on the yoke.

15. Lightly coat the yoke and caliper body contact surfaces, and the pad pin hole, with silicone grease. Assemble the yoke to the caliper.

16. Install the pads.

17. Install the caliper to the suspension arm (28–38 ft. lbs.). Connect the parking brake cable. Connect the brake hose. Apply the brakes a few times to center the pads. Bleed the system.

Types CL11H, CL11HB, CL14B and CL9H

1. See the appropriate procedure and remove the brake pads.

2. Unscrew the mounting bolts and remove the caliper assembly.

3. Remove the pin bolts and separate the caliper body from the mounting support.

4. Using needle nosed pliers, turn the piston counterclockwise and remove it.

5. Pry out the ring from inside the piston. You can now remove the adjusting nut, the ball bearing, the wave washer and the spacers.

6. Installation is in the reverse order of removal. Tighten the caliper mounting bolts to 28–38 ft. lbs. (38–52 Nm.).

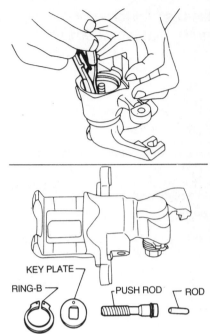

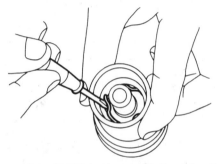

Prying off the CL11H ring from inside the piston. Some rings may be the snap-ring type

Remove the ring "B" with snap-ring pliers, then remove the key plate, push rod and rod

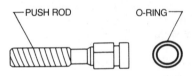

Remove the O-ring from the push rod. Replace the O-ring during installation

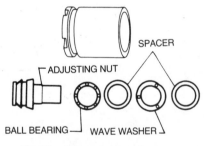

Various CL11H caliper components

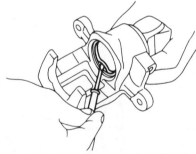

Carefully remove the oil seal, and replace it during assembly

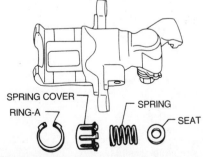

After removing the ring, remove the spring cover, spring and seat

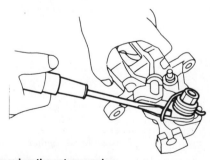

Removing the return spring

Brake Disc (Rotor)
REMOVAL AND INSTALLATION

NOTE: *On front wheel drive vehicles remove the brake caliper assembly and wheel hub assembly. Refer to the necessary procedures in Chapter 8.*

1. Raise and support the rear of the vehicle safely and remove the wheels.
2. Remove brake caliper assembly. Refer to the necessary procedure. Make sure not to twist the brake hose.
3. Remove the brake disc from the vehicle.
4. Installation is the reverse of removal.

INSPECTION

Check the brake rotor for roughness, cracks or chips. The rotor can be machined on a brake lathe most auto parts stores have complete machine shop service. The rotors should be machined or replaced during every rear disc brake pad replacement.

REAR DRUM BRAKES

CAUTION: *Brake shoes contain asbestos, which has been determined to be a cancer causing agent. Never clean the brake surfaces with compressed air! Avoid inhaling any dust from any brake surface! When cleaning* brake surfaces, use a commercially available brake cleaning fluid.

Brake Drums
REMOVAL AND INSTALLATION

1. Raises the rear of the vehicle and support it on jack stands.
2. Remove the wheels.
3. Release the parking brake.
4. Pull off the brake drums. On some models there are two threaded service holes in each brake drum. If the drum will not come off, fit two correct size bolts in the service holes and screw them in: this will force the drum away from the axle.
5. If the drum cannot be easily removed, back off the brake adjustment.
NOTE: *Never depress the brake pedal while the brake drum is removed.*
6. Installation is the reverse of removal.

INSPECTION

After removing the brake drum, wipe out the accumulated dust with a damp cloth.
CAUTION: *Do not blow the brake dust out of the drums with compressed air or lung power. Brake linings contain asbestos, a known cancer causing substance. Dispose of the cloth after use.*
Inspect the drum for cracks, deep grooves,

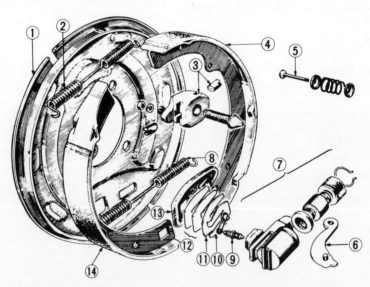

1. Brake disc	8. Return spring cylinder side
2. Return spring adjuster side	9. Bleeder
3. Brake shoe adjuster	10. Lock plate A
4. Brake shoe assembly-fore	11. Lock plate B
5. Anti-rattler pin	12. Lock plate C and D
6. Lever	13. Dust cover
7. Rear wheel cylinder.	14. Brake shoe assembly-after

Exploded view of the rear drum brake—610, 710

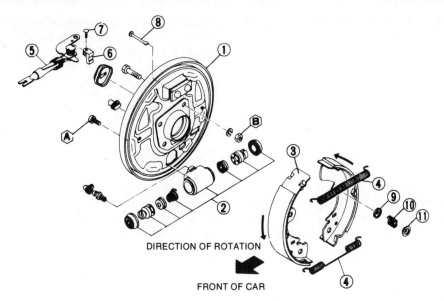

DIRECTION OF ROTATION

FRONT OF CAR

1. Brake disc
2. Wheel cylinder assembly
3. Brake shoe assembly
4. Return spring
5. Adjuster assembly
6. Stopper
7. Stopper pin
8. Anti-rattle pin
9. Spring seat
10. Anti-rattle spring
11. Retainer

Exploded view of the rear drum brake—510; 810 and 200SX similar

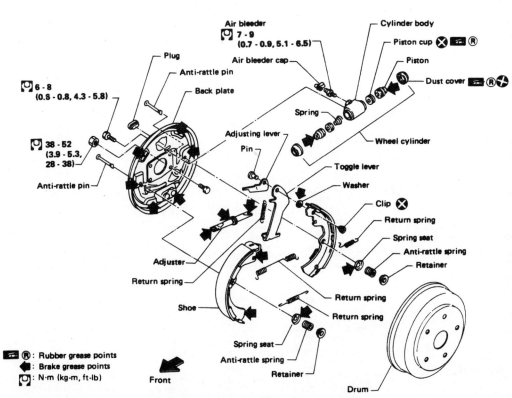

Air bleeder
7 - 9
(0.7 - 0.9, 5.1 - 6.5)

Cylinder body

Piston cup

Plug

Air bleeder cap

Piston

Anti-rattle pin

Dust cover

6 - 8
(0.8 - 0.8, 4.3 - 5.8)

Back plate

Spring

Wheel cylinder

38 - 52
(3.9 - 5.3,
28 - 38)

Adjusting lever

Pin

Toggle lever

Anti-rattle pin

Washer

Clip

Return spring

Spring seat

Anti-rattle spring

Adjuster

Retainer

Return spring

Return spring

Shoe

Return spring

Spring seat

: Rubber grease points
: Brake grease points
: N·m (kg-m, ft-lb)

Front

Anti-rattle spring

Retainer

Drum

Rear drum brakes (LT23B type)—1989 Maxima

roughness, scoring, or out-of-roundness. Replace any brake drum which is cracked.

Smooth any slight scores by polishing the friction surface with the fine emery cloth or have the drum machined (trued) at a machine shop. Heavy or extensive scoring will cause excessive brake lining wear and should be removed from the brake drum through resurfacing.

Brake Shoes

REMOVAL AND INSTALLATION

1. Raise the vehicle and remove the wheels.
2. Release the parking brake. Disconnect the cross rod from the lever of the brake cylinder. Remove the brake drum. Place a heavy rubber band around the cylinder to prevent the piston from coming out.
3. Remove the return springs and shoes.
4. Clean the backing plate and check the wheel cylinder for leaks. To remove the wheel cylinder, remove the brake line, dust cover, se-

curing nuts or plates and adjusting shims. Clearance between the cylinder and the piston should not exceed 0.015mm.

5. The drums must be machined if scored or out of round more than 0.05mm. The drum inside diameter should not be machined beyond 229.5mm. Minimum safe lining thickness is 1.5mm.
6. Hook the return springs into the new shoes. The springs should be between the shoes and the backing plate. The longer return spring must be adjacent to the wheel cylinder. A very thin film of grease may be applied to the pivot points at the ends of the brake shoes. Grease the shoe locating buttons on the backing plate, also. Be careful not to get grease on the linings or drums.
7. Place one shoe in the adjuster and piston slots, and pry the other shoe into position.
8. Replace the drums and wheels. Adjust the brakes. Bleed the hydraulic system of air if the brake lines were disconnected.
9. Reconnect the handbrake, making sure

Brake Specifications

All measurements given are in inches unless noted

Model	Year	Lug Nut Torque (ft. lbs.)	Master Cylinder Bore	Brake Disc ●		Drum		Minimum Lining Thickness ●	
				Minimum Thickness	Maximum Run-Out	Diameter	Max. Wear Limit	Front	Rear
510	1978–81	58–72	0.8125	0.331	0.0047	9.000	9.060	0.080	0.059
610	1973–74	58–65	0.750	0.331	0.0048	9.000	9.055	0.039	0.059
	1975	58–65	0.750	0.331	0.0048	9.000	9.055	0.063	0.059
	1976–77	58–65	0.750	0.331	0.0048	9.000	9.055	0.079	0.059
710	1974–75	58–65	0.750	0.331	0.0047	9.000	9.055	0.039	0.059
	1976–77	58–65	0.750	0.331	0.0047	9.000	9.055	0.079	0.059
810	1977–80	58–72	0.8125	0.413	0.0059	9.000	9.060	0.080	0.059
	1981–84	58–72	0.8125	0.630/ 0.339	0.0059/① 0.0059	9.000	9.060	0.079/ 0.079	0.059
200SX	1977–79	58–65	0.750	0.331	0.0047	9.000	9.060	0.059	0.059
	1980–83	58–72	0.8750	0.413/ 0.339	0.0047/ 0.0059	—	—	0.079	0.079
	1984	58–72	0.938	0.630/ 0.354	0.0028/ 0.0028	—	9.060	—	—
	1985–88	58–72	0.9375	0.630 ②		—	—	0.08	0.08
Maxima	1985–89	58–72 ④	1.0	0.787 ③	0.0028	⑤	⑥	0.079	0.079
240SX	1989	④	.875	0.709 ⑦	0.0028	—	—	0.079	0.079

—Not Applicable
● Second figure is for rear disc
NOTE: Minimum lining thickness is as recommended by the manufacturer. Due to variation in state inspection regulations, the minimum allowable thickness may be different than recommended by the manufacturer. If 200SX is equipped with VG30 engine refer to Maxima specifications.
① 0.0028 in. on 1983 and later, on front and rear
② Rear disc—Min. thickness—0.354; Runout—0.0028
③ Rear disc—Min. thickness—0.354
④ 1986–87 Maxima 72–87 ft. lbs.
⑤ 9.00—1989 Maxima
⑥ 9.06—1989 Maxima
⑦ Rear disc—min. thickness—0.315; runout—0.0028

that it does not cause the shoes to drag when it is released.

Wheel Cylinder

REMOVAL INSTALLATION AND OVERHAUL

NOTE: *Datsun/Nissan obtains parts from two manufacturers: Nabco and Tokico. Parts are not interchangeable. The name of the manufacturer is usually on the wheel cylinder.*

1. Remove the wheel cylinder from the backing plate.

2. Remove the dust boot and take out the piston. Discard the piston cup. The dust boot can be reused, if necessary, but it is better to replace it.

3. Wash all of the components in clean brake fluid.

4. Inspect the piston and piston bore. Re-place any components which are severely corroded, scored, or worn. The piston and piston bore can be polished lightly with crocus cloth.

5. Wash the wheel cylinder and piston thoroughly in clean brake fluid, allowing them to remain lubricated for assembly.

6. Coat all of the new components to be installed in the wheel cylinder with clean brake fluid prior to assembly.

7. Assemble the wheel cylinder and install it in the reverse order of removal. Assemble the remaining components and bleed the brake hydraulic system.

PARKING BRAKE

ADJUSTMENT

Handbrake adjustments are generally not needed, unless the cables have stretched.

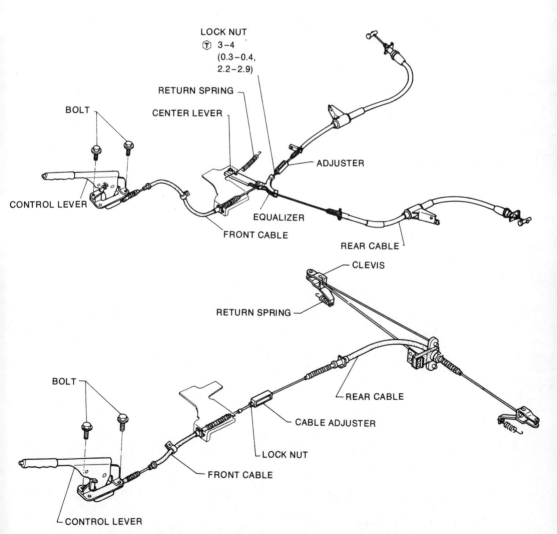

Two types of parking brake cable routing—most models similar

All Models

There is an adjusting nut on the cable under the car, usually at the end of the front cable and near the point at which the two cables from the rear wheels come together (the equalizer). Some models also have a turnbuckle in the rear cable to compensate for cable stretching.

1. Adjust the rear brakes with the parking brake fully released.

2. Apply the hand brake lever so that it is approximately 3–3¼" from its fully released position.

3. Adjust the parking brake turnbuckle, locknuts, or equalizer so that the rear brakes are locked.

4. Release the parking brake. The wheels should turn freely. If not, loosen the parking brake adjuster until the wheels turn with no drag.

Body
10

EXTERIOR

Doors

REMOVAL AND INSTALLATION

Front and Rear

1. Place a jack or stand beneath the door to support its weight.
NOTE: *Place a rag between the lower edge of the door and jack or stand to prevent damage to painted surface.*
2. Remove door without hinge.
3. Remove the door hinge.
4. Installation is in the reverse order of removal.
NOTE: *When installing hinge, coat the*

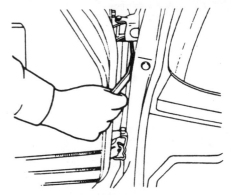

Using special tool to adjust hinge

hinge link with recommended multipurpose grease.

ADJUSTMENT

Front and Rear

Proper door alignment can be obtained by adjusting the door hinge and door lock striker. The door hinge and striker can be moved up and down fore and aft in enlarged holes by loosening the attaching bolts.
NOTE: *The door should be adjusted for an even and parallel fit for the door opening and surrounding body panels.*

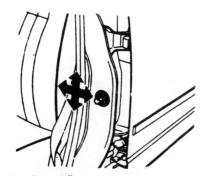

Adjusting door striker

Hood

REMOVAL AND INSTALLATION

1. Open the hood and protect the body with covers to protect the painted surfaces.
2. Mark the hood hinge locations on the hood for proper reinstallation.
3. Holding both sides of the hood, unscrew the bolts securing the hinge to the hood. This operation requires a helper.
4. Installation is the reverse of removal.

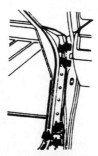

Removing mounting bolts from door

ALIGNMENT

The hood can be adjusted with bolts attaching the hood to the hood hinges, hood lock mechanism and hood bumpers. Adjust the hood for an even fit between the front fenders.

1. Adjust the hood fore and aft by loosening the bolts attaching the hood to the hinge and repositioning hood.

2. Loosen the hood bumper lock nuts and lower bumpers until they do not contact the front of the hood when the hood is closed.

3. Set the striker at the center of the hood

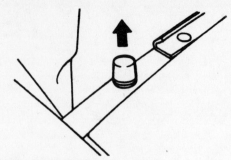

Adjusting hood at bumper rubber

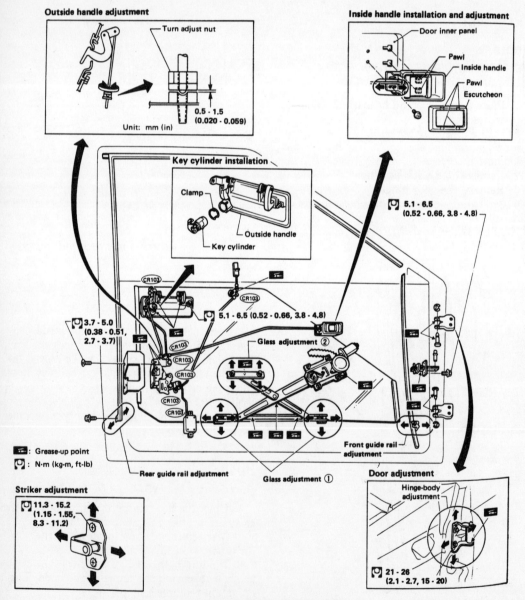

Front door assembly—1988 200SX

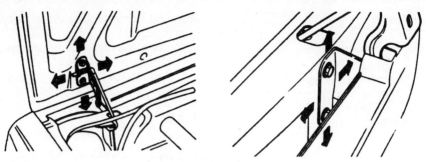

Adjusting hood at hinges

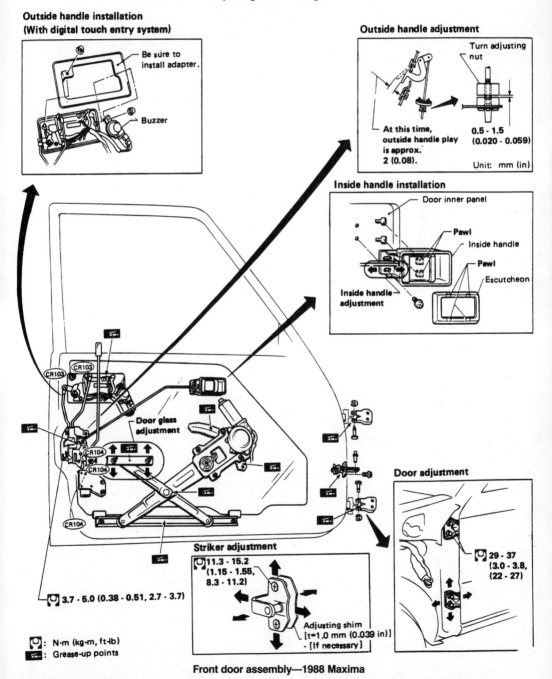

**Outside handle installation
(With digital touch entry system)**

- Be sure to install adapter.
- Buzzer

Outside handle adjustment

Turn adjusting nut

At this time, outside handle play is approx. 2 (0.08).

0.5 - 1.5 (0.020 - 0.059)

Unit: mm (in)

Inside handle installation

- Door inner panel
- Pawl
- Inside handle
- Pawl
- Escutcheon
- Inside handle adjustment

Door glass adjustment

CR103
CR103
CR104
CR104
CR104

Door adjustment

29 - 37 (3.0 - 3.8, (22 - 27)

3.7 - 5.0 (0.38 - 0.51, 2.7 - 3.7)

Striker adjustment

11.3 - 15.2 (1.15 - 1.55, 8.3 - 11.2)

Adjusting shim [t=1.0 mm (0.039 in)] - [If necessary]

: N·m (kg-m, ft-lb)
: Grease-up points

Front door assembly—1988 Maxima

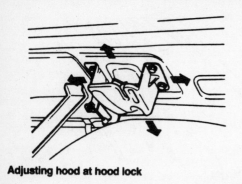

Adjusting hood at hood lock

lock, and tighten the hood lock securing bolts temporarily.

4. Raise the two hood bumpers until the hood is flush with the fenders.

5. Tighten the hood lock securing bolts after the proper adjustment has been obtained.

Trunklid

REMOVAL AND INSTALLATION

1. Open the trunk lid and position a cloth or cushion to protect the painted areas.

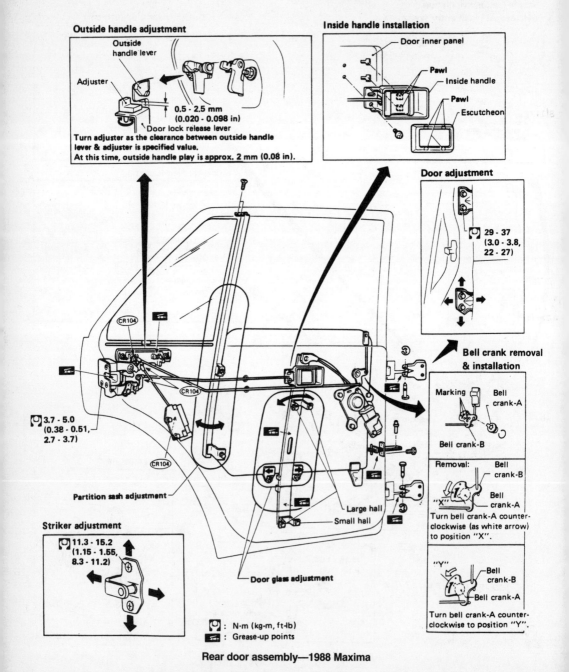

Outside handle adjustment

Outside handle lever

Adjuster

0.5 - 2.5 mm (0.020 - 0.098 in)

Door lock release lever

Turn adjuster as the clearance between outside handle lever & adjuster is specified value.
At this time, outside handle play is approx. 2 mm (0.08 in).

Inside handle installation

Door inner panel

Pawl

Inside handle

Pawl

Escutcheon

Door adjustment

29 - 37 (3.0 - 3.8, 22 - 27)

CR104

CR104

3.7 - 5.0 (0.38 - 0.51, 2.7 - 3.7)

CR104

Partition sash adjustment

Bell crank removal & installation

Marking — Bell crank-A

Bell crank-B

Removal: Bell crank-B

"X"

Bell crank-A

Turn bell crank-A counter-clockwise (as white arrow) to position "X".

"Y"

Bell crank-B

Bell crank-A

Turn bell crank-A counter-clockwise to position "Y".

Striker adjustment

11.3 - 15.2 (1.15 - 1.55, 8.3 - 11.2)

Large hall

Small hall

Door glass adjustment

N·m (kg-m, ft-lb)

Grease-up points

Rear door assembly—1988 Maxima

2. Mark the trunk lid hinge locations or trunk lid for proper reinstallation.

3. Support the trunk lid by hand and remove the bolts attaching the trunk lid to the hinge. Then remove the trunk lid.

4. Installation is the reverse of removal.

ALIGNMENT

1. Loosen the trunk lid hinge attaching bolts until they are just loose enough to move the trunk lid.

2. Move the trunk lid for and aft to obtain a flush fit between the trunk lid and the rear fender.

3. To obtain a snug fit between the trunk lid and weatherstrip, loosen the trunk lid lock striker attaching bolts enough to move the lid, working the striker up and down and from side to side as required.

4. After the adjustment is made tighten the striker bolts securely.

Hatchback or Tailgate Lid
REMOVAL AND INSTALLATION

1. Open the lid and disconnect the rear defogger harness if so equipped.

2. Mark the hinge locations on the lid for proper relocation.

3. Position rags between the roof and the upper end of the lid to prevent scratching the paint.

4. Support the lid and remove the support bolts the the hinge retaining bolts and remove the lid.

5. Installation is the reverse of removal.

NOTE: *Be careful not to scratch the lift support rods. A scratched rod may cause oil or gas leakaged*

ALIGNMENT

1. Open the hatchback lid.

2. Loosen the lid hinge to body attaching

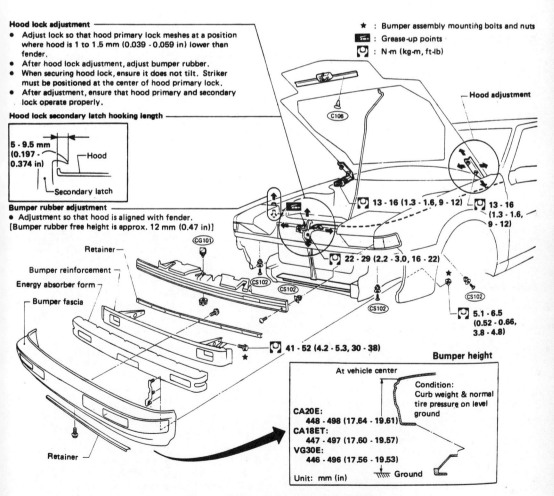

Hood lock adjustment
- Adjust lock so that hood primary lock meshes at a position where hood is 1 to 1.5 mm (0.039 - 0.059 in) lower than fender.
- After hood lock adjustment, adjust bumper rubber.
- When securing hood lock, ensure it does not tilt. Striker must be positioned at the center of hood primary lock.
- After adjustment, ensure that hood primary and secondary lock operate properly.

Hood lock secondary latch hooking length

5 - 9.5 mm (0.197 - 0.374 in) — Hood
— Secondary latch

Bumper rubber adjustment
- Adjustment so that hood is aligned with fender. [Bumper rubber free height is approx. 12 mm (0.47 in)]

★ : Bumper assembly mounting bolts and nuts
: Grease-up points
: N·m (kg-m, ft-lb)

— Hood adjustment

13 - 16 (1.3 - 1.6, 9 - 12)

13 - 16 (1.3 - 1.6, 9 - 12)

22 - 29 (2.2 - 3.0, 16 - 22)

5.1 - 6.5 (0.52 - 0.66, 3.8 - 4.8)

Retainer
Bumper reinforcement
Energy absorber form
Bumper fascia

41 - 52 (4.2 - 5.3, 30 - 38)

Retainer

Bumper height

At vehicle center

Condition:
Curb weight & normal tire pressure on level ground

CA20E:
448 - 498 (17.64 - 19.61)
CA18ET:
447 - 497 (17.60 - 19.57)
VG30E:
446 - 496 (17.56 - 19.53)

Unit: mm (in)   Ground

Body front end assembly—1988 200SX

bolts until they are just loose enough to move the lid.

3. Move the lid up and down to obtain a flush fit between the lid and the roof.

4. After adjustment is completed tighten the hinge attaching bolts securely.

Bumpers

REMOVAL AND INSTALLATION

Front and Rear

NOTE: *Refer to the exploded view of Body Front and Rear End Assembly.*

1. Disconnect all electrical connectors at bumper assembly if so equipped.

2. Remove bumper mounting bolts and bumper assembly.

3. Remove shock absorbers from bumper.
CAUTION: *The shock absorber is filled with a high pressure gas and should not be diassembled, drilled or exposed to an open flame.*

4. Install shock absorbers and bumper in reverse order of removal.

Grille

REMOVAL AND INSTALLATION

1. Remove radiator grille bracket bolts.
NOTE: Refer to the exploded view of Body

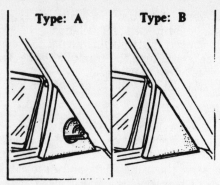

Two types of door corner finisher panels

Front End Assembly. The radiator grille assembly is made of plastic, thus never use excessive force to remove it.

2. *Remove radiator grille from the vehicle.*
3. To install reverse the removal procedures.

Outside Mirrors

REMOVAL AND INSTALLATION

Manual

1. Remove control knob handle.
2. Remove door corner finisher panel.
3. Remove mirror body attaching screws, and then remove mirror body

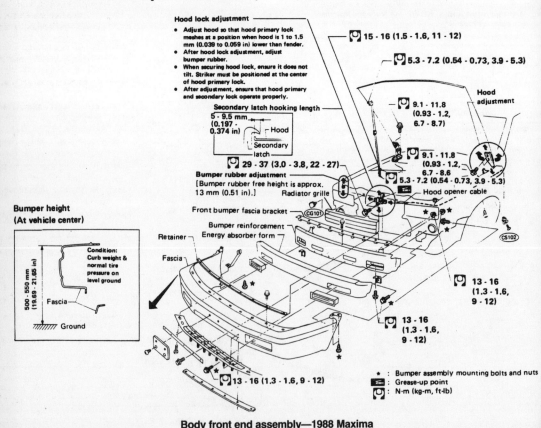

Body front end assembly—1988 Maxima

EASY
STEP-BY-STEP
TIPS FROM PROS

CHILTON'S
AUTO BODY
REPAIR TIPS

Tools and Materials • Step-by-Step Illustrated Procedures
How To Repair Dents, Scratches and Rust Holes
Spray Painting and Refinishing Tips

With a little practice, basic body repair procedures can be mastered by any do-it-yourself mechanic. The step-by-step repairs shown here can be applied to almost any type of auto body repair.

TOOLS & MATERIALS

You may already have basic tools, such as hammers and electric drills. Other tools unique to body repair — body hammers, grinding attachments, sanding blocks, dent puller, half-round plastic file and plastic spreaders — are relatively inexpensive and can be obtained wherever auto parts or auto body repair parts are sold. Portable air compressors and paint spray guns can be purchased or rented.

Auto Body Repair Kits

The best and most often used products are available to the do-it-yourselfer in kit form, from major manufacturers of auto body repair products. The same manufacturers also merchandise the individual products for use by pros.

Kits are available to make a wide variety of repairs, including holes, dents and scratches and fiberglass, and offer the advantage of buying the materials you'll need for the job. There is little waste or chance of materials going bad from not being used. Many kits may also contain basic body-working tools such as body files, sanding blocks and spreaders. Check the contents of the kit before buying your tools.

BODY REPAIR TIPS

Safety

Many of the products associated with auto body repair and refinishing contain toxic chemicals. Read all labels before opening containers and store them in a safe place and manner.

• Wear eye protection (safety goggles) when using power tools or when performing any operation that involves the removal of any type of material.

• Wear lung protection (disposable mask or respirator) when grinding, sanding or painting.

Sanding

1 Sand off paint before using a dent puller. When using a non-adhesive sanding disc, cover the back of the disc with an overlapping layer or two of masking tape and trim the edges. The disc will last considerably longer.

2 Use the circular motion of the sanding disc to grind *into* the edge of the repair. Grinding or sanding away from the jagged edge will only tear the sandpaper.

3 Use the palm of your hand flat on the panel to detect high and low spots. Do not use your fingertips. Slide your hand slowly back and forth.

WORKING WITH BODY FILLER

Mixing The Filler

Cleanliness and proper mixing and application are extremely important. Use a clean piece of plastic or glass or a disposable artist's palette to mix body filler.

1 Allow plenty of time and follow directions. No useful purpose will be served by adding more hardener to make it cure (set-up) faster. Less hardener means more curing time, but the mixture dries harder; more hardener means less curing time but a softer mixture.

2 Both the hardener and the filler should be thoroughly kneaded or stirred before mixing. Hardener should be a solid paste and dispense like thin toothpaste. Body filler should be smooth, and free of lumps or thick spots.

Getting the proper amount of hardener in the filler is the trickiest part of preparing the filler. Use the same amount of hardener in cold or warm weather. For contour filler (thick coats), a bead of hardener twice the diameter of the filler is about right. There's about a 15% margin on either side, but, if in doubt use less hardener.

3 Mix the body filler and hardener by wiping across the mixing surface, picking the mixture up and wiping it again. Colder weather requires longer mixing times. Do not mix in a circular motion; this will trap air bubbles which will become holes in the cured filler.

Applying The Filler

1 For best results, filler should not be applied over ¼" thick.

Apply the filler in several coats. Build it up to above the level of the repair surface so that it can be sanded or grated down.

The first coat of filler must be pressed on with a firm wiping motion.

Apply the filler in one direction only. Working the filler back and forth will either pull it off the metal or trap air bubbles.

REPAIRING DENTS

Before you start, take a few minutes to study the damaged area. Try to visualize the shape of the panel before it was damaged. If the damage is on the left fender, look at the right fender and use it as a guide. If there is access to the panel from behind, you can reshape it with a body hammer. If not, you'll have to use a dent puller. Go slowly and work the metal a little at a time. Get the panel as straight as possible before applying filler.

1 This dent is typical of one that can be pulled out or hammered out from behind. Remove the headlight cover, headlight assembly and turn signal housing.

2 Drill a series of holes ½ the size of the end of the dent puller along the stress line. Make some trial pulls and assess the results. If necessary, drill more holes and try again. Do not hurry.

3 If possible, use a body hammer and block to shape the metal back to its original contours. Get the metal back as close to its original shape as possible. Don't depend on body filler to fill dents.

4 Using an 80-grit grinding disc on an electric drill, grind the paint from the surrounding area down to bare metal. Use a new grinding pad to prevent heat buildup that will warp metal.

5 The area should look like this when you're finished grinding. Knock the drill holes in and tape over small openings to keep plastic filler out.

6 Mix the body filler (see Body Repair Tips). Spread the body filler evenly over the entire area (see Body Repair Tips). Be sure to cover the area completely.

7 Let the body filler dry until the surface can just be scratched with your fingernail. Knock the high spots from the body filler with a body file ("Cheese-grater"). Check frequently with the palm of your hand for high and low spots.

8 Check to be sure that trim pieces that will be installed later will fit exactly. Sand the area with 40-grit paper.

9 If you wind up with low spots, you may have to apply another layer of filler.

10 Knock the high spots off with 40-grit paper. When you are satisfied with the contours of the repair, apply a thin coat of filler to cover pin holes and scratches.

11 Block sand the area with 40-grit paper to a smooth finish. Pay particular attention to body lines and ridges that must be well-defined.

12 Sand the area with 400 paper and then finish with a scuff pad. The finished repair is ready for priming and painting (see Painting Tips).

Materials and photos courtesy of Ritt Jones Auto Body, Prospect Park, PA.

REPAIRING RUST HOLES

There are many ways to repair rust holes. The fiberglass cloth kit shown here is one of the most cost efficient for the owner because it provides a strong repair that resists cracking and moisture and is relatively easy to use. It can be used on large and small holes (with or without backing) and can be applied over contoured areas. Remember, however, that short of replacing an entire panel, no repair is a guarantee that the rust will not return.

1 Remove any trim that will be in the way. Clean away all loose debris. Cut away all the rusted metal. But be sure to leave enough metal to retain the contour or body shape.

2 Grind away all traces of rust with a 24-grit grinding disc. Be sure to grind back 3-4 inches from the edge of the hole down to bare metal and be sure all traces of paint, primer and rust are removed.

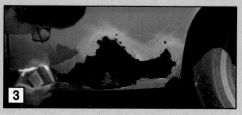

3 Block sand the area with 80 or 100 grit sandpaper to get a clear, shiny surface and feathered paint edge. Tap the edges of the hole inward with a ball peen hammer.

4 If you are going to use release film, cut a piece about 2-3″ larger than the area you have sanded. Place the film over the repair and mark the sanded area on the film. Avoid any unnecessary wrinkling of the film.

5 Cut 2 pieces of fiberglass matte to match the shape of the repair. One piece should be about 1″ smaller than the sanded area and the second piece should be 1″ smaller than the first. Mix enough filler and hardener to saturate the fiberglass material (see Body Repair Tips).

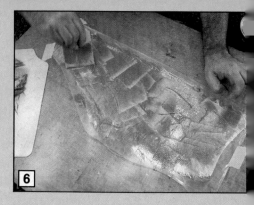

6 Lay the release sheet on a flat surface and spread an even layer of filler, large enough to cover the repair. Lay the smaller piece of fiberglass cloth in the center of the sheet and spread another layer of filler over the fiberglass cloth. Repeat the operation for the larger piece of cloth.

7 Place the repair material over the repair area, with the release film facing outward. Use a spreader and work from the center outward to smooth the material, following the body contours. Be sure to remove all air bubbles.

8 Wait until the repair has dried tack-free and peel off the release sheet. The ideal working temperature is 60°-90° F. Cooler or warmer temperatures or high humidity may require additional curing time. Wait longer, if in doubt.

9 Sand and feather-edge the entire area. The initial sanding can be done with a sanding disc on an electric drill if care is used. Finish the sanding with a block sander. Low spots can be filled with body filler; this may require several applications.

10 When the filler can just be scratched with a fingernail, knock the high spots down with a body file and smooth the entire area with 80-grit. Feather the filled areas into the surrounding areas.

11 When the area is sanded smooth, mix some topcoat and hardener and apply it directly with a spreader. This will give a smooth finish and prevent the glass matte from showing through the paint.

12 Block sand the topcoat smooth with finishing sandpaper (200 grit), and 400 grit. The repair is ready for masking, priming and painting (see Painting Tips).

Materials and photos courtesy Marson Corporation, Chelsea, Massachusetts

PAINTING TIPS

Preparation

1 SANDING — Use a 400 or 600 grit wet or dry sandpaper. Wet-sand the area with a 1/4 sheet of sandpaper soaked in clean water. Keep the paper wet while sanding. Sand the area until the repaired area tapers into the original finish.

2 CLEANING — Wash the area to be painted thoroughly with water and a clean rag. Rinse it thoroughly and wipe the surface dry until you're sure it's completely free of dirt, dust, fingerprints, wax, detergent or other foreign matter.

3 MASKING — Protect any areas you don't want to overspray by covering them with masking tape and newspaper. Be careful not get fingerprints on the area to be painted.

4 PRIMING — All exposed metal should be primed before painting. Primer protects the metal and provides an excellent surface for paint adhesion. When the primer is dry, wet-sand the area again with 600 grit wet-sandpaper. Clean the area again after sanding.

Painting Techniques

P aint applied from either a spray gun or a spray can (for small areas) will provide good results. Experiment on an old piece of metal to get the right combination before you begin painting.

SPRAYING VISCOSITY (SPRAY GUN ONLY) — Paint should be thinned to spraying viscosity according to the directions on the can. Use only the recommended thinner or reducer and the same amount of reduction regardless of temperature.

AIR PRESSURE (SPRAY GUN ONLY) — This is extremely important. Be sure you are using the proper recommended pressure.

TEMPERATURE — The surface to be painted should be approximately the same temperature as the surrounding air. Applying warm paint to a cold surface, or vice versa, will completely upset the paint characteristics.

THICKNESS — Spray with smooth strokes. In general, the thicker the coat of paint, the longer the drying time. Apply several thin coats about 30 seconds apart. The paint should remain wet long enough to flow out and no longer; heavier coats will only produce sags or wrinkles. Spray a light (fog) coat, followed by heavier color coats.

DISTANCE — The ideal spraying distance is 8″-12″ from the gun or can to the surface. Shorter distances will produce ripples, while greater distances will result in orange peel, dry film and poor color match and loss of material due to overspray.

OVERLAPPING — The gun or can should be kept at right angles to the surface at all times. Work to a wet edge at an even speed, using a 50% overlap and direct the center of the spray at the lower or nearest edge of the previous stroke.

RUBBING OUT (BLENDING) FRESH PAINT — Let the paint dry thoroughly. Runs or imperfections can be sanded out, primed and repainted.

Don't be in too big a hurry to remove the masking. This only produces paint ridges. When the finish has dried for at least a week, apply a small amount of fine grade rubbing compound with a clean, wet cloth. Use lots of water and blend the new paint with the surrounding area.

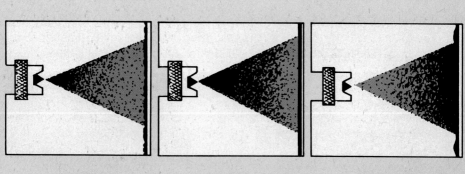

WRONG

Thin coat. Stroke too fast, not enough overlap, gun too far away.

CORRECT

Medium coat. Proper distance, good stroke, proper overlap.

WRONG

Heavy coat. Stroke too slow, too much overlap, gun too close.

Removing mirror mounting screws

Butyl seal

Apply sealer to rear surface of finisher panel

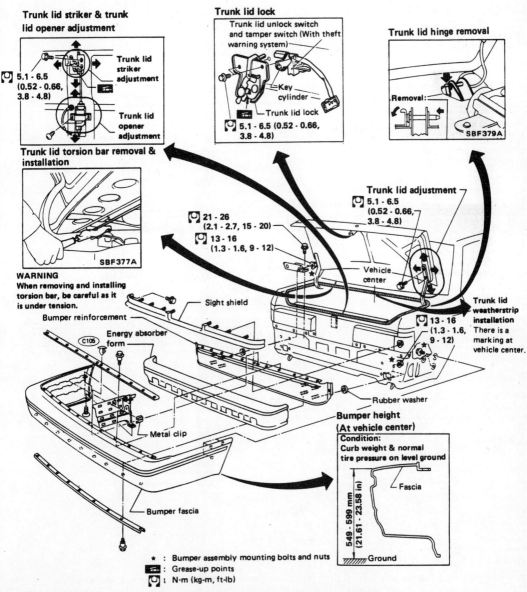

Trunk lid striker & trunk lid opener adjustment

5.1 - 6.5 (0.52 - 0.66, 3.8 - 4.8)

Trunk lid striker adjustment

Trunk lid opener adjustment

Trunk lid torsion bar removal & installation

SBF377A

WARNING
When removing and installing torsion bar, be careful as it is under tension.

Trunk lid lock

Trunk lid unlock switch and tamper switch (With theft warning system)

Key cylinder

Trunk lid lock

5.1 - 6.5 (0.52 - 0.66, 3.8 - 4.8)

Trunk lid hinge removal

Removal:

SBF379A

Trunk lid adjustment
5.1 - 6.5 (0.52 - 0.66, 3.8 - 4.8)

Vehicle center

Trunk lid weatherstrip installation
There is a marking at vehicle center.

21 - 26 (2.1 - 2.7, 15 - 20)

13 - 16 (1.3 - 1.6, 9 - 12)

13 - 16 (1.3 - 1.6, 9 - 12)

Sight shield

Bumper reinforcement

C105

Energy absorber form

Metal clip

Rubber washer

Bumper fascia

Bumper height (At vehicle center)
Condition:
Curb weight & normal tire pressure on level ground

549 - 599 mm (21.61 - 23.58 in)

Fascia

Ground

★ : Bumper assembly mounting bolts and nuts
▭ : Grease-up points
🔧 : N·m (kg-m, ft-lb)

Body rear end assembly—1988 Maxima sedan

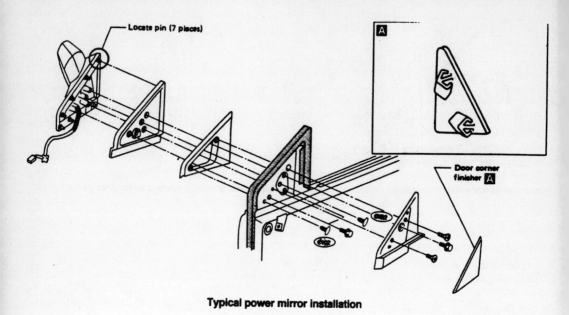

Typical power mirror installation

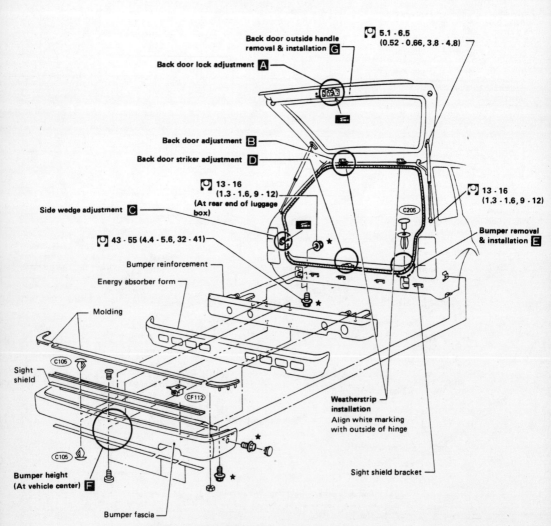

Body rear end assembly—1988 Maxima station wagon

4. Installation is in the reverse order of removal.

NOTE: *Apply sealer to the rear surface of door corner finisher panel during installation to prevent water leak.*

Power

1. Remove door corner finisher panel.
2. Remove mirror body attaching screws, and then remove mirror body
3. Disconnect the electrical connection.

NOTE: *It may be necessary to remove the door trim panel to gain access to the electrical connection.*

4. Installation is in the reverse order of removal.

Antenna

REMOVAL AND INSTALLATION

Fender Mounted

1. Remove antenna mounting nut.
2. Disconnect the antenna lead at the radio.

3. Remove antenna from vehicle.
4. Installation is in the reverse order of removal.

INTERIOR

Door Panel, Glass and Regulator

REMOVAL AND INSTALLATION

Front and Rear

NOTE: *Refer to the exploded view of Front and Rear Door Assembly.*

1. Remove the regulator handle by pushing the set pin spring off.
2. Remove the arm rest, door inside handle escutcheon and door lock.
3. Remove the door finisher and sealing screen.
4. On some models it may be necessary to remove the outer door moulding.
5. Lower the door glass with the regulator handle until the regulator-to-glass attaching

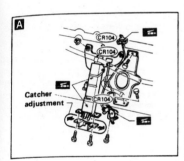
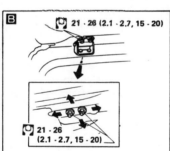
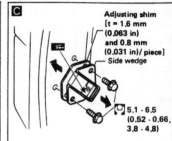

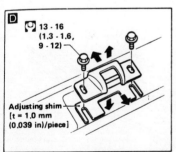
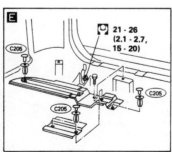
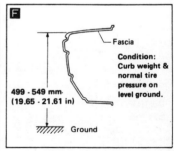

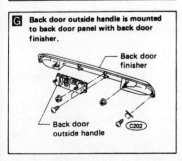

Body rear end assembly—1988 Maxima station wagon

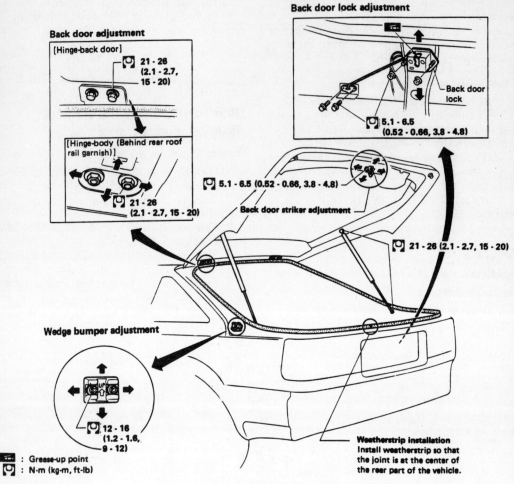

Back door lock adjustment

Back door adjustment

[Hinge-back door]

21 - 26
(2.1 - 2.7,
15 - 20)

[Hinge-body (Behind rear roof rail garnish)]

21 - 26
(2.1 - 2.7, 15 - 20)

5.1 - 6.5 (0.52 - 0.66, 3.8 - 4.8)

Back door lock

5.1 - 6.5
(0.52 - 0.66, 3.8 - 4.8)

Back door striker adjustment

21 - 26 (2.1 - 2.7, 15 - 20)

Wedge bumper adjustment

12 - 16
(1.2 - 1.6,
9 - 12)

: Grease-up point

: N·m (kg-m, ft-lb)

Weatherstrip installation
Install weatherstrip so that
the joint is at the center of
the rear part of the vehicle.

Body rear end assembly—1988 200SX

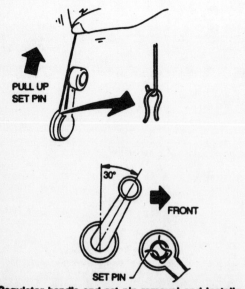

PULL UP
SET PIN

30°

FRONT

SET PIN

Regulator handle and set pin removal and installation

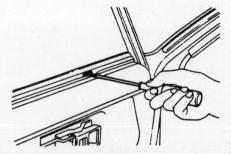

Removing outer door moulding

bolts appear at the access holes in the door inside panel.

6. Raise the door glass and draw it upwards.

7. Remove the regulator attaching bolts and remove the regulator assembly through the large access hole in ther door panel.

8. Install the window regulator assembly in the door.

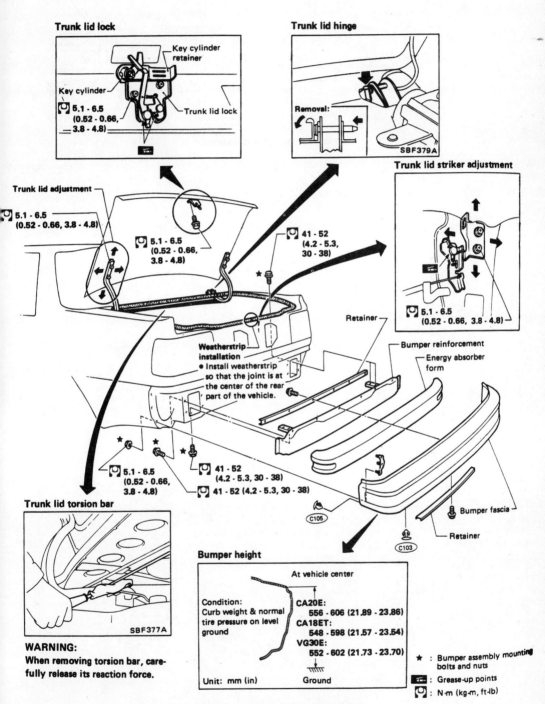

Trunk lid lock

Key cylinder
retainer

Key cylinder

Trunk lid lock

5.1 - 6.5
(0.52 - 0.66,
3.8 - 4.8)

Trunk lid hinge

Removal:

SBF379A

Trunk lid striker adjustment

5.1 - 6.5
(0.52 - 0.66, 3.8 - 4.8)

Trunk lid adjustment

5.1 - 6.5
(0.52 - 0.66, 3.8 - 4.8)

5.1 - 6.5
(0.52 - 0.66,
3.8 - 4.8)

41 - 52
(4.2 - 5.3,
30 - 38)

Retainer

**Weatherstrip
installation**
• Install weatherstrip
so that the joint is at
the center of the rear
part of the vehicle.

Bumper reinforcement

Energy absorber
form

5.1 - 6.5
(0.52 - 0.66,
3.8 - 4.8)

41 - 52
(4.2 - 5.3, 30 - 38)

41 - 52 (4.2 - 5.3, 30 - 38)

C105

C103

Bumper fascia

Retainer

Trunk lid torsion bar

SBF377A

WARNING:
When removing torsion bar, carefully release its reaction force.

Bumper height

	At vehicle center	

Condition:
Curb weight & normal
tire pressure on level
ground
	CA20E:
	    556 - 606 (21.89 - 23.86)
	CA18ET:
	    548 - 598 (21.57 - 23.54)
	VG30E:
	    552 - 602 (21.73 - 23.70)	

Unit: mm (in)	Ground	

★ : Bumper assembly mounting
     bolts and nuts

: Grease-up points

: N·m (kg-m, ft-lb)

Body rear end assembly—1988 200SX

Rear

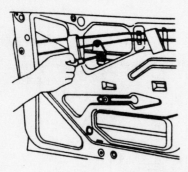

Front

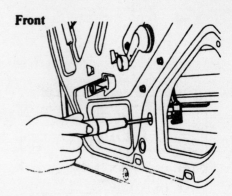

Removing glass attaching bolts

Lumbar support system

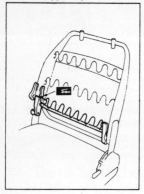

Head rest holder
- Remove holder after rolling back seat back trim.

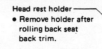

Nylon housing

🔧 13 - 16 (1.3 - 1.6, 9 - 12)

Reclining device

🔧 42 - 54 (4.3 - 5.5, 31 - 40)

🔧 42 - 54 (4.3 - 5.5, 31 - 40)

Walk-in mechanism

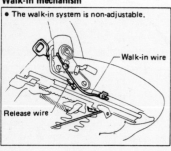

- The walk-in system is non-adjustable.

Walk-in wire

Release wire

🔧 21 - 26 (2.1 - 2.7, 15 - 20)

Sliding device

🔧 21 - 26 (2.1 - 2.7, 15 - 20)

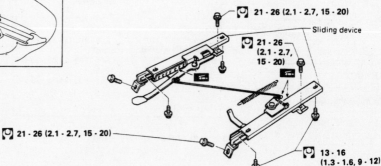

🔧 21 - 26 (2.1 - 2.7, 15 - 20)

🔧 13 - 16 (1.3 - 1.6, 9 - 12)

🔧 : N·m (kg-m, ft-lb)
🔧 : Grease-up point
(Do not apply too much grease as it will drip)

Front seal assembly—1988 200SX

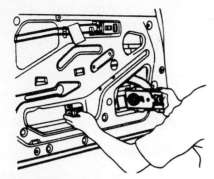

Removing regulator from door

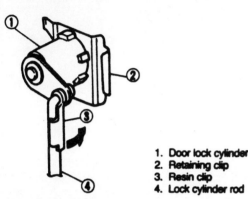

1. Door lock cylinder
2. Retaining clip
3. Resin clip
4. Lock cylinder rod

Typical lock cylinder rod assembly

9. Connect all mounting bolts and check for proper operation.

10. Adjust the window if necessary and install the door trim panel.

11. Install all the attaching components to the door panel.

12. Install the window regulator handle.

Door Locks

REMOVAL AND INSTALLATION

NOTE: *Refer to the exploded view of Front and Rear Door Assembly.*

1. Remove the door panel and sealing screen.

2. Remove the lock cylinder from the rod by turning the resin clip.

3. Loosen the nuts attaching the outside door handle and remove the outside door handle.

4. Remove the screws retaining the inside door handle and door lock, and remove the door lock assembly from the hole in the inside of the door.

5. Remove the lock cylinder by removing the retaining clip.

6. Install the lock cylinder and clip to the door.

7. Install the door lock assembly and handles.

8. Install door panel and all attaching parts.

Electrical Window Motor

REMOVAL AND INSTALLATION

NOTE: *Refer to the exploded view of Front and Rear Door Assembly.*

1. Remove the door panel and sealing screen.

2. Remove the power widow motor mounting bolts

3. Remove all electrical connections and cable connection.

4. Remove the power window motor from the vehicle

5. Installation is in the reverse order of removal.

Inside Rear View Mirror

REMOVAL AND INSTALLATION

1. Remove rear view mirror mounting bolt cover.

2. Remove rear view mirror mounting bolts.

3. Remove mirror.

4. Installation is in the reverse order of removal.

Seats

REMOVAL AND INSTALLATION

Front

NOTE: *On power seat models remove the seat then remove the power seat motor assembly and drive cable. Refer to the exploded view of Front Seat Assembly.*

1. Remove front seat mounting bolts

2. Remove front seat assembly.

3. Installation is in the reverse order of removal.

Rear

1. Remove rear seat cushion mounting bolts.

2. Remove screw attaching luggage floor carpet.

3. Remove rear seat back by tilting forward and pulling straight up.

NOTE: *On hatchback models the rear seat back is remove similar as above.*

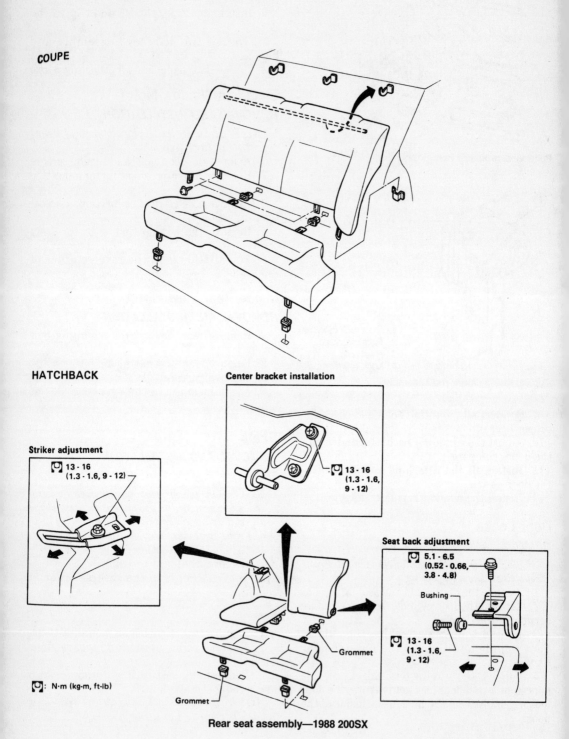

COUPE

HATCHBACK

Center bracket installation

Striker adjustment

13 - 16
(1.3 - 1.6, 9 - 12)

13 - 16
(1.3 - 1.6,
9 - 12)

Seat back adjustment

5.1 - 6.5
(0.52 - 0.66,
3.8 - 4.8)

Bushing

13 - 16
(1.3 - 1.6,
9 - 12)

: N·m (kg-m, ft-lb)

Grommet

Grommet

Rear seat assembly—1988 200SX

MANUAL SEAT

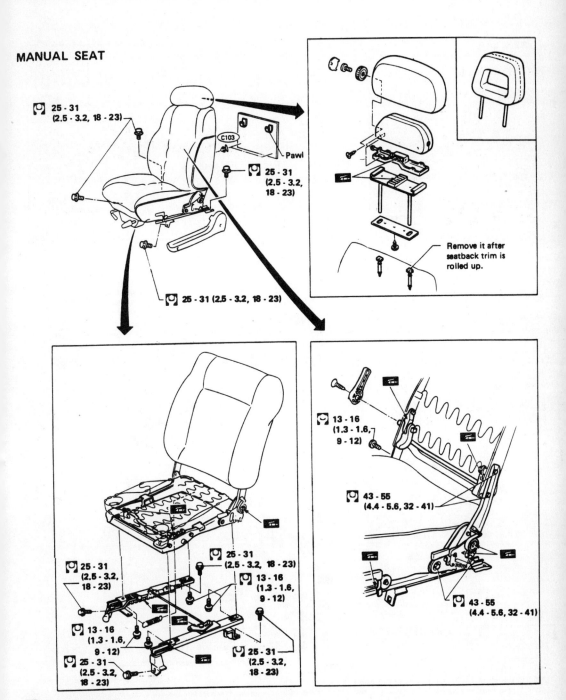

25 - 31
(2.5 - 3.2, 18 - 23)

C103

Pawl

25 - 31
(2.5 - 3.2,
18 - 23)

25 - 31 (2.5 - 3.2, 18 - 23)

Remove it after
seatback trim is
rolled up.

13 - 16
(1.3 - 1.6,
9 - 12)

43 - 55
(4.4 - 5.6, 32 - 41)

43 - 55
(4.4 - 5.6, 32 - 41)

25 - 31
(2.5 - 3.2,
18 - 23)

25 - 31
(2.5 - 3.2, 18 - 23)

13 - 16
(1.3 - 1.6,
9 - 12)

13 - 16
(1.3 - 1.6,
9 - 12)

25 - 31
(2.5 - 3.2,
18 - 23)

25 - 31
(2.5 - 3.2,
18 - 23)

: N·m (kg-m, ft-lb)
: Grease-up points (Do not apply too much grease as it will drip.)

Front seat assembly—1988 Maxima (manual seat)

POWER SEAT

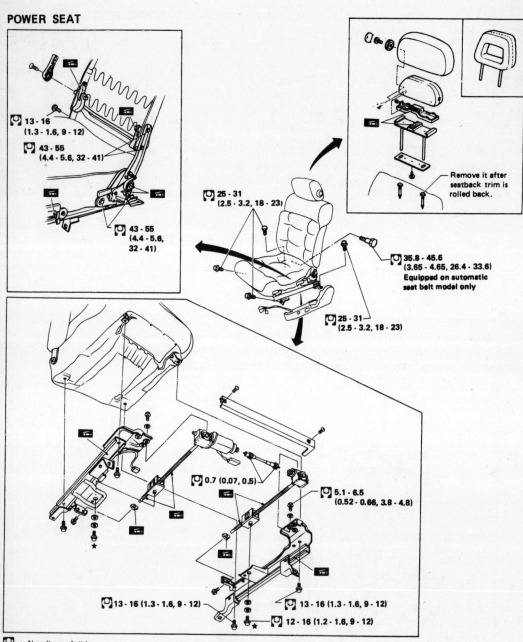

13 - 16
(1.3 - 1.6, 9 - 12)

43 - 55
(4.4 - 5.6, 32 - 41)

43 - 55
(4.4 - 5.6, 32 - 41)

25 - 31
(2.5 - 3.2, 18 - 23)

Remove it after
seatback trim is
rolled back.

35.8 - 45.6
(3.65 - 4.65, 26.4 - 33.6)
**Equipped on automatic
seat belt model only**

25 - 31
(2.5 - 3.2, 18 - 23)

0.7 (0.07, 0.5)

5.1 - 6.5
(0.52 - 0.66, 3.8 - 4.8)

13 - 16 (1.3 - 1.6, 9 - 12)

13 - 16 (1.3 - 1.6, 9 - 12)

12 - 16 (1.2 - 1.6, 9 - 12)

: N·m (kg-m, ft-lb)

: Grease-up points (Do not apply too much grease as it will drip.)

★ : If power seat does not operate because of a malfunction, remove the bolts marked ★ and set free the sliders, then
remove seat mounting.

Front seat assembly—1988 Maxima (power seat)

SEDAN

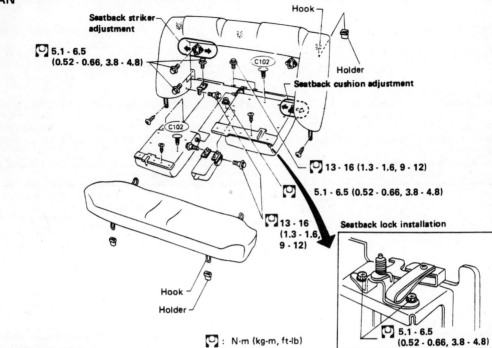

Seatback striker adjustment

🔧 5.1 - 6.5
(0.52 - 0.66, 3.8 - 4.8)

Hook

C102

Holder

Seatback cushion adjustment

🔧 13 - 16 (1.3 - 1.6, 9 - 12)

🔧 5.1 - 6.5 (0.52 - 0.66, 3.8 - 4.8)

🔧 13 - 16
(1.3 - 1.6,
9 - 12)

C102

Hook

Holder

Seatback lock installation

🔧 5.1 - 6.5
(0.52 - 0.66, 3.8 - 4.8)

🔧 : N·m (kg-m, ft-lb)

STATION WAGON

Reclining device

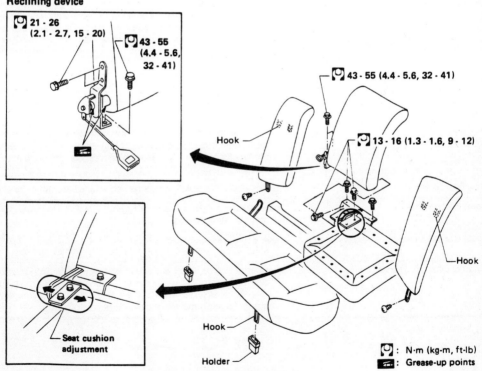

🔧 21 - 26
(2.1 - 2.7, 15 - 20)

🔧 43 - 55
(4.4 - 5.6,
32 - 41)

🔧 43 - 55 (4.4 - 5.6, 32 - 41)

🔧 13 - 16 (1.3 - 1.6, 9 - 12)

Hook

Hook

Seat cushion adjustment

Hook

Holder

🔧 : N·m (kg-m, ft-lb)

🔧 : Grease-up points

Rear seat assembly—1988 Maxima

How to Remove Stains from Fabric Interior

For rest results, spots and stains should be removed as soon as possible. Never use gasoline, lacquer thinner, acetone, nail polish remover or bleach. Use a 3' x 3" piece of cheesecloth. Squeeze most of the liquid from the fabric and wipe the stained fabric from the outside of the stain toward the center with a lifting motion. Turn the cheesecloth as soon as one side becomes soiled. When using water to remove a stain, be sure to wash the entire section after the spot has been removed to avoid water stains. Encrusted spots can be broken up with a dull knife and vacuumed before removing the stain.

Type of Stain	How to Remove It
Surface spots	Brush the spots out with a small hand brush or use a commercial preparation such as K2R to lift the stain.
Mildew	Clean around the mildew with warm suds. Rinse in cold water and soak the mildew area in a solution of 1 part table salt and 2 parts water. Wash with upholstery cleaner.
Water stains	Water stains in fabric materials can be removed with a solution made from 1 cup of table salt dissolved in 1 quart of water. Vigorously scrub the solution into the stain and rinse with clear water. Water stains in nylon or other synthetic fabrics should be removed with a commercial type spot remover.
Chewing gum, tar, crayons, shoe polish (greasy stains)	Do not use a cleaner that will soften gum or tar. Harden the deposit with an ice cube and scrape away as much as possible with a dull knife. Moisten the remainder with cleaning fluid and scrub clean.
Ice cream, candy	Most candy has a sugar base and can be removed with a cloth wrung out in warm water. Oily candy, after cleaning with warm water, should be cleaned with upholstery cleaner. Rinse with warm water and clean the remainder with cleaning fluid.
Wine, alcohol, egg, milk, soft drink (non-greasy stains)	Do not use soap. Scrub the stain with a cloth wrung out in warm water. Remove the remainder with cleaning fluid.
Grease, oil, lipstick, butter and related stains	Use a spot remover to avoid leaving a ring. Work from the outisde of the stain to the center and dry with a clean cloth when the spot is gone.
Headliners (cloth)	Mix a solution of warm water and foam upholstery cleaner to give thick suds. Use only foam—liquid may streak or spot. Clean the entire headliner in one operation using a circular motion with a natural sponge.
Headliner (vinyl)	Use a vinyl cleaner with a sponge and wipe clean with a dry cloth.
Seats and door panels	Mix 1 pint upholstery cleaner in 1 gallon of water. Do not soak the fabric around the buttons.
Leather or vinyl fabric	Use a multi-purpose cleaner full strength and a stiff brush. Let stand 2 minutes and scrub thoroughly. Wipe with a clean, soft rag.
Nylon or synthetic fabrics	For normal stains, use the same procedures you would for washing cloth upholstery. If the fabric is extremely dirty, use a multi-purpose cleaner full strength with a stiff scrub brush. Scrub thoroughly in all directions and wipe with a cotton towel or soft rag.

Mechanic's Data

11

TAX
10.16mm
Liter
Parts
1":254mm
Overhaul

General Conversion Table

Multiply By	To Convert	To	
		LENGTH	
2.54	Inches	Centimeters	.3937
25.4	Inches	Millimeters	.03937
30.48	Feet	Centimeters	.0328
.304	Feet	Meters	3.28
.914	Yards	Meters	1.094
1.609	Miles	Kilometers	.621
		VOLUME	
.473	Pints	Liters	2.11
.946	Quarts	Liters	1.06
3.785	Gallons	Liters	.264
.016	Cubic inches	Liters	61.02
16.39	Cubic inches	Cubic cms.	.061
28.3	Cubic feet	Liters	.0353
		MASS (Weight)	
28.35	Ounces	Grams	.035
.4536	Pounds	Kilograms	2.20
—	To obtain	From	Multiply by

Multiply By	To Convert	To	
		AREA	
.645	Square inches	Square cms.	.155
.836	Square yds.	Square meters	1.196
		FORCE	
4.448	Pounds	Newtons	.225
.138	Ft./lbs.	Kilogram/meters	7.23
1.36	Ft./lbs.	Newton-meters	.737
.112	In./lbs.	Newton-meters	8.844
		PRESSURE	
.068	Psi	Atmospheres	14.7
6.89	Psi	Kilopascals	.145
		OTHER	
1.104	Horsepower (DIN)	Horsepower (SAE)	.9861
.746	Horsepower (SAE)	Kilowatts (KW)	1.34
1.60	Mph	Km/h	.625
.425	Mpg	Km/1	2.35
—	To obtain	From	Multiply by

Tap Drill Sizes

National Coarse or U.S.S.

Screw & Tap Size	Threads Per Inch	Use Drill Number
No. 5	40	39
No. 6	32	36
No. 8	32	29
No. 10	24	25
No. 12	24	17
1/4	20	8
5/16	18	F
3/8	16	5/16
7/16	14	U
1/2	13	27/64
9/16	12	31/64
5/8	11	17/32
3/4	10	21/32
7/8	9	49/64

National Coarse or U.S.S.

Screw & Tap Size	Threads Per Inch	Use Drill Number
1	8	7/8
1 1/8	7	63/64
1 1/4	7	1 7/64
1 1/2	6	1 11/32

National Fine or S.A.E.

Screw & Tap Size	Threads Per Inch	Use Drill Number
No. 5	44	37
No. 6	40	33
No. 8	36	29
No. 10	32	21

National Fine or S.A.E.

Screw & Tap Size	Threads Per Inch	Use Drill Number
No. 12	28	15
1/4	28	3
6/16	24	1
3/8	24	Q
7/16	20	W
1/2	20	29/64
9/16	18	33/64
5/8	18	37/64
3/4	16	11/16
7/8	14	13/16
1 1/8	12	1 3/64
1 1/4	12	1 11/64
1 1/2	12	1 27/64

Drill Sizes In Decimal Equivalents

Inch	Decimal	Wire	mm	Inch	Decimal	Wire	mm	Inch	Decimal	Wire & Letter	mm	Inch	Decimal	Letter	mm	Inch	Decimal	mm
1/64	.0156		.39		.0730	49			.1614		4.1		.2717		6.9		.4331	11.0
	.0157		.4		.0748		1.9		.1654		4.2		.2720	I		7/16	.4375	11.11
	.0160	78			.0760	48			.1660	19			.2756		7.0		.4528	11.5
	.0165		.42		.0768		1.95		.1673		4.25		.2770	J		29/64	.4531	11.51
	.0173		.44	5/64	.0781		1.98		.1693		4.3		.2795		7.1	15/32	.4688	11.90
	.0177		.45		.0785	47			.1695	18			.2810	K			.4724	12.0
	.0180	77			.0787		2.0	11/64	.1719		4.36	9/32	.2812		7.14	31/64	.4844	12.30
	.0181		.46		.0807		2.05		.1730	17			.2835		7.2		.4921	12.5
	.0189		.48		.0810	46			.1732		4.4		.2854		7.25	1/2	.5000	12.70
	.0197		.5		.0820	45			.1770	16			.2874		7.3		.5118	13.0
	.0200	76			.0827		2.1		.1772		4.5		.2900	L		33/64	.5156	13.09
	.0210	75			.0846		2.15		.1800	15			.2913		7.4	17/32	.5312	13.49
	.0217		.55		.0860	44			.1811		4.6		.2950	M			.5315	13.5
	.0225	74			.0866		2.2		.1820	14			.2953		7.5	35/64	.5469	13.89
	.0236		.6		.0886		2.25		.1850	13		19/64	.2969		7.54		.5512	14.0
	.0240	73			.0890	43			.1850		4.7		.2992		7.6	9/16	.5625	14.28
	.0250	72			.0906		2.3		.1870		4.75		.3020	N			.5709	14.5
	.0256		.65		.0925		2.35	3/16	.1875		4.76		.3031		7.7	37/64	.5781	14.68
	.0260	71			.0935	42			.1890		4.8		.3051		7.75		.5906	15.0
	.0276		.7	3/32	.0938		2.38		.1890	12			.3071		7.8	19/32	.5938	15.08
	.0280	70			.0945		2.4		.1910	11			.3110		7.9	39/64	.6094	15.47
	.0292	69			.0960	41			.1929		4.9	5/16	.3125		7.93		.6102	15.5
	.0295		.75		.0965		2.45		.1935	10			.3150		8.0	5/8	.6250	15.87
	.0310	68			.0980	40			.1960	9			.3160	O			.6299	16.0
1/32	.0312		.79		.0981		2.5		.1969		5.0		.3189		8.1	41/64	.6406	16.27
	.0315		.8		.0995	39			.1990	8			.3228		8.2		.6496	16.5
	.0320	67			.1015	38			.2008		5.1		.3230	P		21/32	.6562	16.66
	.0330	66			.1024		2.6		.2010	7			.3248		8.25		.6693	17.0
	.0335		.85		.1040	37		13/64	.2031		5.16		.3268		8.3	43/64	.6719	17.06
	.0350	65			.1063		2.7		.2040	6		21/64	.3281		8.33	11/16	.6875	17.46
	.0354		.9		.1065	36			.2047		5.2		.3307		8.4		.6890	17.5
	.0360	64			.1083		2.75		.2055	5			.3320	Q		45/64	.7031	17.85
	.0370	63		7/64	.1094		2.77		.2067		5.25		.3346		8.5		.7087	18.0
	.0374		.95		.1100	35			.2087		5.3		.3386		8.6	23/32	.7188	18.25
	.0380	62			.1102		2.8		.2090	4			.3390	R			.7283	18.5
	.0390	61			.1110	34			.2126		5.4		.3425		8.7	47/64	.7344	18.65
	.0394		1.0		.1130	33			.2130	3		11/32	.3438		8.73		.7480	19.0
	.0400	60			.1142		2.9		.2165		5.5		.3445		8.75	3/4	.7500	19.05
	.0410	59			.1160	32		7/32	.2188		5.55		.3465		8.8	49/64	.7656	19.44
	.0413		1.05		.1181		3.0		.2205		5.6		.3480	S			.7677	19.5
	.0420	58			.1200	31			.2210	2			.3504		8.9	25/32	.7812	19.84
	.0430	57			.1220		3.1		.2244		5.7		.3543		9.0		.7874	20.0
	.0433		1.1	1/8	.1250		3.17		.2264		5.75		.3580	T		51/64	.7969	20.24
	.0453		1.15		.1260		3.2		.2280	1			.3583		9.1		.8071	20.5
3/64	.0465	56			.1280		3.25		.2283		5.8	23/64	.3594		9.12	13/16	.8125	20.63
	.0469		1.19		.1285	30			.2323		5.9		.3622		9.2		.8268	21.0
	.0472		1.2		.1299		3.3		.2340	A			.3642		9.25	53/64	.8281	21.03
	.0492		1.25		.1339		3.4	15/64	.2344		5.95		.3661		9.3	27/32	.8438	21.43
	.0512		1.3		.1360	29			.2362		6.0		.3680	U			.8465	21.5
	.0520	55			.1378		3.5		.2380	B			.3701		9.4	55/64	.8594	21.82
	.0531		1.35		.1405	28			.2402		6.1		.3740		9.5		.8661	22.0
	.0550	54		9/64	.1406		3.57		.2420	C		3/8	.3750		9.52	7/8	.8750	22.22
	.0551		1.4		.1417		3.6		.2441		6.2		.3770	V			.8858	22.5
	.0571		1.45		.1440	27			.2460	D			.3780		9.6	57/64	.8906	22.62
	.0591		1.5		.1457		3.7		.2461		6.25		.3819		9.7		.9055	23.0
	.0595	53			.1470	26			.2480		6.3		.3839		9.75	29/32	.9062	23.01
	.0610		1.55		.1476		3.75	1/4	.2500	E	6.35		.3858		9.8	59/64	.9219	23.41
1/16	.0625		1.59		.1495	25			.2520		6.		.3860	W			.9252	23.5
	.0630		1.6		.1496		3.8		.2559		6.5		.3898		9.9	15/16	.9375	23.81
	.0635	52			.1520	24			.2570	F		25/64	.3906		9.92		.9449	24.0
	.0650		1.65		.1535		3.9		.2598		6.6		.3937		10.0	61/64	.9531	24.2
	.0669		1.7		.1540	23			.2610	G			.3970	X			.9646	24.5
	.0670	51		5/32	.1562		3.96		.2638		6.7		.4040	Y		31/32	.9688	24.6
	.0689		1.75		.1570	22		17/64	.2656		6.74	13/32	.4062		10.31		.9843	25.0
	.0700	50			.1575		4.0		.2657		6.75		.4130	Z		63/64	.9844	25.0
	.0709		1.8		.1590	21			.2660	H			.4134		10.5	1	1.0000	25.4
	.0728		1.85		.1610	20			.2677		6.8	27/64	.4219		10.71			

AIR/FUEL RATIO: The ratio of air to gasoline by weight in the fuel mixture drawn into the engine.

AIR INJECTION: One method of reducing harmful exhaust emissions by injecting air into each of the exhaust ports of an engine. The fresh air entering the hot exhaust manifold causes any remaining fuel to be burned before it can exit the tailpipe.

ALTERNATOR: A device used for converting mechanical energy into electrical energy.

AMMETER: An instrument, calibrated in amperes, used to measure the flow of an electrical current in a circuit. Ammeters are always connected in series with the circuit being tested.

AMPERE: The rate of flow of electrical current present when one volt of electrical pressure is applied against one ohm of electrical resistance.

ANALOG COMPUTER: Any microprocessor that uses similar (analogous) electrical signals to make its calculations.

ARMATURE: A laminated, soft iron core wrapped by a wire that converts electrical energy to mechanical energy as in a motor or relay. When rotated in a magnetic field, it changes mechanical energy into electrical energy as in a generator.

ATMOSPHERIC PRESSURE: The pressure on the Earth's surface caused by the weight of the air in the atmosphere. At sea level, this pressure is 14.7 psi at 32°F (101 kPa at 0°C).

ATOMIZATION: The breaking down of a liquid into a fine mist that can be suspended in air.

AXIAL PLAY: Movement parallel to a shaft or bearing bore.

BACKFIRE: The sudden combustion of gases in the intake or exhaust system that results in a loud explosion.

BACKLASH: The clearance or play between two parts, such as meshed gears.

BACKPRESSURE: Restrictions in the exhaust system that slow the exit of exhaust gases from the combustion chamber.

BAKELITE: A heat resistant, plastic insulator material commonly used in printed circuit boards and transistorized components.

BALL BEARING: A bearing made up of hardened inner and outer races between which hardened steel ball roll.

BALLAST RESISTOR: A resistor in the primary ignition circuit that lowers voltage after the engine is started to reduce wear on ignition components.

BEARING: A friction reducing, supportive device usually located between a stationary part and a moving part.

BIMETAL TEMPERATURE SENSOR: Any sensor or switch made of two dissimilar types of metal that bend when heated or cooled due to the different expansion rates of the alloys. These types of sensors usually function as an on/off switch.

BLOWBY: Combustion gases, composed of water vapor and unburned fuel, that leak past the piston rings into the crankcase during normal engine operation. These gases are removed by the PCV system to prevent the buildup of harmful acids in the crankcase.

BRAKE PAD: A brake shoe and lining assembly used with disc brakes.

BRAKE SHOE: The backing for the brake lining. The term is, however, usually applied to the assembly of the brake backing and lining.

BUSHING: A liner, usually removable, for a bearing; an anti-friction liner used in place of a bearing.

BYPASS: System used to bypass ballast resistor during engine cranking to increase voltage supplied to the coil.

CALIPER: A hydraulically activated device in a disc brake system, which is mounted straddling the brake rotor (disc). The caliper contains at least one piston and two brake pads. Hydraulic pressure on the piston(s) forces the pads against the rotor.

CAMSHAFT: A shaft in the engine on which are the lobes (cams) which operate the valves. The camshaft is driven by the crankshaft, via a belt, chain or gears, at one half the crankshaft speed.

CAPACITOR: A device which stores an electrical charge.

CARBON MONOXIDE (CO): a colorless, odorless gas given off as a normal byproduct of combustion. It is poisonous and extremely dangerous in confined areas, building up slowly to toxic levels without warning if adequate ventilation is not available.

CARBURETOR: A device, usually mounted on the intake manifold of an engine, which mixes the air and fuel in the proper proportion to allow even combustion.

CATALYTIC CONVERTER: A device installed in the exhaust system, like a muffler, that converts harmful byproducts of combustion into carbon dioxide and water vapor by means of a heat-producing chemical reaction.

CENTRIFUGAL ADVANCE: A mechanical method of advancing the spark timing by using flyweights in the distributor that react to centrifugal force generated by the distributor shaft rotation.

CHECK VALVE: Any one-way valve installed to permit the flow of air, fuel or vacuum in one direction only.

CHOKE: A device, usually a moveable valve, placed in the intake path of a carburetor to restrict the flow of air.

CIRCUIT: Any unbroken path through which an electrical current can flow. Also used to describe fuel flow in some instances.

CIRCUIT BREAKER: A switch which protects an electrical circuit from overload by opening the circuit when the current flow exceeds a predetermined level. Some circuit breakers must be reset manually, while other reset automatically

COIL (IGNITION): A transformer in the ignition circuit which steps of the voltage provided to the spark plugs.

COMBINATION MANIFOLD: An assembly which includes both the intake and exhaust manifolds in one casting.

COMBINATION VALVE: A device used in some fuel systems that routes fuel vapors to a charcoal storage canister instead of venting

them into the atmosphere. The valve relieves fuel tank pressure and allows fresh air into the tank as fuel level drops to prevent a vapor lock situation.

COMPRESSION RATIO: The comparison of the total volume of the cylinder and combustion chamber with the piston at BDC and the piston at TDC.

CONDENSER: 1. An electrical device which acts to store an electrical charge, preventing voltage surges.
   2. A radiator-like device in the air conditioning system in which refrigerant gas condenses into a liquid, giving off heat.

CONDUCTOR: Any material through which an electrical current can be transmitted easily.

CONTINUITY: Continuous or complete circuit. Can be checked with an ohmmeter.

COUNTERSHAFT: An intermediate shaft which is rotated by a mainshaft and transmits, in turn, that rotation to a working part.

CRANKCASE: The lower part of an engine in which the crankshaft and related parts operate.

CRANKSHAFT: The main driving shaft of an engine which receives reciprocating motion from the pistons and converts it to rotary motion.

CYLINDER: In an engine, the round hole in the engine block in which the piston(s) ride.

CYLINDER BLOCK: The main structural member of an engine in which is found the cylinders, crankshaft and other principal parts.

CYLINDER HEAD: The detachable portion of the engine, fastened, usually, to the top of the cylinder block, containing all or most of the combustion chambers. On overhead valve engines, it contains the valves and their operating parts. On overhead cam engines, it contains the camshaft as well.

DEAD CENTER: The extreme top or bottom of the piston stroke.

DETONATION: An unwanted explosion of the air fuel mixture in the combustion chamber caused by excess heat and compression, advanced timing, or an overly lean mixture. Also referred to as "ping".

DIAPHRAGM: A thin, flexible wall separating two cavities, such as in a vacuum advance unit.

DIESELING: A condition in which hot spots in the combustion chamber cause the engine to run on after the key is turned off.

DIFFERENTIAL: A geared assembly which allows the transmission of motion between drive axles, giving one axle the ability to turn faster than the other.

DIODE: An electrical device that will allow current to flow in one direction only.

DISC BRAKE: A hydraulic braking assembly consisting of a brake disc, or rotor, mounted on an axle, and a caliper assembly containing, usually two brake pads which are activated by hydraulic pressure. The pads are forced against the sides of the disc, creating friction which slows the vehicle.

DISTRIBUTOR: A mechanically driven device on an engine which is responsible for electrically firing the spark plug at a predetermined point of the piston stroke.

DOWEL PIN: A pin, inserted in mating holes in two different parts allowing those parts to maintain a fixed relationship.

DRUM BRAKE: A braking system which consists of two brake shoes and one or two wheel cylinders, mounted on a fixed backing plate, and a brake drum, mounted on an axle, which revolves around the assembly. Hydraulic action applied to the wheel cylinders forces the shoes outward against the drum, creating friction and slowing the vehicle.

DWELL: The rate, measured in degrees of shaft rotation, at which an electrical circuit cycles on and off.

ELECTRONIC CONTROL UNIT (ECU): Ignition module, module, amplifier or igniter. See Module for definition.

ELECTRONIC IGNITION: A system in which the timing and firing of the spark plugs is controlled by an electronic control unit, usually called a module. These systems have not points or condenser.

ENDPLAY: The measured amount of axial movement in a shaft.

ENGINE: A device that converts heat into mechanical energy.

EXHAUST MANIFOLD: A set of cast passages or pipes which conduct exhaust gases from the engine.

FEELER GAUGE: A blade, usually metal, of precisely predetermined thickness, used to measure the clearance between two parts. These blades usually are available in sets of assorted thicknesses.

F-Head: An engine configuration in which the intake valves are in the cylinder head, while the camshaft and exhaust valves are located in the cylinder block. The camshaft operates the intake valves via lifters and pushrods, while it operates the exhaust valves directly.

FIRING ORDER: The order in which combustion occurs in the cylinders of an engine. Also the order in which spark is distributed to the plugs by the distributor.

FLATHEAD: An engine configuration in which the camshaft and all the valves are located in the cylinder block.

FLOODING: The presence of too much fuel in the intake manifold and combustion chamber which prevents the air/fuel mixture from firing, thereby causing a no-start situation.

FLYWHEEL: A disc shaped part bolted to the rear end of the crankshaft. Around the outer perimeter is affixed the ring gear. The starter drive engages the ring gear, turning the flywheel, which rotates the crankshaft, imparting the initial starting motion to the engine.

FOOT POUND (ft.lb. or sometimes, ft. lbs.): The amount of energy or work needed to raise an item weighing one pound, a distance of one foot.

FUSE: A protective device in a circuit which prevents circuit overload by breaking the circuit when a specific amperage is present. The device is constructed around a strip or wire of a lower amperage rating than the circuit it is designed to protect. When an amperage higher than that stamped on the fuse is present in the circuit, the strip or wire melts, opening the circuit.

GEAR RATIO: The ratio between the number of teeth on meshing gears.

GENERATOR: A device which converts mechanical energy into electrical energy.

HEAT RANGE: The measure of a spark plug's ability to dissipate heat from its firing end. The higher the heat range, the hotter the plug fires.

HUB: The center part of a wheel or gear.

HYDROCARBON (HC): Any chemical compound made up of hydrogen and carbon. A major pollutant formed by the engine as a byproduct of combustion.

HYDROMETER: An instrument used to measure the specific gravity of a solution.

INCH POUND (in.lb. or sometimes, in. lbs.): One twelfth of a foot pound.

INDUCTION: A means of transferring electrical energy in the form of a magnetic field. Principle used in the ignition coil to increase voltage.

INJECTION PUMP: A device, usually mechanically operated, which meters and delivers fuel under pressure to the fuel injector.

INJECTOR: A device which receives metered fuel under relatively low pressure and is activated to inject the fuel into the engine under relatively high pressure at a predetermined time.

INPUT SHAFT: The shaft to which torque is applied, usually carrying the driving gear or gears.

INTAKE MANIFOLD: A casting of passages or pipes used to conduct air or a fuel/air mixture to the cylinders.

JOURNAL: The bearing surface within which a shaft operates.

KEY: A small block usually fitted in a notch between a shaft and a hub to prevent slippage of the two parts.

MANIFOLD: A casting of passages or set of pipes which connect the cylinders to an inlet or outlet source.

MANIFOLD VACUUM: Low pressure in an engine intake manifold formed just below the throttle plates. Manifold vacuum is highest at idle and drops under acceleration.

MASTER CYLINDER: The primary fluid pressurizing device in a hydraulic system. In automotive use, it is found in brake and hydraulic clutch systems and is pedal activated, either directly or, in a power brake system, through the power booster.

MODULE: Electronic control unit, amplifier or igniter of solid state or integrated design which controls the current flow in the ignition primary circuit based on input from the pickup coil. When the module opens the primary circuit, the high secondary voltage is induced in the coil.

NEEDLE BEARING: A bearing which consists of a number (usually a large number) of long, thin rollers.

OHM: (Ω) The unit used to measure the resistance of conductor to electrical flow. One ohm is the amount of resistance that limits current flow to one ampere in a circuit with one volt of pressure.

OHMMETER: An instrument used for measuring the resistance, in ohms, in an electrical circuit.

OUTPUT SHAFT: The shaft which transmits torque from a device, such as a transmission.

OVERDRIVE: A gear assembly which produces more shaft revolutions than that transmitted to it.

OVERHEAD CAMSHAFT (OHC): An engine configuration in which the camshaft is mounted on top of the cylinder head and operates the valve either directly or by means of rocker arms.

OVERHEAD VALVE (OHV): An engine configuration in which all of the valves are located in the cylinder head and the camshaft is located in the cylinder block. The camshaft operates the valves via lifters and pushrods.

OXIDES OF NITROGEN (NOx): Chemical compounds of nitrogen produced as a byproduct of combustion. They combine with hydrocarbons to produce smog.

OXYGEN SENSOR: Used with the feedback system to sense the presence of oxygen in the exhaust gas and signal the computer which can reference the voltage signal to an air/fuel ratio.

PINION: The smaller of two meshing gears.

PISTON RING: An open ended ring which fits into a groove on the outer diameter of the piston. Its chief function is to form a seal between the piston and cylinder wall. Most automotive pistons have three rings: two for compression sealing; one for oil sealing.

PRELOAD: A predetermined load placed on a bearing during assembly or by adjustment.

PRIMARY CIRCUIT: Is the low voltage side of the ignition system which consists of the ignition switch, ballast resistor or resistance wire, bypass, coil, electronic control unit and pick-up coil as well as the connecting wires and harnesses.

PRESS FIT: The mating of two parts under pressure, due to the inner diameter of one being smaller than the outer diameter of the other, or vice versa; an interference fit.

RACE: The surface on the inner or outer ring of a bearing on which the balls, needles or rollers move.

REGULATOR: A device which maintains the amperage and/or voltage levels of a circuit at predetermined values.

RELAY: A switch which automatically opens and/or closes a circuit.

RESISTANCE: The opposition to the flow of current through a circuit or electrical device, and is measured in ohms. Resistance is equal to the voltage divided by the amperage.

RESISTOR: A device, usually made of wire, which offers a preset amount of resistance in an electrical circuit.

RING GEAR: The name given to a ring-shaped gear attached to a differential case, or affixed to a flywheel or as part a planetary gear set.

ROLLER BEARING: A bearing made up of hardened inner and outer races between which hardened steel rollers move.

ROTOR: 1. The disc-shaped part of a disc brake assembly, upon which the brake pads bear; also called, brake disc.
2. The device mounted atop the distributor shaft, which passes current to the distributor cap tower contacts.

SECONDARY CIRCUIT: The high voltage side of the ignition system, usually above 20,000 volts. The secondary includes the ignition coil, coil wire, distributor cap and rotor, spark plug wires and spark plugs.

SENDING UNIT: A mechanical, electrical, hydraulic or electromagnetic device which transmits information to a gauge.

SENSOR: Any device designed to measure engine operating conditions or ambient pressures and temperatures. Usually electronic in nature and designed to send a voltage signal to an on-board computer, some sensors may operate as a simple on/off switch or they may provide a variable voltage signal (like a potentiometer) as conditions or measured parameters change.

SHIM: Spacers of precise, predetermined thickness used between parts to establish a proper working relationship.

SLAVE CYLINDER: In automotive use, a device in the hydraulic clutch system which is activated by hydraulic force, disengaging the clutch.

SOLENOID: A coil used to produce a magnetic field, the effect of which is produce work.

SPARK PLUG: A device screwed into the combustion chamber of a spark ignition engine. The basic construction is a conductive core inside of a ceramic insulator, mounted in an outer conductive base. An electrical charge from the spark plug wire travels along the conductive core and jumps a preset air gap to a grounding point or points at the end of the conductive base. The resultant spark ignites the fuel/air mixture in the combustion chamber.

SPLINES: Ridges machined or cast onto the outer diameter of a shaft or inner diameter of a bore to enable parts to mate without rotation.

TACHOMETER: A device used to measure the rotary speed of an engine, shaft, gear, etc., usually in rotations per minute.

THERMOSTAT: A valve, located in the cooling system of an engine, which is closed when cold and opens gradually in response to engine heating, controlling the temperature of the coolant and rate of coolant flow.

TOP DEAD CENTER (TDC): The point at which the piston reaches the top of its travel on the compression stroke.

TORQUE: The twisting force applied to an object.

TORQUE CONVERTER: A turbine used to transmit power from a driving member to a driven member via hydraulic action, providing changes in drive ratio and torque. In automotive use, it links the driveplate at the rear of the engine to the automatic transmission.

TRANSDUCER: A device used to change a force into an electrical signal.

TRANSISTOR: A semi-conductor component which can be actuated by a small voltage to perform an electrical switching function.

TUNE-UP: A regular maintenance function, usually associated with the replacement and adjustment of parts and components in the electrical and fuel systems of a vehicle for the purpose of attaining optimum performance.

TURBOCHARGER: An exhaust driven pump which compresses intake air and forces it into the combustion chambers at higher than atmospheric pressures. The increased air pressure allows more fuel to be burned and results in increased horsepower being produced.

VACUUM ADVANCE: A device which advances the ignition timing in response to increased engine vacuum.

VACUUM GAUGE: An instrument used to measure the presence of vacuum in a chamber.

VALVE: A device which control the pressure, direction of flow or rate of flow of a liquid or gas.

VALVE CLEARANCE: The measured gap between the end of the valve stem and the rocker arm, cam lobe or follower that activates the valve.

VISCOSITY: The rating of a liquid's internal resistance to flow.

VOLTMETER: An instrument used for measuring electrical force in units called volts. Voltmeters are always connected parallel with the circuit being tested.

WHEEL CYLINDER: Found in the automotive drum brake assembly, it is a device, actuated by hydraulic pressure, which, through internal pistons, pushes the brake shoes outward against the drums.

ABBREVIATIONS AND SYMBOLS

A: Ampere

AC: Alternating current

A/C: Air conditioning

A-h: Ampere hour

AT: Automatic transmission

ATDC: After top dead center

μA: Microampere

bbl: Barrel

BDC: Bottom dead center

bhp: Brake horsepower

BTDC: Before top dead center

BTU: British thermal unit

C: Celsius (Centigrade)

CCA: Cold cranking amps

cd: Candela

cm^2: Square centimeter

cm^3, cc: Cubic centimeter

CO: Carbon monoxide

CO_2: Carbon dioxide

cu.in., in^3: Cubic inch

CV: Constant velocity

Cyl.: Cylinder

DC: Direct current

ECM: Electronic control module

EFE: Early fuel evaporation

EFI: Electronic fuel injection

EGR: Exhaust gas recirculation

Exh.: Exhaust

F: Fahrenheit

F: Farad

pF: Picofarad

μF: Microfarad

FI: Fuel injection

ft.lb., ft. lb., ft. lbs.: foot pound(s)

gal: Gallon

g: Gram

HC: Hydrocarbon

HEI: High energy ignition

HO: High output

hp: Horsepower

Hyd.: Hydraulic

Hz: Hertz

ID: Inside diameter

in.lb.; in. lb.; in. lbs: inch pound(s)

Int.: Intake

K: Kelvin

kg: Kilogram

kHz: Kilohertz

km: Kilometer

km/h: Kilometers per hour

kΩ: Kilohm

kPa: Kilopascal

kV: Kilovolt

kW: Kilowatt

l: Liter

l/s: Liters per second

m: Meter

mA: Milliampere

mg: Milligram

mHz: Megahertz

mm: Millimeter

mm^2: Square millimeter

m^3: Cubic meter

$M\Omega$: Megohm

m/s: Meters per second

MT: Manual transmission

mV: Millivolt

μm: Micrometer

N: Newton

N-m: Newton meter

NOx: Nitrous oxide

OD: Outside diameter

OHC: Over head camshaft

OHV: Over head valve

Ω: Ohm

PCV: Positive crankcase ventilation

psi: Pounds per square inch

pts: Pints

qts: Quarts

rpm: Rotations per minute

rps: Rotations per second

R-12: A refrigerant gas (Freon)

SAE: Society of Automotive Engineers

SO_2: Sulfur dioxide

T: Ton

t: Megagram

TBI: Throttle Body Injection

TPS: Throttle Position Sensor

V: 1. Volt; 2. Venturi

μV: Microvolt

W: Watt

∞: Infinity

$<$: Less than

$>$: Greater than

Index

Chilton's Repair & Tune-Up Guides

The Complete line covers domestic cars, imports, trucks, vans, RV's and 4-wheel drive vehicles.

RTUG Title	Part No.	RTUG Title	Part No.
AMC 1975-82 Covers all U.S. and Canadian models	7199	**Corvair 1960-69** Covers all U.S. and Canadian models	6691
Aspen/Volare 1976-80 Covers all U.S. and Canadian models	6637	**Corvette 1953-62** Covers all U.S. and Canadian models	6576
Audi 1970-73 Covers all U.S. and Canadian models.	5902	**Corvette 1963-84** Covers all U.S. and Canadian models	6843
Audi 4000/5000 1978-81 Covers all U.S. and Canadian models including turbocharged and diesel engines	7028	**Cutlass 1970-85** Covers all U.S. and Canadian models	6933
Barracuda/Challenger 1965-72 Covers all U.S. and Canadian models	5807	**Dart/Demon 1968-76** Covers all U.S. and Canadian models	6324
Blazer/Jimmy 1969-82 Covers all U.S. and Canadian 2- and 4-wheel drive models, including diesel engines	6931	**Datsun 1961-72** Covers all U.S. and Canadian models of Nissan Patrol; 1500, 1600 and 2000 sports cars; Pick-Ups; 410, 411, 510, 1200 and 240Z	5790
BMW 1970-82 Covers U.S. and Canadian models	6844	**Datsun 1973-80 Spanish**	7083
Buick/Olds/Pontiac 1975-85 Covers all U.S. and Canadian full size rear wheel drive models	7308	**Datsun/Nissan F-10, 310, Stanza, Pulsar 1977-86** Covers all U.S. and Canadian models	7196
Cadillac 1967-84 Covers all U.S. and Canadian rear wheel drive models	7462	**Datsun/Nissan Pick-Ups 1970-84** Covers all U.S and Canadian models	6816
Camaro 1967-81 Covers all U.S. and Canadian models	6735	**Datsun/Nissan Z & ZX 1970-86** Covers all U.S. and Canadian models	6932
Camaro 1982-85 Covers all U.S. and Canadian models	7317	**Datsun/Nissan 1200, 210, Sentra 1973-86** Covers all U.S. and Canadian models	7197
Capri 1970-77 Covers all U.S. and Canadian models	6695	**Datsun/Nissan 200SX, 510, 610, 710, 810, Maxima 1973-84** Covers all U.S. and Canadian models	7170
Caravan/Voyager 1984-85 Covers all U.S. and Canadian models	7482	**Dodge 1968-77** Covers all U.S. and Canadian models	6554
Century/Regal 1975-85 Covers all U.S. and Canadian rear wheel drive models, including turbocharged engines	7307	**Dodge Charger 1967-70** Covers all U.S. and Canadian models	6486
Champ/Arrow/Sapporo 1978-83 Covers all U.S. and Canadian models	7041	**Dodge/Plymouth Trucks 1967-84** Covers all $1/2$, $3/4$, and 1 ton 2- and 4-wheel drive U.S. and Canadian models, including diesel engines	7459
Chevette/1000 1976-86 Covers all U.S. and Canadian models	6836	**Dodge/Plymouth Vans 1967-84** Covers all $1/2$, $3/4$, and 1 ton U.S. and Canadian models of vans, cutaways and motor home chassis	6934
Chevrolet 1968-85 Covers all U.S. and Canadian models	7135	**D-50/Arrow Pick-Up 1979-81** Covers all U.S. and Canadian models	7032
Chevrolet 1968-79 Spanish	7082	**Fairlane/Torino 1962-75** Covers all U.S. and Canadian models	6320
Chevrolet/GMC Pick-Ups 1970-82 Spanish	7468	**Fairmont/Zephyr 1978-83** Covers all U.S. and Canadian models	6965
Chevrolet/GMC Pick-Ups and Suburban 1970-86 Covers all U.S. and Canadian $1/2$, $3/4$ and 1 ton models, including 4-wheel drive and diesel engines	6936	**Fiat 1969-81** Covers all U.S. and Canadian models	7042
Chevrolet LUV 1972-81 Covers all U.S. and Canadian models	6815	**Fiesta 1978-80** Covers all U.S. and Canadian models	6846
Chevrolet Mid-Size 1964-86 Covers all U.S. and Canadian models of 1964-77 Chevelle, Malibu and Malibu SS; 1974-77 Laguna; 1978-85 Malibu; 1970-86 Monte Carlo; 1964-84 El Camino, including diesel engines	6840	**Firebird 1967-81** Covers all U.S. and Canadian models	5996
Chevrolet Nova 1986 Covers all U.S. and Canadian models	7658	**Firebird 1982-85** Covers all U.S. and Canadian models	7345
Chevy/GMC Vans 1967-84 Covers all U.S. and Canadian models of $1/2$, $3/4$, and 1 ton vans, cutaways, and motor home chassis, including diesel engines	6930	**Ford 1968-79 Spanish**	7084
		Ford Bronco 1966-83 Covers all U.S. and Canadian models	7140
Chevy S-10 Blazer/GMC S-15 Jimmy 1982-85 Covers all U.S. and Canadian models	7383	**Ford Bronco II 1984** Covers all U.S. and Canadian models	7408
Chevy S-10/GMC S-15 Pick-Ups 1982-85 Covers all U.S. and Canadian models	7310	**Ford Courier 1972-82** Covers all U.S. and Canadian models	6983
Chevy II/Nova 1962-79 Covers all U.S. and Canadian models	6841	**Ford/Mercury Front Wheel Drive 1981-85** Covers all U.S. and Canadian models Escort, EXP, Tempo, Lynx, LN-7 and Topaz	7055
Chrysler K- and E-Car 1981-85 Covers all U.S. and Canadian front wheel drive models	7163	**Ford/Mercury/Lincoln 1968-85** Covers all U.S. and Canadian models of FORD Country Sedan, Country Squire, Crown Victoria, Custom, Custom 500, Galaxie 500, LTD through 1982, Ranch Wagon, and XL; MERCURY Colony Park, Commuter, Marquis through 1982, Gran Marquis, Monterey and Park Lane; LINCOLN Continental and Towne Car	6842
Colt/Challenger/Vista/Conquest 1971-85 Covers all U.S. and Canadian models	7037		
Corolla/Carina/Tercel/Starlet 1970-85 Covers all U.S. and Canadian models	7036	**Ford/Mercury/Lincoln Mid-Size 1971-85** Covers all U.S. and Canadian models of FORD Elite, 1983-85 LTD, 1977-79 LTD II, Ranchero, Torino, Gran Torino, 1977-85 Thunderbird; MERCURY 1972-85 Cougar,	6696
Corona/Cressida/Crown/Mk.II/Camry/Van 1970-84 Covers all U.S. and Canadian models	7044		

continued on next page

RTUG Title	Part No.
1983-85 Marquis, Montego, 1980-85 XR-7; LINCOLN 1982-85 Continental, 1984-85 Mark VII, 1978-80 Versailles	
Ford Pick-Ups 1965-86	6913
Covers all ¹/₂, ³/₄ and 1 ton, 2- and 4-wheel drive U.S. and Canadian pick-up, chassis cab and camper models, including diesel engines	
Ford Pick-Ups 1965-82 Spanish	7469
Ford Ranger 1983-84	7338
Covers all U.S. and Canadian models	
Ford Vans 1961-86	6849
Covers all U.S. and Canadian ¹/₂, ³/₄ and 1 ton van and cutaway chassis models, including diesel engines	
GM A-Body 1982-85	7309
Covers all front wheel drive U.S. and Canadian models of BUICK Century, CHEVROLET Celebrity, OLDSMOBILE Cutlass Ciera and PONTIAC 6000	
GM C-Body 1985	7587
Covers all front wheel drive U.S. and Canadian models of BUICK Electra Park Avenue and Electra T-Type, CADILLAC Fleetwood and deVille, OLDSMOBILE 98 Regency and Regency Brougham	
GM J-Car 1982-85	7059
Covers all U.S. and Canadian models of BUICK Skyhawk, CHEVROLET Cavalier, CADILLAC Cimarron, OLDSMOBILE Firenza and PONTIAC 2000 and Sunbird	
GM N-Body 1985-86	7657
Covers all U.S. and Canadian models of front wheel drive BUICK Somerset and Skylark, OLDSMOBILE Calais, and PONTIAC Grand Am	
GM X-Body 1980-85	7049
Covers all U.S. and Canadian models of BUICK Skylark, CHEVROLET Citation, OLDSMOBILE Omega and PONTIAC Phoenix	
GM Subcompact 1971-80	6935
Covers all U.S. and Canadian models of BUICK Skyhawk (1975-80), CHEVROLET Vega and Monza, OLDSMOBILE Starfire, and PONTIAC Astre and 1975-80 Sunbird	
Granada/Monarch 1975-82	6937
Covers all U.S. and Canadian models	
Honda 1973-84	6980
Covers all U.S. and Canadian models	
International Scout 1967-73	5912
Covers all U.S. and Canadian models	
Jeep 1945-87	6817
Covers all U.S. and Canadian CJ-2A, CJ-3A, CJ-3B, CJ-5, CJ-6, CJ-7, Scrambler and Wrangler models	
Jeep Wagoneer, Commando, Cherokee, Truck 1957-86	6739
Covers all U.S. and Canadian models of Wagoneer, Cherokee, Grand Wagoneer, Jeepster, Jeepster Commando, J-100, J-200, J-300, J-10, J20, FC-150 and FC-170	
Laser/Daytona 1984-85	7563
Covers all U.S. and Canadian models	
Maverick/Comet 1970-77	6634
Covers all U.S. and Canadian models	
Mazda 1971-84	6981
Covers all U.S. and Canadian models of RX-2, RX-3, RX-4, 808, 1300, 1600, Cosmo, GLC and 626	
Mazda Pick-Ups 1972-86	7659
Covers all U.S. and Canadian models	
Mercedes-Benz 1959-70	6065
Covers all U.S. and Canadian models	
Mereceds-Benz 1968-73	5907
Covers all U.S. and Canadian models	

RTUG Title	Part No.
Mercedes-Benz 1974-84	6809
Covers all U.S. and Canadian models	
Mitsubishi, Cordia, Tredia, Starien, Galant 1983-85	7583
Covers all U.S. and Canadian models	
MG 1961-81	6780
Covers all U.S. and Canadian models	
Mustang/Capri/Merkur 1979-85	6963
Covers all U.S. and Canadian models	
Mustang/Cougar 1965-73	6542
Covers all U.S. and Canadian models	
Mustang II 1974-78	6812
Covers all U.S. and Canadian models	
Omni/Horizon/Rampage 1978-84	6845
Covers all U.S. and Canadian models of DODGE omni, Miser, 024, Charger 2.2; PLYMOUTH Horizon, Miser, TC3, TC3 Tourismo; Rampage	
Opel 1971-75	6575
Covers all U.S. and Canadian models	
Peugeot 1970-74	5982
Covers all U.S. and Canadian models	
Pinto/Bobcat 1971-80	7027
Covers all U.S. and Canadian models	
Plymouth 1968-76	6552
Covers all U.S. and Canadian models	
Pontiac Fiero 1984-85	7571
Covers all U.S. and Canadian models	
Pontiac Mid-Size 1974-83	7346
Covers all U.S. and Canadian models of Ventura, Grand Am, LeMans, Grand LeMans, GTO, Phoenix, and Grand Prix	
Porsche 924/928 1976-81	7048
Covers all U.S. and Canadian models	
Renault 1975-85	7165
Covers all U.S. and Canadian models	
Roadrunner/Satellite/Belvedere/GTX 1968-73	5821
Covers all U.S. and Canadian models	
RX-7 1979-81	7031
Covers all U.S. and Canadian models	
SAAB 99 1969-75	5988
Covers all U.S. and Canadian models	
SAAB 900 1979-85	7572
Covers all U.S. and Canadian models	
Snowmobiles 1976-80	6978
Covers Arctic Cat, John Deere, Kawasaki, Polaris, Ski-Doo and Yamaha	
Subaru 1970-84	6982
Covers all U.S. and Canadian models	
Tempest/GTO/LeMans 1968-73	5905
Covers all U.S. and Canadian models	
Toyota 1966-70	5795
Covers all U.S. and Canadian models of Corona, MkII, Corolla, Crown, Land Cruiser, Stout and Hi-Lux	
Toyota 1970-79 Spanish	7467
Toyota Celica/Supra 1971-85	7043
Covers all U.S. and Canadian models	
Toyota Trucks 1970-85	7035
Covers all U.S. and Canadian models of pick-ups, Land Cruiser and 4Runner	
Valiant/Duster 1968-76	6326
Covers all U.S. and Canadian models	
Volvo 1956-69	6529
Covers all U.S. and Canadian models	
Volvo 1970-83	7040
Covers all U.S. and Canadian models	
VW Front Wheel Drive 1974-85	6962
Covers all U.S. and Canadian models	
VW 1949-71	5796
Covers all U.S. and Canadian models	
VW 1970-79 Spanish	7081
VW 1970-81	6837
Covers all U.S. and Canadian Beetles, Karmann Ghia, Fastback, Squareback, Vans, 411 and 412	

Chilton's Repair Manuals are available at your local retailer or by mailing a check or money order for **$15.95** per book plus **$3.50** for 1st book and **$.50** for each additional book to cover postage and handling to:

Chilton Book Company
Dept. DM
Radnor, PA 19089

NOTE: When ordering be sure to include your name & address, book part No. & title.